HISTORY OF KERALA

HISTORY OF KERALA

WRITTEN IN THE FORM OF NOTES ON VISSCHER'S LETTERS FROM MALABAR

K. P. PADMANABHA MENON

EDITED BY
T. K. KRISHNA MENON

IN FOUR VOLUMES
VOLUME THREE

GYAN

Published by

GYAN

Gyan Publishing House
5, Ansari Road
Daryaganj, New Delhi-110002
Phone: 011-47034999, 9811692060
E-mail: books@gyanbooks.com

Distribution Network
gyanbooks.com
India, USA, Canada, UK, Australia, France

ISBN : 978-81-212-3526-6 (Set)
ISBN : 978-81-212-4665-1 (HB)
First Published, 1937

2nd Impression 2020

Printed at: Gyan Press, Delhi.

History of Kerala Vol. III
Author: K. P. Padmanabha Menon

DEDICATION

TO

MRS. K. P. PADMANABHA MENON.

CONTENTS.

NOTES

Pages

LIST OF ILLUSTRATIONS.

[**Postscript to the Foreword:**—For many of the blocks that have served to illustrate this volume, the Editor is, as on two former occasions, indebted to the Government of Cochin; and for a few of the rest to Messrs. T. Thomas and P. C. Varkki. His acknowledgments are due to Mr. P. I. Cheriyan, the Darbar Photographer, for some photographs, to Mr. K. Narasimha Pai, for a photo of the late Mr. Hari Shenoy, and to Mr. M. S. Menon, for an old print of a Namputiri and his Antarjanam. He is grateful also to Sir C. Sankaran Nayar, Sir M. Krishnan Nayar and Sir K. Ramunni Menon for leave to put in their likeness in this book. He owes it to Mr. N. M. Parameswara Ayyar, the Superintendent of the Cochin Government Press, to state with pleasure that the warm co-operation of the latter and his staff in getting this work through the press has been of great help to him. Finally, he wishes to take advantage of this postscript to record a remark or two which could not, with propriety, be included in the Foreword. The manuscript of this valuable publication was ready about a quarter of a century ago. The Editor had to face considerable difficulty in his attempt to make it up-to-date. To mention but one obstacle in the way—the nearest library for reference lies miles away from his place of residence. This he states not to feed any morbid self-esteem, much less to evoke, by words insiduous, the sympathy of his critics. He welcomes criticism, even violent and unsparing, provided it is correct and merited and supplies something helpful which after all, he trusts, is the true motive and meaning of criticism. Whatever that be, he thinks he has worked hard to carry out the behest of his master and to deliver that patriot's message with its force in no way diminished. Let Malayalis heed it; "bewildered by the rush of the modern world, let them not move from their high seat of vision, forget their ancient prophets, barter their great inheritance, and bow down before the perishable idols of the present age, the unconsecrated gods of a passing hour." Let them, on the other hand, hold aloft the banner of Kerala and live up to the noble traditions of their romantic, their sacred Motherland—*Editor.*]

Mr. & Mrs. T. K. Krishna Menon.
(The Editor of this work and his wi' ,.

(To face p. XI.

FOREWORD

BY THE EDITOR.

There is a class of scholars who believe that Vālmiki's Rāmāyaṇa is an allegorical poem intended to depict the introduction by the Aryans of agriculture and civilisation into Southern India.[1] According to some of these, the whole of South India, by them called Ḍaṇḍakāraṇya, was originally covered by impenetrable forests and infested by Dasyus, Rākṣhasas and Vānaras. But they forget that the descriptions of Janasthana and Kishkindha given in that great epic itself will indubitably disprove their theory. And, as for Lanka, the capital of Rāvaṇa, the poet shows that, from its marvellous splendours of art, architecture and culture, it far outshone the capital of Daśaraṭha himself. Hanūmān was not an ordinary monkey in any case; his learning, tact and firmness marked him out as one fit to carry out a great mission; while Rāvaṇa, as an administrator and commander, was worthy to be Rama's antagonist. To crown all, the name of Maṇṇōḍari, the spouse of the much-maligned Rākṣhasa King, Ravana, the Aryan ladies were asked to daily remember for the extinction of their heinous sins[2] ,—if any.

As Dr. Fleure correctly puts it, the idea of a barbarous Dravidian India on which Aryan Civilisation descended has been fairly widespread, while the number of advocates who plead for the cause of an ancient civilisation

1. Weber's *History of Sanskrit Literature*, page 192. Dutt's *Ancient India*, pp. 209 and 211.

2. (*Ahalya Draupadi Sita*
Tara Mannodari tatha
Panchakanya-smara-nnithyam
Mahapatakanasanam)

of South India is not as great as one might wish.[1] And yet, curiously enough, if one looks at the subject carefully, he will find that the Rāmāyaṇa, the Mahābhāraṭa, Asoka's Edicts, Kāliḍāsa's Raghuvamśa, Sinhalese traditions, the Periplus, Ptolemy's Geography, all these clearly testify to the early existence of prosperous, progressive and independent kingdoms in South India.[2] The Dravidians were in possession of India long before the Aryans came to it, and had developed a civilisation independent of any Aryan influence [3]. Sugrīva, when he sends out his monkey leaders to discover the whereabouts of Sīṭa, directs them to search for her in Viḍarbha, Āndhra, Chōla, Pāṇdya and Kērala countries. Reference is made to Musiris, a great emporium of the Chēra kingdom. [4] In the Sabhā Parva of the Mahabharata, the kings of the Dravidas are incidently adverted to. The description of the *swayamvara* of Ḍamayanṭi, gives the reader of that epic a vivid idea of the grandeur of Vidarbha. [5] And Dandakaranya, by necessary inference, can be seen to have occupied only a limited portion of Deccan .[6]

1. Dr. Fleure in his Preface to Dr. G. Slater's *Dravidian Element in India Culture.*

2. *Dravidian India* by Mr. T. R. Sesha Iyyengar, M. A., p. 185.

3. *Ibid.* p. 119.

4. Chera and Kerala denote the same country. "I have no doubt" says Dr. Caldwell "that the names Chera and Keralam were originally one and the same." Dr. Gundert has thus in his Malayalam Dictionary:—"Keram=Chera=Malabar." "Keralam =Cheram, the country between Gokarnam and Cumari." 'The latitude of the Chera Metrapolis, according to Ptolemy, was 38° 15,' and the ports of Tyndis and Musiris were within his dominions. (*Madras Review* Vol. 1, p. 352. See also *History of Kerala* Vol. I, p. 28.

5—6 *Dravidian India* pp. 16 to 19, and p. 124. Also see Mr. E. B. Havell's *Short History of India*, p. 19. In his *Digvijaya* tour, Sahadeva visits Dravidas, Cholas, Keralas and Pandyas. Again Keralas and Cholas fought on the side of the Pandavas. (Mahabharata, VIII, 22-455-1893. *See History of the Tamils*, by Mr. P. T. S. Iyyengar, M. A., pp. 89-90.)

The Dravidians had well-ordered villages, roads, buildings, tanks and reservoirs.[1] The Dravidian architecture is of indigenous origin and has had its own course of evolution.[2] The art of agriculture existed in Southern India long before the Aryans came to it. Sir John Hewell, in his *Pre-historic Ruling Races*, says that the Dravidians were, of all the great races of antiquity, the first to systematise agriculture. It was a Kerala monarch who supplied rations of rice to the contending armies of the Mahabharatha war.[3]

There can be no doubt that the Aryan civilisation was greatly influenced by the Dravidians.[4] In matters connected with the land tenures, social organisation, village administration and taxation, the Aryans adopted much from the systems of the Dravidians.[5] "As a matter of fact," says Dr. R. Tagore, "the old Dravidian culture was by no means to be despised. The Aryan civilisation acquired both richness and depth under the influence of the Dravidian component. The Dravidians might not be introspective or metaphysical, but they were artists, and they could sing, design and construct."[6]

In the introduction to his *Six Systems of Indian Philosophy*, Professor Max Muller remarks that, in the south of India, there exists a philosophical literature which shows original, indigenous elements of great

1. *Dravidian India*, pp. 54, 123 and 174. See also Baden Powell's *Village Communities in India*, p. 49. Also Dr. R. Mookerjee's article on Village Assemblies in the *Lucknow University Journal*, Vol. I, No. 3. About the National and Village Assemblies of Kerala, see *History of Kerala*, Vol. I, pp. 250 and 259.

2. *Dravidian India*, p. 118, See also *Dravidian Architecture* by Jouvean Dubreial.

3. *Dravidian India*, pp. 125, 127. Also *Siddhanta Deepika*, Vol. V, pp. 169-170.

4. Professor Rapson's *Ancient India*, p. 29.

5. *Dravidian India*, p. 120. Introduction to the *Ambattha Sutta*, *Sacred Books of the Buddhists*, p. 96.

6. *Dravidian India*, p. 117.

beauty and importance.[1] What is Indian religion but Dravidian religion? For the greatest deities of Hinduism were unknown to Vedic Rishis.[2] Siva is *Dakshinamurthy*, a God of the South; and Agasthya, the tradition goes, learned his Tamil from Siva.[3] According to Mr. P. T. Sreenivasa Iyyengar, languages spoken in India in olden times (say 20,000 years ago) were all dialects of proto-Tamil;[4] while Dr. Maclean, though he does not go so far, still holds that there is little doubt that the Dravidian languages are comparatively older in point of time than Sanskrit.[5] I have seen a paper in manuscript on this subject by the late Chattampi Swāmi, whose encyclopaedic knowledge was the wonder and despair of his erudite contemporary scholars.[6] *Samskritham* means, he says, that which is refined. From what, he asks? and he seeks to prove in a variety of ways, that the basis of Sanskrit is Tamil, or, to be more acurate, proto-Tamil. Be this as it may, one fact comes out clearly that the Dravidians developed their language, religion, political organisation and social structure unaided, at any rate, in their early stages, by the Aryans.[7] It is fairly evident that the Dravidian culture had, before the coming in of the Aryans, already attained a high standard of excellence on lines economic, martial and literary in centuries preceding the Christian Era.[8]

1. Pp. XX-XXI.

2. Sir Charles Elliot's *Sketch of Hinduism and Buddhism*, Book I, p. XV.

3. *Dravidian India*, pp. 98 to 101.

4. *Ibid*, p. 79.

5. *Manual of Administration of the Madras Presidency*, pp. 42 and 112-3.

6. A part of it, I know, is with H. H. Thachudaya Kaimal at Irinjalakuday in the Cochin State.

7. Mr. Featherman's *History of Mankind*, Vol. I, p. 3. See *Malabar Quarterly Review*, Vol. V, p. 150 *et seq*. Also *Keralam* by the late Kunhikuttan Tampuran, p. 5, Sl. 16.

8. Dr. A. K. Coomaraswami' *History of India and Indonesian Art*, p. 6.

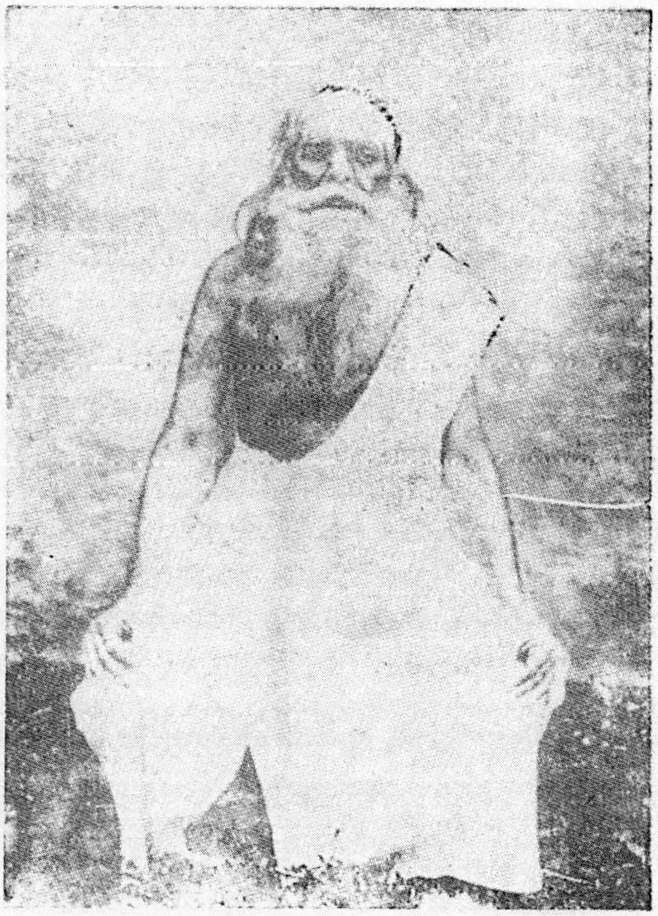

SRI CHATTAMP SWAMI.

(*To face p.* ***XIV.***

The ancient Dravidians were the direct ancestors of the Tamil, Telugu, Malayalam, Canarese and other tribes that occupied the greater part of South India.[1] At first they seem to have been scattered almost all over India until we find them congregated in the south of the Peninsula. Manu, it is significant, classifies them as among the tribes that had once been Kshetriyas. So too *Harivamsa.* While certain other Purāṇas, such as the *Vayu*, the *Matsya* and the *Agni*, claim for them an Aryan Kshetriya ancestry! In any case, we never find them classed as Sudras; and in the whole of the *Tolkappiyam*, there is no reference whatever to the term Sudra.[2] The Dravidians were no doubt called by the Aryans as Asuras, Daityas, Dasyus or Nāgas. But it is equally true that traditions, inscriptions and ancient literature prove in an unmistakable way that the three great Dravidian Kingdoms of Chōla, Chēra and Pāṇdya had, before the advent of the Aryans, attained, in civil and military organisations and in every department of science and art, a high level, and played a grand part in the development of Dravidian culture.[3]

1. A distinguished contributor to the Supplementary Volumes of the *Encyclopaedia Britannica* speaks of South India as "the home of that great, mysterious Dravidian Civilisation." Vol. I, p. 158.

Mr. John Campbell refers to the common origin of the Nayars and Hittites. (See the Jenmi-Kudiyan Com. Report of Travancore, p. 31). For the Basque origin theory, see the same Report, pp. 26 and 62. Ferguson regards them as closely allied to the Newars of Nepal; while there are others who claim for them a kinship with the people in Bengal. (*The Tamils 1,800 years Ago*, p. 46).

2. *Dravidian India*, pp. 21 to 23 and 180. See the Editor's Note on p. 337 in the *History of Kerala*, Vol. III.

3. A perusal of *Dravidian India* by Professor T. R. Sesha Ayyengar, M. A., will amply bear out this statement. The reference is only illustrative, not exhaustive. See the Editor's Notes to the *History of Kerala*, Vol. III, beginning on pp. 162, 167 and 182.

Mr. F. J. Richards is perfectly right when he says that a variety of causes, partly political and partly literary, has tended to the belittlement of Peninsular India's contribution to the history both of India and of the world at large.[1] The experts, he remarks, have failed to take a comprehensive view of the data; and he advises the South Indians that it is time for them to champion for their cause and to assert their claims to recognition. It is not my purpose here to assume the function of an advocate to maintain that cause. The subject is too large for me to handle; but I am sure it will be handled in the years to come by those more competent than myself. My anxious desire is to follow, very humbly as needs must, the ways of a modest annalist who presents in brief outline a few of the relevant materials he has on hand; and I shall consider my labours rewarded if, in so doing, I shall be able to recapture an image of the past and benefit those who wish to work on this subject. Now to proceed with the theme.

Mr. H. R. Hall suggests Sumerians to be a branch of the Indian Dravidians.[2] To quote Mr. Hall:—"It was in their home that the Sumerians developed their culture. There their writing may have been invented and progressed from a purely pictorial to a simplified and abbreviated form which in Babylonia took on its peculiar cuneiform appearance. On their way they left the seeds of their culture in Elam".[3] Provided Mr. Hall's theory holds good, says Dr. Suniti Kumar Chatterji, "It would be established that civilisation first arose in India and was probably associated with the primitive Dravidians. Then it was taken to Mesopotamia to become the source of the Babylonian and

1. *Side-lights on the Dravidian Problem* by Mr. F. J. Richards, I. C. S., M. A., M. R. A. S., F. R. A. I, in the *Quarterly Journal* of the Mythic Society, Vol. VI, p. 156.

2. *The Ancient History of the Near East*, p. 173.

3. *Dravidian India*, p. 58.

other ancient cultures which form the basis of modern civilisation."[1] Sir John Marshall also comes out with the important suggestion that, if the Sumerians were an intrusive element in Mesopotamia, then India may eventually prove to be the cradle of the Sumerian civilisation which, in its turn, formed the bedrock on which the magnificent superstructure of Babylonian, Assyrian and West Asiatic cultures generally rested.[2] Dr. Chatterji, an authority on Comparative Philology distinctly hints that Cretan, Lycian, Sumerian, Elamite, and Dravidian languages might be materially related, and that the Aegean islands, Asia Minor and Mesopotamia might have formed one cultural area.[3]

The recent discoveries at Harappa in Punjab and Mohen-jo-Daro in Sindh prove the existence in India in the remote past of a civilisation and culture closely akin to those of the Sumerians.[4] The materials found in the Indus valley—remains of buildings and temples, pottery and terra cotta, beads and glassware, crude porcelain, bronze and iron articles, and, what is more, inscribed seals and copper coins,—solidly demonstrate the presence of a high culture in ancient India comparable in antiquity and extent with those of Anon and Susa, of Babylon and Crete.[5] The ancient seals, and there are a great number of them, are inscribed with Sumerian writing and associated with buildings and cultural objects of the Sumerian and Phoenician type.[6] In the opinion of Mr. R. D. Banerji and others, the Mohen-jo-Dara and Harappa culture is non-Aryan. The presence of the Brahuis in Baluchistan lends considerable support to the view that the people who built

1. *Dravidian India*, p. 59.
2. *Ibid.* p, 57.
3. *Ibid.* p. 42.
4. *Indian Historical Quarterly*, Calcutta, Vol. I, p. 644.
5. *Ibid.* Vol. VII, p. 177.
6. *Dravidian India*, p. 88.

up this culture were the primitive Dravidians.[1] Sir John Evans is emphatic in his assertion that "Southern India was the cradle of the human race, and the passage-ground by which the ancient progenitors of Northern and Mediterranean races proceeded to the parts of the globe which they now inhabit."[2]

There is a good deal of truth in the remarks of Mr. W. Reade that India, as a land of Desire, has contributed much to the development of man. Open the book of Universal History at what period we may, it is, he says, always the Indian trade which is the cause of the internal industry and foreign negotiation.[3]

The people who were mainly responsible for the early Indian trade were the Dravidians. They formed one of the principal seafaring sections of the Sumerians. The Dravidians of South India lived near the sea and were familiar with it. They became skilled fishermen and boat builders. *Toni*, *Otam*, *Pathemar* and *Kappal* are Dravidian words. There is abundant evidence, writes Mr. Richards, to show that a large proportion of the ancient trade between India and the west was carried on Indian bottoms, and it seems certain that the maritime enterprise of ancient India was in the hands of the Dravidians.[4] They formed the large

1. *Dravidian India*, p. 178. Among the modern Indians as amongst the modern Greeks or Italians, the ancient pre-Aryan type of the head has arrived; and it is to this Dravidian ethnic type of India that the ancient Sumerians bears most resemblance". Professor P. T. S. Iyyengar's *History of the Tamils* pp. 36—7. Mr. C. F. Oldhan in his *The Sun and the Serpant* shows the presence of the Dravidian element in the people of North India.

2. Presidential Address before the British Association for the Advancement of Science, 1897. Mr. E J. Forsdyke, M. A., F.S.A., who contributes the article on Crete to the supplementary volumes of the *Encyclopaedia Britannica*, calls Sir John Evans as "the most experienced and the most active of Cretan explorers." Vol. I, p. 175.

3. *Martyrdom of Man*, 22nd Impression, pp. 40—41.

4. *Mythic Society Journal*, Vol. VI, p. 182.

proportion of the sailors of the Indian Ocean.[1] To them the long chain of backwaters on the west coast supplied a sort of elementary school of navigation.[2] They gave rise to the race of sailors who carried Indian goods in boats to Africa and Arabia in the west and to Malaya and China in the East.[3] Extensive travel by sea in very early times can alone explain the possibility of colonising the Mesopotamian valley on the one side and of the Indian Archipelago on the other.[4] The Dravidians traded with the ancient Chaldeans long before the Vedic language found its way into India.[5] In the words of Dr. Sayce, the commerce between India and Babylon must have been carried on as early as about 3,000 B. C., when Ur Bagas, the first king of the United Babylonia ruled in Ur (Mughair) of the Chaldees.[6] The people of South India used to cross over to the islands of the Indian Archipelago, Java, Sumatra, Borneo and establish colonies there. From Java they pushed on to the mainland and founded the Indian colonies of Siam and Cambodia.[7] In later days, Augustus conquered Egypt in B. C. 30, and he tried to develop a direct sea trade between India and the Roman Empire. Though extensive trade existed from very early times between the Mediterranean Cities and the ports of Kerala, neither the Phoenicians under Hiram, the Jews under Solomon, the Syrians under the Seleucids and the Egyptians under the Ptolemies took the open route. It was the Romans who revolutionised the maritime trade by discovering what Pliny calls a compendious route.[8]

1. *Dravidian India*, p. 131.
2. *Dravidian Element in Indian Culture*, p. 82.
3. *History of the Tamils*, p. 12.
4. *Dravidian India*, p. 36. Also Mr. Hall's *Ancient History of the Near East*, pp. 173—4.
5. *Dravidian India*, p. 131.
6. Dr.R. Mookerji's *Indian Shipping*, p. 85. Also Professor Sayce's Hibbert Lectures, pp. 137—8.
7. *Hindu Colony of Cambodia*, by Mr. P. N. Bose, M. A., p. 2
8. *Cochin State Manual*, Government Press, pp. 35—6.

Subsequently, as a result of embassies sent by the Chera, the Chola and the Pandya Monarchs, the volume of India's trade with Rome expanded to huge proportions.[1] Thus, to quote Professor Sylvan Levi, "The movement which carried Indian civilisation towards different parts of the globe about the beginning of the Christian Era was far from inaugurating any new route. Adventures and traffickers and missionaries, profitted by the technical progress of navigation, followed, under the best of conditions of comfort and efficiency, the ways traced from time immemorial by the mariners of another race whom the Aryans despised as savages."[2] I wonder how the ancient Dravidians came to be treated or even spoken of as savages. Not even the wildest canons of an Aryan poetical license will permit that latitude. To put it mildly and without any warmth of feeling, one has to admit that they had a high civilisation from which the Aryans themselves had to learn much. It is now established beyond question that they knew agriculture, had coins, and used ornaments of gold and silver, and weapons of iron and bronze. They built forts, towns and temples, and worshipped Mother Goddess. Their literature was rich. They built ships, navigated the seas and carried their commodities and their culture[3] to distant

1. *History of the Tamils*, p. 195. Mr. Warrington's *Commerce between the Roman Empire and India*, p. 37. The published researches of Messrs. G. E. Smith, W. E. Schoof, J. W. Jackson, W J. Perry and others give ample proofs of the extreme antiquity of the intercourse between South India and other centres of civilisation. (Vide Dr. G. Slater's *Dravidian Element in Indian Culture*, p. 73.)

2. *The Pre-Aryan and the Pre-Dravidian in India*, translated by Mr. P. C. Bagchi, M. A., p. 125.

3. *Mythic Society's Journal*, Vol. VI, p. 157, quotes the following from Tylor's *Primitive Culture*, Vol. I, p. 1. Culture in its broad sense is "that complex whole which includes knowledge, belief, arts, morals, law, custom and any other capabilities and habits acquired by man as a member of society."

lands.[1] So far as evidence is available, it is now certain that, from the dawn of history, contact existed between South India and the Mediterranean area, the Tigris-Euphrates Valley and China, the three other foci of civilisation. The narratives of the travels and voyages of Alberuni, Marco Polo and Vaseo de Gama in the 11th, 13th and 15th centuries prove the wonderful continuity of this commercial history. In the 3rd century B. C., India sent envoys to the Greek monarchs of Egypt, Syria, Macedon, Cyprus and Cyrene. Canarese passages have been found in a Greek farce written in an Egyptian papyrus. The influence of India on Chinese art and literature has been intense, while the civilisation of Java and Sumatra is saturated with it. The pageant of India's commerce shows that within historic times Peninsular India has been in direct contact with East Africa, Somali-land, Abyssinia, Egypt, Arabia, Babylonia, Indonesia and China, to say nothing of the Makran Coast. The panorama of possible cultural influences is wide.

Let us glance at it for a while, and see if our vision will carry us further into the corridor of time.[2] The vision may not be perfect and the sights may be blurred; but the trial is worth the taking; and it will be the duty of the future historian to rectify the errors or to supplement the information by a comparative study of the materials and scripts now being unearthed in the various centres of the globe.

A little over 100 years, Egypt was a sealed book to the moderns. The Pyramids stood four-square to the sandstorms of the desert and the Sphinx regarded

1. *Dravidian India*, pp. 161—3.

2. "A true historian does not reassemble the past from its broken fragments, he re-creates it........ A historian is as much a creative artist as is a good scientist, his work is as much an act of thought. He does not subscribe to the fantastic theory of an objective past, ascertainable and recordable by mere drudgery, the toil of ants." *The World of Man*. p. 5, by Mr. L. J. Cheney, M. A., Cambridge University Press.

the Nile with the same inscrutable gaze that had puzzled the ancients. It was the Rosetta Stone that for the first time unfolded to us the romance of Egypt. During the Napoleonic war, it was a sapper who secured it, because it was covered with strange writings. It contained the picture-writing of ancient Egypt and the everyday writing of ordinary people. It was the labours of Dr. Young and Mr. Champollion who furnished a clue to the reading of the mystery of the Rosetta Stone, and thus opened to the modern world the way to the ancient knowledge of Egypt.[1]

There were some who thought that this picture-writing which was found in tombs and on old papyri manuscripts represented the oldest writing in the world. But the pictures clearly showed that they are cleverly drawn and indicated training and true artistic perception. That pitch of perfection could have been reached only by time. Professor Flinders Petrie has now established that crude signs preceded the picture-writing. This savant is an authority on ceramics and can deduce amazing facts from a fragment of a broken pot. Thus he has linked the culture of Egypt with that of Crete, far away in the middle of the Mediterranean sea.[2] This view has been confirmed by the excavations of Professor H. Schliemann who pointed to Knossos in Crete as the seat from which the Mediterranean civilisation sprang. His work was taken up by Sir Arthur Evans whose toils were long and unremitting. He found that in that little island, Crete, there flourished a civilisation as old as that of Egypt

1. For materials of this and of the next three paragraphs, I am indebted to the *Romance of Excavations* by Mr. David Masters.

2. At the close of the prehistoric age, the black pottery of the late Neolithic city of Knossos is found in the lowest level of the temple at Abydos. And in the royal tombs of the first dynasty there, many vases and pieces have been found which are clearly of the earliest age of painted Aegean pottery. (Vol. I, p. 237 of Harmsmonth's *History of the World*).

and Mesopotamia, a civilisation that flourished at least 5,000 years ago, that endured the ages before the Phoenicians launched their galleys in the Mediterranean. Mr. Banerji, the Indian who worked at the Indus valley explorations, has concluded that the Indian culture has close connection with Crete and the Aegian region.[1] Striking similarities have been observed between the non-Aryan Indian religion and those of Crete and Asia Minor. The worship of the Mother Goddess is an instance in point. The principal Minoan Divinity was a kind of *Magna Mater*, a great mother.[2] So also in cults and decorative motif and, to a certain extent in the scripts and languages, semblances are marked. It is for these reasons that Dr. S. Chatterji suggests that the Aegean Islands, Asia Minor and Mesopotamia might have originally formed one cultural area. Aegean civilisation was focussed in Crete. It was of such importance as to be considered likely to have exerted its influence on the nascent civilisation in Europe. Even Chinese civilisation was regarded as an offshoot from the Sumerian stock.[3] But we have strayed far away from Egypt. Let us go back to it for a few more moments.

The Egyptians worshipped the Sun for giving them light and the Nile for their life. To the Sun they built a magnificent temple at Helispolis, and the Cleopatra's needle formed an adjunct to that structure. It took years and cost a lot of money in these days for the British for its transport to the Thames Embankment. What a miracle that it was made and set up in Egypt centuries ago. It was a standing monument of their high engineering skill.

1. *Dravidian India*, pp, 36, 41 and 42.

2. *The Rise of Civilisation in Crete*, by Professor F. Petrie in Harmsworth's *History of the World*. When noticing a *Guide to Knossos*, a recent issue of the London *Times* has remarked that the Buckingham Palace could easily go into the palace at Knossos.

The worship of the Sun which formed a feature of the Dravidians was also prevalent in Egypt, Babylon and Peru.

3. See the aforesaid Paper of Prof. F. Petrie; also see p. 261 of Vol. I of the above Harmsworth's History.

The graves of Egypt reveal the rise of Egypt's civilisation. Tombs of stone needed no search; there are plenty of them; of Pyramids alone there are about eighty. Going back, the brick tombs get smaller until they disappear and only the grave remains in which the dead lie doubled up, as are found in some of the funerary urns of South India.[1] The Egyptians believed in another world to which the souls journeyed after they leave their physical bodies. Again, every human being was considered by them to own a double. These notions necessitated the embalming of bodies, their preservation in durable tombs, and the provision for all comforts during the passage of the double to the Egyptian heaven. Hence the pyramids. 1,00,000 men had to slave for 30 years to build one of the pyramids; and Herodotus says that a sloping road for the transport of materials to that took 1,00,000 men 10 years to construct. And about the nature of the supply of the funeral equipment, we can form some idea when it is known that the value of the contents of the tomb of Tutankhamen is computed at £ 3,000,000. There is no wonder therefore that in Egypt grave-stealing was cultivated as a fine art. To rifle a tomb, as a rule, was considered a heinous sin, but the robbers were prepared to undergo sacrifices in the next world for the prospect of a tolerable life in this one. So a constant battle of wits went on in the Valley of the Tombs of Kings between those who desired to see the tombs unmolested and those who desecrated them to abstract their treasures. We shall not tarry over these, except to note that, among the finds, the pottery and the tablets containing inscriptions in Babylonian, Sumerian or the Phoenician cuneiform scripts

1. *Mythic Society Journal*, Vol. VI, p. 165.

Another apparent link with the Mediterranean area is the existence of prehistoric dolmen-graves all over Peninsular India. (See also the Article on *Archaeology* by Mr. A. Govinda Warrier B. A, B. L., in the *Progress of Cochin*, p. 277.)

throw a flood of light on the Dravidian riddle. The reading by Dr. Rawlinson of the cuneiform inscription of Darius at Behistun in Persia and the labours of Mr. Layard among the ruins of Nineveh and Babylon serve a similar end. Mesopotamia was considered the garden of Eden. Letters written in cuneiform characters passed between Egypt and Mesopotamia. The original inhabitants of Mesopotamia was Sumerians. Though they were a peaceful, pastoral people and had a chequered career owing to the waxing and waning ascendancy of Babylon and Assyria, they still stand out in the dim past with a culture far higher than that of their surrounding nations. Materials received as relics from the banks of the Euphrates and the Tigris,—pottery of the best sort, fine statuettes in gold and silver, sealed weights of clay, and laws inscribed on bricks,—all these testify to the high level of their civilisation.[1]

There were extensive intercouse between South India on the one side and Egypt and Babylon and Assyria on the other.[2] The great Egyptologist, Flinders Petrie, after having discovered portraits of Indian men and women at Memphis, remarks, "These are the first remains of Indians on the Mediterranean.....We seem now to have touched the Indian colony in Memphis."[3] There is a marked resemblance between the Mediterranean race and the Dravidian population.[4] The

1. *The Illustrated London News* of November 2 of 1929, of November 29 of 1930, November 21 of 1931, of March 12 of 1932 and of February 11 of 1933, give descriptions of the diggings at Ras Samra, an ancient port on the Bay of Minet-el-Beida, and of the articles recovered. It was a commercial centre grown rich in the 3rd and 2nd millenium B. C. by the export to Egypt and the Aegean of Asiatic produce from Syria and Mesopotamia. Tablets written in the Babylonian, syllabic Sumerian and in the Phoenician cuneiform alphabetic scripts were got from there.

2. *Indian Historical Quarterly*, Vol. I, page 644.

3. *Visva Bharathi* of January 1926, page 368.

4. *The Dravidian Element in Indian Culture*, p 19. *Tamilian Antiquary* No. 8. On the distribution of races round about the Persian Gulf by Mr. J. A. Saldana.

Egyptians, helped by Hiram, the king of Tyre, and the Hebrew king, David, commenced their periodical commercial expeditions to Musiris.[1] Earlier still, Moses refers to the use in large quantities, for religious worship, of cinnamon and cassia, products peculiar to Malabar.[2] The gates of Carthage were made of sandalwood from the same country. The Indian teak was found in the ruins of Ur.[3] It must have reached there in the 4th millenium B. C. when it was the seaport of Babylon and the capital of the Sumerian kings. This particular tree grows in Southern India where it advances close to the Malabar coast and nowhere else.[4] The word Ur itself is the Tamil-Malayalam word Ūr, meaning a town.[5] " "Professor Elliot Smith reminds me", says Dr. Gilbert Slater, "the original form of the Mother Goddess in Egypt was the Divine cow, and that her worship was of extreme importance in Egypt from the 4th Millenium onwards." The adoration of the Mother Goddess and of cows are, so to say, the fundamentals of the Dravidian religion.[6] Again, the sacred Bull in Egypt and the Nimrods' Bull in Assyria find their Indian analogue in Siva's Bull, Nandi. The social institution of the Nāyars, an important branch of the Dravidians, are of the type that the very extant Egyptian literature depicts as there and then disappearing.[7] There is affinity in the scripts that were in use in the different centres. The Sumerian language survives in the script called cuneiform.

1. *Dravidian India*, p. 133.
2. *Malabar Quarterly Review*, Vol. III, pp. 74 *et seq.*
3. *Indian Shipping*, p. 85.
4. Ragozin's *Vedic India*, p. 305.
5. In Southern India, particularly in Malabar, there are several places whose names end in Ur. Chittur, Trichur, Cranganur are all towns in the State of Cochin, where there are many villages with Ur endings—Perumanur, Ariyannur, Pazhayannur, Kattur, Ollur, to name a few at random. (See *Madras Review*, Vol. I, p. 349.)
6. *The Dravidian Element in Indian Culture*, p. 109.
7. *Dravidian India*, p. 167.

The early Sumerian writing was also pictorial[1] and linear. A linear as well as a semi-pictorial form of writing was diffused in Crete at a very early period. The Phoenicians were familiar with the art of Sumerian writing which they modified in some ways. According to Dr. Burnell, the Indian alphabet came direct from Phoenicia.[2] His conclusion is that the South Asoka alphabet and the Vaṭṭeḷuṭṭu alphabet, the most ancient Tamil and almost the present Malayalam character, are derived from the same source.[3] Dr. Buhler says that the Hindu traders may have learnt the language from Mesopotamia.[4] Nicoli Conti speaks of the common use of palm leaves and iron pen for writing, and attributes the rounded style (Vaṭṭeḷuṭṭu) to these materials. Vaṭṭeḷuṭṭu is a modification of Kōle-eḷuṭṭu;[5] and the ancient chronicles preserved in the State Record Rooms and in the archives of aristocratic families in Malabar are written in this character. The Pandyans, it is noteworthy, seems to have got their alphabet from the Cheras.[6]

Orientalists, many of them, are prepared to concede that the Sumerians, the Mediterranean race, are branches

1. *A Sumerian Reading Book* by Mr. C. J. Gadd, Oxford University Press, pp. 8—9. The Sumerian writing was a pictorial system like the Egyptian hieroglyphics, even though obscured by the lineal style of writing. (Page 263 of Vol. I of Harmsworth's *History of the World*).

2. *Elements of South Indian Paleography*, p. 8.

3. *Madras Review*, Vol. I, p. 330.

4. *Indian Paleography*, Appendix to Vol. XXXIII of the *Indian Antiquary*, p. 16.

5. *Madras Manual of Administration* Vol. III, p. 462. Dr. Butler remarks that the letters of the old Indian alphabet are set up as straight as possible. (Vide p. 18 of the *Indian Paleography*). I think that is why they are termed Kole-eluttu (Kole=a stick, straight as a stick.) Perhaps this latter writing was in vogue before the use of the palm leaves and the iron pen. Before the palm leaves, bamboo splits were in use. Cochin state owns such records even now.

6. *Indian Antiquary*, Vol. XXII. p. 58. Dr. M. Collins has shown the existence of a Dravidic subtratums in the languages of North India (*Dravidian India*, p. 77).

of the early Dravidians. They also admit the antiquity of the Dravidian civilisation. Then, why do some of these state, without any qualifying clause even, that the Dravidians got their script from the Phoenicians? I venture to say that the level and the antiquity of culture are in favour of the former; at any rate, all that could be safely predicated is that it is difficult, at this distance of time, to decide who the lenders and who the borrowers were.[1] We shall stop here on this topic, and go on with the general subject.

I referred to the similarities in cultures of several places. The resemblance was so remarkable that scholars grounded it on the tradition that the Indian Ocean was once a continent, called Lemuria, which touched China, Africa, Australia and Comorin. There are vestiges of this culture even in America. Traces of Indian culture have been found in the Phillippines, and some scholars believe that the Maya culture of Central America has an Indo-Polynesian background.[2] In the old world, Mr. Wells writes in his History,[3] before 4000 or 5000 B. C., there were primitive civilisations not unlike this (Maya) civilisation, civilisations based upon a temple, having a vast quantity of blood sacrifices with an intensely astronomical priesthood. The diffusion of cultivated plants affords pregnant evidence of cultural connection. Tobacco, chillies, sweet potatoes, ground-nut, cashewnut, the guava, the papaw have all been introduced from the American continents;

1. The origin of Vatteluttu still remains an unsolved mystery. (*Mythic Society Journal*, Vol. VI, p. 171).

2. *History of India and Indonesian Art* by Dr. A. K. Coomaraswami, p. 156.

3. *History of the World*, by Mr. H. G. Wells, p. 48. It looks as if Mr. Wells is describing a Bhadrakali shrine of old Malabar. Why should I say old? Even now, specimens of this sort exist. See Volume III of the *History of Kerala*, p. 180. I remember to have read in an old number of an American Journal on Anthropology an article from Sir J. Johnstone in which he speaks of a tribe of Indians in the interior of South America, called Nairre, who have structures like Malabar temples.

but, as Mr. Richards puts it, the chain of transmission is so long that their evidentiary value is reduced to a minimum.[1] Not so in the case of China. To the commanding influence which Buddhism exerted over the destinies of China, recorded history bears eloquent testimony; and Buddhism went there from India. The number of Indian scholars who were taken there for teaching that religion and translating works allied to it is legion. China was known to its people as Fien Hsia. Another of its early names was Cathay. The name China Dr. Legge states it got from India through Buddhism. Nothing certain is known of the origin of the Chinese people. Some consider them to be descended from Accadians, relying among other evidence upon the similarity of the earliest Chinese writing to the cuneiform script.[2] Another alternative suggested is that

1. *Mythic Society's Journal*, Vol. VI, p. 163.

Indian maritime activities have to be correlated in due time with the culture developed in Oceania where, in distant New Zealand, traditions survive of a migration from Hawaiki, identified with India. (Page 158 of the Suppy. Vol. I of the *Ency. Britannica*.)

Strabo (A. D. 20) speaks of a hereditary caste in Arabia Felix with customs and practices similar to those of the people of Malabar. (*Malabar Quarterly Review* Vol. III, p. 76. *Christian College Mag*. Vol. V, p. 278.)

In his *Indo-European Folk-Tales and Greek Legends* Mr. W. R. Halliday speaks of the indebtedness of the West to the East and refers to a marked predominance of diffusion from the East of folklore.

2, See the chapter on China by Mr. Max Von Brandt in Vol. 2, beginning on page 709 of Harmsworth's *History of the World*. Canon Taylor in his work on the *Alphabet* shows that the old alphabets of Korea and Japan were of Indian origin. (II, 348 f). Also see Perry's *Children of the Sun*, p. 560. Mr. Von Brandt's remarks on China deserve a wide publicity: "Of the early empires of Western Asia, none survived the dawn of the Christian era. In the west, the civilisations of Greeks and Romans arose and crumbled........But, in the far east, there lives to-day an Empire, vast in extent, painfully populous, a civilisation complex, elaborate, artificial to a degree, and tracing back its unbroken history

the original home of the first emigrants into China was in the valley of the Tarim, where they may have come into contact with Accadian and Indian civilisation.

The worship of the ancestors, and the feudal form of early rule, which one of the ancient monarchs of China attempted to smother by a conflagration of books turn our thoughts to Dravida. It is even hinted that it is the Indian sea-trade with China or Cathay that entailed a chain of ports of call along the Malay Peninsula and the Indo-Chinese Archipelago, in both of which the art and architecture exhibit the profound influences of Dravidian civilisation.[1]

There is an idea abroad that it is not so much the trade but it is Buddhism which is responsible for the Hindu colonies to the east of India. Buddhistic faith, says an Indologist, became the one pure civilising influence in Java, Celebes and the adjacent islands, and also in Burma, Siam and Cambodia. From thence it was carried onwards along the sea-border to China, Korea and Japan.[2] For purposes of argument, I shall for the present grant this. But this will not militate against my contention. For the Jains and the Buddhas wandered to South India in great numbers for the propagation of their religion and in search of lonely haunts for the practice of meditation.[3] The kingdoms of Chera, Chōla and Paṇḍya were in diplomatic relation with Asoka.[4]

beyond the date at which the Hebrew historian fixed the Deluge ....A strange people—a stagnant people to western eyes—as the Chinaman lived in the days of Confucius, so he has lived for 5 times 500 years. So he lives to-day—in all essentials unchanged —apart. But the West is knocking at his gates."

1. Mr. Waddell on the *Sumerian Origin of the Egyptian Civilisation and Hieroglyphics*, p. 70.

Fa Hian speaks of going from Java to Canton with 200 Hindu traders on board. (*Indian Culture in Java and Sumatra* by Dr. B. R. Chatterji, D. Litt., Ph. D.)

2. *Visva Bharathi Quarterly* of 1926 April, p. 68;

3. *History of the Tamils*, p. 143.

4. *Mythic Society Journal*, Vol. VI, p. 165.

Buddhism had a long and glorious innings in Kerala. The Buddhistic Sanyasins went about preaching their religion, built viharas and spent a good portion of their time in curing diseases and spreading education among the people here. The Nayars took to the new faith with eagerness. "Under the kind care and tutelage of the Buddha Sanyasins, the Nayars attained a marvellous degree of scholarship and acuteness in all branches of Indian Sciences. They became religious teachers and preachers [1], and some attained fame as authors as well".

1. See the learned Introduction to *Rasa Vaiseshika Sutra* by Dr. K. Sankara Menon, M. A., L. T., Ph. D., No. 8 of the *Sri Vanchi Setu Lekshmi Series*, Travancore Government Press. Dr. Sankara Menon says 'Bhadanta Nagarjuna, the author of the work, must have been a Buddistic Sanyasin of Kerala, educated and trained by Buddhists. The word Bhadanta occurs in Varaha Mihira's Brahat Jataka......This appellation Bhadanta (= a man possessing white shining teeth. The Buddha Sanyasins are forbidden to chew betel.) is perhaps added to the name Nagarjuna to distinguish him from others who bore a similar or same name. Naga is a common name assumed by Nayars of Kerala. The popularity of the name may be due to the fact that the Nayars of Malabar who were of Dravidian origin were worshippers of Nagas (serpents). That the Nayars of Kerala went, in those ancient days, to such remote educational centres as Vijayanagar, Kashmere, Kasi, etc., can be borne out". It is an Indian monk Nagasena that is sent to China by the Kambujan King Jayavarma (484 A. D.). Re Nagas and Nayars, See pp. 29 and 77 of *Bhasha Sahithya Charithram* by Mr. R. Narayana Panikkar, B. A.

"എങ്കിലൊ അക്കടലുടയവർ നാകത്താന്മാരല്ലൊ ആകുന്നതു, അവൎക്കെല്ലാം ആദികാലത്തെ വരുണൻ ഒരു നൂററെട്ടു കാതം കൊണ്ടു തറമുഴവതും കൊടുത്തു എന്നു ചൊല്ലിയതു."

(ഒരു പുരാതന കേരളോല്പത്തി).

"കൈകത്തിടമെ (കഴുക്ക്) കരുവാനനാകത്താരെ
മെയ്ത്തിടമെ മെനി (അഴക്) യാന നാകത്താരെ
പൊയിത്തിടരെ (കള്ളന്മാരെ) പൊടിയാക്കും നാകത്താരെ
എത്തിരെയും പുകൾ കൊണ്ട നാകത്താരെ
ചിത്തി (സിദ്ധി) മുത്തി (മുക്തി) കൈ കണ്ട നാകത്താരെ

The worship of Gods in Temples was unknown to the vedic religion. The Hindus gradually copied this from the Buddhists who began to build viharas and set up images of Buddha in these for purposes of adoration and meditation. These viharas were also centres of learning, and there was a great university at Matilakam, near Cranganur, where at one time the Viḍval-Sabha [1] was presided over by Ilan-kō-Aḍigaḷ, the author of Śilappadhikārom,[2] and the brother of the great Chera ruler, Sem Kuttuvan. Ilan-ko-Adigal became a Buddhistic ascetic and lived in a Chaitya [3] near Matilakam.

The treatment that is in these days given to lunatics in Ṭiruviḍāi and to lepers in Ṭakaḷi temples in Travancore are reminiscent of Buddhistic times. For Hindu temples do not prescribe or dispense medicines.

But when Buddhism was on the wane, the viharas were converted into temples. Śāsṭha is a Sanscrit synonym for Buddha, and one meets with any number of temples dedicated to Sastha in Kerala, especially in

വില്ലാളി വിരരാന നാകത്താരെ
വിരുതു കെട്ടി പടൈ വെല്ലും നാകത്താരെ
പുല്ലനെ (പുല്ലുപോലെ) വെല്ലാം ഇറക്കം (ത്യജിക്കം) നാക
ത്താരെ

(ഒരു പഴയ പാട്ടു്)

1. The Assembly of the Wise, a sort of witenagemot, to direct studies, to enact laws and even to give the last word on political matters.

2. Manimekhala and Silappadhikaram are two of the Panchamahakavyas, five great epics, of the Tamil literature. The former is by Chittala Chattanar, a great friend of the author of the other work. It describes the circumstances under which the heroine, Manimekhala, the daughter of Kovilan, a rich merchant, renounced the world and took the vows of Buddhism. She comes to Matilakam, near Vanchi, to complete her studies and to worship Kannaki, her step-mother, whose image had been set up in the temple now well-known as the Cranganur Bhadrakali temple. The other kavya commemorates the lives of Kovilan and of Kannaki. See the writer's article on *Matilakam* in Dr. Law's *Historial Review*, Calcutta, Vol. V. p. 138.

3. Chaitya is from chita, a funeral pyre. These Chaityas gradually became places of worship like the graves of Mussalman Saints.

that line of hills to the east of the backwater system where the ancestors of the Nāyars lived.[1]

At the time of the religious revival in Malabar, Nayars accepted the Hindu faith with warmth and devotion; and to-day one will find in Malabar no more pious worshippers of the gods and goddesses of the Hindu Pantheon than the Nayars.

Thus, even if it be the faith and not the trade that carried the Indian culture to Java and other parts, the claim of the Dravidians need not become the less forceful. But I would still contend that it was the trade and the worldly gain and not the faith and the life beyond that made the Dravidians face the risk of voyages in unchartered seas.[2] No doubt, theirs was a peaceful penetration and gradual colonisation and, in latter days, a temple was one of the first steps in gaining their ends.[3]

Our earliest information about Java, writes a competent authority, can be traced to Indian traders. They gave the princes the power to enhance their revenues by trade. They had no small share in the work of political consolidation. Indian culture organised the

1. See the writer's article on the Kilirur Temple in the 1st No. of the 1st Vol. of the *Rama Varma Research Institute Bulletin.* Government Press, Cochin State. "At the time of the revival of Hinduism" says Dr. S. Menon in his Introduction to the *Rasa Vaiseshika Sutra* "many works of Buddhists were burnt and the Sanyasins had to leave Kerala with their works in a body to avoid sharing a similar fate." Both *Keralolpathi* and *Kerala mahatmyam* speak of a severe contest between Buddhism and Brahminism for supremacy in Malabar (*Madras. Review* Vol. VI, p. 344.)

2. Mr. Keul Weule writes in Vol. IV, p. 1421-2 of the Harmsworth's *History of the World*—"All the nations which ventured out on to the Indian Ocean in times known to history were induced chiefly by commercial objects to make such voyages...... The magnet which chiefly attracted navigators into this ocean was the peninsula of India."

3. Page 28 of the *Hindv Colony of Cambodia* by P. N. Bose, M. A.

constitution, made laws and introduced writing, inscriptions and ruins; and the accounts of Fa Hian testify to these. Oldest traces of the Hindus have been found in West Java. There must have been a Kingdom in that part whose monarch was favourable to the new religion. It is possible that the Buddhists then appeared.[1]

The immigrants from India, continues the same writer, seemed completely to have assumed the lead in Sumatra and to have created a feudal kingdom quite in the Indian style.[2] Bāli and Borneo were profoundly influenced by the Indian culture.[3] Malayism is always predominant in the Philippines; and the key to the ancient ancestry of the Australians we find in the still existing trade of the Malays on the north coast of that continent.

Mr. Fournereau has collected the six names of the Indian colonies after the annals of Luang-Phrabang:[4]

(1) Yavanaḍēśa (north of the peninsula, comprising Me-Kong) with Chūḍañagari as capital;

(2) Champaḍeśa (land of Chams, south-east from Hui to sea) with Champāpuri (Annam) as capital;

1. See the Chapter on *The Islands of Malaysia and their Story* in the Harmsworth's *History of the World*, beginning on p. 406.

2. *Dravidian India*, p. 915.

3. *Ibid.* p. 919.

4. *The Indian Colony of Siam* by Mr. P. N. Bose, M. A.

Mr. J. Campbell says that Kera is the land of the Hittites. Some say that Syria is a Greek adaptation of Kera, Etruscan Kara, Japanese Kori (Korea), old Kars. Yet another set of people think that one can hear of the echo of Nayar in Navarese and Naharci, the Scythic Neuri, Nairi of the Assyrians, and the Nahanti, Navatl, or Niquirians of America. (*Report of the Travancore Jenmi-Kutiyan Committee*, presided over by Mr. Justice Raman Thampi, B. A., M. L., pages 46 and 62).

The similarity in the expression of the countenance of the Bengalis and the Nayars, in their custom and manners and in the development of their respective languages and literatures, is remarkable.

(3) Kambōjadēśa (whole of Cambōja or Cambodia with the gulf of Siam as limit);

(4) Śyāmadēśa (north-west—Siam up to Salonen);

(5) Rāmaṇyadēśa (Pegu and part of Burma);

(6) Malayadēśa (same position as now).

Indian contact with Indonesian lands may have been made centuries before the Christian era. Suvarṇabhūmi (Sumatra) is mentioned in the Jāṭakas, the Epics and the Mahāvamśa. Sugrīva refers to Jāva (Yavaḍwīpa) when he sends out searching parties in quest of Sīṭā.[1] Rulers with Indian names (Varma)[2] and using an Indian language are early met with in Champa, Cambodia, Sumatra and even Borneo.[3] Even in such a remote area as Vocanh in Annan, there is an inscription in an early South Indian script.[4] From a study of Maṇimēkhala it may be inferred that, before the Christian era, the Dravidians traded with the islands of Java, Sumatra and also Malaya.[5] An archaic Tamil inscription in Siam tells how the Indian merchants used to go to trade and settle down there in early days. Reference is made in that to Nārāṇam, a Viṣhnu temple, as the refuge of the members of Maṇigrāmam and of the members of the detachment and of the bowmen.[6]

1. *Indian Culture in Java and Sumatra* by Dr. B. R. Chatterji.

2. The term Varma occurs in the names of all the male members of the Ruling Family of Cochin.

3. *History of India and Indonesian Art*, p. 156.

4. *Ibid.* p. 195.

In old Siam, a great literary monk is called Nankitti. It may be a variant of Nanukkutti, a very common name among Nayars. This supposition gains strength when it is remembered that his monastery was called Panasarama, a garden of jack trees. This variety of trees is invariably found in every garden of a Nayar's house.

5. *Sen Tamil*, Vol. 5, p. 419.

6. *Indian Colony of Siam* by P. N. Bose, M. A.

Maṇigrāmam is a seat of the early trading community in Cochin; and Anchuvaṇṇam, an ancient Jewish settlement there, and Maṇigrāmam are mentioned in some old copper-plates. The Takopa inscription in Siam leaves the construction of a temple tank there to the custody of a committee of people known by the name of Sēnāmukham, Maṇigrāmam and Chāppattār. The first of these words perhaps refers to the leaders of the army, while the last word is peculiar to Malabar, and means a class of people who have pledged themselves to the king's cause ; men who have undertaken to die (Malayalam: Chāvaan ēttavar) for their king.[1]

Professor Bloch says that the South Dravidian is the vehicle of an old civilisation. That general remark is borne out by facts. Mr. Pūrṇalingam in his sketch of the Tamil literature states that a corrupt form of Tamil was current in Java, Sumatra and other isles of the Indian Archipelago. All the Alphabets of Cambuja up to the time of Yaśōvarma have been unmistakeably of the South Indian type.[2]

So also the art and architecture of Indo-China and Malayan Archipelago.[3] According to the opinion of accepted authorities, there are many features in the temples that are distinctly Dravidian. The pyramidal

1. From an article on *Evidences of South Indian Culture in Indonesia* by Professor S. V. Viswanath, M. A., in *India and the World*, a Journal edited by Dr. Kalidas Nag, M. A., D. Litt., of Calcutta, Vol. II, p. 76. Lands free of tax used to be given to the families of the Chavettu Panikkars in Cochin. Even now the writer knows of a family who still owns such lands. See also the *Book of Durate Barbosa* Vol. II, p. 48.

2. *Indian Cultural Influence in Cambodia* by Dr. B. R. Chatterji, D. Litt., Ph. D., p. 109.

3. *Art of India and Java* by Dr. Vogel in *Influences of Indian Art*, p. 69. Ferguson, Vol. I, p. 310. *Indian Colony of Siam*, by Mr. P. N. Bose, M. A. In a recent lecture by Countess de Coral-Remusat on *Indian Influences in the Architecture and Decoration of Khemer Temples*", she has fully shown that the art and architecture of ancient Cambodia are largely derived from those of India. (The Hindu of June 26, 1933, p. 6).

character, the profusion of external ornaments in high relief, the edifices akin to the South Indian gōpura, the vimāna, the spirit of toleration indicated by the pictures and sculptures, may be cited to illustrate and to fortify the contention. The temple at Borobudur, which is built on the plan of the Chakra, an instrument most prevelant in connection with the Ḍēvi worship in Malabar, is another instance in point.[1]

The worship of Śiva and the Mother Goddess which commonly prevailed in those parts confirms the Dravidian contact. One of the ports of South Annan, Nhantrang, is towered above by a brick shrine dedicated to Bhagavaṭi.[2] The word Chaṇḍi occurs in almost all the temple structures in Java, indicative of the influence of the non-Aryan Kāli worship. The presence of the caste system, the inheritance in the female line, and the belief in magic points to the same direction. The caste system and the worship of Kāli, Śiva, Vishṇu, Pārvaṭi, Subrahmaṇia and Gaṇēśa are of Dravidian origin. Even now the system of caste is powerful in South India, particularly in Kērala. Luxury, the use of magic, superior architectural skill, and the ability to restore the dead to life, the Sanscrit writings ascribe to Dravidian Daityas.[3] I believe I need not stress this aspect of the question further. I shall, therefore, devote the rest of this paper to consider who among the old South Indians were mostly responsible for the diffusion of the Dravidian Culture.

Mention is made of the Kēralas in the Mahābhāraṭa and the Rāmāyaṇa and also in the Vāyu, Maṭsya and Mārkaṇḍēya Purāṇas.[4] At the dawn of history in Southern India, we see the Chōla, the Kērala and the

1. Professor S. V. Viswanathan, M. A., in *Indian and the World*, p. 159 *et seq.*

2. *Hindu Kingdoms in Hindu China* by Professor L. Finot, Vol. I, p. 603.

3. *The Dravidian Element in Indian Culture*, pp. 50—54.

4. *Malabar Quarterly Review*, Vol. II, p. 11.

Pāṇḍyan Kingdoms sharing the country among them. The Chēra or the Kērala Kingdom had as high an antiquity as the Pandya and Chola States.[1] Megasthenes has left us a descriptive account of these three kingdoms. He refers to Naroe, by which term he calls the Nayars.[2] In the Asoka Edict, Kerala is mentioned not as a subjugated territory but as a *Pratyanta*, bordering country.

Certain areas of the world, remarks Mr. Richards in his paper on the *Dravidian Problem*, are blessed with certain products that are wanted elsewhere. Of these the pepper of Malabar is a sample, and in a sense the History of Europe is the History of the Malabar pepper trade. The Trade and the Trade Routes have continued for milleniums, all that changes is the traders.[3]

Malabar coast afforded one of the most convenient landing places for ships; and Musiris, described by Pliny as *primum emporium Indiae*[4], was one of the famous emporiums much frequented by foreign merchants. It is the Muziris of the Greek geographers, the Muchiri of the Tamil poets and the Kodungallūr (Cranganoor) of modern days. The Egyptians, the Phoenecians, the Greeks and the Romans came to Cranganoor for commercial purposes. The Jews, the Muslims and

1. *Dravidian India*, p. 186.

Dr. Sewell on p. 1 of his *Sketch of South Indian Dynasties* states that these kingdoms were in existence as early as the 4th century B. C. Among certain western savants there is a tendency to modernise everything Indian. Limurike or Damurike has been shown by Dr. Caldwell to represent Dravida or the Tamil-Malayalam Country. (*Malabar Quarterly Review*, Vol. II, p. 12).

2. *Ancient India*, as described by Megasthenes, by Mc Crindle, p. 146.

3. *Mythic Society Journal*, Vol. VI, p. 161,

4. *Malabar Quarterly Review*, p. 352.

Ma Huan (1409) is the first to refer to Cochin. Nicolo Conti (1440) followed him, a century after the formation of the Cochin Harbour,

the Christians alike claim it as their first settlement.[1]

This tract of land, known as Kerala, with *Malaya Parvata* on the one side and *Paschima Sagara* on the

1. There was a Grecian colony of Byzantium on the Malabar coast, while the Romans had in Cranganoor a force of about 2,000 men to protect their trade. There was a temple there erected in honour of Agustus. (*Dravidian India*, pp. 140—1).

Pepper, cassia, sandal-wood, teak, ivory, and gold were exported from there. (*Dravidian India*, p. 143).

Hebrew *Tuki* is the old Tamil-Malayalam *Tokai*. (Dr. Caldwell's *Comparative Grammar of the Dravidian Languages*). So also Hebrew *Ahalim* is Tamil Malayalam *Akil*. The *Algum* tree of Hiram's shipmen, according to Professor Max Muller, is *Valguka*, sandal-wood, which is found chiefly in Malabar. (*Science of Language*, Vol. I, p. 232). Greek *Oryza* (rice) is Tamil-Malayalam *Arisi*, *Ari*; Greek *pepperi* is similarly *pippal* (Dr. Oppert on the *Ancient Commerce of India* p. 37); while the Greek *Zingiber* is *Inchi* (ginger). (*Madras Review*, Vol. I, p. 336). Mr. Warington writes that South India supplies of Rome were sent from Musiris and Nelcyuda (Nilkanda, that is Kallada, near Quilon). Aromatics and spices were the chief plant-products from South India to Rome. Pepper was called *Yavanapriya*, dear to the Romans. It was to them more important than salt or sugar. He refers to an Indian remedy made of pepper, and also to the uses of the gingelly oil and of teak wood of Malabar. (*Commerce between the Roman Empire and India*, see pp. 163, 182, 206, 213 and 214).

Drs. Burnell, Caldwell and Gundert have identified Musiris with Kodungallur (Cranganore), and the doubt now seems to be settled by a consensus of opinion of orientalists of all shades of views. (*Madras Review*, Vol. I, p. 338). Pliny's warning that Musiris port is infested by pirates did not affect the trade or the immigrants. The piratical character of the early Malayalis was notorious. Who knows it may be that the daring engendered by that sort of hazardous and strenuous life that nerved them to go far and to found colonies. (*History of Kerala*, Vol. III, p. 181).

Regularity of monsoons in the Indian Ocean gave impetus to the Roman trade. Hippalos found this and ships began to sail direct to the port of the Musiris. (*Dravidian India*, p. 117). Dr. Oppert, however, considers that Hippalos simply rediscovered the south-west monsoon, which, he says, was known to the Phoenecians. (*Ancient Commerce of India*, p. 28).

other, evolved a culture, unique in its own way.

Almost every ancient civilisation will be found to be bottomed in a river. Here we have the Periyār. The very first river mentioned by Ptolemy in Sera (Chēra, Kērala) country (called by him Dymirike) is the Pseudostomos (false mouth), because the Periyar does not enter the sea direct but loses itself in the back-water, very near Musiris. *Agam* and *Purananuru* sing of the beautiful ships of the yavanas disturbing the white foam of the fair Periyar of the Seralas.[1]

Nāyars and the Nampūṭiris are the two classes of

1. P. 360 of Dr. S. K. Ayyangar's *Some Contributions of South India to Dravidian Culture.* Agam, 149, ll. 7—12. Purananuru, 343, ll. 1—10 Agam describes a Karur town. In the *Keralotpathy*, Karoor is mentioned as the capital of one of the Cheraman Perumals. In the copper-plate of Bhaskara Ravi Varma, Kodungallur is called Makotaipattanam, and this is stated to be the capital of the Cheraman Perumals. The Rev. W. Taylor rightfully assures us that "the Sera Metrapolis was no other than Tiruvanchi, the capital of the Sera Desam, according to manuscripts; and all known traditions, early records and inscriptions point to Tiruvanchikulam, adjacent to Kodungallur, as the capital of the Perumals. (*Oriental Mss.* Preface, p. 13). 'Thiru' only means sacred, and will be seen prefixed to many words. These considerations lead us to look for the ancient site of Karur somewhere near the modern towns of Cranganur and Thiruvanchikulam. (*Madras Review*, pp. 341—2). And we have such a place, in a little interior and elevated locality, called Karurpatanna, now called Karupatanna. Ptolemy calls it *Karoura bassileon Kerabothron*, Karoura the royal seat of Kerabothras (Keralaputra), and places it, as it is even now, near the West Coast on a river flowing into the sea not far from Musiris. (Mc Crindle's *Ptolemy*, pp. 52-53. *Madras Review*, Vol. I, pp. 341 and 351.)

Kunhi Kuttan Tampuran says that the word Namputiri is from the Dravidian root Nampuka=to think, to believe. (*Keralam* p. 9, sl. 30.)

people who are the most early to be seen in Kerala.[1] If one look at them from the points of view of physiogonomy and anthropometry, they look alike.[2] Originally, they were all classed as Kshetryas, and as descendants of Ḍuṣhyanṭa. To a rule of Pāṇini, which Kāṭyāyana thought was not comprehensive enough, he appended supplementary rules about words common to Kṣhetrya tribes, including the Kēraḷas.[3] It is likely that, in later times, those families who took to the study of the vedas became gradually separated from those who took to the arms.[4] Nayars were recognised

1. A good way, long after them, came the other races. Still later, that is, within the period of modern history, came the East Coast Brahmans. Many of them, no doubt, came for trade; but, in the first instance, I am led to believe, they came, some by invitation and others otherwise, to teach Sastras and music in the families of Chiefs and in aristocratic Tarawads. That is how, I suppose, they came to be called Pattars. Bhatta means a learned man. As the letter corresponding to the sound of *ba* is absent in Tamil, *pa* took its place; *ar* is only an honorific suffix —hence Pattar. For analogy, see Pattathanam for Bhattasthanam.

The Ruler of the Cochin State makes, at stated times, presents of purses of money to learned Brahmans who have attained Battasthanam, the position of Bhattas. It is called the Batta sthanam ceremony. Now it goes by the name of Pattathanam.

The first outstanding person we hear of among those who had come from the East Coast is Uddanda Sastri. His period can be correctly fixed. For he was a friend of Chennos Nambutiri to whose *Thanthra Samuchchayam* he contributed, as a bond of friendship, one slokam, descriptive of the bath after sacrifice, *avabhruta-snanam*. That work gives the Kali year of its composition which is 4528, which corresponds to M. E. 602 and A. D. 1427. (കല്യ[illegible]). (See the writer's Introduction to *Kokila-sandesam*).

2. *Jenmi-Kutiyan Committee Report* of the Travancore Government, pp. 52—3.

3. *History of the Tamils*, p. 136.

4. This process of differentiation went on even among the Namputiris and the Nayars. Those who learnt and practised the healing art became Moosads, who were placed in a grade below the Vedic Namputiris; still lower were placed the Moothathus, who officiated in Siva and other temples. Lower still, the

as Kshetryas within historic times.[1] Abbe Du Bois goes further and says that "Amongst those same people (Nayars) again is another class of people called Nambudiris."[2] Some scholars say that the Nampūṭiris and the Nāyars were Nāgas, and that the former first accepted the Aryan cult from the physical or spiritual descendants of Parasurama.[3]

Varthema (A. D. 1502) has recorded:—"The first class of pagans in Calicut are called Brahmans. The second are Naeri who are the same as gentlefolks among us, and they are obliged to bear sword and shield

Elayathus, because they officiated as priests among the Nayars. Similarly, we meet with gradations among the Nayars. The holy thread, a substitute for upaveetham, was never worn except at sacrifices. (See the article on the *Sacred Thread of the Hindus* in the 1923 July issue of the *Viswa-Bharathi*). When Dr. Tagore went to Java and other places, he found the Brahmins, without the holy thread, sitting up aloft and chanting vedic texts and ringing bells. (*Viswa-Bharathi* of January 1928, p. 329.)

The Aryans copied a lot from the Dravidians: For instances, the shaving of the head, leaving a top-knot, the tying of the thali as an important act of the marriage rite, and the wearing of a bit of thread dyed in turmeric. They are considered Dasyu rites (*History of the Tamils* p. 56). They have the whole Dravidian Pantheon. Gods and Goddesses and all as their own now.

1. *Pioneers in India* by Sir H. Johnstone, p. 143. Dr. Annie Besant and Bishop Leadbeater in their *Man—Whence, How and Whither* remarks: "Aryans called the Toltecs, whose philosophy they learned, Nagas (p. 272). Toltec is the third sub race and is of a rich red-brown colour. It is the most splendid and imperial race which long ruled the world (91). It was a warrior race, but its pure type never formed the lower classes anywhere (92). A splendid Toltec civilisation flourished in Egypt at a very remote time (198)."

2. *Hindu Manners and Customs*, Vol. I, p. 17.

3. *History of the Tamils*, p. 93. J. R. A. S. 1910, pp. 625—29. The importance of the sacredotal caste in Kerala began only from the time of Melathol Agnihotri, whose period may be to some extent ascertained by the chronogram (Kalisamkhya 127070) of the day he performed a great sacrifice—*Yejna-Sthanam Surakshya* (യജ്ഞസ്ഥാനംസുരക്ഷ്യം)—(379 A. D.) (*Zamorin's College Magazine*, Vol. V, p. 52).

or bows or lances." Barbosa (A. D. 1516) wrote:—"In these Kingdoms of Malabar, there is another sect of people called the Nayars who are the gentry who have no other duty than to carry on war, and they continually carry their arms with them, which are swords, bows, arrows, bucklers and lances." Ma Huan, a Chinese Muhammadan traveller in the beginning of the 15th century, observed:—"The Nayars rank with the King". [1] Mr. Logan, in the Introduction to his *Malabar Manual*, has remarked:—"I would specially call attention to the central point of interest, as I look at it, in any descriptive and historical account of the Malayāli race—the position, namely, which was occupied centuries on centuries by the Nayar caste in the civil and military organisation of the province. Their functions in the body politic have been tersely described as the eye, the hand and the order". [2] The position of the Nāyars in spiritual matters is evidenced by the prominent part they played in the establishment and management of temples. An inscription on a stone wall of the Ḍwāraka Emperumāl Kōil at Śuchīndram, dated 400 M. E. (A. D. 825), speaks of Pallikkal Nayar as the Śrīkāryakāran of the temple. [3] If the chronicles of ancient Malabar temples are ransacked, it will be found that many of them were either owned or managed by the Nayars. [4]

1. *Royal Asiatic Society's Journal* of April 1896; *Malabar Quarterly Review*, Vol. IV, p. 319.

2. Travancore *Census Report* of 1931, p. 376.

3. *Dravidian India*, p. 376. For other instances, see p. 337 of Volume III of the *History of Kerala*. See also Chattampi Swami's *Pracheena Malayalam*, Chaps. V, VI and VIII.

4. See the writer's article on *Matilakam*, Calcutta *Historical Review*, Vol. V, p. 138. The Editor's Ernakulam *Kshetramahatmyam*; the *Avarodham Grandhavari* of the Kootalmanickam Temple at Irinjalakuda, Chronicles of Vycome, Ambalapuzha, Trivandrum and Suchindrum temples will tell a similar tale.

See the writer's article on a *Desavazhi* on pp. 177—82 of the *All-Kerala Literary Parishat Magazine*, Vol. I, wherein is also given the present state of the attenuated lineaments of a republican village Government of old as it still exists in the Cochin State.

"Smritis permit only marriages in which the wife is one grade below the husband. There are texts in Manu forbidding the marriage of a Brahman and a Sudra woman. In Kerala, Namputiris have been from ancient times marrying Nayar women. Even now, under certain circumstances, they also interdine with the Nayars. During the period of pollution caused by child-birth, Namputhiri women can eat the food served by Nayar woman. In the face of such evidence it seems to be a travesty of facts to include Nayars in the traditional Sudra caste." [1]

Among the distinctive features of the ancient Nāyars, as different from the other Dravidian races, may be mentioned, by way of illustration, their inheritance through females, the absence of the kingly element in the early stages of their society, their worship of Ḍurga, the Mother Goddess, and of the ancestors and Nāgas and their excellence in magic, medicine and architecture.

As Mr. Richards remarks in his valuable contribution to the Dravidian Problem, Mr. Hartland, without embarking on the stormy waters of Primitive Promiscuity, has, in his work on *Primitive Paternity*, given us safe anchorage to the right understanding of the mother kinship. [2]

In his view, marriage was matrilocal before it became patrilocal. At first, the husband's visits were surreptitious; then, his open presence was tolerated, and was permitted to reside occasionally in the wife's house and to take her at times to his family residence. Next, the husband was allowed to take home his wife on condition that she should be sent back for her first confinement. In the last stage of all, the husband is allowed to retain his wife in his own house permanently.

1 Rao Sahib N. Kunjan Pillai, M. A., B. Sc., Ph. D., in the above Travancore *Census Report* of his, p. 377.

2. *Mythic Society Journal*, Vol. VI, pp. 191—2.

He has produced ample evidence to prove this theory. Mr. C. Gopalan Nayar supports him in his able monograph on Wynad. I am sure every knowing Nayar will echo the sentiments of Mr. Hartland. Only in Kerala, the system of Marumakkathāyam was accentuated by the military life of most of the males. [1]

Magic, sorcery and even witchcraft were prevalent in Ancient Kerala. [2] There are even now articles of personal adornment among the Malayalis as protectives against evil influences; and there are families, members of which are regarded as adepts in the performance of magic rites and in the art of exorcism.

Kerala has made solid contributions to the science and practice of *Tachu Sastra* (architecture). Ancient temples and particularly certain Kūṭṭampalams (theatres) exist as finished products of indigenous sculpture and architecture.

The system of Āyurvēḍa as practised in Kerala, says Dr. Sankara Menon, bears the distinct impress of the country. Its growth there stands unrivalled. In a country where war formed part of its political life, it is but natural that in massage, bone-setting and the treatment of cuts and dislocations the Kerala system is seldom excelled. It has also specialised in the treatment of elephants and poison cases.[3]

There are great works written by Malayalis, some of which are not yet published, on magic, medicine and architecture.

That a republican form of Government prevailed

1 *The Book of Durate Barbosa*, Vol. II, p. 45.

2. *Malabar Quarterly Review*, Vol. I, p. 193. *Dravidian Element in Indian Culture*, p. 117. Indian magic must be regarded as a special Dravidian contribution to Indian culture.

3. The Chapter on *Ayurveda* by Dr. K. Sankara Menon, M. A., Ph. D., till lately the Director of *Ayurveda* in Travancore, in the *Progress of Cochin*, p. 385.

in Kerala before monarchy set in, and that, even during the time of the Perumals and the early local rulers, feudalism prevailed there are facts that need not detain us to be detailed or documented.

In South India, Malabar was the head-quarters of the Ṅāgas. It is still the part where Ṅāga worship prevails on a large scale. [1] One of the progressive and highly educated castes of South India, says Dr. Gilbert Slater, is that of the Ṅāyars. In the gardens attached to their houses a cobra (Ṅāga) shrine is invariably found. The Ṅāga worship looks like an organised cult. [2] Some think that the top-knot of a Ṅāyar is symbolical of the serpents' hood.[3]

In the *Hindu Colony of Cambodia* [4] it is stated that, there in Cambodia, originally, there was the Hindu colony of Funan. The Matriarchal system

1. *History of the Tamils*, pp. 92—3.

2. *The Dravidian Element in Indian Culture*, p. 85. The late Kunhi Kuttan Tampuran identifies Nayars with Nagas. (The *Keralam*, pp. 5—6, Sls. 16 and 21). Some scholars think Nayar is from the Sanskrit Nayaka, a military commander, a chief, a leader.

3. *History of the Tamils*, pp. 92—93. There the same work remarks that the speech of Nagas was not Tamil, but it was possible for a Tamil man to master it (*Manimekkalai* XVI, ll. 60—61). The late Mr. T. A. Gopinath Rao, M. A., the author of a scholarly treatise on *Iconography*, (a brilliant Archaeologist and Epigraphist, and the late Superintendent of Archaeology in Travancore), used to come to the writer, now and again, with lists of words picked up in his readings of inscriptions. The ease with which he was supplied with their meanings at first surprised him. He would say that the words are old Tamil words. The writer would add that they are either current Malayalam or are commonly found in old Malayalam works. The late Mr. Seshagiri Prabhu, M. A., a great grammarian, called the parent language of Tamil and Malayalam Proto-Tamil, which he said was neither Tamil nor Malayalam. The *History of the Tamils* says (p. 250), "Early poems on which Agathyanar and Tolkappiyanar and other early grammarians based their researches and rules have perished."

4. By P. N. Bose, M. A., see p. 30.

prevailed there. The first Indian king of Funan married the daughter of a Ṅāga king. A famous race of men descended from him. Through the power of the Ṅāgas, the vast desert became a glorious land. The tradition of the Nāgi ancestors of the kings of Kamboja survived up to the 13th century. [1]

Dr. Chatterji also records in his *Indian Cultural Influence in Cambodia* that Pegu (Hamsāvaṭi) was founded by one who married the daughter of a magician by a Ṅāgi. A later king Jayavarma (484 A. D.) sends Ṅāgasēna the Indian monk to China. [2]

From the existence of numerous tanks and the representation of Ṅāgas in the sculptures of a temple in the capital of Jayavarma, Dr. Chatterji thinks it is probable that it is dedicated to an aquatic deity, very likely to the aforesaid Nāgi ancestress. [3] In Malabar, every temple, every house of note will have their tanks. His further statements about the place and its people only makes the similarity of the two countries all the more pronounced. Ancestor-worship and the worship of the gods in Cambodia are found combined together. [4]

1. *Indian Cultural Influence in Cambodia* by Dr. A. R. Chatterji, Ph. D., D. Litt.

2. On the subject of the Nagas, please see the *Jenmi-Kudiyan Committee Report* of Travancore, p. 22 *et seq.* Agastya is a grandson of Brahma, a son of Pulastya, a brother of Visravas, and an uncle of Ravana and Kubera. He is said to have settled on the Malaya Hill, near Cape Comorin. It is said that it was because of his seafaring habits (for he seems to have gone to Java, Sumatra, Cambodia, Siam and other parts where he is even now worshipped) that he came to be called the *Pitasagara*. Is it because of his Naga connection and sea-voyages that he took his habitat in the south? The tradition is that he could not go to the north lest Vindhyan will raise his height and grow as of old, thus giving a decent explanation for his excommunication from among his Aryan brothers!.

3. Page 87 of the *Indian Cultural Influence in Cambodia*.

4. Vide p. 103. On the same page, the practice of Brahmins marrying Kshetrya Princesses is referred to, a practice peculiar to Malabar.

The common people there did not dare use tiles for the roofs which were thatched. Every one has his or her hair tied up in a knot.... They have only a loin cloth, but when they go out, they use a scarf.[1]

In the other Hindu colonies also, one met with the worship of the ancestors, of the Mother Goddess, of the phallus, of the hereditary caste and of the wealth going to the female line. Siva temples abounded, Tantric form of rituals was common, and the word Chaṇḍi occurs in almost all the names of temple structures in Java.[2] The style of architecture too is distinctly South Indian. Even in sports and pastimes, one finds similarity between Kerala and the Hindu Colonies. The Kaṭhakaḷi is an indigenous form of the dramatic art in Kerala. It is a dumb-show, and the actors have to learn an elaborate system of *Mudras* (signs). They have also to undergo a rigorous course of physical training. The dresses are gorgeous, but there are no scenic divisions..... 3

In Jav̤a, Siam, Bali and other places we meet with this sort of dramatic performances. As in Malabar, even permanent troupes are maintained for this by courts. A spiritual and cultural value is attached to these. Closely attached to this theatre is the ritualistic dance in temples. Balinese and Javanese dances are like the Mōhiniyāṭṭam of Malabar. There are pastimes

1. *Indian Cultural Influence in Cambodia*, p. 228.

In ancient times, the people in Malabar had to get the leave of their Chiefs or rulers to tile their houses. As a rule, they were only thatched.

2. For authority, the writer invites the attention of the readers to the works on Hindu Colonies already referred to.

In the Buddhapada of Sukhodaya in Siam, it is noteworthy that, in the centre of the padas, are two chakras, each with 6 circles and 108 signs. These numbers are significant and shall be referred to when Samghams are remarked upon.

3. Professor T. C. Sankara Menon's paper on *Sports and Pastimes* in the *Progress of Cochin*, pp. 342-3.

Indo and Indonesian Art, pp. 180 and 211-2.

in the Malayasian isles that correspond to our Pāva-Kaḷi (puppet-play) and the Ōlappākūṭṭu. There too, as here, a spiritual significance is attached to these. Curiously enough, even our Blāvēli reading exists in their Yama-paṭa (Javanese *Wayang Beber*). This is a special kind of painting, depicting the reward of good and bad deeds. It is executed on scrolls of canvas. The performer points to the different pictures as he narrates the stories in the form of an explanatory monologue. [1]

Though a military race, the lives of the Nayars, from start to finish, seem to be invested by religion. From birth to death, every act and rite of theirs is touched by it. When they settled down and began to till and toil for livelihood, a part of the barn, kaḷam, was set apart for worship and was called kaḷari. [2] When the necessity for common shrines for the community, settled in different centres, was felt, these were established, and were called Kāvus, [2] where Nayars

1. *Dravidian India*, p. 89. Originally, the painting may have been done on elk's leather (*Milav*), and so *Mlaveli* and then *Blaveli*. The presentation of such scrolls to Sadhus who will go about and give readings is regarded in Malabar even now as of high, spiritual virtue.

2. As the fencing-school was held in front of it, this also came to be called Kalari.

3. Kavu means a grove; a holy enclosure. For these shrines were originally made in shady groves. An inferior fane too then came to be called kavu, e. g., Sarpa-kavu, one for nagas or serpents. It is under these that of old the Tarayogams or Kara-yogams were held. The race of Nayars, warriors, were known as Lokar. They formed the State, the citizens par excellence. The others had no voice in tribal affairs. The Tara or Kara or village was the smallest territorial unit for administrative purposes. The affairs of the Tara was managed by its elders, who were called Taravazhies (cf-Natuvazhies, Desavazhis) which term was afterwards changed into Taravadis. A Taravad means an ancestral house of a landed proprietor; and a Taravadi means a decent member of an ancient, respectable family. Even now the meeting of the Nayar community of Kodungallur (called one less for a 1000—Onnu-Kuray-Ayiram-Yogam) is called *Nizhalil Irikkal*, a sitting in the shade, even though it is convened under the convenient roofs of tiled buildings.

(See also *Keralam*, p. 8, cl. 28).

themselves officiated as priests and where animal sacrifices were also usually conducted. The priests came to be called Kurups, Kurukkals, Uṇṇikal and Adikal. In the process of years, Kāli gradually became Kārṭṭyāyani and Pārvaṭi; Kuruṭi[1] took the place of blood-sacrifices, and Brahmins superseded Nayars as priests. Still the Nayars cling to their old beliefs. Every year, almost all well-to-do houses give offerings to their Dharma-Daivamgal, which comprise ancestors, serpents (ṅāgas), Ayyappan (Śāsṭha), Bhadrakāli or Ḍurgā-Bhagavaṭi and so on. In many families these are repeated on the celebration of the birthdays of their most senior male and female members and on other festive occasions. There are even now 108 Durgālayas in Malabar, temples (Kāvus) dedicated to Ḍurga. They have a history behind them.

In ancient times, Nayars, for purposes of military training and for facility of governance were divided into 18 Samghams.[2] A sangham was a military organisation. It had also a hand in the control of the country's management. For, it was the Naṭṭār, the people of the Nād, country, that administered it before the advent of the Perumals whose rule began in B. C. 113.[3] All complaints then had to be laid before the gate of the Kūṭṭam, (Kūṭṭam-vāṭukkal) which, to start with, was the Paṭakkoṭṭilil, the place where the military leaders of each of the 18 Samghams congregated. Subsequently, when the kings began to rule the land, the procedure was to lodge them at the gate of the palace

1. Water mixed with turmeric and lime, which then had a blood-like look. (See *Mythic Society Journal*, Vol. VI, pp. 173 and 175).

2. See the article on *Sanghams* by H. H. Appan Thampuran in the *All-Kerala Literary Parishat Magazine*, Vol. I, pp. 239—272.

3 See the Kali *Dudurdharam*, which denotes the kali year 2988, which corresponds to B. C. 113.

(Kōvilakaṭṭum-vāṭukkal), the residence of the rulers.

Each Samgham [1] had six systems of training. As the training was usually effected in the fencing-schools held in front of Kalaries [2], there came to be in Malabar 108 Kalaries, and 108 Ḍurgālayas. Every year there used to be held, in a central part of Kerala, Samghakkali [3], a tournament of the experts of the different schools in which the combatants exhibited their skill and courage in movements and in arms. On these occasions, national sports of other sorts and burlesque of various kinds were also presented. The

1. The Tamil Samgham was first started in imitation of a Dravida Samgha. The name Samgha was also given to royal Durbars of ancient times. (*History of the Tamils*, p. 251). This same work does not seem to favour the existence of Tamil Samghams or academies that acted as censors. For, it says, on p. 233, "Nor can we believe that men of different parts of Tamil India, from Musiri to Mylapore, living under Kings warring with one another, could be summoned at the fait of a Madura King and sit, we are not told, how often in the year, in judgment over the works of poets, most of them short odes, a few lines long. The Jaina and Buddha Samghas are bodies of ascetics or religious followers who lived in monasteries and followed a strict code of laws, and practised yogic exercises."

1. See *History of Kerala*, Vol. III, p. 344.

2. Samghakkali, has passed through the names of yathrakkali, Panakali, Sastrakkali and so on.

Its evolution in names and in practices will, so to say, also show the gradual ascendancy which Namputiris gained over Nayars in temporal and spiritual matters. The Pana for the Durghabhagavati is seen superseded by the mysterious recitation of a Vedic text, and the local chief of a Kaimal is being made the butt-end of much clumsy ridicule. No wonder. The old Patayani, a strict scientific military formation, has, in the words of the late Professor Sundaram Pillai, become the modern Pateyni, a disorderly march on Pooram or Vela nights, only to be an item of calculation with abkari renters. (*Sovereigns of Venad*, p. 5).

whole function was a national festival, beginning and ending with elaborate invocations to the Mother Goddess, their tutelary deity [1].

Kumāralayam,
Ernakulam;
29th June 1933.

T. K. KRISHNA MENON.

---

1. "The Dravidian Culture and its Diffusion" is a large subject. I have touched but its fringe. I had to do it here, because this work in general and this volume in particular deal with Kerala and an important branch of the Dravidian stock. My treatment I own has been desultory. But, even at the risk of being considered pedantic, I have given all relevant references, so as to facilitate the work of the scholars who may be making researches in this field; and, to avoid any accusation of a bias in favour of my country, I have used the very words of the authors from whose works I have quoted. I close my labours on this volume with a melancholy interest, as Mrs. K. P. Padmanabha Menon, who was, till the other day, warmly encouraging me in the editing of her husband's work has left her mortal coil. May her soul rest in Peace.

Visscher's
LETTERS FROM MALABAR.

LETTER XX.

Of the Nairs, or warrior caste of Malabar. Their families, occupations, mode of warfare, and numbers.

This letter shall be devoted to a minute account of the Nairs or warriors of Malabar [1], who attained much celebrity during the wars between the Zamorin and the Portuguese. They may be justly entitled born soldiers, as by the virtue of their descent they must always bear arms [2] They constitute the third and last of the honoured castes under the name of Sudras.[3]

Their ceremonies and observances coincide in a great measure with those of Chetriahs: like these they are allowed no lawful wives, and the children always belong to mother's family. Another point of resemblance between these castes is that their corpses are always burnt, a privilege which belongs exclusively to the higher castes ; the members of the inferior ones alone are interred. The ceremonies observed on the birth of a child resemble also in many points those of the Chetriahs. At the age of 12 years a Sudra child begins to learn the laws of his caste, and when he has attained his 16th he first takes up arms.[4]

The Sudras may be divided into two classes [5]: the nobles and the commons. The following are the noble families—Nambedi [6], Nambiar [7], Samandrá [8], Patitsjan [9], or Belerte Nairs, Bellalen or Bellares [10], Wellekoc Tallenairs [11], who are barbers and much esteemed, as they were privileged by Saneratojaar [12]

Intoductory Note Part	1.	On Malabar Castes	pp. 1—25.
Do ,,	2.	On Nambutiris	pp. 26—136.
Do ,,	3.	On Kshetriyas	pp. 136—144.
Do ,,	4.	The Antaralas	pp. 144—161.

1. Note 1, pp. 161—337.
   This is put in as Part V of the Introductory Note.
2. Note 2, pp. 338—342.
3. Note 3, p. 342.
4. Note 4, pp. 343—7.
5. Note 5, p. 347.
6. Note 6, pp. 347—8.
7. Note 7, pp. 348—9.
8. Note 8 pp. 349—352.
9. Note 9, p. 352.
10. Note 10, p. 353.
11. Note 11, p. 353.
12. Note 12, p. 353.

to assist the Brahmins at funeral ceremonies, Vellala Sudren[13], and Sudren. These all subsist on the produce of their own estates and carry on no trade, with the exception of bartering among each other.

Some of them are lords of their own territories, possessing royal power, but most of them merely hold their estates in fief [14] from their prince, whom they are bound to serve in war, and to protect his dominions, for which service they receive no pay, but are maintained when employed out of the country. They generally own Pulleahs, whom they have inherited with their property, and who cultivate the soil.

There are also several Nairs who are employed in constant attendance upon their Rajahs, whose retinue they form. These receive daily pay, more or less of the Rajah's pleasure ; it is well if they get as much as 3 stivers a day a piece [15].

Rasidoors, Governors of towns and provinces, and high Military officers are chosen from this class of Sudras, as they are superior in dignity to the second class.

These inferior Sudras are also Nairs or soldiers, bound to accompany the Rajah at his behest in war [16]; but in time of peace they maintain themselves by certain handicrafts and trades, to which they are called by their birth respectively. Thus there are the

Sakkiara [17]	Musicians in the Pagodas and at Court.
Poodewallen	who have the honour of handing betel to the Rajah.
Andoehellan [19]	Makers of pots and fans.
Tzomboe Kotty [20]	Bargain makers.
Toonen [21]	Tailors.
Noelchottin [22]	Cloth weavers.
Wilsiatte Nairs [23]	Oilmakers.
Jodache [24]	Ploughers.

13. Note 13, p. 354.
14. Note 14, pp. 354—9.
15. Note 15, pp. 359—61.
16. Note 16, p. 361.
17. Note 17, pp. 361—7.
18. Note 18, pp. 367—8.
19. Note 19, pp. 368—9.
20. Note 20, pp. 369—70.
21. Note 21, p. 370.
22. Note 22, p. 370.
23. Note 23, p. 370.
24. Note 24, p. 370.

Wallamneoers [25]	Fishermen
{ Ajari [26]	Carpenters.
Moesjari	Tinkers.
Tataan	Silversmiths.
Kollen	Blacksmiths-

The armies of Malabar are formed of these Sudras. They are expert in the use of arms, and set at nought the lower castes, who being unarmed are unable to protect themselves against their violence. The Pulleahs do not venture to approach them, and get out of their way to escape blows or perhaps wounds [27] for these heroes always carry a naked sword when they are abroad, and even in their houses they must have one at hand as a token of their dignity and office [28]: these weapons vary in form; they are generally straight with both edges sharp. They sometimes have a small weapon called a *Katjanel* [29] besides, which is fastened to the shoulder by a ribbon.

The weapons used in war are various [30]. The most common are swords with which they can do considerable execution, and large round shields made of leather prepared with many colours, resembling the ancient clypei. Sometimes the shields are covered with tiger skins, they are very light and the Nairs are adroit in the use of them. Some are armed with bows and arrows; these are chiefly inhabitants of the mountains. They have also pikemen; their pikes are very small and light, and they are quick in hurling them. They are all foot soldiers; knowing nothing of horsemanship. I have never seen a Malabar on horseback; not even do their princes possess seeds, and indeed they would be of no use in the low flat lands, where the ground is much broken and very marshy, and intersected with streams: and besides this, there are no beaten roads, the whole country being covered with bushes and underwood [31]. It often happens that our troops are obliged to march in single file, and if the natives at such times were wise and active enough they might easily annihilate our regiments by opposing their progress. [32]

Moreover there are few or no horses found here. There are a few of a puny species unfit for riding at Tengepatnam. The wealthy Moors import them from Arabia, and these animals fetch a high price.

25. Note 25, p. 370.
26. Note 26, pp. 370—3.
27. Note 27, pp. 373—81.
28. Note 28, pp. 381—2.
29. Note 29, p. 382.
30. Note 30, pp. 382—5.
31. Note 31, pp. 385.
32. Note 32, pp. 385—6.

The Rajahs keep elephants, which are captured in the mountains and are of immense size, but they are only used for hard work, and in war for transporting baggage. [33]

They have musketeers also among their troops, and they have a good notion of making the barrels of their muskets which they do not bore, but cast. [34] With these muskets they can reach nearly as far as we do with ours; but they are very heavy and their weight is increased by the ramrod being of iron. They take a very sure aim, and the first shot generally hits [35] and often inflicts great mischief, for the wounds are inflicted by the grape-shot of various shapes which they use instead of round bullets are very painful. Their muskets have one great fault, that it takes a long time to load them, so that. European foes, when they have stood the first fire can fall upon them while they are reloading. Besides this, they can never let off more than three volleys in succession, because when firing they place one of the finger nails between the eye and the nose, and by the time the third shot is discharged, all the skin is scratched off that part of the face. Like other barbarous nations [36] they possess but little military science. They do not know how to form ranks, and pay little heed to the commands of their officers. They fight in a confused manner without any order or concert, for which reason they cannot be incorporated into our regiments like the other Indian soldiers, but must form a separate Crops. We beheld in the late war, how much they were terrified by the pikemen of Balise and Java, who led by Europeans made such a furious onslaught upon these Nairs that they were thrown into the utmost confusion. They have another fatal custom, which has cost many lives; Every body slain in battle must immediately be taken away to be burnt, which creates great confusion, and the survivors lose heart at the sight of their comrades thus carried dead off the field.

Again they are ignorant of the science of beleaguering strongholds[37] and they have no materials for cannonading[38] bombs, grenades, and other instruments of war being unknown to them: therefore we have not much to fear from them in this respect, if our forts are but tolerably well protected. We have seen how Anjengo held out against them when almost entirely bereft of garrison. They are better at defending a fort or fortified village, constructed in their own fashion, than at open fight in

33. Note 33, p. 380.
34. Note 34, pp. 386—7
35. Note 35, pp 387—8
36. Note 36, pp. 388—95.
37. Note 37, pp 395—417.
38. Note 38, p. 417.

the field : for, when behind the shelter of their walls they can fire away at their ease through the gunholes, and we are obliged to keep out of range of their firelocks: but, after all, there is not much to fear from them, as they know so little how to handle them. The Rajah's endeavour to entice our men to act as officers of them[39], imagining that every European is well versed in military matters, though, may be, he has never seen a cannon fired.

I think it the wisest way in attacking their forts and paggers to make use of bombs, grenades, and combustibles, both because these missiles strike terror into them and because their fortified villages, being constructed generally of combustible matters (for the houses are built of dry palmyra leaves,) speedily catch fire and are consumed.

The wars which the Rajah's wage among themselves are not productive of much bloodshed.[40] A battle in which 20 lives were lost would be considered a very serious affair. The deaths in the course of a whole war often do not amount to that number, therefore these hostilities excite but little of our attention, though sometimes three or four Rajahs combine together against others. The principal mischief they cause is by hindering the transport of supplies, and very often the whole country is devastated and laid waste, the cattle driven away, and the miserable subjects sorely oppressed. There are sufficient reasons to account for this species of warfare, they possess no walled towns and very few fortified villages ; but all their places are unprotected [41] and open and their territories contiguous to each other, so that the injured party being the weakest in one quarter may be able to inflict reprisal on the aggressor by invading his domains in another.

The death of a Rajah or grandee in war tends to improve the condition of his party. for the enemy who has been the cause of his death must immediately quit the field, and pay a fine either in goods or lands to the family of the slain prince. [42] Thus the Rajah of Mangatti once killed three Parocse princes and was therefore obliged to resign a considerable piece of land. This law is of service in protecting the lives of these princes.

And now let us consider the numbers of these Nairs. According to Malabar calculation there are 3,000,000 of them in this country ; but this is incredible, for although many places are highly populated, we cannot believe that so small a track of land can contain so many hundred thousand, taking into consideration

39 Note 39, p: 418.
40. Note 40, p. 418.
41. Note 41, pp. 418—9.
42. Note 42, pp. 419—20.

besides the numbers of the other castes. But the Malabar Rajahs, like other Oriental monarchs, are fond of exaggerating their importance, and they boast of the number of Nairs and soldiers they have in their country and service, to impress us with the idea of their wealth and power[43].

LETTER XXI.

Account of the Chegos, and other low castes of Malabar.

The lower orders of Malabar are divided into several castes, differing considerably in rank and dignity[1]. We will first notice the Chegos [2] who came in very ancient times to this country, of which they may be reckoned, on account of their long habitation and similarity of religion, as natives. The tradition is that they came originally from Ceylon, where they belonged to the military caste, in consequence of the following circumstance. In the time of Cheramperoumal, a woman belonging to the caste of the washermen, whose house adjoined that of an Ajari (the carpenter caste), being occupied as usual in washing a cloth in water mixed with ashes (which is here used for soap), and having no one at hand to hold the other end of it, called to a young daughter of the Ajari, who was alone in the house, to assist her. The child, not knowing that this was an infringement of the laws of her caste, did as she was requested, and then went home. The washerwoman was emboldened by this affair to enter the Ajari's house a few days afterwards; and upon the latter demanding angrily how she dared to cross his threshold, the woman answered scornfully that he belonged now to the same caste as she did since his daughter had helped to hold her cloth. The Ajari, learning the disgrace that had befallen him, killed the washerwoman. Upon this, her friends complained to Cheramperoumal who espoused their cause and threatened the carpenters; whereupon the latter combined together to take refuge in Ceylon, where they were favourably received by the king of Candy, for whom the Malabars have great veneration. Cheramperoumal was placed in great embarrassment by their departure, having no one in his dominions who could build a house or make a spoon, and begged the king of Candy to send them back, promising to do them no injury. The Ajaris would not place entire confidence in these promises, but asked the king to send with them two Chegos and their wives, to witness Cheramperoumal's conduct towards them, and to protect them. The king granted their request, with the

43. Note 43, pp. 420—422.
1. Note 1, pp. 423—4.
2. Note 2, pp. 424—46.

stipulation that on all high occasions, such as weddings and deaths and other ceremonies, the Ajaris should bestow three measures of rice on each of these Chegos and their descendants, as a tribute for this protection; a custom which still exists. If the Ajari is too poor to afford the outlay, he is still obliged to present the requisite quantity of rice, which is then taken back, to him again; the privilege of the Chegos being thus maintained. From these two couples all the Chegos of Malabar are said to be descended.

This caste comes next below that of the Sudras, but is considered much less honourable. In times of civil war or rebellion the Chegos are bound to take up arms for the lawful sovereign; and some princes employ them as soldiers on other occasions, if they have not a sufficient force of Niars. Their principal occupation is that of drawing *toddy*, which is compulsory on their caste, this operation, as you know, is performed by cutting off the top of the cocoa-palm, and collecting in vessels the juice which exudes from it. The Chegos are sub-divided into two castes: the Chegos and the Twen Chegos.

Next to the Chegos are the *Coelagoeryp* [3], who make bows, arrows shields and other weapons of war, and the *Canniargoeryp*, [4], whose vocation is to teach the art of fencing and the use of weapons; with these we must reckon the *Coetady* [5] or trumpeters.

After these castes follow others still lower in rank, consisting of 1st, the *Cannianol* [6], who are astrologers; 2nd, the *Corwaas* [7] or exorcisers of evil spirit; 3rd the *Cuca Corwaas* [8], snake charmers and diviners; and 4th, the *Poenen Poeloon* [9], who accompany them with tambourines or small drums. These four castes are in some measure distinct, but resemble each other in their strict separation from other castes in their unsettled mode of life, wandering from place to abode and earning their livelihood by exorcisms, jugglery, snake-charming [10], etc., like the heathens in Europe: and in their independence, for they manage their own law suits, punish their own criminals, and are subject to no Prince or Rajah.

Another caste are the *Mocquaas* [11], who inhabit the seashores and subsist by fishing. We cannot wonder that many of

3. Note 3, pp. 446—7.
4. Note 4, pp. 447—8
5. Note 5, p. 448.
6. Note 6, pp. 448—455.
7. Note 7, p. 455.
8. Note 8, pp. 455—6.
9. Note 9, pp. 456—9.
10. Note 10, p. 460.
11. Note 11, pp 460—76.

them have become Romish Christians, as the Europeans have so much influence in those parts of the country.

The slave castes, the members of which belong to individual masters, are: 1st, the *Cannekaas*, who gather the cocoanuts; and 2nd, the *Bettoas*, who make saltpans and collect the salt: these two are the most honourable of the slave castes [12].

Then follow the Pulleahs, who are again sub-divided into several classes; the *Collamary* or smiths; the *Weltoe Carens*, the *Beltoe Pulleahs*, and the *Canna Pulleahs*, whose occupation is agriculture, sowing, planting and cutting the Nely, for which they receive, both from their proprietors and from strangers, one sheaf out of every ten they cut. There is a dispute between the Cannekaas and the the Pulleahs as to which is the higher caste [13], for there is room even among these miserable creatures for pride; the first maintaining that their caste ranks first, whilst the Pulleahs [14] aver that they enjoy more privileges, as for instance that they may employ barbers, and may wear a fillet on their heads and a long garment reaching to the knees, which the Cannekaas may not do.

The Pariahs [15] are divided into two castes; the *Canni Pariahs* and the *Asse Pariahs*. They are regarded as out-castes; their usual occupation is making rice winnows and baskets, and they are also cow-doctors, and have a right to flay the carcases of cows and to keep the hides for themselves. They are permitted to eat the flesh of cows that have died, and often devour it raw.

Besides these there are three jungle castes [16]: 1st, the *Oilare's* [17], who collect honey and wax in the jungles, where these articles are found in great abundance, and are brought down to the coast by merchants and thence exported to other countries. The Ollares wear no clothing, and regard the tiger as their uncle. When one of these animals dies, either naturally or by violence, they shave their beads in token of mourning, and eat no cooked food for three days; they may eat no flesh but that of animals which have been killed by tigers, so that the existence of these wild beasts is of great consequence to them.

The *Wedden*, [18] and the *Naiaddy* [19] are also bushmen who hunt wild beasts and subsist upon their flesh, as well as upon herbs,

12. Note 12, p. 476.
13. Note 13, pp. 476—7.
14. Note 14, pp. 477—512.
15. Note 15, pp. 512—523
16. Note 16, pp. 523—526.
17. Note 17, pp. 526—528.
18. Note 18, pp. 528—529.
19. Note 19, pp. 529—538.
Other Hill tribes p 538.

and roots; so that there are many among these three castes who have never tasted rice.

I have thus given you a brief account of the low castes, who come little if at all under the notice of us Europeans, and are therefore little thought of.

LETTER XXII.

Account of the Pattares and their privileges—of the Canarese, their manner of life, divisions of caste, nuptial and funeral ceremonies, and feasts: and of the Jogis.

The heathens or idolators of Malabar may be divided into two classes; the natives and the foreigners. The latter are of three descriptions[1]: (1) Those who visit the country for trading purposes, and sojourn in it for a long time, who are called *Pattares.* (2) Those who are settled in Malabar, called *Canarese.* (3) Those who merely travel through it, called *Jogis.*

The Pattares[2], who are many thousands in number, are Brahmins, dwelling among and beyond the mountain range. Their native country is the district round Tuticorin, Coromandel, Madura, Kotar and the neighbourhood. They hold themselves higher than the Malabar Brahmins and Namburies, who they say sprang from fishermen elevated to the Braminical dignity by Paroese Raman. The Pattares take no share in the Administration of Government in Malabar,[3] being regarded as foreigners, although they sometimes spend three or four years on this coast. Their occupation consists in trading, and the conveyance of commodities into the interior. They do not deal with the Company or other Europeans, but with the Canarese, Moors and Jews, whose goods they buy. They have erected factories for trading purposes[4] at Quilon, Kully Quilon, Cochin, Trichur, Ponnani and Calicut, where they possess also magazines.

The Rajahs of Malabar have granted certain commercial privileges to the Pattares.[5] The first is exemption, to a great degree, from customs; they pay only half the usual duty for the loads they carry on their heads, and nothing for those they carry on their backs, so that we generally see them laden with two packages. They are restricted however to such goods as they can carry themselves overland. Their second privilege is an allowance of food gratis at any Pagoda they visit, so long as they remain there: in return for this they are bound to sweep and clean the building when required. They enjoy the same privilege at the courts of several Rajahs where they appear in great numbers

1. Note 1, p. 602.
2. Note 2, pp 602—4.
3. Note 3, pp. 604—5.
4. Note 4, p. 605.
5. Note 5, pp. 605—6.

on festival days, and take the opportunity to eat voraciously; on these occasions they receive also a few fanams. Thirdly, the right of carrying their loads is confined to men of their own caste and nation, an arrangement by which many thousands of their poor are supported, no other race being allowed any share in their profits.

The Pattares are sub-divided into three castes[6], which differ but little in rank, though the respective members refuse to eat out of the same dish, or to intermarry with each other. They are called:—

Pandy	Tanlour	
Toele	Pattares or Choolia	Pattares.
Toelegen	Mockeramby	

Their customs resemble those of the Canarese and other Brahmins, of whom we will now speak.

The Canarese[7] who are permanently settled in Malabar, are the race best known to the Europeans; not only because the East India Company trade with them, and appoint one of their number to be their merchant, giving him the attendance of two Dutch soldiers; but also because from the shops of these people in the town we obtain all our household necessaries, except animal food. Some sell rice, others fruits, others various kinds of linen, and some again are money changers: so that there is hardly one who is not engaged in trade. For this purpose their dwellings are scattered all along the sea coast. They are much fairer than the natives of Malabar. The woman are good-looking, and wear a quantity of ornaments, such as gold chains, ear-rings and nose-rings set with precious stones or pearls, and bracelets; in addition to which there is generally a thick silver ring, on one foot, hanging over the ankle. Their hair is twisted in a roll on one side, and sometimes adorned with flowers; and they wear a veil of white linen or silk, thrown over their shoulder, and fastened in front to the dress, which is of the same material. The men are in general well made; they wear white linen tunics, which may either hang loose or are girded up; and like the women they wear rings on their hands and in their ears. The head is shaved, with the exception of a long tuft of hair on the crown which they twist together, and cover with a Roomal or band.

According to their own tradition, the Canarese came from a country called Kasti Bardy, lying in the high lands, between Goa and Bombay, and divided into twelve small provinces, from which they were driven in early times by the Moors or Moguls;

6. Note 6, pp. 606—609.
7. Note 7, pp. 607—608.

they then came down to Goa, and to the districts of Canara or the Concan, where great numbers of this race are found, and nhetce called Canarese [8]. The Portuguese have converted several of them to the Christian confession by violent means, tearing children from the arms of their parents in order to baptize them. As, however, under our Government no compulsion is permitted in matters of religion, we find no one now turn Romanist unless it may be one who has lost caste by the commission of some crime. They are attracted to Malabar for the sake of trade, which they first entered into with the Portuguese, and continue to carry on with the Dutch.

The Canarese in the Kingdom of Cochin live in the vicinity of our towns and forts,[9] but not inside them, for they look upon the Europeans as unclean, and will not eat or drink in our houses. They carry this feeling so far, that if they are shut up in the prisons of the East India Company, they will not touch any cooked food or rice, but only eat a little betel and cocoanuts, which are not reckoned as food; so it is the custom to allow them before sunset to go out of the town under the guard of the Serjeant of justice, that they may bathe and change their dress, and then eat the food their friends bring to them; for, like the Malabar Brahmins, it is against their laws to eat in the same clothing they wear in the town.

There are two classes of Canarese, the *Visnoumattes* and the *Schoumattes*,[10] but there is no more difference between them than there is between two strips of sandalwood. They say that Sancratchar [11] gave some petty laws to the Brahmins of his sect, called Schoumattes to distinguish them from the others; but the distinction is very trifling. Polygamy is forbidden among the Canarese as it is among other Brahmins; widowers may marry five times, but not more. They give their daughters in marriage[12] at the age of eight or nine years; for if they pass their tenth year unmarried, they lose caste, and are not allowed to marry. Parents consequently begin to look out for suitors for their daughters very early, and generally obtain for the purpose the services of their priests, who first sound the inclinations of the bridegroom and his father, and then propose the marriage to them. The feelings of the girls themselves are not taken into account at all, and they are much to be pitied, being driven into matrimony so young, with the dread of their tenth year hanging like a weight over them.

8. Note 8, pp. 610—613.
9. Note 9, pp. 613—614.
10. Note 10, pp. 614—618.
11. Note 11, pp. 618—628.
12. Note 12, p. 629.

When the parents of both parties have agreed together, the young man, accompanied by his friends, repairs to the house of the bride, where he stands before the door, and asks her parents:—" Will you give me your daughter". The answer is given in the affirmative; and then the bride's father takes the bride-groom by the hand, and leads him under a canopy raised before the door for the purpose, and there puts in his hands the money, gold and jewels assigned for his daughter's dowry. The bride-groom now enters the house, where a white linen sheet is stretched between him and the bride, so that they cannot see each other. The bride's father then says:—" My daughter's name is * * *, her parents are called * * * * and come from the province of * * *." If it happen that both parties belong to the same province, they must not marry, fellow provincials being regarded as brethren: if this is not the case, the marriage is lawful, the sheet is removed, and the bride-groom takes the bride by the hand, whilst the priest reads aloud to the newly wedded pair their conjugal duties. The bride is then exhibited to all the guests with her eyes closed and her arms folded, after which she and the bride-groom are seated together on the same bench; a fire is lighted, over which they take an oath to this effect.—" We will live as the Priest has bidden us, and as our parents have lived". Some women now appear and chant a song in honour of the couple, strewing on their heads uncooked rice, which among the rich is mixed with pearl-dust. The nuptial ceremonies last five days, during which time the custom is to place 3 cups, with small holes in them, in a tub of water; as the water runs into the cups, if they sink straight to the bottom, it is a good omen, but if they turn and fall on one side, it is the reverse. They have a way, however, of forcing a good omen out of a bad one, by repeating the experiment till the cups sink down rightly. The whole period of the nuptials is celebrated with great rejoicings, and dancing girls are hired to exhibit their skill. The guests are sprinkled with rose water, a great mark of respect among these people, and presented with flowers. On the sixth day they rest, and on the seventh the newly wedded pair bathe, and the ceremony is concluded.

When a first child is born,[13] they go through various enchantments to ascertain whether the aspect of the Heavens is favourable or not, from which they foretell the infant's future fortunes, the Canarese being, like all the Indian tribes, much addicted to astrology. The father and all his friends must then remain within doors for ten days; on the twelfth they name the child, and take it to the Pagoda to exhibit it before the idol, before which

13. Note 13. pp. 629—631

they do reverence. When the boys of this race attain their tenth year, the thread is hung round their neck with much solemnity, by which ceremony they are consecrated or set apart; the head is shaved at the same time, a tuft being left on the crown, which they must preserve all their lives as a mark of their dignity.

The Canarese, as we have said, maintain themselves by trade.[14] Children of six or seven years old are set to work at it, so that they grow up very sharp and cunning: they have notion of honesty, and no dependence can be placed on their word. If they want to obtain any thing from us, they will keep on asking for it in the most unbushing manner; but nothing can be got from them without the greatest trouble. They defer paying their debts as long as possible, in order to gain interest on the money in the meantime; and when reproached for their dishonesty do not take it amiss, but assent to all that is said, caring little for hard words. They are also very uncourteous; if any one visits their houses they will not even ask him to come in, and think it a great favour if they give him a cup of milk.

The Canarese are more numerous in the kingdom of Cochin than in other parts of Malabar. They dwell at a distance of about half a league from the town of Cochin possessing a bazaar, and shops of all kinds, which are usually closed during the day, whilst their owners are engaged in business in the town, and opened in the evening, when they exhibit their wares for the native purchasers. The women do not mix in trade, but occupy themselves in household cares. They are generally to be seen sitting in their doorways, gossiping together. If a European passes by, they take refuge inside the house but their heads are soon seen peeping out at him; they are not shy of talking with our women, but have very little idea of conversation. Their houses are congregated in clusters, members of the different castes living together.

The solemnities observed on occasions of death and burial are nearly alike among all races of Brahmins. When the Pandyt or physician has pronounced that there is no hope of life, the sick man makes his will, and bestows some presents on his daughters. The priest then comes, and enquires what heinous sins he has committed, exhorting him to repentance ; his head is shaved, and he is washed with cold water for the purifying of his soul, after which he distributes alms and presents the priest with a good milch cow, which he must hold by the tail till he dies. After his demise he next of kin must have their heads shaved and let their beards grow as a sign of mourning. The corpse is covered

14. Note 14. pp. 631—633.

with a white linen cloth, and carried out by four men to be burnt, all the nearest friends and neighbours following it and the eldest son leading the procession and carrying the fire destined to consume it. When the party reach the funeral pyre, which with the wealthy is generally made of sandal wood, the corpse is laid upon it and the son kindles the flame ; on the following day the ashes are collected and thrown into the river. The children of the deceased must remain at home for twelve days after the funeral, the eldest son or next of kin dressing half a measure of rice each day and making it into three balls, which, after they have been set on the ground, are thrown into the water tank to serve as food for the dead man. This ceremony is repeated every month. During these twelve days of the first mourning the survivors may only eat once in the day, and must abstain from betel chewing. the greatest of all penances for an Indian. On the first anniversary of the death they give a great feast in memory of the deceased which is repeated every year, but with less expense.

By the laws of the Canarese sons alone inherit [15] and that in equal shares; the daughters are entirely excluded, and must be content with their marriage portions and whatever their father may have given them in his life-time. Unmarried daughters or widows, however, must be supported by their brothers. If a man has no son, he adopts his brother's son, or any other male next of kin.

The Canarese are divided into several castes, which differ in rank and sanctity, but have similar customs. The Brahmins may follow no manual or commercial occupation, but this last restriction is but imperfectly observed. Most of them are priests, who are supported by the Rajahs or the other Canarese; some are pandyts or physicians. The castes of the Pannekour and the Wannia [16] trade in all things which have not had life. The Sonar [17] are silversmiths, many of whom imitate the workmanship of Europeans very skilfully. The Isuwede and the Curronby [18] carry the merchandize of the other Canarese, and labour in their gardens and farms. The Banda are soldiers; they are not found in Cochin, but are very numerous in Canara and other districts: the Portuguese make use of the services of those who have embraced Christianity.

The festivals of the Canarese [19] differ from those of the natives of Malabar, because among these heathens each nation

15. Note 15, p. 633.
16. Note 16, p. 633.
17. Note 17, pp. 633—34.
18. Note 18, p. 634.
19. Note 19, pp. 636—40

has separate tutelary deities in whose honour they hold special feasts. There are eleven of these festivals annually.

(1) The first is *Isamparocah* or New Year's day which is held in the month of March, when the days and nights are equal; at this season he Canarese make merry and wish each other joy, bathing with certain ceremonies and putting on new apparel; the priests announce, from their astrological observations, which will prove unluckly days in the ensuing year.

(2) *Tirunal* is solemnised in the month of April, when any one who chooses may go to the pagoda seven days in succession and receive food, which it is the business of the wealthy persons of their nation to provide. This feast is held in honour of the building of their Pagodas. At night lamps are lighted, and they make all kinds of rejoicing, and adorn the elephants belonging to the Pagodas with costly housings making their *Sombail* before them.

(2) The feast of *Mantjemy* is held in July in honour of the cobra capella to which they offer milk and sandalwood, placing them in the tree which the reptile inhabits.

(4) *Tzontam Pounon* is solemnised in August, when they wind round their necks a new thread, the token of their high caste; this service is performed for them (whilst they bend in reverence before the fire) by the priests, who receive some fanams in return.

(5) *Astamy* in the same month, is a day of penitence, when they abstain for food and drink for 24 hours, and implore forgiveness for their sins.

(6) *Wine Szoute*, a festival which lasts three or four days, is celebrated in September, in honour of their God Gonnipatti whose image they form at that season, of wood, stone, or silver, according to their means and piety. They affirm that this deity was born on a mountain, having four arms and the trunk of an elephant; and that they were divinely commanded to keep this festival in his honour.

(7) Ten days after this is kept *Tje Hordesje*, a feast of rejoicing for the fruits of the earth. It is celebrated in the pagodas, which are hung round with every species of fruit that can be procured; and, as in the Jewish feast of Tabernacles (at least as kept in this country), the worshippers erect in their villages booths of green palm leaves and suspend various fruits around them. This feast of the Canarese is attended by the Rajah of Cochin in person.

(8) *Mannemy*, the feast of the school children, is a sort of holiday to that class, when they are released from school for nine

days and go about the houses of the Canarese singing and dressed in their costliest attire: they sometimes enter the town on these occasions in their holiday trim.

(9) *Dewaly*, is a feast celebrated at the end of October in memory of an act of divine benevolence, by which they were delivered from a powerful giant called Nabakasser, who had put to death many persons in their country. On this occasion the people annoint themselves at night with oil, and bathe, and in the morning rub their bodies with powder ground from sandalwood; throughout the day they make great banquets, and at night illuminate the lamps all round.

(10) *Terou*, is the feast of pagodas, when their idol *Winke Tapati* is placed on a triumphal car and carried about in state. To assist in drawing this car is regarded as a mark of sanctity, and in some countries the people suffer themselves to be crushed under its wheels; here however they are wiser. The car is drawn on amidst shouting multitudes, to the sound of music and drums, some climbing upon it, others hanging to its sides like burrs, whilst others strew cocoanuts to be crushed under it; the Baya deres dancing around it all the time. This festival takes place at the end of November.

(11) In February is the feast of *Chigma* or Fortune. For ten days before it begins, drums are beaten every evening, and the people adorn themselves with flowers till the period of the full moon, when the festival commences, and is celebrated with great solemnity and many extravagances. Boats full of water colored with turmeric are placed in the bazaars, and the people plunge into them, or sprinkle themselves with the contents, and run about in troops with drummers and trumpeters; in the evening they have exhibitions of giants and giantesses, which are made to dance by persons placed inside them, or of ships, elephants and other works of art. In the meantime, the dancing girls exhibit their skill, the canarese joining in the dance; whilst others carry about long areca trees on their shoulders, running as if they were mad, the old and the idle hurrying about with them, and exhausting their small strength. These areca trees are wound round with *olas* and are finally burnt, in memory of the terrible giant *Kammetja Scressel* who was burnt by their deity.

So much for the festivals of the Canarese. They have a bishop who resides on the banks of the Ganges[20], and who takes a journey once in eleven or twelve years to visit his flock in distant

20. Note 20 pp. 640–42.

countries. He wears no splendid habiliments, but has only a cloth wound around him, a proof of sanctity in the eyes of these benighted people. They are bound, when he comes among them, to give him the tithe of their property, but I will not vouch for their conscientious performance of this duty, however, the bishop always returns laden with treasures to the banks of the Ganges, where he inhabits a large dwelling in which all the pilgrims who flock by thousands to that river receive food and lodging.

The third class of foreigners who are met with in Malabar are called *Jogis*.[21] It is a mistake to suppose that all the *Jogis* are Brahmins; they are composed of persons from various heathen nations who have bound themselves by a vow to wander about as pilgrims either for a term of years, or for their whole lives, gaining their livelihood by mendicancy. They pretend to a peculiar degree of holiness, and the more to impress this upon the people, and to work on their liberality, they wear the scantiest clothing, and disfigure themselves frightfully, covering themselves with ashes, and letting their hair and nails grow to an inordinate length, till they look like monsters. Some carry instruments of torture to castigate their persons, the more to mislead the poor people. They sit idle the whole day with no occupation but tobacco smoking: and when they want something to eat, they merely ask for it, having so little modesty that if it is not given them, they scold in the strongest terms, not sparing the Rajahs themselves. They will sometimes sit down before a man's door and refuse to stir till they have got what they want. I can believe that some may adopt this mode of life from a vain notion of religion, but there is no doubt that most of them are great rogues. European Jews and Christians are sometimes found among them, who join them for the sake of obtaining fine jewels, which are often bestowed on the Jogis by the superstitious people of Bengal, Coromandel, and Golconda: they then sell their acquisitions by stealth, and conceal the money in some secure place as they may not carry it about with them.

With these Jogis may be classed the fakirs, mussulman pillgrims who live in like manner by mendicancy, and in the Mogul kingdom are often the recipients of the splendid presents which are given to the monarch. This coast is annually visited by fakirs from the East Indian islands, on their way to Mecca and Medina, who generally return wearing dark grey cloaks they have received there, garments which are so highly venerated that all their fellow-mussulmans kiss them; and these black mahometans, many of whom look like thorough rogues, are held a great and learned men when they return to their homes.

21 Note 21, pp. 642—49.

NOTES ON

Visscher's LETTERS FROM MALABAR.

LETTER XX.

Introductory Notes. Having in his previous Letters given us an account of the Christians, Jews and Mahomedans inhabiting Malabar, our author proceeds in this to say something of the Hindu population; but, as he seems to confine himself to certain particular sections of the community, without giving us a comprehensive idea of the majority of Hindus inhabiting Malabar, we propose to say a few words here regarding the various sections that comprise the Hindu population of that part of Southern India.

The inhabitants of Malabar may broadly be divided into aborginies and settlers. Under the first head may be classed the Cheřumars, Veṭṭuvars, Pulayars, etc., who are agrestic slaves, and the jungle tribes, known as Kāḍars, Malayars, Pařiars, Kuřichyars, Kuřumbars, etc. Under the second head come the Nambūṭirīs, Nāyars and Ṭiers. The orthodox view in Malabar is that the graduated series of castes and professions that go to form modern Malabar society were brought into the country by Paraśu Rāma and planted there in their full growth. It is indeed unphilosophical to think of a society cropping up all at once in a barren soil, as if by the wave of a magical wand. Much more is it unphilosophical to think of such a society following at his bidding a man, though represented to be an incarnation of Viṣhṇu, to a foreign country leaving behind them their cherished hearths and homes. Such a theory, however acceptable in the eye of the orthodox believer, does not give scope to natural development.

That the various races now inhabiting Malabar are not indigenous to the country is more or less true. They are indeed colonists from foreign climes. But to hold that the whole fabric of Malabar society was by an effort of human exertion plucked by a single individual, root and branch, from its native soil and planted in its full growth in a strange land would be, at the very best, but chimerical. Successive settlements must have been made by immigrants from the north, who, in the onward rush of races, sought 'fresh fields and pastures new' at the extreme end of the Peninsula. It would be difficult at present to ascertain the order in which the various colonies arrived in Malabar.

According to the Jāṭi Nirṇṇaya, a poetical work in Sanskrit dealing with the various castes inhabiting Malabar, said to have been composed by Śankarāchārya, there are seventy-two castes in Kērala, not including the Kṣheṭriyās and Vaiśyās. Of Kṣheṭriyās, it is supposed that there are but few families absolutely pure. The Solar line is said to have become extinct, and of Lunar line there are a couple of houses or so alleged still to exist. The Vaiśyās are, like 'snakes in Iceland', a class that does not exist in Malabar. Barring these, the seventy-two existing castes are said to be made up in the following manner, *viz*:—

There are eight classes of Brāhmans, two classes of Nyūna Jāṭīs or "defective castes"; twelve classes of Anṭarāla Jāṭīs or "intermediate castes"; eighteen classes of Śūḍras; six classes of Śilpi or artisans; ten classes of Paṭiṭa Jāṭīs or "degraded castes", eight classes of Nīcha or "polluted" castes and eight classes of extra castes.

Most of the above have sub-divisions. Thus the eight classes of Brāhmans are divided into:—

(1) Ṭamprākal or Brāhman rulers and high priests.

(2) Āḍhyans—leaders of the aristocracy of Malabar, sacrificers and expounders of the Vēḍās.

(3) Viśiṣhṭa-Brāhmaṇan--distinguished Brāhmans noted for rank, learning and sanctity.

(4) Sāmānya-Brāhmaṇan—ordinary Brāhmans.

(5) Jāṭimāṭrēyan—Brāhman in name; one who is 'barely in the caste'.

(6) Sāmkēṭikan—those who once deserted Malabar but returned soon.

(7) Śāpagrasṭan— the accursed, because they doubted the divine nature of Paraśu Rāma.

(8) Pāpiṣhṭan—the sinful; various faults being traditionally alleged against them.

Of the above, the third class, *i.e.*, Viśiṣhṭa Brāhmaṇan is again divided into:—(1) Akkiṭṭiri, (2) Sōmayāji or Chōmaṭiri and (3) Aṭiṭiri. These attain their position by virtue of the performance of yāgās or sacrifices.

The fifth class, *i. e.*, the Jāṭimāṭrēyans have four sub-classes, *viz.*:—

(1) Aṣhṭa Vaiḍyans or the eight physicians.

(2) Śāsṭrāngakkār—those who obtained arms from Paraśu Rāma to defend and protect Malabar. They practise a sort of theatrical performance known as Yāṭrakkaḷi elsewhere described.

(3) Those who gave up the study of the Vēḍās, either on account of being subject to incurable diseases, *i. e.*, physical disabilities or on account of extreme poverty, and so compelled to seek their livelihood by some other means.

(4) Those who have become slaves to passions and therefore neglected the study of the Vēḍās and sought their livelihood roaming about in various garbs and professions.

The sixth, *i. e.*, the Sāmkēṭikans have six sub divisions amongst them, and they are known as Emprāns or Emprānṭirīs. The six sub-divisions are:— (1) Akkaraḍēśi, (2) Ikkaraḍēśi, (3) Ṭṛppūniṭṭuṛaḍēś (4) Ṭiruvellāḍēśi, (5) Kaṛṇāṭakaḍēśi and (6) Ṭuḷuḍēśi

The eighth class has five sub-divisions, viz:—

(1) Those who received ḍānam (gift) from Paraṡu Rāma—called Grāmiṇīs.

(2) Those Grāmaṅīs who gave permission to assasinate Bhūṭarāya Perumāl, one of the early kings of Kērala.

(3) Those who perpetrated the deed, known as Nampaḍīs.

(4) The Ilayaṭus or priests of the Ṡūḍras.

(5) Those inhabitants of the Payyannūr Grāmaṃ who possibly ejected the idol of Varāhamūrṭṭi.

The two classes of Nyūna Jāṭīs are the Ilayaṭu and the Mūṭṭaṭu, *i. e.*, the "junior" and the "senior." The defect considered in the one being administering to the Ṡrāḍḍha or death-annual ceremonies of the Ṡūḍrās, and in the other, partaking of food served to the god Ṡiva.

The twelve classes of Anṭarāla or intermediate castes, *i. e.*, those who are placed midway between the Brāhmans and Ṡūḍrās and generally known as Aṃpala-vāsīs or temple servants are:—

(1) Aṭikal, slaves, (2) Pushpakan, florist, (3) Nampīṡsan, (4) Puppalli, (5) Pishāroṭi, (6) Vāriar, (7) Chākkyār, (8) Naṃpyār, (9) Ṭiyyāṭṭuṇṇi, (10) Piṭāran, and (12) Nāṭṭupaṭṭar.

The eighteen classes of so-called Ṡūḍrās are:—

(1) Kiriyāṭṭil Nāyar—independent Nāyar.

(2) Illakkār—Nāyar families attached to certain Naṃbūṭiri illoms (families).

(3) Swarūpakkār—servants in Kshetriya houses.

(4) Pāḍamangalam—servants in temples.

(5) Ṭamilpāḍam—those who refused to accept polyandry and Marumakkaṭṭāyam, *i. e.*, inheritance in the female line.

(6) Iṭacheri Nāyar—shepherds and dairymen.

(7) Mārān—drummers and musicians in temples.

(8) Chempukoṭṭi—copper smiths (not the Goa Christian).

(9) Ōḍaṭṭu Nāyar—tile-maker for temples.

(10) Pallichān—palankeen bearer for Rajas.

(11) Maṭavan—servants to Brāhmans and others, down to Aṃpalavāsīs.

(12) Kalamkoṭṭi—potter.

(13) Vaṭṭakkāṭan or Chakkāla Nāyar—oil mongers for temples.

(14) Aṭṭikuruśśi—one who officiates at the funerals of Nāyars. He is also called Chīṭian.

(15) Cheṭṭi—merchant, selling curry-stuffs etc.

(16) Chālian—weaver.

(17) Veluṭṭēṭan—washerman.

(18) Veḷakkaṭṭalavan or Kṣhurakakāran } barber.

The six classes of Śilpi or artizans are :—

(1) Āśāri—carpenter.

(2) Muśāri—brazier.

(3) Kallāśāri—stone-mason.

(4) Ṭaṭṭān—goldsmith.

(5) Kollan—blacksmith.

(6) Īṙchakkollan—sawyer.

The ten classes of Paṭiṭa or degraded classes are:—

(1) Kaṇiyān—astrologer.

(2) Vilkuṙup—bow-maker and painter.

(3) Kuṙup—box-maker.

(4) Ṭōle Kuṙup—maker of shields and other articles of leather.

(5) Vēlan or Maṇṇan—sorcerer; does also washing for classes below Nāyars.

(6) Pāṇan—tailor.

(7) Paravan—lime burner.

(8) Īḻuvan or Chōgan or Ṭīyan } cocoanut-tree-climber and distiller.

(9) Mukkuvan—sea fisherman.

(10) Vālan—river and back-water fisherman.

The eight classes of Nīcha or polluted castes are:—

Of the plains, four, viz. :—

(1) Paṙayan—labourers and basket-makers.

(2) Pulayan—agrestic slaves.

(3) Nāyāṭi—hunters or dog-beaters. They are beggars.

(4) Uḷḷaṭan—wood cutters.

And of the hills four, viz. :—

(1) Kuṟumbar or Kuṟavan.

(2) Malayarayan—hill cultivator.

(3) Mala Vēlan or Vēṭan—hunter.

(4) Kaniyān—also hunters.

The eight extra Jāṭīs are :—

(1) Ammomanmar—the Nambūṭiri inhabitants of Payyannūr Grāmmam.

(2) Nampiḍi with Brahmanical thread.

(3) Do without do do

(4) Puṭuvaḷ

(5) Pilāpilly.

(6) Sāmanṭan.

(7) Karivēlaṭṭu Nāyar.

(8) Veḷḷālars of Ñānnanāḍ.

The above is the scheme of the Jāṭi Niṟṇṇaya. It furnishes us with a list of castes showing the comparative estimate in which the respective castes were held by the early law-givers of Malabar. Beyond this, there is no attempt made to arrange them on any recognised principle. When we proceed to give an account of the origin and history of the various castes, as can be gathered from indigenous works and tradition, it will be seen that the above arrangement is highly conventional, embodying some absurd prejudices and traditions and making the number of castes to accord with theory rather than historical facts and existing circumstances. The classification is altogether faulty. Not simply that there are cross divisions, e. g., Elayaṭu coming both in the Pāpishṭan subdivision of the Brāhmans and in the class of Nyūnajāṭīs which forms one of the main divisions, but also that various professions are jumbled together without any regard to their relative value or position. Thus those who follow the noble profession of medicine and surgery are classed along with common soldiers and theatrical performers and the whole lot is said to be "barely in the caste"—Jāṭimāṭṙēyan—Brāhmans merely in name. Again, Brāhmans who preside at the Śṙāḍḍha or death-annual ceremony of the Nāyars are placed on the same level with murderers, and both come under the class of Pāpiṣhṭan or the 'sinful'. One can understand the sin committed by a murderer, but what is the heinous sin committed by the 'twice-born' individual who unfortunately took it into his head to minister to the spiritual needs of the so-called Śūḍra? Is his brother, the Mūṭṭaṭu or 'the senior', he himself being only an 'Eḷayaṭu' or junior', both together going to form the Nyūna Jāṭi or defective caste, also a sinful man? Apparently he is, for he has committed the unpardonable sin of partaking of food offered to the god Śiva.[1] His duty is to carry the idol of Śiva in procession round the temple, to sweep and clean the shrine, except the *Sanctum Sanctorum*, guard the idol, to administer the affairs of the temple, &c. And these are sinful duties, and on a par with these is placed the other sinful duty of administering to the spiritual needs of a Śūḍra! And Nāyars are classed as Śūḍras!

The castes of Malabar are said to have a racial, marital and functional basis. In their origin, it might have been so. But a classification on these lines can scarcely be satisfactory at present. There has been in course of time such a commingling of races that it is almost impossible to say with any degree of certainty that a particular caste is Āryan or Dravidian. The Nambūṭiri Brāhmans claim to be pure Āryans, perhaps, with some justification. They belong to the Ārya Vaṙṇa or noble race characterised by their broad forehead, regular features and fair colour. Others with coarse feature and dark complexion may be said to belong to the Dravidian family. It is possible and indeed most probable that the Anṭarāla Jāṭīs or the intermediate castes and the Saṃkara Jāṭīs or mixed castes, which name, however, does not find a place in the Jāṭi Nirṇṇaya, are

1. See *Kerala Mahatmyam*, p. 42, para 24.

the result of either mixed marriages or of the illicit connection between the two races. The progeny of women by husbands superior to their caste are known as Anulōmajas, while the issue of all unholy alliances, that is, sexual relations of men of lower castes with women of higher castes go by the name of Praṭilōmajas. A classification on the basis of traditional occupation will be altogether unsatisfactory. For, as remarked by Mr. Risely, " it accords neither with native tradition and practice, nor with any theory of caste that has ever been propounded by students of the subject. In different parts, it proceeds on different principles, with the result that on the one hand it separates groups which are really allied, and on the other includes in the same category groups of widely different origin and status. It is in fact a patch-work classification in which occupation predominates, varied here and there by considerations of caste history, tradition, ethnical affinity and geographical position." As observed by the Cochin Census Reporter, " the struggle for existence in modern times has compelled many castes to give up their time-honoured traditional occupations in favour of more lucrative ones, so that a classification based upon that principle cannot but be defective. All Brāhmans are not priests now, nor are all Kṣheṭṭiyas warriors. A Ṭarakan (Cheṭṭy) is not the only merchant or shop-keeper, nor a Pulayan the only agricultural labourer. A scheme in which the priestly class of Nambūṭirīs (Brāhmans) and Valluvans (the priests of the Parayans), the military class of Kṣheṭṭiyas and and Nāyars, the mercantile class of Vāṇians and Jōnaka Māppilas (Mahomedans) &c., are grouped together on the score of having once followed or now following similar occupations, while it might show to what extent traditional occupations have been given up by castes that once followed them, cannot certainly be regarded as assigning to each caste its exact position in society"[1]

1. Pp. 133—4.

The test of social precedence is no less objectionable. For, though in Malabar the castes are sharply marked off as those 'polluting' and not 'polluting,' whether by contact or by proximity, it will be somewhat difficult, in the face of caste quarrels and jealousies, to found a scientific classification on the degree of pollution imparted—an almost imaginary and vanishing test.

An attempt may, however, be made to classify the castes on the basis of the rules regarding endogamy, exogamy and hypergamy, the period of ceremonial pollution and the performance of purificatory ceremonies which are supposed to determine social precedence. But these, in course of time, have been so elaborated, in an infinite variety of detail, that it would be an invidious task to attempt any exact classification in the order of social precedence, perhaps the only basis left.

The Nambūṭiri Brāhmans of Malabar are very strict in preserving the purity of their race, and to that end they confine their marriages within their own class, so much so that the Vēḍic or Ōṭṭulla Nambūṭiris would not intermarry with the non-Vēḍic or Ōṭṭillāṭṭa Nambūṭiris. Neither will the Makkaṭṭāyam Nambūṭiris intermarry with the Marumakkaṭṭāyam Nambūṭiris of Payyannūr Grāmom. While thus jealously guarding the purity of their own race, they not simply tolerate but, by virtue of their position of influence in religion and society, enforce the rule of hypergamy or women 'marrying up' in castes below them. Thus the Kṣhaṭṛiyas, the class that comes just after them in the Malabar heirarchy of castes, to which belong a large number of Malabar princes, can scarcely claim to have preserved the purity of their race, if they ever did belong to the Hindu caste of Kṣhaṭṛiyas proper at any time. For, according to the Malabar system, the rule of hypergamy begins with these. Their women are, indeed, allowed to go through the ceremonies of Brāhman marriage to their minutest details, but the *pseudo* husband need not continue to be the lifelong helpmate of the woman at whose marriage ceremony he merely officiates. Hence the rule of hypergamy authorises the woman to take for her partner, so long as she pleases, any one of the Nambūṭiri class also of the Brāhman caste generally at present. She is not at the same time prevented from allying herself with one of her own caste. The men may consort with their own caste women as also with women of the Anṭarāla and Nāyar castes. Thus it becomes clear that the pure Kṣhaṭriya blood, if it had ever flown in their veins, must have become altogether diluted at present. However, those of their women who had mated themselves with the Nambūṭiris, generation after generation, must have been the means of improving and purifying the race rather than degrading it, while the very few assorting with mates of their own caste could not have certainly lowered the race. Hence we may say with the authors of the *Malabar Gazetteer* that, "it is clear that, if the expression Kṣhaṭriya is to have any ethnological signification, it cannot be applied with any appropriateness to a class who practise hypergamy and are therefore admittedly of hybrid race", unless it be by agreeing with them when they go further and add that, "racially no doubt Kṣhaṭriyas and Sāmanṭas were originally Nāyars." There are those who say that there is no basis for the statement, so far at any rate as the Kṣhaṭriyas are concerned, unless one holds that, of all the inhabitants of Malabar, the ancestors of the present Nambūṭiris alone belonged to the Aryan race, who made settlements from the north, and that the classes below them were all Dravidians who had preceded them. The theory cannot be said to be altogether incorrect. Nor is it without its supporters. It has been observed by competent authorities that the ruling chiefs of Southern India originally belonged to the aborginal races and that, after the Brāhmans had subdued them by their intellectual superiority, they succeeded in investing them with a halo of political sanctity, in furtherance of their own selfish ends, by supplying them with geneologies tracing their descent from the Solar and Lunar lines of Kṣhaṭṭriyas of the Purāṇic age. "The Aryan immigrants to the South," says Dr. Caldwell, "appear to have been generally Brahmanical priests and instructors rather than Kṣhaṭṭriya soldiers; and the kings of the Pāṇḍyas, Chōlas, Kalingas and other Dravidians appear to have been simply Dravidian chieftains whom their Brahmanical preceptors and spiritual directors dignified with Aryan titles and taught to imitate and emulate the grandeur and cultured tastes of the Solar, Lunar and Agnikula race of kings."[1] Again we read in the *Manual of the Trichinopoly District* that "the Chōla and Pāṇḍya kings are of course held by natives to have been Kṣhaṭṭriyas; but there is no evidence that they have the slightest claim to be considered as such It may appear worthy of remark that their caste title was Ḍēva, the same as that of the Maṟavars at present."[2]

The rule of hypergamy prevails among the Anṭarāla and Nāyar castes also, so that, in its strictest working, one may say with the authors of *The Malabar Gazetteer* that "it is difficult to see what material difference in blood there can be between Nambūṭiris themselves and those lower castes whether styling themselves Nāyar, Sāmanṭa or Kṣhaṭṭriya who follow the Marumakkaṭṭāyam family law and restrict their women folk to Nambūṭiri consorts."[3]

Intensely exclusive as the Malabar caste system affects to be, there are evident traces of accessions to even the superior castes by means of a silent and almost inappreciable process. Even the jealous vigilance of the exclusive Nambūṭiri has not been successful in keeping out other and foreign elements from entering the bounds of his charmed circle. There have been

1. *Comparative Grammar*, Introduction, p. 115
2. See also Caldwell, p. 533.
3. Vol. I, p. 112.

well-known instances of Embrāṇṭiris, who are Brāhmans of Canarese and Ṭulu origin, with whom the Nambūṭiris as a class do not intermarry, slowly and cautiously trespassing into the Nambūṭiri fold. The Nambūṭiris ever watchful of their rights and privileges oppose the Embrāṇṭiris in their sly attempt; but, in spite of their vigilance, the latter have succeeded in many instances in obtaining a firm footing among the Nambūṭiris. Embrāṇṭiris of wealth and position begin by purchasing large Jenmam or free-hold estates and get themselves described as Nambūṭiris in the documents of purchase. They then make a movement towards getting themselves enrolled as belonging to the Nambūṭiri class entitled to participate in the great ceremonies to which Nambūṭiris alone are eligible. In these prosaic days of utilitarian ideas, it is not often difficult to those hovering round the outskirts of the charmed circle to open its closed doors by means of a golden key, specially when such doors are under the lock and ward of those who are not rich and not over-scrupulous in letting in those who are able to grease well their itchy palms.

The Sāmanṭas who claim to be Kṣhaṭṛiyas, or, at any rate, Anṭarālas, must originally have been Nāyars who have raised themselves by restricting their alliances exclusively to the Brāhmans. We learn from early Portuguese writers that the princesses of the Zamorin's family who are Eṛāḍīs by caste were not allowed to consort with any one below the rank of a Nāyar. That even so late as the early years of the nineteenth century, this remained to be the rule appears from what Dr. Francis Buchanan says.[1] And in a suit between the Nilambūr Ṭirumulpād, who claims to be a Sāmanṭa and the Collector of Malabar in 1888, the District Judge of South Malabar held that the plaintiff was only a Nāyar and that there was no distinct caste known as Sāmanṭas.[2]

1. Vol. II, p. 83.
2. Moore's *Malabar Law*, pp. 345—46, Note.

In our own day, we see a process of so-called elevation in caste going on in the upper and middle strata of Nāyar society. As a Nāyar advances in life, amasses wealth, attains a commanding official position and secures sufficient social influence, he begins slowly to drop one by one his associations with those of his own class, arrogates to himself social superiority over them, pretends that the females of his family can consort only with Nambūṭirīs who pander to his idiosyncracies readily, and if necessary, invent for him a respectable pedigree and a family legend which ascribes the origin of the family to some miracle in a by-gone age, and finally the ordinary Nāyar famīly of the other day professes to belong to a superior order of men, calls itself by a curious new-fangled name, and if its wealth and influence continues for a time, is joined by others similarly circumstanced. The non-cohesive character of the Nāyars as a class is nowhere so well-exemplified as in their social life. They would not mess in public, or intermarry with those of their own class who belong to a different sub-division. Nāyar women specially take care not to partake of food cooked by members of her class unless they belong to her circle which is becoming narrower and narrower every day by the process of arrogation above described. So long as Nambūṭirīs are available as consorts, a Nāyar woman need not care to find a partner in her own class. Class for class, Nāyars of different localities will not associate together. Thus Nāyars of Travancore or Cochin or South Malabar will not be permitted to mess or intermarry with the corresponding class of Nāyars of North Malabar who always pretend to be of higher caste than the others. Their brethren in the south never fail to return the compliment! There are certain conventional limits beyond which Nāyar women are not allowed to go. Those of North Malabar are prohibited from crossing the Perumpuḷa river towards the north and the Kōrappuḷa river towards the south. Those of South Malabar and Cochin cannot go beyond Quilon in Travancore on pain of losing caste. Of course these senseless and silly restrictions are wearing away in the light of western education and enlightenment, though in the north it is not very long ago educated Nāyar gentlemen have plucked up courage to break through the shackles forged by custom and take their wives with them beyond the conventional limits. And yet it would not be quite accurate to say that education has always acted as a mitigating or corrective element towards the unification of sub-castes among Nāyars. For, a blind and unmeaning reverence to old musty customs still deter many, even among the educated, from giving their adherence to what is known as Praṭilōma marriage, *i. e.*, marriage of a woman of a higher sub-caste with a man of a lower one, though such alliances, if they do take place, do not necessarily deprive the parties of their legal rights in their Ṭarawāḍs. Yet there are those who insist on the woman being put out of caste. Another meaningless observance to which they still cling tenaciously is the one regarding sitting for meals in the same row or line—what is known as Panṭi Bhōjanam. Different sections of the Nāyar caste sit apart for meals on ceremonial occasions. These and many such senseless customs tend to keep up perennial disunion in the caste.

There are also instances of members of the lower sub-castes rising in the caste scale and claiming to rank with higher sub-castes, as there are also instances of members of a higher sub-caste being degraded and brought below the rank of high class Nāyars. The Chempukoṭṭis (copper-smiths), the Ōḍaṭṭu Nāyars (tilers), the Eṭachēry Nāyars (cow-herd), the Vaṭṭakāṭan (oil-monger) are instances of the first class. These were evidently classes who were of a rank inferior to the Nāyars but who have apparently been raised in the caste scale as a matter of necessity or have themselves risen by reason of their office or profession which was indispensable to Brāhmans and temples. These are allowed to enter the inner precincts of temples, the Elàyaṭu officiates as purōhits at their Śrāḍha ceremonies and they can touch the other Nāyars without polluting them.

The Chālian or the weaver, the Veluṭṭēṭan or the washerman, the Kşhourakan or the barber are all instances of the second class, *viz.*, of those who have lowered themselves from the ranks of Nāyars by taking professions supposed to be degrading. These impart pollution by touch to other Nāyars, are not allowed to enter temples and do not get the benefit of the spiritual offices of the Elayaṭu.

There are also instances of foreign castes trying to get into the fold of the Nāyar class. Among others, the Ṭarakan or Cheṭṭi and the Maṇṇāṭṭi, an altogether new class, may be named as prominent instances.

That the sub-castes are increasing in our own day is evidenced by the gradual increase in their numbers returned by the successive decennial Census Reports.

To classify the Malabar castes by races or to determine the race to which each caste belongs is altogether impossible, seeing that the Nambūṭiris, who may be taken to be pure Aryans, have been for generations together, mingling freely in connubial relationship with all castes below them down to the Nāyars. The Kşhaṭṭriyas, the Anṭarālas and the Nāyars also have been doing this for ages. No castes, perhaps with the doubtful exception of the Nambūṭiris, can pretend to have preserved the purity of their race

The Malabar castes now may be said to fall into the following broad divisions, *viz.*,

(1) The Ḍwijas or the twice-born classes:—
- (a) Brāhmans—Nambūṭiris.
- (b) The Kşhaṭṭriyas.

(2) Anṭarālas—with their sub-divisions
- (a) Nampiṭi, (b) Ampalavāsi, (c) Sāmanṭa.

(3) The Nāyars:—
- (a) Nāyars—proper *i. e.* high class Nāyars.
- (b) Nāyars—low class—whose touch pollutes sub-class (a)

(4) Ṭiyyans, Kammāḷars or artizans and other polluting castes who are not aborginal.

(5) The depressed aborginal classes who are outside the caste system, such as Paṙayars, Cheṙumars, etc.

The above classification is on almost the same lines as those adopted by Mr. M. Ṡankara Mēnōn in his Report on the Census of the Cochin State for 1901.— The following Tables adapted from those given by Mr. Ṡankara Mēnōn give us some idea of the Malayāli caste system according to social precedence as determined by circumstances already mentioned .

It will be seen that the highest place in the scale is occupied by the Malayāli Brāhmans—Nambūṭiris. The Malayāli Kṣhaṭṙiyas, who follow more or less in the footsteps of the Nambūṭiris in the matter of religious observances, bath, ablutions, &c., come next. The Anṭarāla-Jāṭies or intermediate castes, are placed above Nāyars (group No II). The Ampalavāsis are in this group. The Nāyars distinguished as high caste and low caste are placed in group No. III. The remaining castes are arranged according to the degree of pollution by touch or approach which marks each group. In another place a little more elaboration will be made on a few of the points lighty touched above.

Table I.

Group No.	Name of Caste	Race	No. of Divisions
I.	Nambūtirīs and allied castes.	Aryan	10
II.	Antarāla-jātīs or intermediate castes		
	(a) Nampiti	Do.	1
	(b) Ambalavāsi (threaded)	Do.	7
	(c) Do. (unthreaded)	Mixed Aryan and Dravidian	4
III.	Nāyar (a) High caste	Dravidian ?	14
	(b) Low caste	Do.	4
IV.	Kammālans	Dravidian	6
V.	Other polluting castes below them	Do.	10
VI.	Chandalās	Probably aborigines	
	(a) of the Plains		4
	(b) of the Forests		4
			Total 64

Table II.

Purely Malayali Hindu and Animistic Castes arranged in the order of social precedence.

Group No.	Name of Caste	Remarks
1	2	3
I.	Brāhmans and allied classes— (1) Nambūṭiri	I. (1) There are 8 divisions, of which 4 are Vēḍic and 4 non-Vēḍic, that is, those allowed to read and study Vēḍas, and those not. While all males interdine, all the divisions cannot intermarry. Among Nambūṭirīs, infant marriage is seldom resorted to, but widow marriage is prohibited.
	(2) Mūṭṭaṭ	(2) They are Brāhmans degraded on account of partaking of the offerings made to the God Śiva. Nambūṭirīs officiate as priests at marriage and purificatory ceremonies.
	(3) Elayaṭ	(3) They are Brāhmans degraded for having officiated as the priests of Sūdras. They are their own priests. Nos. 2 and 3 pollute each other by touch. Brāhmans, Kṣhaṭriyas or Nampiḍīs will not take water from them. There is no infant marriage or widow marriage among these two castes also.

Table II—(*contd.*)

Group No.	Name of Caste	Remarks
1	2	3
II.	Malayāli Kṣhaṭriyas— (1) Ṭampurān (members of the ruling family) (2) Ṭampān (distant relatives of the ruling family and a few others) (3) Ṭirumulpāḍ	II. The three names denote titles. They follow certain Brahmanical customs in respect of religious ablutions, etc.. Brāhmans are their priests. Brāhman males interdine with them. Groups II to V both inclusive are mostly Marumakkaṭṭāyīs. Among them, Ṭāliketṭu (ceremonial marriage) and Saṃbandhaṃ (real marriage) are two distinct ceremonies. Widows can reunite in Saṃbanḍhaṃ.
III.	Vaiśyas and allied castes—	III. In Malabar sociology, Vaiśyas have been conspicuous by their absence.
IV.	Anṭarāla-jāṭis or castes below the Brāhmans and Kṣhaṭriyas and above the Nāyars (a) Nampiḍi	IV. (a) They voluntarily accepted degradation on account of having murdered one of the Perumāls. Brāhmans are their priests. Their touch pollutes Brāhmans and Kṣhaṭriyas, neither of whom will take water from them. Brāhmans officiate as priests. They wear the sacred thread.

Table II—(*conta.*)

Group No.	Name of Caste	Remarks
1	2	3
	(b) Aṃbalavāsi (temple servant)	IV. (b) Brāhmans, Kṣhaṭriyas or Naṃpiḍīs will not take water from them. Most of the divisions must bathe if they touch one another. [In some parts specially in Travancore, high class Nāyars will not take water from them or eat food touched by them.]
	(1) Aṭikal	IV. (b) No. 1 is degraded on account of having performed priestly functions in Bhagavaṭi temples and used meat and drink as offerings.
	(2) Chākkiyār	No. 2, Chākkiyār, was originally of the Sūṭa caste. Children born of an adulterous Brāhman woman during the period of her criminal intimacy are adopted into this caste.
	(3) Chākkiyār Naṃbiyār	(3) This caste also originated as No. 2. No. 3 does not wear the sacred thread.
	(4) Naṃbiyār or Uṇṇī	No. 4 is degraded by origin similar to No. 2.
	(5) Ṭiyyāṭṭuṇṇi or Naṃbiyār	No. 5 is degraded by profession. The threaded classes have Gāyaṭri.

Table II—(*contd.*)

Group No.	Name of Caste	Remarks
1	2	3
	(6) Pișhāroți (7) Vāriyar (8) Puțuvāl	Nos. 6 to 9 do not wear the sacred thread. Purificatory ceremonies alone are performed by the Brāhmans. Other priestly functions are performed by their own caste-men.
	(9) Mārār	(9) Raised in the social scale by being attached to the temples as drummers and musicians. In some places, Elayads officiate as priests; in other places, their own caste-men do priestly functions.
	(c) Sāmanța (1) Uņițțiri (2) Ațiyōți	(c) They are the children of Nāyar women by Kșhațriya husbands. They and all castes above them abstain from flesh and spirituous liquors. IV and V (a) can go within the quadrangular structure of temples.

Table II—(*contd.*)

Group No.	Name of Caste	Remarks
1	2	3
V	(a) High caste Nāyars	V. (a) Their touch pollutes all castes above them. The use of meat or liquor does not entail loss of caste, but many absolutely abstain from both. Elayaḍs are their priests.
	(b) Low caste Nāyars (1) Chāliyan (2) Velūṭṭēḍan (3) Velakkaṭṭalavan	(b) Their touch pollutes all castes above them. They pollute one another also by touch. The highest Brāhman uses cloths washed by No. 2 without being thereby polluted. Their own sub-castes officiate as priests for Nos. 1 and 2. Nambūṭiris give *Punyaham* or holy water for the purification of No. 3. No. 3 has birth and death pollution for only 10 days, while all high caste Nāyars and other low caste Nāyars have pollution for 15 days. V. (b) can go only within the outer enclosure of temples.

Table II.—(*contd.*)

Group No.	Name of Caste	Remarks
1	2	3
VI	Castes which pollute by approach within graded distances and do not eat beef.— (1) Kallāśāri (Mason) (2) Kollan (Black-smith) (3) Marāśari (Carpenter) (4) Mūśāri (Bell-metal worker) (5) Taṭṭan (Gold-smith) (6) Ṭōlkollan (Leather worker)	VI—Nos. 1 to 5 interdine and sometimes intermarry. No. 6 pollutes Nos. 1 to 5 by touch. The approach of Kammāḷans within a distance of 24 feet pollutes castes above them. A sub-division of the caste known as Kuruppu officiates as priest. They are generally Makkaṭṭāyis. There are relics of the fraternal or adelphic form of polyandry among them. Groups VI to IX both inclusive are mostly Makkaṭṭāyis. Most of the castes have Ṭālikeṭṭu and real marriage as two distinct ceremonies. Ṭālikeṭṭu must take place before the girls attain puberty. Failure entails loss of caste among most of them. These castes have to keep themselves as far away from the outer enclosure of temples as from Brāhmans, Kṣhaṭriyas and Nāyars.

Table II.—(*contd.*)

Group No.	Name of Caste	Remarks
1	2	3
VII	Other castes having distance pollution but do not eat beef.— (1) Īluvan or Ṭiyyan (toddy drawer) (2) Vālan (fisherman and boat-man) (3) Arayan do (4) Mukkuvan do (5) Marakkān do (6) Kaṇiyān (astrologer) (7) Vilkuṛup (maker of bows and arrows) (8) Pāṇan (necromancer) (9) Vēlan (washerman of low castes)	VII. Their approach within 36 feet pollutes groups I to V. Some of the castes in the group itself and in group VI are polluted by touch. Each division has a sub-caste that officiates as priest. They are mostly Makkaṭṭāyis, but some follow Marumakkaṭṭāyam also. There are rare instances of polyandry among some castes, notably Kaṇiyān, Pāṇan and Vilkuṛup.

Table II—(*contd.*)

Group No.	Name of Caste		Remarks
1	2		3
	(10) Puḷḷuvan (singer in serpent groves)		
	(11) Paravan		
VIII.	(1) Kaṇakkan (2) Kūṭan	Agricultural labourers	VIII. They have to keep themselves at a distance of 48 feet from high caste Hindus. They pollute castes in Groups VI and VII also by approach, but within a less distance.
IX	(1) Pulayan or Cheřuman (2) Pařayan (3) Veṭṭuvan	Agricultural labourers	IX. In their case, the distance causing pollution is 64 feet. They are Chaṇḍālas of the plains. Of these, the Pařayans eat teef. Both Pulayans and Veṭṭuvans bathe, if they touch or approach one another. Their status is a point of dispute among themselves.

Table II—(*contd.*)

Group No.	Name of Caste	Remarks
1	2	3
X.	(1) Uḷḷāṭan (2) Nāyāṭi (3) Malayan (4) Kāṭan	X. Uḷḷāṭans and Nāyāṭis are also Chaṇḍālas of the plains but, by religion, they are treated as animists and are therefore placed in this group. Approach within a radius of 64 feet pollutes Brāhmans and castes up to Sūdras (Nāyars) inclusive. They pollute also the polluting castes above them by approach, though only within a less distance. Some of the castes pollute one another by touch or approach among themselves. The Hill Tribes of Kāṭans and Malayans are Chaṇḍālas of the forests (*Cochin Census Report*, page 181).

The Nambutiris.

Introductory Note—Part II.

In this part, I propose to notice at some length some of the important castes omitted by our author. Having sojourned for a long time in such a priest-ridden country as Malabar, where all classes of people who have any pretention to be Hindu devote themselves, body and soul, to contribute to the welfare, prosperity and pleasure of the twice-born classes, where kings and princes, when they ascend the thrones of their ancestors, solemnly swear to protect "the Brāhman and his Kine," it is surprising that our author has given the go-by to the Brāhmans, as a class, altogether. While he has given us interesting and detailed accounts of the Christians, Jews and Mahomedans and has also not failed to notice at some length the Nāyars and the castes below them, he has not a word to say about the Naṃbūṭirīs who are the Brāhmans of Malabar. It cannot be that he was not aware of the existence of Brāhmans in the country. For in Letter No. 22, he gives an account of the Paṭṭers "dwelling among and beyond the mountain range," whose "native country is the district round Tuticorin, Coromandal, Madura, Koṭṭār, and the neighbourhood," and "who take no share in the administration of Government in Malabar, being regarded as foreigners, although they sometimes spend 3 or 4 years on this coast." Speaking of this class of people, he also informs us that "these hold themselves higher than the Malabar Brāhmans, the Naṃbūṭirīs, who, they say, sprang from fishermen elevated to the Brahmanical dignity by Paraśu Rāman." Thus it is evident that our author knew of the existence of a separate class of Brāhmans in Malabar; but the apparent distinction he seems to draw between the Malabar Brāhmans and Naṃbūṭirīs leads us to think that he had but a hazy idea about them, and that, rather than venture to descant upon a subject of which he was evidently ignorant, he thought it wise to let it alone. And this is most likely, for the Nambūṭiri Brāhmans are a peculiarly exclusive class, and it is by no means easy to obtain information which is accurate and trustworthy respecting them, especially for one so placed as our author, a Christian priest. Unlike their brethren of the East Coast who are always pushing forward in the battle of life, the Naṃbūṭiri Brāhmans of Malabar immure themselves within the sacred limits of their households "far from the madding crowd's ignoble strife," attending solely to their interminable ceremonies and ablutions. Untouched by the advance of western education and civilization, these represent today the type of their ancestors, who, centuries upon centuries ago, had left the table-lands of central Asia and had come all the way down to Malabar in search of a new abode.

Name.—The Brāhmans of Malabar are known as Naṃbūṭirīs, Eṃprāns or Eṃprānṭirīs and Pōṫṫīs. Those of the 32 Grāmams (villages) that lie to the north of the Perumpuḻa river are called Eṃprāns, a term said to be made up of the words *En+puran*, meaning "my lord." The Brāhmans of the remaining Grāmams lying between Perinchellūr and Kātamuṟi, and those who have immigrated from the north and live in the Grāmams up to Aṃpalappuḻa and Harippād, are designated Naṃbūṭirīs. The term "Naṃpūri or Naṃbūṭiri" has been variously derived. Some of these derivations are sufficiently grotesque and need not therefore be referred to here. One derivation, perhaps the least objectionable, is said to be from *Nambu* and *tiri*. *Nampu* is taken to mean either 'sacred' or 'trusted' (*Tamil*) and *tiri*, an honorific suffix among Malabar Brāhmans and other castes above the Nāyars, as in Akkiṭṭiri, Naṃbyāṭṭiri and Uniṭṭiri. It is also used as an honorific suffix for Rajas, as in Kuññala Kōnāṭiri, *i. e.* the Zamorin, Vaḷḷuva Kōnāṭiri, the Raja of Waḷḷuvanād, &c. The late Pāchu Mūṭṭaṭu, a well-known Sanskrit and Malayālam scholar and author, derives it from *Na*, the first part of the word, meaning Vēḍa, the whole term implying those who devote themselves to the study of the Vēḍas.

Origin.—It is accepted on all hands that the Naṃbūṭirīs do not form part of the indigenous inhabitants of Malabar. If so, whence did they come? What is their origin? These are questions that are not easily answered. Tradition, as recorded in native annals, such as the Kēraḷa Māhāṭmyaṃ and the Kēraḷōṭpaṭṭi, ascribes the peopling of Malabar with the Naṃbūṭiri Brāhmans to Paraśu Rāma, who is said to have brought colony after colony from the banks of the Narbuda, the Krishna, the Cavery and other rivers. The theory of Mr. Nāgam Ayya, that "the bulk of them came, of course, from the region between the Krishna and thé Godavari rivers," seems more or less correct. Mr. Nāgam Ayya refers to "many points of similarity, large and small, between the Naṃbūṭirīs and their prototype residents of the Telugu country from which they are said to have come," the cumulative effect of which is certainly to favour the probability of this theory being correct, the more so that native tradition also points in that direction. Dr. Subramania Ayyar tells us that he has come across Naṃbūṭirīs who have referred to traditions in their families regarding villages on the East Coast whence their ancestors originally came, and the sub-divisions of the Smārṭṭā caste Vaṭama, Bṛhaṭcharaṇam, Aṣhṭasahasram, Saṃkēṭi, &c., to which they belonged. According to him, even to this day, an East Coast Brāhman of the Vaṭaḍēśaṭṭu Vaṭama caste has to pour water into the hands of a Naṃbūṭiri Sanyasi as part of the latter's breakfast ritual. The low origin attributed to them by Sir W. W. Hunter and others is based on the authority of some Canarese or Maharatta tradition to which reference is made by our author also, which, in fact, has no foundation whatever in history and is resented by the Naṃbūṭirīs as outrageous. This theory makes them Brahmanical fishermen. In support of it, Sir William Hunter draws our attention to their post-nubile marriage, the prohibition of the sacrament of marriage among all but the eldest son in a household, and to the observance of the ceremony of fishing as part of the marriage ritual among the *Yajur* Vēḍic branch of the caste as the relic and record of a pre-Brahmanic age. No doubt the rigid insistence of child marriage under penalty of forfeiture of caste as in other parts is wholly unknown among the Naṃbūṭirīs of Malabar. But this is only in accordance with ancient Hindu Law, while the practice of the Brāhmans on the East Coast is a later innovation forced upon them by the necessities of the times. Mr. Dutt, speaking of the manners and laws of the Buddhist age (B. C. 320 to 400 A. D.) says: "while Manu approves of the marriage of girls at an early age, it is quite manifest, from all we know of the times, that Hindu maidens generally married in early maidenhood. It would seem that the frequent invasion of foreigners in this age and the general insecurity of the times fostered the baneful custom of child-marriage, and the custom became a religious duty after the Hindus had lost their independence." The statement that holy matrimony is prohibited to all but the eldest son of the household is altogether incorrect. There is no such prohibition, but the desire to conserve the joint estate and not to dissipate it among the many members of the family has induced the Naṃbūṭirīs not simply to prohibit partition but also to ordain that only the eldest son of a householder *need* marry. There are Naṃbūṭiri *Illoms* (houses) in Malabar all male members of which do enter into holy matrimony. As to the observance of certain ceremonies by a particular section of them, it is idle to argue from it that it gives us a clue to the origin of the class itself. Any casual reader of Mr. Edgar Thurston's chapter on marriage customs in South India in his *Ethnographic Notes* will be convinced that it is next to impossible to trace the origin of many of the curious customs and observances mentioned by him so as to connect them with the genesis of the classes that observe such customs. At any rate, the peculiar observances of the Naṃbūṭirīs only show that they had separated themselves from the parent stock long before the development of Śāsṭraic customs now obtaining among their brethren on the East Coast.

Notwithstanding the theory that the Naṃbūṭirīs and Nāyars formed parts of a homogeneous Turanian race, the researches of Mr. Fawcett go to show that, as far as anthropometry can be relied on to indicate racial origin, the Naṃbūṭirīs "are the truest Aryans of Southern India."[1] But this statement cannot be said to have disproved the theory, for the period of their arrivals in and colonisation of Malabār it is difficult to determine for certain, and the enquiry already made into the question makes any further discussion unnecessary.

Their location.—The whole country of Kērala was divided into 64 *Gramams* or villages and the Brāhmans who came from the north were settled in these.

The names of these 64 Grāmams are:—

1.	Gōkarṇam	17.	Vellār
2.	Gōmakūṭam	18.	Venṭōṭu
3.	Kāravalli	19.	Vencaṭam
4.	Mallūr	20.	Chengōṭe
5.	Ēppanūr	21.	Kōṭīśvaram
6.	Chēppanūr	22.	Manchīśvaram
7.	Kaṭalūr	23.	Uṭuppu
8.	Kālanūr	24.	Śankaranārāyaṇam
9.	Kariāchira	25.	Koṭṭam
10.	Paiachira	26.	Sivalli
11.	Tṛkkani	27.	Mora
12.	Tṛkkaṭa	28.	Pancha
13.	Tṛkkampāla	29.	Viṭṭal
14.	Tṛchōla	30.	Kumāra Mangalam
15.	Kellūr	31.	Ananṭapuram
16.	Gōmayam	32.	Karṇapuram

1. *Madras Museum Bulletin*, Vol. 3, No. 1, p. 33.

These 32 Grāmams belong to the Ṭulu division. The 32 *Gramams* of the Malayālam division are:—

1.	Pyyannūr	17.	Uḷiyannūr
2.	Perinchellūr	18.	Kaḷuṭṭanāḍu
3.	Karīkkāṭu	19.	Kaṭappūr
4.	Īśānamangalam	20.	Iḷibhyam
5.	Ālaṭṭūr	21.	Śivapuram
6.	Karinṭolam	22.	Aviṭṭaṭṭūr
7.	Tṛśivapērūr	23.	Vennanāḍu
8.	Paṅṅyūr	24.	Kaṭumuri
9.	Śukapuraṁ	25.	Kiṭangūr
10.	Perumanam	26.	Kumāranēllūr
11.	Paṙappūr	27.	Kaviūr
12.	Aiyrāṇikkuḷam	28.	Ēṙṙumānūr
13.	Mūṣhikakuḷam	29.	Anmani
14.	Iringālakoḍa	30.	Anmalam
15.	Aṭappūr	31.	Ṭiruvella
16.	Chengavōṭu	32.	Chengannūr

Caste Sub-divisions:—The Naṃbūṭirīs may be divided into the *vedic* and *non-vedic*, *i. e.*, those who are entitled to study the Vēḍas, Ōṭṭuḷḷavar, and those who have been deprived of that right for some reason or other—Ōṭṭillāṭṭavar. The first of these may again be divided into *Adhyans* and *Asyans* or *Hasyans*. But as the non-vedic section also arrogates to itself this distinction, it does not sufficiently define the position of the vedic class in society. The Āḍhyans of both sections, the vedic and non-vedic, possess the honorific title of Naṃbūṭiripād. The suffix 'pāḍ' means 'one in authority.' The Naṃbūṭiripāds of the non-vedic section have, however, the further appellation of *Gramini Adhyans*. Just as the suffix 'ṭiri' is added to the names of both spiritual and secular magnates to denote their exalted position, the suffix of "pād" is also used for the same purpose of denoting exaltation.

The Cochin Census Report notices certain special privileges in regard to the performance of religious rites and other matters of a purely social nature which serve as the best basis for a sub-division of the Naṃbūṭiris in the order of social precedence as recognised amongst themselves. For this purpose, the privileges may be grouped under two main classes A and B as given in the following statement taken from the Report.

A	B
1. Ēṭu (the leaf of a cadjan Granḍha or book), the right of studying and teaching vēḍās and śās-ṭrās.	1. Āṭu (sheep), the right of performing holy sacrifices.
2. Piccha (mendicancy of family priests), the right of officiating as family priests.	2. Bhikṣha (receiving alms), the right of becoming a Sanyāsi.
3. Ōṭṭu (Vēḍās), the right of studying the vēḍās.	3. Śānṭi (officiating as temple priests), the right of performing priestly functions in temples.
4. Aṭukkala (kitchen), the right of cooking for all classes of Brāhmans.	4. Arañgu (stage), the right of taking part in the performance of śāsṭrāngam.
5. Kaṭavu (bathing place or ghat), the right of bathing in the same bathing place with other Brāhmans, or the right of touching after bath without thereby disqualifying the person touched for performing religious services.	5. Panṭi (row of eaters), the right of messing in the same row with other Brāhmans.

Those who enjoy the privilege of No. 1 in A are entitled to all the privileges in A and B; those enjoying No. 2 in A have all the privileges from 2 downward in A; and those having No. 3 in A have similarly all the privileges from No. 3 downwards in A and B, and so on. Those entitled to No. 1 in B have all the privileges except No. 1 in A. Similarly those entitled to No. 2 in B have all the privileges from No. 2 downwards in B, but only from No. 3 downwards in A, and so on. With the above formula as basis, the various classes of Naṃbūṭirīs may be distinguished as follows:— Ālvānchēri Ṭampurākals, Ashṭagrahaṭṭil Āḍhyans (Āḍyans of eight houses), Agnihōṭris, Bhaṭṭaṭiris, Ōṭikkans, Vāḍḍhyāns, Vyḍīkans, Smārṭṭans, Ṭanṭris, Ṣāsṭrāngakārs. Vaiḍyans or physicians, Grāmaṇis and Ūril Parisha Mūssads.

According to the *Jatinirnnaya*, as we have seen, there are 8 sub-divisions among the Naṃbūṭirīs. They are:—

1. Ṭampurākkal.
2. Āḍhyan.
3. Viśishṭa Brāhman.
4. Sāmānya Brāhman.
5. Jāṭi Māṭrēyan.
6. Sāmkēṭikan.
7. Śāpagrasṭṭan.
8. Pāpisṭhan.

Taking them in order:—

1. Ṭampurākkal.—The term is said to be a corrupt form of the Sanskrit word Sāṃrāṭ denoting spiritual sovereignity. Of this class, there is only one family existing at present, that of Ālvānchēri in South Malabar. There was another family known as Kalpanchēri in the same locality, now extinct. As spiritual sovereigns, they enjoy certain peculiar privileges, *viz.*,

(1) Bhaḍrāsanam.—the chief seat in an assembly.

(2) Brahma-Sāṃrajyam.—Brahmanical sovereignity.

(3) Brahma-Vālcha.—authority in Vēḍic lore and holiness resulting from the study and recital of Vēḍās.

(4) Sārvamānyam.—universal acknowledgment of reverence.

The Ṭampurākal, as he is generally designated is considered higher than all other Brāhmans, and possesses unquestioned supreme spiritual authority over all Nambūṭirīs. He is regarded with great reverence, and the Malabar Rajas perform Sāṣhṭānga ṇamaskāram (prostration) before him. He is the last resort of appeal in caste matters. With regard to the sanctity of the Ṭampurākkal and the origin of the designation itself, Mr. Nāgam Aiya mentions an incident which is interesting. "According to popular tradition," says he, "Āluvāncheri Nambūṭiri on his way home from the *Hiranyagarbham* ceremony, with a gold-cow from the ruling sovereign of Kēraḷa was accosted by a Pulaya (Paṛaya?) thus:—'We are the rightful claimants to dead cows, not Brāhman dignitaries. If this cow should be yours, you had better walk it home'. On this affront being offered, the Nambūṭiri by his great mānṭric power sprinkled water upon the golden cow and gave it life. The wondering Pulaya exclaimed 'you are indeed a Ṭampurākkal', and it is believed that this title of *Tampurakkal* (Sanskrit, *Samrat* meaning sovereign, having reference to their temporal as well as spiritual sovereignity) belongs to them from that time."[1]

The Ṭampurākkals form an endogamous community with the Āḍhyans.

2. Āḍhyans.—There are 8 families of this class which are known together as *Ashtagrahathil Adhyans* or Āḍhyans of the eight houses.

1. *Travancore State Manual*, Vol. II, p. 249.

The names of the Aṣhṭagraham with their chief representatives of the present day are:—

Names of houses.	*Present representatives.*	
1. Kālamkaṇṭam	1. Olappamana	Nampūripād
	2. Varikkāśēri	
	3. Ōṭṭūr	
2. Mēlaṭṭōl	1. Kūṭallūr	
3. Maṭṭūr	1. Pūvuḷḷi	
4. Kulukkallūr	1. Mappād	
	2. Oralāśśēri	
5. Chemmangāṭ	1. Chemmangāṭ Bhaṭṭaṭiri	Nampūripād
6. Pālūr	1. Pālūr Paṭuṭōl	
	2. Panappālūr	
7. Muringōṭṭil	1. Ekāḍaśi Ṭe-kkēṭam	
	2. do Vaṭa-kkēṭam	
8. Vellāngallūr	1. Akkarakkuriśśi	
	2. Mēchēri	
	3. Vālappiḷḷy	

It is related in the 10th chapter of the Kēraḷa Mahāṭmyam that Paraśu Rāma brought from the banks of the Krishna a Brāhman of great sanctity learned in Vēḍic lore, one who was a proficient in the practice of yoga and poor withal, his wife and their 8 children, who were all no less learned than their venerable parent, and settled them in his country of Kēraḷa. The father was installed as Yōgiaṭiripāḍ or Yōgiār or preceptor of all Nambūṭiri Brāhmans, and was authorised to pronounce final judgment on the religious questions referred to him. A house was built for him at Trichur on the side of the western (chira) reservoir or tank. He was given great wealth and was loaded with honours and privileges, some of which are :— the right of (1) going about in a palanquin, (2) being attended by guards armed with swords and shields, (3) having a conch blown when moving about, and (4) having disciples. On the death of a Yōgiātiri, his successor used to be consecrated with great ceremony by the Brāhmans under the orders of the Raja of Cochin. The ceremony was used to be attended by the Rajas and chiefs of Malabar. **The office ceased on the expulsion of the last Yōgiāṭiri, Pāṭāyakkara Naṃbūṭiripād, whose installation into office** by the Zamorin was unauthorised, when, under orders of the Raja of Cochin, he was deprived of his dignity and formally expelled from Trichur, and no one was consecrated to succeed him.

To each of the 8 sons a separate house, endowed with great wealth, was given. They were also honoured with privileges. The beauty of this tradition is, however, marred by the fact that these houses belong to separate gōṭras, and do not constitute exogamous sections. 'The fund of accumulated spirituality inherited from remote ancestors is considered to be so large that sacrifices (yāgās) as well as vānaprasṭa and sanyāsa (the two last stages of a Brāhman's life) are reckoned as being superogatory for even the last in descent.," To them was ordained an austere religious life, one of continued penance and self-mortification. Early bath, repetition of prayers a thousand times, observance of strict fasts, the reading of the Vēḍās, familiarity with Śāsṭrās, but not discussing them in a contentious spirit—these form the daily routine life of one of this class. The eldest son *should* enter holy wedlock in the presence of agni, (fire) and procreate children for the uninterrupted maintenance of a righteous lineage. The others should not have even the thought of carnal pleasures. They should not indulge in the six sins (kāmam) lust, (krōḍham) anger, (lōbham) covetousness, (mōham) infatuation, (maḍam) pride, and (maṭsaram) contentious spirit. They should avoid parānnam, literally, 'food belonging to others', śrāḍha bakṣhaṇam, 'the taking of food at śrāḍha (funeral) ceremonies', and praṭigraham—receiving presents. By the due observance of the above ordinances, they are enjoined to confer merit on the land they live in, and induce the rest to follow the right path. The Āḍhyans have indeed receded a good deal from the path chalked out for them by the ancient sages. They are, however, still strict in the observance of religious services, and engage themselves much in the reverent study of the Vēḍās.

3. Viśishṭa Brāhmaṇa.—There are two sub-divisions of this class, *viz.* :—

(1) Agṅihōṭrīs
(2) Bhaṭṭaṭirīs

To them are prescribed (1) Agṅihōṭram — sacrifice, (2) Bhaṭṭavṛṭṭi—teaching of philosophy, (3) Sanyāsam—asceticism, and (4) having sacrifices, (yāgam) performed by other Brāhmans.

(1) The Agṅihōṭrīs are those who have performed yāgas or sacrifices and are of three kinds:—

(1) Those who have performed the ceremony called Agṅichayanam are known as Agṅichit corrupted into Akkiṭer or Akkiṭṭiri.

(2) Those who have performed the ceremony of Agṅi Āḍhānam are known as Āhiṭagṅi corrupted into Aṭiṭiri.

(3) Those who have performed the Sōma sacrifice are known as Sōmayāji corrupted into Chōmāṭiri.

To these sub-divisions, known as a whole by the term Agṅihōṭri, are assigned the following functions, *viz.* :—The study of the Vēḍās, the teaching of the same, the performance of hōmam or oblation to Agṅi or fire for one's own benefit as well as for the benefit of others; hospitality to guests (Aṭiṭhi Pūja), the offering of libations of various kinds, Viviḍha Ṭarpaṇaṃgal, sacrifices for the propitiation of the gods and the spirits of ancestors, and the performance of yāgams (sacrifices) already named, such as Āḍhānam, Agṅi, Sōma yāgam, etc. Only those who have entered into holy wedlock are qualified to perform these sacrifices. It is also interesting to note that a Nāyar is an indispensable factor in these sacrifices.

The performance of ceremonies by the Naṃbūṭirīs is designed to benefit not only themselves but also all those who inhabit Malabar. It is the vicarious performance of these ceremonies enjoined on them by Paraśu Rāma that relieves the people of Kērala of "the ills that man is heir to." The Kēralōṭpaṭṭi says:—

"Thus in the land created by Śri Paraśu Rāma the Brāhmans should all bathe at dawn of day, and live virtuously, performing religious duties, worship and make offerings of rice to the elements at the Kṣhēṭrams or holy places and Kāvus (or lesser temples), and in order that the sorrow and the sickness which are incidental to mankind might be removed from the people, they were to cause to be performed Īśwara Sēvakal (or worship of God) by

Hōman—offering oblations to Gods by throwing ghee, etc., into consecrated fire;
Dhyānam—meditation on the deity;
Bhagavaṭi Sēva—worship of the goddess Bhagavaṭi;
Puṣhpāññali—worship with flowers;
Anṭi Namaskāram—prostration in the evening;
Ṭṛkāla Pūja—worship at dawn, noon and sunset;
Gaṇapaṭi Hōmam—fire sacrifice to Gaṇapaṭi;
Mṛṭyum-Jayam—prayer or invocation in the name of Mṛṭyu (or god of death) to avert accidents;
Mūññu Lakṣha Sahasṙanāmam—the ceremony of repeating of the 1,000 names of Īśwara three lakhs of times;
Brāhmaṇa Sahasṙa Bhōjanam—distribution of victuals daily to a thousand Brāhmans; and
Mahā Mṛṭyum-Jayam—prayer to Mṛṭyu".[1]

(2) Bhaṭṭaṭiris—These are the repositories of Śāsṭriac and legal lore. They have all the rights and duties of Agñihōṭṙis, except the performing of yāgams or sacrifices. After the study of the Vēḍas, the Bhaṭṭaṭiris are enjoined to learn Ṭaṙka (logic), Vēḍānṭa (religious philosophy or theology), Vyākaraṇa (grammar) and Mīmāṃsa (ritualism). The last is divided into

1. Wilson's *Collection of Oriental Manuscripts*, p. 311.

Bhaṭṭa and Prabhākara Mīmāmsas. It is their duty to teach these to others. They are to discuss religious and sastraic questions in assemblies gathered periodically for the purpose, when rewards are given to those who excel the rest in learning. They are to demonstrate to others the greatness of the Vēḍās and Śāsṭras and the truth of the Hindu religion. They were thus the great religious teachers of Malabar, and had always a large number of disciples around them. Those who teach the Vēḍās are known as Ōṭikkans, and these also officiate as family priests. The Vāḍhyāns or heads of Vēḍic schools, of which there are two, one at Trichur in the Cochin State and the other at Ṭirunāvāya in British Malabar with a branch at Kōṭṭayam in Travancore, are to teach the Vēḍās and to supervise the moral conduct of their pupils. The Vyḍīkans are the highest authorities to decide what does and what does not constitute violations of caste rules and prescribe expiatory ceremonies. There are six families of Vyḍīkans, two for each grāmams of Chōvaram or Śukapuram, Perumanam and Iriññālakkuṭa. The names of these families or Illoms are :—(1) Ṭaikāṭ, (2) Kaṉlingāṭ, (3) Pantal, (4) Perumpaṭappu, (5) Kaymukku, and (6) Cherumukku. The Smārṭṭas are to study the Smṛṭis, and other Śāsṭras relating to law and custom, with the special object of qualifying themselves to preside over Smārṭavichārams or socio-moral tribunals called by the Rajas to investigate cases of conjugal infidelity arising amongst Naṃbūṭiri women. There are six such Smārṭṭas. Their names are :—(1) Paṭṭachōmayār, (2) Mūṭṭamana Bhaṭṭaṭiri, (3) Vellārkkaṭṭu Bhaṭṭaṭiri, (4) Naṭuvaṭṭu Puṭavar, (5) Iruvachchi Puṭavar, and (6) Mēppilly Naṃpūṭiri.

4. Sāmānya Brāhmaṇar.—Under this class come the majority of Naṃbūṭiris from whom the study of the Vēḍās alone is all that is excepted. Their chief profession consists in (1) Archana [performing pūja (ritual worship)] in temples; (2) Ṭanṭram (duty of directing pūja) ; (3) Manṭravāḍam (mystic enchantment);

(4) Purāṇa Pārāyaṇam (the reciting of Purāṇās), (5) Muhūrṭṭāḍi Kālaviśēṣham (astrology—foretelling auspicious moments) &c.

(1) Archakas.—On the East Coast, those who do Pūja to 'self-revealed' (Swayambhu) images are held in low estimation. But, in Kērala, as the land is purified by the performance of ceremonics, and as the images are consecrated and are therefore considered as endowed with great sanctity, no slur is attached to the profession of Pūjāri, (officiating priest), and there are villages the members of which, as well as particular households, who follow the profession without undergoing any degradation in caste thereby.

(2) Ṭanṭrīs.—Among the Āḍhyans, there are certain houses professing Ṭanṭram in temples. They are, by virtue of this office, head-priests of such temples. The religious services of the pagodas are under their direction, though they have no voice in their temporalities. They are the duly constituted Gurus (preceptors) of the temple priests and are the final authorities in all matters of temple ritual. They preside at Uṭsavams, Pṛaṭishṭa-Kalaśams, prescribe purifactory ceremonies, &c. The chief among them is the Taraṇanellūr Naṃpūṭirippād, who, the Kērala-māhāṭmyam says, was appointed Tanṭri of 24,000 temples in Malabar by Paraśu Rāma.

(3) Manṭravāḍīs—Their profession is, after the study of the Vēḍās, to acquaint themselves with the use of Manṭrams (mystic formulas), Yenṭrams (cabalistic figures) and employ them along with Bali(sacrifices), Pūjās (rituals), Ḍānam (gifts), Hōmam (oblations to fire), Rakṣhākaraṇam (protection from evil spirits), Uchāṭanam (exorcism), Vaśīkaraṇam (subjection), Ḍaṇḍanam (punishment), Banḍhanam (binding), Sṭambhanam (causing of stupification) , Māraṇam (destruction), &c. for the protection and well-being of others.

(4) Pouraṇikaṇmar—These recite and expound the Puraṇas, such as the Ramayaṇam, Bharaṭam, Bhagavaṭam, &c., in temples with a view to infuse among worshippers belief in religion and faith in God. These are called Bharaṭa Bhaṭṭaṭiris.

(5) Jōṭish Śasṭrakar.—Their profession is the study of astrology by means of which they are to foretell the happening of eclipses, what effect these have on those who are born under the star on which the eclipses fall, prescribe auspicious moments for ceremonies, &c., and cast horoscopes.

5. Jati Maṭrēyan.—This class is divided into four sub-divisions:—

(a) The Ashṭa Vydians.

(b) The Śasṭrangakar and Gramaṇi Aḍhyans.

(c) Those who have given up the study of the Vēḍas on account of physical or mental incapacity or imbecility.

(d) Those who have done the same having become slaves to the passions.

(a) The Ashṭa Vyḍians—These are physicians by profession. They are said to have become degraded on account of their having had to shed blood in performing surgical operations. What a gross misuse of language to call them Jaṭimaṭrēyans or nominal Brahmans, because they follow the noble profession of medicine and surgery! In Malabar, there are eight houses or illams, the members of which follow the medical profession, and the names of these have already been given. They are also called Mussaḍs and Naṃpis.

(b) The Śasṭrangakar.—These are said to have been the Brahmans who accepted the profession of arms from Paraśu Rama. The Gramaṇi Aḍhyans are those who, it is said, actually received territorial sovereignty from the hands of the sage. These two are supposed to have gone down the scale of Brahmanhood. The physicians, the soldiers, and the kings had other duties to perform, which left them no time to devote themselves to the study of the Vēḍas exclusively, and the Nampūṭirīs in course of time came to look upon them as a class not entitled to the study of the Vēḍas and to be associated with their sacred selves. But it is altogether incorrect to class them as Jāṭimāṭṛēyans; for, according to the Kēralōṭpaṭṭi, the foremost among those who accepted arms from Parasu Rāma was the Eḍappilli Nampiāṭiri or the Eḍappilli Rāja, who is thus both king and soldier. Yet he is at this moment considered Āḍhyan of Āḍhyans and of the very highest authority as a Vēḍic Nampuṭiri, barring Āluvāncheri Ṭampurākkal. Even now, all the above classes have what is called Muṭalmuṛa or reading the Vēḍas or hearing it read once at any rate. The obvious injustice done to these classes requires no comment. Sub-divisions (c) and (d) call for no further notice than the descriptions given of them. According to the Jāṭiniṛṇṇaya, these classes have four Sṭhānams or privileges. These are:—

(1) they can bathe at the same ghat with the Adhyans (Kaṭavu);

(2) sit for meals with them in the same line (Panṭi);

(3) stage (Arangu); and

(4) kitchen (Aṭukkala).

6. Saṃkēṭikanmār. These are the Emprāns or Ṭulu Brāhmans and have 6 sub-divisions among them, *viz.*:—(1) Akkaraḍēsi, (2) Ikkaraḍēsi, (3) Ṭṛppūṇiṭṭuṛaḍēsi, (4) Tiruvellāḍēsi, (5) Carṇāṭakadēsi, (6) Ṭuludēsi.

These, it is said, ran away from Kērala after they were settled there by Parasu Rāma, but returned soon afterwards on hearing of the prosperity and wealth of the country.

Of the above sub-divisions, the first and second were those who were brought by Kulasekhara Perumāl to his country, Travancore, and settled there. The third formed a colony brought by the Raja of Cochin and settled in his kingdom; the fourth formed another colony brought by the Kōlaṭṭunāḍ or Cheracal Raja and settled in his country of Kolaṭṭunāḍ, North Malabar, and the remaining two came to Malabar of their own accord. They are all half Malabar and half Canarese or Ṭuḷu Brahmans in their daily life, customs, manners, etc. Their profession consists in the study of the Vēḍās, performance of services in temples, etc. Of the settlement of the Ṭiruvellaḍēśis we have the following account given us by the late Ravi Vurma Raja, M. A., B. L., in *The Malabar Quarterly Review*:—

"The Nambūris of Perinchallūr Grāmam were wont from time immemorial to assist in the performance of religious ceremonies in Kōlaswarūpam. There arose, for what reason it is not known, a feud between them and the then Kōlaṭṭiri Rajah, and in consequence thereof, the former sternly refused to help the latter in religious ceremonies. This irritated the sovereign, and he resolved to dispense with their services in future and found a separate Brahman community for the purpose. With this view, he went to Mangalore and requested the Ṭuḷu Brahmans there to send some families to his country. They were promised full honours and large estates. To test the sincerity of the Raja, they imposed a condition on him, on the fulfilment of which they promised to go with him, and the condition was to build up the banks of a big tank called Kōṭiṭīrṭham in the midst of the village in six hours, *i. e.*, between 9 p. m. and 3 a. m., when alone it will not be used. Thanks to his splendid resources and firm resolution, the Raja stood the test to the very letter. Thereupon two sets of families, one consisting of 237 and the other of 257 houses, represented usually by the mnemonics, Sāgaram and Samudram, migrated to Kōlaṭṭunāḍ and they are the so-called Ṭiruvallāḍēśis of the present day. Why they are called by this designation I cannot tell. They were given all the privileges which once belonged to Perinchallūr Grāmam Nampūris. Of these latter, however, the members of one family alone, *viz.*, Arippan, stood aloof from their comrades in the quarrel with the Rajah. To this family, therefore, was given the Pourōhiṭṭyam, and the members of the family are even now the hereditary Purōhiṭṭs (i. e., family priests) of Kōlaswarūpam."[1]

7. Śāpagrasṭṭanmār.—These are supposed to have doubted the divinity of Paraśu Rāma, and were consequently cursed by the sage. Hence called 'the cursed ones.'

8. Pāpiṣhṭan.—There are five sub-divisions of this class :—

(1) those who received as ḍānam or gift the sin of Paraśu Rāma incurred by the destruction of the Kṣheṭriya race. They are called Urila Pariṣha Mūssaḍs ;

(2) those Grāmiṇīs who permitted the murder of Bhūṭa Rāya Perumāl ;

(3) those who committed the deed. They are known as Nampiṭīs ;

(4) those who officiate as priests to Nāyars at their Śrāḍha ceremonies called Elayaṭus;

(5) the inhabitants of the Pañṅyūr Grāmmam who destroyed the temple of Varāha Mūrṭṭi, the Boar incarnation of Viṣhṇu.

The two classes of Nyūna Jāṭīs are said to be the Elayaṭu and the Mūṭṭaṭu, i. e., the 'Junior' and the 'Senior'. Their defect consisted in the one administering to the Śrāḍhas or death-annual ceremonies of the Nāyars, and the other partaking of food served to the god Śiva.

Of these, the Mūṭṭaṭus are said to be emigrants from the other coast. There they were a degraded

1. Vol. I, pp. 294-5

class of Brahmans whose duty was to do pūja to the phallic emblem of Śiva and to partake of the offerings to that deity. They were there designated Śiva Ḍwijas. In Malabar to do pūja in a temple is not considered degrading to any class of Brahmans, even to the highest, and so to the Mūṭṭaṭu is assigned the duty of carrying the idol, in certain temples, round the temple in the daily service, to act as guards to the deity, to wash the Śrīkōvil, i. e., the inner sanctum excepting the Gaṙbha Gṛham or the sanctum sanctorum, to prepare and make ready the rice to be offered to the god and do such other services in the temple. That with which the idol is bathed, that with which it is adorned, that which is offered to it—these are the peculiar perquisites of the Mūṭṭaṭu. Their women go by the name of Manayammamāṙ and carry the Maṙakuṭa or umbrella with them, like the Naṃbūṭiri women. Their ceremonies do not differ much from those of the Naṃbūṭirīs. They follow the Makkaṭṭāyam form of inheritance.

The Eḷayaṭus owe their degradation, as already observed, to their officiating as Purōhiṭs to the Nayars. Their profession is to act as such and to live on the perquisites attached to the office. They are their own priests. They also do services in temples of their own and in some others that are the property of Nāyars. They have also certain duties at the Ṭāli marriages of Nāyars. In some places they are called Naṃpiāṭīs. Their ceremonies are the same as those of the Naṃbūṭirīs. Their women are called 'Elōraṃma'. These too carry the Maṙakuṭa and follow the practices of Naṃbūṭiri women. The Eḷayaṭus are Makkaṭṭāyīs and in all respects resemble the Naṃbuṭirīs.

General Appearance.—The Naṃbūṭirīs are a very fair coloured race of men, with well-defined, regular features. They wear the Kuḍumma or tuft of hair in front on the top and not on the back of the head as the Brahmans on the other coast. The Eṃprāns wear it half way between the crown of the head and the back. The Śānkara Smṛṭi prescribes rules regarding the position and extent of the tuft of hair to be left unshaved on the crown of the head. It says that four fingers length upwards from where the hair appears on the forehead, is the place for Ḍēva Śikha, or tuft of the gods, to the extent of four fingers in breadth. Thence receding four fingers length beyond is the place for Pyśācha Śikha or tuft of Pyśāchas or spirits. Four fingers length further is the place for Āsura Śikha, tuft of the Demons. Bhārgava's injunction is that the Brahmans of the southern 32 of the 64 Grāmas should adopt the first and the northern 32 the second.[1] The growth of hair on the head is plentiful, glossy and wavy. The Naṃbūṭirī's tuft occupies an oval patch on the crown of the head, removed more to the front than to the back, and is worn long. It is tied into a knot and thrown behind, the hair spreading on the head. All but the oval patch is shaved. So also the face. But when the Naṃbūṭirī's wife is pregnant, he refrains from the barber. It will be noticed that the Malabar people are peculiar in having their tuft in front. All Hindus but Malayālīs wear it on the back of the head except the Mukkāṇi and Chōlian Brahmans of the East Coast. It has been surmised that Paraśu Rāma's first colony was composed of these Brahmans, and that the tradition of the Sage's having changed the tuft of his newly brought Brahmans for a national purpose is a fiction. Of course we have at present no means of testing the truth of the theory or of the fact. But there is a saying in Malabar "Pūrva śikha paraḍēśaṭṭu niṣhiḍhaṃ", meaning "the front tuft is forbidden in Paraḍēśa" (East Coast). The Naṃbūṭirīs grow their finger nails sometimes very long. After bath, they wear on their foreheads the horizontal Śaivite marks with the Bhasmam or sacred ashes and the vertical Viṣhṇuvite mark with the Gōpichanḍanam (sandal).[2] It has been remarked of the Naṃbūṭirī's general

1. *Sl.* 13 to 16—Chap. 1, Pt. 3.

2. See *Sankara Smrithi*, Chap. IV, Pt. II, *Sls.* 20 to 25.

appearance that "there is about his good old person and his quaint looking dress and jewelry, a Saṭvic (mild and guileless) beauty which the eye delights to dwell on."

The Naṃbūṭiri lady is generally uncommonly fair and handsome. Being strictly ghosha, the women shut themselves up inside their houses and seldom move about except on extreme urgency. They then shelter themselves behind broad round cadjan umbrellas, specially made for the purpose, which are turned against the passer-by. They have long and glossy hair, which is parted at the crown and drawn tight to the ears with a knot at the back. After bath, they put on three horizontal lines on their foreheads with sandal paste. The Āḍhya women put these on in a crescent like form. They apply also eye-salves, which extend as dark lines up to the ears on either side.

Clothing.—The Naṃbūṭirīs are very sparing in their clothing, and do not seem to feel the shame of walking about almost naked, a habit which is not countenanced by the Smṛṭi, which they profess to follow. The Śānkara Smṛṭi, supposed to be a compendium of the ordinances originally laid down by Paraśu Rāma and extracted and expounded by the renowned Vēḍanṭist Śankarāchārya, lays down sumptuary laws for their guidance, and these do not certainly permit them to be scantily clothed. The Naṃbūṭirīs are strict Swadeshies and would not on any account go in for Bilāṭṭi (European) piece-goods as wearing apparel. Manchester piece-goods are taboo to them. They wear a cloth of local manufacture, 4 or 5 cubits in length with a red line border, round their waist reaching a little below the knee. They eschew the use of silk or coloured cloths of any kind, as well as a plain white cloth without a border. Their mode of dressing is peculiar. That of the males is known as Ṭaṭṭuṭukkal, which is done on religious occasions by tying a long piece of country-made cloth round the waist with a portion of it passing between the thighs and tucked in

A NAMPUTIRI AND HIS ANTHARJANAM.

From an old print
By courtesy of Mr. M. S. Menon.

(To face p. 49.

at the front and behind, with the front portion arranged into a number of reduplications. This mode of dressing exhibits a front covered by numerous folds hanging down from the waist to the feet, while the buttocks are left almost exposed. They wear wooden shoes, but are not averse to leather ones, though they will not allow the heel of the foot to be covered. On ordinary occasions, they dress like the Nāyars and seem not to be averse to wear Manchester made mulls. Some affect elegance by tying the cloth round the body below the arm-pits. The Naṃbūṭiri woman, who is called an Anṭar̄janam or Akaṭṭamma, i. e., one who is inside (strictly ghōṣha), also dresses in a peculiar style. While the ordinary Naṃbuṭiri woman dresses in the style called Ñer̄iññuṭukkuka, the Aḍhyan lady dresses in the style known as Okkum Koluṭṭum Vachchuṭukkuka. A white piece of cloth, for coloured ones and silk are prohibited, about 10 cubits in length is fastened round the loins, a portion of it passes between the legs, the whole reaching well below the knee. A gold border to this cloth is allowed. They do not wear the *ravukka*, or half-jacket which is but a recent introduction into Malabar. At home, inside the house, they dress themselves like Nāyar women but, while walking abroad, they cover themselves up with a long piece of cloth leaving only the feet exposed; one end of the cloth is so held up in the hand which holds also the Mar̄akkuṭa, or the covering umbrella already mentioned, as to cover the face and the body completely. Walking abroad, they are always accompanied by a Ḍāsi or Viṣhal, i. e., a Nayar maid, and a Nāyar servant, one of whom walks in front, while the other follows behind, who call out to the wayfarers to move off the road. The Naṃbūṭirīs insist on their women folk wearing about their persons as much clothing as they would persistently deny to Nayar women.

Ornaments.—The Naṃbūṭiri wears but few ornaments on his person. He has finger rings made of gold, and often set with stones. A finger ring of peculiar make is considered sacred and necessary on religious occasions. This is the Paviṭṛam, which is of gold and of the thickness of an ordinary finger ring with an '8'-like figure worked on it, having on each side a dotted pattern, the rest being plain or worked in lines. In place of this, Paviṭṛams made of Ḍurbha grass are put on when performing religious ceremonies. The latter is of course the most orthodox. The Nambūṭirīs bore the ears as other Hindus do, but are prohibited from wearing ear-rings. Those, however, who have performed the Agniyajana and are Agnihoṭrīs, use ear-pendants known as kuṇḍalam or less elaborate ones called kuṇukku made of gold. The Nambūṭirīs sometimes wear round their necks neck-laces of Ruḍrākṣha (nuts of the *Elaocarpus Ganitrus*) or Ṭulasimaṇi mounted in gold. The middle bead of these neckiaces will be generally a Gouri Śankar, representing Śiva and Pārvaṭi curiously worked in gold and set with precious stones.

The proscription against the use of valuable ornaments is even more strict in the case of Nambūṭiri women. The desire for valuable ornaments, a weakness natural to women all over the world, is rigorously suppressed by the ordinances to which the Nambūṭirīs are subject. The Śankara-Smṛṭi ordains, she could wear on both arms only bracelets made of brass or bell-metal. Those made silver are not objectionable; but of gold never. She should never have a nose screw. She should not have her hair plaited. She should not ornament her forehead with dots of beautiful pattern. The cloth round the loins should not be fastened with a gridle. She may wear an ear ornament made of gold called Chiṟṟu and round her neck a string made of cotton thread with a ṭāli hanging by it. She should not wear rings on her toes; neither anklets nor ornaments on the crown of the head.[1] That these rules are not very strictly observed in practice is but natural. For Mr. Fawcett tells us that "in North Malabar

1. Chap. 7, pt. 4.

golden bangles are worn as a rule—*pace* Mr. Logan." Dr. Subramania Ayyar observes that "a peculiar kind of necklace, called cheṙuṭāli, is also worn and beneath this the Āḍhyan women wear garlands of maṇis or gold pieces, along with other jewels, known as Kāśumāla, Pūṭṭāli and Kaḷuṭṭila". The Naṃbūṭiri widow is allowed to wear ornaments except the Ṭāli, and she is not to shave her head as among the East Coast Brāhmans.

A Naṃbūṭiri female before she attains puberty is known as Uṇṇi Kiṭāvu; after puberty till marriage as Peṇ Kiṭāvu. If she remains unmarried after she has come of age, she is called Nanga Piḷḷa, and after marriage she is known as Akāyil Uḷḷaver, Āṭṭēnmār or Akaṭṭuḷḷavar. There is no ceremony on the attainment of puberty. But on the appearance of the menses, the girl has to sit apart in a special place and is held unclean. According to the Śānkara-Smṛṭi, the following rules have to be observed by a woman in her periods. She should not touch the roofing of the house. She should sit apart inside the house specially reserved for the purpose. She should not clean her teeth. If she does this, her children will have blackened teeth or have deceased gums or have irregular teeth. She should not take an oil bath. It will make her children look rough. She should not paint her eye-lashes with lampblack, for her issue will be born blind. She should not adorn her hair with flowers, for her issue will become bald-headed. She should not use sandalpaste, etc., for that will bring on skin disease to her children. She should not sit outside the house at dusk, for her children will then be subject to epilepsy. If she walks on the road at this time, her children would become lame. She should not wear a double cloth, Eṇappuṭaka, i. e., two cloths, round her loins, lest her children become lepers. If she takes her meals from a bell-metal vessel, her children will have to beg for their living. If, on the other hand, she is served with her meals in a plantain leaf, her children will shine with Brahma-Ṭējas, i. e, the effulgent light of the Brahman. But the leaf of the Arayāl (*Ficus Religiosa*), the Pēral (*Ficus Indica*) and the Pilāśa (*Butea Frondosa*) should be avoided. She should have a vessel set apart for her use. She should not touch any other. In no circumstance should she bathe on the third day. If the performance of any ceremony, such as Śrārḍha falls on that day, she should fast on that day and have it performed the next day after the ceremonial bath. This ceremonial bath she can take only after sunrise on the fourth day. She has to wear round her a cloth washed by a Maṇṇāṭṭi or Vēla woman (a low caste washing class) and should be attended by Pariyapeṭṭaval, i.e, a Nāyar woman attached to her Illam. On returning from her bath, the first look she should have must be at her husband's face. She could, after the bath on the fourth day, enter the kitchen[1].

Habitation.—A Nambūṭiri's house is called an Illam or Mana, the one a Telugu and the other a Canarese term meaning house. The Illam is generally situated in the midst of an extensive garden planted with many kinds of trees especially the jack, the mango the areca, the laurel and the plantain, amidst whose cool, luxuriant and shady foliage it rears its roof giving secluded shelter to the inmates. All sorts of edible vegetables and roots are grown in the garden round the house. A tank is an inseparable accompaniment, with bathing shed and ghauts. The Nambūṭiri can cleanse his body and soul only with a plunge-bath, and he generally dips himself twice a day in cold water; for this alone confers the requisite ablutional purity. The inevitable Sarpakkāvu or serpent grove is located in the north-western corner of the compound. The structure of the Nambūṭiri's house is described elsewhere. The furniture is of the simplest description. A few bell-metal pots, pans, and settles for cooking purposes, a few planks wrought after the manner of

1. Part 3, Chapter 12.

A TYPICAL NAMPUTIRI ILLOM.

(To face p 52.

a tortoise, Avaṇapalaka, the Kūrmāsana, for purposes of sitting, several cots, some made of planks of wood, while others are lined with coir rope, and one or two hanging cots attached to the ceiling by chains of iron, skins of leopard or the spotted deer used to sit on during prayers—these form the full complement of a Nambuṭiri's house-hold furniture. Chairs, tables, mirrors, globes, etc., are being slowly introduced into the Nambūṭiri's house. But these are not popular with the orthodox.

Laws of inheritance.—The Nambūṭiris follow the Makkaṭṭāyam system of inheritance from father to son, in contradistinction to the Marumakkaṭṭāyam system, according to which not one's own issue, but one's sister's children inherit property. The latter is the Nāyar system. The Nambūṭirīs follow the Hindu Law as modified by custom. The family property is joint and impartible. The eldest male member is manager, irrespective of his being the son of the last holder, and the junior members have only the right to be maintained in the illam. Their self-acquisitions lapse to the joint family at their death. In fact the archaic Hindu system of succession and inheritance is still kept up in all its integrity. In default of male issue to represent the illam, the last surviving girl is given over in marriage with all her patrimony by a ceremony called Sarvaswadānam (gift of all or everything) after which the son-in-law assumes management of the property in trust for the to-be-born son, to whom it is handed over, if born, on attainment of majority. The lineage is further kept upon failure of male issue by means of adoptions and affiliations of which there are various forms such as (1) Paṭṭu Kayyāl Ḍaṭṭu, (2) Chān Chamaṭa and (3) Āyaṭṭuviḍhi.

(1) Paṭṭu Kayyāl Ḍaṭṭu, i. e., adoption by ten hands—*viz.*, those of the adopter's (father and mother), of the adoptee and of the adoptee's parents or guardians. Generally the boy selected is one on whom the Upanayana, or the ceremony of the investiture

with the sacred thread has not been performed. This form of adoption is the most approved one.

(2) Chān Chamaṭa Daṭṭu.—This means adoption by Chamaṭa, i. e, adoption in which the essential ceremony, besides gift and acceptance of the adoptee consists in putting into the fire or sacrificing a span (Chān) of a sacred plant called Chamaṭa.

(3) Āyaṭṭu Viḍhi Ḍaṭṭu.—This is simply the taking into the family and constituting the adoptee as heir to the adoptor, without any religious ceremony. This is simple affiliation and is generally the form in which widows take in heirs to the last male holder.

The second or the Chān Chamaṭa form confers the right of sonship on the adoptee, though not as efficacious from a religious point of view as No. 1. Such adoptee loses all rights in his natural family except to offer Piṇḍas or oblations to the manes of ancestors and to succeed to the property of that family, in default of other members therein, and becomes a member of that joint family to which he is adopted. As to the third form it is, as already, observed but a mere affiliation, and is practised to a large extent by the Naṃbuṭirīs, but it is difficult to say if the courts would recognise such a custom when the family is represented solely by females.

Neither an eldest son nor an only son should be given or taken in adoption. The degrees of prohibition as regards relationship in cases of marriage also apply to adoption. Neither a sister's son nor a daughter's son should be adopted. But the latter is allowed in extreme cases of necessity, though the former is allowed under no circumstances.[1]

Some 17 houses of Naṃbūṭiri Brāhmans of the Payyannūr Grāmam in North Malabar follow the Marumakkaṭṭāyam system, and are looked upon as of an inferior order. They are called Ammōmanmār.

Food.—The lines of the *Lusiad*,

"To crown their meal no meanest life expires,
Pulse, fruit and herb alone their food requires"

1. See *Sankara Smriti*, pt. 3 of Chap. 6.

are strictly true of the Nambūṭiri's daily food. Their staple food is rice and vegetable curry with condiments known as Uppiliṭṭaṭu (pickles of sorts), and sauce known as Sammanḍhi. To these are added Uppēri or chopped plantains, yams, etc., fried in cocoanut oil, and Pappaḍam or round crisp-flour cakes also fried in cocoanut oil. They like both sour and sweet things, but are afraid of pungent ones. The curries usual among them are the same as those mentioned in our account of the Ōṇam feast. To those may be added Mulaka ṣhyam and Meḷukkupuraṭṭi. Both are favourites with the Nambūṭirīs, the former is a preparation of sliced vegetables boiled in water with salt and chillies and seasoned with cocoanut oil and Karivēppila (a kind of leaf)[1]; while in the preparation of the latter, the water in which the sliced vegetables are boiled is strained off and the slices themselves are seasoned with cocoanut oil over a slow fire. Ghee is not much used. The conjee or rice gruel with accessories is the Nambuṭiri's favourite mid-day meal. Tea and coffee are not prescribed in their Śāsṭrās, and are therefore looked at askance. But of late, the progressives amongst them indulge in these, though on the sly. They are however steadily coming into fashion. They seldom drink cold water. Their drinking water is known as Chukku Veḷḷam. It is water boiled and flavoured with dried ginger, cummin seeds, coriander, etc. The ladies take their meals separately. When there are no strangers, the wife serves meals to her husband. But, if there are guests dining with the Nambūṭiri, the food is served by a Paṭṭar Brāhman or a younger male member of the family. It is served on plantain leaves, which take the place of plates. The Nambūṭiri ladies do not partake of food cooked by Paṭṭar Brāhmans, but the male members of the Illam have no objection to do so. Strictly speaking, the Nambūṭirīs are allowed only one rice meal a day, their supper being confined to fruits;

1. Kariveppu—Bergera Koenigii.

but, in practice, they take rice oftener—not less seldom than twice a day. A widow is confined always to one meal. Certain vegetables, such as the gourd and other articles as palmyra fruit and jaggery, etc., are among those a Naṃbūṭiri is prohibited from eating. The wife takes charge of the leaf off which the husband has dined by holding it by her right hand, the husband touching it by the left before he rises from his seat. This is to indicate that the wife is eating in continuation and not the echchil, or the remains of the victuals which are considered impure.

In the 11th Chapter of the Śankara Smṛṭi, there are certain rules laid down regarding the taking of food by the four orders of Naṃbūṭirīs, viz., the Brahmachāri, the Grahasṭan, the Vānaprasṭan, and the Sanyāsi. The Brahmachāri or the student who has to live in his preceptor's house may take the food he pleases there. To him, that is the purest food, equal to Ambrosia. The Grahasṭa must, before he takes his meals, satisfy the hunger of the Gods, the Piṭṛus (spirits of ancestors), guests, pupils and household divinities. He can take only what is left after these are served. The Vānaprasṭa should, so far as he possibly can, live on air. He can, at any rate, only eat wild fruits and roots that grow in the forest. He should not eat anything that is ground in a mortar. He must satisfy himself with having his food ground by his teeth, i. e., he should not partake of things boiled. The Sanyāsi can have only one meal a day. He must partake only of what he gets by begging. He can drink only water. Then follow rules that are common to all Naṃbuṭiris. No one should take unclean food. Nothing should be taken within six hours of the occurrence of an eclipse of the sun or moon. Food may be taken after bath, when the eclipse is fully over and the surface of the sun or moon is fully visible. If a Naṃbūṭiri comes to know of any untoward thing having happened to a Brāhman or a cow, he should desist from taking his food, till he tries all he can to give them relief, and till he has sympathised with them. He should not take meals at the moment when the king or his own relative is plunged in grief, at the dead of night, at midday, when his previous food has not been well-digested, at dawn and at dusk. No food should be taken with a wet cloth on, or with naked body, or sitting at a window, and not on the floor, or on a broken plank, or on tiptoe, or lying down, or sitting in the lap of another, or from a broken vessel, or from the bare floor, or holding the food in the bare hand without a leaf or vessel. No salt ought to be served before prayers at meals are over. While sitting at meals, children should not be abused. No one should sit by himself for meals. But an enemy, a wife and one who by caste rules is not allowed to sit in the same line should, on no account, be allowed to sit by you. Rice prepared with gingely seed, as well as curds, should not be taken in the night. Milk ought not to be taken in the day time ; food ought not to be taken before performing hōmam (sacrifice), or before one's parents have taken theirs. Remains and refuse of victuals should not be taken. No food should be taken without ghee. Food should not be taken outside a house, or in the view of a great multitude, or in an altogether uninhabited house. The stomach should at no time be over-filled. If the food and Āchārams (observances) are pure, the heart will be pure, and God will bestow grace only on an absolutely pure heart. Otherwise, one will be cast in the darkness of hell and will have to be grieving there.

Occupation.—We know already something regarding the occupations pursued by the eight classes of Nambūṭirīs described above. It is apparent that the original Brāhman families divided among themselves. They assigned the profession of medicine to one class, sorcery and magic to another, astronomy and astrology to a third, and the duty of performing pūjās in temples to a fourth, and so on. The Nambūṭirīs were, according to tradition, brought into Kēraḷa a colonists to people the country, and the socio-economic polity of their patron sage found, for the various classes into which the community was divided, exclusive occupations. While some had the government of the land, others were equipped with arms to protect the country from foreign incursions and internecine quarrels Another set was endowed with spiritual functions and so on. That these exclusive divisions were not strictly maintained till of late is evident. Notwithstanding that those who exercised territorial sovereignty were held not competent to study the Vēḍās, we have the fact that there were territorial magnates among the highest class of Vēḍic Naṃbūṭirīs, to wit, the Rajas of Cheṃpakaśśēry or Aṃbalāppuḷa or Poṙacād and Eḍappiḷḷy. Our author speaks of the Raja of Poṙacād as a spiritual prince. "Paṙūr", he says "is a powerful ecclesiastical Raja." Again, according to him, "the Princes of Poṙacād and Paṙūr, being Brāhmans, have alone the privilege of being seated in the presence of the Raja of Cochin." "The former," it is added "is superior both in sanctity and rank." "The kings who hold the reins of Government at Eḍappiḷḷy on the coast of Malabar and also at Paṙur and Araceri, are certainly Brāhmans," says Bartolomeo.[1] Really the profession of arms did not disqualify any Brāhman from the study of the Vēḍās or detract from his sanctimonious charactēr. The Eḍappiḷḷy Chief, as we have said, was the foremost who accepted arms from Paraśu Rāma and, even so late as the Portuguese period, we see him fighting that nation, espousing the cause of the Zamorin, and leading the Zamorin's land forces as also his navy in the fight at the ford of Cambaḷam. A Brāhman general is known as Naṃbiāṭiri, and the Raja of Eḍappiḷḷy is called by pre-eminence Eḍappiḷḷy Naṃbiāṭiri, while there are still to be found others bearing the title, such as Inḍanṭuruṭṭi Naṃbiaṭiri, Perimpiḷḷiaḷaṭṭ Naṃbiāṭiri, etc. But it is quite true that they never served

1. P. 296.

in the ranks, as fighting units in the armies of the Rajas. Archbishop Meneses, who had an interview with the then Raja of Poṙacād, describes him as a "young man of short stature, but well-proportioned, and distinguished among the Rajas of Malabar for his valour and courtesy." This Prince was accorded the high honour of being styled "Brother-in-arms to the King of Portugal." Meneses observes "that he called himself Nambrache (Naṃbūṭiri), that is, High Priest and was very zealous in his devotions." It will be remembered that the patron saint of the Naṃbūṭirīs, Paraśu Rāma, was himself a Brāhman of the militant type, having fought with and destroyed the Kṣhaṭṛīya race thrice-seven times over. That the study of Vēḍās and the practice of religious austerities are not incompatible with the profession of arms is clearly indicated by the fact that the instructors in arms of both the Cochin and Travancore Rajas are Brāhmans of the Vēḍic class, and these enjoy to the present day the emoluments and privileges attached to their office, though the Rajas have left off the exhilarating study of the use of weapons. In Cochin, the office is hereditary in the family of Pērāmangalaṭṭ Naṃbūṭiri who is officially styled Pērāṃpaṫṫa Paṇikkar. In Travancore, the office is held by Kallaṃṭāṭṭil Kurukaḷ. The suffix Kurukaḷ or Gurukaḷ means preceptor. It is said that, in former times, every Pērāṃpaṫṫa Panikkar had to vindicate his title to his office by having an open fight, sword in hand, with a Royal Tiger and, if he succeeded in killing the animal, he planted, in token of the victory, a post in the inner courtyard of his *Illam* (house). It would appear that some of these posts are still to be seen standing in the yard of his house.

The Naṃbūṭirīs form the landed aristocracy of the country and claim the land in *Jenmam* or birthright, tracing their title to an alleged original gift by Paraśu Rāma. It is only the poorest of them who will consent to act as priests in temples. Those who are landlords do not cultivate the lands themselves but let them out to tenants mostly Nāyars on various tenures. It is seldom that they earn their livelihood by personal exertion. They are such a favoured class that, from royalty downward to the merest peasant, every one would forego even his necessity to pander to their luxury. Instead of scorning delights and living life's laborious days as ordained by the *Sankara Smriti*, they use their utmost endeavour, by deed and word, to impress on others the idea that all excellences in the world are theirs by birthright, and that whatever is low and mean is the portion of the lower orders. In fact, it is the Naṃbūṭiri of all Brāhmans in India, who strictly follows the injunction of Manu, "never serve."

There can be no doubt that the Naṃbūṭirīs associated themselves with the Government of the country even after they had ceased to have any direct control under the early theocratic system of rule that prevailed in Malabar They were the ministers of the Rajas, their judges on the Bench, their generals in the field and above all their spiritual preceptors. It was "the King's Brāhman and high Priest" who received Vasco de Gama at the palace gates and conducted him to the king's presence at the Portuguese Admiral's first interview with the Zamorin.

"The patriarch Brāhmin (soft and slow he rose)
Advancing now, to lordly Gama bows,
And leads him to the throne."[1]

On Della Vella's visit to Calicut in company, with the Portuguese who were sent by the Viceroy to treat with the Zamorin, it was "a prime Brahman and a man of great authority with the king," who, along with the king, discussed matters of high importance with the Portuguese Captain, and Della Vella informs us that the Brāhman told him that he had "sometimes treated of weighty affairs on his king's behalf with the Portugals in

1. In Lusiad.

the enterprise of *Cognale*, and that he was very well known to the Viceroy and the Chief Captains of Goa." We have the assurance of Barbosa that this is no mere boast, for he tells us that "the kings used to employ these Brāhmans as messengers and ambassadors to go from kingdom to kingdom, because they pass in safety in all parts without any one molesting them, though the kings may be at war." Till but recently we have had Nambūṭiri Sarvādhikāriakārs (Prime ministers), Kāriakārs (Governors), Judges and Munsiffs in Travancore and Cochin. Fifty years ago the highest Courts of both these States were presided over by Nambūṭiri judges. But at present in the public service the Nambūṭiri is nowhere. He has not kept pace with the progress of modern times. His Smṛṭi prohibits the study of the language of the Mlēchchās, *i. e.*, the unclean! Hence the Nambūṭirīs never study English, with the result that they have already been far out-stripped in the race of progress by their downtrodden slaves, the Nāyars and other classes. The Malabar Marriage Commission reported that "instead of taking the lead in every intellectual pursuit, as do the Brāhmans in other parts, the Nambūṭiri has become enervated to such an extent that it would be difficult to find more than a few who have mastered the Grammar and syntax of Sanskrit, which is the chief vehicle of their scared texts. Most of them get no further than committing a number of Slōkas to memory. Not only do they refuse altogether to tread the path of knowledge opened up to them by a barbarian government, but it is rare to find one of them who has studied the literature, such as it is, of his own vernacular Malayālam, his mother tongue. He despises Sanskrit, the language in which his sacred lore is entombed which he has ceased to study." There are of course those who stoutly maintain that the Nambūṭiri is not the degenerate being he is represented to be. Mr. Fawcett, for instance, champions his cause in this wise: "It will have been seen that physically he is the best in the land; also that his position among the people is loftier than that of any other Brahmans in Southern India. Perhaps it is for his special sacredness, which is correlative with high position, that the priest of the temple at Baḍaryāśrama in Northern India, as also the priest of the Śaiva temple at Ṭhiruvaṭṭūr near Madras, is always a Naṃbuṭiri. He enters into none of the ordinary pursuits of livelihood, and for that very reason he is able to maintain his high position, and to exercise influence for good which is very considerable." It may be that the people of Malabar accord to the Naṃbūṭiri a position loftier than that of the other Brāhmans of Southern India, but that is the inheritance of ages, and had its origin at a time when the Naṃbūṭirīs were both spiritual and temporal sovereigns of Kērala and when they never failed to fulfil their high functions. No one can doubt that the Naṃbuṭiri is fast losing ground, and that unless he wakes and bestirs himself, he will soon be delēgated to the limbo of oblivion. Haughty aloofness can scarcely confer lofty position, much less special sacredness, and Mr. Fawcet forgets that the priests of Baḍari and Ṭiruvaṭṭur are chosen from among the Naṃbūṭirīs, not because of their "special sacredness" or "high position", but because the temple of Baḍari was founded by the Naṃbuṭiri, Śankara Achāryar, and that the Ṭiruvaṭṭur temple has the reputation of having for its founder Paraśu Rāma, the Patron-Saint of the Kērala Brāhmans. If indeed the dignity of labour is discounted a good deal and indolence and idleness sanctified, the Naṃbūṭiri may well claim to have attained his sacred position by reason of his scorn to enter into the ordinary pursuits of life. The so-called Vēḍic studies of which he is theoretically a life-long student and repository are at present a matter of ancient history recorded perhaps in the tablets of time. The modern Naṃbūṭiri is decidedly a degenerate representative of his illustrious ancestors. The present economic condition of the class is thus well described in the Travancore

Census Report : "As the pre-historic heirs to the entire land of Kērala, the Naṃbūṭirīs live on agriculture. But inefficiency in adaptation to changing environments operates as a severe handicap in the race for progressive affluence for which the initial equipment was exceptionally favourable. The difficulties incidental to an effete landlordism have contributed to making the Naṃbūṭirīs a litigious population and the ruinous scale of expenditure necessary for the disposal of a girl, be it of the most plebian kind, has brought their general prosperity to a very low level. The feeling of responsible co-operation on the part of the unmarried males of a Naṃbūṭiri household in the interests of the family is fast decaying, old maidens are increasing and the lot of the average Naṃbūṭiri man and more especially woman, is very hard indeed. As matters now stand, the traditional hospitality of the Hindu Kings of Malabar which, fortunately for them, has not yet relaxed is the only sustenance and support of the ordition Naṃbūṭiri Brahmin"[1].

Magic and Sorcery—The Naṃbūṭiris are not strangers to magic and sorcery. Their practices in this respect are described elsewhere.

Manners and Customs.—The Naṃbūṭirīs have certain customs or observances which are peculiar to them, and, so far as they differ from those of the other Brāhmans of India, are in a body designated as *Anacharam* or mal-observances. There are 64 of them and are supposed to have been instituted by Śankara Āchārya. The Nambūṭirīs defend them as being based on the authority of the Smṛṭis and Śāsṭrās. These are set forth in the fouth *pada* or part of the bath chapter of *Sankara Smriti*. They are :—

(1) You must not clean your teeth with sticks.

(2) You must not bathe with clothes worn on our person.

1. Travancore *Census Report* for 1901, p. 302.

(3) You must not rub your body with the cloth worn on your person.

(4) You must not bathe before sunrise.

(5) You must not cook your food before you bathe.

(6) Avoid the water kept aside during the night.

(7) You must not have one particular object in view while you bathe.

(8) The remainder of water taken for one ceremonial purpose must not be made use of for another ceremony.

(9) You must bathe if you touch another, i. e., a Sudra.

(10) You must bathe if you happen to approach one of a low caste.

(11) you must bathe if you touch polluted wells or tanks.

(12) You must not tread over a place that has been cleaned with a broom, unless it is sprinkled with water.

(13) A particular mode of marking the forehead with ashes. (otherwise described: put three horizontal lines on the forehead with pure burnt cow dung).

(14) You must repeat charms (*mantrams*) yourself (must not allow some one else to do it for you).

(15) You must avoid cold rice, &c. (food cooked the previous day).

(16) You must avoid leavings of meals by children (or do not eat food which has been left by children.)

(17) You must not eat anything that has been offered to Śiva.

(18) You must not serve out food with your hands (must not touch the food with the hand when serving it).

(19) You must not make use of the ghee of buffalo-cows for burnt offerings.

(20) You must not use buffalo-milk or ghee for funeral offerings.

(21) A particular mode of taking food (not to put too much in the mouth, because none must be taken back).

(22) You must not chew betel while you are polluted.

(23) You must observe the conclusion of the Bramachāri period.

(24) You must give presents to your *guru* or preceptor (the Brahmachāri must).

(25) You must not repeat the Vēḍās on the road.

(26) Yon must not sell women (receive money for girls given in marriage).

(27) You must not fast in order to obtain fulfilment of your desires.

(28) Bathing is all that a woman should observe if she touches another in her menses. (A woman touching another who is in this state should,it is said, purify herself by bathing. A man should change his thread and undergo sacred ablution).

(29) Brāhmans should not spin cotton.

(30) Brāhmans should not wash cloths for themselves (should not wash their own cloths).

(31) Kṣhaṭṛiyas should avoid worshipping the Lingam.

(32) Brāhmans should not accept funeral gifts from Śūḍras (anniversary gifts too).

(33) Perform the anniversary ceremony of your father (father's father, mother's father, and both grandmothers).

(34) Anniversary ceremonies should be performed on the day of the new moon (for the gratification of the spirits of the deceased).

(35) The funeral ceremony should be performed at the end of the year, counting from the day of death.

(36) The ceremony to be performed till the end of the year after death (the Ḍīkṣha: letting the hair grow, apparently).

(37) Śrāḍḍhas should be performed with regard to the stars.

(38) The funeral ceremony should not be performed until after the pollution caused by a child-birth has been removed.

(39) A particular mode of performing Śrāḍḍha by an adopted son (who should do the ceremony for his adopted parents as well as for his natural parents).

(40) The corpse of a man should be burnt in his own compound (on his own *jenmam* land).

(41) Sanyāsis should not look at (see) women.

(42) Sanyāsis should renounce all worldly pleasures.

(43) Śrāḍḍha should not be performed for deceased Sanyāsis.

(44) Brāhman women must not look at any other persons besides their own husbands (should not be seen by men out of the family).

(45) Brāhman women must not go out unless accompanied by women servants.

(46) Should wear only white clothing.

(47) Noses should not be pierced. (Amongst South Indian Brāhmans outside Malabar the noses of women are always bored).

(48) Brāhmans should be put out of their caste if they drink any liquor.

(49) Brāhmans should forfeit their caste if they have intercourse with other Brāhman women than their wives.

(50) The consecration of evil spirits should be avoided (otherwise said to be that worship to ancestors should not be done in temples).

(51) Śūḍras and others are not to touch an idol.

(52) Anything offered to one god should not be offered to another.

(53) Marriage, etc., should not be done without a burnt offering (hōmam).

(54) Brāhmans should not give blessings to each other.

(55) They should not bow down to another (should not salute each other).

(56) Cows should not be killed in sacrifice.

(57) Do not cause distraction, some by observing the religious rights of Śiva, and others those of Vişhṇu.

(58) Brāhmans should wear only one sacred thread.

(59) The eldest son should marry and enter *Grahastasramam* (householder's life).

(60) Ceremony in honour of a deceased ancestor should be performed with boiled rice.

(61) Kşhaţriyas and those of other castes should perform funeral ceremonies to their uncles (deceased).

(62) The right of inheritance among Kşhaţriyas goes towards nephews.

(63) Widows should lead the lives of Sanyāsis.

(64) Saţi should be avoided.

Dr. Subrahmania Ayyar has classed these 64 *anacharams* under six heads :—

(1) Personal hygiene.

(2) Eating.

(3) Worship of the gods and manes.

(4) Conduct in society.

(5) Āsramas or stages of life.

(6) And the regulation of women's conduct.

(1) *Personal hygiene.*—With the Nambūţiri bathing is a most important religious duty, which he has to perform by immersing himself in either a tank or a river. It purifies both body and soul. The mere touch of a Nambūţiri by any other class necessitates

his taking a plunge bath to avoid the impurities. As Camoens observes:—

"Vile were the stain and deep the foul disgrace,
"Should other tribe touch one of noble race;
"A thousand rites, and washings over and over
"Can scarce his tainted purity restore."

The Nampūṭirīs have therefore a large tank or reservoir of water attached always to their houses. Every Nampūṭiri bathes in this tank twice a day at least, and oftener sometimes. As in everything else, there are special rules laid down regarding the bath in the *Sankara Smriti.*[1] According to it, the *Smritis* prescribe four kinds of bath, *viz*, (1) Brāhmam, the sprinkling of water (on a man) on which manṭras have been uttered; (2) Vāyavyam, the application of the dust taken from the hoof of a cow; (3) Āgnēyam, the wearing of sacred ashes; and (4) Vāruṇam, the immersing of oneself in water. Of these, a combination of the first with the last is ordained to the Nampūṭiri *i.e*, one should enter water, dip himself in it and at the same time sprinkle himself with water on which the prescribed manṭras have been duly muttered. It would be tedious to go into details of the rules which prescribe how to dip oneself, how many times to dip, etc. But a Nampūṭiri should never bathe before sunrise.

The prohibition from entering water with the covering waist-cloth on does not really run counter to the injunction of the Sūṭrakāras who say, "bathe not without clothing," for the Nampūṭiri bathes with his *langot*, or undercloth passing between his thighs and covering his private parts. More clothing is indeed desirable. As observed by Dr. Subrahmania Ayyar: "The fastidious sense of bath purity occasionally takes the form of a regular mania, and receives the not in-apt description of Jalapiśāch, or possession by a water-devil which would perpetually raise doubts as to whether

1. Chapter 4, pada 1.

the required degree of personal purity has been secured by the bath in question".

(2) *Eating.*—The rules regarding this have been already noticed.

(3) *Worship of the gods, etc.*—The mode of worshipping the gods and prayers for the souls of departed form the third group of Kēraḷāchāras. The anniversary of a person's death is regulated not by the age of the moon at the time, but by the star, which is unlike the practice on the other coast. Again a birth-pollution has the priority of observances over even funeral duties. A son who has to perform the funeral ceremonies of his father is rendered unfit for that solemn function by an intervening birth-pollution. An adopted son in Malabar is not, as in other parts of India, relieved of the Śrāḍḍha obligations to his natural parents. Sectarian controversies in regard to Śiva and Vishṇu are strictly tabooed. The establishment of Hinduism on a non-sectarian basis was the sacred mission of Sankara's life.

A single triple string (sacred thread) is worn irrespective of civil conditions. This is contrary to the usage of the other coast, where married Brāhmans wear two or three triplets. Sprinkling with water is an essential purificatory act after the use of broom. An isolated rule requires dead bodies to be burned in private compounds, and not in consecrated communal sites, as among the East Coast people.[1]

(4) *Conduct in society.*—Chastity is jealously guarded by the imposition of severe ostracism on adulterers. Formal salutation and even Namaskāras and Anugrahas or prostration before and blessing by, seniors are proscribed. This is a striking point of difference between Malabar and the rest of India, and is probably based on the esoteric teaching of universal oneness.[2]

(5) *Regulation of woman's conduct.*—These are described later on.

1. Travancore *Census Report*, Vol. 1, p. 304.
2. Ibid p. 304, para 4.

(6) *Asramas.*—Of the four Āśramas prescribed for the Brāhmans, the Nambūṭirīs follow at present three only. Even these three all Nambūṭirīs do not observe. The really orthodox among them go through the three stages of Brahmachāri, *i.e.*, the period during which they are engaged in the study of the Vēḍās, Gṛhasṭa, *i. e.*, life as a householder or married man. Sanyāsi, *i. e.*, life as an ascetic. The third stage that of Vānapṙasṭa, *i. e.*, life as a religious recluse retiring into the forest is not practised at present.

(a) *Brahmacharya.*—The period of study begins soon after the Upanayana or the investiture with the sacred thread. The student should live with the preceptor in the house of the latter. With the consent of the preceptor, at an auspicious moment, after performing Pṙāraṃbha Hōmaṃ, initiatory sacrifice, the student must begin his studies meditating on the syllable Ōṃ! Pṙaṇavaṃ and Gāyaṭṙi. The preceptor should teach the student the Ḍhaṙma Śāsṭṙas in the beginning, lest, not knowing the correct way of performing ablutions, he may go wrong, and thus be put out of caste. Various rules are prescribed for the guidance of the student, by which he is enjoined to render absolute and unquestioning obedience to his Guru, to serve him whole-heartedly, to minister to all his wants and desires, and so to conduct himself as to deserve the blessings of his preceptor. He is to study till mid-day. His regimen is regulated with strict regard to extreme abstemiousness. He is enjoined not to be idle, to be absolutely truthful in deed and word, to abstain from causing injury to any living being. His studies are not to be confined to the Vēḍās alone. They are to extend to other branches of knowledge, such as grammar, logic, astronomy, etc. The three Vēḍas, Ṛk, Yajus and Sāma, he ought to study.

Besides studying under the guidance of private instructors or Ōṭikkans, there are public institutions at which the Vēḍas are taught. There are at present two such in Malabar, one at Trichur, and the other at Tiruṅāvāy, both of which are richly endowed, besides

THE VEDIC COLLEGE IN TRICHUR. (To face p. 70.

the one at Ṭirunakkara in Kōṭṭayam maintained by the Travancore Sirkar. These Vēḍic Colleges or Brahmaswam maṭhams are presided over by Vaḍhyāns, or teachers chosen from the Chāngaliōṭ and Eṛakara houses (*Illams*) respectively. At these institutions the pupils are fed and lodged free of cost, and given oral instructions in the Veḍas, Sāstras, etc. The method of study pursued is such that the pupils and teachers look more to the sharpening of the power of retentiveness than to the understanding of the subjects studied. Competitive examinations are occasionally held between the pupils of the two institutions, which are feats of intellectual gymnastics, serving more to test the memory of the pupils than their knowledge of the subject. They are made to repeat at random select portions from the Veḍas which they have to do from beginning to end or *vice versa*, the candidates being in the meanwhile unmercifully badgered and interrupted by a batch of young men who take a special delight in thwarting the endeavours of the candidates to go through the passages correctly. Those who are able to withstand this badgering, and succeed in repeating with exactitute the portions assigned to them are held in high estimation. Kaṭavallur temple, in the Ṭalapilly Ṭāluk in the Cochin State, is the place for these competitive examinations, and the Kaṭannirikkal is considered the blue ribbon of vēḍic studies. There are certain other festive occasions designed specially to promote the study of the Vēḍās. These are the Oṭṭūṭṭu, Tṛsanḍha, Panchasanḍha, and Vrāam at which the Vēḍās are repeated three or five times by experts for a number of days together, or a single day, which are occasions of feasting on a grand scale.

After the period of study is over, the pupil makes the Gurudekshiṇa or present to his preceptor, receives his blessing, and returns home.

The next Āśramam is that of Gṛhasṭa (married life). But in Malabar it is not all that lead this life. Only the eldest son *need* marry or *ought* to marry. The rest are expected to lead a cilebate life, snāṭakavṛṭṭi. This, as we have already observed, is with a view to secure the impartibility of the family property. If, however, the married member has not begotten male issue, or if it is evident that his wife is past bearing, the next brother may marry. To avoid this, the Naṃbūṭiri marries a number of wives in succession. If it is objected that every Hindu is bound to get married, and that the *Smritis* are very clear that no one who has not begotten male issue has fulfilled the purpose of creation, and discharged his debt to the Piṭṛus, the Naṃbūṭiri is ready with his answer. Manu has dclared that "if, of several brothers, one procreates a son, that son is son to all." But he need not take shelter under this doctrine of Manu, for the *Smrities* and *Puranas* have themselves declared that the unmarried, whether males or females, are entitled to higher heavens than the married—only they should lead a celibate and chaste life.[1]

Now the younger members who do not marry, and are supposed to lead a life of celibacy, are for a year or two to stay in their family temples meditating and worshipping. During this period, they are to revise the study of the Vēḍās and try to attain agility in their repetition from any point indicated, to become experts in Kṛamam, Jaṭa, Raṭha, etc., *i. e.* various permutations and combinations of words, sentences and verses from the Vēḍās. They are also to study the Vēḍāngas. Having finished this course, they remove themselves to the Grāmakṣhēṭṛams, *i. e.*, the village temples, which are endowed for the purpose, giving board and lodging to students of the village that resort to them. There they continue their studies for a period of two or three years more. Then and then only are these Naṃbūṭirīs considered fit to take their place in assemblies of the learned. So far they have studied only the Vēḍās and Vēḍāngas. They have now to proceed to other branches of knowledge.

1. Manu, 2, 243-244 and 289; 8, 363. Vishnu, 28—47-p. 113 (Cal. Ed.). Yagnavalkya, Chap. 1, 50 p. 414 (Cal. Ed.) Sri Bhagavat, 2—6—18.

For this purpose, they resort to Sabhā-Maṭhams or endowed institutions, where students are lodged, maintained and taught Śāsṭras, Grammar, Astronomy, Astrology, Mīmāmsa, Vēḍānṭa (Philosophy and Philosophic theology). There were 18 of these institutions in Malabar, each being supplied with pandits, who are masters of Sanskrit lore, capable of imparting it to others, and are styled Bhaṭṭaṭirīs. At these Sabhā-Maṭhams, those students who seek to learn Ṭanṭra Śāsṭra, Yōga Śāsṭra, rituals at sacrifices etc., are taught free of all expenses. The Bhaṭṭaṭirīs themselves will have passed a course of twelve years' study at these institutions before they are installed as teachers. By undertaking the course of studies sketched above, the Nambūṭirīs have been ever known as great scholars. Confining themselves throughout their life to intellectual pursuits, they used to attain a high level of scholarship. The Rajas of Malabar used to give them opportunities to display their scholarly attainments. Annually, assemblies of the learned were held at their courts, where disputations were held in logic and other subjects, and those who came out well were honoured with costly presents. The Zamorins of Calicut used to hold Ṭānams at Ṭali. These were gifts to the learned on the occasion of the Śrāḍḍha ceremony of a deceased ancestor. Seven days before the ceremony, the learned gather at Ṭali, one of the suburbs of Calicut, and display their learning at the assembly in the presence of the Zamorin. The subjects taken up for the test are Grammar, Mīmāmsa and Vēḍānṭa. Those who are accepted as proficients deserving reward hold their place for a period of 12 years during which they get their annual presents. Those who vacate their seats on the expiry of their period are replaced by new comers. At the courts of Travancore and Cochin also such assemblies of the learned are still held on various occasions. But the importance of the assemblies has become attenuated, the test at present is nominal, scholars attending are few and of mediocre attainments, the inducements offered are meagre, and the whole thing has come to be a mere show, a faint shadow of a once brilliant institution—a mere relic of the past. The community has produced distinguished scholars and authors, such as Meppaṭṭūr Bhaṭṭaṭiri, Bhaṭṭaṭirīs of Payyūr Illam, Kākkassēri Bhaṭṭaṭiri, Mullappilly Bhaṭṭaṭiri, Chēnnōss Nārayaṇan Nampuṭiripād, and others. But times have changed, and at present, the Nambuṭirīs, instead of sticking to their traditional profession of study, idle away their time in litigation consequent upon the oppression they practise on their rack-rented tenants. They have left off their traditional moorings and are after modern fashions and tendencies. That they may maintain their culture and look to ideals consistent with it is the prayer of the well-wishers of that great community.

Grihasta-Aśrama.—This is the married life of a householder. The eldest son of the house alone, as we have already seen, marries. With the Brahmans, marriage is a sacrament and a holy sacrament too. Of the eight forms of marriage described by the Smṛṭīs, the Nambuṭirīs follow the Prājāpaṭya form, in which the father gives away his daughter with due honour, saying distinctly "may both of you perform together your civil and religious duties." The father of the girl should in proper time get his daughter married, and he who desires to marry should also look about for a proper match. The rule as to the age of the bride is thus set forth in the Sankara Smṛṭi. "One may marry a Kanya, Rōhiṇi and Gouri, but not a Maḍhyama." A Kanya is a girl of 10 years, Rōhiṇi of 9 years and Gouri of 8 years of age. A Maḍhyama is one who has attained her puberty. Bhārgava has, however, as a matter of sufferance, allowed the marriage of a girl after puberty. The rule is that, by whatever means, one should get one's daughter married before puberty.[1] Otherwise one incurs Bhrūṇahaṭṭyapāpam, *i. e.*, the sin of killing a child in the womb.[2] In practice, the

1. *Sl.* 32, part 1, chap: 6.
2. *Sl.* 30, part 1, chap: 6.

majority of marriages are performed after puberty, so much so, that it has come to be the rule rather than an exception. Thus the large majority of the married Naṃbūṭirīs of the present day are open to the charge of having committed the sin of Bhrūṇahaṭṭya. The father of the bride and of the bridegroom are required to make themselves sure of the position in life and personal qualities of the parties. The wishes of the couple are seldom, if ever, consulted. As it is, the desire to get rid of a girl with a cheap dowry induces fathers to make rather short work of making such enquiries as are contemplated by the Śankara Smṛṭi. Marriage is now a matter of bargain and exchange—a daughter with a small dowry, or a daughter for a daughter. Certain rules are laid down by the Śankara Smṛṭi[1] for testing personal qualities of the bride and bridegroom. The bride should be clean at everything, of good behaviour, of pleasant conversation, handsome, having brothers. She should not be of the same Gōṭra (sect) or be a Sapiṇḍi (i. e, an agnate). She should not be cruel-hearted, lame or maimed, or have abnormal limbs, without hair on her body, or be very hairy, of a talkative nature, or one accustomed to be always looking out through the window. She should be handsome and fair, emitting a good odour, accustomed to smile turning her head a little, should have high and full bosom, and be of good temper. A rather curious and amusing test is then prescribed, called Mṛṭ-Piṇḍa-Parīkṣha, or the test by earth balls. A large square is formed with small squares within by means of parallel lines drawn lengthwise and crosswise. Within these small inner squares, are put powders of different colours.

After worshipping the gods, place in the first row, in the order prescribed, clods of earth, formed into balls, taken from a cow-pen, a place where yāgom (sacrifice) has been formed, a river bed, and a pagoda. In the line below place similarly other balls of earth

1 Chap. II, Parts 3 and 4.

obtained from where four roads cross each other, brackish soil, land scoured (ploughed) by a boar with its tusk, and gravelly soil. Then mutter some manṭras over these, and ask the girl to take from among these one ball of earth. The girl should circumambulate the square thrice and make her selection. How she should fare in her married life may be determined from the selection she makes. If she chooses the ball of earth taken from the cow-pen, the couple will have a number of cows in the course of their married life. If she selects the earth taken from the sacrificial ground, she will be a Ḍharmavaṭi, one leading a devotional life. If she takes the river sand, you may be certain that she is good hearted. If her choice falls on the earth taken from a pagoda, she is sure to be prosperous and wealthy. The choice of any one of the above may be considered as indicating that she would be chaste and pure. But if she has her choice from the second line, it bodes no good. The selection of the clod of earth taken from where four roads cross one another indicates that she would lead a vagabond life, that of the brackish soil shows that she is cruel, that of the ground ploughed by a boar's tusk is indicative of her false character, and that of the gravelly soil forbodes that she will compass the death of her husband.

The bride's father has also to satisfy himself as to the personal qualities of his future son-in-law. Sixteen classes of persons are described as impotents or as hermaphrodites and therefore not eligible for marriage. Another set declared ineligible is composed of those who are insane, dumb, deaf, limping, lame, blind, epileptic, not of noble birth, one who has overstayed the auspicious hour for the marriage ceremony, one who has cut off his tuft of hair (Kuḍummi), and one whom the bride hates. The following circumstances require the special attention of the bride's father with regard to the bridegroom: —

(1) Fully developed manhood.

(2) Youthfulness-adolesence.

(3) Beauty.
(4) Wealth.
(5) Learning or celebrity.
(6) Agreeable conversation.
(7) Charitable disposition especially in the matter of giving food to others.

When the parties are satisfied with the choice they have made, they should consult a learned astrologer, who is interested in both of them equally, who is innocent and not avaricious. He should examine the horoscopes, and find out the conjunctions or favourable symptoms of the intended match. (There are 28 conjunctions of which 8 are indispensable). The agreement of the nativities (Rāśi), of week days (Ḍinaṃ), of planets (Nakṣhaṭṛaṃ), of descent (Gaṇaṃ), etc., between the couple is indispensable. If these agree, the marriage is determined upon, and an auspicious moment for the ceremony is appointed by the astrologer.

A few days previous to the ceremony, what is known as Uḍvaha Kouṭukaṃ is performed, said to be the Vēlippāṭṭu of the present day.

The bride's father should then prepare for the ceremony in a style befitting his position in life. He should put up sheds for the reception of guests, give the house a bright appearance by decorating it in many ways; fumigate the building, walls, pillars, doors, narrow passages, etc., with sweet smelling things, and adorn them with figures drawn in rice-flour-paste. He should hang garlands of flowers at the gate and at the thresh-hold, set up plantain trees with gay looking bunches of fruits. The posts on each side of the main door should be decorated by tying on them the tender leaves of the banyan and mango tree, as well as cocoanuts and arecanuts. The house should be beautified by hanging all round garlands of lotus flower and the flower of the water-lily.

The father is then enjoined to prepare everything that the bride wants, apparently household articles and other things she may want to take with her to her new home. A rich father should give as much wealth as the bridegroom desires, and an indigent one should get as much as he can get by begging, and bestow it on his daughter.[1] So at present, a good deal of bargaining goes on before the match is settled, and the sum generally fixed is Rs. 2,000. Sometimes a higher sum has to be found, and the bride's parents have often to go on an extended begging tour to find the amount. As a result of the present practice, we see old maids pining away without any prospect of marriage, while those professed Benedicts, the junior male members of the family, consort with Nāyar women, forming fugitive alliances with them. In former days the native Rajas seem to have interfered, and fixed the dowry payable at a low rate, and the marriage of the Naṃbūṭiri girls was more general than at present. But progressive ideas scoff at Government's interfering with the liberty of private individuals, with the result that society is very often scandalised by unmarried Naṃbūṭiri women going astray, and a number of men put out of caste irrespective of their innocence or guilt, simply because they are accused of complicity by the peccant woman.

After all arrangements in the house are completed, the bride's father should await the arrival of the bridegroom and party, praying God that the ceremony may pass off satisfactorily. Meanwhile the relatives and guests invited for the ceremony assemble at the bridegroom's house and are sumptuously feasted at the expense of the bride's father. This feast is called Ayani Ūṇu. The bridegroom then leaves his house (receiving the benediction of his elders) accompanied by his relatives and attendants, and goes in procession to the bride's house. Before leaving the house, he should circumambulate a cow, a bull, a temple and a holy tree, repeating mangalasūkṭam, or according to Bōḍhāyana Gṛhya Sūṭra, Swasṭi Sūkṭam. If he meets on the road as omen the bird *cuculus*, a cat, a dog, or an ass, he should

1. *Sl.* 31, part 1, chap. 6.

pass by the left of these. If he meets with bad animals or birds such as a fox, a monkey, a mangoose, or an eagle, he should repeat certain expiatory manṭras and give away ḍānams or gifts. As the auspicious moment for the actual ceremony approaches, the party should reach the house. The bridegroom walks behind the long procession with a consecrated string tied round his waist, and with the ṭāli or wedding necklace, a mirror as an omen of good luck, an arrow for guarding the bride against evil spirits, two pairs of cloths, and a bamboo stick with 16 joints, in his hand. The bride's father meets the party at the gate with greetings. Nāyar women represent the Naṃbūṭiri ladies of the house, who are prohibited from appearing in public. On the invitation of the bride's father, the bridegroom should step into the compound, stretching forward his left leg first, and then walk up to the yard, enter the same stretching forward his right leg first. Having come to the threshold, he should step into the outer verandah by stretching forward his left leg first, and enter the Nālukeṭṭu (the inner precincts), putting forward his right leg first. He who wishes for the prosperity of the house should conform to these rules without fail. After this, the bride's father should make a gift of the girl, with water, to him who has come seeking her hand, according to the rules prescribed by his Gṛhya Sūṭra and the bridegroom should accept the gift with due ceremony. This ceremony is called Uḍakapūrvam. There are, however, other ceremonies preceeding this one.

As the bridegroom enters the house, the bride's father formally invites him "to bathe and come for wedding." The manes are then propitiated by the Nanḍimukham ceremony, and the house purified and fitted for the sacred rite. Then with a lamp in front of him, the father of the bride passes to the central courtyard within the house, and sits facing the east. The Nāyar attendant of the house then waves an earthern pot before him and hands a garland. The father of the bride, who is about to make Kanyakādānam (gift of the girl), the most meritorious of all dānams or gifts, duly slautes the donee, *i. e.*, the bridegroom, touches the head of the donor (father-in-law-elect) as if by way of blessing. The bride's father then walks to the Hōmakuṇḍa or the sacrificial altar in the interior, and a few preliminary rites are gone through. At the auspicious hour, the girl gets duly bedecked and has the ṭāli brought by the husband tied round her neck by the father and not by the husband as in all other ṭāli-tying communities on the East Coast. A Nāyar woman waves a saucer of oil with several burning wicks, known as thousand wicks (Āyiraṭṭiri) before the bride, who appears with her face covered. With the Nāyar woman and her panlight in front, the bride now walks on to the altar. It may be said in passing that the ghosha ladies witness the ceremonies from behind a pardah ,but they join the Nāyar women, at all stages of the ceremony in the peculiar national cheering, known as Vāykkila or Kurava. The next stage of the ceremony is called Mukhadarśanam, or the actual seeing of each other, face to face, of the husband and wife, when vēdic hymns are sung; after this ceremony, the bride's father pours, through her hands, into those of the bridegroom, some water accompanied by the words "sahadharmam charataḥ", meaning 'may you both tread the path of duty together', repeated three times. This is the Udakapūrvam ceremony.

The next ceremony is the Pāṇigrahaṇam or the clasping of hands. The bridegroom clasps the right hand of the bride. In doing so, he should hold the four fingers leaving alone the big finger, having in his mind the desire to have male issue by her. If he desires to have daughters also, he should clasp all the five fingers of the right hand. Upon this, the assembled Brāhmans bestow their benedictions on the happay couple. Then comes the Lajahōmam, or the oblation of fried grains, and circumambulations of the sacrificial fire. After this, the bride is mounted on a grinding stone, and she is exhorted to be as fast-fixed in constancy as the stone on which her husband has placed her legs. This ceremony is called Aśmārōhaṇam. The Sapṭapaḍi, an all-important ceremony with other Brahmans, in fact *the* ceremony which accomplishes and effects the union, is of minor import with the Naṃbūṭirīs. It consists in the walking of seven paces. This terminates the more important ceremonies connected with marriage (Mal : Peṇkoṭa *i. e.*, the giving away of a girl).

Then follows the Kuṭipūkal or the taking of the bride to the bridegrooms's house. The sacrificial fire lighted at the marriage ceremony, known as Oupāsanāgni is carried from the wife's house to the husband's where it is maintained till it is used to light the funeral pyre of the couple at their death. This fire is produced by the friction of two pieces of wood. Before the parties leave the house, the fire is transferred to a Ch maṭa, piece of wood, which is heated in it. The party now proceeds to the wife's house, where the next three days' ceremonies have to be performed. If the journey is by land, the wife should be taken in a palkee borne by Pallichchāns (a class of Nāyar bearers). Friends and relatives should accompany the party. Armed attendants with swords and shields should walk in front. Attendant maids should walk on either side of the palanquin. Nāyars should keep guard all round, so that the lower classes may not approach and pollute the procession, which should be accompanied with music and tom-toms. When the procession passes by sacred places or where four roads meet etc., manṭras should be repeated. If it has to stop on the way, those who come to meet the party should be received and entertained with honour. It should avoid fire places. On approaching the husband's house, the way from the gate of the Illam to the interior court-yard should be spread with Karuka (grass), and Ṭair (curds) etc. A lamp, well-lighted, and a measure of rice and paddy each, should also be placed in the yard. Nāyar women should meet the party as it enters with Aṣhṭamangallyam,

K.

i. e, saucers with eight things in them. The entry should be made at an auspicious moment, the husband leading the wife by the hand repeating manṭras. That night, sacrificial fire should be set up according to the rituals prescribed to the class to which the couple belongs, and maintained without failing. For the next three days, the couple observe fast, avoiding the use of salt; they are forbidden from lying on cots and are prohibited from doing any business. During these days, the guests should be feasted and old couples should be specially cared for. After these three days are over, the Chaṭuṛṭha Snānam, or the bathing on the fourth day, should be performed. In the evening, the couple anoint themselves with oil, bathe and prepare themselves for the Sēkam or nuptials. For the first three days, the married girl is supposed to be given up to the gods.[1] The nuptial room is entered only after the Vyśvaḍēvam ceremony at the sacrificial altar. The couple enter the chamber dressed in the same clothes as on the marriage day at the invitation of the Nāyar woman who had hitherto the charge of the girl from her infancy, who stands at the door and says Akaṭṭēkku Eluṅṅellām, *i. e.*, "your holiness may go in." In some parts, it is the Vāḍhyān or priest who officiates at the marriage who shuts the pair in the room.. It is said that the priest outside and the bridegroom inside following him repeat appropriate manṭras. There is, however, no fixed rule as to the day of the consummation. If the fourth is not an auspicious day, the fifth may be made use of. Any how till the Sēka is over, the Nambūṭiri cannot take part in other ceremonies. On the fourth day of marriage, there is a little ceremony, in which the bride plants a jasmine cutting, the import of which is not apparent, but it is suggested that it symbolises the help she has to give her husband in the discharge of his religious duties. The Yajurvēḍic Nambūṭirīs have another curious little ceremony which, as already observed, has given rise to wild speculations regarding the origin of the Nambūṭirīs.

1. *Cochin Census Report*, p. 139.

On the fifth day, before bathing, a few fish called Maṇṇaṭṭa Kanni, common in South India, are put into a tub of water, and the newly married couple, holding each end of the piece of cloth, play at catching fish—ergo the Nambūṭirīs were originally fishermen. Mr. Nāgam Aiya's explanation of the ceremony seems to be apt. He observes :—

"The same custom obtains among the Bōḍhāyana Sūṭrakārs of the East Coast Brahmins. The popular and correct interpretation seems to be that fishes are caught as emblems of the fertility wished for by the parties of the union. Even otherwise, it is satisfactorily explained by the well-known fact that, in this case, as in others, the Brahmins of Malabar retain with them some of the very ancient customs which pertained to the Āryans in the old country when they left it, among which may be mentioned flesh and fish-eating which undoubtedly existed there though very far back in time. The marrying after puberty, the keeping of the women's hair and the putting on of the sandal paste caste-marks on the fore-head by the widows, the wearing of white clothes among women whose husbands are alive, the marrying on Saturdays, the fixing of a Muhūrṭam (auspicious hour) for the Sanchayanam and other practices of the Malabar colonists to-day represent an epoch of history in the old country now quite forgotten. The Gauda Brahmin of the north, undoubtedly Āryan in his birth and type, eats fish to this day. Thus there is nothing in this ceremonial fishing of the Nambūṭirīs which should shock the sociological student as inconsistent with the community's purely Āryan origin."[1]

The last ceremony in a Nambūṭiri marriage is the Sṭhālīpākam, which is a sacrifice at the domestic altar on the day after the succeeding full moon.

According to the Hindu theory, the sacrament of marriage is as indispensable to females as to males, though passages are to be found in Śruṭis, Smṛṭis

1. *Travancore State Manual*. Vol. II, p. 262.

and Purāṇas which make it clear that marriage is optional with either. In Malabar, the Nampūṭirīs do not follow the Hindu theory strictly. Just as the junior members do not enter into holy wedlock, they allow their females to die old spinsters. But it is said that "tardy retribution" is made to the woman who dies unmarried by having the ṭāli tied round the neck of the corpse while lying on the funeral pile by a competent relative, for the body cannot be burned without this mock ceremony. The Abbe Dubois, in his *Hindu Manners, Customs and Ceremonies*, goes further and observes that he was informed that, among the Nampūṭirīs, " if a girl, who has arrived at an age when the signs of puberty are apparent, die before having had intercourse with a man, caste custom rigorously demands that the inanimate corpse of the deceased shall be subjected to a monstrous connection. For this purpose, the girl's parents are obliged to procure by a present of money some wretched fellow willing to consummate such a disgusting form of marriage; for, were the marriage not consummated, the family would consider itself dishonoured".[1] The learned translator and editor of the Abbe's works, Mr. Beauchamp, in his foot-note, while asserting positively that the custom no longer exists, leaves room for doubt as to whether it did not exist at the time the Abbe wrote, and Mr. Logan simply remarks that the Abbe's account of the strange funeral-pile marriage requires confirmation. Finding that this was news to the Nampūṭiri community, Mr. Justice Nārāyaṇa Mārār sought information from "the greatest living authority among the Nampūṭirīs, on their customs, manners and observances, *viz.*, the Kaimuk Vaidīkan Kṛshṇan Nampūṭiri, a venerable old man nearing eighty, who assured me (says the judge) that not only did the custom not exist at the present day, but there was not even the slightest vestige of any tradition that it had existed among them at any time." Upon this, the learned judge remarks very correctly that "the above serves

1. Vol. 1, pp. 17 and 18.

merely to illustrate the various wild, baseless and fantastic notions that are afloat concerning the people of Malabar."[1]

The injunction of the Śankara Smṛṭi, that the eldest son should marry, does not prevent the other male members from matrimony. The Smṛṭi does not certainly countenance, much less authorise or justify, the present practice of the junior members of the *Illams* roaming at large, sowing their wild oats. It gives them the choice of marriage or absolute celibacy.[2] It says clearly that Bhārgava is of the decided opinion that all brothers should marry. Only he does not compel them to marry as other Smṛṭikārakas.[3] His object is simply to prevent partition in the family.[4] So he says, if the brothers love each other well and are of one mind and desire marriage, it is best that all should marry with a view to increase the family.[5] They are at liberty to take the bath of celibacy or to enter into holy matrimony, but not to lead a wild life. The bath of celibacy means the ceremony by which one undertakes to lead for ever the chaste life of a Brahmachāri or student spending one's days in the service of God. Whoever among the sons that desire to lead such a life should be allowed to take the bath.[6] He who is the father of many sons should allow the bath of celibacy to be undertaken by those among them who are desirous of it and get the rest married.[7] The Smṛṭi then points out that, if after the bath is taken, he who takes it goes astray, the whole family will be doomed to perdition, and that, rather than risk such a contingency, it is better that all should enter into the sacrament of matrimony.[8] O! what a world of

1. *Malabar Quarterly Review*, Vol. I, p. 20.
2. *Sl.* 3, Chap. 5, Part 3.
3. *Sl.* 4.
4. *Sl.* 5.
5. *Sl.* 6.
6. *Sl.* 2.
7. *Sl.* 3.
8. *Sls.* 7 to 9.

difference between precept and practice! Would that there was some means of compelling them to follow the precept of their patron saint strictly!

The Nuṃbūṭirīs practise polygamy to a large extent. Nature has so contrived that there are as many Naṃbūṭiri women as there are Naṃbūṭiri men in the community, and the practice of the elder brother alone marrying in the caste leaves a large number of eligible unmarried females with the result that, more often than not, the eldest brother of an *Illaṃ* has to be a polygamist, some times of the worst type though not so bad as the Kulin Brahmans of Bengal, but bad enough. A number of girls in one family are exchanged in marriage with a number of girls in another to save marriage expenses and dowry. The women are dealt with as mere marketable commodity. The Naṃbūṭiri law as to polygamy is contained in the precepts of the Śankara Smṛṭi. Having enjoined on the necessity of one possessing male issue to save oneself from hell by the offer of piṇḍa, Bhārgava goes on to say: "It will be difficult for even five or ten men to satisfy the sensual passions of a woman, then need I say that it is sinful to marry two or three wives?"[1] "Still if it becomes certain that there is no chance of having a son by the first wife, a second marriage is not objectionable."[2] "If the second wife too bears no son, he may marry a third one. In the lifetime of these three wives, he should not marry any further."[3] But Naṃbūṭirīs of the present day do not often stop here. They marry more and do so more by force of circumstances than from personal inclination.

We have seen that, by custom, the eldest brother alone marries in the caste, and that the others consort with Nāyar women otherwise than with the sanction of marriage. In spite of the injunctions of the Śankara Smṛṭi already quoted enjoining the desirability of all

1. *Sl.* 8, part, 2, Chap. 6.
2. *Sl.* 9.
3. *Sl.* 10.

males marrying, the Nambūṭirīs still invoke the authority of Śankarāchārya for the origin of the practice. They trace it to the 59th of the 64 anāchārams or *irregular* customs already noticed. It is noteworthy that the 59th anāchāram as mentioned in the Śankara Smṛṭi or the Kērala anāchāram, does not warrant the assertion that the eldest brother of a Nambūṭiri Illam alone should marry in the caste. Neither does it authorise the juniors to consort with Nāyar women without the sanction of marriage. It simply says Jyēṣhṭa Bhrāṭa Gṛhī Bhavēṭ, which means only that the eldest brother should accept Grahasṭa-Āśrama or the duty of the house-holder,[1] not that the others should not marry or that they should roam about like a wild bull and debauch the women of another class.

The Smṛṭi writers have absolutely prohibited mixed marriages, *i. e.*, intermarriage between different castes in the Kali age.[2] Though Manu authorises the marriage of a Brahman with women of the other three castes, it will be found that, in almost the same breath, he denounces such union as extremely improper and undesirable.[3] He says that a Brahman who enters into holy wed-lock with a Śūḍra woman thereby becomes degraded to the level of a Śūḍra and quotes Gouṭama as his authority. In verse 17, Manu says that a Brahman who cohabits with a Śūḍra woman goes to hell, and if he procreates children in her, he loses his Brahmanhood. No expiation would wipe the sin committed by a Brahman who inhales the breath of a Sūḍra woman or who begets children in her. Yājñavalkya expressly says that he dissents from the statement that the twice-born men may marry Śūḍra women.[4] Vishṇu prohibits it altogether. So also modern Smṛṭi writers, such as

1. *Sl*: 24, Part IV, Chap. 12.
2. *Udvana Tatwa*; Raghunandana, BK. II, p. 62; *Vyavastha Darpana*, pp. 14-15. See also Steele, p. 26; 1 Strange, 40; General Note to Manu VI.
3. Chap. 3, V. 14.
4. Chap. 1, V. 56.
5. Chap. 26, V. 4.

Śankha [1], Vyāsa [2]. If it is contended that these authorities do not apply to Malabar Brahmans, let us see what the Śankara Smṛṭi, an authority absolutely binding on them, ordains on the subject, Verse 1, Part III. Chapter 2 says:—'No Nampūṭiri should consort with a Nāyar woman even for the satisfaction of lust.' Thus it is clear that the practice of modern Nampūṭiris consorting with Nāyar women has no basis in the Hindu law or in the Śankara Smṛṭi. The Vyavahāra Samudram, a poetical treatise on Malabar (of which Major Walker states that he was informed that it was translated four thousand two years ago!) [3] expressly prohibits a Nampūṭiri Brahman from having sexual connection with a Nāyar female. It says: "Śūdra Kanyaka sangaṭṭey varjjikkēṇam visēṣhaṭa [4]. This work is designed especially for the Malayālīs.

In a recent case that arose in the law courts, the question as to whether there was any law or custom having the force of law which prohibited the junior members of a Nambuṭiri Illam from marrying in their own caste came up for judicial decision and was decided in the negative by the Madras High Court.[5] As a matter of fact, there are many Illams in Malabar, all the members of which marry in their own caste.

The Nampūṭirīs appeal to a Sanskrit work, the Kērala Māhāṭmyam, in justification of the practice. No doubt, chapters 49 and 50 of this work expressly sanctions it and attributes it to divine ordinance. The Kērala Māhāṭmyam says that Paraśu Rāma, who is accepted by the Hindus to be an incarnation of Viṣhṇu, brought eighteen celestial maids from Indra's heaven. Coming to Vṛṣhabhādripura (Trichur), he saluted all the Brahmans assembled at the Maṇḍapam of

1. Chap. 1, Vs. 6-9.
2. Chap. 2, V. 2.
3. *Report on the Land Tenures of Malabar*, 1801, p. 6.
4. *Mack: Ms:*
5. *Mad. Law Jour.*, Vol. XIV, p. 214.

Śrīmūlasṭhānam, and thus spoke to the learned Yōgāchāriar (preceptor ot the Nambūṭirīs):—

"Such of you as are not house-holders may have sexual intercourse with these beautiful women for the sake of your personal enjoyment as well as for the purpose of procreation."[1]

Rāma settled the Ḍēva woman, with her six maids in the midst of the town of Vṛṣhabhāḍri and gave them six houses, to carry on their amorous dalliances.[2]

The Brahmans may have their sexual cravings satisfied as (freely) as the Ḍēvas do in heaven, *viz.*, one woman may be enjoyed by three or four persons in common.[3]

And the Brahmans shall not be amenable to the imputation of adultery; for, are not the celestial beauties so enjoyable in Heavens?[4]

Hence no Brahman shall be guilty of adultery in my land. O! superior Brahmans.[5]

And let the celestial women remain in my Kēraḷam land cohabiting with Brahmans according to their pleasure."[6]

Compared to certain other verses, the verses here quoted are only mild samples of the unblushing impudence of the author of this treatise. Those who have the patience to go through the work can easily see the object with which it is written.

1. Verse 22.
2. Verse 23.
3. Verse 26.
4. Verse 27.
5. Verse 28.
6. Verse 30.

Rāma is said to have proceeded towards the north and settled the woman of the Gandharva tribe with her six maids in the town of Lekṣhmipura (Ṭaliparamba) with similar injunctions as those proclaimed at Trichur[1].

He then settled the woman of the Rākṣhasa tribe with her six maids, who were in the prime of their youth, in Ambica's town (Mūkāmbi) for the daily enjoyment of the Brahmans.[2] In chapter 48, Paraśurāma is said to have ordained that, "among the folk of this land, in this my country, among all castes, amongst all Sāmanṭas and among all other women likewise, let there be no chastity. But as for the wives of Brahmans and of Ḍwijas (twice-born classes), let the rule of chastity stand in regard to them; with other residents, let there be no rule of chastity."

The Kērala Māhāṭmyam was cited as an unerring authority on Malabar law and custom by many a learned witness before the Malabar Marriage Commission, without stopping for a moment to enquire into its authorship, or as to when it was written, much less to ascertain its authority over the land. Its authorship is uncertain. There is no means of knowing when and where it was produced, except that there are versions of it differing one from the other. The Report of the Malabar Marriage Commission observes: "The book would be unworthy of notice, were it not relied on as an authority by many champions of Marumakkaṭṭāyam, and were it not that it correctly exhibits the religious teaching of the Nambūṭiri priesthood even at the present day."[3] Mr. O. Chanṭu Mēnōn, the only dissentient member of the Commission who stood out strongly for Marumakkaṭṭāyam, speaks as follows regarding the Kēralōṭpaṭṭi and Kērala Māhāṭmyam:—"These two books that are supposed to give accounts of the Nāyar institutions are works of Nampūṭiri Brahmans who, from interested motives, have always wished to

1. Chap. 50, verses 2 to 7.
2. Verses 8 to 10.
3. Para 24.

make out that our women do not, and need not, practise chastity." Again he refers to these books as "two recent Nambūṭiri works composed with the evident object of degrading the social status of the Nāyars". Sir T. Muṭṭuswāmy Ayyar says: "Kērala Māhāṭmyam, it is said, is not really an ancient treatise, but it was composed about 150 years ago by a Naṃbūṭiri Brahman." Mr. Justice Moore, in his book on *Malabar Law and Custom*, in a note on a passage quoted from Montaignes' essay on Virgil, in which there is some reference to marriage customs then existing at Calicut, observes: "The third book of the Essays in which this essay is to be found was first published in 1588, *i. e.*, more than 300 years ago, while the Kērala Māhāṭmyam and Kēralōṭpaṭṭi, written by the Naṃbūṭiri Brahmans and frequently quoted as if they were authorities, are certainly not more than 200 years old, if indeed they can honestly claim anything like so respectable an age. There are strong grounds for believing that they are forgeries dating from the closing of the eighteenth or the opening of the nineteenth century."[1] The writer again observes:—"As years passed, sometime about the opening of the nineteenth century, the Kērala Māhāṭmyam and Kēralōṭpaṭṭi were concocted, probably by Naṃbūṭiris, and false and pernicious doctrines as to obligations laid on Nāyars by divine law to administer to the lust of the Naṃbūṭiris were disseminated abroad".[2]

It will not be out of place to mention here that the Aliyasanṭāna system of marriage prevalent in Canara, which is just like the Marumakkaṭṭāyam system of Malabar, is supposed to be based on the authority of a book alleged to be the work of Bhūṭala Pāṇḍya, not dissimilar from the Kērala Māhāṭmyam. No less an authority than the late learned Dr. A. C. Burnell observes of it as follows in a note in his *Law of Partition and Succession*:—

1. P. 63
2. P. 88

"One patent imposture yet accepted by the courts as evidence is *Alya Santanda Kattu Kattale*, a falsified account of the customs of South Canara. Silly as many Indian books are, a more childish or foolish tract it would be impossible to discover; it is about as much worthy of notice in a law court as 'Jack the Giant Killer'. That it is a recent forgery is certain. * * * The origin of the book in its present state is well-known; it is satisfactorily traced to two notorious forgers and scoundrels about 30 years ago, and all copies have been made from the one they produced."[1]

The Kēraḷa Māhāṭmyam is no better. It is a pity that the work had not fallen into the hands of so profound a scholar and critic as the late Dr. Burnell, who would certainly have been able to expose its real character. The Malabar Marriage Commission observes in its Report, " The only copy which the Commission were able to obtain was obligingly sent by the Āḷuvānchēri Ṭampurākkaḷ, a Nambūṭiri dignitary esteemed to be of the highest sanctity, and he informs the Commission that this copy was made 37 years ago, from an older granṭham (palm-leaf book) which through age was becoming undecipherable and which is now lost. No information whatever is forthcoming as to the authorship of the poem or as to its date ; and the language and character in which it is written have prevented the Commission during the short time at their disposal, from submitting it to a critical examination. " And it was not also necessary for them to have undertaken the task, for the teachings of the book, even if it were authentic, were so much out of date, pernicious and subversive of all ideas of morality that they had no hesitation in saying, "The Nāyars will not submit to this teaching much longer." Looked at even from the most orthodox point of view, it is blasphemous to say that Paraśurāma, an incarnation of Vishṇu,

1. P. 12, note.

the preserver of the universe, would promulgate such diabolical doctrines regarding the chastity of women and the moral conduct of the priestly class. The mere statement of the revolting doctrines entombed in this sepulchre of a book is sufficient to condemn it.

It is fortunate for the Nāyars living to the south of Trichur that the Kērala Mahāṭmyam does not touch them or has to do anything with their marriage customs! For, according to it, Paraśurāma, in settling his houries, stopped at Trichur and proceeded northwards, settling the Gandharva and Rākṣhasa maidens at Ṭaliparamba and Mūkāmbi and making a gift of them to "the superior Brahmans" of those localities, "to play with." The Nayars there ought to be thankful to the God for not directing his attention to the south of Trichur and not giving them the benefit of the company of his celestial maidens.

Apart from the Kērala Mahāṭmyam, the authority invoked by the Nambūṭirīs is long established custom. A custom to be recognised by law must be reasonable, and no one will regard as reasonable a usage which condemns a class to live in promiscuity. "Custom," observes Mr. Justice West, "cannot prevail against a recognised general interest of the community." Says Sir Henry Maine: "There would be little evil in the British Government giving to native custom a constraining force which it never had in purely native society, if popular opinion could be brought to approve the gradual amelioration of the custom."[1] Quoting this passage, Mr. Justice West observes: "There seems in reality nothing to prevent this precise process from taking place. The command to be governed by usage is ill-obeyed by an extinction of usage to the extent of every adjudication which recognises it. Such a petrifying process would, in fact, be fatal to social progress, and thus opposed to public policy in the highest sense of that expression. * * As the mind of the community becomes enlightened, its legal convictions will

1. *Village Communities*, p. 72.

change, and this will constitute a change in its common law as that law must, from time to time, be recognised and recorded in the courts. The usage of individuals or of a class cannot, in opposition to the general conviction, on which it rests its validity, rank higher than a practice without binding force."[1]

The effect of this custom on Malayāla society is thus set forth by the Malabar Marriage Commission:—"As regards the effect of this precept on the morality of the Śūḍra women more will be said later on, but it is desirable here to note the effect of the system on the Naṃbūṭirīs themselves. To keep the family property imparitible and to guard against an inconvenient increase of mouths to be fed, the 'Earth-gods' set up a rule that only the eldest son should take a Naṃbūṭiri wife, and that all the junior members should solace themselves by forming fugitive connections with Śūḍra girls. The issue of these fugitive unions following Marumakkaṭṭāyam were no burden upon the Naṃbūṭiri father, but had to be supported by the Kāraṇavan (senior male) of the girl's ṭarawāḍ. The defect in this ingenious arrangement is that it leaves out of sight the natural law from which 'Earth-gods' are not exempt and which so arranges matters that there are as many Naṃbūṭiri women as there are Naṃbuṭiri men. The consequence is that while the Naṃbūṭiri bachelors solace themselves with their Śūḍra loves, the Naṃbūṭiri spinsters, secluded and vigilantly guarded in the privacy of their house, must live and die unmarried.

"In consequence of this custom, the females often enter into wedlock at a very advanced age or die in a state of celibacy, but so tenacious are they of their observances that the corpse undergoes all the ceremonies of marriage".[2] "Many Naṃbuṭiri women necessarily never get a chance of marriage." "In order to get their daughters married at all, a Naṃbūṭiri must be

1. *I. L. R.* 4 *Bombay*, 562.
2. *Census Report of Native Cochin*, 1875—76, p. 35.

rich, for with each of them he has to pay the bride-groom a heavy dowry, and many an illam's resources have been drained in this way."[1]

"The Nambutiri woman, unlike her Brahman sisters on the other coast, may remain unmarried even after attaining the age of puberty, and there are many among them who die virgins at an advanced age. Numerous daughters are considered a misfortune, as their dowry and other marriage expenses will impoverish any but the wealthiest Nambutiris. They do not, however, kill their children on this account"—a forbearance for which they, no doubt, deserve due credit. "The women are guarded with more than Moslem jealousy."[2] An institution which, by debauching the women of one class, condemns the women of another to life-long and enforced celibacy, is not one which justice need hesitate to condemn. If the reform movement set on foot by educated Nayars should eventually have the effect of driving the Nambūtiri bachelor into wedlock with women of his own caste, this indirect consequence of a marriage-law for Nayars is one which no right-thinking person can deplore. What (some persons ask) is to become in such case of the Naduvāli (chieftain) and other aristocratic families, who have hitherto preferred Nambutiri consorts for their females? It can only be suggested in reply that they should follow the example of many of their number and marry in their own caste."

The Commissioner's opinion as to the effect of the system on the Nambūtiri men has already been quoted.

Sanyasa Asramas.—We have already observed that the Nambūtiris of the present day are not in the habit of entering the third stage of life, the Vānaprasta-stama, prescribed for Brahmans by the Hindu system. It requires them to retire into the forest and lead a supremely austere life full of privations and sufferings,

1. *Malabar Manual*, pp. 127—8.
2. *Travancore Census Report*, 1874—75, pp. 213—14.

a by no means inviting prospect to a pampered class. Having nothing to gain in a worldly way by leading such a sort of life, they eschew it. But there are those among them who become Sanyāsis lured into it by extensive estates attached to the mutts of which they become managers by virtue of their position as Sanyāsis of those mutts. This is the last stage of the Hindu scheme of life, that of asceticism. There are mutts said to have been founded by the well-known Śankarāchāriyar, which are richly endowed by the piety of successive generations of Malayali Hindus. There are two such in Trichur, the Ṭekkēmaṭham and the Naḍuvilamaṭham with branch institutions throughout Malabar. These are presided over by Sanyāsis who are disciples in succession from the founder. The estates attached to the mutts are under their management. They have of course to lead an austere life, and to conform themselves to rules which do not differ very much from those of Sanyāsis elsewhere. Those that are peculiar to Malabar Sanyāsis or Swāmiyārs are:—

(1) The Sanyāsis should not have his Bhikṣha or food of alms in all houses. He should accept the invitation only of a Gṛhasṭa Brahman of the highest class.

(2) The Sanyāsis should bathe if he touches or approaches any one whose touch or proximity would cause pollution to a Brahman.

(3) He should bathe if he sleeps in the day time, if he vomits, or if involuntary emission occurs.

(4) He should, as a rule, bathe both in the morning and in the evening.

(5) When he goes out, he should have his attendants walk in front blowing a śank (conch-shell).

(6) He must walk—never use conveyances—a rule more honoured in the breach than in its observance.

A Brahman of the highest class who has performed all the sacraments prescribed, one who has given up all wordly thoughts, one who has got rid of all desires, jealousies and other evils, one who has attained Sāḍhana Sampaṭṭi which consists of (1) Niṭṭyāniṭṭya Vasṭu Vivēkam, (2) Virāgam, (3) Śamāḍi Ṣhalka Sampaṭṭi and (4) Mumukṣhuṭṭvam alone is qualified to become a Sanyāsi.

Sāḍhana Sampaṭṭi, otherwise known as Sāḍhana Chaṭuṣhṭayam, are.—

(1) Niṭṭyāniṭṭya Vasṭu Vivēkam or a clear and doubtless knowledge of the perishable and the imperishable. The term itself has been defined as follows.—A clear and undoubted conviction that Āṭmaswarūpa or the soul alone is imperishable (because he is the seer or the one who sees) and that every other thing is perishable (because they are the seen) is what is known as a clear perception of things.

(2) Virāgam or Vairāgyam is aversion ; repugnance of minds.

Definition.—An aversion to the enjoyments of all the worlds beginning with Brahma lōka and ending with Sṭhāvara lōka (material world), just as one feels at sight of the excrement of a crow, is called Vairāgia or aversion.

(3) Śamāḍi Ṣhalka Sampaṭṭi.—This consists of the six attributes beginning with Śama, to wit,

(a) Śama, (b) Ḍama (3) Paramōparaṭi (d) Ṭiṭikṣha, (e) Śraḍha, (f) Samāḍhānam.

Definition:—

(a) Śama.—The restraining of the inborn tendencies of the mind ever and anon.

(b) Ḍama.—The restraining or controlling the action of the organs of the body, such as the eye, the ear, the tongue or, in other words, the avoiding of prohibited actions.

(c) Paramōparaṭi.—A turning aside from all things of enjoyment, such as sound, sight, taste,etc.,

(d) Ṭiṭikṣha.—Endurance or bearing of every kind of pain or distress arising from such opposites as heat and cold.

(e) Śraḍha.—Reverence and belief in the words of the Upaniṣhads and the Guru or preceptor.

(e) Samāḍhānam.— Fixing of the mind on Brahma, the solitary aim indicated by the Vēḍās.

(4) Mumukṣhuṭvam.—A firm state of mind whose attitude is "O! Brahman, when and how shall I be freed from the bonds of Samsāra."

Ceremonies.—The Naṃbūṭirīs have to observe the Ṣhōḍaśa Samskāras like other Brahmans. These are according to the Śankara Smṛṭi.—(1) Sēkam, (2) Pumsavanam, (3) Sīmanṭam, (4) Jāṭakarmam, (5) Nāmakaraṇam, (6) Vāṭalpurappaṭu, (7) Chōruṇu (8) Choulam, (9) Karṇavēḍham, (10) Upanayanam, (11) Vēḍārambham, (12) Gōḍānam, (13) Samāvarṭ-ṭanam, (14) Vivāham, (15) Oupāsanāgni Swīkāram (16) Āḍhānam[1].

These Śhōḍaśakarmas or the 16 ceremonies correspond with those of the Eastern Coast Brahmans, *viz.*,

(1) Garbhāḍhānam (impregnation rite), (2) Pumsavana (ceremony for male issue), (3) Garbharakṣhaṇa (for securing the unborn infant from danger), (4) Sīmanṭa (hair parting), (5) Jāṭakarma (birth ceremony), (6) Nāmakaraṇa (name giving), (7) Niṣhkramaṇa (carrying the child out), (8) Annaprāśana (food giving), (9) Choula (cutting the hair for the first time), (10) Kēśānṭa (cutting the beard), (11) Karṇavēḍha (boring the ears), (12) Upanayana (initiation), (13) Samāvarṭ-ṭana (returning from the Guru), (14) Building a house, (15) Vivāha (marriage), (16) Aparakriya (funerals).

(1) Sēkam—is the nuptials. It is also called Garbhāḍhānam.

(2) Pumsavanam.—Ceremony performed for the wife in the third month after conception with a view to her being blessed with male issue.

1. *Sls.* 17 to 21, chap. 5, part I.

(3) Sīmanṭam.—This should be performed in the fourth month. Some think that it may be done after the seventh month.

(4) Jāṭakaṙmam.—This should be performed within 36 hours after birth. Correctly speaking, this should be performed before the baby sucks the mother's milk. But this is not indispensable.

(5) Nāmakaraṇam.—This is the naming of the child. It may be done in the third part of the night of the tenth day, or on the 11th or 12th day after birth, but in Malabar it should be done only after the purificatory bath.

The names in general use are those of Purāṇic deities. Some of the more important personal names in use among Nambūṭirīs but which are not used by Brahmans of the East Coast are :—

For males.—Vishṇu, Jayanṭan, Ḍevadaṭṭan, Kirāṭan, Pṙabhākaran, Ḍaṭṭaṭṙēyan, Kaḍamban, Chiṭṙan, Jāṭavēḍan, Bhavaḍāsan, Śṙīkumāran, Bhavaśaṙman, Kubēran, Bhōḍhayanan, etc.

For females.—Śṙīḍēvi, Saviṭṙi, Ganga; the names of demi-goddesses are those generally chosen for females, such as Ḍēvaki, Subhaḍra, Nārāyaṇi, Lakṣhmi, etc.

There are, however, other names also used both for males and females ; but these are either pet names or nick names.

For males.—Pōṭāyan, Nambiāṭṭan, Iṭṭiyāṭṭan, Ṭuppan, Kunchu, Kuññan, Nampōṭan. They are, however, corrupt forms of names already mentioned; for instance, Pōṭāyan is a corruption of Bōḍhāyanan, while Ṭuppan is a corruption of Subramaṇyan, and so on.

For females.—Nangeli, Nangayya, Iṭṭichiri, Pāppi, Uṇṇimāya, Kanka, Cheruṭa, etc. Here again Iṭṭichiri and Cheruṭa are corrupted forms of Śṙī and Sīṭa, Uṇṇimāyá of Uma; Pāppi of Pāṙvaṭi, and Kanka of Ganga.

Nambūṭirīs are generally known among themselves, not by their proper names, but by the names of their Illams or houses. Thus a member of the Malliśśēry Illam is called Malliśśeri. The father of the house is known Malliśśēri Achchan, the uncle as Malliśśēri Aphan, the son as Malliśśēri Makan, *i. e.*, father Malliśśēri, uncle Malliśśēri, son Malliśśēri, etc. In addressing Naṃbūṭiripāḍs, they generally add the term Naṃbūṭiri to the house name, *e. g.*, the Ḍēśamangalaṭṭu Naṃbūṭiripāḍ is generally addressed by them as Ḍēśamangalaṭṭu Nambuṭiri and so on.

(6) Vāṭalpuṙappāṭu.—This is the taking of the child out of the room.

(7) Choṙuṇu.—This is the first feeding of the child with rice, and should be performed in the sixth month.

(8) Choulam.—Tonsure follows either in the third or fifth year. About this time, the child may begin his education. He is initiated by his father in the alphabet on the last day of the Ḍuśara—that is, Vijayaḍeśami.

(9) Kaṙṇavēḍham.—Ear-boring.

(10) Upanayanam.—This is the investiture with the sacred thread performed in the seventh year. After this comes on the Brahmacharya for three years.

This is the most important ceremony in the Brahman's life, for it is this that makes him a Brahman. A Brahman is called a Ḍwija, or twice-born, because, in addition to his natural birth, he is said to be born again after the Upanayana ceremony. A bird is also called Ḍwija, because it has two births, one in the form of an egg and afterwards when the shell breaks and the little bird emerges out of it. Just so, on the performance of the Upanayana, the shell that surrounds the Brahman boy is supposed to be broken. The word is a compound of Upa+Nayana—Upa=near, Nayana=leading. He is said to be led to Brahmajñāna or the realisation of the eternal and universal self. Upanayanam should be performed in the eighth year including the period that the child was in the mother's womb. But if the child has to be taught the Vēḍas

A NAMPUTIRI BOY AFTER UPANAYANAM.

(To face p. 101

early, the ceremony may be performed in its sixth year.[1] Anyhow, he must be invested with the sacred thread before his 16th year[2] on pain of exclusion from caste.[3] In the other countries, boys on whom Upanayanam had not been performed in time are taken into caste on undergoing the expiatory ceremony known Vṛaṭyasṭōma, but, in Kērala, this is not allowed[4]. The boy's father or any other closely related to him or one who is by virtue of learning and nobility suited for the purpose should officiate as preceptor. The Gṛhyasūṭṛa to be observed is that of the officiating preceptor, so that, if the boy belongs to the Aśwālayana Sūṭṛa and his preceptor happens to belong to the Boudhāyana Sūṭṛa, the boy becomes one of the latter class after the ceremony.

The ceremony begins with the payment of Gurudekṣhaṇa to the boy's teacher. A sacrificial fire is made, and the boy stands to the west of it, facing the east, with the father beside him. He holds his right hand up. The sacred thread Yajnōpavīṭam to which the skin of Kṛṣhṇāmṛgam (the black antelope) is attached, is thrown round his shoulders and underneath his right arm, while the boy stands reverently with his eyes closed. The thread is made up of fine country grown cotton (foreign cotton is prohibited) spun by hand. It must be white to signify purity, endless to signify eternal being. It is always triple. The East Coast Brahmans wear six strings after marriage. He is after this led to an open space, and the priest introduces him to the sun and invokes the God to cover the new Brahmachāri with his rays. He then returns to the sacrificial fire and offers certain sacrifices. After a few more preliminary ceremonies, the Guru or preceptor utters into the right ear of his disciple the sacred letter Ōm which is known as the Pṛaṇavam, or the primeval sound, from which the whole manifested creation is believed to have developed and then the Gāyaṭṛi

1. *Sankara Smriti, Sl.* 5, Part 3, Chap. 1.
2. *Sl.* 8.
3. *Sls.* 9—11.
4. *Sl.* 10—12.

Manṭram which the teacher repeats nine times. It runs thus:—"Ṭaṭ Saviṭur Varēṇṇyam Bhargō ḍēvasya ḍhīmahi ḍhiyo yo naḥ prachōḍayāṭ," *i. e.*, "we meditate on the desirable light of the divine Sāviṭri who influences our pious rites." The Guru then instructs his pupil in certain maxims of conduct which he is to cherish and revere throughout the Brahmacharya stage. Addressing the pupil, the Guru says, "you have now become a Brahman: you have become entitled to the study of the Veḍas, perform all the duties that pertain to the Asrama you are about to enter. Never sleep during the day. Study the Vēḍas by resigning yourself to the care of your spiritual instructor." These exhortations, though made in Sanskrit are, explained in Malayalam as well, to enable the pupil to understand, a feature unknown to Brahmans on the other coast. With these words of advice, the preceptor gives him a Ḍaṇḍa or stick, as if to keep him in perpetual memory of what would follow, if any of these direction is disregarded. The boy then goes and makes his obeisance to his parents and to all his relations, after which he is given a brass vessel, the Bhikṣhapaṭra (alms-pot) in which he collects, by a house to house visit, food for his daily sustenance during the Brahmachari stage. He proceeds first to the kitchen of his own house with the vessel in one hand and the stick in the other. The boy making his obeisance in due form to his mother who stands turning to the east, says Bhikṣham Bhavaṭi Ḍaḍāṭu (mayst thou be pleased to give me alms). The mother places five or seven handfuls of rice in the vessel and, after receiving similar contributions from the other elders there assembled, he takes it to the father who is the first Guru, saying Bhikṣhamiḍam or 'this is my alms-collection.' The father blesses it and says, 'may it be good'. After the Gāyaṭrijapa, there is the ceremony of Samiḍhaḍhana which is the Brahmachari's daily worship of the sacred fire, corresponding to the Aupāsana of the Gṛhasṭha, and has to be performed twice every day. After another Hōma in the night, the cloth that covers the Kṛshṇājina and the sacred thread is removed, and the consecration of his food is then done for the first time. In addition to the strap of Kṛshṇājina worn like his thread and the Ḍaṇḍa or the stick of *ficus religiosa* in his right hand, the Nambūṭiri Brahmachāri wears a Mēkhala or the string of Kuśa grass twisted[1]. The Ḍaṇḍa should not be too long or too short, it should not have been burnt in any part, the bark should not have been peeled off, it should not be too thick, nor worm-eaten, its head should not have been broken, neither should it be double headed, it should not be bent, or curved, it should not have been fetched by a polluting caste man, it should have been cut either on a new moon day or on the 8th day of the waning moon, it should not have had contact with polluting objects—such a Ḍaṇḍa should not be accepted[2]. The Brahmachāri does not wear any clothing except the under-cloth which passes between the thighs and covers the private parts. Even with regard to this, the Śankara Smṛṭi prescribes directions[3].

Of the Nambūṭiri Upanayana ceremony, Barbosa writes at the beginning of the 16th century:—"And when these are seven years old, they put round their necks a strap of two fingers in width of the skin of an animal which they call Cresnamergan, and they command him not to eat betel for 7 years, and all this time he wears that strap round the neck passing under the arm; and when he reaches 14 years of age, they make him a Brahman, removing from him the leather strap round his neck and putting on another three threads which he wears all his life as a mark of Brahmin." The rules that were observed in such strictness hundreds of years ago are still observed, and every Nambūṭiri boy goes through his period of Brahmacharya which lasts at least for full five years. During the whole of

1. *Report on the Census of Travancore* (1901), p. 309.
2. *Sls.* 29-32.
3. *Sl.* 20, *et seq.*

this period, no sandal paste, no scents, and no flowers are to be used by him. He is not to take his meals at other houses on festive occasions. He is not to sleep during the day. Nor must he wear a covering loin-cloth in the ordinary fashion. Shoes and umbrellas are also prohibited. [1]

(11) Vedārambham—This is the beginning of the study of the Vedas.

(12) Godānam—A ceremony performed in the 16th year which lasts for one year.

(13) Samavarttanam—This is the ceremony which closed the Brahmacharya period. All signs of austerity are thrown off. He shaves for the first time after Upanayana, puts on ornaments, wears marks with sandal paste, puts on shoes, bedecks himself with sweet scented flowers, etc.

(14) Vivaham—This is the marriage ceremony.

(15 and 16) Oupāsanāgni Swīkāram and Adhanam—Accepting the sacrifical fire and performance of yagam.

Funeral Ceremonies.—When death becomes a mere matter of minutes, some verses from the Taittiria Upanishad are whispered in the dying man's right ear. This is known as Cheviyil Ottu. This done while life is departing, and the particular Mantra is called Karnna mantra (ear-hymn). A bed of Kusa grass, called Darbhāsana, is prepared, and the dying man is placed on it. When life has become extinct, the blood relations of the departed bathe and, with dripping cloths on, place two pieces of a plantain tree, one by the head and the other by the foot of the corpse. The hair on the head and face is shaved a little, and the body is washed with water wherein turmeric (mannal) and Mailanchi, a red colouring vegetable substance, are dissolved. The fore-head is marked with the Vaishnavite Gōpi. So also other parts of the body

1. *Travancore Census Report*, p. 309.

with sandal paste. The body is then dressed in white cloth and decked with flowers and garlands. It is then covered with unbleached cloth which is kept in position by a rope of Kuśa grass. It is then carried to the cremation ground by other Naṃbūṭirīs who are outside the pollution circle of the deceased, the eldest son supporting the head and the younger ones the legs. In some parts, the body is placed on a bier made of bamboos and carried on the shoulders of the nearest relatives. In the south-eastern corner of the Naṃbūṭirīs' compound, the pyre is prepared. A pit is dug and the fuel of a mango tree felled for the purpose is used. Some sandal is also used in the burning. The bier is placed on the pyre, the body uncovered and some rice is scattered over the face by the blood relatives. Small pieces of gold are also thrust in to the Navaḍwāra, or the nine openings of the body, while the priests repeat texts. Fire taken from a hōma or sacrifice (Aupāsanāgni) is placed on the chest and the pyre is lighted in three places. The eldest son acts as chief mourner. He is the responsible ritualist, and the younger ones have to keep physical contact with him while the ceremonies proceed. The performer of the rite carries earthern pots of water round the pyre, and the officiating priest makes holes in it with a knife, and receives water in another pot, which water is then thrown on the pyre. This burning of the dead body is the last Samaskāra or sacrifice that a Brahman has to offer. The mourners as soon as the body is almost reduced to ashes bathe once more, and taking some earth from an adjoining stream or tank make a representation of the deceased by means of Āvāhana manṭrās or texts employed to attract life from one body to another. In all these ceremonies, the Mārān (a class of Nāyar) is an indispensable factor. He has to hand over the Kuśa grass and *Sesamum* seeds for the oblations to be made to the deceased.

On the fourth day, the Sanchayanam or the picking up of the charred bones and their disposal come on.

N

On the 11th day the pollution ceases, when puṇṇyāhaṃ or purification is performed. On the 12th day, Sapinḍī-karaṇa Śrāḍḍha, or the ceremony of the joining the fathers, (after which the dead person passes from the stage of Prēṭa to that of a mane or spirit) is observed. The daily Śrāḍḍha now commences, and the Ḍīkṣha or special observance is kept up for 41 days, more generally for a whole year, during the course of which Śrāḍḍha is performed every day. There are also the monthly ceremonies, Māsikas and the Aṣhṭa Śrāḍḍhās (eight śrāḍḍhas). The first annual anniversary of the death is known as Ābḍika or Māsaṃ, a very important ceremony in Malabar, in the celebration of which money is almost lavishly spent according to the circumstances of the family. After this there is but the annual Śrāḍḍha or the yearly anniversary of the death, calculated according to the lunar year, when not less than three Brahmans are well fed and given presents of money, cloths, vessels, etc.

Caste Government. The majority of Naṃbūṭirīs are followers of the Rig Vēḍa. There are a few Yajur vēḍists and Sāma Vēḍīs. There are also diverse Sūṭras and Gōṭras amongst them The most important of the Sūṭras are Āṣvalāyana, Bauḍhāyana, Āpasṭamba and Kouśika. The best known Gōṭras among them are:—Āngiras, Vasiṣhṭa, Kāśyapa, Bhṛgu, Viśwāmiṭra, Aṭṭri, Bharaḍwāja and Kauśika. There are two Yōgams or unions among them known as Ṭṛśivapērūr yōgam and Ṭiruṇāvāye yōgam. Another division which is or was quasi-political, is into the Paṅṅiyūr and Chowara Kūrs. All caste matters are disposed of by caste officers and assemblies. There were originally 8 Smārṭas or judges attached to the two above-mentioned yōgams. But at present there are only six. The whole caste government rests absolutely with these judges. The office is hereditary and, in case of the extinction of a family, the place is restored by election. Besides these Smārṭas, there are four Kōymas or executive officers, who too are hereditary holders, whose duty is to carry out the orders of the Smarṭas.

If a Nambuṭiri is suspected of being guilty of any caste offence, or when there is a caste dispute in any locality, the matter is brought to the notice of the local Raja or chieftain, and he refers it to the Smarṭa, who has jurisdiction over the locality, who enquires into the question and gives his decision, against which there is no appeal. Minor offences are punished with the infliction of penances such as fastings, ḍanams or gifts or special forms of prayer, etc. But graver ones are visited with excommunication from the caste, which is always a terrible punishment.

In illustration of the method of caste inquiries and punishments a late incident may be referred to. A Nambuṭiri woman of the Cochin State was put out of caste for adultery, after the usual enquiry, and, with her, the alleged paramours, were also excommunicated. Two of the latter obtained from one Muṭṭamana Bhaṭṭaṭiri, a Smarṭa, who had *not* taken part in the inquiry a *pump* or writing to the effect that, as the holders thereof protested their innocence, they were entitled to prove it by undergoing the boiling ghee ordeal at the temple of Suchindṛam. This ordeal had already been stopped long ago by the Travancore Sirkar, within whose jurisdiction the temple is situated. The Nambuṭiri community took exception to the conduct of Muṭṭamana Bhaṭṭaṭiri, and held an assembly of the whole community at Trivandrum during the sexannual ceremony of *Murajapam*, with the consent of the Maharaja, and called on the Bhaṭṭaṭiri to explain his conduct. His explanation being found unsatisfactory, he and those who took part with him, or were connected with him in the affair, were condemned to various penances.

The Bhaṭṭaṭiri was for a period of three years to repeat the Gayaṭri manṭra a thousand times every day and, at the end of the period, he was for 12 days to cook his rice in *Panchagavyam*, *i. e.*, the five products of the cow. After this he was to undergo a peculiar form of solitary penance, and then make a gift of 100 cows to as many Brahmans who were to be fed sumptuously and to whom Pūjas were to be offered—a rather cruel punishment to an old man of more than three score and ten. The other members of the family as a body were to make a gift of 200 cows and undergo 12 Kṛchram. Those who took part in the affair as well as those who had associated with the Bhaṭṭaṭiri and his following were similarly condemned to undergo more or less severe penances.

The proceedings are signed by Āḷuvānchēri Ṭamprākal, four of the six Vyḍīkans, the two Vāḍhyāns, a Smārṭa, and a host of other Nambūṭiris. One of the remaining Vyḍīkans and a Bhaṭṭaṭiri were not prepared to go the extent the others had gone. They held that the *pump* was not warranted and not properly given, and that those concerned need be subjected only to jnāṭi śāsyam, a lesser sort of punishment.

Adultery. The purity of the race is so jealously and rigidly guarded that the least suspicion as regards the conduct of a Nambūṭiri woman forms the subject of elaborate and rigorous enquiry. The Śankara Smṛṭi says that the whole world rests on the chaste conduct of women, and the country where Brahman women are not chaste cannot claim to be properly governed. So the Raja should always be on the look out for suspects and punish them severely. The enquiry is conducted by the Smārṭa, and hence the term Smārṭa Vichāram. No consideration whatever would deter a Nambūṭiri, when once his suspicion is aroused, from courting a formal enquiry into the conduct of a female member of his family, however dear, or however closely she may be related to him. The Smṛṭi ordains that he should at once go with his Vāḍhyān to his relatives, and call their attention, to his suspicions. He should then bring home with him the Vāḍhyān, 5 or 6 Eṇangars (clansmen) who are truthful, well versed in sifting the matter, and arriving at the truth, and who have persuasive tongues. These at first interrogate three of the Nayar maids attending the Illam, who may be expected to know what transpires in the house, and who may be expected to speak out the truth. This preliminary enquiry is called Ḍāsi vichāram. If by this enquiry the suspicion is found to be well grounded, the suspect is at once removed to a shed outside the main building. As it should be outside the Nālukeṭṭu or quadrangle, it is called Anchāmpura, i.e., the fifth house. If there is not a permanent building available, a temporary shed is raised with green-thatch roofing, and therefore called Pachchōlappura. The suspect is thenceforward not called by her name, or as Anṭaṙjanam, but is known as Sāḍhanam or 'the thing', or 'article'.

After this, the Gṛhasṭa, accompanied by his Eṇangars and others, goes before the reigning sovereign and lays before him his suspicions. He should say, "O! sovereign, pray do all that is necessary to be done to relieve me from this difficulty, and thus protect Ḍhaṙma" (justice, religion, etc.). Upon this the Raja should appoint a smāṙṭa (judge) and four Mīmāmsakas or men learned in the law. The Raja should also send a Brahman to represent the sovereign, who should be supplied with a cloth with which he has to cover his head and face when sitting at the enquiry.[1] At present this latter office is known as Kōyma. There are two classes of Kōymas, the Akakōyma (whose office is hereditary), and the Puṙa Kōyma who is appointed for the time being. The business of the former is to preserve order within, and of the latter to watch the whole enquiry as the deputy of the sovereign. The Mīmāmsakas frame the questions and communicate them to the Raja's deputy and the Smāṙṭa in private. This should be done from outside the house, say, at the nearest pagoda. Their one object should be to arrive at the truth.[2] The Smāṙṭa should, after he has fully understood and grasped the

1. *Sl. 8*, pt. 1, Chap. 8.
2. *Sl. 9 to 10.*

import of the questions framed, proceed to the house along with the Raja's deputy and the Gṛhasṭa. He should in the meanwhile pray to the sun and moon, who are ever witnesses to all the thoughts of men, whether good or evil, as also of all that transpires in this mundane sphere, to cause the truth of the matter to be disclosed and demonstrated.[1] It would appear that at present in Travancore alone the Smārṭa conducts the enquiry, while outside that State one of the six Vaiḍīkas accompanies the Smārṭa, who merely acts as the proxy of the Vaidīka, and is authorised and guided by him. On reaching the place where the Sāḍhanam or ' suspect ' is, the Smārṭa pretends not to know that she is within the Anchāmpura, and proceeds to enter the room, when the maid-servant, who stands at the door, prevents him saying that her mistres is inside. The Smārṭa expresses surprise that a lady of the house should be confined there, and asks the reason why. This leads to the examination which, with scrupulous respect to the ghosha observances of the class, is at first conducted through the maid, and the ' suspect ' is made to admit that there is a charge against her. This is the first point to be gained, for nothing further can be done in the matter until the accused herself has made this admission. This point however is not easily gained and the Smārṭa has often to appeal to her own feelings and knowledge of the world and asks her to recollect how unlikely it would be that an Anṭarjanam of her position should be turned out of her house and placed in the Anchāmpura unless there was some cause for it. The Smārṭa sits in the adjoining room, so that neither the judge or the 'suspect' can see each other, though they can hear each speak. The 'suspect' sits near the door and the Smārṭa puts the questions prepared by the Mīmāmsakas. Meanwhile the Raja's deputy sits by the side of the Smārṭa with his head and face covered,

1. *Sl.* 11.

paying particular attention to the questions and answers. If he finds the questions are not put properly, he should at once drop the cover. This will draw the attention of the Smārta, and he should proceed to repeat the questions which the Mīmāmsakas had instructed him to ask. When the Raja's deputy finds that the questions are properly put, he should cover his head and face again. The answers received should be carefully stored in memory and communicated to the Mīmāmsakas in the presence of the Raja's deputy who should act in the same manner as at the enquiry, with regard to the answers. The process should be continued till the innocence is proved or the guilt of the 'suspect' is brought home to her. If she admits the guilt, the purda is removed, and the 'suspect' appears before her judge. Otherwise, till she gives a circumstantial confession, the questioning in camera will go on.[1] Often the enquiry is an expensive one, as it lasts for days and days together, and the Gṛhasṭa has to maintain the whole judicatory staff. It is not enough to confess guilt. She should point out all her paramours, if there be more than one. She should be particularly asked who the first partaker in her guilt was, and then the 2nd, 3rd and so on. She should herself give out the names. Often the questions degenerate into indelicate and obscene forms, yet they have to be asked. The Smārṭa communicates the result of his interrogation to the Mīmāmsakas. All of them should then go in a body to the Raja to whom a detailed report should be made. The Raja's deputy and the Mīmāmsakas should carefully watch that the Smārṭa makes a correct report. If he goes wrong, the Mīmāmsakas should set him right. The Raja's deputy should report to his master if the Smārṭas or Mīmāmsakas have in any way misconducted themselves. The 'suspect,' who has now been thus found guilty, after having made a full circumstantial and voluntary confession, should be "sent out" with the clapping of hands.[2]

1. (*Sls.* 13 to 19).
2. (*Sls.* 19 to 20).

In former days, when the servant accused her mistress and there was other evidence forthcoming, but the accused did not confess, various modes of torture were resorted to in order to extort a confession, such as rolling up the accused in a piece of matting and letting the bundle fall from the roof to the court-yard below. This was done by women, and the mat supplied the place of the purdah. At other times live ratsnakes and other vermin were turned into the room beside her, and even in certain cases cobras, and it is said that if, after having been with the cobra a certain length of time, and she was unhurt, the fact was accepted as conclusive evidence of her innocence.[1] When the enquiry is closed, and the party has assembled at the village temple, the guardian of the woman appears before them and makes his obeisance. The Smarṭa then recounts the whole course of the enquiry, and solemnly pronounces sentence of excommunication. The proceedings then assume a sad and serious aspect. The assembly comes outside the temple and a Paṭṭar Brahman, i. e., one of the East Coast, in a stentorian voice, repeats the substance of the charge and the sentence awarded. A man from the assembled crowd steps forward and snatches her umbrella with which Nambūṭiri ladies screen themselves when going out, as she is no longer worthy to carry it; she has also to divest herself of the brass bracelets worn on her arms. The Ḍāsi or maid, who has hitherto attended her always, is ordered to leave her, and the Smarṭan claps his hands and the assembly joins him in this, in token of her being turned out of caste. He who was hitherto her guardian leaves her, and the Smarṭa hands her over to the Puṛakōyma, or the representative of the sovereign. From this moment she is considered dead and the family performs her funeral rites. She becomes in future to them even less than if she had died. Indeed, if she happens to die in the course of the enquiry, the proceedings go

1. *Malabar* p. 123.

on as if she were still alive and they are formally brought to a conclusion in the usual manner by a verdict of guilty or of acquittal against the men implicated.[1] The members of her family have then to perform certain penances or Prāyaśchiṭṭams, expiatory ceremonies, as prescribed by the Vyḍīkan. After this, a śuḍḍha-bhōjanaṃ, or feast given in token of purification, is held, at which the members of the enquiring committee as well as the other Brahmans sit with the members of the family and take their meals. This brings the matter to a close. Similar ceremonies have also to be performed in the families of her partners in guilt, who are also excommunicated. Every one of them, except the one who, according to the woman's statement was the first to lead her astray, has a right to be admitted to the 'boiling-ghee ordeal', as administered at the temple at Suchīnḍraṁ in Travancore. If his hand is burnt, he is guilty ; if it comes out clean, he is judged as innocent. The order for submission to the ordeal is called a *pampu* and is granted by the president (Smārṭa) of the tribunal. Since this form of ordeal at Suchīnḍram has been abolished by the Travancore Sirkar, and all forms of ordeals put a stop to by all the governments, a *pumpu* is no more of any use. By virtue of the excommunication, the accused men are cut off from their families by the performance of the ceremony of Uḍaka-Vichhēḍam after which their funeral rites are also performed. They possess no longer any rights in, or to, the family and are driven out of it. Here too a śuḍḍha-bhōjanaṃ follows. Though cut adrift from caste and society, the Raja should see that she receives her maintenance so long as she expresses contrition, and leads a proper and decorous life. This is still the rule in the Native States of Travancore and Cochin. The following document shows how the excommunicated adulteress and her *par amours* are dealt with in Cochin after they have

1. Malabar, p. 125. O.

been turned out of caste after the sentence has been pronounced. It refers to the case already mentioned.

Proceedings of the Diwan of Cochin.

Miscellaneous Branch.

Read the following letter, Ref. on C. No. 1230 of 80 of 5th July 1905, from the Sarvadhikariakar (Secretary to H. H. the Raja.)

The charge of infidelity against the suspected sāḍhanam (creature) of Kuriyēṭaṯh Illam of Eyyāl Pravaṟṯṯi, Chemmanṭaṭṭa Muṟi, having been inquired into, she was brought down here and sentence pronounced upon her (Swarūpam Cholluka) on the 31st of this month. As it has been the custom to lodge such sāḍhanam in a secluded locality by the side of a river and give her sustenance and maintain her till her death, the above-mentioned sāḍhanam is sent under custody of policemen, who have instructions to take her to a place near the Ūṭṭupurah (Choultry or Brahman-feeding house) at Chalakkudi, leave her there, and come away. Conveyances should be arranged for the sāḍhanam and the Police constables and maid servants who escort her, to proceed from here to Chalakkudi. Their feeding at the Chalakkudi Ūṭṭupurah should also be arranged for. As soon as the sāḍhanam reaches Chalakkudi, she should be lodged in a house, if there is one close by. Otherwise a house should be built of mud walls and bamboo roofing, with door and lock, and she should be lodged therein, with no opportunity to have any sort of intercourse with any one. She should be given one measure of rice with the necessary accompaniments daily for the rest of her life from the Chalakkudi Ūṭṭupura.

When sentence was pronounced on the above mentioned sāḍhanam, [here follows the names of 65 men, composed of a Nampūṯiripād, Nampūṯiris, Paṭṭars (East Coast Brahmans), Nambiaššans, Vāriārs, Pişhāroṭies, Puṭuvāls, Mārārs and Nāyars] these have been named as partakers of her guilt. These should be prevented from frequenting the neighbourhood of their vīṭu, illam, and maṭham (designation of the houses of Nāyars, Nampūṭiris and other Brahmans respectively) as also from resorting to places, such as temples, illams, etc., where sajjanam (virtuous men) frequent. They should also be prevented from touching tanks, wells, etc., and thus be shut out (discarded). This communication is made under command of His Highness (*Kalpanaprakaram*—according to Royal orders) the Maharaja for immediate action''.

Order, dated 15th July 1905, Ref: on C. No. 2949 of 1080.

Communicated to the two Peishkars (Divisional officers) and the Superintendent of Dēvaswams (temples) and Uṭṭupurahs (feeding houses) who are requested to give effect to His Highness's commands conveyed in the Sarvadhikariakar's letter *at once*.

2. * * *

3. * * *

To

The two Peishkars.

Superintendent of Dēvaswams and Ottupurahs.

Endorsement on C. No. 4051 of 1080.

True copy forwarded to all the Taluks and Dēvaswam Tahsildars, Kāriakārs, etc., etc., etc., for information and guidance.''

There is little or no surveillance kept over them, and they soon manage to quit the place where they are lodged. In the District of Malabar, according to Mr. Logan, the woman thus driven out goes where she likes. Some are recognised by their seducers, some become prostitutes; not a few are taken as wives by the Chetties of Calicut. A few find homes in institutions specially endowed to receive them.

"These last-mentioned institutions", says Mr. Logan, "are of a peculiar character. Perhaps the best known, because it has formed the subject of judicial proceedings, is that of the Miedatta Aramanakal in the Chirrakal Taluk with extensive jungly land endowments. The members of this institution are respectively styled as Mannanār or Machchiyar according as they are men or women. They have baronial powers and keep up a sort of baronial state, for which purpose two hundred Nairs of the Edavakutti Kulam (or clan) were in former days bound to follow the Mannanars when out on active service. The members of the institution are recognised as of the Tiyan (Toddy drawer) caste, and the sons of Machchiyars become in turn Mannanar (or barons). The women take husbands from the Tiyan community. The women who are sent to this institution are those convicted of illicit intercourse with the men of Tiyan or of superior castes. If the connection has been with men of lower castes than the Tiyan (toddy drawer), the women are sent on to another institution called Kutira Mala, still deeper in the jungles of the Western Ghats"[1]

Of late, an attempt has been made to bring about modifications in the inquiry, in deference to the growing impression that the alleged paramours are being condemned to excommunication unheard. on the testimony of an accomplice who, on her own confession, has lost character. The Raja of Cochin, in consultation with the Smārṭas, Vyḍīkans, and other Naṃbūṭiris, has, on the principle of *audi alteram partem*, ruled that the persons named by the woman should also be called on to defend themselves. They are allowed to cross-examine the woman, and produce such evidence as they deem necessary. But, being a socio-religious inquiry, no representation by counsel is allowed. However meagre this privilege may be, one may console oneself with the thought that half a loaf is better than no bread.

The old-world simplicity which pervades the whole course of the inquiry, the idea of preserving intact the purity of the race which impels even the nearest and dearest relative to proclaim from the housetops the

1. Malabar, Vol. I, pp. 125—126.

infamy of a wife, mother, sister or daughter, is characteristic of the Naṃbūṭiris. They believe that, unless the matter is closely enquired into and the guilty excluded from caste, both themselves and the guilty are destined to perdition. Over and above this, they also believe that the world itself is doomed, if an unfortunate woman of their caste goes astray. So in justice to themselves, in justice to the outside world, in justice to the frail woman herself, the Naṃbūṭiri feels compelled to court a formal open inquiry. One may be pardoned in wishing that he may show half this delicacy of feeling with regard to the Nāyar women whom he deliberately debauches. The procedure adopted is equally characteristic of them. The matter is not brought before the sovereign till the guardian and the relatives are satisfied that there is a *prima facie* case for enquiry. Then it is the maid that is approached and, unless the suspicion is supported by her testimony, the matter is dropped. The sentiment of the 'suspect' is so much respected that till she confesses her *ghosha* is respected. Neither the Smārṭa, nor the Mīmaṃsakas nor the Raja's deputy sits in her presence. The feint by which the enquiry is introduced and the extreme unwillingness to proclaim in public that the 'suspect' is out-casted, are also characteristic of the Naṃbūṭiris.

Festivals.—The following are some of the more important festivals observed by Naṃbūṭirīs :—

(1) Ṭṛkkēṭṭa or Gyēṣhṭa star, (2) Upākarmaṃ, (3) Nāgar Panchami, (4) Gōkulāṣhṭami or Aṣhṭami Rōhiṇi, (5), Vināyaka Chaṭurṭṭi, (6) Ōṇam, (7) Makham or Māgha star, (8) Nava Rāṭri or Dassara, (9) Dīpāvali, (10) All the days in the month of Ṭulām, (11) Gauripūja, (12) Ṭiruvāṭira, (13) Aṣṭakālam, (14) Śivarāṭri, (15) Pūram, (16) Viṣhu (17) The new moon day in Karkaṭakam.

(1) *Trikketta*. In the month of Chingam, on the day of the Gyēṣhṭa star, 18th asterism, all the married

male members, as well as all female members, of a family eat before sunrise food prepared in the early hours of the morning. It goes by the name of Ṭṛk-kēṭṭa Paḷayaṭu (old), though it is not really the previous day's food. It will be remembered that Śankara expressly prohibits eating paḷayaṭu, food cooked the previous day.

(2) *Upakarma.* The day in the month of Chingam on which the sacred thread is renewed after Prāyaśchiṭṭam or penance for the sins of the last year.

(7) *Makam.* This is really a harvest festival celebrated for Ḍhānyasamaṛḍhi, or prosperity in grain. A few grains of paddy are taken by the ladies of the house, who anoint them with oil and bathe them in turmeric water, consecrate them with the repetition of certain hymns, and these are then deposited in the Āṛa or store room of the *Illam.* If there are females born under the Makam star, 10th asterism, they should do this. This ceremony comes on in Kanni or August-September.

(10) In the month of Ṭulām (October-November) young unmarried girls perform Gaṇapaṭi Pūja every morning before 4 a. m.

(11) *Gauripuja.* This is the worship of the goddess Gouri, wife of Śiva, on any selected Monday of the month of Vṛschika (November-December). It is known as Ammiyuṃ Viḷakkuṃ Toṭuka, or "touching the grinding stone and lamp." The grinding stone of the house is cleaned and a bronze mirror is placed on it and the married women of the house proceed to worship the goddess whose wedded life is believed to represent the ideal of conjugal happiness.

(12) *Tiruvadira.*—Though this festival is described elsewhere, there are certain features of it that are peculiar to the Naṃbūṭiris. The early bathing and the worshipping of Śiva begins 7 days before Ṭiruvāṭira. On the day previous to Ṭiruvāṭira, they take what is known as Eṭṭangāḍi (8 articles of food).

On the Ṭiruvāṭira day, 6th asterism, only one meal is taken. The husband and wife sit together before a lighted fire and keep night vigils. They also chew a bundle of betel-leaves not less than a hundred and one in number. All this is intended to promote the felicity of married life.

(13) *Ashtakalam.*—On the new moon day of Dhanu (January—February), the Pitrus or manes of ancestors are propitiated by offerings of Piṇḍa and Ṭarpaṇa—oblations of rice and water.

(15) *Pooram.*—In the month of Mīna (March—April) and on the 11th asterism day, the unmarried girls of the *Illam* worship Kāmaḍēva, the god of love, represented by a clay image, for 7 days. After the worship is over, the image is given away to a Brahman along with some money. He deposits it in a well. The flowers used in the worship are placed by the girls at the foot of a jack tree.

(17) On the evening of the new-moon day in the month of Kaṛkaṭakam (July—August), various kinds of sweetmeats are prepared and, before the family partakes of them, a portion of each is placed on the loft of the house for the rats to consume, believing that this will propitiate their master the god Gaṇapaṭi.

The other festivals are described later on, as they are common to other communities also in Malabar.

Their position in caste and society.—The Nambūṭiris occupy both in caste and society a unique position. They are considered by other Malayāli Hindus as Bhūḍēvanmār, god on earth. As such they claim to possess extraordinary powers. They profess to infuse the spirit of God into images made of wood and stone, and vivify these by means of their sonorous manṭrams and incantations and the ringing of their bells. They claim also the power of withdrawing from these self-same images the life they profess to have infused into them, leaving the stone and wood the dead inert matter they really are. They profess to have the power of raising from the lowest rung of the caste ladder to the topmost a Śūḍra, one of the servile-class, and invest him with the extraordinary privileges appurtenant to a Sanyāsi, i. e., one belonging to the highest Āśrama among the Brahmans. Witness the raising of the Thachudaya Kymal—having the power of raising a Śūḍra to Brahmanhood by their Manṭras and ceremonies, they also claim the power of hurling him down from the dizzy height to which they themselves had assisted him to ascend. They are held in high esteem by the Rajas of Malabar. They are a specially favoured people in Travancore, which is their happy hunting ground, their land of grace. The Maharaja of Travancore invites them once in six years for the great Muṛajapam ceremony, celebrated at the capital of the State. The more important members of the community are brought in state with great pomp and circumstance as befits their high sacerdotal position to Trivandrum, where they are sumptuously entertained for a period of 56 days. Their comforts are scrupulously attended to, and all sorts of luxuries are provided for them. On their part, the Naṃbūṭiris are expected to offer up prayers for the long life of the Maharaja and for the wealth and prosperity of the State. The function is unique, and costs the State exchequer between 3 and 4 lakhs of rupees on each occasion. The gathering is generally numerous, and no one leaves the place at the end of the ceremony without being richer than when he went there.

Again, once during the life-time of a Maharaja of Travancore, he has to solemnise two ceremonies which are held to form part of his coronation. He has once to weigh himself against his equal weight in gold, as also to dip himself in Panchagavyam or the five products of the cow, collected in a large golden tub with a lid of gold over it. The gold in both cases is minted into beautiful looking coins, and distributed among the Naṃbūṭiris. These are, however, but special ceremonies for their benefit, while there are other annual, monthly and daily celebrations which go to fill their purses.

Their position in society is not the less unique. Claiming to be free-hold proprietors of all land in Kērala under an alleged gift from Paraśu Rāma, the Naṃbūṭiris lord it over all other sections of the population of Kērala. A Nāyar should not go nearer than six paces to a Naṃbūṭiri; lest his holiness should be polluted by the proximity; a man of the barber caste no nearer than 12 paces; a Ṭīya 36, and so on. A Pulaya, the lowest race, 96 paces [1]. As already observed, the Naṃbūṭiris endeavour in every respect to impress on the other classes how low these are in their view. They are very punctilious in exacting great respect and reverence from those below them. In approaching a Naṃbūṭiri, one of these classes, whether male or female, must uncover to the waist as a token of respect. "His person is holy; his directions are commands; his movements are processions; his meal is nectar; he is the holiest of human beings; he is the representative of God on earth."[2] One has to debase oneself in his presence in the same degree as he is exalted. Thus he should only be addressed a Ṭampurān and Ṭirumanass, i. e., "Lord" or "holy mind", while the person addressing him styles himself Aṭian, i. e., "foot servant" or 'slave'. His food is Ambrosia, while, of the other, it is but Kallari, "gritty rice". While his house is Illam or Mana, the other lives in a Kuppa Māḍam, or "dung heap". While his coppers (chempu cash) are Rupees (silver), the other's Rupees are but coppers. While the Naṃbūṭiri "sports in water" (bathes-Nīrāṭṭu Kuli), the other has "to drench" himself or to get himself "wet" (nanayuka). The Nāyar's cloth is but an "old rag" (Palanṭuṇi, more often Aṭiṭhōle, *i. e.*, covering bark or skin), even if fresh from the loom, whereas the Naṃbūṭiri's is

1. See footnote 3 on p. 429 of the second volume of this work on "Malabar untouchability".

2. *Travancore Census Report for 1874—75, p. 191.*

Parivaṭṭam "daily washed cloth". The Nāyar can only treat himself to the black water in which rice has been washed (Karikāḍi), whereas the Nambūṭiri tastes his "Ambrosia" (Amṛṭaṭṭu); while the one calls his sleeping "lying flat on the ground" (Nilampoṭhuka), the other enjoys his rest like a Raja (Paḷḷikuṛuppu). The Nambūṭiri's death is called his Ṭīppeṭal, or "entering fire," while the other "commits a mistake" in dying, "Kūṭṭam Piḷachu". A Nambūṭiri's illness is Śīlāima, or Ālasyam, *i. e.*, uneasiness, weakness, while a Nāyar should speak of his illness as Paṭukāl, *i. e.*, 'stiff limbs'. A Nambūṭiri does not get shaved but he gets beautified 'Chanṭam Chārṭṭ". He is never angry, but only "his sacred mind is dissatisfied" (Ṭiruveḷḷakēṭu.) He does not clean his teeth; he cleans his "sacred pearls" (Ṭirumuṭhuveḷakkuka). Nor does a Nambūṭiri laugh—not he; he, however, deigns some times "to display his superior pearls," and so on.

With all this caste haughtiness, arrogance, and self-assertion, a Nambūṭiri, who is true to his traditions and leads a life of piety and unworldliness, and who keeps himself strictly within the śāstraic ordinances that regulate his life, is as a rule so simple, gentle, and benevolent, that all around him do not in the least grudge to render submissive obedience to him.

Games, recreations and pastimes. Boys generally have a game called Panṭukali with a foot ball made of coir or pack thread. This game will be found described elsewhere. The elders play at cards, also chess or Chaṭuranga. They have also games known as Ēḷu Nāyum Puliyum, Paṭinanchu Nāyum Puliyum, Irupaṭṭeṭṭu Nāyum Puliyum, i. e., 'seven dogs and the leopard,' 'fifteen dogs and the leopard,' and 'twenty-eight dogs and the leopard'—no doubt a relic of early hunting days when they must surely have indulged in that exhilarating pastime. A large square is drawn on the ground with small ones within, described by means of lines drawn horizontally and vertically. The leopard is represented by a stone larger in size than those that represent the dogs. The play consists in moving the stones from one small square to another so that, while the dogs endeavour to surround and corner the leopard, the latter attempts to dodge the former. The success consists in so bringing the dogs as to form a thick phalanx, two abreast, round the leopards. Evidently the play represents hunting the leopard by setting the dogs at the beast. Two other kinds of pastime are Kampiṭṭāyam and Pakiṭa, games at dice.

The Nampūṭiris take delight in Kaṭhakaḷi, or the national drama of Malabar, and the Ōṭṭam Ṭuḷḷal, or a kind of ballet dance. We shall have to speak of these in our notice of the Nāyars. It is sufficient to mention here that they are good connoisseures of these plays, which they study well, and fastidiously criticize the slightest fault or failure in performance. They attend these plays night after night, and support and patronize them to a large extent.

The next important recreation of the Nampūṭiris, one to which a religious turn is given, is the Yāṭrakaḷi or Śāsṭranga Kaḷi or Sangha Kaḷi. It is said to have had a historic beginning, and is performed by the Sanghams, or associations composed of the non-vedic Nampūṭiris, who took to the profession of arms. Kṣhaṭṛiyas also take part in these performances. There are in Malabar 18 of such Sanghams or associations, and every non-vedic Nampūṭiri and Kṣhaṭṛiya household is attached to one or other of these Sanghams. The names of the more prominent of these associations may be mentioned:—(1) Kanṭāran, (2) Pōrkkuṭaṭṭan, (3) Paḷḷikkuṭachchaṭṭira, (4) Nēmūr, (5) Chowāram, (6) Ṭaṭṭamangalam, (7) Vēḷapparampan, (8) Kiḷaviṇiyar, and (9) Paṭuṭōḷ.

Local chiefs, no matter to what caste they may belong, are patrons of one or more of these associations. Each association has one or more temples presided over by its patron deity. Their favourite divinities are Śiva, Bhaḍṛakāḷi, Śāsṭa, and Subṛamaṇṇya. There are three office-holders in each Sangham, (1) Wākyavṛṭṭi, (2) Parișha, and (3) Guru. The first two are hereditary office-bearers, and none but an Ōṭhan, or one of the vēdic class, is eligible for the first. The third is the Guru or instructor. The Wākyavṛṭṭi is the President or chief of the association, while the Parişhakkāran holds charge of the yāṭrakali paraphernalia, such as swords, shields, dresses, etc.

On occasions of marriages, māsams or the first annual ceremony after death, Upanayanam (investiture of the sacred thread), Chōrūṇu (first rice-giving), when the ceremony is intended to be celebrated in a grand style, these Sanghams are formally invited to give a performance, and they do not object to attend even Nāyar houses for the purpose. In Travancore, when the Sanghams are invited to attend and perform at a ceremony in the Royal Household, the party is formally received with all honours at the entrance by the Maharaja in state, sword in hand.

The functions and performances of the Sanghams, when attending ceremonies, are various and last for 2 or 3 days. They are:—(1) Nālupāḍam (meaning literally 4 steps or 4 stanzas). This is an antique dance performed round a lighted brass lamp with the recitation of certain stanzas, supposed to have been originally taught by a Ṛshi of old. This takes place of an evening, and is followed by the recitation of a few hymns in praise of their household divinities and especially of the God Śiva, the saviour that manifested himself at Ṭṛkkāriyūr. These hymns enshrine the legendary origin of the whole function. The story goes that the early Brahman theocracy of Malabar had installed at Crānganūr a Perumāl or king called Bāṇa Perumāl, whom they had invited from Bāṇapura. During the reign of this prince, certain Boudha (Budhist) missionaries arrived in Malabar and succeeded in persuading him to follow their tenets. The Perumāl required the Brahmans to adopt the new religion. Alarmed at this, they retired in a body to Ṭṛkkāriyūr, but

SAMKHAKKALI.

(To face p. 124.

found that, even in that hilly tract, they could not avoid the defiling contact of the Boudhas. They began to concert measures to get the new-comers expelled from Kērala, and assembled for consultation the headmen of the community. While thus engaged, a Maharṣhi (Saint) named Jangama came there who, on being appealed to, prescribed certain penances. The Brahmans were instructed to take out a lamp from within the temple to a room built on the Western ghaut of the temple tank, and pray to Śiva in terms of a hymn which the Maharṣhi taught them. This hymn is called Nālupāḍa (four feet or parts of a Slōka), said to be extracted from the Sāma Vēḍa. It is in praise of one Supreme Being (Brahma), and is sometimes styled Jangama gānam, or the song of Jangama. While repeating the hymn, they are to circumambulate the lamp before-mentioned. The deity ordered to be worshipped was Śiva as he had manifested himself at Ṭṛkkāriyūr. The Brahmans were told that, if they continued the observance every day, they would ere long find a means of getting rid of their troubles, and would also be able to purify themselves from the sin occasioned by Sankara Bhōjanam (mixed meals) and Aspṛśya sparśanam (touch of those who are not to be touched), etc. While they were following these instructions strictly, there arrived on the 41st day six learned men from the East Coast (Paraḍēśa), whose names were:—Bhaṭṭa Āchāryan, Bhaṭṭa Bāṇan, Bhaṭṭa Vijayan, Bhaṭṭa Mayūran, Bhaṭṭa Gōpālan and Bhaṭṭa Nārāyaṇan. With the help of these learned men, the Nambūṭiris were able to convince the Perumāl of the folly he had committed; and the Perumāl proposed a public discussion between the Śāsṭries newly arrived and the Boudha missionaries, to which the former agreed on condition that, whichever party was defeated, should be expelled from Kērala with their tongues cut off. The challenge was accépted, and a protracted discussion followed with the result that in the end the Boudhas were worsted and had to be expelled from the country.

Ever after this, the sacred hymn of Nālupāḍa has been sung with the circumambulation of the lamp by the Naṃbūṭiris for the attainment of a variety of objects, every one of which they expect to secure by this means. It is also said that, while this sort of worship was going on at Ṭṛkkāriyūr, Śiva Bhūṭams or saints or angels attending on the God were found amusing Pārvaṭi, with quips and cranks, and that an Aśarīri (a voice, not proceeding from a body, i. e., from heaven), was heard to say that such frolics must thereafter form part of the worship of Śiva. The story cannot be dismissed as altogether legendary, for, according to Professor Wilson, it refers to the confutation of the Boudhas of Malabar by Kumārila Bhaṭṭa, a northern Brahman. He thinks that the event must have occurred, if at all, before the time of Śankara. Such public discussions also were not of rare occurrence at the time; for we have an account of a great public disputation the Chinese Pilgrim Huien Tsiang had with a learned Brahman at the great University of Naḷanḍa.[1]

(2) The second function performed by the Sangham is in cooking and in serving the meal for the feast. Even the highest grade of Naṃbūṭiris partake of food cooked by them. It will be remembered that the Nālupāḍam was originally described as a means of purifying them from the defilement caused by Sankara Bhōjanam or mixed eating, so that, after the observance of the Nālupāḍam, they emerge purified.

(3) Towards evening, they assemble in a large shed, erected for this purpose, and sing merry songs, sitting round a copper cauldron, one of the cooking vessels, placed upside down, upon which they beat time with their hands. One of the party then jumps up, takes hold of one of the feast spoons made of cocoanut shell with a bamboo handle, and runs up and down acting the part of one possessed.

(5) On the night of the performance, they are treated to a sumptuous meal, during the course of

1. *Wilson's History of India*, Vol. 3, p. 273.

which they sing in loud tones songs known as Kaṙi-slōkams, so called because they are devoted to the description in detail of how the curries of a feast are to be cooked and served. Each one calls, by means of these songs, for any particular preparation he likes, no matter whether it is forthcoming or not.

(5) This is followed by a torchlight procession to the Kaḷam or hall, where the main performance is to take place, with the singing of songs in the Vanchip-pāṭṭu or boat-song metre. At this stage, they have their sacred thread hanging vertically round the neck (Apavīṭa), and not diagonally as in the orthodox fashion. In the centre of the hall there will be placed a well lighted brass lamp, a Paṙa (a Malabar measure) filled with paddy, a number of cocoanut bunches, and plantain fruits and flowers. The Brahmans sit round the lamp in a circle and recite verses in praise of Śiva, specially of his manifestation at Tṛkkāriyūr.

(6) Then follow dumb-shows and feats of swordmanship. Each in turn exhibits his skill in the use of the sword and shield, the arms that Paraśu Rāma had supplied his Naṃbūṭiri army with.

(7) At the end of the above show, the host appears on the stage, and the effects caused by any evil spirits that may have attached themselves to him is sought to be removed by an exorcism which consists in waving a lighted torch before his face, and a prayer is made to the Goddess, Bhagavaṭi, to shower on the host health, wealth, and prosperity.

(8) The whole function is then brought to a close with a variety entertainment. Comic and humorous performances are given. There is much mimicry, cracking of jokes, recital of droll stories, etc. Figures in peculiar dress appear, and their quips and cranks keep the audience laughing. A local chief in the person of an oddly dressed figure is represented on the stage. He is called Kymal, and the Naṃbūṭiris make mock submission to him, and twit him with the

oddities of his rule over the neighbourhood. The one great blemish that mars the otherwise innocent entertainment is the coarse and indecent element that is present in many items of the performance. At the end of the performance, invited guests give away customary presents to the performers. Towards early morning the host performs what is called Vachchunamaskāram. The Brahmans that compose the association sit together on the ground in a circle, and the host places before them the fee due to the association, makes three rounds of the assembled Brahmans, and finally performs Sashṭāngam (prostration), and receives their blessings.

As observed by a recent writer, "few people whose real home is not Malabar will be able to appreciate and enjoy the play. A great East-Coast Pandit (we believe it was Uḍḍaṇḍa Śāsṭrikal), once in the employ of the Zamorin of the day, when asked about the merits of the performance, is reported to have said, "it is the mental aberration of the people of Malabar."

Ēlāmaṭṭkali, or the 7th amusement, is another source of recreation enjoyed by the Nambūṭiris. It is so called because of its alleged introduction by the 7th Nambūṭiri Grāma in Kērala. It is but the yāṭrakali in miniature, shorn of the religious accompaniments of the latter. There is the sitting round the lamp and recital of songs in praise of Śiva, but the performers need not necessarily be Brahmans, nor need there be any set religious formalities observed. The party round the lamp simulate the proceedings of a court of justice, and hold a mock trial. The presiding judge is known as Kallūr Nāyar, who will be assisted by a Bhaṭṭaṭiri. There are two who serve as bailiffs to execute the judge's order. Then follows an interrogation by one of the party addressed to another who has to answer it. It is in fact a competition in quick-wittedness and memory held between two parties, into which the assembly will have been previously divided. The questions and answers are in the form of verses sung to long drawn tunes. A specimen of a question and answer may be given here. The interrogator asks Eṅṭila, Eṅṭinkōl, Eṅṭinkāya. The interrogated answers Kaṇṭila, Ṭākkōl, Sūkshikkāya. It will be observed that the second portion of each word in the question and answer correspond. Beyond this, the answer is altogether meaningless and absurd with reference to the question. The query is Eṅṭ-ila—what leaf? Eṅṭin-kōl—what stick or twig? Eṅṭin-Kāi—what fruit? The answer is Kaṇṭilla, has missed. Tā-kkōl, keys; Sūkṣhikkāya, carelessness. When put together, the answer would stand thus:(I have) missed (my) keys (because of my) carelessness, which of course is no answer to the question (of what) leaf, (of what) twig,(of what) fruit (were you speaking)? The answer being absurd, the person answering is reckoned to have committed an offence. The questioner would then address the President in these terms: "What punishment should be awarded to Mōrppala Kēśavan who has committed this offence in the presence of this assembly composed of Kallūr Nāyar, Bhaṭṭaṭiri and representatives of the 64 Grāmams (villages), O Kallūr Nāyar?" The President would then solemnly pronounce sentence by saying, "Let him be raised up." and the bailiffs would at once pull up the offender who should then play the fool. When he has finished entertaining the assembly with his fooleries, a question of a similar nature as above is asked, and another comes out with an equally absurd answer, and the same process is gone through again. In this manner, each one of the party has to perform some part before the play ends. Typical characters are represented on the stage, and the assembly is kept in a constant roar of laughter. The characters introduced generally are Iṭṭikaṇḍappan Nāyar, Prākkaḷ, Muṭṭi or old woman, Paṭṭar or East Coast Brahman, Naṃbūṭiri, Paṇḍāram and so on.

Religion. The Naṃbūṭiris are vēḍic Brahmans. In their migration from the north, they seem to have brought whith them the religion of the Vēḍas. They are strict observers of the injunctions contained in the Śruṭis, Smṛṭis, Gṛhya Sūṭras. There is little or no sectarian differences among them. Though there are Śaivite and Vaishṇavite Naṃbūṭiris among the community, there is not that bigotted exclusiveness which is characteristic of sectarian differences on the East Coast. The Saivite worships Viṣhṇu as much as the Vishnavite would worship Śiva. They observe almost all the religious ceremonies of the East Coast Brahmans, of course with local colouring. All the Puraṇic deities are devoutly worshipped. They are at the same time no strangers to the wonderful teachings of the renouned Vēdantist Śankara, who was himself a Naṃbūṭiri Brahman. For all that, the religion of the Naṃbūṭiris must be admitted to have been influenced considerably by its Dravidian surroundings. With this difference, it stands in strong contrast with the religion of the masses, which is but an elevated form of the early Dravidian religion refined and ennobled by an intense admixture of Brahmanism. The life of the Naṃbūṭiris is but one round of religious observances. He has but little time to spare for worldly concerns, if he only keeps up to the life sketched for him. While believing in the highest form of Vedantism, his religion is elastic enough to take within it the lowest forms of animism, fetishism, ancestor-worship, and what not. All things animate or inanimate, organic or inorganic, are believed to be permeated by the divine spirit and are therefore objects of veneration. Thus animals, birds, trees, plants, and flowers are all worshipped. The cow, the snake, the Brahmani kite, the Ṭuḷasi plant (ocymum sanctum) the banyan tree (ficus religiosa), the Bilva or Kūvaḷa (Ægle marmelos), the lotus flower, are all worshipped with fervour. The Navagrahas or the nine planets, and among them the Sun and the Moon specially, are worshipped almost daily.

Rules of good conduct.—The following are a few rules of good conduct prescribed by Śankara Smṛṭi for the Nampūṭiris to observe and they afford us an insight into their ideals of life and good manners:—

1. He who is anxious of his own welfare should not insult others.

2. Do not jeer at those who have an organ wanting, or who have an abnormal addition of one, or are deformed, and those who belong to low castes, or are illiterate, or are afflicted with diseases.

3. Brahmans should never serve low class men, nor should they abandon their study of the Vēḍas.

4. Your dress, your whole outward appearance, should be suited to your position in respect of caste, the particular stage of life, (such as Brahmachāri āśramam) your age, nobility of birth, wealth, fame, time, place and circumstances ; you should reject all that is despicable.

5. Be constantly pondering over the meaning of the texts of the Śāsṭras.

6. If you can help it, do not wear old, dirty, or torn clothes.

7. Never say 'may' to those who beg alms of you.

8. Do not learn the language of mlēchhas, i. e., those who speak a provincial dialect or a language other than Sanskrit.

9. Do not look at one's own excrement.

10. Do not look at your own image seen reflected in oil or in water.

11. Do not look at the face of your angry Guru, preceptor.

12. Do not see your wife while she is eating.

13. Do not gaze at a woman who is nude, or one who is in her menses, or one without her bodice on.

14. Do not look at the private parts of female children, or

15. On the copulation of animals.

16. Do not throw impure matter into the fire.

17. Do not warm your feet over a blazing fire.

18. Do not clean your feet with Ḍaṛbha, holy grass.

19. Do not place your foot on a bell metal vessel.

20. Do not place one foot over the other.

21. Do not break clods of earth.

22. Do not draw lines on the ground.

23. Never tear your hair or nails with your teeth.

24. Avoid all kinds of gambling.

25. Do not wear clothing or shoes already worn by another.

26. Do not wear a sacred thread which has once snapped. The sacred thread should always be worn in the prescribed manner.

27. Never serve food to a Śūḍra before you have yourself partaken of it.

28. Rice offered to the gods and to the manes should never be given to a Śūḍra.

29. You should not teach a Śūḍra letters.

30. Do not eat rice prepared with sesamum.

31. A Brahman should never act as the Purōhiṭ or priest of a Śūḍra.

32. Do not speak to a woman who is in her menses.

33. Do not wake those who are sleeping.

34. If you see a cow grazing on another's land, do not drive it away, nor inform the owner of the land of the fact.

35. Do not remove a calf which is being suckled.

36. Do not live in a country governed by a Śūḍra.

37. Do not reside in a place full of men not inclined to charity, or where there are no good doctors, or where you cannot get water.

38. Never do any unnecessary act.

39. Never utter obscene words, nor do a dishonest act.

40. Do not speak ill of thyself or use words which may wound the feelings of another.

41. Take due time for your morning, mid-day and evening prayers.

42. Do not play with sharp edged weapons.

43. Do not touch your ears, eyes, etc., unnecessarily.

44. Do not touch your impure organs unless it be to wash them clean.

45. An act which is perfectly legitimate in itself and which is sanctioned by the Śāsṭras as well, should be avoided if the people of the country are against it.

46. Prayers should be recited and sacrifices offered on sacred days such as Sankrānṭi, i.e., the first day of the month, the new moon day, etc., for obtaining absolution from sins.

Such are in short a few rules of good conduct (Saḍāchāram). In other matters, act as men of virtue and righteousness generally do.

Concluding remarks. The Naṃbūṭiris are a simple, polite, hospitable race, leading an inoffensive and religious life. The prayers and sacrifices they offer are not exclusively for their own benefit, their office in this world being to lead an intensely religious life for the salvation of themselves as well as the other classes that inhabit Malabar. The characteristic features of the Naṃbūṭiri have been described to be " his faith in God and resignation to His will, hospitality to strangers, scrupulous veracity, punctiliousness as regards the ordinances prescribed, and extreme gentility in manners ". In regard to his anxious fidelity to truth, it has been observed that " he rarely gives a decided answer, being fearful he should state what is not exactly the truth ". " Whatever be their faults", observes Mr. Elie Reclus, " the Naṃbūṭiris have at least one virtue, that of perfect veracity. They answer questions put to them with great deliberation, being always scrupulous to tell the exact truth in all respects". Absorbed in their religious exercises, they are innocent of all worldly guile and not seldom fall victims to intrigue and fraud. They are loath to do harm to others and never indulge in vituperation or even the use of harsh language. Till of late, they lived in the most amicable relations with their tenantry. A degree of tension between the two is however observable to be growing as the result of stagnation on one side and progress on the other. They have not changed with the times—at any rate for the better. Indeed the modern Naṃbūṭiri is "not the unadulterated specimen of goodness, purity, and piety that he once was ", but the Naṃbūṭiris have not so far degenerated as to merit the unsympathetic critcism, that " they are arrogant and oppressive, vindictive and grasping," that " they will turn aside sooner than tread on a worm or any other insect, but think the murder of a slave no crime, should he provoke his death by too near an approach to one of their bigotted race, or by showing them any impertinence ".[1] We have a much more true and correct account of the religious Brahmans from Mr. Forbes who, writing in the end of the 18th century, observes that they have " the absolute and entire management of everything relating to religion. Occupied by no secular concerns, they spend their days under the sacred groves of their temples in superstitious ceremonies and listless indolence, or the study of the sacred volumes, treatises on astrology, medicine and fabulous legends; they inculcate benevolence to man, and kindness to the animal creation, and are

1. Dr. Day, p. 306.

reverenced by the inferior tribes, who swear by their heads and treat them with filial affection.[1]" Mr. Grose, writing about the same period, contrasts the Brahmans of other parts of India with those of Malabar, and remarks that though, in Malabar they "are in the same or greater esteem and have more the lead of affairs, they retain more of the humanity and disinterestedness of their primitive institution."[2] There is nothing to induce one to believe that, between the time of Messrs. Forbes and Grose and that of Dr. Day, a change, infinitely for the worse, had come over the community to justify the observations of the latter. We may close our account of the Naṃbūṭiris with the following quotation from Mr. Fawcett. "The moral element certainly enters largely into the life of the Naṃbūṭiri. And, if it be true, as there seems little reason to doubt, that a religion may be classed high or low according as it does or does not influence the morals of a people, we must class the religion of the Naṃbūṭiri high, for his whole life, his moral life we shall say, is dominated by it. A peace-loving people, and devoted to their religion, the Naṃbūṭiris are beyond doubt. Long may they remain as they are, untouched by what we hear called "progress", but which is really *change*—for better or worse, who knows? Long may they be what they are, the only undisturbed vestiges of Vedic Brahmanism".[3] Indeed it is not possible to echo the sentiments of Mr. Fawcett all through. All the same there is much that is loveable in the character of the Naṃbūṭiris.

One can, however, scarcely admire the moral conduct of a class that, by enforcing celibacy on its junior members, allows these to marry the women of another class bound to them by ties of absolute dependency, religious and social. The result of this is ruinous to themselves. The community that abstains from marriage amongst

1. Vol. I, p. 236.
2. Vol. I, p. 242.
3. P. 85.

themselves is destined to become extinct sooner or later and as a matter of fact successive decinnial censuses show their numbers steadily diminishing. The haughty aloofness so characteristic of the old-world Naṃbūṭiri stands in the path of his progress. The Naṃbūṭiri has yet to realise full that the world around him is changing and that he alone stagnates. It is, indeed, gratifying to note that the more far-seeing members of the community are beginning to realise their forlorn position and are trying to mend matters before it is altogether too late. They have recently formed themselves into associations to consider the best means of breaking through old effete customs and place themselves in the path of progress. The desirability of all male members of an *Illom* marrying in the community, the cutting short of exhorbitant demands as dowry from the bride's father, the English education of the younger members of the community, the cancelling of the prohibition against Naṃbūṭiri females travelling by railway—all these and more have come under the consideration of a large section of the rising generation. A few of the more prominent members of the community have taken themselves with commendable alacrity to agricultural and industrial pursuits, and the profession of trade is also not being neglected. They are, slowly realising the truth of the adage that 'Union is strength' and they have founded associations such as the 'Kērala Jenmi Sabha' and started organs of their own such as the 'Jenmi' and the "Yōgakshēmam". No doubt the outlook for the future is not altogether without hope.

III. The Kshetriyas of Malabar.

The Kṣheṭṭiyas of Malabar do not form a large community. They are said to have been brought into Malabar by Paraśu Rāma. According to the Kēraḷa Māhāṭmyam, Rāma is said to have brought certain Kṣheṭṭiya families of the Sōma Vamśa or lunar race from Āṭyapura, whence he brought his first colony of Brahmans. At present the Kṣheṭṭiyas live scattered throughout the country from Trivandrum in the south to Cannanore in the north.

The Malayāli Kṣheṭṭiyas are known in the country by various names, the most comprehensive one being Kōvil or Kōyil, meaning a "Royal residence", as well as a temple. The theory is that these Kṣheṭṭiyas were originally brought into Kēraḷa for the purpose of ruling over tracts assigned to temples by the Brahmans, and to supervise and govern the pagodas and other religious institutions. The Raja of Cochin, one of the prominent Kṣheṭṭiyas of Malabar, still describes himself officially in kānom deeds as "Gangāḍharaṭirukōviladhikārikaḷ", i. e., 'Gangāḍhara the prosperous manager of pagodas', a circumstance that lends colour to the theory of the Kēraḷa Māhāṭmyam. The Portuguese historians give the name of the reigning Raja of Cochin on the arrival of Vasco de Gama in Malabar as Uṇṇi Rāma Kōil Ṭirumulpād.

The titles used in addressing them are :—

(1) for male, Ṭampurān also Kōyil Ṭampurān; for female, Ṭampurāṭṭi.

(2) Ṭampān; Ṭampāyi, Ṭampāṭṭi.

(3) Ṭirūpād also Kōvil Ṭirūpād or more correctly Ṭirumulpād; Nampiṣhṭāṭiri.

(4) Bhaṇḍāraṭṭil or Paṇḍāraṭṭil.

Of these terms the first, Ṭampurān, is a compound of Ṭam+pirān, meaning liege lord, and the same idea also pervades the other terms.

The Travancore Census Report points out that there is an old Sanskrit verse which describes 8 classes of Kṣheṭṙiyas as occupying Kērala from very early times, namely (1) Bhūpāla or Mahā Rāja, (2) Rājaka or Rājas, (3) Kōvilṭampurāns, (4) Pūrvan or Ṭampān, (5) Śṙipurōgama or Ṭirumulpād, (6) Bhaṇḍāri or Paṇḍāraṭṭil, (7) Ṭirumulpāṭ, (8) Chēṭa or Sāmanṭa. Of this list, the 5th are waiters at the Rāja's Palace, meaning that they are upper subordinates serving the first and second classes, while the 7th perform *udvahaka* or wedding ceremonies of Nāyars. Both these are however identical. Mr. Logan speaks of the Kottayam and Paṙappanād chieftains as having been Rajaputs or foreign Kṣheṭṙiyas, and observes that the former of these chieftains used sometimes to be called the Puṙanāt (foreign) Rājas.

Personal names :—

Kōil Ṭampurāns—males—Rāja Rāja Vaṙma,
Rāma Vaṙma,
Kērala Vaṙma,
Ravi Vaṙma,

Tampurans. In the Cochin Royal family, the first name above given is not used, but another, Gōḍa Vaṙma, comes in. In Travancore, however, in addition to the ordinary names prevalent among Kōil Ṭampurāns, names such as Māṙṭṭāṇḍa Vaṙma, Āḍiṭya Vaṙma, Uḍaya Vaṙma are also used. It will be noticed that, though the Kērala Māhāṭmyam tells us that the Kṣheṭṙiyas introduced into Malabar by Paraśu Rāma belong to the lunar race, the personal names borne by their descendants now indicate their descent from the solar line. Almost all those names with the exception of Rāma and Kērala are those of the Sun. The suffix Vaṙma denotes that they are Kṣheṭṙiyas just as the term Śarma denotes a Brahman. Of the two exceptions the name Rāma was borne by the most prominent of the solar line, Śri Rāmachanḍṙa of the Rāmāyaṇa, an incarnation of Vishṇu, while Kērala is but another name of the Malabar country.

Tampans and Tirumulpads. These use the same names as other Kṣheṭṙiyas. The title of Vaṙma is uniformly added to their names.

Kōil Ṭampurāns—females—Aṃba, Aṃbika, Aṃbālika.

Ṭāmpurāns—females—In Travancore—Lakṣhmi, Pārvaṭi, Gouri.

In Cochin—Aṃba, Aṃbika, Aṃbālika.

Ṭampāns and Ṭirumulpāḍs—females—In addition to those in use among Kōil Ṭampurāns, the name of " Subhaḍra " also is used.

The usual names adopted as nicknames in household conversation are :—

Kōil Tampurāns—males—Kuṭṭan, Kuññuṇṇi, Cheṟuṇṇi and Cochappan.

Ṭampurāns.

In Travancore—males—Kuññaru, Kuññappan, Kuññōman, Kuññuṇṇi Uṇṇi, and Aṃpu.

In Cochin—do—Kochuṇṇi, Kuññuṇṇi, Kuññikiṭāvu, Kochaniyan, Kuññan, Kōmar.

Ṭampāns and Ṭirumulpāds also use the above names.

Kōil Ṭampurāns.—Female,—Kuññikuṭṭi, Kochukuññi, Kuññikkāvu, Ikkāvu and Aṃmu.

The rest use the following names. Kāvu, Ikkāvu, Kuññipiḷḷa, Maṃku, Ikku, Kunji, etc.

Koil Tampurans.— Tradition says that they are descendants of Rajaput emigrants from the north who had originally settled in and near Beypore in South Malabar. It would appear that about 300 M. E. a few of them were invited to settle in Travancore and form marital relationship with the female members of the Royal house of Vēṇāḍ or Travancore. These then resided at Āṟṟingal in the Cherayinkīl Taluk and the new-comers were provided with residence at Kiḷimanūr 6 miles from Āṟṟingal. About 963 M. E., a fresh colony of Kōil Ṭampurāns arrived in Travancore, having run away to escape the oppression of Tippu Sulṭān. The then sovereign of Travancore welcomed them and accommodated them in the palace of the Ṭekkenkūr Rāja at Changanāssēri, who had not long before been subdued by Travancore. A few years after, this colony divided itself into different branches and spread itself within central Travancore.

Tampurans. Those resident in Travancore form an endogamous community, and live in 7 families, distinguished by the localities they live in, viz., Māvēlikkara, Eṇṇakāt, Mariapilli, etc. They are all related to one another more or less closely, and have community of pollution. They belonged originally to Kōlaṭṭunād, and most of them are but recent immigrants to Travancore, having run away from Tippu Sulṭān. But one family, that of Puṭuppilli Kōvilakam, had already come to Travancore in the 5th century M. E., to supply members for adoption to the Travancore Royal Family which was then about to become extinct. It is from these houses that the Travancore Royal line is kept up by occasional adoption.

In Cochin, letting the reigning family alone, a few of the more important families, among Ṭampurāns, may be mentioned:—

(1) Chāliūr and Vaṭakkēkōvilakam, closely related with the Royal house of Cochin, form one group having community of pollution.

(2) Paṭiññāttyēṭaṭṭu Swarūpam (the house of the Crānganūr Raja) and Airūr Swarūpam form such another group.

Tampans and Tirumulpads.—Ṭampān is but another form of Ṭampurān. It is said that, when these were divested of their ruling power by the Ilayaṭaṭṭu Swarūpam, they fell from the status of Ṭampurāns into that of Ṭampāns. The Ṭirumulpāds seem not to have had any territorial sway as such. But most of the Ṭampurāns or Rajas are of this class.

The members of each of the above classes of Kşheţŕiyas are held to have community of pollution, so that there can be no marital union between them. In Cochin, all the houses belong to Viśwāmiţŕa-gōţŕa though the Śasţŕas, it would seem, deny goţŕa to the Kşheţŕiyas, who were to adopt the gōţŕa of their purōhiţs. Notwithstanding this, the titular Raja of Pańţalam, who claims to be descended from Kulaśē-khara of Madura, is a follower of Bhāŕgava gōţŕa. According to the *Travancore Census Report*, "The Rajas, like the Koil Ţampurāns, belong to the Yajur Vēḑa section of Ḑvijas, but follow the Suţŕa laid down by Bouḑhāyana. Their gōţŕa is that of Bhāŕgava, i. e., of Paraśu Rāma, the uncompromising Brāhman of the Hinḑu Purāṇa."[1] It would also appear that, even with the difference of gōţŕa, scriptural marriage between these and any other Kşheţŕiya of Viśwāmiţŕa gōţŕa is not allowed. Tradition and the Kerala Mahāţmyam say that the Malabar Kşheţŕiyas are the progeny of Kşheţŕiya women consorting with Brāhmans, so that they have to be classed as a Saṃkara or hybrid caste as known to the Śāsţŕas, wherein such progeny is styled *Moordhavasikshtan*, i. e., son of a Brāhman and a Kşheţŕiya. But, as between such Kşheţŕiyas as have no community of pollution, the Nāyar system of union, known as Saṃbanḑḑham, is not prohibited. Any sexual relation on the part of males with women of superior caste, or with those below a Nāyar proper, and of females with men of a caste inferior to theirs, will entail excommunication from caste.

The Kşheţŕiyas of Malabar take after the Naṃbūţiris so far as their religious ceremonies, ablutions, habits of cleanliness, discipline, food and drink are concerned. They have the Saṃskāras as with the Brāhmans. The Upańayana or the investiture with the sacred thread takes place in the 16th year and, along with it Choulam or tonsure which always precedes the

1. P. 289.

investiture. The priest at the same time initiates the boy into the Gayaṭrī manṭra which he is entitled to repeat only 10 times over on each occasion. Other hymns necessary for the performance of daily oblations are also taught, but not the Vēḍa as a whole. With the Kōil Ṭampurāns, Samāvarṭana or the close of the pupilary stage is performed on the 15th day after Upanayanam. After this the boy undergoes the mock journey to Benares, but is stopped and reminded of the Ḍharma or duty of a Kṣheṭriya, i. e., to protect and govern. He is then given a sword, symbolic of his function in society. With the Ṭampurāns or Rājas, Samāvarṭana takes place on the 4th day, and instruction in arms follows. With the Ṭirumulpāds and Ṭampāns, the Samāvarṭana comes on any auspicious day after the 4th day of investiture with the sacred cord, when he makes obeisance to his elders and his priest, and receives their blessing and the kāraṇavar or the senior male member of the family hands him a sword in token of his profession, that of military service. They are entitled to hear portions of the Vēḍas read to them.

Marriage. With the females, this is an essential ceremony, which, after all, is only a mere formality without the legal or social incidents of marriage following. Its meaninglessness is accentuated by the fact that the couple need not and cannot claim as a matter of right to consort together. The essential pre-requisites of scriptural marriage are also dispensed with. No regard is paid to the Gōṭra, Sūṭra, or Charaṇa of the so- called bridegroom, nor are the horoscopes of the couple consulted. The ceremony is gone through between the ages 7 and 14. It lasts for 4 days. The bridegroom is chosen from among Naṃbūṭiris and Ārya Paṭṭars. In the Cochin Royal family, the choice is confined to Naṃbūṭiris. At the end of the ceremony, the bridegroom is given a fee called Vara Ḍekṣhiṇa. The same bridegroom can perform the office to more than one girl. The Naṃbūṭiris act as Purōhiṭs. One item in the programme of marriage of a Kōil Ṭampu-rāṭṭi is called Ḍīkṣhạ Virippu, which consists in the bride being confined to a special room, in which is spread a white cloth with a carpet over it on which she has to sit. In the families of the Ṭampurāns or Rājas in Travancore, the bridegroom is always a Kōil Ṭam-purān.

The above of course is not their real marriage, which comes on later when the free choice of a part-ner is allowed. Their own caste-men with whom there is no community of pollution, Naṃbūṭiris, Emprāns, foreign Brāhmans, etc., are all eligible as husbands. Re-marriage is allowed and is of frequent occurrence. So also divorce which takes place on the parties separating when they cannot agree. There are no religious ceremonies attending these unions, and the issue have no sort of claim to inherit the property of the father. The Kṣheṭṛiyas follow the Marumakka-ṭṭāyam system of inheritance.

Funerals. On the death, the body is cremated and pollution is observed for 11 days. The funeral ceremonies of the Kṣheṭṛiyas are performed in the manner of Brāhmans of the Aśwalāyana school. An-nual Śṛāḍhas are also performed. As followers of the matriarchal system, the order of precedence in the offering of cakes and oblations at Śṛāḍhas is as fol-lows:—

(1) Mothers, (2) mother's brothers, (3) brothers, (4) mother's sisters, (5) sister's children, (6) mother's mother, (7) sisters, (8) mother's conventional husband, and (9) the Brāhman that acted as con-ventional father, the Āchārya who performed the string investiture ceremony. Another authority gives the order as follows:—(1) mother, (2) brothers and sisters (among whom precedence is according to seniority by age), (3) mother's brothers, (4) mother's sisters, (5) mother's mother, (6) sister's children, (7) mother's conventional husband, and (8) Āchārya. According to another reading (5) and (6) exchange places.

In the matter of dress, ornaments, &c., they do not differ much from Nāyars.

IV. The Antaralas

Our author does not mention the Anṭarāla Jaṭis as a class, though he names one of them, the "Poodewallen" as one of the "inferior Śuḍras". As already mentioned, there are twelve sub-divisions among the Anṭarālas or those who come between the Brāhmaṇs and the Śuḍras, not reckoning the Kṣheṭriyas. They are generally temple servants.

As regards the origin of the Anṭarālajāṭies as a separate class and the *rationale* of their occupation, I cannot do better than quote the observations of the *Travancore Census Report.*—

"All these castes are not connected with pagodas, nor do the Muṭṭaṭus, who are mainly engaged in temple service, come under this group, strictly speaking. The *rationale* of their occupation seems to be that, in accepting duty in temples and consecrating their lives to the service of God, they hope to be absolved from the sins inherited from their fathers. In the case of ascent from lower castes, the object presumably is the acquisition of additional religious merit. Some details of traditional origin have been referred to below in regard to the chief divisions. But there is no guarantee of their authenticity. At the same time, it is quite conceivable that the fear of even conventional sins was very great in the early unsophisticated ages of Malabar Hinduism. All considerations of sentiment and interest were then freely and spontaneously subordinated, and in their altruistic desire to keep up the purity of caste, persons whose offences would not otherwise be known except to the great Searcher of Hearts, did not probably hesitate to come forward and accept the mandate of public conscience with a cool self-sacrifice rarely surpassed in the history of human society. To form a self-contained community, therefore, for the fallen of various kinds, and to prevent them from infecting the general mass, various subsidiary and intermediate castes were organized as by a natural process, rules more in keeping with a relatively weak moral sense were prescribed, and every detail was so planned as to afford sufficient scope for its gradual strengthening. Society attached no stigma to these castes; and one did not look upon his traditional origin with any more sense of mortification than one would feel at the possession of an evolutional defect. Each member believed that, by serving out his term of life in accordance with the canons prescribed, he would be returned to the position from which his distant progenitor fell. The moral effect of such an object-lesson on society in general was, of course, great. Viewed from the economic aspect, the occupations ordained for these intermediate castes seem to have been so arranged as not to disorganize society with reference to the division of labour and the contentment and harmony that characterised its working. The object and aim of the scheme of Indian castes is, as generally admitted, to enable society to keep up, by heredity, progressive skill and fitness in all the functions on which universal happiness depends. Its further object seems to be to keep out from the world's arena the chances of one occupational class trespassing on another and thus creating feelings of unhealthy rivalry.

"The industrial Śūḍra, as the foundation of society, was to be kept undisturbed by adverse influx, the exchanging Vaiśya should not be demoralized by the letting in of possible competitors, and the hereditory protector of internal order and the external peace should not be handicapped by the admission of evolutional tyros into his ranks. The delinquent Brahman cannot be retained in the Brahmanic function without lowering the standard of his caste. He had, therefore, to be allotted other functions. Temple service of various kinds, such as garland-making for the Puṣhpakan, Vāriyar and others, and popular recitation of God's works, for the Chākkiyār, were found to hold an intermediate place between the internal functions of the Brahmans and the external functions of the other castes, in the same sense in which the temples themselves are the exoteric counterparts of an esoteric faith and represent a position between the inner and the outer economy of nature. Hence arose probably an intermediate status with intermediate functions for the Anṭarālas, the intermediates of Hindu Society The Kṣheṭṛiyas having commensal privileges with the Brahmans come next to them in the order of social precedence. In the matter of pollution, periods which seem to be in an inverse ratio to the position of the caste are in vogue. The Brahmans observe 10 days, the Kṣheṭṛiyas 11 days and the Śuḍras of Malabar (Nāyars), 16 days. The Aṃpalavāsis generally observe pollution for 12 days. In some cases, however, it is as short as 10 and in others, as long as 13 and even 14, but never 16 days.'[1] *The Cochin Census Report* divides the Anṭarālajāṭies into three sub-groups—(a) Naṃpiṭis, (b) the Aṃpalavāsis and (c) the Sāmanṭas. While the *Jatinirnaya* places the Naṃpiṭis among the Pāpiṣhṭan or sinful Brahmans, some class the Sāmanṭa as a degraded class of Kṣheṭṛiyas. Strictly speaking, they are of the intermediate class, for the one comes below the Brahman and the other below the Kṣheṭṛiya. The Naṃpiṭi and the Sāmanṭa are noticed below in connection with our author's reference to them.

The term 'Aṃpalavāsi' means one who lives in a temple. It is a group-name and is applied to castes whose occupation is temple service. But all those whose occupation is temple service do not come under this caste group, e. g., the Muṭṭaṭu who is a Śiva Ḍwija and the Mārān who is a Śuḍra, though some are inclined to class these also as Aṃpalavāsis. The Aṃpalavāsis are classed as Anṭarālas from their occupying an intermediate position between the Brahmans and Kṣheṭṛiyas on the one hand and the Śuḍras on the other.

1. Census Report, pp. 259—260.

AMPALAVASI LADIES.

(To face p. 147.

While according to some they are fallen Brahmans, according to others they are those who have risen from the rank of Ṡūḍras.

The Travancore Census Report mentions the following as included in the generic name of Aṃpalavāsis:—

(1)	Naṃpīṡṡan	(8)	Pilāppaḷḷi
(2)	Pushpakan	(9)	Naṃpiyār
(3)	Pūppaḷḷi	(10)	Pishāroṭi
(4)	Chākkiyār	(11)	Vāriyar
(5)	Brāhmaṇi or Dēvaṃpaḍi	(12)	Nāṭṭupaṭṭan
		(13)	Ṭiyāṭṭuṇṇi
(6)	Aṭikaḷ	(14)	Kurukkaḷ
(7)	Naṃpiṭi	(15)	Poṭuvāls.

Of these, *the Cochin Census Report* makes mention of Nos. 2, 4, 6, 10, 11, 13, 15 and adds two more, viz., Chākkiyār-Naṃpiyār and Mārān.

Most of these classes have their origin in sexual relations between members of the higher and lower castes and are therefore Anulōmajas or Praṭilōmajas. They may broadly be divided into (1) those that wear the sacred thread and (2) those that do not wear the same. Aṭikaḷ, Chākkiyār, Naṃpiyār or Pushpakan and Ṭiyyāṭṭuṇṇi belong to the first, while the Chākkiyār—Naṃpiyār, Pishāroṭi, Puṭuvāl, Vāriyar, and Mārān belong to the second class. They have separate and distinct duties to perform in temples.

Nampiyassan—Pushpakan, Pūppaḷḷi and Brāhmaṇi form a sub-group of the Aṃpalavāsi caste known generally as Pushpakan or Uṇṇi. The term Pushpakan is sufficiently indicative of their occupation, viz. preparing flower garlands for the temples. Pushpakan is literally 'a florist'. They sweep the inner premises of temples, clean intensils, gather flowers, string them together into garlands to adorn the idols in their daily worship. As to their origin, the *Kerala Mahatmyam* says that they are the descendants of a Brahman woman conceived while her mother was in menstrual impurity.

The social and religious ceremonies observed by all the members of this group are similar to those of the Brahmans. The Upanayana is performed between the 8th and 16th year. They are to repeat the Gāyaṭri ten times at each Sanḍhya, morning, noon and evening. All Puṣhpakans are supposed to belong to the same Goṭra; yet they inter-marry. Divorce is permitted and the divorced woman can form Saṃbanḍham with a Brahman. The issue of the latter union inherit along with those of the regular marriage. Their caste government is in the hands of the Naṃbūṭiri Vyḍīkas. Birth and death pollutions last for 11 days. For all usual ceremonies, they have priests of their own caste. For the more important ones, Naṃbūṭiris officiate. Their women are called Brāhmaṇis. These sing at the marriage of Nāyars songs appropriate for the occasion. They also have to sing in Bhagavaṭi temples. They wear the same jewelry like the Naṃbūṭiri women, but dress more or less like Nāyar women.

Chakkiyar.—(See note to Letter).

Aṭikals.—These belong to a class of degraded Brahmans, the degradation being caused by their having officiated as priests in Bhadrakāli temples, and worshipped the goddess with offerings of flesh and liquor or what was supposed to be equivalent to these. *The Travancore Census Report* refers to an interesting tradition regarding their origin.

"Aṭikaḷ (literally slaves or servants):—Tradition states that Śankarāchārya, to test the fidelity of certain Brahmans to the established ordinances of caste, went to a liquor-shop and drank some stimulants. Not recognizing that the obligations, from which adepts like Śankara were free, were none the less binding on the proletariat, the Brahmans that accompanied the sage made this an excuse for their drinking too. Śankara is said to have then entered a foundry and swallowed a cup of molten metal and handed another to the Brahmans who had apparently made up their minds to do all that may be done by the Āchārya. But here they begged to differ, apologized to him as Aṭiyāls or humble servants and accepted social degradation in expiation of their sinful presumption."[1]

They practise sorcery and certain objectionable forms of exorcism and the worship of evil spirits. They perform the Upanayanaṃ and are entitled to repeat the Gāyaṭri ten times. They ape their own priests. They observe the birth and death pollutions for 11 days. Their women are known as Aṭiyamma and are not ghosha. They wear the same jewelry as the Naṃbūṭiri women. There are both Makkaṭṭāyies and Marumakkaṭṭāyies amongst them.

Thiyyattunni or Thiyyati Nampiyars.—In Bhaḍrakāli temples the Ṭiyyaṭṭuṇṇies have to paint in fantastic colours the image of Kāli, chant appropriate songs in praise of the Goddess and the miraculous deeds she had performed, and perform propitiatory worship. Their services are in constant requisition during the prevalence of small-pox. Houses occupied by small-pox patients are never reoccupied by the rest of the household till the Ṭiyyāṭṭuṇṇi performs his ceremonies within them. Similar ceremonies are performed in Bhaḍrakāli temples also. These are known as Tiyyāṭṭu or 'fire dancing'. Brahmans and their own caste-meṇ consort with their women. They follow either form of inheritance. In some parts Elayaṭūs act as their priests. As a thread-wearing class, they perform the Upanayanaṃ. They observe birth and death pollutions for 11 days. Their women are very much like the females of the Puṣhpakan class, in the matter of dress, ornaments, etc.

Pitarans.—These also perform priestly services in Kāli temples and resemble the Aṭikaḷ.

Nampitis.—It is scarcely correct to class the Naṃpiṭis among the Aṃpalavāsis. (For particulars regarding them, see Note to Letter.)

Plappilli.—This is a class peculiar to Travancore, and it is impossible to understand how they came to

1. pp. 262—3.

be classed among the Ampalavāsis though they certainly come under the Antarālajāti. The word Plāppilli is by some considered to be a corrupted form of the Malayālam Balāl Talli meaning 'forcibly ejected' and a tale hangs thereby. In the palmy days of the Ampalappula or Chempakaśśēri Raja, somewhere about the year 808 M. E. (A. D. 1623), the Nambutiri attendant on duty on the Raja, who was himself a high class Nambūtiri, was entitled to anything placed before the Royal presence as a present. When a distant ancestor of the Plāppillis was on duty, a dead fish, beautifully tied up and covered, was placed before the Raja, and the Nambūtiri attendant unwittingly removed it. When the contents of the packet became known to the court, he was excommunicated. The Brahman and his two wives removed themselves to a village near Alleppey called Kallērcōde where the Raja gave them some land. The caste does not now consist of more than a hundred and odd members all told. A few of them are said to have proceeded to Chālakkudi in the Cochin State. The Plāppillis have the Upanayanam which is performed in the 16th year, and other ceremonies like the Nambūtiris. Till about 50 years ago, the Elayatus acted as their priests, but now Nambutiris and Potties act as such. They have the tāli-tying marriage like all Marumakkattayies, an Arya Pattar taking the part of the *pseudo* bridegroom. On attaining maturity, their women consort with Brahmans. The male members consort with Nāyar women. Their birth and death pollution last for 10 days. In the matter of dress, both males and females dress like Nambutiris. So also with regard to ornaments. Their tāli is not the Cheru tali of the Nambutiris but is known as Kumpalattāli. Of late however their women have been adopting refined fashions. They follow the Marumakkattāyam system of inheritance. Offerings are made in honour of departed ancestors on new-moon days, but no oblations of water (Tarpanam) are made.

Nampiyar. The term 'Nampiār' is applied to four classes of people, one of which belongs to the Nayar caste and is noticed elsewhere in a Note to Letter XX, while the other three are Ampalavāsis. These are (1) the Chākkiyār-Nampiār proper, (2) the Ṭiyyāṭi Nampiār or Ṭiyyaṭṭuṇṇi, and (3) the Pushpaka-Nampiār. The last two have been already noticed.

The first one is noticed below in connection with his companion the Chakkiyar.[1]

The Pishāroṭi, Puṭuvāl and Vāriyar may be grouped together, as all of them have the same profession, that of sweeping and cleaning the temple and supplying it with flower and garlands for Puja. The rice offerings made in the temple partly go to them as their perquisite.

Pisharoti. In Travancore, those of this class that live to the south of Quilon are called Aloṭi, while those that live to the north are known as Pishāroṭis. They are said to have hda their origin from a run-way Sanyāsi novice who, while at his term of noviciate felt the prospect of an austere life cheerless, and so escaped from his preceptor. He is said to have allied himself with a Vāriyar woman, and descendants of their issue are the Pishāroṭis. A Sanyasi novice is known as Pishāra and, as the progenitor of the Pishāroṭis ran away, (Pishār+oṭi=ran) he and his descendants are said to have been called Pishāroṭis. The late Professor Sundram Pillay of Trivandrum, writing in his *Early Sovereigns of Travancore*, rejects this tradition and the derivation based thereon, and traces the Pishāroṭis to the temple officials of the Buddhistic period. He says, "I would allow again the Buddhistic monk, Bhaṭṭaraka to go through his slow evolution of Bhaṭṭaraka Ṭiruvaṭi, Baḍava Ṭiruvaṭi, Bḷāra Ṭiruvaṭi and Pshāra Ṭiruvaṭi, before I identify him with our modern Pishāroṭi, whose puzzling position among the Malabar castes, half monk and half layman, is far from

1. See Note 17 to letter XX.

being accounted for by the silly and fanciful modern derivation of Pişhārakal+Odi, Pişhārakal being more mysterious than Pişhā roți itself".[1] Referring to this, Dr. Subrahmania Ayyar observes in *the Travancore Census Report* thus: "As far as we could gather from early and medieval Travancore inscriptions, there appears to have once existed an officer called Pițara Țiruvați attached to every important temple, the nature of whose duty cannot now be ascertained. He received large perquisites, and to the Bhațțaraka of Nelliyur extensive paddy lands were given. If Bhațțaraka, the Țrețayuga type of an apostate Brahman, be the original Pițāra, then Pişhāroți may be a contraction of Bhațțaraka Țiruvați". At the same time, it must be said that the usually accepted derivation is wholly improbable".[2]

The Pişhāroțis act as their own priests. They have however to accept their Puṇṇyāham or holy water for purification from the Naṃbūțiris, whose superior sanctity does not allow them to sprinkle the water on the Pişhāroți. He has to receive it on his head, while it is dripping from the roof of his house over which the Naṃbūțiri pours the holy water. Instead of the Upanayana and Gāyațri, he is initiated into the Vaishṇavite manțra or Aşhțākşhara. They are bathed with consecrated water, soon after which, they dress themselves in the fashion of the orthodox Brahman and set out on a mock journey to Benares, as a sign of the conclusion of the Brahmachāri period. Their women are called Pişharasyārs and they undergo the marriage ceremony before or after puberty. Pāṇigrahaṇam or the taking of the bride's right hand in that of the bridegroom is the most important portion of the marriage ceremonial. The bridegroom performs the Hōma and ties the țali round the bride's

1. Page 17.
2. Prge 264.

neck. After this they are at liberty to form Sambanḍham with Brahmans and Kṣheṭriyas.

Their funeral ceremonies partake of the nature of those of the Sanyāsis. The dead body is never cremated but buried in a sitting posture in a pit with salt, ashes and sand to the accompaniment of a hymn which says "may water go with water and air with air," i.e., "may this body made up of the five elements, may the Panchabhauṭika Śarīra resolve into their component parts in nature." As in the case of a Sanyāsi who is a Jīvanmukṭa, one liberated from the bondage of the flesh though alive in body, a dead Piṣhāroṭi is believed to leave no subtle body needing to be entertained with any *post mortem* offerings. A few rites are however performed; but they are more in prayerful memory (witness the Āradhana Śrāḍha of Brahman Sanyāsis) than in satisfaction of a real want felt by the soul of the departed. On the 11th day, a ceremony corresponding to the Ēkōḍiṣhṭa Śrāḍha of the Brahman is performed. A knotted piece of Kuśa grass representing the departed soul is taken to a neighbouring temple where a lighted lamp symbolical of Mahāvishṇu is worshipped and prayers offered by the Brahman for the absorption of this soul in His divine substance. This ceremony is repeated at the end of the first year. The asterism of the death is commemorated every successive year by certain rites. For these and other ceremonials the priests are taken from their own castes. Their funeral ceremonies and observances lend colour to their origin from the original run-away Sanyāsi novice.

They are followers of the Marumakkaṭṭāyam system of inheritance. The women wear ornaments known as Pallaṭṭali and Enṭram and Kuḷal. But the ear-ornaments are exactly the same as those of the Nāyars.

Variyars. Regarding the origin of the class of Vāriyārs, many suggestions more or less speculative are made. Some would say that they are called

1. Travancore Census Report pp. 264-6. T.

Vāriyars because Paraśu Rāma created them from Vāri, Sanskrit for water, which again is explained to mean that these men, originally Nāyars, were purified by Paraśu Rāma by subjecting them to a plunge bath to qualify them to serve as temple servants. Some say that they are called Vāriyars because their profession is Vāruka, *Mal*: to gather by sweeping, their traditional employment being sweeping and cleaning the temple precincts. Another suggestion is that the term is a corruption of the Sanskrit Parāśava, the sŏn of a Brahman duly married to a Śūḍra woman; the progenitor of the class is said to have been a Brahman so married. The tradition recorded by the Kēraḷamāhātmyam is thus set forth in the *Travancore Census Report*.

"A young Brahman girl was once married to an aged man. Not confident in unaided human effort, especially under circumstances such as were hers, she devoted a portion of her time every day to preparing garland for the use of the diety at the nearest temple. The pious girl conceived. But the over-scrupulous old Brahman welcomed the little stranger by first getting the mother thrown out of caste. Her flower-garlands could no longer be accepted, but nothing daunted, she worked as usual and made a mental offering of the garlands she prepared, and, as if by an unseen hand, the garlands became visible on the person of the diety. The people were then struck with shame at their unkind treatment of the God-blessed innocent, but felt at the same time unprepared to take her back. The Vāriyar caste was, it is said, constituted accordingly. The child born of this woman was brought up by the Āīvāncēri Ṭamprakkaḷ and was accommodated in his Paṭippura (an out-house at the entrance gate). However fanciful these derivations appear, one who enters into the condition of society at the time and the high level of religiousness, absolute and conventional, which was attained by some, would perhaps hesitate before he rejects any as primarily and wholly absurd."[1]

There are 8 sub-divisions among the Vāriyars.

1. The Oṇāṭṭukara Vāriyar.
2. The Ṭekkuṃkūr Vāriyar.
3. The Vaṭakkuṃkūr Vāriyar.
4. The Iḷayeṭattuṅāṭ Vāriyar.
5. The Aṭaṭīni Vāriyar.
6. The Aṭaṭiṅṅaṭṭa Vāriyar.
7. The Paṭippura Vāriyar.
8. The Chēlayil Kuṭiya Vāriyar.

" The first four classes are based on territorial distribution and represent the four principalities north of Vēṇāt, extending from Eṭava in the south to nearly Parūr in the north. Iḷayeṭaṭṭuṅāṭ under the Koṭṭārakara Raja, Oṇāṭ under the Kāyaṃkuḷam Raja, Ṭekkumkūr under the Ṭekkuṃkūr Raja at Changanāśśēri and Vaṭakkuṃkūr under the Vaṭakkuṃkūr Raja near Eṭṭumānūr. The Raja of Ōṇāṭ or Ōnāṭṭukara, being the most puissant, the Vāriyars who were his subjects naturally became recognized as the highest among their class.

"In the light of the tradition connecting the first female progenitor of the Vāriyar caste with the Paṭippura of the Ālvāncheri Ṭampṛākkaḷ, the name Paṭippura Vāriyar may quite correctly be applied to the whole community of Vāriyars. But in practice the Vāriyar attendants of the Ālvāncheri Ṭampṛākkaḷs alone are called by that name. Even to-day a Paṭippura Vāriyar walks in front of the Ṭampṛākkaḷ as his trusted orderly. These Vāriyars employ their own priests and do not mix even with the Ōṇāṭṭukara Vāriyars.

" The Aṭaṭīni and the Aṭaṭiṅṅāṭṭa sub-divisions have been accounted for by the following tradition. The Nāyar chieftain of Kavaḷappāṟa, while travelling, met a group of Vāriyars and mistaking them for Brahmans

1. P. 266.

alighted from his palanquin to do them the usual obeisance. He soon found out his mistake and by way of unreasoning revenge forced them to eat the cakes (*ata*) they had with them, in the presence of himself and his palanquin bearers. The descendants of those that had to undergo social degradation by so eating became Aṭaṭṭni Vāriyars (Vāriyars that ate the cake) and the descendants of those who ran away and successfully evaded the eating in this heterodox fashion came to be designated Aṭaṭinnāṭṭa Vāriyars".

Manners and Customs. The Vāriyars along with the Pushpakans and Pishāraṭis are, by Paraśu Rāma's appointment as it were, the three garland making castes of the Malabar temples, the Kurukkals in South Travancore being the fourth. The technical name of the Vāriyar's office is Kaḷakam (from Kaḷukuka, to cleanse) of which there are two kinds, the Mālakeṭṭu Kaḷakam (garland-making service) and the Talikkaḷakam (sweeping service). The scope of the Vāriyar as a sort of general assistant to the Brahmanical priest is so varied and extensive that the term 'Kaḷakam' seems undoubtedly a misnomer. Some of the Vāriyars are skilled in astrology, and most of them are learned in Sanskrit, and, like the Pishāraṭis, are often invited to teach in the families of Malabar noblemen.

The house of a Vāriyar, like that of the Ampalavāsis, has no special name and is simply called Vāriyam. If there be more than one, they are distinguished by the names of Vaṭakkēvāriyam (Northern Vāriyam) and Ṭekkēvāriyam (Southern Vāriyam), They resemble the Pishāraṭis in many respects. But they are strict Śaivites, Śūlapāṇi Vāriyar being one of the commonest names, just as the Pishāraṭis are devoted adherents of Vishṇu. We never hear of a Nārāyaṇa Vāriyar. In the place of the Kalaśam Oḷikkuka purification that the Pishāraṭi goes through before his initiation into the Ashṭākshharamantra. the Vāriyar has a ceremony called Śivaḍīkṣha. Dressed in the orthodox Brahmanical style and decorated with the Śaivite marks of Vibhūṭi (holy ashes) and Ruḍrākṣham, the Vāriyar goes like a Brahmachāri for Bhikṣha (alms) on which the pupil had to live under the ancient system, and walks seven steps in a northerly direction as a symbol of Kāśiyāṭra or journey to Benares for post-graduate study. This terminates his Brahmachārya stage and makes him thenceforward a Gṛhasṭha.

The Vāriyars with the exception of the Ōṇāṭṭukara sub-division are all matriarchal in their system of inheritance. There are two distinct types of marriage in vogue among the latter :—(a) Keṭṭukalyāṇam like that of the Nāyars where the marriage is a mere ceremony, and (b) Kuṭivaikal (settling in life) which confers full civil rights on the wedded wife and her issue. The latter form comes in very conveniently whenever a family tends to become extinct, and is also resorted to when the female members are few. In these cases, the newly arrived wife has the same rights in the family as if she were a born member. Pollution is generally for 12 days.

A Vāriyar performs the Śrāḍha for his parents and his maternal uncle. The offerings are addressed to his deceased ancestor as the servant of Śiva, and member of the Gōṭra of Kailāsa (the residence of Śiva), Kailāsa Gōṭrōṭbhavāya Śivaḍāsāya, being the Saṃkalpam.

The Vāriyar, it may be added, is referred to in the Kēralōṭpaṭṭi as Kailāsavāsi or dweller in mount Kailāsa. This only indicates his devotion to Śiav. To the Ilayaṭu, his sometime priest, the Vāriyar is a hated foe. The former will not even drink from a well situated in the house of the latter.[1]

The Naṭṭupaṭṭan is similar to Ṭiyyāṭṭuṇṇi or Ṭiyyāṭi Nampiār.

1. Travancore Census Report, p. 267—268.

Kurukkal. This class of Aṃpalavāsis is peculiar to Travancore, and we have the following interesting account of them in *The Travancore Census Report*:

"*Kurukkal.* The Kurukkals are very probably of Tamil origin, having been originally brought down from the Tamil country for the purpose of temple service. Their customs and manners bear out this view. The Vāriyars who are the recognized temple-servants of Malabar, are not indigenous to Vēṇāṭ and the relations that must have been frequently strained between the Vēṇāṭ and the Ōṇāṭ Rajas, where alone the Vāriyars were found, must have raised a necessity for importation. Further, the Kōlaṭṭuṇāṭ family which is the present-stock of the Travancore Royal House have had differences with the Naṃbūṭiri Brahmans of the Perinchellūr Grāmaṃ and the Vāriyars, at least one large section of them, being the hereditary servants of the Ālvānchēri Ṭampṛākkal were not readily available for service in Travancore temples. The men imported had already been priests at the non-Brahmanical temples, such as at Manṭaikkāṭ in South Travancore. In the *Keralolpathi*, Kurukkals are referred to as Chilaṃpāṇṭis and Aṭiyārs or hereditary servants at the shrine of Śrī Paḍmanābha Swāmi.

Manners and Customs. The dress and ornaments of the Kurukkals are very much like those of the Naṃpūṭiri Brahmans. The women wear the Cheruṭāli round their necks, and Chuṭṭu in the lobes of their ears. Tattooing is in great favour. The line of inheritance is maternal. The house of a Kurukkal is called by the same name as that of a Śūḍra, i. e., Vīṭu. The Kurukkals have priests among themselves. Their caste government is in the hands of the eight trustees, called Yōgakkār, of Śrī Paḍmanābha Swāmi's temple. The Ṭiru Ōṇam day in the month of Chingam is to them, as to the East Coast Brahmans and allied castes, an important religious festival called Upākarma. But the ceremonial at a Kurukkal's Upākarma is not apparently much more than the renewal of the Upavīṭa (sacred thread).

A curious account of the circumstances connected with their change into the Marumakkaṭṭāyam from their original Makkaṭṭāyam system is current in tradition and may perhaps be referred to.

The Ṭaraṇanallūr Nampūrippāṭ is the Ṭanṭri or the chief ecclesiastical functionary of Śri Paḍmanābha's temple at Trivandrum. One of the temple yōgakkār, wishing to secure this office for himself and his family, prevailed upon the Kurukkal, whose business it was to convey the formal intimation about the dates of temple festivals to the Ṭaraṇanallūr Nampūrippāṭ living several miles from Trivandrum, to deliver it at such a time as would make it impossible for him to reach Trivandrum, in time for the occasion. The Ṭanṭri's absence from his duty on the appointed day would, the Pōtti is said to have calculated, so displease the Maharaja as to lead to a vacancy in the office in question. All these plans were duly carried out, but not with the desired result. The Nampūrippāṭ's phenomenal piety towards Vighnēśvara helped him to tide over all obstacles and enabled him to cover the whole journey in a single night. But the Kurukkal was cursed for having thus colluded in an unworthy act, and the supposed conversion of the old Makkaṭṭāyam into Marumakkaṭṭāyam, tradition connects with this curse. But judging from the way in which the system of inheritance in an immigrating community has changed by long residence into that of the country into which they have so immigrated, all this explanation may not be quite necessary. From a copper plate document which, however, is not forthcoming, the change, it would seem, was as recent as 907 M. E. (1732 A. D.)

Ceremonials. For the Nāmakaraṇa and Annaprāśana there are no special manṭras to be recited. Every thing is done by the family priest. The day previous to the Upanayana, the family priest performs the puṇyāha and ties the praṭisara string round his right wrist. On the second day is the tonsure. On the third day, the sacred thread is worn and the Gāyaṭri hymn is first recited. For four days from the third day, the Samiḍāḍhāna or worship of the sacred fire is observed. Ten Gāyaṭris may be recited each time. The marriage ceremony or rather the Ṭālikeṭṭu of the girl is performed between the ages of 8 and 12. Before the auspicious moment arrives, the Brahmaṇi is called to sing her songs. If the person who ties the Ṭāli happens to live with her as husband and continues to do so till he dies, her sons observe pollution and make funeral offerings. When a Kurukkaḷ girl attains puberty, there is exhibited all the gaiety and merriment, often of a rough unedifying kind, found among Tamil Brahmans. No Puṃsavana or Sīmanṭa is observed, but in its place the puḷikuṭi ceremony of the Nāyar caste is celebrated. Neither at the tonsure nor at the funeral ceremonies is the assistance of the Mārān required. This, it may be remarked, is a notable point of distinction from the indigenous highcastes of Malabar. Pollution is observed for 12 days. On the 13th day, they undergo a puṇyāha ceremony at the hands of their own caste men.[1]

The Cochin Census Report, as already observed, includes the Mārān among Aṃpalavāsis but remarks that they are Śūḍras; but, properly speaking, they ought to be classed along with Nāyars. Their claim to be classed with Aṃpalavāsis "is their close connection with services in temples, and the absence of free interdining or intermarriage with Nāyars." But, in the South, the Nāyars generally do not accord to the Mārān the privilege of interdining or intermarrying with them. They arrogate to themselves social superiority over the Mārān who in turn puts forward his own superiority.

1. Pages 269—270.

SIR C. SANKARAN NAYAR.

(Formerly — Advocate-General & High Court Judge, Madras; Member of Governor-general's Executive Council and of the Council of the Secretary of State; once President, Indian National Congress).

(To face p. 161.

They are drummers and musicians in temples. In the matter of marriage (both Ṭālikeṭṭu and Sambanḍham), inheritance, period of pollution, etc., they follow customs exactly like those of Nāyars. In some parts, the Eḷayaṭus officiate at their Śrāḍhas while, in some other parts, their own castemen do so. Similarly with regard to the tying of the Ṭāli.

V. The Nāyars.

In this letter our author proposes to give a minute account of the Nāyars or "Warriors of Malabar". But, as his account is, at the best, but meagre and indifferent, it is deemed necessary to add to it further details, to enable our readers to have a correct idea of the class of people who played a very important part in the social and political drama of Southern India.

1. The Nāyars form the most important section of the Malabar population and hold a position in caste next to the Brahmans and the Kṣheṭṛiyas. The Vaiśias, or the trading class, find no place in the socio-religious economy of Kērala. The Anṭarālajāṭies or Ampalavāsis claim superiority to the Nāyars, which is contested in certain quarters, and some of them also demand a higher position in virtue of their office in temples and their strictly vegetarian diets. Malabar is often styled the land of Nāyars, and there can be no doubt that, in various respects, they may be said to form the most distinguishing feature of the district.

Origin of the Caste. No two opinions agree as to the origin of the Nāyars. While a few take them to form part of the aboriginal inhabitants of Maḷabar, the more correct view seems to be that they were early settlers from the north. "The Nairs of Southern India" says Sir Harry Johnston "were really a warlike, aboriginal tribe which had forced themselves to be recognized as a twice-born caste—practically equivalent to the Aryan Kshatriyas and Rajaputs"[1]. One theory goes to say that,

1. Pioneers in India, note on page 143.

long before the Aryans left their common home in the plateau of Central Asia, several sections of a race seem to have progressed southwards and overrun South India. A certain section of the population of Southern India is regarded ethnically as being Dravidian or Turanian, and, in common with them, the Nāyars are also considered to belong to the Turanian race. It has been suggested that "both the Brahmans and the Nairs of the Malabar coast are of homogeneous descent and of a primeval Turanian race"[1]. The Rev. W. Taylor observes that "the Nairs are the descendants of the aboriginal inhabitants of Kerala who probably were brought into some measure of civilization by the colonist Brahmans, yet retaining so much of their own manners as to be a people inclusive of mixed tribes very different from genuine Hindus"[2].

1. Native Life in Travancore, p. 179.

2. The word Dravidian indicates a linguistic rather than a racial section. The principal Dravidian languages are Tamil, Telugu, Canarese and Malayalam. Malayalam is the language of Cochin, Travancore and British Malabar, and is spoken of by some ten millions of people. "The main racial element in the Dravidian population" says Dr. G. Slater, "is a branch of the Mediterranean race." The people of this class seem to have come to India through Baluchistan by way of Mesopotamia, before the dawn of the Sumerian civilization. (Pp. 19 and 27 of *The Dravidian Element in Indian Culture*). On the other hand, Dr. S. Konow thinks that "There is no indication that the Dravidians have entered India from outside or superseded an older population." According to him, they form the aborigines of the Deccan, whence they appear to have spread over part of Northern India. (*His article on Dravidian in the 11th Edition of Ency. Britanica.*) That is also the view expounded by Prof. T. R. Sesha Iyengar in his *Dravidian Iudia.* (Pp. 59—60). "That our view of South India being the probable home of civilization is not entirely a baseless fabric of a dream receives support from Dr. Chatterji who says "It would be established", provided Hall's theory of Sumerian origins be true, "that civilization first arose in India, and was associated probably with the primitive Dravidians. Then it was taken to Mesopotamia to become the source of the Babylonian and other ancient cultures which form the basis of modern civilization." * * * According to Sir John Evans (*Presidential address of the Br. Assn. for the Advancement*

Some distinctive features of the Nāyar community are pointed out as indicating their racial origin, such as (1) that the family is founded on a matriarchal basis; (2) that they are serpent worshippers to a large degree;

of Science, 1897, on Science of Man), Southern India was probably the cradle of the human race. Investigations in relation to race show it to be possible that Southern India was once the passage ground by which the ancient progenitors of northern and Mediterranean races proceeded to the parts of the globe which they now inhabit." "The Dravidian race," says Sir H. Risley "the most primitive of the Indian types, occupies the oldest geological formation in India, the medley of forest-clad ranges, terraced plateaus and undulating plains which stretches, roughly speaking, from the Vindhyas to Cape Comorin" * * * "To the general rule that Dravidian languages belong to the South of India, there is one remarkable exception. Brahui is isolated and far separated from its kin, having its locale in Baluchistan. The tribes that speak Brahui resemble to a considerable extent the people of South India in physical characteristic and temperament, and show a marked contrast to their neighbours so that it is clear that, in their case, affinity of language is the result of affinity of race. (Pp. 14 and 15 of Dr. Slater's book, referred to above.). In the words of Dr. E. Thurston, there is practical agreement among linguistic authorities as to the Dravidian affinities of the Brahui language. Dravidian culture was evolved in India, and mainly under the stimulus of the Indian environment, though not without the operation of important external influences". (P. 27 of Dr. Slater's book.). "Proofs in abundance of the extreme antiquity of intercourse by sea between South India and other countries of civilization............are conveniently summed up by Mr. W. J. Perry in his *Children of the Sun*." (P. 73 of Dr. Slater's book; also see p. 21 of the *Jenmi-kudiyan Report of Travancore*). There are those who claim a greater antiquity for Dravidian than for Aryan civilization. "The very character of the Tamil language," says Dr. Slater " the perfection with which it has been developed into an organ for precise and subtle thought, combined with the fact that it represents a much earlier stage in the evolution of inflexional language than any Indo-Germanic tongue, suggests, though, of course it does not prove, the priority of the Dravidians in attaining settled order and regular Government. The late 'Chattambi Swami has written a small paper on the antiquity and perfectness of the Tamil language. There he incidentally remarks that Samskrtam, the Sanskrit language, has been refined and polished by Tamil* * Some scholars want us to believe that the

and (3) that the kingly element was wanting in its earlier stages. The institution of the family on a matriarchal basis is, as shown by Mc' Lennan and others, incidental to certain early stages of social evolution, in every part of the world, for instance, among the

great Epic Ramayana is only an allegory to describe the march of Aryan civilization into the dark Dravida lands, while others maintain that it is intended to indicate the introduction of agriculture into Southern India. But the Epic belies both these contentions; at any rate, it does not conclusively prove them. For, there is clear, internal evidence in that work to show that, in spite of hills and forests which exist even to this day, civilization had reached a high stage in South India and though the poet calls the non-Aryans Vanaras and Rakshasas, there were amongst them many who were great in the arts of war and of peace. To speak of less ancient times, there is the authority of Mr. J. F. Hewitt who has the following remark in his *Ruling Races of Prehistoric Times*:— "The Jewish and Roman Codes could never have grown up unless the seeds from which they sprang had been sown by the Indian Dravidians, the pioneers of international trade." "Amongst the elements of Dravidian origin," says the historian of Indian and Indonesian Art, Dr. Koomaraswamy, "are probably the cults of the phallus and of the Mother-goddesses; Nagas, Yakshas and other nature spirits; and many of the arts". "The enrichment of civilization consequent upon the constant and lively interchange of ideas and experiences with the myriad races of the ancient world, the higher degree of material prosperity that followed in virtue of this extraordinary commercial enterprise, and the remarkable outburst of literary and intellectual activity, which is the outcome of that prosperity, these along with a distinct non-Aryan alphabet, a highly cultivated language exclusively Dravidian, a polished literature composed on Dravidian lines and independent of Sanskrit models, an indigenous system of medicine, and an advanced civilisation independent of Aryan influences are among the factors that entitle the ancient Dravidians to a high place among the nations of antiquity." (Pp. 150—1 of *Dravidian India* by Prof. Sesha Iyengar.) Mr. Sivaraja Pillai, the Reader in Tamil to the Madras University has, in an appendix to this *Agastya in the Tamil Land*, a "Testimony of Scholars" re. Dravidian Civilization. A few sentenees from that shall be extracted here:—

The reason why the Aryan irruption was so different in Southern India from what it was in the north appears to be that, when the Aryans penetrated to the south, there existed already well organised communities and kingdoms" (Dr. Bhandarkar's *History of Deccan*, p. 10). "The development of the early stages

Orinoco Indians, among most of the Australian savages in Ceylon, New Zealand, in parts of Africa, etc. The remarkable system of tracing succession and inheritance through females is not strange to early society and it exists even now in some parts. Col. Yule observes that this custom exists, or has existed, also in Canara, among the aborigines of Hispaniola and tribes of New Granada and Bogota, among the Negro tribes of the Niger; among certain sections of the Malayas of Sumatra, in the Royal family of Tipara, and among the Kasias of the Sylhet mountains

of the grantha character is very difficult to trace, for the reason that the north Indian civilization, when it got far down in the Peninsula as the Tamil country, found there a people already in possession of the art of writing and apparently a cultivated language." (Dr. Burnell's *Elements of South Indian Palaeography*). "This extension is everywhere marked by the spread of Sanskrit and its dialects. It received a check in Southern India, where the older civilization and languages remain predominent even to the present day". (Prof. E. J. Rapson's *Ancient India*, p. 9). "Apart from the language, there is a general culture which is characteristic of the Dravidian race and, after the elimination of the pre-Dravidian, a racial type emerges with finer features than those of the aborigines, and the conclusion seems evident that this was due to an immigrant people who reached India before 2,000 B. C." (Dr. A. C. Halldon's *Races of Man*).

"The ancient kingdoms of the far south, although rich and populous, inhabited by Dravidian nations not inferior in culture to their Aryan rivals in the north, were ordinarily so secluded from the rest of the civilised world including Northern India, that their affairs remained hidden from the eyes of other nations; and native annalists being lacking, their history previous to the year 800 of the Christian Era, has almost wholly perished." (Dr. Vincent A. Smith's *Early History of India*, p. 7).

"But although the Dravidians were not the earliest settlers, and although they have not been exempt, and that in no small degree from external influences, it is from them that the civilised part of the Deccan derives its characteristic features in language and institutions. Among the latter may especially be noticed its monetary system and the coins in which it is expressed." (Sir Walter Elliot's *Coins of Southern India*, p. 2).—Editor.

(both east of Bengal); in a district of Ceylon adjoining Bintenne; in Madagascar; in the Fiji Islands; and among the Hurons and Natchez of North America."[1] The prevalence of the custom amongst people living so widely apart shows that its existence was almost universal in early society, and its survival among the Nāyars may be taken as indicating dimly their origin. But, as observed by Lubbock, "different races in similar stages of social evolution often present more features of resemblance to one another than the same race does to itself in different stages of its history."[2]

A Scythian origin of the Nāyars has also been recently propounded. This is based more or less on the prevalence of serpent worship amongst them, and a fancied resemblance between the terms Nāgar (serpent) and Nāyar. The argument is that a Scythian race, known as the Ṭakṣhakas or serpents, probably because their totem was a snake, or more probably because they were snake-worshippers themselves, settled in Northern India and sent down colonies to the south. They were also known by the tribal name of Nāgas (serpents, again). It is said that about the 5th century B. C., while the Nāgas were yet ruling in the north, Vijaya, a son of the king of Magadha, sailed towards Ceylon and established himself there. Vijaya and his successors seem to have had frequent intercourse with the Peninsula, and it is most likely that the present day Nāyars are the descendants of the original Nāga settlers. Another step in the argument is that "the term Nair or Nāyar, which seems the more correct form, is only a corruption of Nāgar, Nagars or serpent worshippers, the gutteral 'g' being softened into the 'y' sound by a process well known to philologists." With regard to the serpent cult, we shall be able to show later on that it was almost universal throughout the whole world and that it has still its votaries in many parts. James Ferguson has shown

1. A Note in his Wonders of the East.
2. Origin of Civilization.

in his work on *Tree and Serpent Worship* that the adoration of the snake as divine is a practice once common to all the tribes belonging to the Turanian race, not only of India, but of far distant countries such as Lapland and Finland. The Hindu religion, as practised even now, and on the East Coast, is no stranger to Serpent worship. The great Serpents Ṭakṣhaka, Āḍi Śēṣhan, Vāsuki are all worshipped by modern Hindus. The temples of Madura, Srirangam and other places contain images of serpents which are objects of daily worship. Catching similarity in sounds and names is often unsafe to base an argument upon, and yet the identity of the Nāyars with the polyandrous Tibetans has been suggested on the similarity of the words Nāyars and Newars. So also with regard to the similarity between the words Nāgar and Nair, or Nāyar. The transition from the one to the other by the softening of the gutteral 'g' into the 'y' sound being more fanciful than real. If we are to appeal to the phonetic variations, may we not suggest that they favour the derivation of Nāyar from Naicker (Tamil) or Nāyakar (Sanskrit). Some do indeed contend that the Nāyars are Aryans, and that the term Nāyar is but another form of the Sanskrit Nāyaka.[1]

It was not only among non-Aryan races that the kingly element was wanting in their earlier stages. The original settlements of the Aryans themselves in Northern India were republican. In the time of Buddha, we see village republics abounding in the north. In some instances, the Governments were also aristocratical in form. Buddha himself was a prince of a country which was governed by an absolute

1. Surgeon-Major C. F. Oldham has shown in his *The Sun and the Serpent* that the solar and the lunar lines of kings were Nagas or serpent-worshippers, that Ravana was a Naga, and that Indra and his celestial set has marriage relations with Nagas. Agasthya's descent from Naga ancestors and Vasishta's connection with Nagas are also shown in it. (See also the Jenmi-Kutiyan Report of Travancore pp. 22 and 23.)—Ed.

monarch. But the Vaffis or Vrafis, the Kṣheṭṭiya inhabitants of a neighbouring province, formed a republic. Many such other republics are also spoken of. These republics were gradually absorbed into the monarchies that lay contiguous to them, and the political growth of the country was arrested. The same process took place in the south. In Malabar, the Government the Brahmans introduced was an oligarchical one. The Kēralōṭpaṭṭi tells us that the Brahmans had soon to give up this and to adopt a monarchical form, only the kings were to be elected, holding office for a definite term. This again ceased before long, when the last of the elected princes assumed absolute power, and is alleged to have taken upon himself to divide the country among his relatives, friends, and dependants.

Linguistic evidence would tend to show that the Nāyars belongs to the Dravidian race family. Speaking of the Malayalam language, the mother-tongue of the Nāyars, Dr. Caldwell observes that "it claims to be placed next to Tamil in the list of Dravidian tongues, on account of the peculiarly close relationship it bears to Tamil in which it abounds." He therefore calls it a "very ancient and much altered offshoot" of Tamil. On the other hand, Dr. Gundert the eminent Malayalam scholar, holds that "the two languages (Tamil and Malayalam) of old differed rather as dialects of the same member of the Dravidian family than as separate languages." Both scholars however agree in giving it a Dravidian origin. Notwithstanding the copious introduction of Sanskrit that has taken place in recent years, the Dravidian element still predominates in the language in its most elemently form. Words expressive of near relationship, of the most absolute rights of property in land, etc., are all distinctly Dravidian.

It is contended by some that the Nāyars colonised Malabar along with the Brahmans, and that they are of Aryan descent. Their physical features, the colour of their skin, their position in the social scale, their being associated with the Brahmans in all important Brahmanical ceremonies, the military order to which they belong, all these are pointed out as unmistakable proofs of their Aryan descent. The latest suggestion regarding the Aryan origin of the Nāyars comes from Mr. Fawcett [1], though he takes care to add that "it is not yet time to say whether they are or are not 'Dravidians.'" He observes, "To the ordinary visitor their outward appearance, customs, habitations, mode of life generally, are very different from what he sees in the Telugu or Tamil countries; for Malabar, 'the west coast', is as unlike the rest of the Presidency as Burmah. The only other district of the Madras Presidency which resembles Malabar is Ganjam, more particularly the northern part of it, where the people are almost entirely Aryans. The resemblance between these, the Uriyas of Guntur and thereabouts, a fine fighting stock, and the Nāyars of Malabar is very striking. It is not, perhaps, a mere coincidence that in these two furthest remote corners of the Presidency alone, the people at large are to be seen wearing umbrella hats to protect them from the sun." In the cast of features, in the habits and customs, many have noticed a close resemblance between the Bengalees and the Nāyars. There is a remarkable similarity even in the development of their literature.

1. Madras Museum Bulletin Vol. III, No. 3, p. 187.

2. The report of the Jenmi-Kudiyan Committee has the following remarks on this question: "The Coorgs and the Marathos who are treated as Sytho-Dravidians, do not differ in essential respects from the Nayars, and there is sufficient warrant for the conclusion that the Coorgs and the Nayars are racially connected" (p. 19). In another part of the Report (p. 26), it says: "Serpent worship, recognition of kinship in the female line, strong attachment to national customs, love of power; sense of political independence, manliness and martial spirit characterise the Basques. The description of the Basque in whom these attributes predominate could, word for word, be made applicable to the Nayar in his palmiest days. Communal rights in family

The question whether the Nāyars are of Aryan or of Dravidian origin is, one of considerable doubt and difficulty. In physical features, one may contend, it is difficult to say for certain that the Nambūṭiri or the Nāyar differs materially from his brother of the East Coast. The colour of the skin, he will say, is no sure index of the race to which a man may belong. It is perhaps the most evasive of tests applied to determine a race. If it shows anything at all, it tells you at once of his occupation. Among those that inhabit Malabar, we have in fact almost every grade of colour. The Nambūṭiri Brahman, who never exposes himself to the tropical sun unless well clothed and sheltered beneath his broad and shady umbrella, who, as Jenmi, or freehold proprietor of the land, is not unfrequently rich, and who, by the privilege of his class need not and has not ever earned his bread by the sweat of his brow, is seldom if ever brown; he is oftener a dingy white. His wife who seldom stirs out of her house is also, as a rule, often fair. The well-to-do Nāyar whose main occupation, at present, is to supervise the cultivation of the land by praedial slaves, is brown, but is by no means black as, these, his workmen. He leads an easy life, lives in a substantially built house placed in the centre of a shady garden filled with the jack, mango, and areca-nut trees, the cocoanut and the talipot palm whose feathery foliage affords shelter from the fierce rays of the scorching sun. But the slave who, for time out of mind, has been working in the fields from morning to night, exposed to the incessant rays of a tropical sun, as well to rain, wind, and storm, is invariably black. Even among the aborigines those who live in forests, and who do not toil and moil day and night, like the slaves of the plains, are, at times, of a shade fairer than these aggrestic slaves. Of the Mala Aryans of the Travancore hills the Revd. Richard Collins says, "They are undoubtedly a purely Dravidian people, but are as fair as the

property are said to be the characteristic feature of the Basque society as of the Nayar society."

high caste Hindus, proving that the aborigines of India were not black from race peculiarities, but only sometimes black through circumstances".[1] But this process of reasoning will apply not only to the Nāyars but to the Nambūtiris as well.

The Nambūtiri Brahmans of Malabar regard the Nāyars as socially superior to the Tamil Śūdras and they associate the Nāyars with themselves even in important Brahmanical ceremonies. The Brahmans have ever been chary of according any privileges to the Śūdras. The Aryan authorities are very unfavourable to their reception into the Vedic circle. "A Brahman must not touch a Śūdra. He is commanded not to hold converse with him by some writers. For the touch of a Śūdra, no end of penances are prescribed. Even when the privilege of performing certain rites was conceded to Śūdras, it seems to have amounted to little more than the performance of ceremonies without the recitation of texts. And here again a kind of distinction appears to have been drawn by which the Śūdras were divided into two classes. The *Sat* Śūdras and the *Asat* Śūdras, *i. e.*, the good and the bad. But, on a critical examination, very little substantial difference will be perceived. They are still the servile class, standing on the borders, as it were, of the Aryan community, but not forming an integral portion of it. They were, indeed, provided for in a speculative way by the Arya code; but they had the ban of their class as a mark of exclusion from the regular Aryans."

Under these circumstances, the fact that the Malabar Brahmans conceded to the Nāyars privileges that are denied to the Śūdras, generally, certainly requires explanation. The arguments of the advocates of the Śūdra theory appear plausible, but are not convincing. They say that the Nambūtiris must have been impelled by very strong political and economical motives to make such important concessions. On their arrival in Kērala, they found the Nāyars in

1. Mss. Eut. p. 225.

authority, whom they subdued by sheer force of intellect. They were, however, wise enough to secure the adherence of the conquered by allotting to them a position in the caste hierarchy which was practically one next only to that of the Brahmans themselves as will appear afterwards. The Nāyars had also to be employed in the supervision of the cultivation of the land. The Nambūṭiris in the process of years, seem to have imposed on them the belief that all the land in Kērala was a free-hold gift to the sacerdotal class by their patron Saint Paraśu Rāma, whom, they thought it convenient to style an incarnation of Vishṇu, the second God-head of the Hindu Trinity. To enjoy ease and plenty, the land they had thus appropriated to themselves had to be cultivated. The Nāyars were selected to supervise the cultivation.

It was therefore the interest of the Brahmans to hold the Nāyars close to them and, in order to do so, they were humoured with the idea that they were altogether outside the pale of what the Aryans chose to call the 'servile class'. But they seem to have taken special care not to admit them within the charmed circle. In associating the Nāyars with them, the Nambūṭiris had other objects also to serve. They wanted to secure a strict entail of their properties so that they might never be reduced to indigent circumstances, or their estates be frittered away by frequent partition. For this object, they ruled that only the eldest son of a Nambūṭiri family need enter into holy wedlock, and it was ordained a privilege for Nāyar females to allow the younger brothers of a Nambūṭiri family to consort with them.

It will be pertinent to the present enquiry here to point out the proposition propounded by Baden Powell as a reason for the respect shown by the Nambūṭiris to the Nāyars. He considers that Nāyars are the Kshetriyas of Malabar. "The Brahminic historians, true to their own theory, make out that the land all belonged originally to the Brahmans. But inasmuch as military duty,

SIR M. KRISHNAN NAYAR.

(Formerly the Chief Judge of the High Court of Travancore, and then the Diwan there. Now a Member of the Executive Council of H. E. the Governor of Madras).

(To face p. 173.

police and executive rule are foreign to Brahman life, we always find that the Kṣheṭṛiya rulers from a Raja to a Ḍēśamukhyan are an essential part of the system, and accordingly we find the Brahminic history assigning the ruling and protecting duties to the Nāyars as representing the Kṣheṭṛiya element. The Kēralōṭpaṭṭi records the tradition that Paraśu Rāma gave the Nāyars the executive power (lit: the "the eye, the hand and the giving of orders") so as to prevent rights from being curtailed or suffered to fall into disuse. This clearly means that they were to hold the executive power. But whether from jealousy among themselves or from the comparatively equal power of the other castes, no local chief was allowed to elevate himself into a central ruler or sovereign. At first, we learn, the country being allotted into 64 ṅāds or unions, that the Nāyars of the ten and-a half ṅāds furnished a force for military and executive duty. An elected council of four managed the whole, acting for twelve years. This sort of republican rule, however, failed to give satisfaction. We find that, after a time, Brahmans were sent to the adjoining kingdoms for a ruler; and for a long time the curious feature is presented of a chosen king ruling for twelve years only (if he lived so long) and then retiring. It was at a later time that the king became permanent."[1] Dr. E. Thurston also has the following in his *Castes and Tribes of Southern India*[2]:—"The original Nāyars were undoubtedly a military body, holding lands and serving as a militia." But this by the way.[3]

1. Land Systems of British India, Vol. III, p. 158.

2. Vol. V, p. 283.

3. The following facts collected by M. R. Ry. Rama Varma Elaya Raja Avl., Chirakkal, in his brochure on the *Nayars of Malabar* (Rama Varma Grantha Series, No. 4, published by Mary Memorial Press, Kuthuparamba, N. Malabar) will serve as an interesting contribution for the solution of the problem in which we are engaged. In the *Bhugola Purana*, one of the well-known Puranas, there is a description of Kerala. There it is stated that the Nayars were originally Kshetriyas and that, out of fear for Parasu Rama who was an inveterate foe of the Kshetriya race,

A review of the various circumstances above set forth leads some only to conclude that the facts adduced to prove the Aryan origin of the Nāyars are not in themselves sufficient to support the theory. It is, say they, therefore, perhaps safe to hold for the present at any

removed their holy thread. They were learned and skilled in the use of arms.

"നതെചിധാഃ ബാഹ്യചരാഃ പൂർവ്വം ക്ഷത്രകുലോത്ഭവാഃ-"
"സന്ത്രസ്താഃ ക്ഷത്രധർമ്മാം സ്താൻ സർവ്വാൻസന്ത്യജ്യ ശ്ശൂദ്രവൽ
ബ്രാഹ്മണാന്തികമാഗത്യ ബാഹ്യം ചേതഃസവിക്രമം."
"ആയുധാക്ഷരവിദ്യാസു കുശലാസ്സർവ്വപാരഗാഃ."

The Nayars were very pleased to meet the Brahmans, while they were equally glad to meet the Nayars and to find them adepts in the art of administration.

"അതിവിസ്മയവന്തസ്തേ നായകാഃ പൂർവ്വസംഗതാൻ
മഹീദേവോത്തമാൻ ദൃഷ്ട്വാ ജഹർഷുർബ്ബാഹ്യചാരിണഃ
ജഗൽഭരണനൈപുണ്യവിക്രമാനവലോക്യതാൻ
ഭൂദേവസത്തമാശ്ചൈവം തദാമുമുദിരേ ബഹു."

It is also stated in *Brahmanna Puranam* that it was the Nayars who protected the sacrificial halls from the approach and poullution of *Mlechchas*. Some of these Nayars who distinguished themselves in this defence were honoured with the title of Samanthas.

We find references to Kerala soldiers in the *Bhishma* and *Karna Parvas*. In the latter, they are described as high, broad-chested, long-armed and large-eyed.

"പാഞ്ചാലാനത്ഭുതസ്യാംശ്ച കേരളാംശ്ച പ്രഭദ്രകാൻ
ഭീഷ്മഃ പ്രഹരതാം ശ്രേഷ്ഠഃ പാതയാമാസ മാർഗ്ഗണൈഃ"
"വൃതാഃ വ്യൂഹേന മഹതാ പാണ്ഡ്യശ്ചോളാസ്സകേരളാഃ
വ്യൂഢോരസ്കാഃ ദീർഘഭുജാഃ പ്രാംശവഃ പൃഥുലോചനാഃ.[3]"

(Also see the article on the "Sacred Thread of the Hindus" by Pandit Vidusekhara Bhattacharya in the July (1923) number of the *Visva Bharati* Quarterly).

The acid test about the status of community is, in Malabar at any rate, the nature of its connection with recognised temples. In the dawn of Kerala history, so to say, one finds that the great temple at Mathilakam was being controlled by the Tekketath and Vatakatath Veetil Nayars. So was the case of many other well-known temples. And, in spite of the lapse of time and the vicissitudes of fortune through which they have passed, one can still notice vestiges of the Nayar proprietorship over some, of Nayar authority over others of even temples now owned by Sirkars.

rate that they are of Dravidian origin. To this position few will demur. But serious objection is raised by their protagonists only when certain Brahmans, *albeit* learned, make frantic attempts to make out that the Nāyars are Śūdras. As to the three points raised above, they will be answered in the course of this note. For the superiority of Aryan racehood as such is a gratuitous assumption in the opinion of some eminent ethnologists. Historical accuracy requires that no race should be classed with certainty as Aryan or Dravidian unless it can be done so on clear and cogent proofs.

The curious similarity between the manners and customs of the Nāyars and the Newars of the Himalayan ranges of Nepal may also be noticed in connection with the race question. Col. Kirkpatrick, who points out this similarity, observes that "it is remarkable enough that the Newar women like those among the Nāyars, may in fact, have as many husbands as they please, being at liberty to divorce them continually on the slightest pretence"[2]. Dr. Bunchanan Hamilton also remarks, "In fact there are no two tribes in India, except the Nāyars and the Newars, who are known to have the same strange notions as to female chastity, and that, coupled with their architecture and other peculiarities, seem to point to a similarity of race which is both curious and interesting, but how and when the connection took place I must leave it to others to determine. I do not think that there is anything in the likeness of the names, but I do place faith in the similarity of their architecture combined with their manners and customs"[3]. This striking similarity in the style of architecture is noticed prominently by Ferguson in his *History of India and Eastern Architecture*. The similarity is most marked in the District of

1. "The name Dravidian races fits only the Tamils, Telugus and Canarese." F. Ratzel in his *Races of Mankind*. Vol. 3, p. 359.
2. Nepal, p. 175.
3. Account of the Kingdom of Nepal, pp. 29. 42. 52.

Canara, and Ferguson says that he "cannot offer even a plausible conjecture, how or at what time a connection existed between Nepal and Tibet and Canara".[1] We shall have presently to refer to the all but universal prevalence of loose marital relationship between the sexes in the early stages of society all over the world which, we believe accounts for the strange notions as to female chastity among the Newars in the extreme north and among the Nāyars in the extreme south of India. As to the similarity in the style of architecture, we know that Buddhist and Jain Missionaries had extended their proselytising endeavours to the south of India so early as the period of the great Emperor Asoka, who mentions the kingdom of Kērala in one of his edicts as one of Pratyantas or neighbouring Kingdoms of his Empire. It has been doubted whether Asoka was a Buddhist or Jain in religion. Whether Buddhist or Jain, the emissaries of the great Emperor seem to have brought Kērala within the sphere of their master's influence.[2] The similarity we notice in the architecture in the north and in the south is that both are in the Jain style. A close observer will be impressed with the striking similarity between the temple architecture of Malabar and Canara, and the temple architecture of China, and it is a matter of known history that till but recently China had extensive commercial transactions with the West Coast of India.

If the Nāyars were not the original inhabitants of Kērala, but were settlers from outside, when and whence did they come? The theory of the Kērala Māhātmyam is that they were brought by Parasu Rāma along with his colonies of Brahmans. Various circumstances tend to show that they were in Kērala long before the arrival of the Nambūtiris. The *Mahatmyam*

1. p. 278

2. See the articles by Mr. T. K. Krishna Menon on Matilakam in Dr. Law's Historical Quarterly Review of Calcutta (Vol. V, p. 138) and on the Kilirur Temple in the Rama Varma Research Institute Bulletin (Vol. I, No. 1), Government Press Cochin.

would have us believe that the Nambūtiris found Kērala, at the time of their settlement, entirely uninhabited. This is far from being likely. The probabilities are that the immigrants found Kērala occupied by an early colony of agricultural settlers. The Nambūtiris themselves have never been known to be agriculturists, and the Vyśias, the lowest section of the twice-born, who were cultivators by profession, find no place in the caste economy of Kērala. The existing agricultural classes seem not to have any connection whatever with Aryan Vyśias, and the fact that almost all, if not all, agricultural terms are of non-Aryan origin is a matter of great significance.

Dr. Caldwell argues from the Malayalam words denoting 'East' and 'West', *Kizhaku* meaning 'beneath' and *melku* meaning 'above', that the Malayālīs must have come from the Tamil country east of the Ghauts since there they had the low level of the oceans on the east and the high level of the Ghaut mountains on the west. He observes that the Malayālīs had emigrated at an early date from the east, and this was the reason for the people of the two coasts having languages akin to each other. To this argument, Dr. Gundert answers that, "if the analogous progress of the Aryans to the south be considered, it will appear probable that the Dravidians, like the Aryans, formed settlements on the West Coast first and afterwards crossed over to the Eastern." This argument would appear to prove too much. For, as observed by Dr. Caldwell, "it would require us to regard the whole Tamil people as immigrants from the Western Coast, and the Tamil Language an offshoot from Malayalam. The geographical and philological difficulties in the way of both these suppositions appear to be insuperable." Successive batches of immigrants seem to have converged towards Kērala from different parts, and at different times, and become so mingled that it is not possible at present to differentiate the various elements that went to form the Nāyar community. The evidence of language may tend to show that, while a considerable portion of the community consists of the descendants of Tamil immigrants, there are among them those whose ancestors belonged originally to the Telugu, the Canarese, and other groups of the Dravidian stock. We have already shown that the Nambūtiris emigrated from the banks of the Krishna, the Godaveri and other rivers, and it is most likely that their followers brought with them their language which made permanent additions to the Malayalam tongue, e.g., *Thantha*, (father), *Illam*, (house), *Thalla*, (mother), *Ulli*, (onion), are evident modifications of the Telugu words *Thandri*, *Illu*, *Talli*, and *Uelli* respectively. Similarly we find Canarese words such as *Mana* (house) in the Malayalam language.

The occupation of Kērala by the early Dravidian tribes must have taken place in almost pre-historic times, and all theories regarding the time when and the region whence they came must be purely conjectural. Wanting historical records, one can only try to trace survivals of rudimentary features common in communities inhabiting different parts which may possibly afford a clue to a common origin. On the authority of Baden Powell's observations regarding the Kolarian tribes of Chota Nagapur, the *Cochin Census Report* seeks to find some similarity between them and the Nāyars. That writer has observed that "those people (the Kolarians of Chota Nagapur) were organised in tribes and they established the territorial divisions still known as *Nad*". He further notes that "the Chota Nagapur country is admirably adopted to secure the preservation of old tribal forms of settlement, since it is fertile within and unaccessible to enemies from without, and it does not lie in the track of many of the greater military movements known in history. Here we have distinct evidence that the Kolarian population was in part let alone, and in part, combined with (or supplemented) by Dravidians, and all came under later Dravidian rulers." Having quoted these passages of Mr. Baden Powell, the Census Reporter remarks, "Except for the fact that tribes that settled in Kēraḷa came also under Aryan supremacy, all the conditions and circumstances above set forth are strictly true of Kēraḷa. In the same connection he observes, that those tribes made small territories for tribal sections locally known as Paṙah. In the Agricultural and Land Revenue language of Kēraḷa, no word is more familiar than the word parah, which is here applicable to a plot of agricultural land measuring 2/25 of an acre." The analogies pointed out are too slender to construct a theory upon, though the similarity in the use of the terms Ṅāḍ and Paṙah are seductive enough to induce one to detect some sort of identity, illusory though it be, between the two races. The Census Reporter goes on to observe that there are other features of tribal and village systems of Kēraḷa that seem to correspond in many respects to the mixed Kolarian and Dravidian systems of Chota Nagapur. What these are he does not unfortunately tell us. An inquiry into these will certainly be very useful and is likely to lead to important and interesting historical results.

Hemmed in on three sides by natural barriers, the sea in the south and the west and the mountains of the ghauts on the east, the north was the main route left free for colonists to enter Kēraḷa. Of course the break in the chain of mountains that occurs here and there along the line of the ghauts served as openings for the migration of adventurous tribes from the east, though difficult. It is difficult, almost impossible, to fix with any amount of accuracy the period of the original settlement. We have observed that the Brahmans found, on their arrival in Kēraḷa, the Nāyars in possession of the country; in fact they were the ruling race. If so, they must have settled in the land long before the Nambūṭiris, the period of whose emigration has been shown to be anterior to B. C. 300. If the Narāe of Megasthenes have any reference to the Nāyars of

Malabar, they must have colonised Kērala some time before the period of Megasthenes.

It would seem that, after settling in Malabar, the Nāyars had thrown out colonies into different parts of the globe'.[1] Miquel Balboa attributes the settlement of Southern Chile to pirates from the East Indies, whom he calls Naiyres, and Bandelier in a note adds that "the Nayres were originally from Malabar; I am informed by Dr. Berthold Laufer the distinguished student of eastern Asiatic Anthropology." Balboa traces the career of these people over nearly like the whole eastern world, making a part of them finally land near the southern extremity of America. According to him, they were "the origin and trunk of the Indians of Chile, from whom also descended the Cheriguanaes or (rather) Chiliganes. By these were made those strange fortifications that in Ayavira and Tiagnacs (and in other parts of this section of the world) are seen etc.[2]

"After the 'Nāyres' had conquered the austral regions, they penetrated inland and were never afterwards heard

1 "Dravidian culture can be affiliated not only to the Asura or Mundari, but to foreign cultures like the Sumerian Chaldean, Aegean, Etruscan and Egyptian ** The high status of Dravidian women probably accounts for the conception of mother goddess. Among other non-Aryan accomplishments of the Vedic age, which also answer to the Dravidian, may be mentioned magic and medicine and excellence in architecture.

The greatest achievement of the Dravidian was in the art of navigation. The Indian ship was very like the Egyptian as we see it in a fifth dynasty painting, a long and wall-sided vessel with the stern and stem highly raised, and with oars arranged in banks. The Dravidian paddle was round, not spade-like in form as in ancient China, or very long as in ancient Egypt. There are words in the Dravidian languages for boats of all sizes—the raft, the dug-out and the decked vessel. There are words there for the oar, sail, mast and anchor. There are Sanskrit borrowings of several nautical terms from Dravidian languages". (Pp. 10 and 11 of Indian Culture through the Ages". Mysore University series, Vol. I. by Prof. S. V. Vencateswaran, M. A.). Though the word Dravidian is here used, the statements apply more to Kerala than to any other part of ancient Dravidian India. *Ed.*

2. Chap. 19, fol. 251.

from. Their intrusion on these our Indies is conjecture, for the reason that old Indians state they have it from ancient traditions of their forefathers, who told them that from that part of the world there came these pestiferous tyrants [the Nayres], and those of Chile say the same, pointing out that they came from this side of the straits which we call of Magallen." Commenting on the above, Bandelier remarks, "This passage is confused. In the first place, Balboa says that nothing was known or learned about the 'Nāyres' after they had once penetrated inland, yet he attributes to them the contribution of ancient edifices near Ayaviri (probably the remains of Pucara are meant) and Tiahnanco. Again, he intimates that the Nāyres were the original inhabitants and settlers, whereas he also states that the Indians of Chile spoke of them as ruthless invaders. All this shows that he has arranged, but not objectively rendered, the traditions claimed by him to be original and primitive. What might possibly be gathered from his statements is that there existed in his time, among the Indians of Chile, lore, perhaps ancient, relative to landings on the southern Chilean Coast of people coming from the direction of Asia. This is said with very proper reserve."[1]

We have had occasion to notice the notorious piratical character of the early Malayālīs, of which we have accounts on record, from the days of the early Greek Geographers to those of European travellers of the 17th and 18th centuries, only that the later pirates happen to be Māppillas (Moors) rather than Nāyars. However that be, there are undoubted indications which go to show that the Malayālīs had ventured to go abroad and form colonies. We have already referred to traces of colonies made by the Hindus in Arabia and elsewhere and especially in the island of Socotra at the mouth of the Gulf of Aden as also

1. *American Anthropologist*. N. S. 1925 pp. 257—267.

to traces of Malayāli settlements mentioned by Strabu in Arabia Felix.[1]

1. The following extracts from the Report of the Travancore Jenmi-Kudiyan Committee may be perused with advantage in connection with the subject we have been considering—(page 31 et seq.):—

"Mr. John Campbell in his work on the Hittites has made some interesting observations, which appear to throw a flood of light on the genesis of Kerala and the origin of the Nayars. He says that the Niquirians of Nicaragua are Southern Nahuatl (*h* being modified into *v* and *tl* into *r*). The greatest of the Hittite families, which the Assyrian and, before them, the Egyptian inscriptions held to represent the whole of the Hittite people, was that of the Assyrian Nairi and the Egyptian Naharina. Their capital was Khupascai, the Thapascus of the classical geographers and the Tipsach of the Hebrews. In India, the prefix *Khu* or *Tha* was lost, and the Pisachas came to be representatives of the Khupascians. These Pisachas were associated with Rakshasas and Nagas who were Nairritas. An ancient document classifies the Etruscans of Italy in the same category, making their tribal divisions Tusci, Naharci and Japusci; and the Basques of the Pyrenees reproduce the nomenclature in their divisions of Navarre and Guipuscoa. In the Navarese and Naharci, the Scythic Neuri of Herodotus may be found, as well as the Nairi of the Assyrians and the Nahuatl, Navatl or Niquirians of America.

"It is stated further on that Syria is a Greek adaptation of the Native Kera, probably identical with the Basque Herri, the Etruscan Kara (country) which survives in the Japanese Kori (province), but finds its modern exponent in Korea, anciently called Karo, meaning the land. Kera, therefore, is the national land of the Hittites, *the* country in contradistinction to all other parts of the earth * * *

"Mr. Jagadish Chatterji of Kashmir seeks to prove that the so-called Aryan invaders of India are a composite race made up of several tribes, who dwelt about the region of the Black Sea, Asia Minor and elsewhere, and who brought into their new colony names of places, persons and things connected with their earlier abode. * * * He also holds that that composite race consisted also of other elements which went to make up the nationalities of the Babylonians, the Egyptians, the Afghans and the Hebrews, and that some of the ancestors of these races as well as of the Chinese had their common home, along with the Aryans, in and about Pontes and Armenia * * *

"Mr. John Campbell's book on the Hittites shows that the Hittites migrated in all directions. That they were Turanians

Their caste position. We have already observed that the Nambūṭiris have accorded to the Nāyars a position in the caste scale that the Brahmans of the East Coast have not accorded to the Śūdras there, and that to this they were, according to some, compelled by political and social necessity. On entering Kērala, the Brahmans found the Nāyars in possession of the country. They were, as described by the Kēralōṭpaṭṭi, the people of the 'eye', the hand, and the 'order', and it was their duty to preserve the rights of the people from being curtailed or infringed. The social and political organisation of the Nāyars which created and maintained these rights and privileges will be noticed later on. In fact, the Nāyars were in the words of

is clear. The Etruscans and the Basques belong to the same stock. The names Navarrese, Naharci, Nairi, Neuri, Nairritas and News may be connected with them * * *

"That Cheran Chenkuttuvan led an expedition up to the Himalayan regions and that a Karnataka dynasty reigned in Nepal are historical facts. This dynasty was established with the help of the Newars who had warlike instincts like the Nayars. At this distance of time it is difficult to localise Nayera from which Newars are said to have been drawn. The Indica of Megasthenes, describing the valley of the Indus and the adjoining parts, says: "Next follow the Narae enclosed by the loftiest of Indian mountains, the Capitalia". It is said that Capitalia is Mount Abu and that Narae recalls the name of Nayar, which the Rajput chronicles apply to the northern belt of the desert. * * Nayar in Rajputana might, for aught we know, have been the first Indian home of the Nayar branch of the Dravidian race, and they might have, after their immigration into Malabar, applied the name to themselves * * * It may be asserted that no Karnataka king is likely to have enlisted soldiers from an unknown region, but Karnataka or Kanara, which was under Chalukyan kings, might have supplied the soldiers who helped Nanya Deva to overthrow the last Malla or Rajput King of Nepal. It is well-known that long afterwards the Vijayanagar dynasty drove out Nayars from Kanara. * * * Ahichhtra in India is the place from which Brahmans are said to have been brought into Malabar by Mayura Varma. It is not very far fom the desert, the northern belt of which is styled Nayar in the Rajput chronicles. * * Alichhatra was evidently a stronghold of the Nagas, chief among whom were the Madras, the Gandharas, and the Balhikas". *Ed.*

Mr. Logan "the ruling race" who, under the system of the Aryans, ought to belong to the Kshetriya caste. The Brahmans were indeed their intellectual superiors, and had, by the sheer force of their intellect, obtained complete ascendancy over the ruling race. But they had to depend upon the Nayars to defend the country against aggressions from without. They themselves were but few in numbers, and were not apparently a fighing class. As observed by Mr. Logan, "they had no sufficient body of 'protectors' of their own race to fall back upon, so they had perforce to acknowledge as 'protectors' the aboriginal ruling race—the Nairs—whom they designated 'Śūdras' but in reality treated as Kshetriyas. If their 'protectors' were called Śūdras (servile classes), then the classes below Śūdras would not have any footing in the original Aryan organisation * * * The real facts seems to have been that the Aryans who introduced the political system of caste into Malabar were unwilling to raise even the aboriginal ruling race to the dignity of the pure Kshetriya caste of Aryans. Very possibly they were Khsetriyas themselves who introduced the system. And yet the state organization required that there should be a protector or Kshetriya caste, so they solved the difficulty by inventing a term—Nayen, plural Nayar (Skt. leader, soldier), and by applying it to the caste whom they constituted 'protectors', and yet treated as Śūdras (servile class)." "In this way it was", adds Mr. Logan, "that the Nairs came to be treated as outside the caste system altogether"—a unique position which finds no parallel in the Hindu religious or political system elsewhere. We have seen that the Nambūtiris had also constituted the Nayars 'supervisors' and 'trustees' of their landed estates, so that their most important, most consequential, and most acceptable function in the body politic was the protection of the land and its people—the function accorded by the Hindu political system to the Kshetriya caste. This theory is no new one started by Mr. Logan. Before him Dr. Gundert defined the Nāyars as the Śūḍras of Kērala, raised to the rank of Kṣheṭṛiyas by their intimate connection with the Brahmans. The French traveller Thevenot, writing half a century before Visscher, observes of the Nāyars that "they had a great conceit of their nobility because they fancied themselves to be descended from the sun". All Kṣheṭṛiyas claim descent either from the sun or the moon. In 1409, Ma Huan, speaking of Cochin, observes: "The Nayars rank with the King." The Brahmans themselves accord this position to the Nayars. In a Sanskrit work called *Kerala Kshiti Ratna Mala* (A garland of gems of the land of Kērala) the author says:—

"Some of them (the Nāyars) are superior warriors even amongst warriors. All the gods take to them. (verse 115.)

Though these warriors be *Kshetrya-Sudras*, they should be honoured even by the Brahmans (verse 116).

Even the mightiest lord should get up on seeing them, *i. e.*, should not sit in their presence out of respect for them. The life of those who rule over the land rests on the weapons (of warriors), and to those who possess such weapons they are preceptors (verse 117)."

In a recent work in Malayalam, entitled *Prachina Malayalam* or 'Ancient Malabar', a native scholar of great learning and ability strongly combats the view that the Nāyars are Śūḍras. He is of opinion that they are the descendants of the original Ṅāgas and are Dravidians, and are really Kṣheṭṛiyas.[1].

Their organisation. In giving an account of the National Assemblies of Malabar, we have shown how the country had been divided into Ḍēśams and Ṅāds for purposes of civil and military administration. These divisions were the result of the evolution and development of society and not of the arbitrary act of any particular

1. (See *Cochin Tribes and Castes* by Rao Bahadur L. K. Anantakrishna Ayyar, Vol. II, p. 2; also Dr. C. F. Oldham's '*The Sun and Serpent Worship*, Chap. VII, pp. 162-5.); (see also the Editor's note at the end of this Note on Nayars).

person or group of persons. We may reasonably presume that the early settlers had organised themselves into tribes, and appropriated to themselves land suited for cultivation. Each tribal section grouped itself into clans under the lead of the elder or the more competent among them, and took possession of such land as they could lay hand on, 'clearing waste by expelling the owners or by enslaving them'. Even at the present moment we see this process going on, of course in a lesser degree. Squatters settle on patches of waste land in the interior, clear waste, cultivate it, and finally have the land assessed as theirs in the Government registry. But at present there is no scope for colonies making such settlements as in the good old days. The lands appropriated by the several tribes, sections and clans came to be known as ṭaṟās, a Dravidian word meaning originally a foundation. It is possible that such of those who were unable to occupy any land took to professions other than agricultural. In course of time, the ṭaṟās or villages had to be multiplied as the tribes and clans increased in number, and began to occupy and bring under cultivation new localities. It is significant that, throughout Kēraḷa, the Nāyars are divided into sections known by the same caste names irrespective of the localities they inhabit. Another peculiar feature with them is that each family (ṭaṟawād) is known by a separate name, and where one family branches off into different sections, they take care not to drop the original family name. In Kēraḷa, the feeling of kinship is diffused over a very wide circle, wider perhaps than anywhere else in India. All property is joint, the family indissoluble, however large, however distant in blood relationship the head may be from the youngest member. The family is founded on a matriarchal basis. 'The heirs of a given ancestor and their heirs in turn continue to live together upon the common inheriance, with a common dwelling and a common mess. A ṭaṟawād has its Eṇangans or *Machampikkar* families allied to it, between whom marriage and social communion is allowed. These with their several branches may be taken to form a clan. Two or more such clans having the same social status go to make a tribal section or Jāṭi or sub-caste. The Ṭara was the Nayar territorial unit of organisation for civil purposes, and was governed by representatives of the caste, who were styled Kāraṇavars or elders. There seems to have been four families to each ṭara. Originally the Nāyar community seems to have been grouped into the "six hundred", the "five hundred", the "five thousand", etc., each of these being perhaps sections composed of as many individuals or as many families, most probably the latter. A further grouping was that of the ṭaras into Ñāds. There being four families to a ṭara, 150 ṭaras went to make a Ñād of the 'six hundred', and so on. We have already referred to the division of the land into Ḍēṣams and Ñāds for military purpose. These divisions and the functions allotted to each subsisted almost up to the British occupation of Malabar, and in some instances seem to have lingered longer. For Mr. Logan observes, in connection with the measures adopted by Major Macleod, first Principal Collector of Malabar, and his assistants, to whom Government had committed all power both civil and military, the latter being further authorised to punish "by summary process, crimes of every description", until the military power of the company shall have subjected the refractory people of the Province:—"The *tara* organisation of the Nayars, *albiet* crushed by the Mysorean supremacy, was not altogether dead, and it only needed some acts of palpable injustice to rouse the whole community into violent opposition to the new race of rulers" [1].

Personal names. Generally the personal names employed used to be exclusively Dravidian, but these are fast going out, being replaced by names of Sanskrit origin, derived from Puranic sources, and therefore Āryan.

1. Page 538 of his *Malabar Manual.*

Males.	*Females*
Kunchu	Kavu
Kunnan	Kurumpa
Chattu	Kali
Otenan	Tuli
Kōmappan	Ichi
Iksha	Kunchi
Rairu	Kunnīppilla
Tenchu	Tai
Manchu	Ikkāvu
Panchu	Kunnikkāvu
Koman	Nangeli
Ikkoman	Ittuli
Ittikoman	
Ittikandappan	
Kōppu	

Pet names.	*Pet names.*
Ammunni	Ammu
Appunni	Ammini
Kuttan	Kāyi
Appu	Pāppu
Kuttappan	etc., etc.
Ponnu	
etc., etc.	

At present, the names of Puranic deities, such as, Raman, Krishnan, Sankaran, Madhavan, etc., for males, and Parvati, Lakshmi, Devaki, Kallyani, Narayani, etc., for females, are common.

Titular suffixes.—In Travancore, Pillai, Chempakarāman, Tampi. These are peculiar to Travancore.

Pillai was once a title of distinction granted as a mark of royal favour. The conferring of the title is known as *Tirumukham Kodukkuka*. Before the title was conferred, an enquiry was made as to the caste, the social position, etc., of the person to be honoured with it. It was held in such high esteem that even a Brahman Dewan, Sanku Annāvi, sought for and obtained the dignity. The person honoured has the term *Tirumukathu Kanakka* prefixed to his name. If Nāyars, both males and females are styled Pillai.

Chempakaraman.—This is a titular distinction higher than that of Pillai, and may be said to correspond to the knighthood of Western nations. It was instituted by Maharaja Mārttāṇḍa Varma as a distinction to be conferred on those who have rendered meritorious services to the State. The ceremony of investiture will be found described in the *History of Travancore*.[1] The title is sometimes conferred on the family in perpetuity. The recipients are styled *Thirumukham Kanakku Chempakaraman* so and so.

Tampi.—This used to be a title conferred by the sovereign in recognition of meritorious services of an exceptional nature and may be compared with that of Prince, and is higher than that of Chempakarāman. At present, it is the distinctive suffix attached to the names of the Nāyar sons of the sovereigns of Travancore. As such, they have certain privileges, such as riding in palanquins, appearing before the king without a head-dress, etc. The Maharaja's consorts are usually selected from Ṭampi families and, if the choice goes beyond these families, the consort is adopted into one of these before or soon after the alliance. The sons of the Maharaja have the title 'Śrī' prefixed and 'Ṭampi' affixed to their personal names, *e. g.*, 'Śrī Nārāyaṇan Ṭampi'; other male members of the family are called simply Ṭampies so and so. The daughters are known as 'Ponnammas' and other female members as 'Ṭamkachies'. The consort herself is Amma or Ammachi.

We shall now enumerate the various titular suffixes in general use throughout Malabar. These are Kaṛṭāvu, Kuṛupp, Kaimal, Uṇṇiṭṭān, Valiyaṭṭān, Nampiār, Kiṭāvu, Nayanār, Achan, Mēnon, Mēnōkki, Mūṭṭān, Paṇikkar, Paṭanāyar, Maṇavālar, Perimbrar, Paṭiar, Prālar, Arimbrar, Taravanār Maṇṇaṭiar. These titles are more or less indicative of the traditional professions of the individuals bearing them.

1. Page 180.

Of these the first nine indicate nobility and the rest more or less profession.

Karthavu.—The word means 'one who does', *i. e.*, 'he who rules'; cf. 'Karta', used in Bengal to mean 'manager of a joint family'.. It also appears to have been used by the old Madura Kings as a title[1]. In Malabar it is a title formerly conferred on Nāyar feudal chieftains by their suzerains. They are generally high class Nāyars.

Kurup.—This is a title of honour. But there were also Kuṙups who were chieftains. cf. 'Goreyph' or Kuṙup of Travancore mentioned by our author in his 9th letter. Kāraṇāṭṭu Kuṙup, a dignitary of Travancore, is one of the members of the Śri Paḍmanābha Swāmi Temple Yōgam at Trivandrum.

Kaimal Perhaps from *Kai*=hand meaning power; cf. 'Kai', 'Kan' and 'Kalpana'='the hand', 'the eye' and 'the order' said to be the distinguishing prerogatives of the Nayars according to the *Keralolpatti*. They were the feudal chiefs of the Malabar kings and are very often mentioned by the Portuguese writers such as Barbosa, Castenheda and others. Both these writers mention, as also Purchas, that, between the death of one Zamorin and the swearing in of his successor, the Government of the country is conducted by some Kaimals. It was at one time their prerogative that one of them should always be in exclusive charge of the treasuries of the Malabar Rajas, the Rajas themselves having no power over them except through the Kaimal in charge. "Neither could they," says Barbosa "take anything out of it (the treasury) without a great necessity and by the council of this person." Captain Alexander Hamilton also speaks to the same effect with regard to the Rajas of Cherakkal. The Kaimals as feudatories had independent governments of their own, they being obliged only to follow the Rajas into the field of battle with an allotted number of fighting men. These also belong to the highest class of Nāyars.

1. See Ethnographic Appendices, p. 131.

Unnithan and *Valliathan* are also noblemen of a lesser order but belonging to the highest class of Nāyars. These seem peculiar to Travancore just as Kiṭāvu and Nayanār and Nampiār are peculiar to Kōlaṭṭnād, modern N. Malabar. Some of them were also territorial magnates, such as the Iruvālinād Nampiārs.

Achan —The word means 'father'. It is the title of a few Nāyar chiefs such as *Mangat Achan* and *Paliat Achan* who were hereditary Prime Ministers and Commanders-in-Chief of the Zamorin and the Cochin Rajas respectively. The circumstance that they are styled Mēnōns by the Rajas in ordinary conversation and correspondence shows that they were originally of the commonality since ennobled by those Rajas. The eldest member of the Palghat Raja's family bears the title of Achan.

Panikkar.—Probably from *Pani* work. These were fencing masters whose gymnasiums were known as *Kalaris* ,half schools and half shrines.

Menon and *Menokki.*—These were the writers of the Rajas and their supervisors—the latter term *Menokki* means literally 'one who supervises', *mal:-mel-nokki.* We have an interesting description of the Zamorin's writers given by Barbosa. In Travancore, the corresponding title is Piḷḷai. These titles of Piḷḷai and Mēnōn are now commonly used by Nāyars indifferently. The other terms do not require any special notice as they are known only locally.

Sub-divisions.—There have been and there are an ever increasing number of sub-divisions in the Nāyar community. The Nāyars it has been observed are more a tribe than a caste. Bhattacharya reckons them as such in his work on *Hindu Castes and Sects.* The Nāyar community is an elastic and expansive body. At the same time, within the community as already pointed out, there is a tendency to split into smaller sections with new caste pretentions. It is somewhat difficult to define who a Nāyar is, but it may be said generally that a Malayāli who attaches, or is entitled to attach, any one of the titles already enumerated to his own name, who follows the Maru makkaṭṭāyam law of succession, and may enter the temples of Kērala where Brahmans and Nambūṭiris officiate as priests, without polluting them, belongs to one of that class of Malayālis now known by the name of Nāyar.

According to the Jāṭinirṇṇaya, the Nāyars are divided into 18 sections or sub-divisions. These are

(1) *Kiriattil Nayar.*—Said to be the descendants of the first of the 3 classes of females brought to Malabar by Paraśu Rāma, viz., *Deva, Gandharva,* and *Asura* maidens. Their peculiar privilege is that they are exempted from serving the Brahmans. To this class belong the chieftains of Malabar known as Nampiyār, Kaṛṭṭāvu, Kaimaḷ, Paṇikkar, Uṇṇi, Uṇṇiṭṭan, Māṭampi, Ṭampi, &c. Their profession was the bearing of arms, direction of State affairs. They were statesmen, accountants, generals, &c.

(2) *Illakkar.*—These can act as servants in Brahman houses. Every *Illam* or Brahman house has its *Pariyappaṭṭavar* or Nāyars who are attached to it. The males of these Nāyar houses are servants of the Illam and the females act as maids to the Nambūṭiri ladies. They hold properties of the Illam and receive perquisites for the service. The Nāyar women have to escort the Nambūṭiri ladies when they go out and have to warn off the low *cannile* on the road from approaching the holy presence of their mistress. They have to attend them at their ceremonial baths after the monthly periods and while confined after child-birth. These Nāyars consider these duties as honourable and pride themselves in being the *Pariyappattavar* of wealthy, influential and highly placed Nambūṭiris. As they are attached to an *Illam*, they are called *Illakkar.*

(3) *Swaroopakkar.*—Also called *Charnavar* servants in Kṣheṭriya houses. Under this class comes

literally those attached to the inside and those attached to the outside, the one performing menial duties within the house and are domestic body-servants while the others are the retainers of Kşheţriyas. Another explanation for this division is that the Akaţţu Charnnavar have duties within the Yāgaśāla or sacrificial shed of the Nambuţiris while the duties of the Puraţţucharnnavar are confined to the outside of the shed. The latter always take social precedence of the former.

(4) *Padamangalam.*—Servants in temples.

(5) *Tamilpadam.*—General servants. This class seems not to be recognised, or to have no existence, in Cochin and in Malabar.

(6) *Etachery Nayar.*—These are shepherds and dairymen. It seems that, of the several castes of Nāyars, Eţachēry is the only one from which a man belonging to the Chārna caste may take a wife, unless it be from his own caste, without social degradation to both parties.

(7) *Maran.*—Drummers and musicians in temples. A class of Mārān known as Aşţikurichi are attendants at ceremonies of Brahmans, Kşheţriyas, and high caste Nāyars. Members of the former class abstain from fish and meat, and therefore claim superiority over those of the latter class.

(8) *Chempukotti*—Copper utensil makers.

(9) *Odathu Nayar.*—Tile-makers of temples.

(10) *Pallichan*—Palanquin bearers for Rajas and Brahmans.

(11) *Matavan* or *Puliath Nayar.*—These are said to be servants to Brahmins and others down to Ampalavāşis. But there is a class known as *Pulikel* Nāyars or *Matavars*, to be found in the hilly parts, such as those of the Kurumbranad Taluk of Malabar and the Koţţārakkarai and Māvēlikkara Taluks of Travancore, who are clever archers.

(12) *Kalamkotti.* Potters.—These are also known as *Kuśavans* and Anṭūr Nāyars.[1]

(13) *Vattakadan or Chakkala or Chakingal Nair.* Oilmongers for temples.

(14) *Astikkurichi or Cheetikan,*[2] is subordinate to Maran and performs funeral rites for Nāyars.

(15) *Chettis or Vyaparis* are merchants selling curry-stuffs and other goods. Barbosa mentions the *Barbares* or Vyaparis as a caste separate from Cheṭṭīes. Regarding *Barbares,* Barbosa says:—"In Calicut and in all Malabar these are merchants. They deal in all sorts of goods, collect pepper and ginger from the Nayars and cultivators in the interior and frequently buy them in advance in exchange for cotton stuffs and other goods that come from beyond the sea. They enjoy much freedom; crime among them being punished by their chief men and not by the king. If the offender deserves death they kill him with dagger or lance thrusts."[3] Of the Chetties he says,—"They are considerable merchants. They deal in precious stones of all sorts, and in pearls, coral and other very valuable merchandise; and in gold, silver, either bullion or corn which is a great article of trade amongst them, because they rise and fall many times".[4] Evidently Barbosa is not referring to the Nāyar Cheṭṭies or Vyāpāries. Probably foreign Hindu merchants trading in Malabar at the time were called by local names.

(16) *Chaliyan. Weaver.*—Regarding the weavers Barbosa says:—"These are called Chālians. They have no other business except to weave cloths of cotton, and some silk, which are of little value, and are used by the common people. * * Many of these are the sons of Nāyars, and so they are very fine men in their figures; and they bear arms like the Nayars and go to the wars and fight very well."[5]

(1) See note 19 of Letter XX.
(2) Also Asthikurichi and Cheethiyan.
(3) P. 134 (4) P. 144 (5) P. 136.

(17). *Veluthetan.* Washerman.— Barbosa says: —"These are called Maṇṇaṭṭānmār and their business is only to wash the cloths of the Brahmans, Kings and Nayars and they live by this business and they cannot adopt other employments, nor can their descendants."[1]

(18). *Velakkethelavan* or Kṣhavurakkāran.—They are barbers who work for the higher classes of Brahmans and Nāyars. The last four classes, though classed as Nāyars, are yet not allowed to touch them, and are considered to belong to the polluting class. It is, however, curious that the cloths washed and handled by the Veluṭṭēṭan are not prohibited as polluting, though his touch would be. These cloths are received in pagodas for the use of the idols and are worn by even the highest Naṃbūṭiri Brahmans.

The first 14 sub-divisions form the class of high caste Nāyars, who have in course of time split themselves into a large number of sub-sections, and the process of division, as already observed, is still going on. From the schedules of the *Travancore Census Report*, we see that in that State there are over a hundred and thirty such sub-sections. *The Census Report for Malabar* (*1881*) also shows 138 sub-divisions of the Nayar caste. Who knows that this tendency to divide and sub-divide is not "a device to secure a certain degree of division of labour, technical training and development of aptitude for particular crafts."[2]

Appearance and Physical features—As a class, they are a fine race. "They are strong of limbs", says Linschoten, "of colour altogether blacke, yet verie smooth, both of haire and skinne which commonly they annoynt with oyle, to make it shine. Of face, bodie and limbs they are altogether like men of Europe, without any difference, but only in colour, the men are commonly verie hairie, and rough on the breast and on their bodies". Ralph Fitch observes, "the men be tall and strong .... of a reasonable stature, the

1. P. 135.
2. See On Malabar Untouchability on p. 429 of the History of Kerala Vol. II; also the Editor's Paper on the System of caste in his Speeches and writings, 2nd Ed. p. 59.

women little, and all blacke". Captain Nieuhoff says that "they are generally well proportioned, though of a brown or olive colour. Pyrard who saw them in their prime observes, "They are the handsomest, most shapely, best proportioned men I ever saw. They are of a dusky olive colour, and all tall and lusty". Early in the 19th century, Colonel Welsh has described the Nāyars as "a race of beings equally superior to the rest of the population in stature, features, strength and beauty of limbs". "With their olive-brown complexion, dainty extremities, graceful figure, noble bearing, and distinguished carriage", says Mr. Elic Reclus, "they are a gracious race which, according to Richard Burton, singularly resembles the portraits given at the close of the last century as representative of the Pacific Islands". "A well nourished Nair is perhaps one of the finest in all India", says Dr. Subramania Iyer. "The women are distinctly fair as well as well favoured. Many are very handsome. The colour of the men is fair or very nearly so, but darker than the Nambootiri. As a rule, they have a plentiful growth of hair on the head, both men and women, which they take great pains to preserve long and glossy. The climate of the country, the nature of their occupations, and the surroundings of their habitations contribute in no small degree to secure to them a healthy appearance and strong physique. But it is to be deplored that the race is fast deteriorating in physique. The Nairs no longer lead the active and hardy life of their ancestors. The enervating influences of an alien civilisation have sapped their powers of physical endurance. They are fast losing their virility, and the race has at present gone so far down that it has been remarked that, in regard to strength and endurance, the average Nair of to-day stands inferior to his analogue on the opposite coast".

Dress and Ornaments.—The Nāyars have always been a scantily clothed race. Perhaps the earliest notice we have of the dress of the Malayalees is that of Marco Polo in the 13th century. He observes, "Now in all this province of Malabar there is not a tailor, for the people go naked at every season. The air is always so temperate that they wear only a piece of cloth round the middle. The King is dressed just like the others, except that his cloth is finer, and he wears a necklace full set with diamonds, etc. He wears also round three parts of his body both of his arms and legs bracelets of gold, full of goodly stones and pearls."[1] This description of the dress of the average, uneducated Malayalee is as true to-day as when it was written seven centuries ago, except that the Kings of Malabar have dispensed with the bracelets that used to encircle their arms and legs.

Not long after Marco Polo, Ibn Batuta describes the King of Calicut, "the great Zamorine" coming down to the beach to see the wreck of certain junks, "his clothing consisted of a great piece of white stuff rolled about him from the navel to the knees, and a little scrap of turban on his head, his feet were bare and a young slave carried an umbrella over him"[2]. Friar Jordanus' description does not differ much from the above.

The Chinese traveller Ma Huan (1409) thus says of Cochin:—"The King wears no clothing on the upper part of his person; he has simply a square of silk wound round his loins, kept in place by a coloured waist-band of the same material and on his head a turban of yellow or white cotton cloth. The dress of the officers and the rich differs but little from that of the King."

Abdur Razak, (1442), speaking of the people of Calicut, observes that they "have the body nearly naked; they bear only bandages round the middle called *Lankoutah*, which descend from the navel to above the

1. Vol. I, p. 320
2. IV, p. 97

knee * * * * This costume is common to the King and to the beggar". [1]

In the year 1498, the Zamorin is described, on the occasion of his granting audience to Vasco Da Gama, as wearing "a short coat of fine calico strewed with branches and roses of beaten gold. The buttons were great pearls and the holes of gold thread. About his middle was a piece of white calico which reached to his knees". [2].

Barbosa also observes that the Kings of Malabar "sometimes clothe themselves with short jackets open in front, reaching half way down the thigh, made of very fine cotton cloth, fine scarlet cloth, or of silk and brocade."

Della Vella says, "The King and all others, as I have said, commonly go naked; only they have a cloth where-with they are girded, reaching to the mid leg: yet, when upon any occasion the King is minded to appear much in majesty, he puts on only a white vestment of very fine cotton, never using either cloth of gold or silk; others also when they please may wear the like garment, but not in the King's presence, in which it is not lawful for any to appear otherwise than naked, saving the cloth above mentioned".

Varthema writing of Calicut says, "the dress of the King and Queen and of all the others, *i. e.*, to-say, of the natives of the country is this:— they go naked and with bare feet, and wear a piece of cotton or of silk around the middle and with nothing on their heads. All pagans go without a shirt. In like manner, the women go naked like the men".

Ralph Fitch quaintly says, "the King goeth incached as they do all". He adds that both men and women had only "a cloth bound about their middle hanging downe to their hammes; all the rest of their bodies be naked".

1. Major p. 17
2. *Astby* p. 32

Linschoten and Caesar Fredrick both give the same description as Varthema and Fitch. Linschoten observes "they go all naked, only their middle covered, the women likewise have but a cloth from their navel downe to their knees, all the rest is naked". And Caesar Fredrick says, "these men go naked from the girdle upwards with a cloth rolled about their thighs, going bare-footed".

In the 16th century, Sheikh Zeen-ud-deen observes that the "Nairs have their bodies, for the most part exposed, wearing only a covering around their middles. In this custom, both men and women, and Kings and nobles, without exception agree".[1]

In the 17th Century, Tavernier says, "the people go quite naked, only wearing a cloth which covers his private parts. The King himself is in that respect like the least of his subjects, save that he wears a little gold in his ears".[2]

Della Vella speaking of the people of Calicut observes, "As for clothing, they need little, both men and women going quite naked, saving that they have a piece either of cotton or silk hanging down from the girdle to the knees, and covering their shame; the better sort are wont to wear two either all blue or white stripped with azure, or azure and some other colour, a dark blue being most esteemed amongst them". But, according to Neiuhoff, the men wore "a large piece of calico wrapt round their middle, which reached down to their knees, and was drawn through betwixt their thighs, and tied together behind above their buttocks". At the interview which Della Vella had with the Zamorin, there were present two little princesses of the Royal house aged about 12 years each; and of them he says, "they were all naked (as I said above, the women generally go) saving that they had a very small blue cloth wrapped about their immo-

1. *Tohfut* p. 65
2. Vol. 2, p. 247

desties". While this surprised the foreigner, the princesses themselves were in their turn not a little surprised to see the visitors bundled up as it were in a mass of clothing. For, Della Vella observes that "one of them being more forward could not contain, but approaching gently towards me, almost touched the sleeve of my coat with her hand, made a sign of wonder to her sister, how we could go so wrapped up and intangled in clothes, as we seemed to her to be; such is the power of custom that their going naked seemed no more strange to us, than our being clothed appeared extravagant to them." The King himself "was naked having only a piece of fine, changeable cotton cloth, blue and white, hanging from the girdle to the middle of the leg."

We have a fine description of the get-up of a Nāyar warrior of the higher class going forth to have single combat with his opponent in one of the well known Ballads of the North, Vaṭakkan Pāṭṭus (വടക്കൻ പാട്ടുകൾ). Speaking of Tachchōli Oṭēnan preparing himself for battle it says,

"And went to dress—a full dress.
He wore god-of-serpent's head earring
in ears,
Combed down his hair,
And wore a flower of gold over the crown.
A silk cloth round the loins,
A gold girdle over it,
Gold ring on four fingers,
A bracelet worked in with scenes
From Ramayanam and Bharatam
High up in his right arm,
A gold-handled sword in his right hand,
And a tiger-fighting shield in his left hand".

The dress of the men cannot be said to have improved much. For they still satisfy themselves with wrapping round their middle a piece of cloth between 4 and 5 cubits in length and 3 cubits in breadth. It hangs down to the ankles. They also throw on their shoulders a shorter piece which serves as a towel. Both men and women use only white cloths, and are scrupulous about these being clean and well washed. This is their ordinary dress. Their official or ceremonial dress, when attending Durbars, etc., is altogether different. Broad cloth dress suits and boots with a turban on their heads have become the ruling fashion. Formerly their official dress consisted of white flowing petticoats, a turban on their heads, the nether limbs being sometimes enclosed in white trousers or covered with two fine pieces of cloth one worn over the other, the feet being left bare.

The dress of the women did not as we have seen differ from that of the men. They simply wound round their middle a longer piece of cloth hanging down but seldom going below the knees. They felt it no shame to expose their charms by leaving the upper portion of their body above their waist uncovered. It is the custom of the country and no one feels it to be wrong. "It is not only the vulgar," remarks Forbes, "who are thus sparingly clothed; for the first princesses wear only a finer muslin, with costly jewels." Captain Alexander Hamilton, in giving an account of a visit he paid to the Kurumbarnad Raja whom he calls 'Onnitree', speaks of the "Queen and daughters of the Raja as all naked above the navel, and they were bare footed". Reference may also be made to Nieuhoff's description of the attire in which the Queen of Quilon gave him audience.

Speaking of the dress of the women of Malabar, Grose says, "the women of those countries are not allowed to cover any part of their breasts, to the naked display of which they annex no idea of immodesty, which in fact ceases by the familiarity of it to the eye. Most Europeans at their first arrival experience the force of temptation from such a nudity on the basis of the ideas to which their education and customs have habituated them: but it is not long before those impressions by their frequency entirely wear off, and they view it with as little emotion as the natives themselves, or as any of the most obvious parts of the body, the face, or hands".

"In some parts of Malabar, this custom is however more rigorously observed than in others. A Queen of Attinga, on a woman of her country coming to her presence, who having been sometime in an European settlement, where she had conformed to the fashion there, had continued the concealment of her breasts, ordered them to be cut off, for daring to appear before her with such a mark of disrespect to the established manners of the country." [1]

1. Vol. I, p. 244.

Otto Rothfeld, F. R. G. S., I. C. S., has the following remarks about Nair women in his *Women of India*:—

"Nowadays it is the women who have won the higher fame. Seldom in any country can there have been a womanhood that has received such universal eulogy. From the earliest histories of Malabar to the latest writings of French tourists, the chorus of praise has been a monody....... This careful cleanliness and a certain grave sort of neatness are indeed recurrent in every description. The bath is to them a very article of faith and they bathe not daily, but, almost it might be said, hourly...... A scrupulous cleanliness and a fastidious neatness—a total impression of almost hieratic purity—this exhales from the Nair woman like an emanation." (Pp. 82—3).

"The dress is simple in the extreme, a simple white cloth that reaches from the waist to the knee. This for long ages has been the sole honoured dress of the Nair lady, above all fear as she is and above reproach..... Sometimes, however, especially in these later days, and when she travels to other provinces, she throws a cloth over her shoulders and bosom, with a certain shyness, as of something coquettish and immodest." (P. 84.).

Mr. F Fawcett's words on the subject of dress in his *Nayars of Malabar* (pp. 197—8) bear repetition here:—

"The dress of men is very simple; ordinarily one cloth round the loins, the ends overlapping a foot or two in front. It is not tucked between the legs, which is the fashion practically all over India (of women too in many parts of Malabar), but hangs straight to the ground. It should touch the ground, or very nearly do so. Wearing a cloth in such fashion carries with it dignity to the wearer."

Custom required Nāyar women in Travancore to remove the cloth covering the upper part of their body in the presence of the Royal Family. But this was abolished by a Royal Proclamation in 1856. However, it is still thought to be a mark of respect not only for women but also for men to throw off the upper garment in the presence of their elders or superiors. The Malabar women have, no doubt, made some advance in the matter of dress. At present, a Nāyar woman ties round the loins tightly a long piece of cloth with one end passing between the legs and tucked fast to the waist behind. This reaches below the knee. Another and finer piece of cloth is worn over this, and it goes down almost to below the ankles. Over the upper part of the body a bodice or a sort of half-jacket, called *Rowkkai*, is worn, and when going abroad another piece of fine cloth is thrown over the shoulders covering the bust. This is the dress of the younger ones. The older women still stick to the former practice of simply throwing a piece of cloth over their shoulders when going abroad. In North Malabar and in South Travancore the long piece of cloth first mentioned is simply wound round the loins without the end being passed between the legs.

"In Malaber, where there is prevalent the idea that no respectable woman covers her breast, there has crept in lately, chiefly among those who have travelled a feeling of shame in respect of this custom of dress. Dress is, of course, a conventional affair, and it will be matter for regret should false ideas of shame supplant those of natural dignity such as one sees expressed in the carriage and bearing of the well-bred Nair lady."

No doubt these words will be welcome to men and women of an old, dying generation. But the modern girl, whether in or out of the school, will resent such sentiments as these, and will even be roused to anger if she were told that her ancestors went about with the upper parts of their bodies always uncovered. She has already begun to bob her black curly hair, to take to high-healed shoes and to aprons. No one wants her to go naked as of old, but it will be an evil day if she abandon the simple grace of her clean pearly white dress and ape alien fashions. *Ed.*

That old ideas regarding the dress of women are changing, giving place to new, is evident from the fact that recently[1] some young Nāyar women of Trivandrum protested to the authorities that their sense of decency prevented them from attending to their duties in the great temple at Trivandrum with their bosoms uncovered as custom required. When the image of Śri Paḍmanābha Swāmi is taken in procession round the temple every day, as also when it goes out to the sea beach at Trivandrum for Ārāṭ (bath) on the last day of the Uṭsavam, a bevy of Nāyar girls have to carry lighted brass lamps in front and in rear of the God. The custom was that, however bejewelled they might present themselves on the occasion, they should on no account have their bosoms covered. Of late the younger members of the sex seem to have revolted against this injunction and refused to appear in public with bare breasts, feeling it a shame to do so. Their attendance at processions gradually fell off, till at last there were only a few elderly women who could be persuaded with difficulty to be present at these processions. Latterly even these refused to attend. Representation had to be made to His Highness the Maharaja,[2] who, with the good sense that always characterised his acts, ordered that these women might thereafter attend the procession wearing such garments as they pleased.

As we have already observed, the practice of wearing the *Rowkkai* or bodice having become general in Malabar, Nāyar ladies had never thought it out of place in going with it to worship in temples till an unpleasant incident occurred in the temple at Ṭṛppūṇiṭṭurai, the seat of the Ruling Family of Cochin. A young decently dressed Nāyar woman of respectability chanced to be in the temple when a Princess of the Raja's family passed by. She was called on by the overzealous royal attendants to remove her upper garment to show respect to

1. The author wrote this about 25 years ago *Ed.*
2. H. H. the late Sri Mulam Thirunal Maharaja.

TWO NAYAR LADIES.

(To face p. 204.

royalty. Naturally the woman refused, and it is said that the cloth that covered the upper part of her body was attempted to be snatched away by some one. Whether this be so or not, she complained of the outrage to her guardians, and her karanavan presented a written complaint to His Highness the Maharaja.[1] No reply was forthcoming and the complainant presented himself in person and prayed for redress. He could get none. The incident gave currency to a rumour that H.H. the Raja had ordered that no Nāyar woman wearing the *Rowkkai* or bodice should be admitted within the inner precincts of temples under Sirkar management, with the result that those frequenting these temples for worship began to drop their *Rowkkai* when so employed. Rather than give up worshipping in temples, they had to reconcile themselves to the idea of going back to their old form of dress in attending them, still holding on to the new method on other occasions. It was indeed hard to believe that so enlightened and advanced a prince as H. H. the Maharaja of Cochin, who has always shown a commendable anxiety to brush aside nasty, old, meaningless forms, would countenance, much less order, such an undesirable backward step, and the Superintendent of Devaswams, *i. e.* the official head of the temple department, was approached with a view to ascertain the truth of the rumour. To an enquiry made as to whether any orders had been received or issued preventing the temple authorities from admitting into the inner precincts of Sirkar temples Nāyar women wearing the *Rowkkai*, the then Superintendent, a very intelligent Brahman gentleman and a graduate of the Madras University, made the following reply:—"I may tell you that no *written* order has been received by me prohibiting Nāyar ladies from entering the inner precincts of a temple with their *Rowkkas* on, and that the Wadakkunnatham (Trichur) Devaswam officers have not been doing anything without direction. But I understand that, after the Ṭṛppūṇiṭṭurai

1. H. H. the ex-Maharaja.

incident, no Nāyar lady has been found entering the inner precincts with her *Rowkkai*, and that this practice appears to have been followed *without any extraneous influence*.* From what transpired at Ṭṛppūṇiṭṭurai, I for one am led to think that it would be well that *Rowkkas* are discarded when a Nāyar lady enters the inner precincts of the temple, and if you do not mind to set up an example which is opposed to the current spontaneous practice". Still more recently a demi-official intimation seems to have gone forth to managers of Sirkar temples to exclude Nāyar women wearing 'Jackets' from the inner precincts of temples. This occasioned some trouble in which the Diwan seems to have interferred and, though the prohibition has not been formally recalled or cancelled, it is more honoured in its breach than in its observance.

The ingenious, but scarcely ingenuous, terms in which the above letter is couched leaves in one's mind no doubt that a more or less veiled attempt is being made by the authorities to bring into practice once more the old order of things. One can only desire that, in a matter like this, where a highly desirable reform, conducive to the advancement of morality and decency, has had its origin spontaneously from within the society affected by it itself, no external official influence should be exerted to retard the advancing tide of progress.

The incident above mentioned reminds one of what was known as the "Upper cloth" question in Travancore about the year 1859 when the women of the Shannar converts to Christianity in South Travancore claimed to wear a costume similar to that of the Brahman women. The higher classes opposing this, disturbances arose to the detriment of public tranquillity. The Missionaries set up a strong agitation on behalf of the fair sex and approached the Madras Government with a memorial. Sir Charles Trevelyan, who had then recently arrived as Governor, chivalarously espoused the

* The italics are not in the original letter.

cause of the oppressed women and wrote thus to the Resident, General Cullen:—

"I have seldom met with a case in which not only truth and justice, but every feeling of common humanity are so entirely on one side. The whole civilised world would cry shame upon us if we did not make a firm stand on such an occasion. If anything could make this line of conduct more incumbent on us, it would be the extraordinary fact that persecution of a singularly personal and delicate kind is attempted to be justified by a royal proclamation, the special object of which was to assure to Her Majesty's Indian subjects, liberty of thought and action so long as they did not interfere with the just rights of others. I should fail in respect to Her Majesty, if I attempted to describe the feelings with which she must regard the use made against her own sex of the promise of protection so graciously accorded by her.

"It will be your duty to impress these views on His Highness the Raja, and to point out to him that such prohibition as those conveyed in the Circular Order of May 1814, and in the proclamation of the 3rd February 1829, are unsuited to the present age, and unworthy of an enlightened Prince."

Not content with having despatched this strongly worded letter, His Excellency sent a more strongly worded verbal message through the Assistant Resident, Captain Heber Drury, who happened to be at Madras at about this time. "During an interview with H. E. the Governor", says Captain Drury, "he alluded among other things to the upper cloth question, and said, 'you have just come from Travancore I believe.'" I replied in the affirmative. 'You are of course aware' he continued, 'that communications have latterly been going on between the two Governments about female converts being required to wear the upper cloth.' I said I knew that discussions had taken place upon the question and that great opposition was shown by the higher castes. 'Well' he said 'when you return to

Travancore, you may tell the authorities that the affair shall be carried out on behalf of the women *even at the point of the bayonet.*' Strong words these I thought. But as the bearer of so important an injunction, I never hesitated in my duty of delivering it. Happily no bayonet was eventually required."

The dress of the Malayāli women has been very often the subject of much adverse criticism at the hands of unsympathetic foreigners. It has been denounced as immodest and unseemly. After all, dress is but a conventional affair. Ideas of modesty too are altogether relative and conventional, and, as observed by Professor Westermarck, it is not the feeling of shame that has provoked the covering, but the covering that has provoked the feeling of shame.

Westermarck observes:—"In a State where all go perfectly nude, nakedness must appear quite natural, for what we see day after day makes no special impression upon us. * * * Several travellers have noted that there is nothing indecent in absolute nakedness when the eyes have got accustomed to it. 'Where all men go naked, as for instance in New Holland' says Forster, 'custom familiarizes them to each other's eyes, as much as if they went wholly muffled up in garments.' Speaking of a Port Jackson woman who was entirely uncovered, Captain Hunter remarks, There is such an air of innocence about her that clothing scarcely appears necessary." With reference to the Uaupe's, Mr. Wallace records his opinion that 'there is far more immodesty in the transparent and flesh coloured garments of our stage dancers than in the perfect nudity of these daughters of the forest.' Describing the naked savages of Tierra del Fuego, Captain Snow says, 'An eminent historian has well observed that 'drapery may be more alluring than exposure;' and strictly speaking, so it is. Familiarity with the naked savages of different lands would, I believe, do more to

1. *Life and Sport in Southern India* by Col. Drury p. 215.

lessen particular immorality and vice than millions of sermons probably ever will or can * * * More harm, I think, is done by false modesty by covering and *partly* clothing than by the truth in nature always appearing as it is, as it is with savages of wild lands who do not clothe. This gives one, I believe, less impure and sensual feelings than the merely mixing with society of a higher kind." [1]

In his *Ethnographic Notes* Mr. Edger Thurston illustrates this by referring to the difference in behaviour of the native females of Malabar and the Tamil women of the East Coast. " A Tamil woman ," says he, " young or old and wizened, going along the high road with breasts partially uncovered by her ample body cloth, will, when she sees a European coming, pull the cloth over them from a feeling of shame in the presence of the foreigner, which is absent in the presence of her fellow countrymen. So too a Tamil or Toda woman, when undergoing the process of measurement at my hands, is most particular in arranging the upper garment so as to conceal her breasts, whereas a Malabar woman has no hesitation in appearing with breasts completely exposed, or in throwing off the slender wrapper which may cover her shoulders, and considers the exposure in no way immodest. There is but little relation between dress and conduct. If there be any, the observation made by the keen sighted Abbe' Dubois shows that in one instance at least it is not the most decently clothed that leads a most virtuous life. The learned Abbe, says 'of all the women in India, it is especially the courtesans (dancing girls or Devadasis) who are the most decently clothed, as experience has no doubt taught them that for a woman to display her charms damps sensual ardour instead of exciting it, and that the imagination is more captivated than the eye." That the idea indicated was not foreign to the women of Malabar would appear from what Mr. Elic

1. P. 192—3, *History of Human Marriage.*

Reclus says of the Tiyya women, "The women, however modest and discreet, will wear no garment above the waist; they are not prostitutes, they say, that they should cover their bosom. English ladies who engage them as nurses, have tried over and over again, in the name of British decorum, to make them wear a neckerchief but have encountered the determined resistence which they themselves would have offered had they been asked to promenade the highways unclothed."[1]

Almost all the mediaeval travellers tell us that the Nāyars, both men and women, used to grow their hair long and have it tied up on the top of the head. The women still grow their hair long and throw it tied in a knot behind, or make a beautiful looking chignon of it and place it coquettishly on the top or on the side of the head. The men have only a front tuft now, grown as long as possible, generally tied in a knot and placed on the left side of the head. This is known as the *Kudumi*. In the 16th century, Linschoten informs us that "they weare their haire as long as it will grow, tyed on the top or crowne of their heads with a lace, both men and women." So also Coeser Fredrick who says "they have their haire very long and rolled up together on the toppe of their heads." Vasco da Gama found the Zamorin "with a long dark hair all gathered up and tied on the top of his head with a knot made in it." Barbosa says, "they wear their hair tied upon the top of their heads, and sometimes Galician Casques." Tavernier observes that "the Malabaries allow their hair to grow like that of women, which they twist round the head with a small cloth having 3 points tied above."[1] Della Vella says, "Both men and women wear their hair long and tied about the head; the women with a lock hanging on one side under the ear becomingly enough as almost all Indian women do, the gallantest that I have seen in any other nation. The men have a lock down the crown of the head, sometimes a little inclined on one side; some

1. Vol. I, p. 170.

of them use a small coloured head band, but the women use none at all." Captain Hamilton speaks of the Raja Onniteree wearing "no ornament on his head, but a very beautiful head of hair hanging over his shoulders. His Queen and daughters were in the same habit only their hair was tied up behind." About the latter part of the 18th century, the men began to have their heads shaved bearing the front tuft on the crown of the head which they allow to grow long. They began also to have their faces shaved clean without having any beard or mustaches. Barbosa tells us that in his day the Nāyars used to "shave their beards and leave the mustaches very long, and after the manner of the Turks." That the people were not averse to wear long beards as they seem to be now, is evident from Della Vella's description of the Zamorin with whom he had an audience. He says, "His (*i.e.*, Zamorin's) beard was somewhat long and equally round about his face." The habit of wearing mustaches and whiskers continued till but recently in Travancore, and the mustache is once more coming into fashion there. In the Cochin State and in the Malabar District as also in Travancore, the fashion of cropping the hair on the head in the European style, and having the chin shaved close, is steadily making progress. Here too an unwritten order, or at any rate an order not duly published, of the Cochin Darbar at one time prohibited the admission into temples of those who have their hair cropped and are without their tuft. This injunction also was but seldom enforced by local authorities who seem to be partial towards this change in fashion.

Both men and women used to have their ears bored and wear them long, the larger the opening the greater the beauty! Coeser Fredrick tells us, "The Nair and their wives make great holes in their ears and so bigge and wide, that it is incredible, holding this opinion, that the greater the holes bee the more noble they esteeme themselves. I had leave of one of them to measure the circumfrence of one of them with a thread and within that circumfrence I put my arm up to the shoulder, clothed as it was, so that it was monstrous great. Thus they do make them when they be little, for then they open the ear, and hang a piece of gold or lead thread, and within the opening, in the hole they put on certain leaf that they have for that purpose, which maketh the hole so great." This is confirmed by Linschoten, who says, "The lappe of their ears are open, and are so long that they hang down to their shoulders, and the longer and wider they are, the more they are esteemed by them and it is thought to be a beautie in them." "They have horrible great ears with many rings set with pearls and stones in them," says Fitch. "They take singular pride," says Nieuhoff, "in having long ears, which they perform by art, they bore holes through the ears of both boys and girls, which they fill up with palm-tree leaves rolled together." This custom seems to have continued till the first half of the 18th century, for Grose, voyaging about this time, has the following observation, "Most of the Malabars, male and female, are particularly fond of having their ears hang almost as low as their shoulders, which is effected while they are young by boring the lobes of them, and introducing a slip of a brab tree leaf spirally folded and renewed in proportion as the whole grows wider and wider from the constant elasticity of its straightness, and when arrived at its utmost, they adorn them with ear pendants, heavy enough one would imagine to burst the gristle, in the upper part of which they also stick jewels of value according to their circumstances." At present the men do not elongate the lobes of their ears though they still bore them as any other caste Hindu. The women have not yet left off "long ears," though the tendency is to narrow the holes on the lobes. Another habit that has gone out of use is the growing of finger nails. At one time the idea was current among the Nāyars, as among the Chinese, that the long nail was a sign of their being gentlemen. We learn from Linschoten that "The Nayros weare the nails of the hand very long, whereby, they show that they are gentlemen, because the longnesse of the nails doth let and hinder men from working or doing any labour". "They say likewise that they doe it, the better and faster to gripe a thing in their hands and to hold their rapiers, which some Portugals and Mesticos doe likewise use and hold the same opinion with the Nayros, whereof there are many in India which let their nails grow for the same cause." Thus it was not mere vanity that impelled them to grow their nails. They seem to have had an eye to utility as well. Taverneir limits the growing of the nails to the left hand, and also refers to additional reasons as to why they observed the habit. "I may say," observes he, "that the Malabaries in general carefully preserve the nails of their left hands * * * * *. These nails which are sometimes half a finger long, serve them as combs, indeed they have no others." If the modern Nayar has given up the habit, the Nampūtiri has taken it up. "The Nambootiris", says the *Travancore Census-Report*, "are passionate growers of finger nails, which are in some cases more than a foot long and serve useful purposes."

Ornaments. We learn from Marco Polo that in his day the Kings of Malabar wore a necklace full set with rubies, etc. "He wears also round 3 parts, both of his arms and legs, bracelets of gold, full of goodly stones and pearls." Friar Jordanus also refers to the Malabar Kings wearing on "their arms gold and silver rings and on the neck a golden collar with a great abundance of jems." Vasco da Gama found the Zamorin rather elaborately got up for the interview he had with the prince. The Zamorin whom Della Vella interviewed "had divers bracelets on his arms, pendants at his ears, and other ornaments with many jewels and rubies of value." The King of Quilon with whom Albuquerque formed a compact from the beach at Quilon "was dressed in slik embroidered with an upper robe of gold muslin; he wore rings of considerable value, and had on his head a crimson velvet cap highly ornamented with jewels, and long chains of pearls and brilliants hanging from the top of his cap with his hair flowing loose upon his shoulders". The exiled Raja of Cochin who sought and obtained the assistance of the Dutch and who lived with them at Quilon is described by Captain Neiuhoff as "being commonly clad in white calicoe with his hair tied in a knot on the top of his head, rings on his fingers and a gold chain hanging down before him." Of the then reigning King of Torcad Nieuhoff says, "he was adorned with many jewels of diamonds and rubies which he wore on his hands, arms and ears according to the Malabar fashion." A predecessor of this prince who paid a visit to Archbishop Menezes is described as being gorgeously apparelled and covered with gold and jewels.

Of the Nāyars in general, Barbosa says, "Their ears are bored, and they wear in them very precious jewels and pearls set in gold, and on their arms from the elbows upwards gold bracelets, with similar jewels and strings of very large pearls. At their waists over their cloths they wear jewelled girdles three fingers in width, very well wrought and of great value." According to Linschoten, the ordinary Nāyar is distinguished from their chiefs by the ornaments worn by the latter. "The principallest or the chiefest of those Nayros, which are leaders or captaines of certain numbers of Nayros, wear a gold or silver bracelet or ring, about their arms, above their elbows, as also their Governours, Ambassadours, and Kings, whereby they are known from other men". Captain Nieuhoff also remarks that "for persons of the chiefest rank, if they will be admitted, in the number of the Nayros, must have the King's peculiar leave for it and are afterwards distinguished by a gold ring they wear on the right arm or by a buffalo's horn." "Both sexes," says Della Vella "have their arms full of bracelets, their ears of pendants, and their necks of jewels." At his interview with the Zamorin, the ladies of the Royal household were present. "No less full" says Della Vella, "were the higher cloisters round about of women, who stood there to behold us, amongst whom stood apart in the most eminent place the Queene, sister to the King, a woman of ripe age, clothed in blue cotton as to her lower parts and abundantly adorned with jewels". Captain Nieuhoff, who had an audience with the Queen of Quilon in March 1664, observes, "she had a guard of above 700 soldiers about her, all clad after the Malabar fashion, the Queen's attirement being no more than a piece of calicoe wrapt round her middle, the upper part of her body appearing for the most part naked, with a piece of calicoe hanging carelessly round her shoulders. Her ears, which are very long, her neck and arms were adorned with precious stones, gold rings and bracelets, and her head covered with a piece of white calicoe."

Captain Alexander Hamilton who visited Onnitree in his palace describes him as "a man of good aspect about 40 years of age, of an olive colour, his dress was only a silk lungi or scarf made fast by a girdle of gold plate about his middle that reached to his knees with great jewels of massy gold set with rubies, emeralds and pearls hanging at his ears but no ornaments on his head."

Before we proceed to refer to the ornaments that are now in use, it will be interesting to quote here two passages, one describing the get-up of the Zamorin on the occasion of Vasco da Gama's first audience with the King, and the other describing how the Nāyar women of Barbosa's time adorned themselves.

The appearance of the King at this interview is thus described: "The King was sitting in his chair which the factor" (who had proceeded Da Gama with the presents) "had got him to set upon; he was a very dark man, half-naked, and clothed with white cloths from the middle to the knees, one of these cloths ended in a long point on which were threaded several gold rings with large rubies which made a great show. He had on his left arm a bracelet above the elbow, which seemed like three rings together, the middle one larger than the others, all studded with rich jewels, particularly the middle one which bore large stones which could not fail to be of very great value. From the middle ring hung a pendent stone which glittered; it was a diamond of the thickness of a thumb; it seemed a priceless thing. Round his neck was a string of pearls, and all full of rubies, in the middle was a green stone of the size of a large bean, which, from its showiness, was of great price, which was called an emerald; and according to the information which the Castilian afterwards gave the Captain-Major of this jewel, and of that which was in the bracelet on his arm, and of another pearl which the King wore suspended in his hair, they were all three belonging to the ancient treasury of the Kings of Calicut. The King had long dark hair all gathered up and tied on the top of his head with a knot made in it; and round the knot he had a string of pearls like those round his neck, and at the end of the string a pendant pearl, pear shaped and larger than the rest, which seemed a thing of great value. His ears were pierced with large holes with many gold ear-rings of round beads. Close to the King stood a boy, his page, with a cloth round him: he held a red shield with a border of gold and jewels and a boss in the centre, of a span's breadth, of the same materials, and the rings inside for the arms were of gold; also a short drawn sword of an ell's length, round at the point, with a hilt of gold, a jewellery with pendant pearls. On the other side stood another page, who held a gold cup with a wide rim into which the King spat; and at the side of his chair was his chief Brahman who gave him from time to time a green leaf closely folded with other things inside it which the King ate and spat into the cup." [1].

Barbosa's description of the bejewelled Nāyar women is as follows:—"They assemble in the King's house, very much adorned with jewelry, gold belts,

1. *Malabar* P. 298.

pearls and many bracelets of gold, and many rings with precious stones, and ankle rings of gold on their legs and dressed from the waist downwards with very much silk stuffs and others of very fine cotton, and from the waist upwards bare, and anointed with sandal and perfumes and their hair wreathed with flowers and rings of gold and precious stones in their ears, the feet bare as they always are accustomed to do."

With the latter description may be compared the account of the dress of the southern Malabar women of the latter part of the 18th century, as given by Forbes:—"The dress of the Malabar women is similar to that of the other sex; their black glossy hair, tied in a knot on the middle of the head, is copiously anointed with cocoanut oil and perfumed with the essence of sandal, mogrees and champakas; their ears, loaded with rings and heavy jewels, reach almost to their shoulders, this is esteemed a beauty; instead of a small gold wire in the orifice, as is practised in the other countries, a filament from the cocoanut leaf, rolled around, is placed in the incision, the circles are increased, until the orifice sometimes exceed 2 inches in diameter, the ear is then healed, and, being stretched to the perfection of beauty, is filled with rings and massy ornaments. Round the waist they wear a loose piece of muslin, while the bosom is entirely exposed; this is the only drapery of the Malabar women, but they are adorned with a profusion of gold and silver chains for necklaces, mixed with strings of Venetian and other gold coins; they have also heavy bangles or bracelets; a silver box, suspended by a chain on one side, forms a principal ornament, and contains the areca or betel nut, with its appendages of chunnam, spice, and betel leaf. Their skin is softened by aromatic oils especially among the Nairs and Tetees, who are peculiarly attentive to cleanliness in their persons." [1]

The men do not at present indulge much in the use of ornaments. Most of them except certain clans

1. Page 249.

wear ear-rings or Kaṭukkans. These are made of gold generally, and as many as six are worn in each ear by people about Palghat. Ear-rings set with precious stones such as diamonds and rubies as also with pearls are in use. Gold rings set with precious stones adorn their fingers. A girdle made of gold or silver round the waist, to which the *langoti* is tied, is also of common occurrence. Beyond these the only ornament now worn is a watch and chain by those who have to don official costume.

The fair sex, as among all classes, is particularly partial to personal ornamentation. There are ornaments for the ear, the nose, the neck, the arms, the waist, the ankles, but none to adorn the head or the forehead as among the Tamil women. The ear ornament is, in the south, the Ṭakka, made of gold, cylindrical in form with a circular face, in some cases set with precious stones. These are inserted in the large holes made in the lobes of the ears. In the north its place is taken by the Ṭōṭa. This is "a two-lipped bi-converse disc holding the inside of the ear-lobes in its circumfrential groove." On the front surface, sometimes, precious stones, such as rubies and diamonds, are set. Otherwise they are elaborately carved with leaves and flowers. The Ṭōṭa and the Ṭakka are also going out of fashion with the abandonment of the elongated ear-lobes. Preference is given to the Kammal which requires only a mere punching of the lobe. The left nasal cartilege is bored and a nose screw inserted to which is attached a pendant. The former is known as Mūkkūṭṭi, and the latter as ñāṭṭu; both these are set with stones. There are certain classes or clans of Nāyars among whom the women do not bore the nose or wear a nose ornament, saying that it is *infra dig*. For the neck there are various sorts of ornaments. Some of them are the Nāgapaṭam (snake's hood) from the shape of its gold pendant, the Nālupanṭi, a necklace elaborately worked in four strings, the Kaṇṭaśaram, the Arimpu Maṇi, the Mampu Māla, the Ṭanḍum Mōṭiram, the

Enṭṟam Kol̄al, the Pūṭṭāli, etc. All of these, however, are displaced or are in course of being displaced by the Aḍḍiyal and Paṭakkam, the simple gold thread to which a small crescent shaped ornament set with precious stones is attached and the Pachchakkal Ṭāli or necklace set with green stones. These have become the fashion of the day. Bracelets of various designs made of gold are worn round the arms. Some of these are set with precious stones. The old patterns that were thick and profusely carved have given place to plain ones. The Kāppu and Gulusu have also been adopted. The Kachappuram or Arañjāl, made of gold or silver in chain pattern worn round the waist, has given place to gold and silver Zones or Uḍḍyāñam of the East Coast. No anklets are worn by Nāyar women in the middle countries. But in the south and in the north, the younger folk are taking to the Pāḍasaram and the Kolusu. Elderly women satisfy themselves with a thick gold thread to which is attached a Ṭāli or ñāli pendant set with stones. They may have a finger ring or two. Those who are religiously inclined wear round their necks Ruḍrākṣham or Ṭulasi mounted in gold in the shape of necklaces, the pendant to which in the case of Ruḍrākṣham being what is called *Gouri Sankar* (Śiva and Pāṟvaṭi.)

Habitation and Furniture. We have given elsewhere a description of the houses inhabited by the Nāyars in general. It will not be uninteresting to quote here a fine description of a Nāyar house of the better class given by Col: James Welsh in his *Military Reminiscences*.

"On the 20th of September, I left Calicut for the residence of my Wynad friend Kalpilly Canarahmenoen,[1] which is about 12 miles distant in a south-easterly direction and six from the sea-shore."

"In the middle of a most fertile and extensive valley, the estate of my friend stands conspicuous for cultivation. His house is on the western side of a long

1. Kanara Menon's house was near Feroke, near Calicut.

range of paddy ground, the property of his family, and two of his brothers are the principal farmers. Being nearly square, the whole compound is surrounded with a high mud wall, covered with shrubs at the top to protect it from the violence of the rain, having one entrance to the eastward, through a very neat upstair building, the lower part being the portico and situated in the centre of the wall. There are also two separate houses beyond this, and various smaller buildings surrounded by a well-stocked garden. This place of abode in peaceful times is common to all the Nāyars of rank and property in Malabar; and the saying so common in England, that 'every man's house is his own castle', is completely verified here, for this and many other Nayars houses, might be defended by 20 resolute men, against thousands without guns, and even four days against field pieces only. On the top of the *porte cochere*,[1] I took up my abode for four days." [2]

As for their furniture, this is but scanty. Speaking of the Kings of Malabar, Barbosa says, "when they are in their houses they always sit on high benches; these benches are very smooth, and are slightly smeared once every day with cowdung, and they keep there a stand very white and 4 fingers high and a cloth of brown wool undyed, after the manner of

1. Purathu Kacheri=out-office.

2. "The general picture of grave and simple purity of the women of Malabar is heightened by their houses, each aloof and separate with a certain quiet dignity in its own grounds. A bathing-tank and a garden, these are the first conditions of every household; and the garden is luxuriant with the great rough stems of the jack-fruit tree, the graceful areca and cocoanut palms and the bright green broad leaved banana plants. * * The house itself, with its large household all related through the female line, has its kitchen and store-room, an open court-yard and a large dining hall, and apartments for men and women segregated entirely one from the other. In such houses, a certain quiet discipline and an instinctive order, from being a duty, becomes a constant habit. Comfort and tranquility, if they are to be had, exact self-effacing restraint and gentle deference to other's wishes and requirements." Mr. Otto Rothfeld's *Woman of India*, pages 83 and 84.

A TYPICAL NAMBUTHIRI ILLAM (HOUSE).

a carpet of the size of a horse-cloth folded in 3 folds; and upon this they sit, and they lean upon pillows, round and long, of cotton, of gold and silk and they also sit on carpets of cloth of gold and silk but they always keep under them, or near them, that cloth of brown wool, on account of their sect, and for state. And frequently they happen to be lying on couches and cushions of silk and very fine white sheets, and when any one comes to see them they bring him this brown woollen cloth and put it near him, and when he goes out, a page carries the cloth folded before him for state and ceremony."[1] Barbosa is evidently referring to Pulpāya, a kind of very fine mat in variegated colours and designs made of a sort of grass. They are of very soft texture and a speciality of Malabar that is much admired.

Bartolomeo's account of the furniture used by the poorer class of Nāyars in their households is true of the generality of Nayars of that sort even today. He says, "Their whole furniture consists of a *Kattila*, or bed-frame, on which a mat is placed; a few flat dishes of copper or brass; a *Kindi*, or brass drinking vessel with a spout; a pot or kettle, in which they boil their rice: a *Vilacca*, or round lamp of iron or brass, fastened to a chain, by which it can be suspended in the middle of the hut; and a large wooden mortar, in which they pound their *Nella*, or unshelled rice."[2] He remarks that "though the Indians see daily before them the furniture and cooking utensils of the Europeans, they have never yet thought proper to make use of them. The customs prevalent among them three thousand years ago still remain unchanged." However the long felt want of change has now begun to set in.

Chairs, tables, sofas, and almirahs, cups, saucers, china and glassware are of common use. The old brass lamps have given place to kerosine lights, specially

1. Pages 104—105
2. Pages 155—6

because cocoanut oil has gone up in price. While the poor people use kerosine fed tin lights, the higher classes use glass lamps and shades. Amongst the educated classes who have had the benefit of western ideas tolerably well furnished drawing rooms of European pattern are common.

Food and drink. As a class the Nāyars are not strict vegetarians, though those who affect superiority ostentatiously avoid flesh meat. Varthema says of the "Pagans" of Calicut that they do not eat flesh without the permission of the Brahmans. He adds that "the other classes of the people eat flesh of all kinds, with the exception of cow-beaf." Varthema tells us that hog's flesh was served at a Hindu ruler's public feasts while the Mahomedan Chinese traveller Ma Huan speaks of a potentate making a bargain with the Mahomedans that he would leave off the use of hog's flesh if the Mahomedans of that place, on their parts gave up eating beaf. Of their food and the mode of taking it, Varthema says "The said Pagans eat on the ground in a metal basin and for a spoon make use of the leaf of a tree (the jack tree) and they always eat rice and fish and spices and fruits. The two classes of peasants eat with the hand from the pipkin, they hold the hand over the pipkin and make a ball of rice, and then put it into their mouths."

We have an accurate description of the food of the Malabar people and the way in which they take it given us by Fra Bartolomeo. We make no apology for quoting it here *in extenso*. "The Indians (meaning Malayalees), after the manner of all the oriental nations, never eat at noon. In the morning, before they go out to labour, they generally take their *cangi* or beverage, consisting of water in which a certain quantity of rice has been boiled till all its mealy, nourishing, and cooling particles are dissolved. After this breakfast they proceed to their labour and continue it without interruption till about 4 o'clock. An hour after or sometimes later, they take their evening meal; go to sleep at sun-set, and rise next morning at break of day. This mode of life is perfectly agreeable to the nature of man, for whom the elements and heavenly bodies were created. It not only saves the Indians a great deal of oil, but secures to them agreeable repose and preserves their bodies healthful. The day and the night are almost always of the same length near the equator, and therefore they seldom or never depart from the above regular course. The women are obliged to cook and to place the dishes on the table. The husband and wife never eat together, for the Indians consider it as indecent and contrary to that respect which is due to the former. The consequence is, that their meals are very short: and that nothing takes place in the presence of the rest of the family which can offend against decency or good manners. At table they use merely the right hand; for the left, with which they wash the lower part of the body etc., they look upon as unclean. The rice is served up on a broad banana leaf, which supplies the place of a dish, and near it is placed the *Karil* (curry), that is, soup which consists of herbs fruit, pepper and cardamoms. It is exceedingly well prepared; has a delicious smell and a pungent taste. This soup they pour, at different times, over the rice, which in very small morsels they put into their mouth with the right hand. If they have no *Kail* or spoon they employ in its stead a *Mava* (jack or *Pilava*?) leaf rolled together. When their meal is finished, they throw away their dish and spoon, because leaves of the like kind may be everywhere found. Persons of condition, however, employ at their meals vessels of copper and brass, which they keep remarkably clean, and which are always washed after they have been used. They eat along with their rice sour milk and butter or herbs which have been baked in butter or oil. The King of Travancore has generally at his table fifteen different kinds of soup, which are varied from time to time. He eats also preserved nutmegs with his rice, which of itself has an excellent and aromatic taste.

During their meals, the Indians sit down on a mat spread out on the floor, and according to oriental custom, place their legs across each other under them. They drink nothing but water; and when they wish to quench their thirst, they pour it from their Kindi, or drinking vessel, directly into their throat, without letting it touch their lips" [1]

On occasions such as the celebration of marriages, anniversaries of births and deaths, etc., the Princes, chiefs and the wealthy men of Malabar give grand entertainments to the public. We have a rather amusing description of such feasts given us by Grose. He says, "The Princes and chiefs of the Malabar dominions, and especially the Zamorin of Calicut, often on particular occasions, and festival days, make entertainment to which the whole country round is invited, and where the quantity rather than the quality of the victuals provided, inflames the charge of them, being chiefly rice, the pea-like grain of dhall, with the sauce of turmeric, cocoanut, and other vegetables, all which articles, are in those parts extremely cheap, and the beverage is never but pure water. They are however, literally speaking, cramming matches, for it is not uncommon for some of the guests, tempted by the free cost of them, to overcharge their stomachs, so as to die under it this is treated by the rest as a matter of pleasantry, and when they mean to celebrate the magnificence of any such feast they do it by telling the numbers that burst at it."[2]

The Nāyars seldom indulge in rich food. Rice is their staple food and it is taken at least twice a day. The water in which it is boiled is strained, and the rice is served on a plantain leaf or a metal plate. The higher classes use a little ghee at morning meals, which generally come off before mid-day. Ordinarily the rice will be accompanied by curries made of vegetables or meat, sauces, pickles, and pappaṭams, etc. All

1. Pages 158—59.
2. Vol. I, p. 257.

these are served along with the rice on the plantain leaves. The course of the meals is first to mix a portion of the rice with ghee and dhall, make it into small balls, and put them into the mouth with the right hand, the left hand being strictly forbidden. Then the remaining portion of rice is similarly dealt with, it being mixed with the curries served, each curry being used separately. After this is over, rice is served a second time. This is mixed with curds or butter-milk, well macerated, made into balls and taken as mentioned before. Pickles and sauces are used more freely with this second course. A small and elegant brass vessel with a spout holds the drinking water which is always boiled along with a little coriander, cummin seeds, dried ginger,etc. The vessel is always placed on the left side and, as occasion requires, it is taken with the left hand, and the water poured into the mouth through the spout, which should on no account touch the lips. The ordinary meal ends with a draught of drink. On festive occasions, besides a large number of curries, sauces, etc., there are *Payasams*, *Prathamans*, fruits, etc., served. *Payasams* and *Prathamans* are various kinds of sweet puddings, and these are served as the last course. Fruits, though served along with the curries, are generally taken last. The evening meal or supper comes on between 7 and 9 *p. m.*, and is almost of the same kind as the morning one, only less elaborate and of course less heavy. Before the regular morning meal people used to have a light breakfast, taking *Kanji* or rice gruel early in the morning. Among the higher classes, imbued more or less with western ideas, the morning *Kanji* has given place to tea, coffee, or cocoa, and lunch has also come into vogue. About three in the evening, tea, coffee, or cocoa, is taken with something solid, such as bread or biscuits. Friar Jordanus has, in the beginning of the 14th century, remarked that "the people of this India (Malabar) are very clean in their feeding."[1]

1, Chap. 4.

Barbosa assures us that, in the early part of the 16th century, the Nāyars were not addicted to spirituous liquors. But whether introduced by the Portuguese or not, the vice of drink gradually insinuated itself till at last it came to have a firm hold on Malabar and, in Travancore, had to be interdicted on pain of forfeiture of property. Fra Bartolomeo says, "in the year 1787, Rāma Varma, the King of Travancore, issued an order by which the use of *Tagara* that is, palm-brandy, was prohibited, under pain of the confiscation of property. At *Pullingune* (Pulinkunnu) a woman was condemned to the besom, and her house confiscated, because, contrary to this prohibition, she had sold *Tagara* (ṭāvaram). The contempt which the Indians entertain for the Europeans arises chiefly from the latter being so much addicted to drinking. For this reason also they are called Ciandeler or Nisher; that is contemptible, impure, unclean people". When Forbes wrote, the Nāyars of Travancore abstained from intoxicating liquors. The use of all sorts of intoxicants is strictly prohibited by the Hindu religious laws.

We do not know if opium and bhang were in use in Malabar before they were imported by western nations, but Pyres, writing from Cochin to King Emmanuel of Portugal in the year 1516, enumerates "the opium of Egypt and Cambay and Cous [*i. e.*, Kūch Behar] in Bengal", adding that "the Kings and Lords eat of it and even the common people". According to Barbosa, opium was imported into Calicut from Cambay and Aden. In the year 1711, Lockyer tells us that the price of opium at Calicut was "160 fanams per candy". In 1726, Alexander Hamilton notes, "The Chief of Calicut for many years have vended between 500 and 1000 chests of Bengal opium yearly up in the inland countries where it is much used". The Nāyars who fought the Dutch at the seige of Cochin are said to have been primed with intoxicants. "They use *amfion* very greedily. They take the quantity of the bigness of a pea, this they either mix with arrack or chew it alone. When they are to attack, they take a good quantity of it", says the Dutch Captain Nieuhoff. The first article of the treaty entered into by Captain Nieuhoff on behalf of the Dutch East India Company and the Kings of Marta, Singnaty, Gouree, Travancore, and Barruyetta Pole (all in modern Travancore), on the 21st February 1664, provides that "Nobody shall import, sell or exchange any Amfion (opium) into these countries, except the Dutch East India Company". Fra Bartolomeo informs us that in his day the *Amochie*, "Nairs who have resolved to sacrifice their lives to serve their King, their country, or any person whose cause they have undertaken to espouse", used to be intoxicated with opium dissolved in lemon juice or any acid solvent. He adds that, "when prepared in this manner and taken, it renders men bloodthirsty, converts them into savage beasts, and inspires them with such fury, that they would rather suffer themselves to be cut to pieces than give up the weapon which they have in their hands."

"Formerly," continues Bartolomeo, "there were a great many of these *Amochie* on the coast of Malabar, but since the king of Travancore prohibited the natives from drinking cocoanut brandy, called *Tagara*, to smoke *Kangavu* (Bhang), and to use opium prepared as above mentioned, such ravenous animals in the human form became uncommon; and should any one venture, in so horrid a manner, to disturb the tranquillity of the public, he would be instantly punished with death. Some persons however, who were at *Civacada* (Chowghat) during the war against Tippu, assured me that they had seen several *Amochie* among his troops; but it is certain, beyond a doubt, that he forbade the use of opium to his soldiers, because the *Amochie* in their fury spare neither friend nor foe, but destroy every person who comes in their way."[1]

At present, though intoxicants are not in general use among the Nāyars, it cannot be denied that both arrack and opium are consumed by the lower orders while, among the higher classes, and more specially

1. P. 407.

among the English educated, a glass of brandy and soda is steadily coming into general practice. What is to be deplored is that the habit, once confirmed, does not stop with a single glass, and the difference between drinking and getting drunk is seldom kept in view. We have had instances of many a bright career being cut short too early by a too free indulgence in spirituous liquors; and, unless the pernicious habit is nipped in the bud, it will indeed be a national calamity.

Occupation. We have in the prior volumes already referred to the traditional occupation of the Nayars, as 'protection' which involved 'fighting' and 'supervision'. The Portuguese Virgil, Luis de Camoens, has, in his epic poem, *The Luciad*, a few lines concerning the Nayars with whom he came in personal contact three-and-a-half centuries ago.

"Polias the labouring lower class are named;
By the proud Naires the noble rank is claimed;
The toils of culture and of art they scorn;
The Warrior's plumes their haughty brows adorn;
The shining faulchion brandish'd in the sight,
Their left arm wields the target in the fight;
Of danger scornful, ever armed they stand
Around the King, a stern barbarian hand."[1]

Johnathan Duncan, a Governor of Bombay, who visited Malabar in 1792—3, thus observes with reference to these lines: "These lines....contain a good description of a Nair, who walks along, holding up his naked sword with the same kind of unconcern as travellers in other countries carry in their hands a cane or walking staff. I have observed others of them have it fastened to their back, the hilt being stuck in their waist band and the blade rising up and glittering between their shoulders."

"The Nairs, the Nareae of Pliny[2] were the swordsmen, the military caste of the west coast of India. There

1. Mickle's translation, London, 1798.
2. Nat. Hist. VI, 21,

SOME OF THE WEAPONS OF THE OLD NAYAR WARRIORS.

(To face p. 229.

are small sects or castes intervening, but, broadly speaking, the Nairs rank after the Nambutiris in Malabar, and they occupy the same position in the Native States of Cochin and Travancore".[1]

Caesar Fredericke who was in Malabar in 1563 writes of them in the same strain. "These men go naked from the girdle upwards, with a clothe rolled about their thighs, going barefooted, and having their haire very long and rolled up together on the toppe of their heads, and always they carrie their Bucklers or Targets with them and their swordes naked".[2]

Dr. E. Thurston has, in his *Caste and Tribes of Southern India*, this extract on the subject from Duarte Barbosa.[3] "The Nairs are the gentry and have no other duty than to carry on war, and they continually carry their arms with them, which are swords, bows, arrows, bucklers and lances. They all live with the Kings, and some of them with other lords, relatives of the Kings, and lords of the country, and with salaried governors, and with one another. They are very smart men, and much taken up with their nobility.... These Nairs, besides being all of noble descent, have to be armed as knights by the hand of a King or Lord with whom they live."

"The only British General of any note—Sir Hector Munro—who had ever to face the Nairs in the field thus wrote, in the Tellicherry Factory Diary of 1761, of their modes of fighting: "One may as well look for a needle in a Bottle of Hay as any of them in the day time, they being working behind sand-banks and bushes, except when they are marching towards the Fort, and then they appear like bees out in the month of June.... Besides which, they point their guns well and fire them well also."[4]

1. Mr. Fawcett's "Nairs of Malabar", p. 1.
2. P. 207 in Sir H. Risley's "The People of India."
3. P. 288, Vol. V.
4. Logan's Malabar Manual, p. 140.

Men who exposed to certain death on great occasions been called Amoucos by the Portuguese; and Barbosa alluded to the practice as a prevalent custom among the Nāyars. These two extracts from Hobson-Jobson, of Yule and Burnell are to the point:[1] "The King of Cochin hath a great number of gentlemen which he called Amochi, and some are called Nairi these esteem not their lives anything, so that it may be for the honour of the King".[2] "If the Prince is slain, the Amochi who are numerous would avenge him desperately. These are soldiers who swear to defend the King's life with their own."[3] The Malayalam term for these men is Chāvēttu-viruttikkār. These were given lands free of tax for undertaking to defend the King with their own lives. The Nāyars formed a huge militia, and, till regular standing armies were organised, were entrusted with the protection of the land. While not fighting, they engaged themselves in agricultural and other occupations. In their capacity of supervisors or *Kanakars*, it was their duty to see the lands of the Brahmans demised to them properly cultivated. In the 16th century, Linschoten speaks of the "Nayros" as "Noblemen or Gentlemen" which are soldiers that do only warre and handle arms." Pyrard de Laval speaks of them as "lords of the land living on the pension allowed them by the King." Nieuhoff describes them as "descended from noble families and brought up to the ware" In Nieuhoff's time, there were learned men among them, but no traders; for he observes, " some apply themselves to philosophy, but especially astronomy, but never to traffick or any handicraft trade". He adds, "Those Nayros, who are watching at the town gates and serve for conductors to travellers, are the poorest of all, yet will they rather follow this employment than a trade which they look upon as below their

1. 2. A. D. 1566. M. Caesar Fredericke in Purchas.

3. P. Vincenzo Maria N. Viaggo ail 'India Oriental del P.' pp. 237—2.

quality." "Nairs of the ancient type were so many Spartan warriors," says Mr. Elei Reclus, "so many knights of a court of Love. All knew at least how to read and write, but the chief part of their education was carried on in the gymnasium and the fencing-school where they learnt to despise fatigue, to be careless of wounds, and to show an indomitable courage, often bordering upon foolish temerity." Again, "war and gallantry! Love and battle! My sword and my mistress! These were their devices and they were ticklish sticklers for the point of honour." These words briefly but characteristically describe the Nāyars of the chivalrous times of old. In these days of peace, the Nāyar has settled himself down into a family man, engaging himself in various walks of life. We have already seen that various occupations of life were assigned to various classes in the social hierarchy, and that these really determined the original sub-divisions. Thus there are, (1) Illakkār or servants of the Illoms, or Brahman houses; (2) Swarūpakkār, or servants of Kṣheṭriya houses; (3) Pāḍamangalakkār or temple servants; (4) Tamil Pādakar, miscellaneous employees; (5) Eṭacheri Nāyars, or dealers in dairy produce; (6) Mārans, or temple musicians; (7) Aṭṭikkuruchies, or undertakers; (8) Chempukoṭṭies, or copper smiths; (9) Ōṭaṭṭu Nāyars, or tile makers, (10) Kalam Koṭṭis, or potters; (11) Vaṭṭakāṭans, or oil mongers; (12) Pallichans, or bearers of palanquins; (13) Cheṭṭīs, or traders in vegetables and other domestic necessaries, (14) Chālians or weavers; (15) Veluṭṭēṭen, or washerman, and (16) Velekaṭṭalavans, or barbers. There are some more sub-divisions representing other professions. Thus every profession necessary for the enjoyment of life in a village is assigned to a sub-division. With the advance of civilization on lines other than those originally sketched by men of old, there has been a disruption of professions. The members of the various classes above enumerated do not at present follow the professions traditionally assigned to them.

The rigorous exclusiveness of the caste system is such that, while it will not stand in the way of members of one caste or sub-divisions of a caste training themselves and adopting in life some profession outside the socio-religious arrangement peculiar to it, it will on no account allow any member of a caste or a sub-division to trespass upon the profession of another caste or sub-division. For instance, a Puṭuvāl or Vārier may train himself and exercise the profession of a lawyer, and so may a Nāyar. But the Nāyar will on no account be allowed to adopt the traditional profession of a Vārier or Puṭuvāl, that of temple service. In the same way, a Nambūṭiri and a Veluṭṭeṭan may both exercise the profession of medicine, but neither of them can exercise the traditional profession of the other. The Nambuṭiri can be no more a washerman than a Veluṭṭēṭan a priest. Thus at present the Nāyars have taken to all such professions as would not involve degradation of caste. Despite the rigours of the caste system and the peculiarly superstitious rules that are enforced by certain native rulers of Malabar,—witness the excommunication from caste recently of a Nāyar gentleman in the Cochin State, who had proceeded to England and had distinguished himself in the University of Cambridge—those Nayars who can afford it, make themselves bold to cross the ocean and proceed to England, Japan and other foreign lands for purposes of education. Of late, caste rules seem to sit somewhat lightly on them, and they have shown an adaptability to circumstances that is a good sign of the way to progress. The following extract from the *Cochin Census Report* fairly represents their present condition:—"Their general intelligence, independence of character, and adaptability to circumstances have not been less admired by foreigners who have come across them. Their present condition may be best described in the words of my predecessor in office, who wrote as follows in 1891:

"No class of the community is availing itself so much of the benefits of modern education as the Nairs,

SIR K. RAMUNNI MENON, M. A. (CANTAB)
VICE - CHANCELLOR OF
THE MADRAS UNIVERSITY.

(To face p. 232.

who are fast becoming conspicuous in every literate walk of life. In every department of the State and in all the learned professions, they form a respectable majority, and the only people who successfully compete with them in this respect are the Brahman immigrants from the other coast. While a large number of the Nayars have thus exchanged the sword for the pen, a still larger number have exchanged it for the plough. Excepting Government service and the learned professions, agriculture and domestic service are almost the only pursuits in which they are largely engaged. Among them there are extensive landholders and substantial farmers, but a large body of them are comparatively poor, and are either petty farmers or agricultural labourers. Domestic servants in well-to-do caste Hindu families are almost wholly Nayars, but none of them are artisans, weavers, or potters."

Home life habits and manners. The peculiar constitution of the Nāyar family is such that it consists of the common ancestress and her descendants in the female line including sons and daughters. Inheritance and succession to property is always in the maternal line descending through females. In the following illustration M stands for mother, S for son and D for daughters.

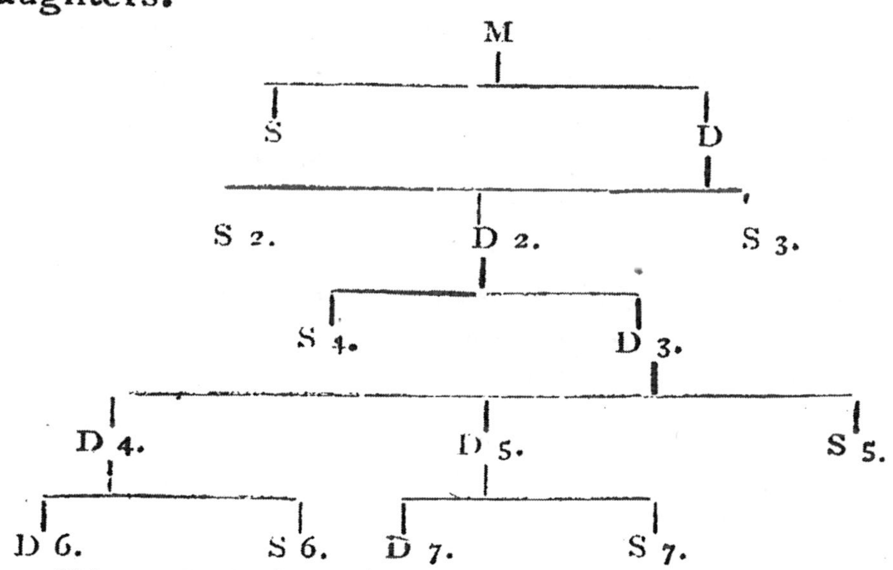

Though descent is traced from the mother and goes down through daughters, the family is controlled and governed by the Kāraṇavar, that is the senior male, who represents the family or Ṭarawād. His position is such that it has been judicially declared that "a Malabar family speaks through its head and, in courts of justice, except in antagonism to that head, can speak in no other way." A mother and an elder sister are always honoured members, who take an active part in the internal government of the family, and are not seldom consulted in the management of the Ṭarawād property. It has been so from early days. "These Nairs", observes Barbosa, "show much respect to their mothers and support them with what they gain * * * They also have much respect for their elder sisters whom they treat as their mothers." The younger female members too are treated with much consideration. The elder male members do not mingle in their company, or hold free conversation with them. Nayar women were never *ghosha* and were never shut up in the innermost recesses of the Zenana. So long ago as the 16th century, Sheik Zeen-ud-deen has observed "Neither do they (the Nāyars) conceal their women from the sight of any one ; for whilst the females of the Brahman caste are kept veiled from sight, the Nairs adorn their women with jewels and fine clothes and bring them to their great assemblies." We learn from Forbes that Nāyar women used to attend the Ōṇam tournaments. As we know from Della Vella, at the interview which the Portuguese Captain had with the Zamorin, two of his nieces were present besides the female members of the Zamorin's family viewing the scene from the gallery. Captain Alexander Hamilton, on paying a formal visit to King Onnitree, was received by the King, his "Queen" and grown-up daughters. Hamilton says, "The Queen had a cheerful countenance, very affable to us and others who had the honour to stand near her, distributing betel and arrecca with her own royal hands, to strangers who came as we did to compliment the prince, her husband—" the occasion was "a visit paid him by all his tributaries and friends to wish him many happy years, it being his birthday." Unlike the Nambūtiri women, they move about freely just as the East Coast Brahman women do.

In a well-ordered Tarawad of the orthodox type, the domestic concerns are controlled by the eldest female—generally the mother. The younger females attend to the cooking, the keeping of the house scrupulously clean, etc. The elderly women get up early in the morning before dawn, see the house swept clean, and sprinkled with water in which a little cowdung is mixed. A brass lamp well cleaned and burnished is lighted and kept in front of the *Ara* or granary in the centre of the house, and is not removed till sun-rise. The children of the house also get up early, clean their teeth, wash their faces, rub sacred ashes on their forehead, breast, and shoulders, and keep on repeating prayers till dawn, the elderly ladies leading them in the repetition of the prayers. By dawn the yards around the house will also have been cleaned by those employed for it and sprinkled with water and cowdung. Then comes the cleaning of the kitchen. Before cooking begins, the floor and the ovens are smeared with cowdung, the ashes and rubbish of the previous night are all removed, and the cooking vessels and other utensils well washed. The morning *Kanji* is first cooked and served. Meanwhile, those who attend to the regular cooking work bathe themselves and generally go and worship in the nearest temple. As soon as they return, they proceed to their work. The chief meal of the day is served between 10 and 12 a. m., the supper between 7 and 9 p. m. The males of the family return to their own houses from those of their wives early in the morning. It has to be remarked here that generally the females live with their mother in their own houses and are there visited by their husbands. In the mornings, after taking *Kanji*, they go about their business and return in time for meals. Both men and women bathe before their meals, especially when they have had occasion to touch or approach any of the lower classes. As Linshoten observes, " when they are once touched by any polayans or by any other nation except Nayros, they must (before they eat or converse with the Nayros) wash and clean their bodies with great ceremonies and superstitions." For this purpose he says " in every place where they dwell, they have a pit or well digged, wherein they hold water, which standeth openly in the way, where every man passeth by, wherein every morning when they rise they wash themselves * * *. It must be in a place where the water standeth in pit or well, and by their Brahmanes conjured with many words and ceremonies, otherwise it were of no virtue but wholly unprofitable."

An oil bath is a peculiar feature of a Nāyar's daily life. Those who can afford it anoint their bodies and heads with oil of sesamum every day. Some have medicated oils of great value for their heads known as Kāchiya Eṇṇā, literally boiled oil, and Koïampu for their bodies. Many use these on alternate days, while the great majority anoint their bodies twice a week on Wednesdays and Saturdays. After anointing, they wash themselves and rub their skin with a plant called Incha (Acacia Intsia) the rind of which has alkaline properties which remove all filth and the oil. For washing off the oil on their head, they use the leaves of various plants, herbs and creepers which possess the property. This ablution and friction strengthen the body and at the same time prevent too violent perspiration.

The children also are bathed in the morning and taken to the temple for worship, and, after they have had their *Kanji*, are either sent to the nearest pyal school, or are taught by an Aśān or tutor employed for the purpose in their houses. The course of instruction takes them through the alphabets, elementary grammar, arithmetic, and a little Sanskrit. Those who are inclined to pursue the higher course of Sanskrit will have to look for it elsewhere. In rich families, there will be provision made for advanced studies too. After the mid-day meal, the males, especially the elders, retire for a short siesta. The Kāraṇavar would, after the siesta is over, take his seat at the portico or Pūmukham of the house and the Ananḍravers or juniors would respectfully stand in his presence. No junior takes his seat before his senior. The family affairs are here discussed and audience given to tenants who have business to transact. The day's business being over, they separate, each wending his way. The women, after their mid-day meal is finished, employ themselves in domestic matters; the younger ones spending their time in singing and dancing (Kaikoṭṭik-kaḷi) or reading the vernacular renderings of the Purāṇās such as the Bhāgavaṭam, Rāmāyaṇam, Bhāra-ṭam, etc. Towards evening, the house is once more swept clean and sprinkled with cowdung and water; so are the yards. The lamps are cleaned and lit, and the women and children wash themselves in the tank and proceed to the temple in gay attire. On their return, the children sit in front of the lighted lamp along with the elderly women, and go on reciting prayers for an hour or so. Then follows the reading of the Rāmāyaṇa or Bhāgavaṭa in Malayālam. This is read out in a long-drawn, loud, musical tone, and the children follow the lead in turn. When this is over, the children take their supper, and retire to rest. By this time the males will have, after their ablutions, come ready for their supper, and they are served. Supper over, the Kāra-ṇavar calls the servants of the house and orders them to see that the outer doors of the house are shut and secured, and enjoins on them the necessity to keep a watchful eye during the night. By this time a servant with a light, generally a torch made of dried cocoanut leaves, will be ready to accompany the Kāraṇavar to his wife's house, which, under ordinary circumstances, is situated not far away. Before leaving, the Kāraṇavar will see that the Anandaravars get his orders as to what they are to do the next day. The Anandaravars, one by one, then leave the house, each taking a light, to go to his wife's house. Meanwhile, the husbands of the women of the house will be gradually dropping in. By 10 p. m. the whole house would have taken supper, and retired to rest.

The Nāyars, both men and women, have the inveterate habit of chewing betel. The Kāraṇavars of the old school carry about them, wherever they go, their *chellam* or betel-box made sometimes of silver but generally of bell-metal. The habit of chewing betel is still prevalent. Though it colours the teeth, giving to them a dark, reddish hue, the betel is so much relished that even the English educated Nāyar feels it difficult to withstand its allurements. Nieuhoff informs us that "all the Malabars have black teeth, occasioned by the continual chewing of the leaves of the betel."; "A few fine leaves of the betel vine are smeared with chunnam rolled up and put into the mouth first. Then pieces of arecca nut sliced with a knife follow. After these are slightly masticated, a piece of tobacco is put in and the whole thing is chewed. The saliva excited would be of reddish black colour and is spat out. Camphor and other aromatic ingredients are also added at times. Though the habit of chewing betel is still in the ascendant, great care is taken to remove the colour caused thereby by constantly cleaning the teeth. Every morning, as a part of the ablutions of the day, the teeth and tongue are cleaned. The material for cleaning the teeth is usually burnt husk of paddy, which is a fine cleanser. After cleaning with this, the leaves of the mango tree rolled up are sometimes used in the place of a brush and finally a short piece of the stock of the cocoanut tree on which the flower grows. The tongue is cleaned with the midrib of the cocoanut leaf split into two so as to give it a sharp edge.

Village life. In the account of the National Assemblies of Malabar, an attempt has been made to portray the village organisation of the Nāyars. A Nāyar village or Ṭara consists of a number of houses situated, not in a line on both sides of a street as on the East Coast, but lying detached in the midst of gardens. In Johnson's *Relations of the Famous Kingdoms in the World* (4 to 1611) we read, "They (the Nairs) inhabit no towns, but dwell in houses made of earth environed with hedges and woods, and their ways as intricate as into a labyrinth". Though some early British administrators asserted that the Hindu village did not exist in Malabar, Sir Thomas Munro seems to have felt, and felt truly, that this could not have been the real state of things in a Hindu State. His enquiries at the spot led him to conclude that Malabar was "in the earliest times divided like the other provinces of India into districts and villages, the limits of which, but more specially of the villages, remain unchanged to this day."[1] These villages had their own organization for agrarian, social, civil and administrative purposes. They were in fact miniature republics so far as their civil life was concerned. Of course, there was the greater division of the country into Ḍēsams and N̄āḍs under Ḍēśavālies and N̄āṭuvālies for political purposes. The rights and function of these officers are noticed elsewhere.

The villages were self-contained. There was the headman or Aśān or Pramāṇi. etc., and the hereditary village servants or Chēru Jenmakar, the village Panchayats or Kūṭṭams, the Kāval or village Police with the village watchman or Kāvalkār. Each of them had its functions well defined, with its rights and privileges. Fees in grain was allotted to each functionary as remuneration for the work he had to do.

The village organisation was based on a system of mutual help, each household helping the other in the general routine of life with money and labour. Thus, at the thatching season, a householder whose house has to be thatched invites the other householders of the village on the day previous to the thaching, he having

1. Logan's Malabar, p. 88.

provided himself in the meanwhile with the requisite quantity of cocoanut tree leaves with which houses in Malabar are generally thatched. The villagers assemble early in the morning at the house to be thatched and commence work under the direction of the headman. The owner of the house provides them with chewing materials, *pan supari*, chunnam and tobacco. As the sun gets hot, the workmen leave their work for the time and are supplied with rice Kanji with suitable accompaniments on a fairly large scale. They refresh themselves with these and rest for a while till the sun goes down and the heat is abated when they resume work. By dusk the thatching will be finished and the workmen leave to the nearest tank where they wash themselves and assemble again at the house to partake of the sumptuous repast prepared for them, after which they leave for their own homes.

The members of the village help each other at marriages, funerals and other ceremonies with funds as well as labour. At marriages, when the ceremony is resolved on, the Āšān or headman of the village is informed of it. He, along with a few leading men of the village, go to the house at which it is to be celebrated and prepares a list of things wanted. The men of the village lend their assistance in the performance of the ceremony at all its stages till it is over and finally contribute in money towards its expenses.

In the case of funeral ceremonies, it is the duty of the villagers to see the dead body cremated and they do this uninvited. In some parts the articles necessary for the celebration of the sixteenth day ceremony are wholly contributed by the men of the village.

Every village will have a temple of its own, generally a Bhagavaṭi Kāvu, where special ceremonies such as Maṇḍalam Pāṭṭu, Bhadrakāli Pāṭṭu, Ṭiyyāṭṭu, Muḍiyēṛṛu, Ṭālappoli, etc., are celebrated at the expense of the villagers. The headman levies from each householder a small amount annually, known as Oṛṛa · ri,

A KAVU: A TEMPLE FOR A GODDESS.

(To face p. 240.

KANIAN ASTROLOGERS.

(To face p. 241

towards a common fund from which the expenses for common ceremonies at the village temple are met. " There are some village temples exclusively owned by Nairs where all the Karakkars (villagers) assemble on special occasions. A very peculiar socio-religious ceremony performed here is the Kuttam. This is a village council, held at the beginning of every month for the administration of the communal affairs of the caste, though at the present day (as all traces of communal life has been or in the course of being wiped off) a sumptuous feast at the cost of each villager in rotation, and partaken of by all assembled, and a small offering to temple, are all that remains to commemorate it."[1]

In some cases the villagers own lands in common which they cultivate in rotation. This is known as Oṭi pakarcha. For a more detailed account of the village organisation and its functions, reference may be made to the account given of National Assemblies.

The Cheṟu Jenmakkār of the village already mentioned are entitled to hereditary rights and perquisites within the village. They are:—

(1) The Kaṉiyān or astrologer who has to be consulted on every ceremonial occasion from birth to death, to cast horoscopes, and to find Muhūrṭams or auspicious moments for the performance of all kinds of ceremonies or feasts.

(2) The Asari or carpenter.—He is the architect and builder of temples and houses in the village. He presides at the dedication of houses; presents himself with his handicraft in the form of tops vessels, bows and arrows, etc., at Oṇam and Vishu at the houses of prominent villagers, and he has to be given grain or a piece of cloth. At the annual temple festival, it is his privilege to prepare the flag staff on which the temple flag is hoisted announcing the

1. *Castes and Tribes of South India*—Thurston.

opening of the festival. The carpenter is entitled for this service to certain perquisites.

(3) The Ṭaṭṭān or goldsmith makes the Ṭāli, a small piece of gold ornament in the form of the leaf of the pipal tree, which is tied round the neck of the bride at her marriage. He too is entitled to certain perquisites.

(4) The Malayan or Conjuror.—His services are requisitioned for exorcism, devil feast, etc.

(5) The Veluṭṭēṭan or washerman.—He has to wash for the village as also for the temple. He has to newly wash for the temple every day the cloth with which the idol is adorned during the festival days. He is entitled to get, at the birthday celebrations of the villagers, prepared rice and curries. Again when feasts on a large scale are held, the boiled rice that remain in the Ṭaṭa or place where it is stored, after serving the guests, is his perquisite. He has also to supply māṟṟu or washed cloth to the Nāyars on ceremonial occasions, such as at purificatory bath after Pula or pollution, Śrāḍḍhas, etc.

(6) The Vēlan, who is a low class washerman, does not wash for the higher castes. But his women supply cloth washed by them to Nāyar women to wear at the ceremonial bath after the monthly periods. These have to wear the cloth while bathing in order to be purified. It is the Vēlan who has to sing certain songs at the ceremonies on the occasion of the appearance of the first menses. Cloth washed by him has to be worn to cast off Pula during the ceremonial and purificatory bath. He has also to provide the villagers with umbrellas (Olakkuṭa) made of palmyra leaves, for which he will be paid by them.

(7) Vilakkaṭṭalavan, or barber. He has to shave the villagers and is entitled to perquisites at the first shaving or tonsure and at birthdays when the rice and viands served for Gaṇapaṭi in front of the lamp form his perquisite. It is the barber woman who acts as

VELANS' DANCE.

(To face p. 242.

accoucher or midwife to Nāyar women at their delivery.

(8) The Kuśavan or the potter.—He has to supply the villagers with pots and pans as also Ṭṛkkākara Appan or conical or pyramidical figures for pūja during the Oṇam; for this he gets rice and curry-stuffs from each household.

(9) To the above may be added the Eḷuṭṭaśśan, Aśān or village schoolmaster. This individual need not necessarily belong to any particular caste. He may be a Nāyar, Kaṇiyān, Paṇikkar or a Kaṭupaṭṭan. In some parts and especially in middle Kērala and in the north, the Eḷuṭṭaśśans generally belong to the last class. The term Eḷuṭṭaśśan means 'father of letters' or 'master of letters', and his calling is peculiarly popular in Malabar. Every village will have more than one Eḷuṭṭaśśan with schools of their own, while families capable of employing one keep one for themselves.

In Malabar, the education of the children both males and females commence very early. They are initiated into the mysteries of the Malayalam alphabet at the earliest in the third year of their age and at the latest not later than the seventh year. For this ceremony an auspicious hour is fixed by the village astrologer generally on the Vijayadaśami day which falls on the last day of the Navarātri or Saraswaṭi Pūja which comes on in the month of Kanni (September—October) or Ṭulam (October—November). That day is peculiarly favourable for the purpose, for it is dedicated to Saraswaṭi, the goddess of learning. The occasion is known as *Vidyarambham* or the 'beginning of learning'. The village schoolmaster or in his absence any other qualified man is invited to initiate the child in the study of the alphabet. After the Pūja to Saraswaṭi is over, in a conspicuous part of the house will be placed a bell-metal plate with a quantity of rice spread on it with a lighted lamp on each side of it along with a measure of paddy and rice. The child to be initiated is seated in front of the plate facing towards the east. Gaṇapaṭi is invoked and offerings made to the God. The Āśān or Eḻuṭṭaśśan sits by the child and, after offering prayers to God, traces on the child's tongue with a gold coin, generally a Vīrarāyan Fanam, the divine invocation *Hari—Sree—Ganapathaye—Namah.* After this, the teacher takes hold of the child's right hand and makes the child write the letters of the alphabet on the rice in the plate. A feast is given to friends and relatives invited and the ceremony closes. This ceremony is known also as Eḻuṭṭinu Iruṭṭal, *i. e.*, sitting to be initiated into letters.

Thenceforth the child is either taught at home or sent to one of the village schools. These institutions are held in low, long thatched sheds put up in an open space with little or no furniture. The children squat on the bare floor in a line with milk-white sand spread before them on which they trace the letters of the alphabet repeating them loud as they go on. The Āśān seated at one end in a raised position supervises the work. Lessons are set to advanced children the previous evening which they learn by heart and they repeat them in turn to the teacher. The lessons are written on Ōlas or palmyra leaves with an iron style, and the leaves are strung together on a thread. The students generally assemble at seven o' clock in the morning and are sent home at 10, to assemble again at two in the afternoon. The lessons are kept up till 5. The evening lessons of the advanced students consist in the reading of the Malayalam rendering of the Purāṇas, specially of the Rāmāyaṇa. Of Prose studies there are none, for the reason that the language can boast of no Prose literature except what is of very recent growth. In the evening the students had home-work to do which consisted in repeating the names of the goddesses and gods, in reciting Kīrṭṭanams or praises in verse of the several deities of the Hindu Pantheon and in conning multiplication tables, etc. The Malayalam can boast of a splendid hymology.

Discipline is rigorously maintained in schools and the Aśān is a terror to the students. These have to march to the school in single or double file, with hands folded crossing the breast, holding the bundle of cadjans on which their lessons are inscribed in their arm-pits and with a cocoanut shell containing sand slung to their shoulder. They are enjoined to keep silence on the road and march on directly to the school. They go back after school hours in the same way. The Aśān is expected to have an eye over their general conduct also. The punishments he awards to delinquents are often severe. The students are made to stand with their legs crossed, to hold their ears with their hands crossed on the breast so that the right ear has to be held by the left hand and the left ear by the right. In this position they are ordered to bow down, so that the knees of their hands may touch the ground. This sort of bowing (*Mal.* Ēṭṭaṃ) has to be undergone often a hundred or thousand times if not more. Again the rod is freely used and never spared; sometimes the point of the iron style is employed as a goad. Knocks are not seldom given on the finger joints with the iron style. Like his English prototype of old, Dickens' Squeers, the Aśan employs his pupils to do all sorts of work for him. The students wearied by all this trouble sometimes skulk, play the truant and do not hesitate even to leave the village.

The studies are stopped for about 12 days in the month in two instalments known as Anaḍhyāya commencing with Ḍwāḍaśi or the 12th day after the waxing or the waning moon. Ḍwāḍaśi and the day following are only half holidays to enable the students to revise their old lessons. The period of study is known as Swāḍhyāyam.

The course of study consists first in writing on sand the letters of the alphabet and learning them. After this the student is made to write short sentences on Ōla with the iron style. He is then made to commit to memory short verses (Ashṭakams) in praise of Gaṇapaṭi, Saraswaṭi, Rāma, Kṛshṇa, etc. Simple lessons in arithmetic are added on, specially the multiplication tables. All this takes up about two years' time, and, when the student is found to be well grounded in the three R's, he goes in for higher branches as a stepping stone to the study of Sanskrit.

The girls undergo the same course of instruction as the boys. They are further taught short poems inculcating moral principles. They learn Śīlāvaṭi Pāṭṭu, Paṭṭu Vṛṭṭam, Paṭiṅṅālu Vṛṭṭam.

The advanced courses for boys and girls consisted in the study of Kāvyams, Alamkāram and Nāṭakams in Sanskrit. Some studied any of the Śāsṭrās too, such as astronomy, logic, grammar and āyurvēḍa. Girls used to specialise in music, Irupaṭṭuṅālu Vṛṭṭam, etc. In addition to these, they are taught to recite Malayalam poetic renderings of the Purāṇas such as the Rāmāyaṇa and the Mahābhāraṭa. They are also taught at home Ṭiruvāṭira Kaḷi or Kykoṭṭikaḷi, a kind of dance with the clapping of hands to the accompaniment of appropriate songs. According to modern experts in physical culture, this is one of the best forms of bodily exercise suited for females. The village schoolmaster is generally remunerated in kind. He gets from each house a quantity of paddy per mensem or per annum as he desires. Otherwise, on the Ḍvāḍaśi day when the fortnightly holidays commence, each student pays him an anna or two. He receives presents of cloths on Ōṅam and Viśhu days with a Rupee or two added. The annual celebration of the Navarāṭri also brings him presents. On the last day of the festival, Vijayaḍaśami, the pupils have to renew their lessons. The Āśān's pupils, past and present, present themselves before him, and give him handsome gifts after prostrating at his feet. This is known as Guru Dakshiṇa.

We have a good account of Education in Malabar in the eighteenth century by Fra Bartolomeo as he found it then:—

"The education of youth in India is much simpler, and not near so expensive as in Europe. The children assemble half naked under the shade of a cocoanut tree; place themselves in rows on the ground, and trace out on the sand, with the forefinger of the right hand, the elements of their alphabet, and then smooth it with the left[1] when they wish to trace out other characters. The writing-master, called Agian, or Eluttacien, who stations himself opposite to his pupils, examines what they have done; points out their faults; and shews them how to correct them. At first, he attends them standing; but when the young people have acquired some readiness in writing, he places himself cross legged on a tyger's or deer's skin, or even on a mat made of the leaves of the cocoanut tree, or wild ananas, which is called Kaida' (The Kaida of Rheede Hort. Malab. as well as the *Keuraathrodaetylus*, and the *Pandanus odoratiffima* is not a wild ananas, but a plant, the male flowers of which have a farina of an exceedingly agreeable smell. In Arabia and India people bestrew their heads with it, as we do ours with perfumed powder. F.), plated together. This method of teaching writing was introduced into India two hundred years before the birth of Christ, according to the testimony of Megasthenes, and still continues to be practised. No people, perhaps, on earth have adhered so much to their ancient usages and customs as the Indians.

"A schoolmaster in Malabar receives every two months, from each of his pupils, for the instruction given them, two Fanom or Panam. Some do not pay in money, but give him a certain quantity of rice, so that this expense becomes very easy to the parents. There are some teachers who instruct children without any fee, and are paid by the overseers of the temple, or by the chief of the caste. When the pupils have made

1. This is not correct. It is done by the right hand itself.

tolerable progress in writing, they are admitted into certain schools, called Etupalli.[1] where they begin to write on palm leaves (Pana), which, when several of them are stitched together, and fastened between two boards, form a Grantha, that is, an Indian book. If such a book be written upon with an iron style, it is called Granthavari, or Lakya, that is, writing, to distinguish it from Alakya, which is something not written.

"When the Guru, or teacher, enters the school, he is always received with the utmost reverence and respect. His pupils must throw themselves down at full length before him; place their right hand on their mouth, and not venture to speak a single word until he gives them express permission. Those who talk and prate contrary to the prohibition of their master are expelled the school, as boys who cannot restrain their tongue, and who are consequently unfit for the study of philosophy. By these means the preceptor always receives that respect which is due to him; the pupils are obedient, and seldom offend against rules which are so carefully inculcated. The chief branches taught by the Guru are: 1st, the principles of writing and accompts: 2nd, the Samscred grammar, which contains the declensions and conjugations; in Malabar it is called Sidharuba; but, in Bengal, Sarasvada, or the art of speaking with elegance: 3rd, the second part of this grammar, which contains the syntax, or the book Vyagarana: 4th, the Amarasinha, or Brahmanic dictionary."[2]

This system of education, specially of primary education, continued in Malabar till the disruption of society caused by the commotions consequent on the invasions of Hyder and Tippu. The State took no part in the education of children till then. For some time after Tippu's expulsion from Malabar everything was in confusion till the British established their supremacy on the coast. The States of Travancore and Cochin soon came under British dominion

1. Eluttupalli—a pyal school.
2. Pages 261—263.

and the administration of those States began to be improved on the lines adopted in the territories directly under the rule of the Hon. East India Company. The education of the youths of the country attracted the early attention of the States. Formerly Nāyar youths, after undergoing their primary education in the village schools as already sketched, either passed on to the Kalaries for being trained in gymnastics and the use of arms, or took to the study of Sanskrit under competent teachers. But the pacification of the country and the restoration of order under the protecting aegis of the *Pax Britannica* rendered the exercise of arms unnecessary, and left a large number of youths with no work to do. The village schools had also disappeared for some time with the result that the people came to be illiterate. At last, in the year 993 M. E. (1818 A. D.) the States of Travancore and Cochin resolved, under the auspices of Col. J. Munro, the then British Resident and Diwan, to introduce a system of free compulsory education under State control. Schools were established in all the villages, and guardians of children between the ages of 5 and 10 were enjoined on pain of punishment to send them to schools to be instructed in reading, writing, arithmetic, astronomy and poetry. In course of time, this system was slowly dropped along with many other useful institutions.

Occupations and morals. So early as in the beginning of the 14th century, Friar Jordanus has observed that the people "of this India" referring to the west coast, "are true in speech and eminent in justice". Ibn Batuta had also noticed the stern justice of the king of Quilon. Some time after Jordanus, Rabbi Benjamin has remarked that the nation is quite trustworthy in matters of trade.[1] Nieuhoff, writing half a century after, between the years 1653 and 1670, observes, "They are not much inclined to vice, sodomy, and incest; nay, the boys and girls tho' they converse together daily and that without cloths, you shall seldom

1. *Asher*, p. 138.

observe in them either in word or in action anything that savours of uncleanliness". Similarly, while Forbes, in the latter half of the 18th century, after having lived at Anjengo for some time, and having had ample opportunity to form a correct opinion, observes of the Nāyars that they are "seldom guilty of debaucheries," and are "not subject to many of those passions which enslave the civilised Europeans," Walter Hamilton writing, in the early part of the first half of the 19th century, with reference to the people of Travancore, tells us, on the authority of two successive British Residents, that they are a people "abandoned to vice and corruption," and that "in no part of the world, are men to be found to whose habits and affections the practice of vice, through all its debasing, loathsome, and hideous gradations seems so familiar." [1] Hard words these! But Hamilton does not stop to enquire how far the vision of these two successive British Residents had been blurred by the political events that had recently transpired in Travancore, one of the incidents being the open and unconcealed attempt to murder one of these Residents, the inhuman punishment meted out to which by the local British authorities called forth the strongest condemnation of the Governor-General Lord Minto. Referring to the passages quoted above from Friar Jordanus and the Rabbi Benjamin, Col. Yule remarks: "There are many other passages of this kind. It is curious, however, that with reference to the very district of Travancore which now includes Quilon where the Bishop's experience must have chiefly lain, two English Residents have borne testimony lamentably opposed to his account of the character of the people in former times." The gallant Colonel prefaces the above comment by an observation which, perhaps, supplies a satisfactory explanation for the change in the character of the people. He says referring to Jordanus' observation, "This is a remarkable testimony to the character of the Hindoos

1. Deser. Hindoostan, Vol. II, 315.

when yet uninjured by foreign domination or much foreign intercourse."[1]

Both Linschoten and Nieuhoff refer to the revengeful character of the Nāyars. The former says, "They are also very full of revenge, so that whomsoever, they fight against their enemies either by water or land, and that they chance to be thrust into the body with a pike, they are not presently therewith content to lie down, but if they cannot speedily pluck the pike forth, they will not spare to pull forth with both their hands and draw it through their bodies, therewith to set upon them that gave them the wounds, and to be revenged on them". Referring to the Amucos, Nieuhoff says, "They oblige themselves, by most direful imprecations against themselves and their families, calling heaven to witness that they will revenge certain injuries done to their friends or patrons, which they certainly pursue with so much intrepidity that they stop neither at fire nor sword to take vengeance of the death of their masters, but like madmen run upon the point of their enemies' swords, which make them be generally dreaded by all."

Nieuhoff's account of the Nāyars is scarcely complimentary. "Very bold and brave they are," says he, "nevertheless very civil and meek in their conversation, according to the custom of the country; notwithstanding which they are mightily addicted to robbing upon the high way and will kill the travellers unawares, unless they be well upon their guard." He adds that on this account the Mahomedans dwelling in the country take along with them while travelling convoys or guards of Nāyars for protection. Nieuhoff's testimony is that the Nāyars are "extremely covetous and will venture at anything for a small sum." He describes them as "a very haughty" race, pretending "to dispute the rank with the Portuguese which occasioned no small disturbance." They are "strict observers of the times, which are neglected by the common people, for they

1. Col. Yule's Note to para 26 Chap. IV. *The Wonders of the East.*

will not converse with any of the inferior orders, except the Brahmans. They scarce even laugh, and that not but upon extraordinary occasions; and if they see others laugh, they will look downward." Linschoten speaks of them as "verie arrogant and proud." Sonnerat, in 1774 says, "they are besides known by their insolent haughtiness."[1] Buchanan observes, "their submission to their superiors was great but they exacted deference from those under them with a cruelty and arrogance rarely practised but among Hindus in their state of independence." But all this is now past history. A concatenation of circumstances, has, within the course of a few centuries, brought about a thorough change in the character of the people, and we shall have occasion later on to consider the national characteristics of the present Nāyars.

Festivals. The chief festivals of the Nāyars are the Ōṇam, Vişhu and Ṭiruvāṭira, which are all described elsewhere. There are of course many other festivals of minor importance which do not call for notice. Nieuhoff speaks of a strange feast. He says, "The Brahmans have, under pretence of a religious worship, introduced a feast, which furnishes them with a certain opportunity of being revenged of their enemies. It is a custom among the Malabar Kings once every year viz., at the time of the new moon in October, to remember the blessings they suppose they have received from their idols, by a solemn sacrifice, which is performed by setting certain houses on fire such as are appointed by the Brahmans. This is commonly performed in the night time, without the least forewarning given, so that sometimes not only the house, but also the inhabitants with all their goods are burnt, nobody daring to quench the flame. This they call the sacrifice of fire and blood". There is no trace at present of any such festival, and it is possible that the Dutch Captain has mistaken some annual bonfire for the festival described by him.

1. *Voyage to the East Indies*, 1774—1781.

NAYARS TUNING THEIR BOWSTRINGS BEFORE THEY PLAY ON THEM DURING THE ONAM FESTIVAL.

(To face p. 252.

Religion. The religion of the Nāyars will be found discussed elsewhere, and need not detain us here.

Ceremonies. Marriage—Marriage among the followers of Marumakkaṭṭāyam Law of succession may mean either what is called Ṭāli Keṭṭu Kallyāṇam, which is a mere formal ceremonial, or Sambanḍham, which latter alone creates the relation of husband and wife between the parties. While the former is an essential ceremony with females, the males have no corresponding ceremonial.

The details of the ceremony of Ṭāli Keṭṭu Kallyāṇam vary in different localities, though in essence they agree. It is needless to refer to the details as they exist in Malabar, Cochin and Travancore separately. *The Report of the Malabar Marriage Commission* has embodied in it a correct description of the ceremony as it obtains in the British Districts of North and South Malabar; and *the Census Reports of Travancore and of Cochin* give us a description of it as it is observed in the Native States. In effect it is an imitation of the marriage ceremony of the Naṃbūṭiris with the religious portions, such as the recital of vedic texts, performance of *homas* or sacrifices, etc., omitted.

It is held essential that the ceremony should be gone through before the girl attains puberty, but in practice this is not always observed. The ages 7-9-11, odd numbers as usual, are considered auspicious. A number of girls may go through the ceremony at the same time, and obvious considerations of economy induce even infants at their mother's breasts to be produced to go through the innocent ordeal. The same individual may act as the pseudo-husband to a number of girls at the same time or in succession. He has only to wash his hands after tying the ṭāli round the neck of one girl and before doing the same with another ! With some the person tying the ṭāli is an Eṇangan or clansman, with others a Ṭirupād or Kṣheṭriya, a Neḍungāḍi or Sāmanṭa, or an Ārya Páṭṭar, or what not. Even the mother may do and has done this to her daughter.

The ceremony opens with the fixing of a post for the pandal or shed in which the Kallyāṇam (marriage) is to be celebrated. This is known as the Poluṭūṇi-ṭuka, and is done at an auspicious hour prescribed by the village astrologer, and is followed by Polūṇel Pulunguka, or the boiling of paddy for the ceremony. To the first ceremony in particular, the male members of the village are invited, and treated to a sumptuous feast, followed by the distribution of the inevitable *Pan Supari*. If the ṭāli-tier is not an Eṇangan, he is brought in procession, performs his office, receives some remuneration, and is courteously dismissed. But if he is an Eṇangan, his horoscope has to be compared with that of his proposed pseudo-bride, and be found to agree.

The marriage itself begins with the Ashṭamangalyam (a procession to the marriage pandal with the eight auspicious things), and Pāṭṭiniruṭṭal (seating for song) at the latter of which a Brāhmiṇi, not a Brahman woman, but a Pushpiṇi, *i.e.*, an Ampalavāsi woman of the Nampiyār caste, sings songs based on Puranic texts, an account of the Subhaḍra-Vivāham or the marriage of Arjuna with Subhaḍra being the most popular. On the first day, before the girl takes her seat for Brāhmiṇi Pāṭṭu, she is bathed, clothed in rich stuff, and decked with jewels. Hence forward she is provided with a separate room, where she sits aloof, being one who has to undergo the ceremony. In some parts a string is tied to her left arm as a symbol indicating that she had resolved on a particular act. This is called Kāppu Keṭṭuka. The girls, with other female members of the family to attend on them, come out in procession to the pandal, where the Brāhmiṇi sings, dressed in gay attire and decked with costly ornaments. After taking 3, 5 or 7 rounds of this, a cutting of the jasmine plant placed in a brass pot, is carried on an elephant by the Elayaṭu (a low class

Nambūṭiri) the family priest, to the nearest Bhagavaṭi temple, where it is planted on the night previous to the ceremonial day, with tom-toms, pop guns, and the joyous shouts of men and women. A few hours before the tying of the ṭāli, this cutting is brought back in procession. As the auspicious moment draws near, the girl is brought out of the room. She is made to worship the sun either from the ground or from a raised platform put upon posts and gaily decorated with festoons, etc. A bow and arrow takes a prominent part in this worship. The ṭāli-tier is then brought in procession with the usual tom-tom beating, the firing of pop-guns, and the shouts of a joyous crowd. He is received at the gate by a few female members of the house with Ashṭamangalyam, and is seated on a bench or stool in the pandal. His feet are washed by a male member, the uncle or brother of the girl. Meanwhile the girl is clothed in new cloths, called Manṭravaṭi, and is brought into the pandal with her face and head covered with rich cotton or silk cloth with an arrow and a looking glass in her hand. If there are more girls than one to undergo the ceremony, they are seated screened off one from the other. Money presents are made to Brahmans and the Elayaṭu, and the latter hands over the ṭāli; a thin piece of gold shaped like the leaf of Aśwaṭṭa (*Ficus Religiosa*) tacked on to a string, to the ṭāli-tier. The village astrologer calls out Muhūrṭṭam, Muhūrṭṭam (auspicious moment, auspicious moment) and the string is tied round the neck of the girl amidst the din of tom-toms, pop-guns, and the shouts of a gay gathering. If there be more girls than one, and only one ṭāli-tier, he goes through the tying in turn washing his hands in the interval, and as each one has her ṭāli-tied, the screen between her and the next one is removed. The girls are then carried inside the house by their brothers.

When an Enangan ties the ṭāli, the ceremonial is somewhat different. On the appointed day, the boy selected is invited to a house close to that of the girl, where he is fed with his friends by the Kāraṇavan of the girl's family. The feast is called Ayani ūṇu, and the boy is thenceforth called Maṇavālan or bridegroom. From this house he is taken in procession to the bride's, accompanied by men armed with swords and shields shouting a sort of war cry. The Ṭirupād's procession is also of a like nature. The ceremony generally lasts for four days, and where the Maṇavālan is a casteman the boy and the girl are required to remain in a separate room under a sort of pollution for 3 days. On the 4th day they bathe in the neighbouring tank or river, holding each others' hand and return in procession. They find the doors of the house shut against them, and the Maṇavālan has to force them open. He then takes his seat in the northern wing of the building, and sweets are served to the couple there by the women of the house. The girl then serves meals to the boy. They eat together and proceed to the pandal for the last ceremony, in which a cloth is severed into two parts, and each part given to the Maṇavālan and the girl separately in the presence of Eṇangans and other friends. The severing of the cloth is indicative of a separation or divorce. And the solemn farce comes to a close. The divorced wife has, however, to observe the death pollution on the demise of the Maṇavālan.

In cases where the family is poor and is not in a position to afford the useless and meaningless luxury of having an Eñangan or Ṭirūpād to tie the ṭāli, the girl's mother performs the office, and this is often done in the presence of the idol in the village temple. The retention of the ṭāli is not at all obligatory. It may be broken the moment it is tied, of course that would be unseemly or indecorous, but never sinful, by any means.

The headman of the village is an important factor on the occasion of a marriage ceremony. In a conspicuous part of the marriage pandal, he is provided with a seat on a cot, generally lined with coir yarn, on which a grass mat, a blanket, and white cloth are spread, one over the other. Before tying the ṭāli, his permission is solicited and, with his consent, the ṭāli is tied. He is paid in Cochin 4, 8, 16, 32 or 64 puṭṭens (a puṭṭen = 10 ps.) per girl, according to the means of the family. He is also given rice, curry stuffs and betel leaf and nuts.

The local chieftain's permission has also to be obtained. A member of the family visits the Raja or chief with presents and solicits leave to have the ceremony-performed. Certain special privileges, such as worshipping the sun from a platform, sitting on a grass mat, having an elephant procession, drumming, firing of pop-guns, serving of particular articles of food, etc. have to be obtained from the local chief or ruler of the State, if one is anxious to have them, and the privileges have to be paid for.

The description of the ceremony we have endeavoured to give sufficiently points to its real character. It is purely ceremonial in its nature, being merely a caste rite. The man tying the ṭāli is at once dismissed with a present. The ṭāli itself need not be retained. A single individual may perform the office to many simultaneously or in succession. The vicarious office may even be undertaken by the mother—all these point to what the ceremony really means—a mere nothing—simply an occasion to squander hard earned wealth.

It will be found from Mr. Thurston's *Ethnological Notes* that, among many castes and tribes in various parts of the Madras Presidency, customs resembling the *Tali-Kettu-Kallyanam* are prevalent.

"As a religious ceremony", said the late Justice Sir T. Muthuswamy Ayyar, "the Kettu Kallyanam is taken to give the girl a marriageable status," or, as Mr. Elie Reclus quaintly observes, "the nuptials (referring to this ceremony) are here interposed only to emancipate the woman, and introduce her into the world". "But in relation to marriage", continues Sir

AG.

T. Muthuswamy Ayyar, "it has no significance, save that no girl is at liberty to contract it before she goes through the Tali Kettu ceremony. * * *. A ceremony, which creates the tie of marriage, only to be dissolved at its close, suggests an intention rather to give the girl the merits of a Samskāra or religious ceremony than to generate the relation of husband and wife." Sir T. Muthuswamy Ayyar describes the Keṭṭu Kallyāṇam as an "essential caste observance preliminary to the formation of sexual relation, and is analogous to the ceremony of Samavartana prescribed for Brahman bachelors who desire to terminate the Brahmachari Asramam or the status of a vedic student and enter on Grahasta Asramam or the status of a married man." "The Tali Kettu now is no marriage in itself," observes Mr. Rama Varma Raja of Parapanad, a member of the Malabar Marriage Commission; "it is a preliminary purifying ceremony analogous to Samavartana in point of capacitating to marry." "In my opinion" says Mr. O. Chandu Menon, another member of the Commission, "The Kallyanam is a mere preliminary ceremony something like a Samskaram among the Hindus which makes the person who undergoes it, eligible to marry."

The witnesses examined before the Malabar Marriage Commission characterised the Keṭṭu Kallyāṇam as a "mock marriage", a "fictitious marriage", "meaningless ceremony" an "empty form", a "ridiculous farce", an "incongruous custom", a "pretence", a "waste of money", and a "device of becoming involved in debt."[1].

What then is the origin of this mock ceremony? Some writers on Kērala trace it as a remnant of the old days when they say, polyandry was a recognised institution in Malabar.

In seeking to ascertain the origin of the Marumakkaṭṭāyam institutions now extant in Malabar, it becomes necessary to go back to their early stages and examine the conditions of society which gave rise to

1. Para 30 of the Report.

them. If, in doing so, we find that the Nāyars belonged originally to a stock that practiced polyandry or even promiscuity in an early stage of its history, one need hardly be ashamed of it. Bachofen, Mac Lenan, and Morgan have shown that polyandry and kinship through females are phases or stages in the evolution of all human societies. Of course there is the opposite theory of Sir Henry Maine, as eminent an authority as any above named, that the origin of society is in patriarchal families, that polyandry and kinship through females are of temporary duration, liable to be brought about at any stage in the progress of a society by peculiar circumstances under which it may be placed.[1] There is yet another theory started by Laterneau who in his *Evolution of Marriage* maintains that there is no warrant to consider this form of conjugal union as having been general, but that it is an exceptional form brought about by necessity in a good number of gross societies. Westermarck says in his *History of Human Marriage* that it is safe to hold with Max Muller that we can neither assert nor deny that in unknown times Aryans ever passed through a *metrocratic* stage. Mr. Andrew Lang, after an examination of the nature of the evidence in support of the theories of both Mac Lenan and Sir Henry Maine, observes, "The Aryan races have very generally passed through the stages of scarcity of women, polyandry, absence of recognised male kinship, and recognition of kinship through woman."

Of the non-Aryan races there can be no question that they had to pass through the several stages before the final one of paternal kinship was reached. The maternal family and inheritance in the female line need not necessarily be the result of polyandry. It may be, and probably is, one of the many causes that conduce to bring it about. Among the Tibetans, the Todas, the Ainos of Japan and other races that practice polyandry and have hardly any system of settled marriage,

1. Early Law and Custom, p. 202.
2. Custom and Myth, p. 275.

inheritance is through males and not females. So also among some of the aborginal tribes in North America, the Pacific Islands in Australia and Africa where the son, as a rule, takes the father's name and becomes heir to his property, though marriage amongst them is in the lowest stage.[1]

The Scythians had practised polyandry as a recognised fact, and 30 millions of respectable people of Scythian origin practice it in Tibet. Herodotus says, of the Agathyrsi, a Scythian people, "They have their women in common that they may be all brothers of each other." Aristotle alludes to similar promiscuity among the Lybians. "They have their women in common, and distribute the children by their likenesses to the men." Diodorus Siculus reports the same manners among the Troglodytos, and the Ichthyophagi on the coast of the Red Sea. The Auseis are said by Herodotus to have lived like cattle with no permanent cohibitation. Among the ancient Greeks themselves, it is said that the women of Attica abandoned themselves to unchecked vice, and the male parentage of children could not be ascertained. The polyandry of Draupadi as related in the *Mahabharata* is an instance of its practice among the Aryans of India. Among the ancient Hindus, before the time of Śvēṭakēṭu, "women were unconfined and roamed at their pleasure." Among the Egyptians and Chinese promiscuity was the rule before the institution of marriage by Menes and Tohi respectively. Ceasar's description of the manners of Britain at the period of the Roman conquest coincided generally with the alleged practice reported to exist in Malabar, not only in the lower, but among the higher classes, with the exception regarding filiation. Ceasar says: "Ten or twelve men have wives in common, and chiefly brothers share with brothers, and fathers and children". "Sir William Temple", remarks Wilks, "who has some curious observations on these associations of ten or twelve families of our ancestors, relates the apology made on

1. Westermarck, p. 98 *et seq.*

the subject by a British lady who had been admitted to some intimacy with Julia Augusta in the time of Severus, "We do that openly with the best of our men which you do secretly with the worst of yours"[1]. The area over which some form of polyandry extends may be traced, as observed by Mr. Mac Lenan in his *Primitive Marriage*, "to points half round the globe". Thus there is ample evidence to show that the family as known among the civilised nations of the present day was evolved out of a prior state of polyandry and promiscuity.

It has been argued that polyandry and its corollary descent of property in the female line were introduced into Malabar by the Naṃbuṭiri Brahmans for their own selfish ends, and that the Keṭṭu Kallyāṇam ceremony indicates a period when marriage as elsewhere in India was a religious sacramental institution. That Brahman work, the *Kerala Mahatmyam*, deals with the matter in question in chapters 48 to 51. Paraśu Rāma is said to have ordained that "among the folk of this land in this my country among all castes, among all Samantas, and among all other women likewise, let there be no chastity. But as for the wives of Brahmans and of Dwijas (twice-born), let the rule of chastity stand in regard to them; with other residents let there be no rule of chastity". It is impossible to believe that a fiat like this, even with the impremature of the divine authority of Paraśu Rāma would lead a community to give up their social customs and manners of such vital importance, and adopt others abhorrent to all principles of morality, religion and social life, simply to please another community. We read in the *Keralolpathy* that the Naṃbūṭiri Brahmans themselves refused to renounce their old customs and adopt new ones to please their patron saint, and that only the Payyanūr grāmam adopted the Marumakkaṭṭāyam system. "It requires", as remarked by Mr. Justice Narayana Marar, "more than the proverbial grain of salt to take in the

1. Mysore, vol. 2, pp. 122—3.

assertion that the Nāyars, who followed the monoandrous and patriarchal system before the advent of the Brahmans, assumed the polyandrous and matriarchal system at their instance. It means that while you were living with your wife and children as a family, in the modern acceptation of the term, involving the right in them to succeed to all your property on your death, you were told that you should no more regard the tie of the family as permanent, nor your wife and children as your successors, and that your property should go after your death to your sister and her children, these in their turn abandoning all their right to succeed to their husband and father though the change were highly detrimental to them, and you and the others quietly accepted it. Those who will bestow some little thought on the matter will readily realize the monstrosity of this theory and agree with me, I hope, in my difficulty to accept it."[1]

This is the conclusion that that eminent jurist Sir T. Muthuswamy Iyer has arrived at. The learned judge observes that "a handful of Brahmans, who must have settled in Malabar in small groups from time to time, could not have succeeded in uprooting the national institution of marriage, if any, even if they had attempted to do so."

Another theory propounded is that the Nāyars were not polyandrous when they settled in Malabar, but that they deliberately adopted it as suitable for their military habits. The theory had its advocates from early times. The Malabar system first became known in Europe through the works of Barbosa and Castenheda, both of whom give a description, however meagre, of the *Tali Kettu Kallyanam*. Speaking of the members of a northern family, Barbosa says, "The nieces or sisters, from whom has to proceed the lineage of the Kings, are held in great honour guarded, and served, and they possess revenues for their maintenance. And when one of these is of age to bring

1. Malabar Quarterly Review, vol. 7, p. 30.

forth, on arriving at about 13 to 14 years, they prepare to make festivity and entertainment for her, and to make her *enceinte*, and they summon some young men, a noble and honourable person, of whom there are many, deputed for this, and they send to fetch him that he may come for this purpose. And he comes, and they give him a great entertainment, and perform some ceremonies, and he ties some gold jewel to the neck of the damsel, and she wears it all her life in sign of having performed those ceremonies in order to be able to do with herself whatever she chooses; because, until the performance of this ceremony, she could not dispose of herself. And the before mentioned youth remains with her for some days, very well attended to, and then returns to his land. And she sometimes remains in the family way, and sometimes not, and from this time forth for her pleasure she takes some Brahman, whosoever she likes best and there are priests among them, and of those she has as many as she likes." Castenheda's account is the same.

Montaigne, whose *Essays* were first published in 1558, not long after Castenheda's work appeared in print, was inclined to think that the Malabar system was devised to maintain the military habits of the people. What the Malabar Kings wanted was an "army of bachelors as King Ceteways of Ashantee". Montaigne says in his *Essay* upon some verses of Virgil:—

"Those of Calicut made of their nobility a degree above humane. Marriage is interdicted, and all other vocations except warre. Of concubines they may have as many as they list, and women as many lechardes without jealousie one of another. But it is capital crime and unremissible offence to contract or marry with any different condition; nay, they deeme themselves disparaged and polluted if they have but touched them in passing by."

Castenheda himself has written, "This strange law prohibiting marriage was established that they might have neither wives nor children, on whom to fix their love and attachment, and that, being free from all family cares, they might more willingly devote themselves to warlike service."

There are eminent advocates of this theory. Montesque assigns the following reason for the polyandrous system of the Nāyar ladies. "The origin of the custom is not difficult to discover. The Nairs are the tribe of Nobles, who are the soldiers of the nation: in Europe, soldiers are not encouraged to marry; in Malabar, where the climate requires greater indulgence, they are satisfied with rendering marriage as little burthensome as possible, they give one wife amongst many men; which consequently diminishes the attachment to a family, and the cares of house-keeping; and leaves them in the free possession of a military spirit."[1]

Mr. Warden, Collector of Malabar (1804 to 1816), in a report to the Board of Revenue, gave the same explanation of the origin of polyandry and the Marumakkaṭṭāyam system. "The profession of arms by birth" subjecting the males of a whole race to military sevice from the earliest youth to the decline of manhood, was a system of polity utterly incompatible with the existence amongst them of the marriage state."

That the Nāyars were essentially a military race has been more than once mentioned.

Whatever merits the above theory may have, it would be hazardous to express any dogmatic opinion regarding the Malabar system. The materials are scanty, and one has to keep in view that one is apt to be prejudiced by one's experience of other systems which have no affinity whatever to the Malabar system.

It has however been pointed out that the Nāyars belong to the Dravidian race. The Dravidians were, and some of them still are, a polyandrous race. It is

1. Quoted by Forbes in his *Oriental Memoirs*, Vol. 1, p. 248

most likely that after entering Malabar they retained for some time more their polyandrous ways under the stress of adventitious circumstances rather than that they deliberately adopted it as suitable to their military organisation or that the Brahmans imposed it on them.

The loose habits that form the basis of the system have been given up long ago and, if this lingers at all, it does so only in nooks and corners far from the ken of civilized life. The opinions expressed by the Nambūṭiri landlords and others of the same class before the Marriage Commission give expression to the old-fashioned Malabar custom which they would be the last to condemn whether out of self-interest or out of veneration to its reputed divine origin. There is indeed much truth in the observation contained in the report of the Marriage Commission about the Marumakkathayam Hindus, "They are all or nearly all of them are better than their custom." Mr. Fawcett, dealing with the question, observes, "But it must not be imagined that the goddess Lubricity reigns supreme in Malabar. It seems perhaps to have been indicated that she does—such is however not the case." He observes that he has not known any admitted instance of polyandry among the Nāyars of Malabar at the present day.[1] Mr. Wigram, who was a District Judge in Malabar for a long time, wrote in his treatise on *Malabar Law and Custom* in these terms on this topic: "Polyandry may now be said to be dead and, although the issue of a Nayar marriage are still children of their mother than of their father, marriage may now be defined as a contract based on mutual consent and dissoluble at will."[2] Mr. Logan,

(1) *Nayars of Malabar*, p. 241.

(2) "Polyandry, plurality of husbands, if it ever existed as an institution in Malabar, must certainly have died out by this time (the time of Vatakkan Pattukal—the Ballads of the North); for we find not a single instance of any such practice throughout the pages of any one of these songs. It has often seemed to me that

whose acquaintance with Malabar entitles him to make an authoritative statement on questions connected with the country, observes in his *District Manual* that female chastity in Malabar is as good as elsewhere though marriage is not a legal institution, "that nowhere is the marriage tie, albiet informal, more rigidly observed or respected than it is in Malabar; nowhere is it more jealously guarded or its neglect more savagely avenged". Commenting on this, Mr. Justice Muthuswamy Iyer remarks that "the system of enforced privacy in the case of women and their early home training lend weight to Mr. Logan's remark as a correct description of the case in North Malabar and also generally in South Malabar." Constancy was not unknown even in the days of Barbosa and Castenheda. In fact constancy was never the exception, for Barbosa observes, "and many of them for honour's sake do not change them." "What then," asks Mr. Fawcett, is the meaning of the assertions of the exponents of the orthodox view that the women need not be chaste and so on? The question is not an easy one to answer, but I think we may say with confidence that this orthodox view has been in some measure propounded by the Nambūṭiris for their own gratification. I have myself known several tragedies arising out of unfaithfulness, and I believe the old-fashioned code of custom admitted the right of the husband to kill his wife's lover if he could, and also to kill his wife." "As a matter of fact," says Mr. Fawcett, "lubricity has no more followers in Malabar than elsewhere."

The reason for the introduction or adoption of the Ṭalikeṭṭu Kallyāṇam, which was an imitation of Brahman marriage, perhaps with a view to ward off the

this charge of polyandry laid at the door of the ancient women of Kerala, is the result of a huge misunderstanding. The system of living in tarawads, the respect paid for the wives of elder brothers, all militate against this supposition." From an article on Women in ancient Kerala by Mr. K. Achyuta Menon, B. A., B. L., Govt. Advocate, in Vol. 3. No. 3, pp. 124-25 of the Teachers' Magazine, Trichur.

calumny attachable to unrestricted intercourse, having vanished, one would have expected that the ceremony itself would cease to exist. *Cessante ratione cessat lex ipsa.* But it still lingers, and Kāraṇavers of Malabar families still vie with one another as to who would squander most borrowed money on this meaningless ceremony and encumber their family property. The explanation offered by Mr. Fawcett seems to be apt.

"The ceremonies surrounding marriage and death seem to be those in which human feelings are deepest and, consequently, in these, more than in any others, we see relics of a long gone past; much of the ceremonial being now apparently meaningless, and handed on after the manner of all ceremonial, for no obvious purpose, long after the original signification has been forgotten. Amongst all races of the world it is the same. These form perhaps—for the ceremonies connected with death are interwoven with primitive religious ideas—the closest links between our earlier ancestors and ourselves. The institution of marriage itself is not easily liable to change or even modification, and thus it is, perhaps, that it, the product of a bye-gone age, is not always suited to the wants of the age in which it is found. It is rarely up to date. It is invariably blended with superstitions and restraints which people believe they believe, and the relations between the sexes are rarely natural, i. e., rarely free from restraints which are souvenirs of the past and which are resented in the present. Of course amongst primitive peoples changes in respect of marital connexions, as also in respect of death ceremonies, are imperceptible. They must be very small indeed in even an immense period; and in their case there is not that unsuitability to the time in which they exist, which is apparent amongst those societies more liable to change".[1]

Keṭṭu Kallyāṇam has never been considered as real marriage, the ceremony which creates the conjugal

(1) Mr. Fawcett's Nayars, Govt. Museum Bulletin, p. 228

bond at any time, though it is often spoken of as marriage both by European and Indian writers. For the real ceremony we have to look to the Sambandham or cloth giving ceremony. Among the early writers Barbosa and Castenheda and, among the later, Messrs. Bunchanan, Mateer, Logan, Elie Reclus, Herr Starke and Nagam Aiya refer to the Keṭṭu Kalyāṇam as marriage, but only as a mere formal ceremony. Buchanan says, "The female Nairs, while children go through the ceremony of marriage both with Nambudiries and Nayars, but here (North Malabar) as in the south the man and wife never cohabit." [1] The Rev: S. Mateer writing of Travancore says:— "In early youth, the girl goes through the ceremony of marriage by having the Ṭāli or marriage cord, tied round her neck, but this is not followed by co-habitation." Again "There is indeed a ceremony called 'marriage,' which is performed in the infancy or childhood of every (Nayar) girl; but it is the merest pretence, never consummated as a marriage, and conferring no connubial claims or obligations on the nominal bridegroom, who has thenceforth no further connection." Again, "But the mere ceremony of marriage does not make her a wife unless the same man should also 'give cloth' and cohabit with her. The trifling ceremony of "giving cloth" is rarely omitted in any case of co-habitation." [2] "Every Nayar girl" says Mr. Logan "is married in one sense at a very early age".... ... "the strange thing about it all is that the girl is not really married to the man who performs the ṭāli-tying ceremony." [3] Herr Starke speaks of it as "a wedding ceremony which has been degraded into a mere formality.[4] Mr. Nagam Aiya refers to Keṭṭu Kallyāṇam as the "formal ceremony of tying a tali round the neck of a girl," while he mentions "Sambandham or

1. Vol. 2, p. 165.
2. *Native Life in Travancore*, p. 172.
3. *Malabar Manual*, p. 135.
4. *The Primitive Family. Its rise and Development.*

Pudavakoda (literally 'cloth giving') as the ceremony of actual alliance as husband and wife." [1]

Sambandham or, to give its full form Guṇa-Ḍōṣha Sambandham, is the institution that denotes real marriage. It means the contracting of relationship for participating in good and evil, almost exactly the gist of the marriage service in the Church of England. Throughout Malabar, including Cochin and Travancore, the word is fully understood to mean marriage. A full account of the Sambandham ceremony is given by the late Sub-Judge Mr. O. Chandu Menon in a Memorandum attached to the Marriage Commission Report. He says:—

" The variations of the Sambandham are the Pudamuri, Vastradanam, Uzhāmporukkuka, etc., which are local expressions hardly understood beyond the localities in which they are used, but there would be hardly a Malayali who would not readily understand what is meant by Sambandham tudanguka (to begin Sambandham). The meaning of this phrase, which means 'to marry', is understood throughout Keralam in the same way, and there can be no ambiguity or mistake about it".

"It is thus found that Sambandham is the principal word denoting marriage among Marumakkathayam Nayars. It will also be found on a close and careful examination of the facts that the principal features of this Sambandham ceremony, all over Keralam, are in the main the same. As there are different local names denoting marriage, so there may be found local variations on the performance of the ceremony. But the general features are more or less the same. For instance, the examination, prior to the betrothal, of the horoscopes of the bride and the bride-groom to ascertain whether their stars agree astrologically; the appointment of an auspicious day for the celebration of the ceremony; the usual hours at which the ceremony takes place; the presentation of the danam (gift) to the

1. *State Manual Vol. I.* p. 352.

Brahmans; the sumptuous banquet; the meeting of the bride and the bride-groom, are features which are invariably found in all well-conducted Sambandhams in all parts of Keralam alike. But here I would beg to state that I should not be understood as saying that each and every one of the formalities above referred to, are gone through at all Sambandhams among respectable Nayars, and I would further say that they ought to be gone through at every Sambandham if the parties wish to marry according to the custom of the country. I would now briefly refer to the local variations to be found in the ceremony of the Sambandham, and also particular incidents attached to certain forms of Sambandham in Malabar. I shall describe the Pudamuri or Vastradanam, as celebrated in North Malabar, and then show how the other forms of Sambandham differ from it. Of all the forms of Sambandham, I consider the Pudamuri form the most solemn and the most fashionable in North Malabar. Of course my description will be borne out by the evidence that is before us. The preliminary ceremony, in every Pudamuri, is the examination of the horoscopes of the bride and bride-groom by an astrologer. This takes place in the house of the bride, in the presence of the relations of the bride and bride-groom. The astrologer, after examination, writes down the results of his calculations on a piece of palmyra leaf, with his opinion as to the fitness or otherwise of the match, and hands it over to the bride-groom's relations. If the horoscopes agree, a day is then and there fixed for the celebration of the marriage. This date is also written down on two pieces of cadjan, one of which is handed over to the bride's Karanavan, and the other to the bride-groom's relations. The astrologer and the bride-groom's party are then feasted in the bride's house, and the former also receives presents in the shape of money or cloth; and this preliminary ceremony, which is invariably performed at all Pudamuries in North Malabar, is called Pudamuri Kurikkal, but it is unknown in South Malabar.

"Some three or four days prior to the date fixed for the celebration of the Pudamuri, the bride-groom visits his Karnavans and elders in caste to obtain formal leave to marry. The bride-groom on such occasions presents his elders with betel and nuts, and obtains their formal sanction to the wedding. On the day appointed the bride-groom proceeds, after sunset, to the house of the bride accompanied by a number of his friends. He goes in procession, and is received at the gate of the house by the bride's party, and is conducted with his friends to seats provided in the tekkini or southern hall of the house. There the bride-groom distributes presents (danam) or money gifts to the Brahmans assembled. After this, the whole party is treated to a sumptuous banquet. It is now time for the astrologer to appear, and announce the auspicious hour fixed. He does it accordingly, and receives his dues. The bride-groom is then taken by one of his friends to the padinhatta or principal room of the house. The bride-groom's party has, of course, brought with them a quantity of new cloths and betel leaves and nuts. The cloths are placed in the western room of the house, called padinhatta, in which all religious and important house-hold ceremonies are usually performed. This room will be decorated and turned into a bed-room for the occasion. There will be placed in the room a number of lighted lamps, and Ashtamangaliam, which consists of eight articles symbolical of Mangaliam or marriage. These are rice, paddy, the slender leaves of the cocoanut tree, an arrow, a looking-glass, a well-washed cloth, burning fire, and a small round wooden box called 'cheppu' made in a particular fashion. These will be found placed on the floor of the rooms aforesaid as the bride-groom enters it. The bride-groom with his groom's man enters the room through the eastern door. The bride, dressed in rich cloth and bedecked with jewels, enters the room through the western door, accompanied by her aunt or some other elderly lady of her family. The bride stands facing the east with the Ashtamangaliam and lit-up lamps in front of her. The groom's man then hands over to the bride-groom a few pieces of new cloth, and the bride-groom puts them into the hands of the bride. This being done, the elderly lady, who accompanied the bride, sprinkles rice over the lit-up lamps, and the head and shoulders of the bride and the bride-groom, immediately leaves the room, and he has to perform another duty. At the tekkini or southern hall, he now presents his elders and friends with cakes, and betel leaf and nuts. Betel and nuts are also given to all the persons assembled at the place. After the departure of the guests, the bride-groom retires to the bedroom with the bride.

"This is an unvarnished account of a 'Pudamuri'. Next morning the Vettilakkettu or Salkaram ceremony follows, and the bride-groom's female relations take the bride to the husband's house, where there is a feasting, etc., in honour of the occasion.

"Uzhamporukkuka or Vidaram Kayaral is a peculiar form of marriage in North Malabar. It will be seen from the description given above that the Putamuri is necessarily a costly ceremony and many of the people resort to the less costly ceremony of Uzhamporakkuka or Vidaram Kayaral. The features of this ceremony are to a certain extent the same as Putamuri, but it is celebrated on a smaller scale. There is no cloth giving ceremony. The toasting is confined to the relations of the married couple. The particular incident attached to this form of marriage is that the husband should visit the wife in her house, and is not permitted to take her to his house, unless and until he celebrates the regular Putamuri ceremony. This rule is strictly adhered to in North Malabar, and instances in which the husband and wife joined by Uzhamporukkuka or Vidaram Kayaral ceremony, and with grown up children being the issue of such marriage undergoing the Putamuri ceremony some 15 or 20 years after Uzhamporukkuka, in order to enable the husband to take the wife to his house, are known to me personally.

"The Sambandham of South Malabar and the Kidakkora Kalyanam of Palghat have all or most of the incidents of Puṭamuri, except the presenting of cloths. Here money is substituted for cloths and the other ceremonies are more or less the same. There is also the Salkaram ceremony wanting in South Malabar, as the wife is not at once taken to the husband's house after marriage".

The Sambandham ceremony as it is celebrated in Travancore is thus described by Mr. C. V. Raman Pillai in his answers to the questions of the Travancore Marumakkathayam Committee. He says:—

"Formerly the bride used to be chosen by the guardian of the bride-groom. In those days, horoscopes of marriageable girls used to be obtained and returned. Now-a-days, the bride-groom himself often makes the choice, and no importance is attached to horoscopic concurrence. However, the horoscope is received in the generality of cases. The orthodox cloth-giving ceremony is celebrated thus: After the preliminary private arrangements, an elderly representative of the bride-groom, accompanied by a few friends and relatives, go to the bride's house where her guardian and relatives receive them and treat them to pan supari.

"At an auspicious hour, the bride's horoscope, placed on a plate, is delivered to the senior gentleman of the bride-groom's party. A small feast generally follows. The bride-groom's party consults the astrologer who fixes an auspicious day for celebrating the ceremony, and intimation of this is given by the bride-groom's party to the bride's. Both parties issue invitations to relations, friends and villagers. The bride-groom's party, and their guests meet at a common place and proceed to the bride's residence where they are received by the party. Music is provided to entertain the guests by those who can pay. The wedding of Sita in the *Ramayana* is recited in a prominent place in the house. In the most commodious portion of the house, not reserved for females, arrangements are made for the ceremony. At the western end, a small plank is placed and a white cloth spread on it, other draperies and ornamentations being super-added according to the status of the bride-groom. The following ornamentations are adopted in all ceremonies.

(1) Nilavany, *i. e.*, ornamental diagrams with rice flour and saffron mixed in water.

(2) Well-lit lamps in front of the plank.

(3) Nira Para, *i. e.*, a large grain measure decorated with Pookulay (areca nut flower).

"A Machampikāran (Eṇangan) sits on the right lamp side with the cloths to be presented placed on a plate. At the auspicious time, the important gentlemen and relatives present are called into the room and the rest flock round according to the accommodation. The bride-groom makes presents to the Brahmins and then bows to his senior relatives and takes his seat on the plank facing eastward. The bride makes gifts to the Brahmins in the inner apartments or sometimes in the marriage hall; of course she has to be shoved into the presence of the bride-groom, though modern young women sometimes make their appearance with a military jauntiness. The bride in all cases is escorted by an elderly relative by marriage. The bride too makes a worshipping bow to the seniors present. The plate with cloth is passed on to the bride-groom by the Machampikaran, and the former, continuing in his sitting posture, raises and streches the plate with both his arms. The bride, standing, bows to the bride-groom, receives the plate, makes it over to the escorting lady and retires. The bride on retiring, immediately wears the presented cloths and appears before the ladies assembled. The husband is then served sweet rice by the wife amidst the Kuravas (cheers) of the ladies. A grand feast follows or precedes according as it suits the hour fixed for the ceremony. The invitation to the females for the ceremony is limited to close relatives and friends. The bride-groom provides presents in cloth also to the entire household excepting the mother of the bride. Now-a-days, there is tom-tom and music arranged for the reception of the bride-groom and to play while the ceremony takes place, but presents to Brahmins are dispensed with.

"A well-understood code regulated the taking of the bride to the bride-groom's house, the first return of the bride to her own house and the first visit of the mother to the daughter in her husband's house; but all this is discarded now."[1]

Mr. Justice Moore, in his edition of *Malabar Law and Custom*, observes that there was nothing analogous to the Puṭamuri prevalent in Malabar from A. D. 1550 to 1800, and that this may be fairly presumed from the absence of all allusion to it in the works of European writers from Castenheda to Buchanan. He says that it is not easy to understand how it came about that such a custom, differing so completely from the state of things described by them, never came under the notice of any of the travellers. It has to be borne in mind that the European writers were naturally prone to look on the question with a prepossessed mind. They were altogether strangers to the idea of marriage except as a religious sacrament conferring secular rights and, where on enquiries they found that what passed off for marriage in Malabar carried with it no religious merit or conferred any secular right, they naturally enough stopped short of proceeding with their inquiries further. Even if they did proceed further, as one is inclined to think was done in the case of Barbosa, the moment it was found that the union between the sexes did not lead to the conferring of rights to property, enquiries must have been dropped

1. (App. B to answers sent by interrogatory witness No. 43, Mr. C. V. Raman Pillai, pp. 24—26).

as to its real nature and the ceremonies by which it was effected. Barbosa could view the woman from his standpoint only as a concubine or mistress. Speaking of the Malabar Rajas, he observes : —

"These kings do not marry, nor have a marriage law, only each one has a mistress, a lady of great lineage and family, which is called Nayre, and said to be very beautiful and graceful. Each one keeps such a one with him near the palaces in a separate-house, and gives her a certain sum each month or each year, for expenses, and leaves her whenever she causes him discontent, and takes another * * * * And many of them for honour's sake do not change them, nor make exchange with them, and they seek much to please their king, for that honour and favour which they receive. And the children that are born from these mistresses are not held to be sons, nor do they inherit the kingdom, nor anything else of the king's, they only inherit the property of the mother. And whilst they are children, they are favoured by the king like children of other people, whom he might be bringing up, but not like his own, because since they are men, the children are not accounted for more than as the children of other mothers. The king sometimes makes grants of money to them, for them to maintain themselves better than the other nobles. The heirs of these kings are their brothers, or nephews, sons of their sisters, because they hold these to be the real successors, and because they know that they were born fron the body of their sisters. These do not marry, nor have fixed husbands, and are very free and at liberty in doing what they please with themselves."

These travellers seem to have confined themselves mostly to the coast, and their enquiries do not often extend to the interior. They were therefore at considerable disadvantage in obtaining accurate information, and when the enquiries themselves did not, and could not, extend to subjects beyond their comprehension, one need not at all be surprised at their silence on matters concerning the inner social life of the people. The remarks of the Fra Bartolomeo on the disability of the European travellers to travel along the high-road in the interior part of the country shows the difficulties they laboured under in obtaining correct information. "The Europeans dare not use it (the high-way), lest the Brahmans should be polluted by them. For this reason the Europeans must pass along the sea-coast which is inhabited only by the fishermen, and people of the lowest castes. Hence it happens that few Europeans have the least knowledge respecting the interior parts of the country, though they talk a great deal of their travels in India."[1]

Of the interior parts of Travancore and Cochin, and for that matter of Malabar generally, these writers seem to have known little or nothing. In Travancore we have a record of the conflict between the patriarchate and the matriarchate, which came to ahead when the Kunju Tampies, sons of a deceased King of Travancore of the early part of the 18th century, openly laid claim to succession to the throne in preference to the nephew, who was heir according to Malabar Law. This at any rate shows that, about the year 1730, *i. e.*, the period when the event occurred in that part of Malabar, people were disposed to acknowledge paternity and to base claims on the same. It is well-known that Maha Raja Rama Varma of Travancore, known throughout India as the Rama Raja, had wedded three ladies, provided each of them with a separate house known as Nagercoil, Aramana, and Ṭiruvattar, indicating the localities whence the choice was made, and ruled that henceforward members of the Royal house could choose their consorts only from one of these three houses. If the choice fell outside one of these families, the consort-elect had to be adopted into one of them before she was formally recognised as Ammachi (or Royal consort). Various privileges were accorded to them, and they and their issue received State recognition. Even before this, the sons of the

1. (p. 148.)

Rajas of Travancore received the title of Tampies with the honorofic of Sri (something like the Sir of English knighthood) prefixed to their personal names while the daughters were called Ponnammas. The ceremonial forms observed by the male members of the Travancore Royal family in taking a consort are not those of yesterday or the day before, but are those that have been handed down from generation to generation. The ceremony itself is known as Pattum kachcha Iduka or Pattum Parivattam Kodukkuka, *i. e.*, the presenting with silk and cloth, and is the exact counterpart of Pudamuri (cloth giving) Sambandham.

Tradition also points to formal matrimonial alliances formed by the early Malabar Rajas and the provision made by them for their children. Mr. Logan refers to an account preserved in the *Keralolpathy* of "three women (one Kshetrya and two Sudras), strangers from some northern land being stranded in a boat on Mt. Deli. Cheraman Perumal took all of them to wife apparently, and on the descendants of the Kshetrya woman he conferred the title of Elibhūpan (King of Eli) with 'heirdom to Kingdom', and he built for her the Elott King's house at the foot of Eli Mala (Mount Deli)." "This tradition' adds Mr. Logan "relates undoubtedly to the northern Kolattiri family the second most ancient seat of the family having been at this particular King's house under Mount Deli". "The descendants of the other two (the Sudra) women became, respectively, the ancestresses of the Nerpett and Chulali dynasties." Mr. Logan is inclined to think further that it is not at all improbable that the Kshetrya lady with whom Cheraman Perumal formed matrimonial alliance and who was the founder of the Northern Kolattiri Kingdom belonged to the stock of the great southern feudatory the Travancore (South Kolattiri) Rajas. This he believes explains the relationship, admittedly acknowledged, even at the present day between the two families. Two other instances are also in point. The Keralolpathy explains how the Ñīlēswaram dynasty holding the Malayali portion of South Canara sprang from a matrimonial alliance between a prince of the Kolattiris and a lady of the Zamorin's house. The Kadattanad family had also a similar origin. The principality of Kadattanad was carved out of the Kolattiri Kingdom as an appanage for the wife and children of one of the Kolattiri Rajas."

Although the Sambandham union has in it all the elements of a valid marriage, courts of law have hitherto refused to recognise it as legal, or at any rate as having a sanction more than social. The question as to whether a Marumakkathayam Sambandham has any of the characteristics of a legal marriage has not up to this come before the Madras High Court. But the legal nature of similar sexual unions among the followers of the Aliya Samtāna system has been discussed in several decisions, and the High Court does not seem disposed to accord to it any legal character. Such a union, the learned Judges remarked, "was in truth not marriage but a state of concubinage, into which the woman enters of her own choice, and is at liberty to change when and as often as she pleases." Again "the customary cohabitation of the sexes under Aliyasantana law appears to us to do no more than create a casual relation, which the woman may terminate at her pleasure, subject perhaps, to certain conventional restraints among the more respectable classes, such as a money payment, and the control of relations, etc., which may be prescribed as a check on capricious conduct".

The Malabar Marriage Commission has placed on record its opinion that "Marumakkathayam was and still is destitute of the institution of marriage". Regarding mixed Sambandhams it has been remarked that, "whatever view be taken as to Sambandham among Nayars, it is difficult to see how the sexual connection between a Brahman male and a Nayar female can be characterised as anything better than

1. Malabar, vol. 1, pp. 234—5.)

concubinage". Sir T. Muthuswami Ayyar, the learned President of the Commission, was not prepared to accept the above view. In a Memorandum annexed to the Report of the Commission, that eminent jurist observes:—

"It is clear then that, in the course of social progress, the majority of the Marumakkathayam Hindus have engrafted forms of marriage on their ancient practice, but these forms are resorted to as overt acts whereby the intention to marry is manifested, and that the sexual relation thus constituted in the majority of cases endures for life. This being so, the point for consideration seems to be, whether it is legislation on the customary basis or on the basis of the Brahmo Marriage Act (the so-called undenominational Law) that will, by enlisting the sympathies of the people, more effectually help on social progress. The Report, however, overlooking this consideration, mixes up notions of the ancient polyandry with the present social marriage customs, and does not discriminate between a legal marriage and a social marriage. Further, by introducing other side issues, the Report throws a cloud over the relations of the sexes as it now exists, and states that 'Marumakkathayam was and still is destitute of the institution of marriage'. If the marriage customs are so bad as to render the sexual relation sanctioned by them nothing better than what it was in the primitive stages of the Marumakkathayam society, how are we to account for the admitted improvement in its moral tone, and how can legislation on the rigid line of the alternative scheme be recommended? Our colleague, Mr. Chandu Menon, in his interesting Memorandum, describes the marriage customs in detail, and they are accepted in the Report as accurate. But the Report states that, because a Nambutiri Brahman who goes through 'Puaamuri' does not consider it a marriage binding upon him, therefore it cannot be regarded as marriage in any other case. A Brahman may not look upon any marriage other than vedic as binding upon him; but that is no sufficient reason for concluding that, as between Nayars, it is not regarded as binding either. On the other hand, that the Nambootiri Brahmans themselves are compelled to go through the same formalities of wedding proves that, owing to social progress, the Nayar women insist on giving the union the character of a marriage.'

The question came up for decision in the Travancore High Court in a suit in which the issue of a Nāyar woman who had contracted a Puṭamuṙi Sambandham with a junior member of a Nambūṭiri Illam sued the father for maintenance, from him personally and from his Illam properties (20 T. L. R., p. 65). The maintenance was decreed by a majority of the Judges who seem, however, not to have agreed on the grounds of their decision. The appeal was heard by three Judges, Govinda Pillai, Hunt and Padmanabha Ayyar, J. J. who were divided in their opinion with regard to the legal effect of the union. While Mr. Justice Padmanabha Ayyar held it "not a valid marriage", Mr. Justice Govinda Pillai thought it "fit for legal recognition," and Mr. Justice Hunt was of opinion that "it is a matrimonial union recognised by custom in Travancore and acceptable to both Nambootiris and Nayars and is a valid marriage in law". Both Govinda Pillai and Padmanabha Ayyar, J. J. tested the validity and legality of the union by the principles of Hindu Law, forgetting, for the moment that, at least one of the parties to the union, was not a follower of that law. The Nāyar wife was a follower of the Marumakkaṭṭāyam system which, in no sense, forms part of *Sastraic* Hindu Law. It is based wholly on immemorial usage, and it was usage that was pleaded in justification of the validity and the legality of the union.

Dealing with the legal effect of a Sambandham union as between Nāyar males and females, Mr. Justice Govinda Pillai observes, "it is a well known fact that such unions are looked upon by the community concerned as sacred as marriage among other classes. In

AJ.

pursuance of the moral sense of that community, the Sambandham union is fit for legal recognition." Again, speaking of a Sambandham union between a Nambūtiri Brahman and a Nāyar female, the learned Judge says "Sanctified by the practice of a thousand years, the usage has been invariable, imperative and definite and thus has all the necessary elements of a valid custom." "Both parties to such a union consider it as legitimate and proper." After this pronouncement, it is difficult to understand why legal recognition could not be given to such a union.

Public opinion is everywhere and at all times the source of all law, and custom is the most concrete expression of public opinion, and it is through judicial recognition that custom becomes incorporated with the law of a country where it prevails. No political legislation is needed to legalise the custom; mere judicial sanction is enough. Where the law is unwritten, judicial legislation can give legal effect to notions which have a prevailing preponderance in the community. "Whatever disadvantages attach to a system of unwritten law", observed Chief Justice Sir Alexander Cockburn in *Wason* vs. *Walters*, "and of this we are fully sensible, it has at least this advantage, that its elasticity enables those who administer it to adapt it to the varying conditions of society and to the requirements and habits of the age in which we live, so as to avoid the inconsistencies and injustice which arise when the law is no longer in harmony with the wants and usages and the interests of the generation to which it is immediately applied." Mr. Justice Hunt who appears to have approached the question with a perfectly open mind has pointed out in his judgment, rightly enough, that "The chief difficulty that Christian and Hindu writers have to contend with in discussing Malayalee marriages is the inherent prejudice or conservatism of men to whom marriage is in the nature of a sacrament, approaching the subject in any other light but that alone." Most of the members of the Malabar Marriage Commission will be seen to have been altogether unable to soar above this inherent prejudice. "The parties do not plight troth and do not call God to witness their union, so there is the absence of a religious element in it. There is no permanency in the union, and such a contract is a contradiction in terms. No rights to property flow from it, and such a union cannot be dignified with the name of marriage", and so on. But those who argue in this line forget that a legal and valid marriage can arise out of a civil contract, that the sanction of religion is not a *sine qua non* of its validity, that the pronouncing of the words of divorce by a Mahomedan once a month for three successive months is not far removed in simplicity from the Malayalee form of divorce, that, in view of the fact that the contract at its inception is intended to be a life-long one, in one sense, every marriage that is dissolved is a contradiction in terms, and that the relation of property to marriage is but an accident, being the creation of man, having nothing to do with natural law.

In most uncivilised countries and (latterly in many) civilised ones, marriage is regarded as a civil contract and no religious ceremonies need be interposed, nor is the presence of a priest even necessary to give it validity or legality.[1] Religious ceremonies are but unnecessary adjuncts. In Buddhist countries, marriage is a civil contract. In China, the only ceremony that bears any semblance of religion is the prostration that the parties make before the altar on which the ancestral tablets are arranged. Among the Hebrews, they have no religious ceremony and there is no trace of a priestly consecration of the contract, either in the scripture or in the Talmud. With the Mahomedans also, it is a mere civil contract, though concluded with a prayer to Allah. In Greece, it was generally, though not always, contracted at the Divine Altars. Among the Romans, marriage was purely a civil contract, and so it remained in the time of Justinian.

(1) Westmark's *History of Human Marriage*, p. 424.

The founder of Christianity had not prescribed any ceremonies in connection with marriage but, in the earliest times, the Christians of their own accord asked for their pastor's benediction. The Emperor Leo the Philosopher, A. D. 886, appears to have been the first who declared ecclesiastical benediction necessary to marriage; but his constitution was in force only in the Eastern Empire. Among the early barbarian codes no mention is made of this ceremony, and in the *History of Gregory of Tours* marriage is treated as a civil contract.[1] Before the decree of the Council of Trent, in November 1563, marriages contracted without ecclesiastical benediction were recognised as legal and valid throughout Christendom. The dogma that marriage was a religious sacrament was gradually developed and finally declared by the Council of Trent though not unopposed.[2] With the Roman Catholics, it is still a sacrament. After the Reformation, it ceased to be thought of as a sacrament but continued to be regarded as a divine institution. The French Revolution brought about a change. Since then, civil marriage has gradually obtained a footing in the legislation of most European countries in proportion as liberty of conscience has been recognised. In France, marriage before a civil officer has to be performed before the religious ceremony to consecrate the union, and any minister of public worship who proceeds to the religious ceremony before the civil marriage, is liable to severe punishment under the Penal Code. The French system has lately been adopted in Germany and Switzerland. The law of England recognises as legal and valid a marriage celebrated in the presence of the Registrar of the District and of two witnesses or at the office of the Superintendent—Registrar of the District and of two witnesses upon making the declaration and using the form of words prescribed. In Scotland, marriage is a civil contract constituted by the mutual

(1) Mackenzie's *Roman Law*, 6th edition, page 108.
(2) do., p. 109.

consent of the parties. No doubt some sort of religious ceremony is interposed but as remarked by Lord Mackenzie, "These religious forms, however, are not essential to the validity of marriage, any further than may have been rendered necessary by the positive institutions of any particular State, for it belongs to the secular power alone to determine what forms, if any, shall be required in addition to the consent of the parties, in order to constitute a valid marriage." Blackstone observes "The intervention of a priest to solemnise this contract is merely *juris positive* and not *juris naturalisant divine*".

The Hindu Law regards marriage as a religious sacrament, the only one prescribed for Śūḍrās. But it has to be borne in mind that, though the Nāyars have been brought within the pale of the Hindu religion, they are not the followers of the Hindu Law; nor can they be classed with Śūḍrās or styled as such. They are seen to belong to the Dravidian race and, if classed at all, would belong to the Kṣheṭriya denomination, and are governed in their civil life by usages and customs some of which at least are contrary, if not abhorrent, to the principles of Hindu Law.

Here we may mention the main features of the Puṭamuri form of Sambanḍham as prevailing throughout Kērala and test their efficacy to constitute the conjugal bond among Nāyars.

The main features of the ceremony are :—

(1) The consent of the parties, or, in case of the one or the other or both being minors, of their guardians.

(2) The ceremonious delivery of the bride's horoscope by the bride's people to the bride-groom's.

(3) The selection of an auspicious day for the ceremony in consultation with an astrologer on his finding the horoscope of both parties to agree.

(4) The sending of a formal invitation in writing of the auspicious day by the bride-groom's party to the bride's.

(5) The bride-groom's procession to the bride's house.

(6) The reading of a portion of the *Ramayana* or some other sacred book.

(7) The presentation of cloth by the bride-groom to the bride in the presence of villagers, friends and relatives invited to attend.

(8) The placing of well-lit lamps and *nira para* in front of which the ceremony takes place.

(9) The distribution of *dakshina* (gifts) to Brahmans.

(10) The serving of sweet rice to the husband by the wife.

(11) And the grand wedding feast given to the guests and to the poor.

The most essential of these is, of course, the presentation of cloth in the presence of villagers, friends and relatives and in front of lighted lamps and *nira para.* The assembling of the villagers for the bride-groom's procession and the grand wedding feast gives publicity to the fact of the union. The reading of the *Ramayana* or other sacred book, the presence of the lighted lamps and the distribution of *dakshina* to Brahmans lends a religious colour to the ceremony, while the serving of sweet rice by the wife to the husband is symbolical of their future joint living and messing.

In primitive societies, marriages are contracted with no ceremonies whatever. Among the Eskimo, visited by Captain Hall, there is no wedding ceremony at all, nor are there any rejoicings or festivities. The parties simply come together and live in their own *tupic* or *igloo.*[1] According as marriage was recognised as a matter of some importance, the entering into it came, like many other significant events in human life, to be

(1) Westermarck, p. 417.

celebrated with ceremonies. Very commonly, it is accompanied with a wedding feast.[1] Among some people, the social meals that the boy and girl eat together is the most important part of the ceremony. As instance we may mention the Sontals, the people of the Malay Archipilago (among whom this is the chief and most wide-spread marriage ceremony), the Horas, the Hindus, the Erethonians and the people of Ermland in Prussia. Amongst certain Brazilian tribes, the ceremony consists in the couple drinking brandy together. A similar custom is observed in Scandinavia and Russia. In Japan the ceremony consists in drinking a fixed number of cups of wine. In Assam the interchange of the betel-leaf constitutes marriage.[2] In Croatia, in Austria, the bride-groom boxes the bride's ears.

As society advanced in civilization, the religious element was imported into the marriage ceremony and it came to be celebrated with religious observances, either with or without the intervention of priests. This perhaps accounts for the reading of sacred books and the distribution of *danams* or *dakshinas* to Brahmans. For all that, the presentation of cloths creates or constitutes the conjugal bond and the Sambandham marriage is a civil contract complete in itself and does not stand in need of the adventitious aid of religion for its validity.

The next objection raised against the validity of the Sambandham union is the want of permanency. Permanency, however desirable, can scarcely be considered as an essence of marriage. What we have to look to is the intention of the parties at the time of the commencement of the union. In human marriages every degree of duration is met with, from unions which, though legally recognised as marriages, do not endure long enough to deserve to be so called to others which are only dissolved by death. As a general rule, human marriages are not necessarily contracted for life. We

(1) Westermarck p. 419. See also Laterneau.

(2) In certain parts of Kerala too, the presentation of betel-leaf plays an important part in marriages.

have instances of strange forms of marriages, such as experimental, temporary, partial, conditional, free, etc., some of which are recognised as valid even in this civilised age. Among the Jews, says Laterneau, in Morroco, the Rabbies consecrate temporary marriages for three or six months according to agreement. The man only engages to acknowledge the child if needful, and make a certain donation to the mother.[1] Such temporary marriages are not unknown in India. They are designated *Mutaa* in the Mahomedan Law and are regarded as lawful by the Abkari Shias. They are contracted for a fixed period of time as for a day, a month, or a year, or for any other specified period. Declaration and acceptance are considered sufficient to effect the union. The parties become absolutely separated upon the expiration of the period. The Right Hon'ble Sir Syed Ameer Ali, lately a Judge of the Calcutta High Court, and then a member of the Judicial Committee of His Majesty's Privy Council, tells us that this peculiar institution is not altogether unknown among Western Communities also and refers us to Hepworth Dixon's *New America*.[3] The facility afforded for divorce both by civilised and uncivilised nations makes it clear that permanancy was never considered an essential element of the marriage union. Even in Roman Catholic countries where the Church holds marriage indissoluble and condemns divorce, she has allowed a good number of cases of nullity of marriage; and in Spain, Portugal and Italy, a husband can demand a judicial separation *a mensa et thoro*, though the marriage contract cannot be dissolved.

The last objection raised is that the Sambandham union does not give rise to rights of property and that children do not inherit their father's effects. The relation of property to marriage is but an accident. It is the making of man and has nothing to do with

(1) Vide *The Evolution of Marriage*, p. 67.

(2) I. L. R. 8 Calcutta, 736; 14 Calcutta, 276.

(3) See his Mahomedan Law, Vol. II, p. 353).

natural law. We have instances of strict marriage existing with the entire exclusion from inheritance, of all daughters, as under the Hindu Law and the Mosaic law; of all daughters and sons, except the first, as under the English Law of primogeniture, or the last, as under the system known as "Borough English," and of all children, as among the Naṃbūṭiris of the Payannūr Grāmam in North Malabar. There is also inheritance without marriage, as in the case of illegitimate children under the Hindu Law (Ḍāsīpuṭra), the Roman law, the *Code Nepolean*, the Mahomedan Law (children by a female slave) and the law in some States of America.

Among the ancient Egyptians and among the modern Chinese and Japanese, by custom, illegitimate children have the same legal rights as children of the wedded wife. Even where the children inherit their father's estate, all systems of law do not give equal rights to them. The Mahomedan Law distributes a man's estate between sharers, residuaries, etc., and gives only half the son's portion to a daughter. The law of Moses gave the eldest son a double share. The law of the *Twelve Tables* distributed the father's property equally amongst the sons and daughters. So also in America. The same law is applied in respect of moveables in Scotland. In Denmark, half the estate goes to the eldest son and the other half is distributed among the remaining children, males and females alike. Mr. F. Fawcett, writing in the *Madras Museum Bulletin*, of the Nāyar system of marriage and property rights, claims it as a merit that the two have no relation with one another. "The marital relation amongst the Nairs is more than commonly natural," says Mr. Fawcett. "The most obvious reason for this being so," he thinks, "is that they are less influenced by considerations of property than elsewhere. The desire to maintain 'property within the family is the curse of all natural relations, between the sexes'" "What strange customs" asks Mr. Fawcett "has it not put on mankind? We have some strange examples of these in Southern India as when a woman is married to the door-post of the house and the house-owner begets children on her to inherit his property, or when a man marries his child to a woman, and himself begets children on her and the individual who stands in the position of father may be but a few years older than the son. But we need not look further than Europe for anomalous customs which inhibit the working of the law of natural selection. Malabar is fairly free from such unfortunate customs and it is perfectly fair to say the marital relation amongst the Nairs is more than commonly natural." [1]

A real insight into the state of some primitive societies that still exist will reveal the circumstance that the relationship between marriage and inheritance is a mere accident, and that rights to property need not necessarily follow marital relationship. Similarly the fact that inheritance runs through the mother who owns all property and that descent is reckoned through the female line need not necessarily show laxity of morals. Mr. Frederick Monson writing in the *New York Craftsman* of the Hopi community of cliff-dwellers in Arizona observes:—"The Hopi women are excellent specimens of primitive humanity. The young women are well formed and strong and of irreproachable character. They own the houses, as well as build them and all family property belongs to the woman, who is acknowledged as head of the household. Inheritance therefore is always through the mother, and descent is reckoned through the female line. In spite of the liberty and importance enjoyed by the Hopi women, their reserve and modesty are surprising. They are as quiet and shy as if their lives had been passed in the utmost seclusion and subject to the dominance of man. Their whole lives are devoted to the care of their children, and the matrimonial customs of the

1. Vol. III, p. 229.

Hopi are of a grade which, if generally understood, might make civilized law-makers and writers of civilized countries stop and think. It is marriage from the point of view of the woman, not of the man. It is a striking example of the principal effect of woman-rule, and it must be admitted that it is dominated by the highest order of purity as well as common sense." "They are," says Mr. Monson, "a people without gaols, hospitals, asylums or policemen, and crime is almost an unknown thing among them."[1]

To the objection that outsiders do not look upon Nāyar Sambandham as valid marriage, the obvious answer is that what we have to see is not what others think of it but how the people themselves view it. In the words of Lord Brougham in the suit of *Warrandar vs. Warrander* "The laws of each nation lay down the forms and solemnities, a compliance with which shall be deemed the only criterion of the intention to enter into the contract".

There can be no doubt that the marriage customs of Malabar, Cochin and Travancore are entitled to legal recognition as they carry with them all the necessary elements of a valid custom. "Custom is crystallised common sense." It is consensual law. As observed by Browne, a large portion of the laws of all nations was "at one time in an amorphous form of heterogeneous custom............... All laws have been in practice before they were put in words..........The legislature is second in time to the executive, custom went before law, and indeed law is nothing but agreed-upon-usage." In Malabar, indeed, "Custom is King."

The Madras Government, in their letter to the Indian Government recommending legislation, observes thus with regard to the marriage customs of Malabar:—"It appears to Government that the case may be briefly stated as follows:—The classes governed by

1. *Review of Reviews* for 1907, p. 611.

Marumakkathayam Law form sexual connections which are at the time of commencing them, intended to be permanent until the death of either of the parties, and which, in the great majority of cases, are so; these connections are publicly formed and socially recognised and are accompanied by ceremonies of a characteristic kind which have nothing in them of a religious element, but which otherwise are as much marriage ceremonies and entitled to the same respect as marriage ceremonies elsewhere."

The Malayalees are so well impressed with the validity of the custom which regulate Sambandhams that the attempts of those who attach importance to English ideas on the subject of marriage to bring about a change by providing a statutory form by legislation have fallen flat on the country. Act IV of 1896 passed by the Legislative Council of Madras, entitled "An Act to provide a form of marriage for persons following the Marumakkathayam or Alya Santana Law," has not hitherto been a success. The figures furnished by the Registrar-General show that the Act has as yet had but little practical effect in Malabar or South Canara. What is wanted is not a new statutory form of marriage but a legislative recognition of the customary form now in vogue with penalties attached to derelictions of marital duties. There is no denying that a marriage law is an important aid to national progress and the provisions of the Travancore 'Nair Regulation' are likely to be more acceptable to the people than the statutory form prescribed by the Madras Act. The enlightened State of Cochin also has given legislative sanction to the customary form of marriage that is prevalent in the country.

In the joint family system, such as that of Malabar, it is nothing but essential that there should be strict rules preventing sexual relations within certain specified degrees of relationship. But before dealing with these, it will be well to consider the question of mixed marriages, i. e., marriages between members of different castes. The evidence given before the Marriage Commission shows that custom permits a man to cohabit with a woman considered to be of a lower caste than himself. Thus the twice-born may consort with Nāyar women. Nāyars may consort with women of sub-divisions held to be lower than their own, but not with women of sub-divisions whose touch would impart pollution. But women of higher classes can in no case consort with men of a lower class without being put out of caste.

As Camoens, the Portuguese bard, sings of Malabar in his *Lusiad*,

"The haughty nobles and the vulgar race
Never must join the conjugal embrace".

This is called the rule of Anulōmaṃ and Pṛaṭilōmaṃ. Dr. Gundhert derives Anulōmaṃ from anu=with+lōman=the hair=going with the hair or grain. So pṛaṭilōmaṃ means going against the hair or grain.

According to this usage, a Nāyar woman consorting with a man of a higher caste follows the hair, purifies the blood, and raises the progeny in social estimation. By cohabitation with a man of a lower division or caste, she is guilty of Pṛaṭilōmaṃ, and, if the difference of caste were admittedly great, she would be turned out of her family to prevent the whole family being boycotted.[1]

But in the course of centuries, society has softened down many of these restrictions considerably, and at present, though marriage within the same sub-division is most approved of, society winks at and condones alliances which offend against the rule of Pṛaṭilōmaṃ. This is specially so in the northern parts of Travancore, in Cochin, and in parts of South Malabar. As such unions would in the long run tend to the fusion of

1. *Marriage Commission Report*, Para 17.

sub-castes and the unification of the various sub-divisions of Nāyars into one composite whole, it is highly desirable that these should be encouraged. It is significant that the parties to such unions do not forfeit their rights in their ṭaṛawāds.

The Nāyars are an exogamous race, and marriage is prohibited within the supposed blood kinship as denoted by the family name and community of pollution. Such marriage, among many backward races, is reckoned incestuous, and is punishable with death. "Wide prohibitions of marriage are archaic, the widest are savage, the narrowest are modern and civilized." Where there has been a disruption of the joint family system, the very strict rule as to prohibited degrees, which had previously prevailed, will be found to have been given up. As a matter of fact, according to Professor Westermarck, we find the rule that prohibits marriage between kindred more extensive among those who retained the family system, than among those who gave it up.[1] The true reason of the prohibition will be found in the unwillingness of men to marry their sisters and mothers and such women as they consider in the light of sisters and mothers. And where the family centres round the mother, as in the case of a Nāyar ṭaṛawād, the prohibited degrees will naturally be reckoned with respect to relationship with her. Thus we find in Malabar the rule that persons descended from a common female ancestress should not intermarry. Those of the same ṭaṛawād, *i. e.*, those who have community of pollution, can never intermarry, but this prohibition does not of course extend to the children of a brother and sister, who are members of different ṭaṛawāds. Marriage between the children of a brother and sister is the most fitting marital union; that between the children of two sisters is incestuous. A man may marry a woman of his deceased wife's ṭaṛawād, even his late wife's sister, but it is not in harmony with social sentiment.

1. *History of Human Marriage*, p. 36.

The Nāyar system allows of polygamy though the Nāyars do not generally practise it. In Travancore the witness examined by the Marumakkattāyam Committee said that it is very exceptional for a Nāyar to have more than one wife. "The practice, at least among all decent sections of the Nāyar people," says *the Travancore Census Report*, "is one of strict monogamy".[1] The tendency is towards monogamy, and even those who are for the retention of the institution do not hesitate to condemn it as being against good morals.

The Nāyars have hitherto enjoyed a system of free divorce at the instance of either husband or wife. Under that system "there is no dragging on under a bondage intolerable to both." Though there was this freedom, it never led to perpetual change. So long ago as 1503 A. D., Barbosa had observed that "Many of them for honour's sake do not change them." "The right to divorce at will," says *the Travancore Census Report*, "is sparingly exercised. Even the remarriage of widows, except at tender ages, is considered not quite the proper thing, if it could at all be helped."[2] Again, we read in *the Travancore State Manual*, "The theory is that the marriage connection lasts during pleasure and is dissoluble at will; but, as the Sambandham is always an affair carefully arranged and settled after consulting the wishes of both parties, divorce is a very rare occurrence. Permanent attachment is always the rule".[3] With regard to British Malabar, *the Marriage Commission Report* observes, "They are all or nearly all of them better than their custom, and the majority (as we are told and believe) cleave to one woman for life."[4] So also Mr. Fawcett in *the Madras Museum Bulletin*[5]. "It may be thought this liberty induced perpetual change;

1. Part II, p. 301
2. Vide p. 331.
3. Vol. 2, p. 358.
4. Para 48.
5. Vol. 3, No. 3, p. 287

so it is as well to state here that it does nothing of the kind. Mere arbitrary divorce is very rare. Permanent attachment is the rule." Sir T. Muthuswamy Ayyar observes in his Memorandum, "The basis on which the duration of the marital union rests is that the couple should get on together well, and that, if they fail, it must cease. Hence the husband or the wife may, in theory, divorce the other at will. But, in practice, neither does so, except for a cause which commends itself to his or her family and to the society in which they move. Arbitrary divorces appear to be rare."[1]

Inheritance and succession. The joint family system of Malabar of course involves descent of property in the female line. The basis of the system is that the tarawād estate is held in trust for the support of the females and their descendants in the female line. The property is impartible and the family indissoluble except by consent of all its members, "As in all Hindu Law," observes Mr. Justice Holloway, "so in the archaic form of it which exists in Malabar, the first conception of a family is of an indissoluble unit, a mere aggregate with no separate rights, living under one head, united more especially by their connection with the same *sacra*". And Mr. Mayne, in his *Hindu Law*, observes:—"In Malabar and Canara, at the present day no right of partition exists. In some cases, when the family has become very numerous, and owns property in different districts, the different branches have split into distinct tarwads, and become permanently separated in estate. But this can only be done by common consent. No one member, nor even all but one, can enforce a division upon any who object." Again, "In Malabar and Canara, where the property is soluble, the members of the family may be said rather to have rights out of the property than rights to the property."

1. Para 16, VII.

Under such a system no question of inheritance can arise except in the case of the separate property of an extinct divided branch, or the self-acquired property of a junior member, which he has left undisposed of at his death, in which case the Karanavan takes it by inheritance on behalf of himself and the other members of the Tarwad to which he belongs.

The senior male member is by law the Karanavan, and notwithstanding the theory that the Tarwad property is vested in the females, he is as such entitled to its entire possession, and is absolute in its management.[1] His powers of management may, however, be limited by contract,[2] and he may delegate it, but, so as not to introduce a stranger.[3] He is the natural guardian of every member within the family.[4] The office is not one conferred by trust or contract, but is the offspring of his natural condition.[5] Till recently it was held that he could not renounce his right to his karanavanship, because it was thought that karanavanship, as recognised in Malabar, is a birthright inherent in one's status as the senior male member of a Tarwad. He could not renounce it as it was the result of his natural condition.[6] This theory is however now exploded, for he could now renounce his right of management.[7] *Prima facie* he is the only person who can represent the family in suits. "A Malabar family speaks through its head and in courts of justice, except in antagonism to that head, can speak in no other way." It is his right and duty to manage alone the property of the Tarwad, to take care of it and to invest it in his own name (if it be movable), either on loans on Kanam or other security, or by purchasing in his own name lands, and to

1. I. L. R. 2 Madras 328.
2. I. L. R. 8 Madras 381.
3. I. L. R. 12 Madras 219.
4. 7 M. H. C. R. 179.
5. I. L. R. 1 Madras 153.
6. C. M. H. C. R. 145.
7. I. L. R. 28 Madras 182.

receive the rent of the land. He can also grant the land on Kanam by his own act or on *otti* mortgage. He is not accountable to any member of the Tarwad in respect of the income of it, nor can a suit be maintained for account in the absence of fraud on his part. He may be removed by suit for *mala fides* in his acts, or for incompetency to manage, and for other causes such as physical and mental disabilities incapacitating him from transacting Tarwad affairs, etc. He is interested in the property of the Tarwad as a member of it to the same extent as each of the other members. All the members, including the Karanavan, are entitled to maintenance out of Tarwad property.[1] His powers of alienation are restricted. Alienations by a Karanavan, whether in the form of gifts, sales or mortgages, are invalid, unless made with the assent, express or implied, of junior members.[2]

The main rights of the junior members are:—(1) a right of succession, in order of seniority, to the management of the *Tarwad* as Karanavan; (2) right of maintenance by the Karanavan out of the Tarwad property; (3) the right to object to any improper administration of the Tarwad property by the Karanavan, and to see that the property is duly conserved for the use of the Tarwad.[3]

Of late a species of property known as *Puthravakasam* has sprung into existence. It means property given by way of gift by a man to his wife and children, either in the name of all of them, or in that of one only. With regard to such property it has been held that it does not lapse to the main Tarwad on the death of the person in whose name it stands, but that it would do so after all the beneficiaries have passed away. But it has at the same time been held that they

1. I. L. R. 2. Madras 328.
2. 1 M. H. C. R. 248.
3. 18 Travancore L. R. 31.

have no individual rights in such property, unless the grant expressly directs it, and that all the donees take it in a body, they being but joint tenants and not tenants in common.[1]

Testamentary power. Doubts have been expressed as to whether a member of a Malabar Tarwad had power to devise property acquired by him, though the power of making wills was at one time thought to be inherent in the followers of Marumakkathayam under the customary law of the country.[2] So far back as 1843, Mr. Strange as Judge of the Provincial Court held that a Marumakkathayi had the power and his view was upheld by the Sadar Court. The point is now set at rest by the passing of Madras Act V of 1898 which declared that every person governed by the Marumakkathayam Law of inheritance may by will dispose of property which he could legally alienate by gift *iner vivos*. A Regulation passed by the Travancore State enables all Hindus in that State to dispose of by will half of their own self-acquisition, and under the recent Nair Regulation, the Nairs are empowered to dispose of by will the whole of their self-acquired or separate property. So is the case in Cochin. In both the States, even before the passing of the respective Nair Regulations, this right was in existence. Even before the passing of the Wills Act, the Madras High Court had held that the last surviving member of a Malabar Tarwad could make a valid testamentary disposition of not simply self-acquired property, but also of Tarwad property.[3]

Adoption. When a Nair family stands the chance of becoming extinct, the lineage is kept up by means of adoption or rather affiliation. Such adoptions or

1. I. L. R. 16 Madras 201.

2. See the fifth Report of the Select Committee of the House of Commons on the affairs of the East India Company 1812, p 133.

3. I. L. R. 22 Madras p. 9.

affiliations are also made for other purposes. There is in the earlier Reports an almost complete absence of mention of cases of adoption among Nairs. The earliest case to be found is one of 1808, and it has been doubted if adoptions were not of recent growth. Mr. Holloway as Judge of Tellicherry, spoke of the "singular and unheard of process of Nair adoption" in 1858, and in 1861 the same learned Judge went to the extent of speaking of the "ludicrous absurdity of adopting a nephew." These remarks only show how meagrely equipped the learned Judge was with regard to the customs and observances of the Marumakkathayam Malayalees, and it was Mr. Justice Holloway as Judge of the High Court of Madras, who laid the foundations of Malabar Law as at present applied to the people by judicial tribunals. It may be asserted without any fear of contradiction that adoption is consistent with Malabar usage, and that, so far as existing records go, the Royal families of Cochin and Travancore would have long ago become extinct but for the adoption of females to perpetuate the succession. In Cochin we have records to show of successive adoptions of both females and males in the 16th and 17th centuries, and in Travancore the earliest adoption of which we have records at present is that of the 14th century.

The adoption of nephews by Nairs was a matter of constant occurrence dating back to centuries on centuries.[1]

"In the event of the failure of rightful heirs" says Sheik Zeen-ud-deen writing in the 16th century[2], "or of any scarcity of them, they (the Malayalees) make choice of a stranger (provided he be a person advanced in age) to succeed, instead of the son, or

1 I. L. R. 12 Madras p. 126.

2. See Hough's History of Christianity in India Vol. 1, p. 109.

brother, or nephew; and after this adoption they make no distinction between him and a lawful heir. And this custom prevails with all the pagans of Malabar, whether in the succession to kingdoms and high dignities, or to the most inconsiderable patrimonies; a perpetuity of heirs being thus secured to them."[1] A fee levied on the grant of sanction to adopt by the ruling power has been a source of revenue in Malabar for time out of mind.[2] A summary of the law and custom as to adoptions prevailing in Travancore may be extracted from the Travancore High Court Reports.[3]

"The object of adoption among the Sudras is purely secular, being either the perpetuation of the Tarwad and the conservation of its endowments, or else its advancement in the social scale, this last being known as *Jathi Sreshtatha* adoption. It is the case that Sudra adoption has some resemblance to the Krithrima form of adoption recognised by the Hindu Law; that there are three kinds of adoption among the Sudras, namely, of a whole family, of a few females, and of a few males and females; that there is no limit of age or number; that, generally, the parties should be of the same caste; that in Travancore, the adoption of a person of a lower order into a higher order is permissible; and that the confirmation by a Royal Neet, issued upon payment of Adiara fees, is necessary to confer validity on adoption."

"Where one or more members only of the Tarwad, and not the entire family, are adopted into a new one, the adoptees forfeit their rights in their natural family in the absence of special reservation to the contrary; but if the adoption be wholesale, the adoptees retain their full rights in their old family, though they may acquire new rights in the new Tarwad; the properties

1. Tohfut-ul-Mujahideen p. 66.
2. Selections from the Asiatic Journal Vol. II, p. 661.
3. Vol. II, p. 666—7.

of the adoptees held in their own right should be viewed as separate or self-acquired property; the adoptive Karanavan can have no more right over the property of his adoptive Seshakars than the natural Karanavan over that of his natural Seshakars; and the Royal Neet was not intended to confer upon his adoptive Karanavan any rights in the natural Tarwad of his adoptive Seshakars."

"The Adiyara fees are, as a rule, to be paid by the Tarwad of the adoptee or adoptees. Where the adoption is of one's own children—which is preferred—the Adiyara fee is to be equal to one-third of the gross value of the property of the adopter, but where those to be adopted belong to a strange Tarwad, the fee is to be equal to one-half of the adoptee's property; and sometimes an extra fee is levied when the parties are not of the same grade".

The law will not be found to differ much in other parts of Malabar.

It may seem strange, but none the less it is true, that the law as administered in Malabar by the courts is different from the law as observed by the people. In Malabar there is no express or written law; neither is there any written record of customs. Instead of enquiring as to what the custom or usage was with regard to any particular question coming before them, the earlier judges plunged headlong into a discussion of theories arguing them out to their logical conclusion. They seem to have aimed more at the attainment of logical perfection with regard to abstract theories than to the ascertainment of facts as they existed in the concrete. In courts of law impartibility of family property is the rule prescribed, and the family itself is, as we have seen, indivisible; and yet, in daily life, there is scarcely any family in the country whose means could afford to do so that has not divided itself and partitioned its property. So early as 1810, the Provincial Court of the Western Division decided in favour of partibility.

The native judges, who may be presumed to be conversant with the customs and habits of their brethren, were invariably inclined to favour the view. But with the highest court of appeal the necessity to "consistently carry out the doctrine that all rights to property are derived from females", stood in the way of admitting the right of an individual to demand his share. This is accentuated by the observations of Mr. Justice Holloway in *Munda Chetty* v. *Timmaju Hensu*. "Decisions dividing family property have also been passed in Malabar, and it is one of the claims of our late colleague, Mr. Justice Strange, upon that respect which we all feel for him, that he successfully resisted the attempts of lower courts, also acting upon their own views of expediency, to introduce foreign admixtures into a law of which, whatever may be thought of the policy, none can deny the consistency with the theory upon which it is based".[1]

To Mr. Justice Holloway, as we have found, a Nair adoption was "a singular and unheard of process;" and the adoption of a nephew a "ludicrous absurdity", and yet adoption is a matter of daily practice and has been so for a long time, and is at present recognised by courts.

With regard to marriage, we have shown by what process of reasoning the Malabar Marriage Commission came to the extraordinary conclusion that the institution of marriage was, and is, entirely absent from the Marumakkathayam system. The Madras High Court could not give legal recognition to such cohabitation as obtains in Malabar under Sambandham union, because "it founds upon it no rights of property or inheritance".[2] And what is more extraordinary still is the observation of their Lordships of the Privy Council coming as it does after the report of the Marriage Commission that

1. 1 M. H. C. R. p. 380.
2. I. L. R. 6 Mad. 374.

"the Nairs are persons amongst whom polyandry is legally recognised," a statement, the correctness of which is, to put it mildly, in its naked form, open to considerable doubt.

So also with respect to the separate and self-acquired property of an individual member left undisposed of at his death. The courts held till but recently that it lapses to the family. The usage amongst the people is that such property goes to the nearest kin of the deceased acquirer.

The result of this theorising and speculation is that the progress of the community is arrested in all directions. It is the common experience of all that compulsory non-division by no means helps the economical or social progress of the people. The non-recognition of individual rights in the members of the family and its corollary, the doctrine of lapse regarding separate and self-acquired property, act as a dead weight retarding industrial advancement. There is always a conflict between inclination and duty in the minds of the members of a Tarwad, and most prominently in that of the Karanavan or manager. The junior members do not feel any responsibility for, till they are called on to administer the affairs of the Tarwad in their turn as Karanavan, they have only the right of bare maintenance in the Tarwad house, however rich the estate may be. It is not incumbent on the Karanavan to educate them, much less to start them in life.[1] Secure of their means of subsistence, they become the drones of the family, scarcely fit to assume management when their time comes. Consequently the family property falls into the hands of incompetent managers who allow it to go to rack and ruin. In the onward march of time the conditions of society have considerably changed. New ideas have been infused and new forms have taken root. The joint family system has loosened its hold on the people, and the desire to possess individual rights in

1. 8 Mad. Law Journal, p. 294.

property is steadily gaining ground. In fact Malabar society has left its old moorings, and it is undoubtedly the duty of judicial tribunals, so far as lies in their power, not to allow it to drift for itself and work its own salvation, but to guide and pilot it to a safe haven.

The law of property in Malabar being based altogether on usage, it would have been well if the judges who administered that law had allowed more weight to the views and wishes of the people as manifested by usage than to their own notions of a perfect system of Marumakkathayam Law which is nowhere expounded in writing. In this connection I am tempted to repeat the observations already made that public opinion is everywhere and at all times the source of all law, meaning private law, and custom is the most concrete expression of public opinion, and it is through judicial recognition that custom becomes incorporated with the law of a country where it prevails. No political legislation is needed to legalise custom, and mere judicial sanction is enough. Where the law is unwritten, judicial legislation can give legal effect to notions which have a prevailing preponderance in the community. In Malabar the law is unwritten. The observations of Chief Justice Cockburn in *Wason* v. *Watters*, already quoted, regarding the advantages of a system of unwritten law which gives scope for judicial legislature apply with great force to Malabar.

It is evident from the observations made above that the beneficial growth of customary law in Malabar to suit the necessities of a progressive and advancing society has been unfortunately arrested by courts of law that were and are not altogether well informed as to the conditions of the society to which the law applied.

Birth : *Ante-Natal and other ceremonies.* The first ceremony generally observed, specially among

AM.

women of the higher and well-to-do classes, is that of *Bhajanam*. This may last for 7 or 12 days, and is observed in the 7th month of pregnancy. It is a sort of penance. The pregnant woman bathes and worships in the temple every morning, and keeps on circumambulating the shrine till the mid-day Pūja is over, partakes of a small quantity of butter over which the temple priest has muttered holy manṭṟaṃs, returns home and has her breakfast. She is during the period holy, does not touch any one, even those of the household, because, if she does so, she has to take a dip bath before she can eat. In the evening also she attends the temple, takes her rounds, and performs her worship. At the end of the period, a ceremony is performed in the temple at which offerings of various kinds are made. Even after the Bhajanam is over, till delivery, the pregnant woman continues the worship in the temple. It will be observed that this gives her very good physical exercise of a mild character.

Pulikuti. This is performed in the 9th month and is a ceremony which can on no account be dispensed with. The day and the hour are fixed by the village astrologer. A twig of the Aṃpaḻaṁ (*Spondias Mangiefera*) tree is planted in the Naṭumuṟṟam, (middle courtyard,) on the morning of the day. At the auspicious hour the pregnant woman, after having bathed and attired herself in a set of new unbleached cloths, sits facing eastward in a particular portion of the house (Vaṭakini or northern wing.) The Ammāyi, *i. e.*, the maternal uncle's wife, goes and plucks a few leaves from the planted twig and squeezes a few drops of its juice into a cup and hands it over to the woman's brother, or as in some parts to her husband, who drops the juice into the mouth of the woman with his right hand over which is held a country knife (pisṡānkaṭṭi) which he grasps in his left hand. This he does three times, and the woman drinks the juice. It is essential that either the knife should have a gold handle or that the brother should wear a gold ring on his right hand ring-finger. In the absence of a brother, some near relation may officiate. In South Travancore, it is a Māran who officiates in the absence of a brother, and the woman is made to stand on a plank facing the east. After she has swallowed the juice, a test is applied to ascertain the sex of the child in the womb. Packets of grains of different sorts are placed before the woman and she is asked to select one of these, and it is supposed that the selected packet will indicate the sex of the child. As an adjunct to the ceremony, a sumptuous feast is given to the friends and relatives of the family who have been invited for the occasion. The whole expense has to be borne by the husband. On the evening some perform a sort of exorcism called Bali Uḷiyal as a safeguard against evil eyes.

Delivery. A barber women officiates as midwife at the delivery. The pregnant woman is taken to a room, known as confinement room, set apart for the purpose,—generally a small, dark ill-ventilated one. She is attended by her elderly female relatives. The messenger who goes to fetch the midwife has to take with him a knife, and should, so far as possible, be accompanied by some one else. This is to avoid the contingency of evil spirits decoying the messenger and turning themselves into the form of the midwife and devouring the fœtus or the new-born babe and doing injury to the mother. The midwife, as soon as she comes, rubs the abdomen of the patient with medicated or simple gingelly oil, which is followed by a hot water fomentation. She is made to walk about the room for some time, and is then made to sit on a footstool or on a low wooden bench (*Kottotam*) in a reclining position her back supported by a companion, generally an old woman. Lying on her back her head is raised and the thighs are stretched wide apart. She is often made to hold herself on to a rope tied to a beam of the room. The midwife sits in front facing her, ready to receive the child. A doctor versed in European methods of treatment is the last person to be called in. All sorts of expedients possible are resorted to before this is done. If the labour is protracted and the pain is severe, it is so because the patient is possessed, and the village astrologer with his companion the sorcerer is called in. Expiatory ceremonies and propitiatory offerings follow. Charms are tied to the person of the patient. If the delivery is complicated by the presentation of an arm or a leg of the babe, it is pushed in, or hot splinter or a pointed pin is used in expectation of its being drawn in, as at sometimes happens. When all expedients fail, a doctor is sent for. Soon after the delivery of the placenta, the umbilical cord, measured generally up to the chin of the child, is cut and tied with a few strips of an alkaline fibre called *Incha*. The mother and child are bathed sometimes in warm water. The child is placed on the bare floor and the father or another relative sprinkles on it some cold water or water of a tender cocoanut with a gold ring. It is believed that the temperament of the child is determined by that of the person who does it. The mother, and the other members of the family observe pollution for a period of fifteen days. On the fifteenth day, the *Cheethikan* or *Attikurussi* sprinkles on the woman a liquid mixture composed of the five products of the cow (*Panchagavyam*) to which gingelly oil is added, and the Vēlaṭṭi (low class washerman) purifies all clothing by sprinkling on it a mixture of ashes and water. The Vēlaṭṭi also supplies cloth washed by her for wear before the purificatory bath. The delivered woman then takes a plunge bath in a tank or river, after which she is purified. The other members of the Tarwad need only bathe themselves to be purified. During these 15 days, none of them can enter the inner precincts of a temple.

Treatment. High caste patients generally bathe in warm or cold water immediately after delivery. The mother is given a decoction of Neem bark, or other drugs and medicinal herbs, mixed with jaggery. From the fourth day after delivery, the delivered woman begins her regular bath, but has oil rubbed all over on the 7th, 9th, 12th, and 15th day. Whenever she washes her body, she undergoes a course of shampooing with hot water and green leaves of a number of plants boiled in the water. The leaves of many hedge plants are plucked and put into the water. The boiled leaves and water are supposed to possess medicinal properties to remove any slight swelling or pain and to promote free circulation. In many cases, the women of the village undertake these soothing processes by turns as a matter of love and duty towards their neighbour, the midwife herself offers her services in several others. The delivered woman continues to take native medicine for varying periods of 28, 56 or 90 days. The miscellaneous group of drugs called Pĕṟṟumarunnu (delivery medicine) consists, among other things, of pepper, aloes, garlic, cloves, cardamoms, cinnamon, coriander, and anise. The native druggist has only to be asked for Pĕṟṟumarunnu. He knows it all. He has learnt from his father or other relative the ingredients required. He packs up a pinch of most of the drugs in his shop, and there is the medicine. All these are powdered and mixed up with gingelly oil, and a pretty large dose of it is taken twice a day before meals. The Brahman midwife has her own electuary, the ingredients of which correspond more or less to the group of drugs mentioned above. During the period, the patient takes complete rest, and is put on diet. She is prohibited from drinking water, and complete abstinence from chillies, butter-milk, tamarind, etc., is rigidly enforced during the period of convalescence. Even the poorer classes go through almost the same course of treatment but only for a shorter period. Now-a-days, the more well-to-do sections are content with the *Dhanvanthara* decoction or some electuary prescribed by a native physician, rest and diet. In towns, the hospital treatment, or English treatment as it is called, is freely resorted to, chiefly by the younger generation, in view of the liberty it allows as regard food, drink, etc..[1]

First Birth-day. This is celebrated on the 28th day after birth, and is known as *Irupathettu purannal.* This will be the first recurring day of the star under which the child was born. On that day the child is fed with a spoonful or two of milk with sugar and a slice of plantain fruit. This is done by the Karnavan. In some parts the child receives its name on this day. The ceremony winds up as usual with a feast to friends and relatives, the necessary expenses being met by the father of the child.

Choroon or Rice-giving. This is the first rice giving to the child, which is celebrated with great ceremony in the 6th month after birth. Till then the child is fed not with rice, but with the flour of dried plantains boiled with sugar or jaggery. Mellin's food and Nestle's food are now frequently used by the well-to-do people. The rice-giving ceremony is not unfrequently performed in some temple of celebrity. The child is placed in the lap of its maternal uncle or father sitting facing the fane. A plantain leaf is placed in front in which boiled rice, which has been previously offered to the deity of the temple, is served along with tamarind, salt, chillies and sugar. At the auspicious hour fixed by the village astrologer, the uncle or father, as the case may be, puts into the mouth of the child a mixture of tamarind, salt and chillies, and then some rice, and lastly a little sugar. If the child has not already been named, the father or uncle calls the child by its proposed name three times in its ear. After this the child is fed with rice, the staple food of the Nāyars. Till then the child is not adorned with ornaments of any sort. But just before the rice is given, it is decked with ornaments provided by the father and the *bandhus* (relatives). It is indispensable that the bandhus, especially the Ammāyi (the maternal uncle's wife), should adorn the child with

1. *Cochin Census Report*, p. 222.

bracelets, rings, necklaces, etc. Till the first rice-giving, the child is given a sort of medicinal preparation consisting of Vayambu (*Acorus calamus*), *Eloeoearpus lanceolatws*, gallnuts, coral, gold, and silver.

The succeeding ceremonies, such as the boring of the ears, which is done either at the end of the year or sometimes later, the first cutting of the hair, initiation into letters, etc., are all of minor importance. It will have been observed that all the ceremonies observed by the twice-born are also observed by the Nāyars, but, with this important difference, all have to be performed without the recitation of manṭras.

First Menses. When a girl attains maturity, there is regular festivity for full four days. This is called Ṭiranṭukuli, i. e., bath after first menses. When the fact is known, the girl is accommodated in a room where a brass lamp will be kept burning, and which will be decorated by a pot with a bunch of cocoanut flowers. She holds in her hand a Vālkaṇṇāṭi, *i. e.*, a looking glass, with a handle, wrought of bell-metal. She is visited by the females of the neighbourhood as also by relatives, the latter presenting her with elegant new cloths. On the third day, the Karakkār or Ḍēśakkār, *i.e.*, the villagers, are invited to a luncheon of milk and rice porridge, or *Palkanji*. On the fourth day comes on the purification. The girl is anointed with oil and decked with imitation ornaments made of the tender leaves of the cocoanut tree. In the company of a number of young maidens she is brought out of the room to an ornamental pandal in front of the house and seated there. Here the Maṇṇān or Vēlan sings certain songs, after which the party proceeds to a tank to bathe. The girl wears a cloth washed by the Vēlans, with which she bathes. After the bath is over, the Vēlans sing once more. In some parts this bathing takes place in a tank at a distance, and the girl, decked in all sorts of gay attire and covered with jewels, is brought to her house in procession with music and tom toms with no end of shouting. In the afternoon, the Vēlans have one more turn of singing their curious songs, this time the last. The girl in company of female relatives and friends resorts to the pandal, and the Vēlans sing standing at a distance. In the course of the singing, they call on the friends and relatives of the girl to make presents of cloths, which are cheerfully given. The Vēlan of course gets his other dues and perquisites of money, rice, paddy, oil, betel leaf, etc. The never-to-be-left-out feasting follows; the invited guests, and the poor are sumptuously entertained and with the usual distribution of *pan-supari* the ceremony ends. In some parts the last ceremony of the Vēlans' singing is put off to some other day. If so put off, the girl is prohibited from going to temples, etc., till that is over. At the subsequent monthly periods, as they recur, the Nāyar woman confines herself for three days to a neat place in a secluded corner of the house where she is not likely to touch or be touched by others. For these three days she is prevented from wearing ornaments, decking herself with flowers, using perfumes, eye-salves, etc. She should not touch anything in the house. Food is served apart by a female member of the family. The orthodox view is that she should neither clean her teeth nor bathe for these three days; at any rate she should not do either on the third day. On the fourth day she should bathe after sunrise, wearing a cloth supplied by a Maṇṇān or Vēlan woman.

Birth-day. A Nāyar celebrates his birth-day with joyous feasting; of course only those who can afford to do so. He bathes in the morning, worships in the village temple, makes offerings to the deity and gives a sumptuous feast to friends, relations and neighbours. The completion of one's sixtieth year, or as it is called Ṣhaṣhṭyabḍapūrṭṭi, is a great event which is attended with offerings to the deity, presents to

Brahmans, and feasting them, as well as relatives, friends, etc.

Death and succeeding ceremonies. The ideas entertained by the Nāyars as to the terrors of death, etc., are described elsewhere. As death approaches, relatives and friends gather round the dying man and watch him. Ḍānams, *i. e.*, gifts to Brahmans, consisting of two pieces of a particular kind of cloth called muṫi and some money, varying from 10 as. to 3 or 4 Rs. representing the value of a cow, per head, are given away. Brahmans repeat the Sahasṫanāmaṃ, or the thousand names of the God Viṣhṇu in the hearing of the dying individual. At intervals the Rāmāyaṇa and the Bhāgavaṭa are read out in a loud tone so that the dying being may hear. The friends and relatives one by one pour into the mouth of the patient a little water, if possible the water of the sacred river Ganges, by means of a Ṭuḷasi leaf, holding in the hand a gold ring or a piece of gold, the idea being that the water should touch the gold ere it enters the mouth. As life departs, the Yāṭrā Ḍānam, *i. e.*, the parting gift, is made. Certain brass vessels, pieces of cloth, and some money are placed near the death-bed, and a Brahman, sitting close by, receives them from the dying individual, his hands touching the same. Soon after this, the body is taken down from the bed and laid on the floor before life is altogether extinct with the head placed towards the south. If possible, the last breath is spent on a Ṭuḷasi plant. The eyes are closed and the corpse covered with a cloth, or a piece of silk. The toes are tied together with a strip of cloth. The relatives go round the body three times, and prostrate at the feet. All round the body, in fact all along the way to the cremation ground, cocoanuts cut into halves with lights burning in them are placed. Lamps are lighted where the corpse is laid. Of course there is loud wailing. The Ḍēśakkārs or villagers assemble, for it is their function to see the body cremated. A mango tree is cut for fuel, and the funeral pyre is prepared in the compound in which the house is situated, for a Nāyar is very particular that his body should be burned in his own ground. A small pit about the size of the corpse is dug, three long pieces of the plantain tree are placed crosswise, one at each end and one at the middle. Upon this the pyre is raised. By the time this is prepared, the body will have been removed to the front yard of the house, and laid on a long plantain leaf. In some parts this is done in the Naṭumiṯṯam or central yard of the house. Here it is washed and anointed, and the usual marks are made with sandal paste and ashes and neatly clothed. Some rice and a piece of gold are put into the mouth. The body is then covered up with new cloths tied at the ends, and in the middle with shreds torn from the covering cloth. It is then carried by the male members of the family, who are junior to the deceased, to the funeral pyre, which is always situated towards the south of the house, that being the direction towards which the souls of the departed are supposed to go. The corpse being placed on the pyre with head towards the south, the senior ananṭaravan, *i. e.*, the next one in age after the deceased, tears a piece of cloth from the one with which the body is covered and ties it round his waist. Sometimes shreds torn from this are distributed to the other juniors, who have to join the senior in the ceremonies. After this the mourners place on the pyre pieces of fuel, sandalwood, etc. In this the sons of the deceased man also take part. The fuel is then piled over the body and the whole set fire to by the chief mourner, the senior ananṭaravan. By the time the body is wholly consumed, the mourners will have gone to the nearest tank and bathed. They return dripping and perform *Bali* or oblation at the foot of the pyre. The chief mourner brings a pot of water which he carries round the pyre three times, another from behind making incisions in the pot so that the water may spill on the pyre. On completing the third round the pot is dashed on the ground close by where the head of the corpse had been placed. The oblations follow this. and consist of raw rice, water, and gingelly seeds. Some fire is taken from the pyre with which a heap of paddy husk, placed where the head of the corpse had rested after removal from the bed, is lighted, this being removed only after Sanchayanam, or the picking up of the calcined remains from the pyre. The party then proceed to make the Uḍaka Kṛiya, or libation of water, a ceremony which has to be repeated for seven days continuously. It consists in dipping oneself in water, and offering oblations of raw rice, gingelly seed, and turmeric on a husked cocoanut placed on a stone at the water edge of a tank. Three turns of this have to be taken by each. The women need not perform this. After this is over, the mourners bathe once more, and return to the front yard of the house which will have been cleaned and smeared with cowdung. Here a small shed made of green cocoanut leaves is made, within which three pieces of green cocoanut stalk are planted. A tender cocoanut with the rind on it is also placed within. The Chīṭikan or Aṭṭikuṛiśśi who officiates as Purōhit or priest will have prepared the necessary materials for oblation, *viz.*, a few grains of gingelly, some turmeric, etc. The mourners boil or rather half boil some rice in a vessel placed on the stalks planted in the shed—at any rate they make a show of this here—the rice being actually boiled outside. A Kūṛśam, or representation of the deceased, is made and placed in front of the shed, and the oblations are offered there, the Chīṭikan or Chīṭiyan giving directions as to the method, in which the offering is to be made. The half-boiled rice is made into balls and offered. The mourners in turn sit on their haunches with the left knee touching the ground while making the oblations. They sit facing the south and wear a Paviṭṛam or ring made of plantain leaf twisted into a peculiar shape on the ring finger. The women offer sitting on their feet facing the east. They offer the half boiled rice without making them into balls. When the whole thing is over, the rice balls (piṇḍās) are gathered up and placed in the open on the southern side of the house at a place which had been previously smeared with cowdung for the crows to feed on. If a large number of crows gather and eat them up, the *manes* are supposed to be pleased. On the 3rd, 5th or 7th day, the Sanchayanam, or the picking up of the calcined bones, comes on. These are picked up by the mourner, his mouth being covered up, by means of sticks cut from a particular tree called Neḷuku, and gathered in a vessel made of the green bark or film of the areca branch. They are washed in milk in a half burnt pot, which is buried in a corner of the yard, until they are consigned to the Ganges or thrown into the sea at Rāmēśwaram. Till then a lamp is lighted every day over the place where the pot lies buried. The oblation ceremony described above is repeated every morning till on the 15th day when something more elaborate has to be performed. On that day the death pollution ceases, for a Nāyar's death pollution, as prescribed by the Śāstras, extends to 14 complete days or 900 Nāḷikas or Indian hours. On the 15th day, the Chīṭigar purifies the family by sprinkling on its members a mixture made up of the five products of the cow to which is added gingelly oil. After this a plunge bath is taken, on return from which the mourners sit to have their last turn with the Chīṭiyan. This day's oblations are in a more elaborate form, the Purōhit taking his food previously prepared by the mourners, while giving his directions regarding the ceremony. Lighted lamps with rice, paddy, etc., are placed at the spot. The Chīṭiyan has his oil bath and is dressed in new clothes in the peculiar style of the Brahmans. Towards the end of the ceremony, the chief mourner gathers the Piṇḍa in a bell-metal vessel, in which a representation of a Ṭēru or chariot is placed with lighted wicks. He is asked to take the vessel in both his hands and raise it up to the level of his head three times, the idea being that the soul of the deceased is being sent up to the heavens in a chariot. He then carries it to the tank and going waist-deep throws it behind overhead. This ceremony is called Piṇḍam Iṭṭu Kuli *i. e.*, the bath after depositing Piṇḍas. After this he bathes and returns home. At the threshold he is met by a female member of the house with Aṣhṭamangalyam, *i. e.*, a plate in which are placed eight auspicious things. She throws some rice on his head, and makes a mark on his forehead with lamp black. In many parts, specially towards the north, it is the Eṇangan (one of the same clan) who takes the place of the Chīṭiyan in many of the details given above. It would seem that in the north no ceremony is observed between the 7th and 14th day after death. All these 15 days the chief mourner is always armed with a knife so that the departed may not harm him even for any defects in the performance of the ceremonies.

The 16th day ceremony or Piṇḍam or Paṭināṟu-aṭiyanṭaram, is a grand affair. It is the funeral repast, and was perhaps originally designed as a compensation for the trouble taken by the villagers, friends and relatives, in getting the body cremated. After the cremation is over that day, in some parts, mostly in the south, the villagers gather in front of the house and place in the yard the spades, axes, and other implements used in gathering fuel, digging the pit, etc. The male members of the family go round them three times, after which the company disperse. For the 16th day feast or Paṭināru, the villagers, friends, and relatives are invited to attend, and the two latter from far and near make it a point to attend. But, before the feast, there are other and more important ceremonies to be gone through. After the Chīṭiyan or Eṇangan, as the case may be, has eaten in the house on the 15th day, all may freely come in and go out without fear of pollution; for, before that, any man from outside coming into the house has to take a plunge bath before he can eat. The Chīṭiyan hands over the mourners to the Elayaṭu, the regular Chīṭiyan Purohit of the Nāyars, a low class Nambuṭiri Brahman, who is supposed to have been degraded for officiating at a Nāyar's Śrāḍha. In aristocratic houses, it is a Nambuṭiri that officiates and not an Elayaṭu. Early in the morning of the 16th day, five of these Elayaṭus perform Puṇyāham, *i. e.*, purify the house, after which they prepare for the Bali or offering to the soul of the deceased. Some raw rice is boiled; gingelly seeds, oil, curds, Kaḍali Palam (a sort of plantain fruit), honey, molasses, Anjanam (sulphurate of antimony) are all used at the offering. Instead of the Ṭulasi used by the women, the men use the small leaves of a plant called Cheṛula. A lamp (Nilavilakku) is lighted in front of which is placed a plantain leaf containing a few plantain fruits and molasses. A (*parah*) measure of paddy and an Eḍangali (10 of which go to make a para) of rice with a cocoanut are also placed in front of the lamp. The women, who have to join in the Bali, sit, in a row facing the east, each having a Kindi or brass vessel with a spout filled with water and a small piece of plantain leaf, on which are placed gingelly seed, the leaves of the Tulasi plant, (*Ocymum sanctum*) sandal paste, and some boiled rice. At the directions of the Elayaṭu, they make libations of water, water mixed with sandal paste, water mixed with gingelly seed, offer the Ṭulasi leaves and finally make an oblation of the boiled rice, all the while wearing on the ring finger of the right hand a Paviṭram, ring of peculiar form made of plantain leaves. The men make these offerings in turn, the eldest leading the way, sitting on his haunches with the left knee touching the ground facing the south. They wear their loin cloth in a peculiar fashion called Ṭaṭṭuṭukkal, have on the ring finger of the right hand a Paviṭram made of the Kaṛuka grass (*Agnostis linearis*). On the right hand side is placed on a plantain leaf, the materials already named. Two brass Kīṇḍies or vessels filled with water are placed in front of them. On the left hand side is another plantain leaf with the boiled rice. Some Kaṙuka grass is spread in front of the performer on which the offerings are made. Libations of water, of water mixed with gingelly seed, water mixed with sandal paste are made 3 times and 5 times in turn, each of the mourners has to go through three courses. At the third course, the Piṇḍa or rice formed into balls is offered. In forming the balls, milk, honey, plantain fruit, molasses, gingelly seeds and ghee are mixed with the rice. Each of the mourners pour on the Piṇḍa offered by him gingelly oil, *Anjanam* (antimony sulphurate) mixed in water, and curds. He also places on it a thread. The idea is perhaps that the soul of the deceased is supplied with all that it wants in its passage to the other world. There is yet another course in which the younger members only touch the eldest while he invokes the attention of the manes of three generations of his ancestors in the ascending scale and offers oblations to them. Finally the soul of the departed is assimilated by a process of will power with the supreme one, or the universal soul, after which the rice balls are given to the crows. The last ceremony is known as Sapiṇḍīkaraṇa, in which one of the members, who is to observe Ḍīkṣha or penance for a year, does not take part. He has to lead a holy and abstemious life for one full year, growing hair abstaining from flesh, meat, sexual connection, etc., and continue performing Bali every day.

Zeen-ud-deen notes this custom. He says "Upon the death of any great person or near relative, as a father or mother, or elder brother, amongst the Brahmans of Malabar or of a mother, or maternal uncle, or elder brother, amongst the Nayars, and their connections, the men of both these castes will abstain for a whole year from associating with women and from eating animal food; during this time, also, neither shaving their hair, nor cutting their nails, but rigidly enduring these and such mortifications, out of reverence to the memory of the dead."[1]

This sort of penance should continue till the Māsam, or the first annual ceremony, when it is concluded, the Elayaṭu officiating at the Bali as described above. Gifts of money, cloth, and umbrellas, etc., are made to Elayaṭus, and the whole ceremony is wound up with a grant feast to friends, relatives, villagers and Brahmans. The poor also receive their share. Ever after this, there is the Śrāḍha or annual offer of oblations made till the Gaya Śrāḍha is performed. For this, one has to go on a pilgrimage to the well known shrine of Vişhṇupāḍa at Gaya. Here Pinḍa is offered at the foot-print of Vişhṇu, and at the foot of the Akṣhaya Vaṭa Vṛkṣha. At the former, the soul of the deceased is believed to get absorbed into Vişhṇu, and at the latter the offerer is supposed to realise that he has performed his duty towards the departed by receiving at the hands of the Gayāvāli, or Purōhit, *Suphalam*, flowers, ashes, etc. Instead of going to Gaya in North India, the Malayalees need go only to Tiruvallam, a few miles South of Trivandrum, which is the place assigned for them by Paraśu Rāma, for the performance of the last Śrāḍha.

The object of the Śrāḍha ceremony is explained by Professor Monier Williams in the following way: "The Hindus fancy that a man has three bodies; and sometimes the attempt is made to puzzle Christian preachers by catechising them on this point. The first is the sthūla sarira, or gross body, which is burned; but the soul quits with the linga sarira, or subtle body, sometimes described as having the size of the thumb, and hovering near the former. The departed spirit has now no real body capable of enjoying or suffering anything, so that it is restless, uncomfortable, and impure. If funeral rites are not performed, it may become a foul, wandering ghost, disposed to take

1. P. 62.

revenge for its misery on all living creatures by malignant acts.

The object of the Śrāḍha is to soothe the troubled spirit by libations of consecrated water, and to furnish it with an intermediate body, by which alone it can obtain gaṭi, or progress onward to other births, and emancipation. The first piṇḍa offered endows it with the rudiments or basis of a body; the next day another piṇḍa supplies limbs, and so on. When the soul receives a complete body, it becomes a piṭṛu (ancestor), and is held to be a ḍēva or deity, and practically worshipped as such in the Śrāḍha ceremonies, which continue to accelerate its progress onwards to a temporary heaven, and then through various stages to bliss, to final union with the supreme".[1]

On the day of the death, the Banḍhus, i. e., those who are allied by marriage, bring Paṭṭiṇikkari, i. e., some raw rice, and Paṭaṛṛukāya, a sort of plantain fruit, intended to be used for the first meal of the family of the deceased. Condolence visits are made by relatives (Kaṇṇōkkukāṇuka, seeing eye to eye) when they bring with them quantities of beaten rice (*aval*), fried rice (*malar*), tobacco, and plantain fruits. In some parts there is a custom of all those who are related by marriage to the ṭaṛawāḍ of the deceased combining and giving a good feast to the inmates of the house and to the neighbours who are invited. This feast is called Paṭṇi Kanji. In south Travancore, there is a system of mutual aid, by which all articles required for the 16th day ceremony are supplied by the villagers, these being in their turn aided when the occasion comes.

Amusements and recreations. The amusements and recreations described elsewhere are all participated in by the Nāyars. The Kaṭhakaḷi or Drama and the Oṭṭam Ṭuḷḷal were favourite pastimes till but recently. Now they are thought to be fit more for the study than for the stage. Their place is now taken up by the

1. Indian Antiquary of July 1876.

Ñāṭakam or Drama proper. The Kaṭhakaḷi or Malayalam Drama is more than 300 years old, and was brought into existence by the Koṭṭārakkaray Raja. It was originally known as Rāmanāṭṭam, as opposed to Kṛṣhṇāṭṭam, designed and introduced by the Zamorin. The first was so called because the earliest theme theatrically represented dealt with the story of Rāma, while the latter took its name from the circumstance that it treated of the story of Kṛṣhṇa. Both are dumb shows; the characters representing by means of signs made by the hand, by facial contortions, and gestures, the story sung in long drawn songs by the Bhāgavaṭar or songster standing behind. These dramas are written in mixed verse and *quasi* prose, slōkas and paḍams. The claim of the last to be styled poetry is questionable. None the less, both are sung by the Bhāgavaṭar. The accompaniments of the song are an Elaṭṭālam or a circular plate of bell-metal gong, on which strokes are made with a stick to keep time, a muḍḍalam (a long finger drum), a cheṇṭa (Kettle drum), and Kaimaṇi (a pair of small circular bellmetal pieces). The play lasts for 8 or even 10 hours in the night. The characters, representing Kings, Asuras, Rākṣhasas, monkeys, birds, etc., put on fantastic dresses, paint their faces in hideous fashion, wear head pieces of peculiar make, each character having its own distinctive dress and appearance. There is a very little attempt at representation of scenery. The acting and the actors literally act—takes place in a panṭal or shed in the open, so that all who may resort to it may see the play. All the three classes Nambūṭiris, Kṣheṭṛiyas, and Nāyars take part in these plays. The following criticism of the Kaṭhakaḷi by Mr. T. K. Krishna Menon will be found to correctly represent the attitude of modern educated Malayalees towards their national drama.

"They, by means of appropriate gestures, convey to the audience the meaning of the prose portions, when they are sung to the accompaniment of the beating of drums and other instruments. No doubt some of these

CHARACTERS OF THE MALABAR DRAMA (Kathakali).

[To face p. 322.

OATTANTHULLAL.

pieces when sung by clever singers without the accompaniment of the discordant sounds of drums and metal gongs bring with them such charm and inexpressible delight to the hearer as may

'Dissolve one into ecstasies
Or bring all heaven before one's eye'.

But, as at present performed, these dramas serve no purpose whatever. Speaking generally, there is considerable dissatisfaction prevalent among the English educated Malayalees towards this institution of Kaṭhakaḷi. It is high time, they say, either to mend or to end it".

The Ōṭṭam Ṭuḷḷal is a singing performance of stories generally taken from the Purāṇas, and done into verse of a peculiar form, introduced for the first time by the distinguished Malayalam poet Kunchan Nampiār (A.D. 1705—1770). We may quote here with advantage Mr. T. K. Krishna Menon's observations on the Ṭuḷḷal. "Ṭuḷḷal, literally dances, are sung to the accompaniment of music, pantomime, and dancing. There are three classes of Ṭuḷḷals: Ōṭṭam, Śīṭankan, and Paṛayan; but, as the poems of the first class predominate, the poems of the other classes are also termed Ōṭṭams. They are based mostly on the episodes of Bhāraṭam and Rāmāyaṇam. Ōṭṭam Ṭuḷḷal as the name indicates (oattam=running) consists of a variety of rapid metres, well suited for amusing narratives. The pure Ōṭṭam is more vigorous than Śiṭankan while the Paṛayan is the best suited for the pathetic style".

The performer of the dance dresses in a peculiar style with a curious head piece on, has tinkling bells attached to his waist and ankles, and sings while dancing. The song is taken up by those standing behind, who use the gong and long finger drum to keep time. It generally lasts for a couple of hours. In the good old days these songs used to be sung by the Nāyars while on their march to battle.

Hunting is a favourite source of recreation, especially in rural and hilly districts. The Nāyar women amuse themselves by Kaikoṭṭi-Kaḷi or Ṭiruvāṭirakaḷi, a sort of dancing with appropriate songs, specially during the Ṭiruvāṭira season in January, when they also enjoy the Ūlinjāl or swinging to and fro, for which there are special songs in the south. At other times they have very little amusement or recreation, unless it be in reading the vernacular renderings of the Purāṇas etc.

General education. Malabar is perhaps the most literate country in all India, specially with regard to the female sex. The Nāyars are as a class literate; both boys and girls receive the rudiments of education early in life. Speaking of the ' Nāyars of ancient type", Mr. Elie Reclus says, "All knew at least how to read and write".[1]

The children receive their elementary education at the village schools already described in the primitive manner sketched before except in remote corners, as yet untouched by the hand of so-called reform or shall we say revolution, the village schools have now given place to institutions subject to Government inspection conducted on lines sketched out by the grant-in-aid code. The course of study now runs in a different groove. At present the young pupils go from these primary vernacular schools into the English School and pursue their English studies. The Nayars have always shown an admirable aptitude for the study of Sanskrit, and, in spite of the uncompromising orthodox attitude of the Nambuṭiris, they always managed in the past to learn the higher branches of Sanskrit literature from Ampalavāsies and East Coast Brahman Śāsṭries. Nieuhoff tells us that in his day the Nāyars applied themselves to "philosophy and specially to astronomy". They are at present paying considerable attention to the study of English and have succeeded in attaining proficiency in various branches of knowledge. There are among them graduates in Arts, Law, Medicine, Engineering, etc.

1. Page 145.

of the Madras University. Many have obtained European University degrees in various branches of knowledge, while others have come out as Baristers-at-law. The girls too are gradually taking to English education; and there are among them many graduates of the Madras University. There are numerous girls' schools all over the country, with a girls' college at Trivandrum [1], not to mention the high schools maintained by the Native States and the missionary bodies.

National character. We had already occasion to speak of the national character of the race as it appeared to the 16th and 17th century travellers. Before referring to the character of the modern Nāyars, it may not be out of place to notice what is recorded of the Nāyars by the 18th century writers as well.

Two Dutch Governors of Cochin, Gollenesse in 1743, and Moens in 1781, have left us their impressions of the Malabar people; and they are not altogether of a flattering nature. The former observes:—

"Promises are with them very frail ties easily broken if their interests required it and so you cannot look too much about and before you with them and not the slightest trust can be put in their promises. Their many and binding contracts made with the Company, but never kept by them are indisputable proofs of my statement. What can you do with men who, when they are embarrassed or beaten, willingly submit to the terms and conditions of the conquerors, but who have no intention of observing them except as long as they feel the force to which they must bow, and whose good faith and obedience vanish as soon as it is withdrawn from this coast? They are in no way excitable, but very composed; outwardly polite but their heart full of bitterness, they are masters of the art of sounding a person without his noticing. I have often found that when the Signatty wish to obtain something from the Company, he proposed the very opposite, solely with the intention of discovering my sentiments. If rejected

1. There is one at Ernakulam too.

his proposal, he had gained his point; if I granted his request, he would produce so many engines directed to the gaining of his object, that I often found myself in a real quandary scarcely knowing how to repulse the attack.

"They are particularly phlegmatic and redicule the hasty temper of Europeans; and, if you have dealings with them you should treat them according to their own ways. This need not prevent you occasionally using, if necessary, strong language and earnest admonations, but that again will accomplish little unless a good number of soldiers impart weight to your words.

"All transactions with them are very much delayed by their numerous festival days and ceremonies; one must put up with this and there is no remedy; but their lucky and unlucky days which always occur according as their interests demand and just as is convenient to them, are intolerable".[1]

Governor Moens observes:—"In general I must note about the Malabaries that they hav e the characteristics of all other Indian races, viz., they are distrustful, cunning and much attached to their old custom with which they cannot be made to break even if their own welfare should suffer. In particular they are lazy, unashamed, untrue to their word and mendacious in the highest degree, which one must always remember, when one has anything to transact with them."

The condemnation of the character of the Malayalees by the Dutch carries along with it its explanation also. The Dutch, a powerful western nation, had come to Malabar to deprive the Malayalees, a much weaker nation than themselves with little or no resources to withstand the gratuitous onslaughts made on them of their country, their independence and their wealth. In achieving their object, the Dutch had never stopped to enquire of the justice, equity or morality of the means

1. *The Dutch in Malabar*, pp. 51 and 171.

they thought fit to employ. The weaker party had of course to defend itself and the sense of self-preservation had perhaps suggested methods which are not absolutely defensible from a moral point of view. The remarks of Mr. Galletti, the translator of the memoirs quoted above, regarding Gollenesses' statement that the Malayalees very often failed to keep their contracts are very apt. In a note Mr. Galletti observes: "This should not be taken seriously. In a frank passage in his memoir of 1761, Commandeur Caspar de Jong observes that much rubbish was talked about the non-observance of contracts and treaties by native princes. These treaties were sometimes obsolete, sometimes curiously interpreted by the Dutch. Similar charges of not observing treaties could just as easily be brought against the Dutch themselves".

Forbes says, "The Nairs of Malabar are equally brave as, and more energetic than, most of the warlike Hindus. The national characteristics of both people are otherwise very similar. A mild climate and the peculiar tenets of their religion inspire meekness, temperance, and listlessness; they abstain from intoxicating liquors, are seldom guilty of debaucheries, and not subject to many of those passions which enslave the civilized Europeans. Strangers to patriotism, and the blessings of liberty, the Malabars, as well as the Northern Hindus, are governed by fear; loyalty and affection form no part of their political system. Amongst such a people ambition has no scope, every man is confined to his own caste, follows the profession of his ancestors, is married in childhood to his equal, and never rises higher than the limited sphere in which he was born: there may be exceptions, but they are very uncommon.

"Civilization, as far as the Malabars are susceptible of it, has long attained its height. Egypt, Assyria, Persia, Greece, and Rome, from the pinnacle of grandeur, perfect in the fine arts, and the luxury of opulence, have dwindled to a name: the Malabars seem to have been for some thousand years in the same state of mediocrity; on such a system, no new designs in building, no alteration in manners or dress, no improvements in art or science are to be expected.

"That the heat of the Torrid Zone debilitates the body, enervates the mind is very obvious; to this cause may be attributed the want of curiosity, enterprize, and vigour, among the Malabars; their inclinations are chiefly passive; indolence constitutes their happiness, and you cannot impose a severer task than mental employment: with the exception of the warlike Nayars, they pass days, months and years, in swinging in their verandahs or under the shade of a tree chewing betel and singing dismal ditties without a reflection on the past or a plan for the future. From this habitual indolence they become incapable of exertion; and thus the laws, manners and customs, are the same at this day as they were a thousand years ago."[1]

Forbes found in conversing with "the Malabars more suspicion and jealousy than among any other people in India: they were very cautious of giving information; and deemed most common questions intrusive." We get an explanation of this from the writer himself, when he adds, "it was therefore impossible from such a people to obtain much knowledge either of a religious or political nature." Forbes was employed by the English at Anjengo, then a power aspiring to empire in India, who were quietly gathering in the meshes they had thrown round the Peninsula and tightening their grasp on it. The people were naturally reticent in giving information to those who they had ample reason to believe were attempting to subdue them. Grose, writing sometime previously to Forbes, speaks of the "Malabars" as "a civilized race." He says, "The Malabars have in general even a certain politeness, and especially a shrewdness of discernment of their interests, which those who deal or treat with them are sure to experience (as perhaps

1. pp. 242—4.

Forbes did.) Like most of the Orientalists, they are grave, know perfectly well how to keep dignity; and are grave observers of silence (which gave occasion to Forbes to regard them as a suspicious class), especially in their public functions. They despise and distrust all verboseness in their management of state affairs. Their harangues are succinct and pathetic. A King of Travancore (the Great Martanda Varma-1729 to 1758) for example, on two ambassadors being sent to him by the Naick of Madura, a neighbouring prince, and one of them having made a prolix speech and the other preparing to take it up and proceed in the same manner where the other had left off, austerely admonished him in these few words, 'Do not be long, life is short.'

" Lord William Bentinck" says Mr. Logan, "wrote in 1804, that there was one point in regard to the character of the inhabitants of Malabar, on which all authorities, however diametrically opposed to each other on other points agreed, and that was with regard to the 'independence of mind' of the inhabitants. The 'independence of mind' was generally diffused through the minds of the people. They are described as being extremely sensible of good treatment, and impatient of oppression; to entertain a high respect for courts of judicature, and to be extremely attached to their customs. Agriculture is considered as an honourable occupation, and the rights of landed property and the division of the produce of the soil between the landlord and tenant are perfectly defined and confirmed by immemorial usage."

"The independence of mind" says Mr. Logan "which is here referred to by Lord William Bentinck, and which has been noticed by every district officer then and since, could only have been the slow growth of a steady political system, and there can be no doubt that this territorial organization of the Nairs into supervising and protecting agencies was the system which produced and (for India) unexpected results."[1]

Mr. Thomas Harvey Baber, who was for 30 years in Malabar, in his evidence before the House of Lords in 1830, said, in answer to a question about the advisability of introducing the system of trial by jury in Malabar, "I should say decidedly that the people of Malabar were the most intelligent and best informed of any natives I have ever met with that they were more strict observers of truth than the other inhabitants of Hindustan". He said that he attributed this peculiarity to their keen sense of honour and high notions and spirit of independence. "The Nairs or military class of Malabar," says Col. Wilkes, "are, perhaps, not exceeded by any nation on earth in a high spirit of independence and military honour."

In estimating the national character of a people it is necessary to previously study their social and political condition, their antecedents, and the gradual growth and evolution of the peculiar characteristics that mark off the particular class from others. A failure to properly do this has caused Dr. Day in Cochin and the Rev. S. Mateer in Travancore to leave behind them an estimate of the character of the Nairs which in many respects is as incorrect and unsympathetic as it is untrue and unmerited. According to the former, "the Nairs are a proud and warlike race, arrogant to inferiors, subservient to superiors, profuse in promises, and slack in their performance. They occasionally officiate as accountants, but their statements must be received with caution, and additional testimony is generally advisable. Their security is always requested in writing, otherwise it cannot be greatly relied on."[2]

Other writers of a more recent date nave left more pleasing accounts of them. To mention one or two only, Col. Heber Drury, writing in 1889, describes them "as singularly docile and gentle", while

1. Malabar, vol. 1, pp. 267—8.
2. Day's Land of the Perumals, p. 315.

Walter Hamilton refers to them as "the polite Nair." The Travancore Census Commissioner, Dr. Subramania Ayyar, who has a lifelong, intimate acquaintance with the people, one who could, as such, speak with authority observes, "The additional features of the ancient Nāyars have undoubtedly been sweet frankness, reverence to authority, uncalculating hospitality, patient industriousness, and manly affection; and, though with the altered conditions of external life, these features possibly have undergone some modifications, none with any pretentions to familiarity with Malabar and its people could fail to be struck with love and regard for this good and interesting community."

Economic condition. The present economic condition of the Nāyars requires the anxious consideration of the community. They have left their old moorings and are drifting whether they themselves seem not to know. They lost their traditional occupation—fighting. They are no longer the brave soldiers they once were. As observed by Col. Drury, "Whatever may have been said or believed of their bravery and courage as a warrior race in earlier days, can hardly apply to their descendants in the present day. They are singularly docile and gentle and the appellation given to them of 'born soldiers' must be received reservedly." With Tippu's invasion of Malabar and the havoc he created there, the fabric of society was rudely shaken, and on his expulsion from the country the British assumed supremacy. The old Rajas, who had fled from their possessions, returned and were placed in despotic power under the protecting aegis of the new suzerain, but without the checks imposed on them by the ancient constitution. They abused their trust, with the result that there was constant rebellion. The British assumed direct authority, and set themselves to put down the Nāyars and break their political system. This brought about the Pyche or Cottayam Raja's rebellion which exercised the powers of so great a soldier as Col. Sir Arthur Wellesley, who subsequently came to be known as Duke of Wellington. The Nāyars were disarmed, and measures were concerted to destroy their power altogether. Ever after this, they have been an enervated, effiminate, docile, gentle race. The policy that dictated this emasculation of a manly and virile race, which has for aeons and aeons of ages maintained with pride the reputation of being "born soldiers," "best soldiers in the world," of whom it has been remarked that more brilliant soldiers have never been seen and their pride was no trifle"—is, indeed, questionable. However that be, there is the official declaration made by Mr. Logan in the *District Manual of Malabar* that "the martial spirit of the Nayars in these piping times of peace has quite died out for want of exercise. The Nayar is more and more becoming a family man * * * * With a large increase of their numbers, and with comparative poverty for the large body of them, the race is fast degenerating" [1] a circumstance that certainly calls for immediate attention.

The Nāyars were agriculturists in addition to being warriors. Of course all Nāyars were not fighters; but in the early days all fighting men were Nāyars. They were also the Kāṇakar or supervisors of the lands of the Nambūṭiris. and they had themselves lands of their own. Ibn Batuta, travelling from Calicut to Quilon in the early part of the fourteenth century, says "In all this space of two months' journey, there is not a spot free from cultivation. For everybody has here a garden, and his house is placed in the middle of it: and around the whole of this here is a fence of wood, up to which the ground of each inhabitant comes." [2] In the 16th century, we learn from Barbosa, that "they lived in their estates which they fenced in." Pyrard, at the beginning of the 17th century, informs us that "the Nayars are all lords of the land and live on their revenues or on the pension allowed by the king." The lands were actually cultivated by the slave class, such

1. Pages 138.
2. Pages 165—6.

THRESHING CORN

as the Pulayas, etc., the supervision being done by the Nāyars. The Nāyar Brigades of Travancore and Cochin, the only surviving remnants of the old fighting Nāyars, now a body of nominal warriors employed exclusively as guards of honour and watchmen, even now add agriculture to their other profession. While off duty, they engage themselves in cultivating their lands to supplement their scanty pay. Even in the matter of agriculture, at present competitions is keen, and the conditions of cultivation have altered greatly. With the disorganization of the traditional arrangements of professions and industries, a large number of hands have been thrown on land as the only means of obtaining a livelihood. Population has increased to a large extent, and, the people not having enterprise or capital to open up new areas of cultivation, waste lands are seldom taken in hand, while the existing holdings are being parcelled out into innumerable small subdivisions. The result is gradual pauperization. The soil is getting exhausted. Little or no manure is used. The live-stock is deteriorating; the area of pasturage is shrunk, the increase of population has caused all available land to be occupied for habitation, though not for cultivation. Both animal manure and leaf manures are scanty. The forest laws and salt duty sit heavily on the agricultural classes. No common pasture land is reserved, and grazing fees have to be paid to Government for pasturing cattle. The duty on salt is so heavy that it cannot be made available for cattle. Leaf manure cannot be cut without extra fees being paid. Apart from them, there are special causes operating towards the degeneration of the Nāyars. Pride of caste, pride of lineage, pride of profession, an overweening and self-complacent idea of their own importance and superiority as members of society—these have in no small degree contributed towards the bringing into existence of their present condition. They are averse to manual labour of any kind, they think it degrading. A false idea of dignity deters them from undertaking enterprises that will in the long run advance them as a nation. "The toils of culture and of art" as observed by Camoens "they scorn." They have yet to learn the truth what Pope says that

> "Honour and shame from no condition rise
> Act well thy part and there all honour lies."

They have not in them the genius of commerce. They have never taken kindly to the mercantile profession, and they do not like to be merchants or traders. But they stick close to agriculture. What nation has prospered as mere agriculturists and quill-drivers? Though theoretically living a corporate life, corporate action is foreign to them. Want of union among themselves, being the heritage of the joint family wherein a state of perpetual disunion prevails, and want of confidence in others, prevent them from united action and stand in the way of their entering into large undertakings. They seem not to understand that confidence begets confidence. Home sickness and superstition born of the 'absolutism of caste and precedent' are among other causes which have deterred their progress. Their unnatural system of family life, and their laws of inheritance are, in a way, partly responsible for their present condition. The family hangs on them as a heavy millstone, of which any one with a sense of duty in him cannot disencumber himself. There is always a conflict between inclination and duty and, of course, with men of honest principles, the sense of duty must prevail. They have been made weak by 'time and fate.' They have not the patience to suffer and the perseverance to command success. They have not the will 'to strive, to seek, to find and not to yield.'

The Nāyars have from early days served the Governments of the country as accountants, writers, magistrates, judges, governors, etc., and this sort of unproductive official and professional labour has come to be looked upon as higher than agricultural and industrial persuits. They forget that other classes whom they are pleased to designate as lower are gradually

THE LATE MR. T. SANKUNNI MENON, C. S. I.
(He was Diwan of Cochin for about 19 years).

(To face p. 334.

coming up, and that there are influences at work which they cannot stop. The Christian missionary, with his proselytizing and educational labours, has been abroad now for some time, and even the Cherumas and Pulayas have improved under his philanthropic instruction. It is not for us to consider how far the missionaries are right in dislocating traditional arrangements as to the exercise of the various profession of the country. But there can be no doubt that they have conferred the boon of education on the submerged classes, and have elevated them in the social ladder. It is indeed gratifying to see that these classes are pushing forward ever and anon. Unlike the Nāyars, they "scorn delights and live life's laborious days" and are never averse to turn their hands to honest labour to earn an honest penny. The Nāyars have yet to realise the dignity of labour and the spirit of self-sacrifice, how to sink the individual in the nation, and unless prompt measures are adopted to improve their present condition, they will be swamped by the more enterprising classes, such as the Īluvas and Native Christians, both of whom are exhibiting a highly commendable spirit of enterprise, indicating the way to prosperity and affluence—a notable object lesson to the Nāyar community. Let us hope with Dr. Subramania Ayyar that, "with the large number of cultured and still monied men, there is no reason to fear that an early diagnosis will not be made and prompt remedy adopted. Under present circumstances, agriculture must be largely supplemented by industries of all sorts, so organised as to leave intact the independent, self-reliant habit of the earlier people, who would not object to do any kind of work if at their ancestral acre. Material want is the chief enemy of religion, morality, and general character, and all efforts of improvement should go forth in that direction under the ennobling stimulus of internal harmony and universal love."[1]

1. Travancore Census Report, Part 1, p. 30.

After the Nāyars come, the six classes of Śilpis or artizans.[1]

Then follow the Paṭiṭas of whom there are ten classes:—

(1) Kaṇiān, (2) Vilkuṟup, (3) Kuṟup.[2] They are like the Paṇikkars or teachers of gymnastics. (4) Ṭōlekuṟup.[3] They are curriers and work in leather. (5) Vēlan. Low class washermen known also as Maṇṇān who supplies Māṟṟu or cloth washed by them which the higher classes have to wear when being purified from ceremonial pollution caused by death and birth in the family and by menses in women. The following account from Purchas refers to them:—"Another sect is called Manantamar, which are laund..ers, nor may they or their posterity be of other function: nor may they mingle themselves with any other generation. They have idol ceremonies and temples by themselves. Their brethren or nephews are their heirs."[4] (6) Pāṇan. These are tailors. (7) Paravans. These are akin to Muckavas and live on the sea-coast. They collect shells and prepare lime. (8) Īluvan.. (9) Muckavaṇ. (10) Vālan.

After these come the eight classes of Nīcha or polluting castes.

(1) Paṟaya (2) Pulaya (3) Nāyāḍi. (4) Ullāṭan (5) Kuṟumpar (6) Malayar] (7) Vēlan (8) Kaṇiān.

Next comes the eight extra castes, *viz*:—

1 Ammamār. This class is included among the Nambūṭiries from whom they differ only in their system of inheritance which is Marumakkaṭṭāyam.[5] (2) Nampiṭi with sacred thread (3) Nampiṭi without

1. For remarks on these and on many of the other classes given below, see notes in this and in the next chapters.

2. This class includes those in Note 3 to Letter XXI.

3. This class includes those in Note 3 to Letter XXI.

4 Puchas Pilgrimage p. 628.

5. For an account of this class, see note on Nambutiries.

sacred thread. (4) Puṭuvāḷ[1] (5) Pilāppiḷḷi[2] (6) Sāmanṭan (7) Karivēlaṭṭu Nāyar—a special class of Nāyars attached to the Rajas of Kōlaṭṭuṅād and Travancore as body-guards. In all respects they are the same with the other Nāyars. (8) Veḷḷaḷans. They are the inhabitants of Nānjaṅād, a class of Tamil Śūḍras who have adopted the Marumakkaāṭṭyam system of inheritance and who, in other respects, are more Tamilian than Malayali.

1. See note under the head Putuval among the Antaralajatis.

2. See note under the head Pilappilli among the Antaralajatis.

[One of the surest of the tests to ascertain the status of a class of people within the Hindu fold is to look for their connection with the old, well-known temples. This is all the more so in the caste-ridden and priest-ridden Kerala.

The subject, though of absorbing interest from social and historical points of view, is vast, and I shall refer only to a few instances to serve the purpose of this note.

The Thachudaya Kaimal had "entire management and control of the whole of the Irinjalakkuda temple concerns and endowments." He exercised even sovereign rights over the Devaswam Samketams. Even on several spiritual affairs his word was law. As in the case of Brahmans, he is given by the officiating priest *theertham* and *prasadam* in his hands. He has the right like them to get on the *sopanam*, ring the bell and worship. The Ernakulam temple, the temple chronicle says, originally belonged to Thoosath Kaimal. In the Vaikam temple, on the annual *ashtami* night, Karukayil Kaimal is brought in in a palanquin with the appropriate music and drumming, to the front of the procession of the Deity, and is even furnished with the money from the temple funds for the offering of his *Kanikam* to the Deity. In the Ampalapuzha temple, Valiyamadathil Panikkar still officiates, with his golden capped cane, as the protector of the yearly *Utsavam* at the time of the *Sribhoota Bali* when not even Brahmans are permitted to stand so near as he to the *Tanthri*. Still further south, in another famous shrine, before the flag is hoisted for the Utsavam, leave and protection are sought for the conduct of that ceremony from a Kurup who never appears on the scene. Even the most ancient and historic temple of Matilakam, where the *Vidval Sadas* of the Nambutiris and the Parliament of the Perumals met, was managed by the Tekkeydath and Vatakkeydath Nairs. These facts unmistakably prove that Nayars are no Sudras. *Ed.*]

AQ.

2. **Nayars.** *Born Soldiers—always bear arms.* Most of the early travellers note this circumstance. Barbosa tells us that "in these kingdoms of Malabar there is another set of people called Nayars, who are the gentry and have no other duty than to carry on war, and they continually carry their arms with them."[1] According to Varthema, the second class of Pagans in Calicut, "the Nairs are the same as the gentle folks amongst us; and are obliged to bear sword and shield or bows and lances. When they go through the streets, if they did not carry arms they would no longer be gentlemen."[2] In 1563, Garcia describes the Nāyars as "those who are the knights," while, a few years later, Castenheda refers to them thus, "The men of warre which the King of Calicut and the other Kings have, are Nayres, which be all gentlemen." Again "they are all gentlemen who follow no office of employ but that of fighting when needed." Gasper Correa says that when Vasco de Gama's ships lay at anchor at Calicut, there came on board "a servant of the king, a gentleman of birth, whom they call Nair." Not long after, Camoens, the soldier poet, who had accompanied Cabral to India in 1553, described the Nāyar in this epic poem. That description has already been quoted in the prior note.

Linschotten (1583) says, "Of these Malabares there are two manner of people, the one noblemen or gentlemen called Nayros, which are Soldiers, that do only weare and handle Armes." He adds, "They are verie good and stout soliders and would set upon a man verie firecely." In Johnson's *Early Relations of the most Famous Kingdoms of the World* (1611), we read "it is strange to see how ready the soldier of this country is at his Weapons. They are all gentlemen and termed Naires." In 1609, Pyrard de Laval speaks of them as "lords of the land ...... the best soliders in the world and courageous, extremely skilful in the use

1. p. 124.
2. p. 142.

BOATS OF OLDEN DAYS.

(To face p. 339.

of arms, with limbs so agile and supple that they can throw themselves into every imaginable posture, and thus avoid or cunningly parry every possible stroke whilst at the same time they spring upon the foe". In 1623, Della Vella speaks of the inhabitants of the Kingdom of Calicut and the inland parts "specially the better sort," as "Gentiles of the race of Nairi, for the most part by profession soldiers sufficiently swashing and brave." The Dutch Captain Nieuhoff (1653—70) says "The Nayrs are descended of noble families and brought up to the war * * * and are very bold and brave. They are the best wrestlers in the world and are very nimble on foot." Dr. Fryer (1672) says, "The second form is that of the Nobiles, who are bred soldiers and therefore called Naires." Orme (1755) remarks that "the people of this denomination (*i. e.*, the Nairs) are by birth the Military tribe of the Malabar coast." [1]

Of the capacity of the Nāyars to fight, various authorities have borne testimony, though they have at the same time pointed out the defects in their organisation and in the methods of their warfare. Of the more recent ones, M. Mahe de La Bourdonnais, the celebrated French soldier who bore the brunt of many a Nāyar onset in 1725, thus described them: "Les Nayars sout de grands hommes basanes, legers et vigoureux: Ils n' out pas d' autre profession que celle des armes, et seraient de fort bons soldats, s'ils etaient disciplines: mais ils combattent sans ordre, ils premnent la fuite de's qu'on les serre de pres avec quelque superiorite; pourtant s'ils se voient presses avec vigueur at qu'ils se croient en danger, ils reviennent a' la charge et ne se rendent jamars."[2]

To the remarks already quoted of Sir Hector Munro, the hero of Buxar, who was perhaps the only British General of note who had ever to face the Nāyars

1. Vol. 1, p. 400.
2. Logan p. 137.

in the field, Mr. Logan adds, "They were brave light troops excelling in skirmishing, but their organisation into small bodies with discordant interests unfitted them to repel any serious invasion by an enemy even moderately organised."

Col. Wilkes observes, "The Nairs or military class of Malabar are perhaps, not exceeded by any nation on earth in a high spirit of independence and military honour; but, like all persons stimulated by that spirit without the direction of discipline, their efforts are uncertain, capricious and desultory." Referring to the defence the Nāyars made against Hyder's invasion of Malabar in 1766, Wilks says "Hyder had not before engaged so brave or so formidable an enemy; their concealed fire from the woods could neither be returned with effect; nor could the troops of Hyder be prevailed on to enter the thickets and act individually against them. In every movement through the forests with which the country abounds, bands of Nayars rushed by surprise upon the columns of march, and after making dreadful havoc were in a moment again invisible." [1]

That, when well-disciplined and properly led, they can be depended upon to fight bravely is evidenced by the testimony of the English officers under whom the detachment of the Travancore army fought Hyder in Tinnevelly and Calicut in the last war with him, which was to the effect that they were "universally allowed to have behaved remarkably well". Detachments of the Travancore army were also employed by the English against Tippu, and these also seem to have acquitted themselves creditably.[2]

The undisciplined guerilla nature of warfare so dear to the heart of the Nāyar was, not long after the final cession of Malabar to the British, used with great effect against the English by the redoubtable Pyche

1. Pp. 289—91.

2. Mr. P. S. Menon's History of Travancore, p. 205.

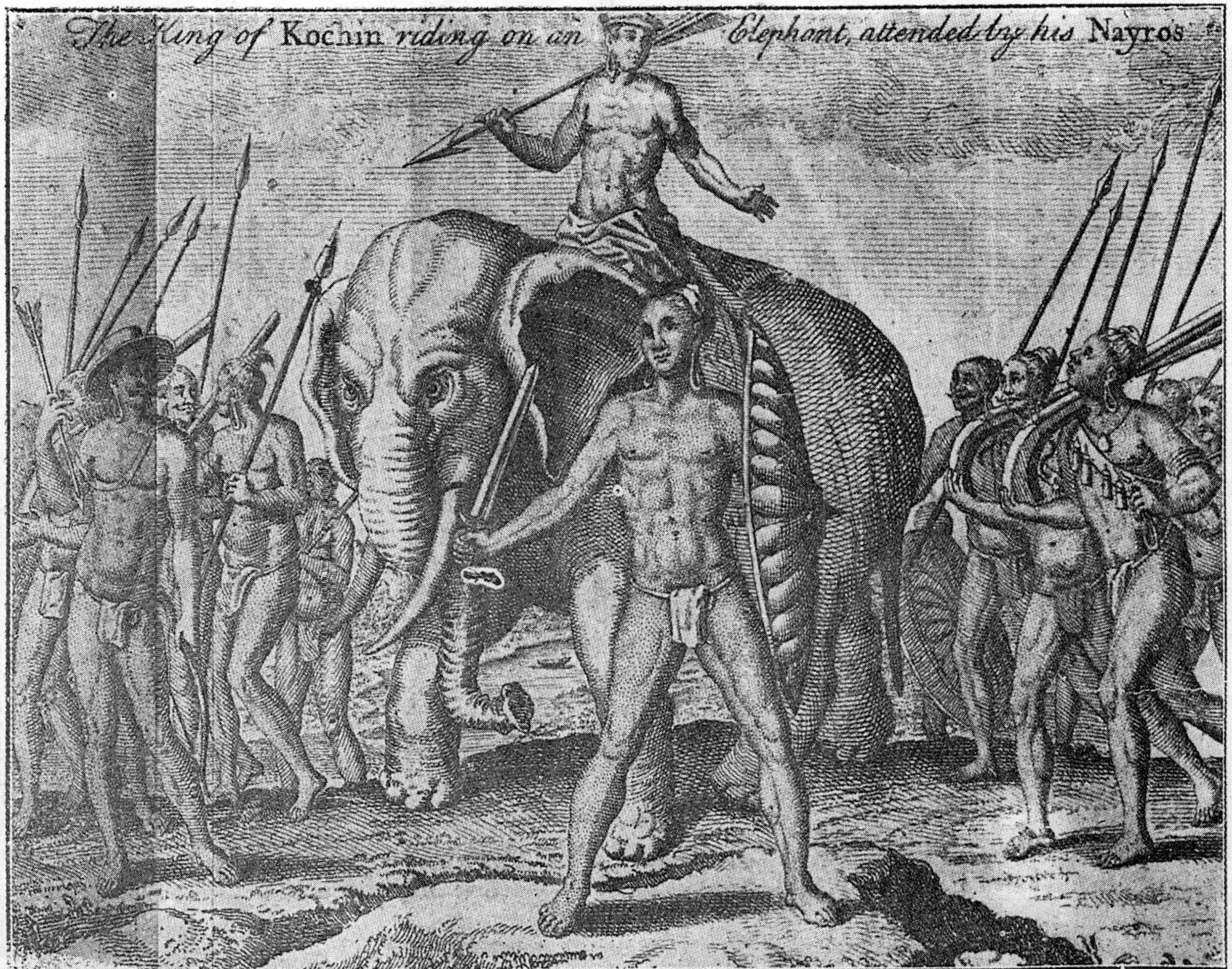

THE NAYAR WARRIORS OF ANCIENT TIMES.

Raja who set up a general commotion which let the country ablaze with revolt and taxed the energy and resources of no less a general than Sir Arthur Wellesly who afterwards came to be known as the Great Duke of Wellington. For full nine years, the revolt was kept up till the Fabian policy of Mr. Baber reduced the resources of the Raja and drove him to the interior of the forests of Mysore whither he was hunted by Captain Clapham and 50 sepoys and bagged.

Early in the 19th century, Col. Welsh speaks of the Nāyars as "Habituated from infancy to the use of arms, and fond to excess of the wild sports of the field, they are the soldiers of the country, without the trammels of pay or discipline; and from their natural habits and being inured to every kind of fatigue and danger, have known to make the most surprising marches and perform feats of utmost daring."[1]

Deterioration had however set in even before the time of Hyder's invasion of Malabar. This drove the Nāyars to desperation. They defended their hearths and homes as long as they could. But the power pitted against them was so superior and the Native Princes were so helpless that they had to give up the struggle and retire into the forests harassing the enemy from there. Tippu completed the work started by Hyder. He devastated the country with fire and sword carrying away an immense number of prisoners, both men and women, and converting to Islam whoever he could lay hold of. The few Nāyars who escaped him fled to Travancore. Tippu's regime in Malabar had completely broken the backbone of the Nāyar military organisation, and the British on their attaining supremacy put forth their best endeavours to keep the Nāyars down. The result was that those who were erstwhile a class of superior fighting men lost heart and were gradually reduced to mere agriculturists and family men. Col: Welsh, marching on Trivandrum on the occasion of the 'Nayar war' in 1809 says, "that the

1. Military Reminiscences.

enemy had proved far below our expectations". He however adds, "yet there were some exceptions. A native officer in the lines being fired at by a soldier of the 69" cut him down and was killed by another soldier, a few others also stood on both sides and refusing to surrender, were put to death on the spot". This deterioration has been steadily going on and Captain Drury, writing in 1858, contrasts the half-eftiminate disposition of the present-day Nayar with the martial valour of his ancestors, so justly celebrated by earlier writers. He remarks, aptly enough, that "the description of a Nayar given by the early writers more fittingly represent a Parthian houseman, or Roman athlete, than the worn-out, modern-day specimen of this once manly race."[1]

3. **Nayars form an honoured caste.** According to the Hindu religion, there are four castes; the Brāhmans, the Kṣheṭṛiyas, the Vyśias, and the Śuḍṛas. The first three are styled the twice-born; for, according to Manu, all are born Śuḍṛas but are re-born as Bṛahmans, Kśheṭṛiyas, and Vyśias by the performance of ceremonies. *Jenmana Jayate Sudra Karmana Jayate Dwija*, *i. e.*, by birth all are born Śuḍras, by the performance of ceremonies persons are re-born as Bṛāhmans. The Śūḍṛas thus form the fourth and not the third class as mentioned by our author. In one sense, our author's statement may be justified; for in Malabar, according to the *Keralolpathy*, the Vysia class does not exist. The Nāyars are classed by some as Śūdras; but it should be observed that their position in the caste scale is quite different from that of the Śūḍṛas of the East Coast. The Nāyars really form an "honoured caste", for they are indispensible associates of the Naṃbūṭiri Brahmans in most of their important religious ceremonies such as yāgam (sacrifice), etc., besides being 'protectors' and 'fighting men'[2].

1. Madras Journal of Literature and Science, vol. 19, p. 205.
2. See Introductory Notes on Nayars, and the foot-note at its close on p. 337.

4. **Military training.** Like the Spartan youths of old, every Nāyar lad had to undergo from his boyhood a severe course of bodily training in the gymnasiums or *Kalaris* which were attached to every village. These were presided over by a Paṇikkar or Kuṛup, *i. e.*, the fencing master, who trained the youth in the skilful use of arms as also to fence, box and wrestle. "In general when these Nayars are of 7 years of age", says Barbosa, "they are immediately sent to school to learn all manner of feats of agility and gymnastics for the use of their weapons. First they learn to dance, and then to tumble, and for that purpose they render supple all their limbs from their childhood, so that they can bend them in any direction. And after they had experience in this, they teach them to manage the weapons which suit each one most. That is to say, bows, clubs, lances, and most of them are taught to use the sword and buckler, which is of more common use among them. In this fencing there is much agility and science, and there are very skilful men who teach this art, and they are called panikkars; they are Captains in war."[1] De Barros gives the same account, and remarks "that the pupils regard their master as a father on account of the instruction he gives them." Castenheda observes that, "the maisters which teach them be graduates in the weapons which they teach, and they are called in their language Panycaes (Paṇikkars)." Purchas too gives a similar account. He says that their masters "teach them to run, leap, fencing, and managing of the weapons, and anoint them with the oil of Gergelin to make their sinew pliant for all winding and tumbling gestures. They begin to go to school at 7 years old."

We have a fuller description given by Johnston (1611 A. D.) in his *Relations of the most famous Kingdoms of the World*. "It is strange to see how ready the Soldiour of this country is at his weapons;

1. P. 128.

they are all gentlemen and termed Naires. At 7 years of age they are put to school to learn the use of their weapons, where, to make them nimble and active, their sinews and joints are stretched by skilful fellows and anointed with Oyle Sesamus. By this anointing they become so light and nimble that they will winde and turn their bodies as if they had no bones, casting them forward, backward, high and low, even to the astonishment of beholders. Their continual delight is in their weapon, persuading themselves that no nation goeth beyond them in skill and dexterity."

Nieuhoff says, "The children of the Nayros are from the seventh year of their age exercised in arms, and trained up to the wars. They annoint the limbs of their young children every day with a certain oil, to make their joints pliable; for when they are forced to fly, they put their greatest confidence in the agility of their bodies, and will in an instant turn back upon their enemies and attack them in the rear; besides that in their flight they throw their javelins backward with great dexterity, and as soon as they have thrown their darts, they know how to shelter behind their shields"

The training given at the *Kalari* has been thus described:—"On an auspicious day, after propitiating the family Deity by suitable offerings, and giving the *Guru* his *dakshina* (presents), the young boy is given the first lessons in gymnastics. A certain prepared oil is rubbed over the body to give flexibility to the muscles and he is to take exercises till he perspires profusely. These first exercises are meant to give adaptability to the various limbs for different postures, dexterity in long and high jumps and endurance in sustained physical efforts. When he has perspired fully, he is required to lie down flat on a mat and the Āsān' begins to pass his hands or feet over the several parts of his body. This is called Ṭirummal. It requires great skill and a strong constitution, ability to hold the breath for a long time to undertake this work. When the operator uses his feet, he supports his hands on a rope tied end to end overhead. It is wonderful to see him with this flimsy support standing wholly on the body of the patient and moving his feet swiftly over it without giving the slightest pain. This which goes by the name of *Kachchakettal*, derived from the practice of tying a long and narrow sheet of cloth round the waist and which is the only wear during the process, is preliminary to the study of both games and military tactics. This treatment makes the body athletic and strong and removes the torpidity of the muscles and internal organs by allowing the blood to circulate more freely, and for this reason it is often resorted to as a cure by the weak and invalids. Girls also have to undergo this process if they intend to take to dancing and other cognate professions. The season best adapted for *Kachchakettu* and usually adopted for the purpose is the cold weather *i. e.*, after the south-west monsoon has set in, when (as the saying goes) the Māṟāṉ (drummer) lays by his drum, and the toads take to the key. So long as one desires to be an athlete or a dancer or a soldier, he is bound to undergo this annually for a few days. When the body has become sufficiently elastic, the young athlete is taught the methods of fencing, balancing, jumping and all those arts of attack and defence which pertain to physical skill.[2]

The Paṇikkar teaches 18 kinds of fencing exercises, *viz.*,—

(1) *Othiram*
(2) *Katakam*
(3) *Chatulam*
(4) *Mandalam*
(5) *Vrithachakram*
(6) *Sukankalam*
(7) *Vijayam*
(8) *Viswamohanam*
(9) *Thiryangmandalam* or *Annyonnyam*

1. Fencing-master.

2. *Malabar Quarterly Review*, vol. IV, p. 221.

(10) *Gadaya-Kheta-gahwaram*
(11) *Sruthanjayam*
(12) *Sowbhadram*
(13) *Patalam*
(14) *Purajayam*
(15) *Kaya-vridhi*
(16) *Sila-Khandam*
(17) *Gada Sastram*
(18) *Anuthamam*

All Nāyars were not necessarily soldiers. There were those who followed other occupations. As Barbosa observes, "they have to be armed as knights by the hand of the King or lord with whom they live, and until they have been so equipped, they cannot bear arms, nor call themselves Nayars, but they enjoy the freedom and exemption and advantages of the Nayars in many things."[1] Not only are they prevented from wearing weapons in spite of their being trained to their skilful use from the age of 7, they are also prohibited from entering into combats before being knighted. The process of conferring knighthood is thus described by Purchas, on the authority of early Portuguese travellers. "He (the Nāyar) is dubbed or created by the King who commandeth to gird him with a sword, and, laying his right hand upon his head, muttereth some words softly, and afterwards dubbeth him saying, '*Have a regard to keep these Brahmans and their kine*'. These are the two great commandments of the Brahman Law. The King sometimes commits this ceremony to their Panicall (Paṇikkar) or master in the feats of arms, whom they ever honour as their father, and, next to the King most reverence"[2] "The Nayars were in ancient times," say Days, "the Militia of the country and held their lands on military tenure, liable to be called out at any time for active service. The Raja of Cochin was the head of this Militia in his own country

1. P. 128
2. 627

and under him were Namburi commandants. When each was able to bear arms he presented the Raja with a nuzzur and received weapons in return. They were trained to warfare from infancy"[1].

The institution of Kaḷaries or gymnasiums, at which the Paṉikkars or fencing-masters imparted physical training and the knowledge of the use of weapons to the Nāyar youth said to have been originally organised by Paraśu Rāma, continued to exist in full working order till the British occupation of Malabar. They were half gymnasiums, half chapels where the Paṉikkar or Kuṟup worshipped and propitiated his tutelary goddess. The Kaḷaries or fencing-schools were invariably in front of or at least in the vicinity of temples dedicated to Bhaḍra Kāli. Fra Bartolomeo, writing in the latter part of the 18th century, in referring to the physique of the Nāyars, says, "The frequent use of the cold bath, repeated rubbing the body with cocoanut oil, and the juice of the Ingia (Incha) plant as well as their exercises which have a great resemblance to the Juvenelia, and which I have often seen in Malabar, all contribute to increase their strength and agility."[2] In the opening years of the 19th century, Buchanan describes the defence of the country as resting "entirely on such of the Nayars as received arms from the Tamuri" (Zamorin).[3]

5. **Division into two classes.** That the classification of Nāyars given by our author is not strictly accurate is clear from the detailed account we have already given of them. Here we shall make an attempt to identify the classes named by him.

6. **Nambidi or Nampidi.** These do not strictly speaking, belong to the Nāyar class. They are degraded Brahmans or Nampūṭiris. Of these, there

1. 316.

2. 261.

3. Vol. 2. p. 84.

are two classes, the thread-wearing and the threadless. To their origin we have already adverted. Though cast out of the pale of Brahmanhood, they were given tracts of land over which they ruled, and were accorded privileges akin to those of the Naṃbūṭiris. Those entitled to wear the sacred thread, have Gāyaṭri, *i. e.*, the most important Manṭra of the Vēḍas for the propitiation of the Sun-God. Naṃbūṭiri Brahmans officiate as priests at their marriage ceremonies, śrāḍḍhas, and purification at the end of birth or death pollution, which lasts for 10 days. They follow the Marumakkaṭṭāyam Law of inheritance. The Ṭāli is tied by their own castemen. Naṃbūṭiris or their own caste men unite themselves in Sambanḍham with Naṃpiṭi women. They are not allowed to sit in the same line with Naṃbūṭiris at feasts and eat with them. In Travancore, Elayaṭus perform the required priestly functions to those who are not allowed to wear the sacred thread. Their women are called *Malpaḍs* in Malabar and Cochin, *Mantàlu* in Travancore and, among their men, the chief is known as *Karanavapad*. The Ainikūr Naṃpiṭis, or the five families of Naṃpiṭis already enumerated, are historically and socially the most important; the eldest male member possesses the honorofic title of *Kakkat Karanavapad*, enjoying special privileges at the hands of the Cochin Raja, as they were once the heads of the Cochin Militia. These belong to the thread-wearing class, while the Vēnganāṭṭil Naṃpiṭi, otherwise known as the Kollangōde Naṃpiṭi, belongs to the threadless class.

7. **Nampiar.** This term is applied to four classes of people, of whom one alone belongs to a sub-division of the Nāyar class. The three others belong to the Aṃpalavāsi or temple servant class, who range between the Naṃbūṭiris and Nāyars. The Nāyar Naṃpiārs were once chiefs of territories, and were a very influential body, especially in North Malabar. The Iruvālināḍ Naṃpiārs wielded great power in

Malabar, and the English East India Company entered into political and commercial engagements with them.

8. **Samandra.** These belong to the Anulōmaja or mixed class, who are frequently considered to belong to the Nāyar class. The *Jatinirnaya* does not mention this community. It is said that Paraśu Rāma, the organiser of Malabar, did not aim at anything like completeness in his division of castes, but that Śankarāchāryar, who made modifications, subsequently established a distinct class known as Sāmanṭan, a lower section of pure Kşheṭṙiyas. As to their origin, tradition traces them to those prudent Kşheṭṙiyas who fled into the forests, giving up their sacred thread to escape the fury of Paraśu Rāma, the Brahman warrior. In those uninhabited regions they seem to have forgotten their Sanḍhyāvanḍanam prayers, and came to be reduced to the position of Śūḍras. Thus they came to be called *Samantrakas*, *Samuntus*, *i. e.*, those having no Manṭṙa at all. But as Mr. Stuart rightly observes, "neither philology nor anything else supports this fable". If they are without Manṭṙas, they ought to be Amanṭṙakas and not Samanṭṙakas. Another account regarding their origin is that the Perumāls, who came to rule over Malabar, consorted with high class Nāyar women, and their issue were given chiefships over varying extents of territory. These were called Sāmanṭas.

There are various sub-divisions and designations among them. (1) Aṭiyōṭi, (2) Uṉṉāṭiri, (3) Paṉṭāla, (4) Ēṙāṭi, (5) Vallōṭi, (6) Neṭumgāṭi, (7) Uṉiṭṭiri, (8) Ṭirumulpād and (9) Karṭṭāvu. Numbers 4, 5 and 6 derive their names from the localities they originally occupied, *viz.*, Ernad, Valluvanad, and Neduganad. Of these, Ernad and Valluvanad were important territories at the commencement of the Malabar Era, and the chiefs of these are found cited as witnesses in the Syrian Christian Copper Plates. The Zamorin was the ruler of the Ernad territory, and belongs to the Ēṙāṭi class and was often styled as *Eradi Tirumulpad* in old days. The other designations by which the class is known are (1) Ṭirumulpād, *e. g.*, the Ṭirumulpāds of Nilamboor, Manchery and Amarampalam; (2) Kaṛṭṭāvu, as those of Chuntampattai and Cherplasseri, all in British Malabar. These designations are only honorofic, and do not indicate the caste or class to which they belong. In Travancore their women are generally known as *Kovilammas*, or ladies of Palaces. An *Unnyatiri* woman is known as *Pillayatiri*. They wear the three special ornaments of the Kṣheṭṛiyas, *viz.*, the *Cherutali*, the *Entram* and the *Kuzhal*.

Of the sub-divisions above mentioned, the *Unnyatiris* regard themselves as a higher class than the others as they employ an Āryapaṭṭar to tie the Ṭāli at their marriages and not a Ṭirumulpād or Kṣheṭṛiya as the rest do. The *Unittiris* and the *Unnyatiris* do not differ much and are almost the same. The word *Unittiri* means a venerable boy, and is merely a title of dignity. The word *Atiyoti* is sometimes traced to the word *Atiyan* or slave or vassal. There is a tradition that the Raja of Kadatanad sought the aid of the Kōlaṭṭiri, who agreed to restore him to his lost possessions on his subjecting himself as a vassal of the Kōlaṭṭiri Raja. Hence the term Aṭiyōṭi, a slave or vassal. The word Paṇḍāla comes from Bhaṇḍāraṭṭil, meaning, 'in or belonging to the Royal treasury.' These were at one time ruling chiefs of small territories. It is significant that most of the Malabar Rajas are Sāmanṭas.

As to their occupation, the more important of them who were once ruling chiefs, are still great landlords, though with faded glory, exercising considerable influence and authority in the community. The lesser class occupy themselves as personal attendants on the male and female members of Royal Families and a few have taken to the learned professions.

Their houses, specially those of the higher order, were till recently known as Koṭṭārams or Palaces while those of the commonality are called Maṭhams. The personal names generally given to males among them are: Rārichan, Kōvuṇṇi, Kēluṇṇi, and to females Ikkāvu, Iṭṭuṇṇi, Nankuṇṇi, Paṭṭuṇṇi, Iṭṭiyāchchi, Kāvu, Kunjikuṭṭi and Iṭṭilāchchi. Important names among them are Kuṭṭan, Appu for males and Ammu for females. Their sect mark consists of three parallel horizontal lines of ashes or Bhasmam on the forehead, breast, arms, and on the shoulders. Their caste government rests with the Naṃbūṭiri Vaiḏīkans, and a lower class of the Naṃbūṭiris act as their priests. They follow the Marumakkaṭṭāyam system of inheritance and succession.

As soon as a child is born, it is taken to the maternal uncle who gives it a little honey on a gold ring. The other ceremonies are the Nāmakaraṇa (the naming of the child), the Nişhkṙamaṇa (taking the child out) both of which are performed along with Annaprāśana (rice-giving). The Gaṇapaṭi Pūja and Puṇṇyāha follow the Niśhkṙamaṇa. The maternal uncle gives the name of the child after formally seeking the permission of the Brahmans assembled. The tonsure takes place only in the 16th year.

For females, the age for the Ṭālikeṭṭu marriage is from the 7th to the 12th year. On the day previous to the marriage, the maternal uncle and, in his absence, the brother of the girl ties the Pṙatisara or string of vow round the waist. During the Muhūṙṭṭa or auspicious moment for tying the Ṭāli, Brāhmaṇipāṭṭu (song by a Puşhpaka woman) is sung. The Ṭāli is tied by Ṭirumulpāds, who are Kşheṭṙiyas, and are brought in procession. The Brahmans perform the Puṇṇyāha, Gaṇapaṭi Pūja, and the sacrifice to the fire. After these come the Mukhaḏaṙśana, or looking at the face, followed by Mangalyaḏhāraṇa or tying of the ṭāli. The son-in-law has to perform the Aupāsana, unaccompanied by vedic hymns, and, during the four days of the marriage, the bride and bridegroom are not allowed to bathe. The Sambanḏham, or the real union of man and woman in matrimony, comes later on, when the Kōvil-ammamār are wedded to Brahmans or Kṣheṭṭriyas. During pregnancy, in the sixth month after conception, the Puḷikuṭi is observed. The Kṣheṭṭriyas do not observe this ceremony though the Nāyars do.

In his *History of Travancore*, Mr. Shangunny Menon points out that there is considerable difference between those who are known as Sāmanṭas and Samanter. In the *Kerala Mahatmyam* and the *Halasya Mahatmyam*, Kṣheṭṭriyas are called Sāmanṭas, and allusions to the King of Chēra and Kēraḷa are often made as Sāmanṭas. While the Samanten is the creature of Śankarāchāriar, the Sāmanṭa had existed long before him.

9. **Patiṭsjan.** If this word stands for Paṭiṭan, or one who is degraded or fallen, then there is, according to the *Jatinirnaya*, a class which is composed of seven sub-divisions, who are reckoned as coming below Nāyars. These are referred to by our author in Letter No. XXI. But the disjunctive "or" shows that our author must have used the word Patitsjan to indicate a class of Nāyars whom he calls "Belerte" Nāyars. Now Day notes a class called Veliāt Nayars or Paḷḷichāns and Gundhert also mentions the word Veliaṭ Nāyar, another name by which Paḷḷichāns are designated. The Paḷḷichāns are bearers of the palanquins of the Brahmans and Malabar chieftains. They are also employed to carry swords and shields before the chieftains when they go out. They are said to be lapses from a higher order of Nāyars. In Travancore, there is a class known as Veliyaṭṭu Nāyar. They are also called Kallūr Nāyar and Matavar, also Puliyaṭṭu Nāyar and Puḷikka Paṇikkar. They are believed to have been good marksmen in ancient days. They help the Aṭikal, a class of temple servants, by drawing the image of Bhaḍrakāli, and are useful to the Chākyār in carrying his accoutrements and ornaments. As their ceremonies, mode of living, etc., are the same as those of other Nāyars, no separate account of them is called for.

10. **Bellalen or Bellares.** Lower down in the same paragraph we see our author mention another class of Vellāla Śūḍran. In some parts of Malabar, the highest order of Nāyars goes by the name of Vellāymakār who, in other parts, are called Illakkār. But there is a distinct class known as Nānchināt Vellālas, who were originally *Pandi Vellalas* of the East Coast, but who, on becoming subject to the Travancore king, adopted some of the characteristic customs and manners of the Malayalees.

11. **Wellek Tallenairs.** Properly Velakkaṭ + Ela + Nāyars, *i. e.*, a low class among Nāyars who are barbers by profession,so called because it is their right to get the leaf (Ela) placed before the lamp (Velakkaṭ). In Malabar, it is the practice to have a plantain leaf placed in front of a lighted lamp on which will be served all the viands prepared for a feast on festive days, such as one's birthday, Ṭiru Ōṇam, etc. This lamp and plantain leaf, with the viands, occupy a prominent position in the dining hall, generally facing the chief member of the house, or of him whose birthday is being celebrated. The viands on the leaf are supposed to be placed there for the benefit of the God Gaṇapaṭi. Just before the diners leave their places, the lamp is removed towards the north, but never towards the south, and the leaf with the viands is claimed by the barber. Hence he is called *Velakkat + ela + avan*, or he who takes the leaf spread before the lamp. Another derivation suggested is *Velukkatalavan*—he who shaves the head clean.

12. **Saṇeratojaar.** Stands for Śankarāchāriar whose name will be found to be more correctly given by the author in his letter XXII as Sancaratchar[1].

[1] It will be superfluous to write a long note on Sankaracharya here, as there are numberless books that treat of him and of the grand system of Philosophy of which he is the founder. But it may not be generally known that he was a native of Cochin; for, till the middle of the eighteenth century A. D. (945 M. E.), when Kalati, his native place, was given over to Travancore, it formed an integral part of the Cochin State. *Ed.*

13. **Sudren.** A high order of Nāyars who are found in Cochin and British Malabar; they are supposed to be those who followed the Naṃbūṭiris when they emigrated into Malabar, and who are still attached to Naṃbūṭiri Illams.

14. **Some lords, but most hold estates in fief.** Malabar from very early times was governed on feudal principles.[1] From its original conquest and colonisation by Paraśu Rāma through the period of the Brahman theocracy and the Perumāl Viceroyalty, and even

1. The theory that some propound that Parasu Rama made free gifts of lands in Kerala to the Nambutiris alone, and that these form the original landed proprietors there, will neither stand the test of reason nor of actual facts. If this theory is true, one should expect the whole of Kerala to belong to Tulu, Kanarese and Malabar Brahmans. But there are several of these who do not own an inch of Jenmam land; and even those that have Jenmam lands have them not in a block or even near their family residences.

Malayadri Mahatmyam, after giving the boundaries of Malabar as Payasvini (Kanjirottu pula) in the north, Kanya Kumari in the south, Malaya mountain in the east and ocean on the west, says that the country was named " *asiprasthanam* (asi=sword), because it is always governed by Naka chiefs, who invariably bear swords in their arms, and because the use of swords and deftness in such use mark out this region." *Sahyadrikandam*, another Brahminical work, describes Malabar as the land "where thrive Sudra Kings called Nayakas who give away to suppliants all their wealth."

As late as 1502, Varthema writes: "The first class of pagans in Calicut are called Brahmans, the second are Naeri who are the same as gentle folks amongst us. They are obliged to wear sword and shield, or bows or lances. When they go through the street, if they did not carry arms, they would no longer be gentlemen."

History will bear out the fact that Malabar was for a long period "parcelled out among an incredibly large number of chieftaincies and principalities most of which were controlled by Nayar chiefs called Rajas, Samantas, Matampis, Natuvazhies, Desavazhies, Kaimals, Kartavus and Kurups." "Many of these are even to-day full proprietors of *tanatu* holdings. In North Malabar there are more Nayar jenmies than Nambutiri jenmies. There are several Taluks in Travancore where jenmam property of Nambutiris

after the disruption of the petty Kērala empire and its distribution into an infinitesimal number of small states, all along, the political and social government of the country was based on feudal principles. In its social aspect, feudalism prevails to no inconsiderable extent even now. The complicated system of land tenures that still exists in Malabar unerringly points to its feudal origin. From very early times, perhaps even before the advent of the Brahmans, there had existed a complete military organisation on feudal lines. The unit was the Ḍēśam presided over by the Ḍēśavāli. A number of Ḍēśams constituted a Ñād, presided over by a Ñātuvāli or local chieftain, who was again subject to the Raja. In the early years of the 19th century, Mr. Warden, Collector of Malabar, in reporting to the Revenue Board, observed that "each state was partitioned into graditions of military divisions from the *Naduvazi* to the *Desavazi*. Every division and sub-division was designated by the allotted quota of Nāyars it was required to

is the exception rather than the rule." Even in Cochin, the families of Paliyam and of Mannatiars, and of a great number of ancient Nayar families in Chittur and elsewhere, not to speak of those of Karthavus and Kaimals, tell the same tale.

"That the ancient form of Government in Malabar was republican or oligarchical, admits of no doubt. The Nayars, a race of hereditary warriors, were predominant in the national councils. They as well as the Nambutiris moved harmoniously together and were mutually dependent." They were on terms of great confidence too. It is idle to contend that one class alone appropriated all the lands. On the other hand, it is easily seen that both were jenmies from time immemorial.

The downfall of Buddhism and the ascendency of Brahminism, the fact that, in later days, Brahmaswam lands became tax-free like Devaswam lands, the confiscation of lands by powerful rulers against whom the chiefs rebelled and, above all, the necessity the members of the warrior class felt for finding a protecting hand for their lands when they had to absent on war service, these gave rise to Kanom and other allied tenures, which, in a great way, are responsible for the disproportionate accumulation of lands in one class. (Vide pp. 49 to 52 of the Report of the Jenmi-Kudiyan Committee of Travancore.) *Ed.*

bring into the field". He adds that "the designations of the different military divisions, large and small, held their dignities as hereditary in their respective families and had appropriate titles of distinction. They were not always in attendance on the Raja's person. If not required on particular state duties or religious services, they were only called out for defensive and offensive warfare". From the days of the Perumāls, the country had been parcelled into a congeries of petty lordships organised into hierarchies beginning with the slaves, who were attached to the lands, and ending with the Raja, who sat at the apex of the system, and held social and political sway over the territories ruled by them. The greater chiefs never maintained any standing army. They always called on their vassals to attend on them at the head of their retainers to follow and fight for them whenever required.

The origin of feudalism in Malabar may be traced to the pre-eminence of the women in the family, the unsettled state of the country in early days, and the dangerous commotions of the times, which made it indispensable for the weaker members of the community to place themselves under the protection of the stronger ones. This is sufficiently evidenced by the nature of the land tenures of Malabar. The whole land is said to be the free-hold of the Naṃbūṭiri Brahmans, who derive their right from an alleged gift by Paraśu Rāma. There is no foundation for this unqualified statement. How the lands passed over to the Brahman theocracy which governed Malabar in early times is clear enough. Holding these lands in freehold, the Brahmans seem to have carved out lesser tenures in favour of their tenants such as, Aṭima, Anubhavam, Kāṇam, Paṇayam, etc. When intertribal wars and convulsions within the community were frequent, the tendency would be for the stronger to absorb the weaker, and one can well understand why owners of landed estates thought it more secure to place them in the hands of the more powerful, and take them back on under tenures in return for which their liege lords undertook to protect them. Thus a number of big landlords came into existence, and some of them were able to secure political authority also over certain defined areas. The feudalism of Malabar resembled the corresponding continental system of Europe in the 13th and 14th centuries, rather than the one introduced into England by William the Conqueror. The petty chieftains more or less exercised the right, not simply of taking up arms between themselves, but also were so far free and independent as to wage war against their own feudal heads themselves. In Letter IX, our author, in noticing the tributaries of the Cochin Raja, "who were considered the pillars of the kingdom", *viz.*, Porcad, Berkencoor (Wadakenkoor) Paroor, and Mangati (Alangad), observes "these princes are independent, but are bound to respect the Raja as their chief, who settles the disputes of the kingdom, and whom they must assist against the common enemy. They may, however, have private wars amongst themselves, and even against the Raja."

The descendants of the early Nāyar chiefs still maintain and assert some sort of authority, socially at any rate, in spite of British supremacy, over their tenantry, and even the British Government, in assuming political power over the many states, have left to its whilom rulers their position as heads of society. The *Ayyayira Prabhu Karta*, or the lord of the five thousand, and the *Patinayira Prabhu* or the head of the Polnad ten thousand, and other chiefs and communities of a similar description, represent the original feudal chiefs, who were heads of 5,000 and 10,000 and of the early military organisation. We learn from the *Keralolpathy* that the last Chēramān Perumāl, in partitioning his petty empire, allotted to each a number of Nāyars who were to serve them as soldiers. Thus to the greater chiefs of Kōlaṭṭunād and Ṭṛppāppūr, *i. e.*, Cherakkal and Travancore, were allotted 350,000 men each, and a proportionately lower number to the lesser chiefs. Mr. Graemme, the Special Commissioner sent to Malabar, has pointed out that a chief who could not muster a hundred Nāyars was not entitled to be styled a Nāṭuvāli and the head of any number below that was only a Ḍēsavāli. Land tax, as such, was altogether unknown, and each of the chiefs, from the Raja to the Ḍēsavāli was possessed of lands cultivated by slaves attached to the soil, out of which he maintained himself. Other sources of income distinctly traceable to a feudal origin have already been referred to as perquisites claimed by the Rajas and chiefs. With the advent of the British power, the old system crumbled mainly with regard to its political aspect. The chiefs still retain much of their social power, and lord it over their poor tenantry to a large extent. In the interior parts, no marriage can be celebrated, no house can be raised to a second story or tiled, no one can ride in a palanquin, no woman can bear gold bracelets, no one can style himself a Mēnōn or Paṇikkar, or do a thousand other little things, without the consent, often times evidenced by the writing of the local chiefs, who have to be paid heavily for the grant of these privileges. The tenants have to address their lords in honorofic terms, such as, Ṭampurān or Ṭampurāṭṭi, or Prince and Princess, and, in referring to themselves, use abject and debasing phraseology such as *Adiyan* (your slave). While the lord's food is 'honey and nectar', the tenant's is but 'gritty rice', the lord's house is 'a palace', his own, a 'dung heap' and so on. The lord sits in judgment in matters of social derilictions, and sees his orders carried out in their integrity by a system of boycotting which is essentially oppressive and grievous. Under his command no member of the community would minister to the social wants of the condemned delinquent, who is practically cut off from all society and friends. The village washerman will not wash his cloths, the barber will not shave him, he will not be allowed to worship in the village temple, the priests will not attend to any of his ceremonies, etc. Thus it will be observed that the descendants of the old feudal chiefs are still a power, more for evil than for good, in Malabar, despite the overpowering authority of the British Government. The power is waning, but still it is there.

The territorial lords mentioned in this paragraph are generally styled *Karthavus*, *Kaimals*, *Nambiars*, etc., in case of their being Nāyars.

15. **Nayars in attendance on Rajas.** In addition to the Nāyars forming the Militia of the land, on whom rested the defence of the country in the absence of any regularly constituted standing army, the Rajas always kept by their side a number of them as retainers to attend on their persons. Barbosa tells us that "these people accompany their lords day and night—little is given them for eating and sleeping, and for serving and doing their duty, and they sleep upon a bare bench to wait for the person whom they serve, and sometimes they do not eat more than once a day. Many of them content themselves with about 200 Maravedis of rice (this may be estimated for the value of rice 150 to 200 Maravedis the 4 bushels or 90 lbs.) each month for themselves and the servant that attends them, and they have small expenses for they have little pay."[1] Again, "these Nāyars whom the King has received as his, he never dismisses, however old they may be; on the contrary they always receive their pay and rations, and he grants favours to whomever has served well, and if some years should pass without their being paid, some four or five hundred of these aggrieved rise up, and go in a body to the palace, and send word to the King that they are going away dismissed, to take service under another King, because he does not give them food. Then the King sends to beg them to have patience, etc., that he will send and pay them immediately. And if he does not immediately give them a third part of what is due, and an order for the payment of the rest, they

1. Page 126.

go away to another King wherever it appears to them that they can best suit themselves; and they engage with him, and he receives them willingly and gives them food for 13 days, before he has them enrolled for pay. And during this time this King sends to enquire of their King if he intends to send and pay them, and if he does not pay them, then he receives them in his pay, and gives them the same allowances which they had in their own country, from which and from their King; in such a case they remain disnaturalised. And many undertake, but few perform this, because their King grants them a remedy, and holds it to be a great disgrace should they go. When these Nāyars go to the wars, their pay is served out to them every day as long as the war lasts; it is 4 *taras* per day each man, which are worth 5 Maravedis, (*i. e.* 20 Maravedis a day about 3 times the peace allowance. Ramusis says 40 *Cas* a day which are 40 Maravedis; the Lisbon Edition has 4 *taros* a day) with which they provide themselves * * * . The King is obliged to maintain the mother and family of any Nair who may die in the war, and the names of those persons are at once written down for their maintenance. And if these Nairs are wounded, the King has them cured at his expense, besides their pay, and has food given them all their lives or until they are cured of their wounds."[1] The Revenue accounts of the States of Travancore and Cochin used to show lands registered in the names of those who have died in the wars of their country, by way of provision made for the maintenance of those they have left behind them. These tenures were called Chāvēttu Virithi, *i.e.* 'provision for the family of the killed.'[2] Varthema observes, "To the said Naeri he (the king) gives pay to each, 4 *Carlini* the month, and in time of war he gives half a ducat and they live on this pay."[3]

1. P. 130—1.

2. More correctly, provision made for undertaking to be killed in the defence of the King.

3. P. 151.

'Rasidoors'. Day calls these *Ragidoors* a Portuguese term—probably it stands for the Malayalam Kāriakkār, *i.e.* Governor or Administrator.

16. **Inferior Sudras.** Not only the inferior Śūdras but latterly also Chōgas and Syrian Christians, when they came on the scene, were bound to answer the command of the Raja to accompany him in his wars. According to Bartholomeo, the military forces of king Mārttāṇḍa Varma of Travancore consisted of, besides 50,000 men disciplined in the European manner, 100,000 Malabar Nāyars, and also Chōgas, armed with bows and arrows, spears, swords and battle axes.[1] Hough says that the Syrian Bishops and Archdeacons were always attended by armed retainers, and we read that, when their Archdeacon George was summoned by Archbishop Menezes to appear before him in Cochin in A.D. 1599, the Archdeacon was attended by two Christian chiefs and 3,000 of their followers, armed with swords and shields who had taken an oath to defend him to the last extremity, even to the indiscriminate massacre of all who should oppose him.

17. **Sakkiara.** This stands for Chākkiyār. These are not Nāyars. They belong to the Antarāla-jāti or intermediate class, which is below Brahmans and Kshetriyas, and above Nāyars. Their name Chākkiyār is said to indicate the traditional function of the caste in Malabar society. The word Chākkiyār is supposed to be derived from *Slaghyavakkiakar* *i. e.*, those with eloquent words, and their occupation is story-telling in temples at festivals, etc. Another derivation suggested is, that the word is a corrupt form of *Slaghyar* or 'men of respectability. This derivation cannot be correct, for their origin belies the respectability of the class.

Among these there are two classes, *viz.*, those who are allowed to wear the thread, and those who are not. While the former are known as Chākkiyārs, the latter

1. P. 175.

are called Naṃpiyārs The Naṃpiyārs, it will be seen, closely associate themselves with the Chākkiyārs.

It is said that the Chākkiyārs belonged to the Sūṭa castes who, according to Manu, were Pṛaṭilōmajas, or the issue of the marriage of a female of a higher caste with the male of a lower one.

Besides being allowed to wear the *Poonu Nool* or sacred thread, they can also repeat the Gāyaṭri ten times, having already gone through the Upanayana Samskāra. The girls either marry into their own caste, or enter into the Sambandham form of alliance with Naṃbūṭiries. The Chākkiyār may choose a wife for Sambandham from among the Naṃpiyār women, who are known as Nangiyārs. The Naṃbūṭiries do the purification of house and person after birth or death pollution; but will not officiate as their priests. They observe birth and death pollution for 11 days. Their women are known as Illaṭṭammamār, and the ornaments they wear do not differ from those of the Naṃbūṭiri women.

Their occupation, as already observed, is story-telling in temples. This is known as *Chakkiyarkoothu* and is a permanent institution in Malabar. The more important temples of Malabar have a separate building attached to them called Kūṭṭampalam, where generally at Utsavams or annual festivals, and, occasionally, at other times, the Chākkiyār by means of oral lectures expound stories taken from the Iṭihāsas and Purāṇas. The Vēdas being considered the special property of the twice-born class, the rest have to satisfy their spiritual cravings with the pabulum supplied by the Purāṇas, which contain the story of the Avaṭāras or incarnations of God. The non-regenerate classes are prohibited even from hearing the Vedas read. But the Purāṇas are not tabooed. The Naṃbūṭiries themselves would not, of course, in their priestly pride, condescend to minister to the spiritual enlightenment of the despised classes and so they have delegated this duty to those who have fallen from their society. Hence, it has devolved on the Chākkiyārs to expound to the non-regenerate classes the mysteries of the Purāṇa. This is done by public recitations from special adaptations called *Prabamdhams* composed by authors of eminence like Mēppaṭṭūr Nārāyaṇan Bhaṭṭaṭiripād, are very popular. In the course of his narration and exposition, the Chākkiyār culls apt passages from other works as well. Several episodes are brought in by way of illustration. There are eminent Sanskrit scholars and eloquent speakers among them, and it is no exaggeration to say that the marvellous flow of their words and the telling humour of their utterances often keep the audience spell-bound. By custom, they enjoy complete immunity from retort or punishment. The law of libel and slander cannot reach them. They are placed beyond the provisions of the Penal Code. They criticise men and measures without reserve, not directly of course, but by introducing current matters in hints and suggestions, by way of illustrating their texts. In olden days, when the editor and reporter were still in the womb of time, they assumed the role of critic and exponent of public opinion, and made their discourses, the vehicle of imparting instructive lessons, political, religious and moral. Custom has not always secured them immunity against the dangerous facility of speech possessed by them. It is said that, in one instance, an eminent minister of the State of Travancore thought it necessary to deport a Chākkiyār, as it was thought that his discourses were likely to lead to political agitation.

There are eminent actors also among them. Part of their occupation consists in performing pieces taken from the Sanskrit Drama. But they have to perform in dumb show, not being permitted to speak. This is known as *Anguliyangam Kooth i. e.,* performance by show of hands, in which a single Chākkiyār has to act the part of all the characters of the play. Except to the initiated, it is an exceedingly dull and uninteresting affair. Yet it is thought meritorious for votaries to have such shows acted at their cost in certain temples of renown. In what is known as *Kootiyattam*, (acting together) or performance by several Chākkiyārs, a number of them take part and the play usually selected is the *Naga-nandam*.

We have a fine description of a Chākkiyār Kūṭṭu of the ordinary kind given us by Mr. Nagam Ayya in the *Travancore Census Report* for 1891. "The Chakkiyar Koothu is one of the chief elements of enjoyment in a temple Utsavam, affording intellectual recreation to the middle-aged and the old that frequent it on such occasions. When the bustle of the morning *poojah* is over and the visitors have been sumptuously fed and the noon *Seeveli* (the procession of the God round the pagoda inside the premises) is done, there is perfect stillness within the pagoda for about three or four hours in the afternoon which is broken only by the Chakkiyar's performance called Koothu. The Chakkiyar is generally a middle aged man well versed in Sanskrit and Malayalam. The theme of his discourse, which usually extends over a space of three hours, is generally one of the scenes of the Ramayana or the Mahabharata, such as the birth of Rama, his marriage to Janaka's daughter, Hanuman's visit to Seeta and the burning of Lanka, *Panchali Swayamvaram*, *Subhadra-haranam*, or the great *Rajasuya Yagam*, or Krishna's mission from the Pandavas to Duryodhana for the partition of the Raj. The Chakkiyar is well up in the art of humouring his audience. The one that I heard is particularly a great master of that art, being considered one of the very ablest performers in Malabar. He is well read and can himself compose in Sanskrit or Malayalam. The delivery is extempore and the Chakkiyar himself told me that he knows by rote about 15,000 Sanskrit slokas. He is a man of genius and can, therefore, adjust himself to his audience

A CHAKYAR IN ROBES.

(To face p. 364.

at a moment's notice, whether that audience consists of Princes, Nambudiri dignitaries, or the common people. He keeps them spell-bound for the span of three or four hours, during which he is continually speaking without a pause. He is something like the great orators of Britain who are said 'to enchant and enchain their audiences'. The performance is considered religious, for the recital never takes place outside the walls of a temple. One portion of the pagoda is specially dedicated for the Chakkiyar's Koothu and is known as the Koothambalam. This is generally a structure of great architectural value in the big temples. One of the prettiest Koothambalams in the country will be here described. It is 52 feet long by 38 feet broad. The centre of this is a raised dais 14 feet square supported by massive pillars and the wood panelling above is worked with elaborate designs representing scenes in the Ramayana and Mahabharata and other Puranas. In one place there is Vishnu riding on his favourite vehicle Garuda; in another is Brahma on his swan. Here Parameswara is represented on his Nandi bull proceeding on a tour of blessing his votaries, and there is Sasta on the back of a tiger.

Carvings of snakes, swans, boars and other animals are found upon the beams; Mahishasuramardanom, Narasimha (the Lion God), Dhanwantiri (one of the subsidiary incarnations of Vishnu), and Darika Vadham also are scenically represented. All the scenes of the Bhagavata from Devaki's marriage with Vasudeva up to the annihilation of Kamsa, including the intermediate Leelas of Krishna, are most beautifully engraved upon the side-panels,—some of them such as Krishna's birth, his shifting by night to Nanda's house, Poothanamokshanam, Kaliyamardanam, Aghasuravadham, Devaki's and Vasudeva's imprisonment and distress, Krishna's amorous intrigues with the shepherd girls, his stealing butter and ghee, his lifting up a mountain (Govardhanoddharanam), Sakatasuravadham, killing the washerman, the elephant and the Mallakas, and the granting of Kubja's request, being fully elaborated. Again you have the scene of Anantasayanam and the ten avatars of Vishnu also fully shown. In the centre are engraved on a big scale the forms of Brahma and the Ashtadikpalakas, while the pillars are filled with many quaint figures of gods and goddesses. In the centre of the raised dais sits the Chakkiyar on a wooden throne, like Soota of old before the Rishis, and delivers his performance. The seat is a three-legged stool far older than the one upon which the two Kings of Brentford are said to have sat. The dress of the Chakkiyar is also of a very antiquated fashion, but I thought his crimson cloth turban with its gold rim and silk embossments in the centre was very pretty. On his right sat his pretty wife, known as the Nangyar, in her simple and neat white dress and with her pretty knot of hair in front sounding the cymbal in her hand. Her presence is indispensable in a "Chakkiyarkoothu". She was the only person I noticed who kept serenely still when the audience was roaring with laughter or ringing with cheers. The etiquette is that the Nangyar should not break silence during the Koothu. Behind him sat the drummer with his drum called the '*milavu*, which was sounded once in 15 minutes or so and which produced a dull and antique sound. The instrument evidently has not undergone any change since it was originally invented in Parasurama's time. I do not think anything similar to it exists in any other part of India. The Chakkiyar criticises men in authority and their measures in terms of scathing sarcasm whenever he gets an opportunity for doing so, or when he feels sufficient confidence in the good sense and tolerance of the officials who listen to him. Even princes and nobles are not spared. His Highness the late Maharaja once listened to a performance by this same Chakkiyar in one of the Koothambalams attached to a most important pagoda in North Travancore. This Koothambalam was in a very neglected condition. The roof was riddled with holes. Wishing to draw His Highness' attention to the wretched condition of the roof, the Chakkiyar quietly remarked in the course of his performance that the occasion (the Chakkiyar was then describing a marriage scene in the Puranas) was not only honoured by the presence of the august Maharaja and his officials, but even by the moon and the stars resplendently shining through the roof. This had a most wholesome effect, for the building was taken in hand the next. day and put into in order. But he is neither vulgar nor offensive in his criticisms. He utters nothing base. He has a charming manner of pointing out foibles, for he is a most amiable critic, but he is more happy in detecting excellences and praising them. This was probably the method adopted for conveying public criticism in ancient days, and was, I believe, more effective than the Newspaper press of modern times on account of the agents being more qualified and the occasions more select. The Chakkiyar is also a very contented gentleman, for he gives you this magnificent performance for the small sum of three rupees and a quarter, which is generally paid by one of the audience, the remaining hundreds of spectators enjoying the amusement gratis. The performance continues for several nights during the Ootasavan season, and is given in nearly all the big temples of the country. The Chakkiyar Koothu is one of the most popular institutions of the land".

18. **Pooduvallen.** This stands for Puṭuvāl, who is an Ampalavāsi, or temple servant, and belongs to the non-threaded class. It is not easy to understand where our author got his information that the "Pudewalen" had the honour of handing betel to the Raja, unless it be that it so happened that the attendant of the Raja, whom our author knew, and whose duty was to hand the betel, happened to belong to the Puṭuvāl caste.

The Puṭuvāl resembles the Nāyar in many respects. The word is said to be derived either from Poṭu+āl=common man, or Puṭu+āl=new man. The derivation perhaps indicates his origin and occupation. The original Puṭuvāl or Poṭuvāl was most probably the new man introduced by the ūrālers or trustees of a temple as their common agent to manage temple affairs. He is a temple-servant, and as such has to do duties of a miscellaneous nature—from keeping the stores to sweeping the temple precincts. He is called Poṙa Puṭuvāl (outside Puṭuvāl) in contradistinction to Aka-Puṭuvāl (inside Puṭuvāl), or Mūṭṭaṭu. He also collects flowers and makes garlands for daily worship just as the Vāriyar and Pushpakan. The women are called Puṭuvārasyārs. They observe birth and death pollution for 12 days and follow the Marumakkaṭṭāyam rule of inheritance.

In Travancore, the term is applied to two different classes of people having wide social differences, *viz.*, Māla-Puṭuvāls (makers of garlands in temples), and Cheṇṭa Puṭuvāls (drummers). It is curious that a Puṭuvāl of the former class has to shave the Ṭachuṭaya Kaimal of Irinjalacuday, an ecclesiastical dignitary who has the management of the Kūṭal Māṇikkam temple at his inauguration into office. The Kaimal is nominated by the Maharaja of Travancore, and is by birth a Nāyar of the Kuṙuppu class, and raised to the sacerdotal dignity and social privileges of a Brahman by means of an elaborate purification and ordination ceremony known as Avarōḍham. It is at this ceremony that the Puṭuvāl has to shave him.

19. **Andoekellan.** The Āndār Nāyars, according to the *Keralolpathy*, are potters. The class derives its name from Andoor, a fief under Calicut.[1] Their occupation is to make pots and pans for temples, and supply the Nambūṭiris with bricks and other articles made of potter's clay required for yāgams or sacrifices. They are also known as Kuśavans. Barbosa notices them as 'Kujavan'. Speaking of the Kuśavans, Barbosa says:—"There is another set of people among the Indians of Malabar

1. Vide Rev. Dr. Gundert's Dictionary, p. 82.

which is called the Kuśavan, and is separated from the Nāyar on account of a fault which he committed. If any of the soldiers deserts his rank or throws away his arms or is guilty of any such act of cowardice, must we not degrade him to the rank of an artizan? Decidedly. For this reason they remained as a separate caste or sect. Their business is to work at baked clay, and tiles for covering houses with which the temples and royal houses are roofed: and by law no other persons may roof their houses except with palm branches. Their idolatory and their idols are different from those of the others: and, in their houses of prayer, they perform a thousand acts of witchcrafts and no ceremony; they call their temple pagodas. They are separate from the others. Their descendants cannot take any other sect nor any other occupation. In their marriages they follow the law of the Nāyars. The Nāyars may cohabit with their women, provided they do not re-enter their houses without washing themselves from the sin, and putting on a change of clean garments."[1] Here we have almost direct evidence of the process by which castes were formed or at any rate replenished to which we have already referred. This also shows the method by which men belonging to higher sub-divisions are degraded and cast into lower sub-divisions for reasons which have nothing to do with religion. The term Kuśavan is now commonly used as a term of reproach to mean 'stupid', and this meaning must have been attached to it because of the reason which brought about the degradation of the class.

20. **Izomboe Kotty**. This is Chembukoṭṭi, or those who work in copper *i. e.*, copper-smiths. The Malabar Gazetteer gives a curious account of how a Chembukoṭṭi was able to raise the status of his class. "The latter (Chembottis) are said to have originally formed part of the Kammalan or artisan community. When the great temple at Taliparamba was completed, it was purified on a scale of unprecedented grandeur, no less than 1,000 Brahmans being employed. What

1. P. 135.

was their dismay when the ceremony was well forward, to see a Chembotti coming from the Sri Kovil, where he had been putting finishing touches to the roof. This appeared to involve a recommencement of the whole tedious and costly ritual; and the Brahmans gave vent to their feelings of despair, when a vision from heaven reassured them. And thereafter the Chembottis have been raised in the social scale and are not regarded as a polluting caste."

21. **Toonen.** Tailor or Chāḷiyan who is also a weaver.

22. **Noolchottin.** Nūl Cheṭṭi or cloth weaver. This class is scarcely a Malayali one. The Malayali weaver is the Chāliyan.

23. **Wilsiath Nayars.** These are known as Vaṭṭakāṭans, whose occupation is oil making.

24. **Jodacheri.** These are Iṭacheri Nāyars, known in South Travancore as Paṇṭāris. They are herdsmen, and engage themselves in selling butter, milk, and curds.

25. **Wallamneoers** or Vālanmārs. These do not belong to the Nāyar caste. They are a lower section, and, in occupation, are fishermen, and are not allowed to approach the higher classes. Both their touch and proximity are held to be polluting.

26. **Ajari, Moojari, Tattan, Kollan.** These four together with a fifth, Kallan or Kallāśāri, go by the name of Kammālars. The *Jatinirnaya* would add a sixth also viz., Ṭachan or Īrchakollan, *i. e.*, those whose work is to fell trees and saw timber. In fact these are only sub-divisions of the same caste and not different castes, each class being distinguished by the materials in which it works. They are all artisans.

The Āśāri is the carpenter, or worker in wood.
The Kallan is the worker in Kallu or stone.
The Mūśāri is the brazier and coppersmith.
The Ṭaṭṭān is the worker in gold.
The Kollan is the blacksmith—worker in iron.

BELL - METAL (MUSARI) WORKERS.

face p. 370.

In Malabar, unlike on the other Coast, the Kammālans are a polluting caste, and do not wear the thread, though they sometimes have the privilege of doing so, when working in the inner precincts or the *sanctum sanctorum* of a temple. Their generic name is Paṇikkan, meaning worker, and they feel honoured by having Paṇikkan added to their names. Those among them who are learned in *Thachu Sastram*, (science of architecture) architectural lore, in calculating formulae, etc. go by the honorific title of Mūṭṭāśāri.

The Syrian Christian Copper-plate of the 9th century makes mention of the carpenters as a distinctive class in Malabar society. Of the various privileges granted by the Perumal to Joseph Rabban and Iravi Corttan, the headmen respectively of the Jewish and Syrian Christian Communities, "Lordship over the oilmakers and the five kinds of artificers (Aymvazhi or Aymkudi Kammalar) that is the carpenter, blacksmith, goldsmith, brazer and tanner," is one.[1] They are said to have had a common origin. They are supposed to be emigrants from Ceylon. Belonging to the artisan class, their services are always in much requisition, with the result that they command higher wages than ordinary labourers, and are therefore able to maintain a higher position in society. All the five or six subdivisions have similar manners and customs. They follow the Makkaṭṭāyam law of succession. Traces of polyandry are still to be found among them in some places. It is of the Tibetan, fraternal or adelphic form. A number of brothers have a common wife, who lives with them in their house, the children are their children and inherit their property. The practice of a brother or cousin marrying the widow of an elder brother or cousin also prevails among them, though both practices are said to be dying out. In the Cochin State, instead of the Ṭachchan, the Ṭōlekollan, the worker in leather forms the sixth sub-division, the Ṭachchan coming

2. Logan's *Malabar*, vol. I, p. 269.

under the head of Mara-Āśāri or carpenter. There the first five sub-classes interdine, and have no objection to intermarry, but the Ṭōḷekollan is held to be of a lower and degraded class. The Ṭachchans also are not allowed the privilege of touching the other classes. They have the *Talikettu* ceremony apart from the real marriage, and this is generally performed before attaining puberty. But all connection between the Ṭāli-tier and the girl is at once formally severed by a ceremony called *Vazhippu* in Travancore. In regard to the Ṭālikeṭṭu ceremony, they follow the observances of the Īluvas. The wedding ornament is known as Minnu (that which shines). Their jewelry resembles that of the Nāyars, with the exception of the nose-screw and its pendant, Mūkkuṭṭi and Gnāṭṭu. If, after marriage, the girl is not brought home to the husband's house and adopted into his family by an open declaration of the priest and the class men assembled on the occasion, she will have to return to her maternal house after her husband's death, and her children do not inherit his property, nor do they become members of his family. Their priests come from the Kuṛuppu sub-division, who officiate at marriages and funerals. They bury their dead and observe pollution for 16 days. They worship Kāli, Māṭan, and other divinities and offer animal sacrifices. On the completion of a building in which they have taken part, the Marāśāri, Kallāśāri and Kollan perform what is called Kuṭṭi-pūja and a fowl or a goat is sacrificed to propitiate the devils who might have dwelt in the wood that supplied timber and other materials for the building. They have distance pollution.

There is a tradition current amongst them that they went back to Ceylon in a body from Malabar, as one of the Perumals pressed them to marry into the washerman caste. They did so, however, only after taking revenge on those who wanted to bring about a fusion of the Kammālar and washerman caste by com-

ASARI WOMEN.

(To face p. 372.

passing the death of a large number of them assembled in a marriage shed which the Kammālars contrived to so build as to come down on the head of the occupants without notice. It seems that the Perumāl and his successors offered all sorts of inducements to them to return, as Malabar was without any artisan class. They refused and, on the Perumāl pressing the King of Kandy, who is said to have been in high esteem with the ruler of Malabar, that Prince, out of international courtesy, prevailed on some of the Kammālar class to return to Malabar, sending along with them some of the Īḷuva caste, who, it is said, belonged to the ruling class in Ceylon. The Īḷuvers were enjoined by the King of Kandy to see that the Kammālas were not ill-treated by the Malabar King. Thus they were placed under the protection of the Īḷuvas, and it is added that this explains why even now the two classes have great sympathy for each other. The tradition is referred to by our author in his next letter.

27. *The* **Pulleahs** *do not venture to approach them.* This refers to the custom of distance pollution observed in Malabar. This has been noticed by early travellers. It exists to some extent even at the present day but only in certain rural parts. According to this system, the Malayalis distinguish two kinds of pollution, that by proximity and that by contact.[1] The Brahman allows the Kṣheṭriya freely to touch him without any fear of contamination except when he is engaged in his priestly and religious functions. The Nāyar touch is polluting to the Brahman and the Kṣheṭriya always, while the high class Nāyar in turn feels himself polluted by the touch of any of the lower classes.

The prescribed distance at which the classes below the Nāyar should stand with respect to one of the higher classes is as follows.—

Kammālars	24 feet.
Īḷuvas and sub-class	36 feet.
Kaṇakkan, etc.	48 feet.

1. Please see note on *Malabar Untouchability* on p. 429 of the second volume of this work.

Pulayan	64 feet.
Ullāṭan	72 feet.

Other kinds of pollutions observed in Malabar may also be noticed here. During pollution caused by the death of a relative, those who are subject to it are not allowed to touch even their own castemen. Women even of equal caste rank pollute, if at certain times they come within certain distances, and this custom prevails even among the lowest classes, e. g., a newly confined woman has to stand at a distance of 18 feet and a woman in menses at a distance of twelve feet.

Another curious custom is that, while the Malayali would not allow his Hindu brethren, such as those above described, to approach him without feeling himself polluted, he does not object to the proximity of the Mahomedan, the Christian and the Jew; only their touch is considered polluting. The orthodox Malayali objects to the touch of even the East Coast Hindu. The Nampūṭiri Brahman should take a plunge bath, change his sacred thread, and undergo other penances, to get rid of the pollution caused by the touch or approach of a low caste man. The Nāyar satisfies himself however with dipping himself in a tank or stream to wash off his pollution. The belief in the efficacy of the plunge bath to remove pollution is referred to by Barbosa, Linschoten, and other early travellers.

In describing his journey through Malabar, Ibn Batuta (A. D. 1324) makes mention of the caste exclusiveness of the Malayalees. He says "The whole of the way by land lies under the shade of trees and, at the distance of every half mile, there is a house made of wood in which there are chambers fitted up for the reception of comers and goers whether they be Moslems or infidels. To each of these there is a well out of which they drink; and over each is an infidel appointed to give drink. To the infidels he supplies this in vessels; to the Moslems he pours it in their hands. They do not allow the Moslems to touch their vessels or to enter into their apartments, but if any one should happen to eat out of one of their vessels they break it to pieces".

The following quotation from Logan's Malabar is instructive on the subject, "Pollution, however acquired, by the near approach of a low caste man or by touch can only be washed out by complete immersion in water. Even to use hot water seems to be against the canon. And great are the perplexities of the strictly conservative, and noteworthy are some of the devices by which the better castes try to turn the flank (so to speak) of this law, now that greater freedom in moving about the country is necessitated by modern requirements. The water must be in a natural tank or stream, even Ganges water, if confined in a tub, would perhaps fail to wash away pollution. The strictly orthodox are sometimes driven to emptying big kettles of boiling water into the stream above the place of bathing in order that the health of the bather may not suffer when on a journey in a cold climate. The orthodox fashion is to hold the nose with finger and thumb and dip completely under the surface when nothing more loathsome has to be washed off than the polluting touch of a European's friendly shake of the hand. This bath is necessary before the food can be partaken or a sacred place entered or several other acts performed. The highest castes are naturally the greatest sticklers for this observance and, although British freedom has made inroads on the Hindu custom in this respect, chiefly through the influence of education and extended knowledge, it is too soon yet to look forward to the final extinction of this anomalous system".[1]

The experiments resorted to at times to keep within the ordinances of custom are many and curious; sometimes they border on the ludicrous. Once a certain Raja had to be attended on his sick bed by a European doctor who felt his pulse and thereby caused touch pollution.

1. P 118.

Before taking any medicine or nourishment, the pollution had to be washed away by a plunge bath. But the condition of the patient would not allow this. The expedient adopted was to cause the Naṃbūṭiri attendant of the Raja, who had sat by the side of the royal patient, in close contact with him while the doctor was feeling the Raja's pulse, to undergo the plunge bath, and to renew the Raja's dress. This vicarious bath of the attendant is supposed to have removed the definement caused to his royal master, by the touch of the doctor. Of course the Raja had to undergo the Puṇṇyāham or the sprinkling on his body of holy water on which sacred Mānṭrams had been repeated. Another device generally adopted is to hold a palm-leaf umbrella over the head of the patient and to pour water over it and, as the water drips from the edge of the umbrella, a few drops are made to fall on the body of the patient.

The orthodox form of bath which it is supposed would cleanse all impurities of body and soul contracted by contact with, or too close proximity with lower classes, consists in entering water and immersing oneself fully in it. The person bathing, after cleaning his body, dips himself facing either towards the East or the North. The East is preferable. The South should always be avoided. The more orthodox mutters some prayer, takes some water in the hollow of his hands and throws it upwards towards the Sun before he dips himself. He makes an effort to realise within his mind that the water in which he immerses himself is that of the holy river Ganges—Mother Ganga. Absorbed with this idea, he stops his nose with the thumb and the forefinger of his right hand and plunges himself into the water. He dips himself a number of times before wiping off the water from his body. After the latter process is gone through, he marks his forehead with ashes of cowdung, making three horizontal lines. This he does on his breast and shoulders and in every joint.

The record of early travellers attest to the fact of the Pulayas and other lower orders being prohibited from approaching the higher classes. Early in the 15th century, Ma Huan, the Chinese traveller, says that the Mukkuvas, when they happen to go abroad, have on meeting with a Brahman, a Nāyar or a Cheṭṭi to prostrate themselves at once on the ground, and dare not rise until they passed by. Barbosa observes, speaking of the Nāyars, (it is all the more so of castes above them), "When they go anywhere they shout to the peasants that they may get out of the way where they have to pass; and the peasants do so; and if they did not do it, the Nairs might kill them without penalty. * * * When these Nairs order any work to be done by the peasants, or by anything of them which they take between man and man, they are not exposed to another penalty on touching one another than the not being able to enter their houses without first washing themselves and changing their cloths for others that are clean."[1] Castenheda says that the higher classes cry out *hoo, hoo*, when walking by the road so that the lower classes may keep off.

We read in Purchas that, "if one of the common people touch a Nayro it is lawful for the Nayro to kill him: and he is also unclean and must be purified by certain washings and for this cause they cry as they go in the streets, *Po, Po.*"[2]

Varthema remarks that these two last classes of people, that is to say, the Poliar and Hirava, "may not approach either the Naeri or the Brahmans within 50 paces, unless they have been called by them, and they always go by private ways, through the marshes, and when they pass through the said places, they always go crying out with a loud voice and this they do in order that they may not meet the Naeri or the Brahmans, for should they not be crying out, and any of the Naeri should be going that way and meet any of the said class, the above mentioned Naeri may kill them without

1. Page 130
2. Page 628.

incurring any punishment, and for this reason they always cry out."[1]

We have the same account given us by Linschoten (1588—89), who says, "As these Nayros go in the streets, they (use to) crie *Po, Po,* which is to say, take heede (look to yourself or) I come, stand out of the way, for that the other sort of people called Polyees that are not Nayros may not once touch (or trouble) one of them; and therefore they always crie, because they should make them roome and know that they come, for if any of the Polyas stand (still), and not give them place, whereby he should chance to touch (their bodies), he may freely thrust him through, and no man ask him why he did it. And when they are once touched by the Polyas or by any other nation except Nayros they must (before they eat or converse with other Nayros) wash and cleanse their bodies with great ceremonies and superstitions." Again "as the Nayros goe in the streets and they hear him call, they step aside, bowing their arms and stooping with their heads down to the ground, not daring so much as once look up before the Nayros be past."[2]

Thevenot (1666), the French traveller, observes that "the Nairs had a strong aversion to a low-caste people known as Poleas. If a Nair felt the breath of Polea, he fancied himself polluted, and was obliged to kill the man and make certain ablutions in public with great ceremony. If he spared the Polea and the matter reached the ears of the Raja, the Nair would be either put to death or sold for a slave. The Poleas in the fields were obliged to cry out "Po, Po," incessantly in order to give notice to any Nairs who might chance to be in the neighbourhood. If a Nair responded, the Poleas retired to a distance. No Polea was allowed to enter a town. If a Polea wanted anything, he cried for it with a loud voice outside the town and left the money at a certain place appointed

1 142—3.
2 Vol. I p. 378, etc. Hakluyit Society's Publication.

for the traffic. Some merchant then brought the commodity that was called for, and took away the price of it."[1]

Grose, voyaging about the years 1753 to 1764, refers to the aversion shown by the higher classes to the lower, and gives an instance of the cruel results to which it leads.

"But the Brahmans and Nayros, the nobles of the Malabar Coast, could not without horror think of seeing the lowest castes, whom it was even a profanation to come within reach of their breath or touch, raised to any equality with them." * * *

"In some parts this nicety extends even to civil distinctions as, on the coast of Malabar, where it is made capital for a Nair or noble of that country to approach so near an inferior caste as to receive a wound that should draw blood from him. It is not many years since that, near Ponnany, the residence of the Zamorin of Calicut, an extraordinary accident of this nature happened. A Nair happened to have a sort of struggle with a Thyvee, or land-tiller, when as in half jest, half earnest, they grappled each other, the Thyvees' sickle by chance wounded the Nair who no sooner saw his own blood, than he loosed his hold, and entreated the Thyvee to make off as soon as possible, and to keep the accident a secret for both their sakes. It happening, however, to take air, the Nairs assembled upon it, and one of the elders getting up and exposing the case, they instantly fell upon the poor Nair and hacking him to death with their sabres, served him, as it is said of the porpoises, when one of their species is wounded, whom the rest whilst he bleeding, instantly tear to pieces: after which and groaning over him, they proceeded, by way of revenge for this sacrifice to which they had been thus compelled by their law, to the exterminating of the whole tribe of the Thyvees in the village of which the author of the

1 Wheeler's History of India Vol. 4, p. 479.

mischief was an inhabitant. Yet even in this they showed that, in the midst of their wild superstition, they could remember equity; and as they were well informed how the thing had passed, care had been taken to pre-advise the Thyvees of what was intended, that they might timely save themselves, till the day particularly set for the massacre was over, after which it was not lawful for them to revive the procedure, so that when the storm was over, they might without danger return to their habitations. However, if a woman in that country lies with one of an inferior caste, they do not indeed, put her to death, but as being *ipso facto* degraded. She is seized and sold as a slave."[1]

Captain Hamilton in the latter part of the 17th century writes, "If a Poliar or Tivye meet a Nair on the road, he must go aside to let his worship pass, lest the air should be tainted, on pain of severe chastisement if not death. But the Pulachies are in a much worse state. * * * If accidently they see any one coming towards them, they will howl like dogs, and run away, lest those of quality should take offence at their breathing the same air that they do".[2]

The description above set forth is not as true now as it may have been when it was written. For to-day even the Pulayas, Pariahs, Ullāṭans and Nāyadis have access to public roads, markets, hospitals, courts, and offices as any other race. They have also schools started for them and have admission in other schools as well, where they are taught free and are supplied with books and cloths and with a meal a day.

Except for the proselyetising endeavouts of Christian Missionaries, little or nothing was done in early days to improve the social position of these submerged classes. Christianity, as well as Mahomedanism, afforded them considerable liberty, and many sought refuge within the fold of those religions. But it is

1. Voyages Vol, I, pp. 188—9.
2. Pinkerton's Voyages, Vol. 8, pp. 738—9.

surprising to note the tenacity with which these lower classes have all along held firm to the faith of the fore-fathers in spite of the over-powering disabilities with which Hinduism, or rather Brahmanism, handicapped them, and the advantages they derived by a mere change of religion. The allurements offered by a change of faith—personal liberty, freedom of action, prosperity in life, and a thousand other worldly blessings—seem to count for little with these rude, illiterate men, when it comes to a question of the giving up of the faith of their ancestors. But there can be little doubt that, unless the Hindu religion can devise some means to take them into its bosom, alleviate their sufferings, and elevate them to the position of civilised human beings, Mahomedanism and christianity will in the long run absorb them. There is enough work here for Hindu philanthropists.

28. **These carry a naked sword.** Till but recently, the Nāyars always carried their arms with them wherever they went. Says Camoens in the *Lusiad*

"The shining faulchion brandished in the right
Their left arm wields the target in the fight."

Barbosa tells us that, in his day, the Nāyars had "no other duty than to carry on war, and they continually carry their arms with them, which are swords, arrows, bucklers and lances." According to Varthema, "when they go through the street, if they did not carry arms they would no longer be gentlemen." Linschoten observes "The Nayros must (in all places) where they go and stand, weare such armes as are appointed for them and always be readie at the Knight's commandment (to do him service): some of them always do bear a naked Rapier or Courtelas in their right hands, and a great target in their left hands."

So also says Pyrard who saw in Cochin Nāyars walking about the streets armed with sword and shield and making a ringing noise. "You see the streets of all the towns on the Malabar Coast" says Nieuhoff "full of Nayros, with their arms always about them tho' many of them dwell in the countrie." Jonathan Duncan, one of the Bengal Commissioners to Malabar in 1792—93, and who was afterwards Governor of Bombay, after quoting the lines above quoted from the *Lusiad* observes, "These lines contain a good description of a Nair, who walks along holding up his naked sword with the same kind of unconcern as travellers in other countries carry in their hands a cane or walking-staff. I have observed others of them have it fastened to their back, the hilt being stuck in their waist band and the blade rising up and glittering between their shoulders."[1]

29. **Katajanel** or Kaṭuṭṭila a sword with winding edge.

30. **Various weapons of war.** Early travellers speak of their using bows, arrows, swords, shields, spears, pikes, and other arms of offence and defence. The use of fire-arms was also not altogether unknown to them. Abdur Razak in 1442 says, "in one hand they hold an Indian poignard, which has the brilliance of a drop of water, and in the other a buckler of ox-hide, which might be, taken for a piece of mist."[2] In 1514, Gasper Correa, describing a "Servant of the King (*i.e.* the Zamorin), a gentleman of birth, whom they call Nair "says, "He had a very thin round shield with slings of wood and vermilion, which glittered very much, and a naked sword with an iron hilt; the sword was short, 27 inches long (a Flemish ell), and broad at the point." Describing an audience with the Zamorin, he adds, "close to the King stood a boy, his page: * * he held a red shield with a border of gold and jewels, and a boss in the centre of a span's breadth of the same material, and the rings inside for the arm were of gold, also a short drawn sword of an elb's length, round at the point, with a hilt of gold and jewelry with pendant pearls."[3]

1. Asiatic Researches Vol. 5, pp. 10—18
2. Page 17.
3. Pp. 151, 193, 194.

Castenheda says "They are armed with bows and arrows, spears, daggers, of a hooked form, and targets". Besides mentioning the 'naked Rapier or Coutelas' and 'the great Target' which a Nāyar should always carry with him, Linschoten says, "There are some that carrie a Bow and a venemous Arrow upon their shoulder, wherein they are very expert, others carry long Pikes, some pieces, with the Match ready lighted and wound about their armes." Of their targets or shields he says "Those Targets are verie great, and made of light wood, so that when they will they can cover their bodies therewith: they are so well used thereunto, that they esteeme it nothing to beare them, and when they travel on the way, they may be heard a great way off, for that they commonly make a great knocking with the hilt of their Rapier against the Target because they would be heared."

Nieuhoff observes, "Their arms are bows, arrows, javelins, swords and shields; these are very large, which they use with the utmost dexterity to cover their bodies. On the hilt of the swords they have small plates of metal, which make a noise when they are fighting, and serves to animate them." They were expert bow men "who drew the bow with such skill that their second shaft often split the first."[1] Ralph Fitch (1583) observes that they are "good archers with a long bow and a long arrow, which is their best weapon: yet there be some calivers among them but they handle them badly."

"On the hilts of their swords", says Baldeus in 1661, "they wear certain pieces of metal, which making a noise as they move, serve them for certain musick. They are very dexterous in defending their bodies with their shields, and, consequently better at warding blows than at firing, for they commonly fire too high".

In addition to the citations already made, we may refer to what Dr. Freyer says regarding their weapons,

1. M. Elie Reclus, Primitive Folk, p. 146.

"They are all bred soldiers, and therefore called Nairos, the one part of them wearing naked swords, rampant, in one hand, and a Target made of Buffaloe's hide lacquered and curiously painted in the other, with which they defend themselves as assuredly as with an iron shield, the rest of them walk with a spiked lance barbed, as long as javelin, and poised at the But-end with Lead; at darting of which they are very expert."

Wilkes, describing the Nāyars in their fight with Hyder, says, "their peculiar weapon is an instrument with a thin but very broad blade, hooked, tōwards the edge like a bill-hook or gardener's knife, and about the length of a Roman sword which the weapon of the chiefs often exactly resembles. This hooked instrument, the inseparable companion of the Nair whenever he quits his dwelling on business, for pleasure, or for war, has no scabbard, and is usually grasped with the right hand, as an ornamental appendage in peace, and for destruction in war. When the Nair employs his musket or his bow, the weapon which has been described is fixed in an instant, by means of a catch, in the waist belt, with the flat part of the blāde diagonally across his back; and is disengaged as quickly whenever he drops his musket in the wood, or slings it across his shoulders for the purpose of rushing to close encounter with this terrible instrument."[1] Dr. Buchanan, in the early years of the ninteenth century, wrote, in his *Canara and Malabar* "both Nairs and nland Mapillas pretent to be soldiers by birth and disdain all industry. Their chief delight is in parading up and down fully armed. Each man has a firelock, and at least one sword; but all those who wish to be thought men of extraordinary courage carry two sabers".

The military dress of the Nāyars was very scanty. Castenheda says "they go entirely naked and barefooted, wearing only a piece of painted cotton cloth, which reaches from the girdle to the knees and a cloth or

1. Vol. 1, p. 290.

kerchief on their heads". According to Varthema, this kerchief was of silk and of vermilion colour. Says Captain Nieuhoff, "They attack their enemies quite naked, their privities being only covered". Later on in the 18th century, Wilkes observes that "the military dress of the Nairs is a piece of short drawers". After the Travancore Raja constituted a standing army disciplined and armed on the European model under General Lanoy, that army was clothed as the sepoys of the European Powers in India.

31. **Country covered with bushes, etc.** Malabar was never known to have had horses. As observed by our author in the previous paragraph, the nature of the country was such that horses would be of no use there, whether as beasts of burden or as cavalry for war. So early as the 14th century, Ibn Batuta has remarked that "no one travels in these parts upon beasts of burden, nor is there any horse to be found except with the king, who is therefore the only person who rides. When, however, any merchant has to sell or buy goods, these are carried upon the backs of men, who are always ready to do so (for hire). Every one of these men has a long staff which is shod with iron at its extremity and at the top has a hook. When, therefore, he is tired with his burden, he sets up his staff in the earth like a pillar and places the burden upon it, and when he has rested, he again takes up his burden without the assistance of another." More than five centuries have glided by since the Arab traveller wrote, and yet the modern tourist will be struck with the exactness of the description, as he sees the present day carrier in Malabar pass by with his burden.

32. (*a*) **Obliged to march in single file.** That the natives were not altogether blind to this advantage is evident from what Captain Nieuhoff says of the Dutch attack on Quilon and its defence by the Nāyars. The Nāyars gave them a warm reception. Speaking of the attack on Captain Polman's

company of firelocks, Nieuhoff, says, "here you might have seen them fight like desperate men, the engagement was very terrible considering the number of men on both sides." "They had however in the meanwhile attacked our rear several times, because our heavy cannon could not come up soon enough with us, by reason of the narrowness of the way; the enemy making use of this advantage attacked us very furiously, but were bravely repulsed by the help of our field pieces, which being charged with small shot, were discharged among them with such success, that many of them remained dead on the spot, and by this means we kept them so long in play, till we received a reasonable reinforcement.

33. **The elephant** abounds in the Malabar forests and there are magnificent specimens of them almost in abundance. They are caught in pits, and are used for various purposes, such as for dragging timber from the forests, for transporting baggage, as also for ceremonial processions, when they are decked in gorgeous trappings. They were in former times also employed in war. "Those on the animal's back, comfortably supplied with arrows and missiles of all sorts, shot them off with telling effect—and no less evil glee—on the enemy."[1]

34. **They make musket-barrels, and take sure aim.** Baldens informs us that "they (the Nairs) make their gun barrels, own gunpowder, and matches." Muskets and cannon were not altogether unknown to Malabar before the arrival of the Portuguese. It is said that Vasco da Gama's ships had cannon of a kind, but such weapons were quite unknown on the African coast, while on the Malabar Coast, though not unknown, they were not in use. Early in 1503, two Milanese lapidaries, Joa Maria and Piero Antonio, who understood gun founding, deserted from the Portuguese for the Zamorin's service. They cast a number of guns

1. Varthema, p. 151.

ELEPHANTS ARRANGING LOGS.

[To face p. 386.

and trained many artificers, before they were killed in a riot a few years later, on suspicion that they were going to desert from the Zamorin and go back to the Portuguese. Varthema made their acquaintance at Calicut. In 1505, four Venetians reached Malabar in the Red Sea ships in order to cast artillery,[1] and from this time the knowledge of the art remained in India.[2] It is noteworthy that when Da Gama visited Calicut a second time in 1502 and bombarded it, the Zamorin had, as an eye witness (Thomas Lopes) states, only two inferior pieces in position; those who worked them had no idea of aiming and they took long to load. In the following year, when the Zamorin attacked Duarte Pachecco with all his forces, he could only bring some iron-guns that shot stones as hard as a man could throw them. "The balls of the enemy," says Castenheda "though cast of iron, had no effect than as many stones thrown by the hand."[3] According to Linschoten, they carried with them "some Pieces, with the Match ready lighted, and wound about their arms, and have the best Lockes that possibly may be found in all Europe, which they knew so well how to use, that the Portugals can have no advantage against them." Captain Nieuhoff tells us "Since the Portuguese and Dutch have got footing there, they have also learned the use of firearms to that degree, that they will turn right and left, and give a volley of shot with the same order as the Europeans do." Again, "The Malabars have great store of artillery, muskets and pikes; nay their arms were in more esteem than those of the Portuguese, only they did not know the art of hardening their armour. They now make very good and strong gun-barrels and gunpowder."

35. **First shot hits.** Baldeus remarks that the Nāyars commonly fire too high though according to

1. *Castenheda* II, p. 12.
2. Whiteway's *Rise of the Portuguese Pow r*, p. 37.
3. *Castenheda*, I, p. 68.

Sir Hector Munro, who had occasion to encounter Nāyar troops in the field, has observed that "they point their guns well, and fire them well also."

36. **Barbarous Nations.** Our author calls the Malayalees a barbarous nation. But let us hear the estimate formed of them in particular, and of the Hindus in general, by an English man who had the capacity and willingness to compare them with the Portuguese one of the most civilized European nations of the time with whom they came in contact. After referring to the combined testimony of a Persian (Abdul Razak), an Italian (Varthema), and a Frenchman (Pyrard de Laval), to the religious tolerance, the strict administration of justice, the commercial probity and the universal contentment of the people and the high state of civilization to which Calicut had attained in spite of a century of desolating war, Mr. Whiteway observes that these lead to the irresistable conclusion that "The Indians of that day were more civilised than the Portuguese." In nothing was their relative civilization more shown," says Mr. Whiteway "than in their treatment of prisoners of war. The Portuguese killed with the most horrible tortures or enslaved all prisoners whom they could not hold to ransom. They even flung the dead bodies of their captives on the shores and watched them to extort a ransom from any one who showed an interest in the corpse.[1] On the other hand, the Portuguese who were captured were in the early days treated with the greatest humanity. Malik Aiyaz, one of their bitterest opponents, wrote to Almeida that, while the fighting was in progress, it was the duty of either side to do all they could to conquer the enemy, but, once the enemy was conquered, he must be treated as a brother and what is more, he practised as he wrote; for he treated his Portuguese captives, with the greatest kindness and after the defeat of D. Lourenco at Chaul he sought for

1. Correa III, p. 835.

his adversary's body to give it a decent burial.[1] Things changed somewhat in later days when the natives of India had been educated by their Christian adversaries; still as late as 1559, when St. Thome was held to ransom for the intolerant acts of some Jesuits and Franciscans, the Raja of Vijayanagara kept such faith with the Portuguese, that as one of them says such humanity and justice are not to be found among Christians [2].

"There are traces that the better side of the Indian nature struck the more savage Portuguese with astonishment. Two pictures may be given from one voyage of Martin Correa up the coast in 1521 of which it was said, as it was of many others that it was an unnecessary expedition as the people they robbed were but poor people who neither followed the sea nor did evil to any one. Landing at one place, Correa marched up country with 25 men till he came to a large country house. * * * Here among the captives Correa took was an old man past work who offered £3 for his liberty and asked that, as he had no friends, he might be allowed to fetch the money himself. Correa more in jest than in earnest, gave him his liberty and made him swear on his sacred cord, for he was a Brahman, to bring the money back. A few days later, to the amusement of the Portuguese, the old Brahman returned with half the money and 8 fowls in lieu of the rest —all that he had been able to scrape together. To the credit of the Portuguese they refused to take anything from him."[3]

"They were completely ignorant of the religious and social systems with which they were brought into contact and they made no attempt to understand them. They took all Indians, except the Mahommadans, to be Christians and they actually in this belief worshipped

1. Barros, pp. 2—9.
2. Correa, II, p. 68. The anecdotes are from Castenheda VI Chapters 2 and 3.
3. Whiteway p. 20.

in a Hindu Temple at Calicut.[1] Pedro Alverz Cabral sent some converted fishermen as envoys to the Zamorin not knowing that the Zamorin would not even look on them. This same Commander considered it a personal insult that the Zamorin should have asked that the Nair hostages should be allowed on shore from the ships to eat, else they should be starved.[2] The Zamorin was of course referring to a strict caste rule. In 1504, Durate Pacheco, who had been some time in the country, almost quarrelled with his faithful ally, the Raja of Cochin, when he said he was unable to make some low caste men Nairs. Several instances of the Zamorin's honesty are given by Mr. Logan.[3] The Cochin Raja's refusal to give up the handful of Portuguese left with him on the departure of the Admiral to Europe, though he was much pressed to do so by his own ministers and the Portuguese themselves, so that he may save himself and his country from the infuriate Zamorin, is a fact recorded in history. Of this incident Faria-y-Souza writes "The King of Calicut envying the advantage he of Cochin made of our trade, got together 50,000 men at Patana, 16 leagues from Cochin, with other preparations of war. The people of Cochin fearing that power were for delivering up the Portuguese to him of Calicut, who demanded nothing more. But Tirumumpara, King of Cochin, refused and went out with 3 of his nephews and small force to meet the enemy. At the first charge he was forsaken by some of his nobles, yet assisted by the Portuguese, valiantly maintained a pass, till his nephews were killed, whereof one was General, he was forced to fly and secure himself in the Island of Vaipi, near to and more tenable than Cochin, which was burnt, and he persisted in not delivering up the Portuguese; *a notable example of fidelity in a heathen scarce to be paralleled among Christians.*"[4]

1. Page 30.
2. Castenheda I—35.
3. Vol. I, p. 278.
4. Portuguese Asia, vol. I., p. 10.

We are here not concerned with the comparative merits of the two civilizations. Our object is simply to point out that the Malayalees were not the 'barbarians' that our author wants to make out. That Mr. Whiteway does not stand alone in his view that the Hindus, while yet unaffected by foreign influence, were a highly civilized race is evident from the remarks of Col: Yule, already quoted.

One or two passages quoted from Portuguese and Spanish writers themselves may throw some light on the question. Referring to the magnanimous conduct of Mahomet Anconii, on whose head the Portuguese had placed the crown of Quiloa, in sending for the son of the late King Alfudail and resigning it to him, Faria -y-Sousa observes:—"This example in a heathen might confound the inhuman insolence and barbarity in Christians (at least those who pretend to the name), who wade through seas of blood, rend the most sacred bonds of consanguinity and alliance; spoil Provinces, oppress the good, exalt the wicked, make honesty, treason, and perjury, duty and religion, a property to work their ambitious cursed ends, to wit, to snatch sceptors and crowns from the hands and heads where the eternal Providence has most worthily placed them".[1]

It is claimed for the Portuguese that "their administration generally strove more to propogate religion than to increase trade"; and it is said that it would be wrong to neglect the intentions of an administration in judging of its success and failure. Now let us hear what a minister of state said to Philip IV of Spain on the point. "It is a vain conceit", he said, "if it please Your Majesty, that the world has entertained of the zeal of the Portuguese upon account of the conversions that have been made by them in the Indies; for it was covetousness, and not zeal, that engaged them to make all those conquests. The conversions that have been made there were effected by the Divine power, and the

1. Portuguese Asia, vol. 1. p. 88.

charity of a few particular Friars, *the Government and Crown having no other aim therein, but the robbing of kingdoms and cities*: and there were always the greatest conversions where there was most to gratify their covetousness. - But where there was nothing to be had there the people were obdurate, and not to be wrought upon. And so we see their zeal expired quickly in all places, where it was not animated by covetousness, and they who had nothing else to say but, **Lord Open unto us**, were not thought fit to enter into Heaven".[1]

The testimony of Faria is also to the same effect. Towards the close of his *Asia Portuguese*, he observes as follows:—"It is remarkable that, among all the persons who have gone to the Indies, whether as Governors, captains or merchants, of which sort most of them were in truth, there has not been one that has raised a family of any consideration, out of the goods they have got in these parts either there or in Portugal though there have been several of them that have got there one, two, three or four millions. Now that nothing considerable of all these vast treasures should anywhere appear, must be for one or both of these two reasons; first that whereas God permitted the discovery of this country, only for the propagation of His name and the true worship (but not by such barbarous methods as the forementioned, I venture to say,) these travellers have, for the most part, persued the ends of a sacrilegious covetousness, committing many acts of injustice to fill their coffers, instead of having any regard to religion; the other is, because the most of those riches were gained by the injust means of tyrannies, robberies and all sorts of insolence, of which you have many instances in the foregoing history."

St. Francis Xavier found the Portuguese on his arrival at Goa, May 6th, 1542, in a most demoralised condition. In the words of Hough, "Though Goa

1. See the passage cited at pp. 158—159 in Hough's History of Christianity in India, Vol. 1.

abounded in priests and monks, with a Bishop at their head, yet their admonitions had been long disregarded by men intent on the acquisition of wealth, and the indulgence of their passions. Xavier must have felt, that it would be in vain to endeavour to convert the heathens to a religion, the moral character of whose professors was so inferior to their own. He therefore set himself vigorously to work to reform this state of things." That this is not an exaggerated or prejudiced statement is evident from the observations of Father Coleridge, the Saint's biographer, who says, "The majority of the Portuguese, even after the reform introduced by him, and much more before that time, seem to have been much in their lives and conduct as to merit the severe language in which many writers speak of them * * * * and, indeed, the lives of the majority of the Christians were such as to scandalize and revolt them (the natives). Many of the Portuguese led the most licentious lives, as too many of the European officers and officials do at the present time."[1]

Hough, after quoting a long extract from a contemporary Mahomedan writer to be found at pp. 20—21 of the 5th vol. of the Asiatic Researches and supplementing it with the text of Hidalcaon's (Adil Khan's?) protest against the conduct of the Portuguese addressed to the Viceroy, Don Luis d' Ataide, remarks:—"In these transactions the Christians and the Mahomedans seem to have changed characters, the Mahomedan writing like a Christian, and the Christians behaving themselves like Mahomedans."[2]

Hough's chapter on a "Comparative view of the Syrians and Portuguese in India in the 16th century," will be found interesting reading in this connection. He derives his information regarding the early Syrian Christians of Malabar from writers such as Antonio

1. *The Life and letters of St. Francis Xavier, 3rd Ed. Vol. 1, p. 124.*

2. Vol. 1, pp. 268—69.

AX

Gouvea, who wrote in Portuguese the history of Archbishop Meneze's attempt to subdue the Syrian Church and of the famous Synod of Diamper, and Vincente Marie de Sainte Catherine de Siene, who was sent to Malabar, with three other friars of his order, by Pope Alexander VII, in the year 1656,—writers "who were not likely to invest the Syrians with imaginary virtues, nor to attribute to them favourable qualities which they did not possess: and it is equally improbable that they should describe the Portuguese as inferior to them in morals and religion, could they have discovered a fair pretext for giving their countrymen a superior character." Hough's information regarding the Portuguese of the period is derived from Vincenzo Maria, the Carmelite Missionary.[1] To the testimony of the Italian Missionary, Hough adds those of Linschoten, Tavernier and other travellers, all Portuguese and Italians, and therefore interested in giving the best account they could of this people.

The result of the comparison is much to the advantage of the Indian. In very many, if not in most, respects the Indian was superior to the Portuguese. Speaking of the courteous manners of the Indian, Hough observes.—"They are also regarded as one cause of that suavity observed in their general deportment, which is so agreeable to strangers. In these respects, they may read an important lesson to Christians boasting greater light, and a higher degree of civilization." Hough refers to the remarks of Vincent Marie de S. Catherine de Siene on the pacific character of the Syrians in the year 1656 under extreme provocation, that "he was unable fully to express his admiration of what he observed. For he says, that he could not help contrasting it with the frequent assassinations that he was accustomed to see or hear of both in Italy

1. Lib ii, C. 18, pp. 202—203—*La Christianita* che vine, etc., La Croze, pp. 87—89,—where the other Italian and Portuguese authorities are all given.

and in all the colonies of the Portuguese in India." Hough's conclusion, after the comparison instituted by him on the testimony of European writers themselves, apart from the question of religion, may be set forth in his own words: "With all their ignorance and imperfections, they were to the Portuguese as light to darkness, as salt to clay."[1] Even if we doubt the impartiality of Hough on account of his hostility to the Romish Church, his conclusions on the present question can scarcely be impeached as they are based on the statement of facts by contemporary Portuguese and Italian writers belonging to the Roman Church who can in no way be suspected to have any bias in favour of the Indians or against the Portuguese.

37. **Ignorant of the science of beleaguering strongholds.** Before the arrival of the Portuguese the Nāyars had to fight only their own class people. The Malabar Rajas never ventured to cross the Ghauts and extend their conquests beyond the borders of their own country. Their quarrels were confined among themselves. So that they had no occasion to improve upon their own methods of warfare, much less imitate or learn the improved methods of others. There was, however, some close connection between the Hindu Empire of Vijayanagara and Malabar. We learn from Mr. Robert Sewell's work on Vijayanagara that, from about 1336 to 1570 A. D., Malabar formed a portion of the Vijayanagara Empire, and that large drafts of soldiers from Malabar, presumably mostly Nāyars, took part in the final defence of Vijayanagara, when that city was sacked and destroyed by the Mahomedans in 1565.[2] We know from inscriptions that the Vijayanagara Kings had conquered Travancore about this time, and had exacted tribute from that King. Notwithstanding this, we see no reason to think that the Nāyars had occasion to study the art of war as practised by others.

1. Vol. 1 pp. 318 to 332.
2. *A Forgotten Empire*, p. 201.

European arms of precision were all but unknown to them. "They were innocent of castrametation, tactics, or discipline. Of that rigour of discipline—the key-stone of what an army might accomplish, of the value of order and arrangement in the disposition of troops; of the skill which sets large numbers of men in motion or aids the evolution of cavalry (which never formed part of their armament), of sieges, convoys: or pitched engagements, they knew next to nothing. Their first wars were therefore rather of the petty skirmishing type, and indeed consisted of the combat of chiefs, of ambuscades, and surprises, of forays at harvest time, ravaging the enemy's country, and racking the inhabitants till they give up their hoards; of burning, pillage, and rapine. No sooner did the rival parties meet, than they fell to reproaches and bravado." This description of Whiteaway tallies almost exactly with what we read of wars and battles in the *Ramayana* and the *Maha Bharata*, where, though we often see mention made of the disposition of armies in various forms, the single combat between chiefs of each party takes the most prominent place. The description of such combats contained in the *Katha-Kali* or the Malayalam Drama, no doubt, reflects the practice as it obtained in Malabar, and it is indeed significant that the characters, as soon as they appear on the stage, and prepare themselves to fight, fall to reproaches and bravado. Hence perhaps the contemptuous remark of Couto that "the Hindus in India fight more with their tongues than with their hands". But it was not long before the Europeans learnt that the Hindus were capable of fighting with their hands as well, and took advantage of it by availing themselves of their services to subdue their brethren.

We have an interesting description of "the fighting of the Nairs" given us by Varthema, which gives us some idea of the mode of Malayalee fighting in the pre-European days.

"In general they practise every day with swords, shields, and lances. And when they go to war, the King of Calicut maintains constantly 1,00,000 people of foot, because they do not make use of horses, only of some elephants for the person of the King. And all the people wear a cloth round the head made of silk and vermilion colour, and they carry swords, shields, and lances, and bows. The King carries an umbrella, instead of a standard, made like the stem of a boot: it is formed of the leaves of a tree, and is fixed on the end of a cane and made to keep off the sun from the King. And when they are in battle, and one army is distant from the other two ranges of a cross-bow, the King says to the Brahman, 'Go into the camp of the enemy, and tell the King to let 100 of his Naeri come, and I will go with a 100 of mine.' and thus they both go to the middle of the space and begin to fight in this manner. Altho' they fight for 3 days, they always give two direct blows at the head and one at the legs. And when 4 or 6 on either side are killed, the Brahmans enter into the midst of them and make both parties return to the camp. And the said Brahmans immediately go to the armies on both sides and say, *Nur Mauezar hanno*. The King answers *Matile* that is, 'Do you not wish for any more?' The Brahman says, 'No' and the adverse party does the same. And in this manner they fight one hundred against one hundred, And this is the mode of fighting. Sometimes the King rides on an elephant and sometimes the Naeri carry him; and when they carry him they always run."[1] The Kings never spared themselves. Castenheda observes, "when these Kings are at war with each other, they often go personally into the field, and even join personally in fight upon occasion." Sheik Zeen-ud-deen observes, "In their wars they have seldom recourse to treachery: but, fixing upon a certain day with their enemies when to decide their quarrel by arms, they

1. P. 151.

regard any treacherous departure from this engagement both as base and unworthy."[1]

Their method of fighting was faulty. No doubt, as observed by Castenheda, "they march in a very regular and warlike manner." Their fighting was very irregular. Among large bodies of men fighting in masses the fire-arms of the Portuguese did great execution, causing the death of large numbers of men. They are nimble on foot and their extraordinary agility made them the terror of every combat. Personally they are brave and of great courage. On the smallest provocation they devoted themselves to death, and having done so, one would hold his ground against a hundred. [2]

We gather from Varthema himself that this mode of warfare was soon giving way before an enemy of a different type from their own class of men. For, speaking of the fighting at Cannanore, at which Varthema himself was present, he observes: "Their fighting was in this wise: two or three thousand men come on at a time and bringing with them the sounds of diverse instruments, and with fireworks (apparently hand grenades, rockets ,etc.), and they ran with such fury that truly they would have inspired with fear ten thousand men."[3]

Mr. Whiteaway in his work on the *Rise of the Portuguese Power in India*, gives us the following account of the weapons of the Nāyars and their methods of warfare:

"In arms and methods of warfare the Hindu of the extreme south, where the Mahomedans had not yet penetrated, is behind his contemporary in Europe. * * * Chiefly, perhaps, because they had then met no serious enemy, and had only fought their own caste-fellows and co-religionists, war had become with them a game governed by a series of elaborate rules, and to break one

1. Tohfut-ul-Mujahideen, p. 62.
2. Primitive Folk, p. 146.
3. P. 281.

of these rules involved dishonour, which was worse than death.[1] Their arms were lances, swords, and shields, and much taste was displayed in lacquering and polishing, till neither sun nor rain affected them, and they glittered 'like a looking glass'. The swords were of iron and not steel, some curved, some short and round, the point was never used: from the handle about ⅓ of the length was strengthened by an extra backing of iron; there were no hand guards, only a small piece of elaborately moulded iron that hardly covered the fingers; the iron work carried numerous little brass rings that rattled in sword play. For armour they wore coats wadded with cotton, that came to the elbow and mid thigh; on the sword arm there was a gauntlet of similar material. On their heads they wore caps, also wadded with cotton, with flaps that covered nearly the whole face and neck."

"There was neither night fighting nor ambuscades. All fighting was in the day time when the sun had well risen; the opposing camps were pitched near each other, and both sides slept securely. At sunrise, the soldiers of both armies mingled at the tank, put on their armour, ate their rice and chewed their betal, gossiped, and chatted together. At beat of drum, either side drew apart and formed its ranks. It was creditable to be the first to beat the drum, but no attack was allowed until the other side had beaten theirs. The armies were formed in close columns. In the front were the swordsmen who, with their shields touching each other and the ground, advanced stooping low, at a very slow pace. Behind the swordsmen were archers, who fired along the ground to hit the enemy in the feet; with these archers were others who threw, also, along the ground, either clubs of heavy blackwood or circles of iron with sharp edges like quoits; where these weapons touched a bone they broke it, or at least knocked a man over and made a gap in the ranks; in the rear of all

1. See Correa I. 354 III 37. and 765; Varthema, p. 150; also Jordanus 20.

were the lancemen with lances and javelins. The fighting was always in the open plain and they advance—all stooping—very slow, now gaining ground, now losing, so that sometimes a whole day was spent in advances and retreats. When the drum beat both sides rose to their feet and fought no more that day. The drum could only be beaten when both sides were halted, and it was a point of honour not to beat it unless some advantage could be claimed. All the strategy was directed to capturing and defending the camp, and scribes were in attendance to write down the different turns of the battle. At times, when the ranks on one side broke, the slaughter was very great, but after the drum sounded the two sides mingled together, and there was no bad blood, even when a man killed his own brother. In certain cases, when a relative died or a vassal rebelled, the leader of the side that desired a suspension of hostilities, after the ranks were formed, advanced, stuck his javelin in the ground, leant his sword and shield against it, and stood apart; the leader on the other side imitated him and a truce ensued. This artificial system broke down very quickly under the stress of fighting against the Portuguese. Thus it had always been the custom for the Zamori to sound a trumpet that it took 4 men to lift to warn his enemy in the morning of an intended attack. In 1536 he nearly surprised the Portuguese by abandoning the custom suddenly.[1] * * It was a maxim with the Portuguese that footmen did not count, their only defensive weapon was a shield and the bowmen had not even that.[2] None of the battles, however, described by the Portuguese historians—and they are numerous and told in great detail—sound much more than magnified street brawls. The interest of this description of the methods of fighting in Southern India, transmitted to us by the Portuguese writers, is enhanced by the evidence it affords that these methods were introduced

1. Castenheda VIII, 144
2. Castenheda II, 16.

from Northern India by the Brahmans, to mitigate the ferocity of the races whom they converted to the Hindu religion. The earliest form in which they are found is in the six rules agreed to by both sides in the great war of Bharata, celebrated in the *Mahabharata*, which embody some of the most artificial of the customs. It may be, as some have said,[1] that these six rules were introduced into the poem by Brahmanical writers, at a later period, to give them an historical sanction in the eyes of subsequent generations; but the same could hardly be said of their inclusion in the laws of Manu, where they are also found [2]. But whether this view be correct, that is, whether they actually governed the fight on the plain of Kurukṣhēṭra or not is of little importance; the great fact is the proof that these passages in the Portuguese writers give, that the Brahman carried with him in his civilizing advance over India such influence that he could impose his humanizing rules on the savage races over which he established his yoke; rules, too, which, although they have left their traces to the present day in the chivalrous tone of some Hindu races, notably the Rajputs, laid those adopting them open to the attacks of outsiders, who could reap every advantage from the artificial system that bound their adversaries * * * *". [3]

"It was a point of honour with the latter (*i. e.*, the Zamorin) never to change the direction of his march when once that had been finally settled. During Pachecco's defence of Cochin against the hordes of the Zamorin, a night attack was planned (by the Zamorin) on the advice of the Italians, but it was contrary to the genius of the Nairs, and of the Zamorin's force one half furiously attacked the other half in the darkness of the night.[4]"

1. Talboys Wheeler's *History of India*, Vol. 1, page 283.
2. See Dr: Oppert's *Sukarneethi*, Madras Journal of Literature and Science.
3. Pages 33 to 37.
4. Whiteaway, p. 98.

It will not be out of place here to make mention of the war songs and the martial music of the Nāyars. Varthema has told us that they marched to the strain of "diverse instruments," that, when the King goes to battle, he either rides on an elephant or is carried by the Nāyars who always run, "and many instruments sounding always accompany the said King." He also tells us that in battle "it had always been the custom of the Zamori to sound a trumpet that it took 4 men to carry to warn his enemy in the morning of an intended attack." "Their warlike instruments were many and of divers sorts," says Castenheda, "and made a noise as if heaven and earth were coming together."

From Fra Bartolomeo we learn that the instruments which they used with their vocal music consisted of the large drum known as *Perumpara*; the small drum, *Tudi*; two clarinets, *Kuzhel*; a kettle drum beaten upon with pieces of iron; two copper or brass basons, and a couple of cow's horns. "During the song," says Bartolomeo, "they frequently clap their hands; often change their tone and voice, according as the circumstance may require; sing sometimes in *piano* and sometimes *forte*; and either let the tone issue through the nose or force it out between their teeth with the greatest violence and by quick and repeated clapping with the tongue. All this gives it the character of a Bacchanalian and warlike music, which imitates the noise made by people who are engaged in battle". [1]

There is no means at present of knowing what war songs were used by the Nāyars during, and before, the Portuguese period, as unfortunately no record of them exist. It is probable that the ballads relating to the deeds of Tachcholi Mēppayil Kunhi Othēnan, the mythical feats of Vaikelēri Kuññi Kēlappan, and others known as Tachcholipat, were very popular. One cannot, however, say that these were sung on the march, for their strains seem to be more languishing than martial[2]. But it is certain that they were very popular

(1) Page 370.

(2) Rao Sahib Kavitilakan Ullur S. Parameswara Ayyar.

as ballads describing the exploits of heroes whose memory the people loved to perpetuate. Such ballads used to be composed till recently. There is one commemorating the deeds of the Palassi Raja and his rebellion against the English, (1797 to 1805 A. D.), another about Tippu Sultan and so on. As a specimen of these ballads the following few lines from the original *Tachcholipat* together with a translation of the whole poem, as given by Mr. Logan, may be quoted.[1]

"Oṭayoṭṭidaṭṭile Kaṇḍaṣṣeri
Lōkanar Kāvil Kavuttanay
Kāvur vaññum pulaññu vello
Nammalā Kāvilum pova veṇam
Tachchōli Meppayil Kunni Oṭenan
Ṭaṇē chamayam chamayavuṃ chaiṭu
Tanṟe idaṭṭeṭum Valaṭṭeṭumāyi
Munnile pokuñña Kaṇḍasseri
Valiyē maṭhakkāran Kuñni Oṭēnan
Iruvarum Kuṭiyallō poruññaṭa."

"To his squire Odayōttidattil Kandāssēri (Chappan)
Said Tachchōli Mēppayil Kunhi Odēnan,
"For the Lokanar Kavil Kavut,
"Which day of ceremony has come and dawned,
"We to that temple must go".
Tachchōli Mēppayil Kunhi Odenan

M. A., B. L., has published as No. 5 of the *Sri Mulam Malayala Bhasha Grandhavali* (Travancore Government Press) a work called *Padappattu* (war-song). It seems that a part of the transcription of its mss. was completed on some day in the December of 1746 (23-4-922 M. E.) It is a *Kilippattu*. 'The poet refers to the fact that a number of war-songs were current in his day. The poem opens with a description of the several branches into which the ruling family of Cochin was divided in the 17th century, the adoptions made from those branches, and the internecine struggles to which such adoptions led and the consequent troubles to which the ruling family became a prey'. It details the Cochin-Calicut wars. It is very doubtful whether these songs or the *Vadakkan pattukal* (Ballads of the North) were ever used as martial music. *Ed.*

1. Pages 96 to 101.

His apparel he put on
His sword and shield he took in his right and left,
In front walked Kandasseri,
In the rear the nobleman Kunhi Odēnan,
Together proceeded in company.
Said dear Kunhi Odēnan
To his wife Kāvile Chāthōth Kunhi Chīru,
"Till I go and come
"Don't you go down the gate steps;
"Do caress child Ambādi;
"Give him milk when thirsty
"And rice when hungry".
So Tachcholi Meppayil Kunhi Odēnan
Took leave of Kōvile Chāthoth.
Odayottidattil Kandāssēri
Took a lance made of the first-rate cocoanut tree;
Armed with it,
They proceeded together;
Walked (the whole distance) in one march.
On arriving at the Lokanar Kāvu
It appeared as if it had been fenced with men on all four sides.
All the Ten Thousand Nāyars had assembled;
Also the Princes of the Four Palaces,
The reigning Raja of Kadattanād,
The heir apparent of Puramēri,
And the Raja of Kuttipuram,
Had put in their royal presence.
Tachcholi Mēppayil Kunhi Odēnan
Went and ascended the entrance steps,
Walked straight up to the Tachchōli's seat—
The platform under the Banian tree—
Where the good fellow sat, and amused himself,
Gazing at the comers and
Looking all round about the temple.
While thus sitting,
The Mathilūr Kurikkal with his disciples—

The two and twenty youngsters—
Arrived at the Lokanār Kāvu,
Went to the Goddess' divine presence,
Most devoutly worshipped with clasped hands,
And, after worshipping, left the temple
To occupy a seat on the Tachchōli's platform,
On the south part of which they went and sat.
This with his own eyes Kunhi Odēnan saw,
And he thus exclaimed:
"Lo! Odayottidattil Kandasseri!
"What (a) strange (thing is) all this!
"On the platform under our Banian tree
"What Nayar cometh to take a seat?
"Make haste and see who he is"
Thus said Meppayil Tachcholi Kunhi Odenan—
A very jealous Odenan—
"What Nāyar art thou
"That went to the Banian tree?"
Odenan seeing this with his own eyes
Rolled his jet black eyes in burning rage,
Shook his legs in excitement,
Clenched his fists in anger,
And spoke thus: "Odayōttidattil Kandāssēri!
"Go home quick, and get
"My silver-handled gun;
"In our western chamber it stands
"Full loaded with two bullets and two plugs.
"Hasten thou and come soon.
"One word more to you! Kandāssēri!
"The Porātara Peacock
"With its young brood
"Is perching upon our Banian tree.
"I'll shoot them dead one by one"
This one word was said.
At once Kurikkal said,
"Hark! My beloved youths!
"We must start at once;
"We must go to our Porātara".
So the Mathilūr Kurikkal and pupils

Proceeded back with their heads covered and hung down in disgrace.
Again said the Kurikkal,
"We should not wait to see the Kavut".
Thus the Kurikkal left at once
With his two and twenty pupils.
When descending the steps,
The Kurikkal shouted loud and challenged :—
"My good fellow, Tachcholi Kunhi Odēna !
"If the tenth and eleventh of Kumbham shall come,
"If God will spare my life,
"I pledge my word to be at Ponniyāt.
"There under the Banian tree
"In single combat could we test our supremacy.
"That day let us meet again !"
Thus the Kurikkal declared the war,
In the midst of the Ten Thousand,
And proceeded back on his way.
The sight-seers trembled
At this throwing down and taking up the gauntlet.
A stillness prevailed like that after a heavy rain.
A panic spread
Over all assembled.
Tachcholi Koma Kurup (elder brother of Odēnan),
On this very news coming into his ears,
Beat his breast and exclaimed in tears :—
"Alas ! You saucy fellow !
"Is it at a mountain that you are throwing a pot ?
"On Thursday in Kumbham next
"You have agreed to enter the lists."
The Kurup hastened on to interpose:
The Kurikkal, on his way from the temple,
Is accosted by the Kurup,
Whom the Lord Kurikkal treats with contempt,
Spits on his face with betel juice,
And says to the Kurup:
"Get thee gone ! What (an) unmanly thing !

"What meanest thou by untimely interposition ?
"If God spares me
"I will make him atone for it".
Thus saying the Kurikkal went his way to Porātara
Tachchōli Kōma Kurup
Went however to the Lōkanār Kāvu
He was met by his brother,
Who was returning having seen the Kāvūt
They walked home straight
On their way the Kurup wept,
Beating his breast, shedding bloody tears,
And thus addressed his brother :—
"My beloved brother ! how impudent you are !
"You have engaged to fight on the 10th and 11th Kumbham!
"What do you think of doing next ?"
Immediately replied Kunhi Odēnan,
"Brother! Why do you weep?
"Am I not a man like himself ?
"Is it enough always to give ?
"Can't I receive it once ?
"Let it happen as fate wills it !
"Why cry for it !!"
"Hear me," said the Kurup,
"In whose charge do you leave me ?
"Am I not in my dotage ?
"If fate should call me away any moment,
"To perform the funeral rites
"No male exists in our family."
Thus saying they were going
The Kurup further observed ;
"My dear brother Odēna !
"Your nice little face of ripe areca-nut color
"How came it to be changed into a new pot's color?"
By this time they reached the Tachchōli Mēppayil house
Their sister Tachchōli Unnichīra

Seeing them come,
Brought a gindy pot of water (to wash hands and feet with)
And asked her dear brother to partake of Kanji;
But Kunhi Odēnan said he must bathe
So he bathed, dined, and spent that day there.
The next morning dawned,
And the Kōma Kurup said:—
"Brother Tachchōli Mēppayil Kunhi Odēnan !
"The fatal 10th and 11th of Kumbham
"Are drawing closer and closer.
"On Thursday week, in Kumbham next,
"At Ponniyāt Banian tree, you must
"Go to fight the duel.
"Your friends in all
"You must go and call—
"Kottakal Ahamad Marakkār,
"Vadakkara Pidigayil Kunhi Pōkkar—
"To them you must go, and tell particularly
"That they should accompany you personally.
"Again, Etachēri Odēnan Nambiyār
"And Panangātan Chandu Kurup
"Must also be requested
"To accompany you to Ponniyāt.
"Hear me again, Kunhi Odēnan !
"There is Payyampalli of Katirūr Tara,
The Kunhi Chandu of that house
"You must also take along with you".
They were all accordingly invited.
Chandu, on being asked said :—
"Odēnan ! don't you go this year to Ponniyāt.
"You have an evil time of it,
"And I shall not come with you".
At once returns Kunhi Odēnan,
Walking hastily through Ponniyāt Kalam field,
Crossing the Ponniyam and Puttalam rivers,
And passing the Chambāt Puncha land,
Arrives at his Tachchōli Mēppayil house
Bathes and takes his food,

And spends the day there.
Next morning he went to Lōkanār Kāvu;
Bade the priest to open the shrine
And light up lamps on each side of the idol,
And caused the musicians to beat tom-tom.
The treasure-box was brought out,
And the idol in procession marched out.
At this juncture
A Nambuṭiri youth received divine inspiration,
And pronounced the oracle:—
"You should not go to Ponniyāt this year,
"Your evil star is in the ascendant;
"I can do nothing for you."
When this was heard
Odēnan prostrated himself before the Goddess
And prayed:—"O! noble Goddess!
"When I go to Ponniyāt
"You must stand on my right.
"I have no other help
"But my mother Goddess"!
The oracle then gave him leave
To stay in the arena till noon,
And not to remain there longer;
And further assured him
That if he looked up to the Banian tree
He would see the Goddess herself in the disguise of a yellow bird.
But after noon she would not be there,
And therefore he should not be there.
Kunhi Odēnan then from his waist cloth took
Sixteen silver Fanams, which in the sacred box he put
Thus worshipping, he returned
With his attendant Odayottidattil Chāppan
To the Tachcholi Meppayil house,
And told his brother Koma Kurup.
All that the oracle had said.

AZ.

"Don't you then go this year," says Kōma Kurup
But Odenan replies—
"Should I die even, it matters not;
"I must go to Ponniyat to-day."
Remonstrance had no effects—
Either brother's or others,
"Let us go," says Odenan to Kandāssēri,
"To Kāvile Chāthoth house."
Thither they went accordingly
And saw his wife Chīru.
Taking the child Ambādi in her arms,
And looking at the husband she cried:—
"Oh! my daring husband!
"You have engaged to fight
"At the Banian tree in Ponniyat:
"To whose care will you entrust us?"
"Dear Chīru," says Odenan in reply,
"Am I going to die?
"Is not man equal to man?"
Bathing and eating he spent that day there.
Next day broke;
Kunhi Odēnan rose
And proposed to go to Meppayil house
Then Chīru prepared milk kanji,
Which Odenan took and went home.
In taking leave of his wife, he told her:
"My dear Kunhi Chīru,
"Till I come back
"Don't you stir out of the house."
When words like these were heard,
Beating her breast, she cried.
"Why do you cry, my dear?" said Odēnam,
"I am not going to die;
"I shall come very soon."
Thus saying, he took leave of her.
When descending the gate steps
Her eyes were full of tears
Which were flowing by the breast in bloody drops.
He walked straight to his Tachchōli Mēppayil house,

Where, in the west room, he found
That his brother was still in his bed.
He sat on the bed
And placing his feet on his lap
And rubbing them gently
He waked his brother from sleep.
"Who is this at my feet?" asked the brother;
"I am, I am, my brother," was the answer.
So and so he passed that day there.
The next day came,
And the eventful Thursday came.
There came then the Kōttakkal Ahamad Marakkār
And his followers,
Vadakara Pīdigayil Kunhi Pōkker
And his followers,
Edachēri Odēnan Nambiyār
And his followers,
Kallēri Kunga Kurup
And his followers,
Panangātan Chandu Kurup
And his followers,
All in a body assembled
Numbering about five hundred.
Tachchōli Mēppayil Kunhi Odēnan
Took an oil bath. and rubbed over his body
A mixture of perfume, sandalwood and musk,
And sat down for dinner.
A Kadali plantain leaf was spread.
His sister Tachchōli Unichira
Served him the dinner—
Fīne lily-white rice,
A large quantity of pure ghee,
An eleven kinds of vegetable curries.
He fed himself sumptuously on all these
And washed his hands and mouth after it.
He then sat in the south verandah.
Kandāssēri Chāppan, his squire,
Served him betel to chew.

Chewing and chatting he sat there for a while;
After which he rose and opened his west room,
Where he stood in devotion to family Gods,
And offered them vows if success he got,
And beseeched them to stand on his right.
He then prostrated himself before them,
And went to dress—a full dress.
He wore God-of-Serpent's head earing in ears,
Combed down his hair,
And wore a flower of gold over the crown,
A silk cloth round the loins,
A gold girdle over it,
Gold rings on four fingers,
A bracelet worked in with scenes,
From Rāmāyaṇam and Bhāraṭam
High up on his right arm,
A gold-handled sword in his right hand
And a tiger-fighting shield in his left hand.
When coming out thus dressed, he looked
Like melted gold of ten and a half touch!
Like the rising sun in the east!
Like the setting moon in the west!
He took leave of his brother Kōma Kurup
By falling prostrate at his feet,
Who then blessed him thus—
"May God help you!
"May you gain the victory!"
Odayōttidattil Kandāssēri
Took a spear—a tiger-spear—
And led the way on;
All in a body went on;
Numbering about five hundred.
They proceeded on in one single march
From Kadattanād to Ponniyāt.
They halted not on the road,
They drank not when thirsty,
They sat not to chew betel.
Fatigued as they were by the march,

They came to the Peringalam river.
And they crossed the river.
Through the Chambāt Punja field,
And through the good village of Chambāt,
They made a rapid march.
They reached the mango grove
For tightening girdles above.
From under the Ponniāyt Banian tree
The noise of the crowd assembled,
The sound of swords clashing upon targets
Were heard, and Odēnan said
To his brother and comrades
That Kurikkal and his party had taken the field.
Odēnan, from his waist cloth,
Took sixteen silver Fanams,
And, presenting the same
To Kōttakkal Ahamad Marakkār,
Prostrated himself at his feet.
In the name of Allah he blessed him:
"The plot you stand in," said he
To Odēnan, "shall be the Kalari—
"The seat of the God of war."
In like manner did he receive blessings
Of Kallēri Kunga Kurup and
Of his brother Kōma Kurup.
With the latter's permission,
Odēnan tied his girdle
One end to a mango tree
The other to his loins.
In one pull the tree's leaves came down,
A second pull brought down the branches.
Then took he in his right and left
The sword and shield.
And ran off, crossing the new river,
To the Ponniyāt Banian tree,
Where, in formidable array, people stood;
But to Odēnan and his party they gave open way.
On his glaring at them

The Mathilūr Kurikkal and pupils were startled.
Leaving his waist dagger behind,
Odēnan jumped into the arena
Like a cock running to fight
And combat ensued.
It was then about noon.
Odēnan took his enemy's sword seven times.
On looking up to the tree at these times
He saw the yellow bird—
The Lokanār Kāvu Goddess.
On looking up again,
It was in vain
And Odēnan retired from the arena instantly,
And marched home triumphantly.
But, as ill fate would have it,
When Ponniyam new river was arrived at
He found his dagger had been lost.
At once sayeth he—
"Hark! my brother!
"I left my dagger in the arena
"And I forgot to take it.
"What shall I do now?"
"If that is lost," replies the brother,
"I shall give you another like it,"
"It's all true, my brother,
"But go and take my dagger I must."
The brother's remonstrance had no effect.
Odēnan ran back to the arena;
The Kurikkal seeing this said
To Chundanga poylil Māyan Pakki—
"The Tachchōli, who went away, is coming again;
"Now he will not allow us to survive."
Hearing words to this effect,
Pakki took up his gun, and
Loaded it with two shots,
And concealed himself behind a tree.
At Odēnan coming near,
The Mappilla, taking good aim, shot

At Odēnan's forehead.
He fell down on his knees,
But would not let his mean enemy escape.
He threw his sword at him,
Which cut not only the tree
But Pakki himself into two.
Tearing off his silk turband,
Odēnan dressed his wound on the forehead.
The Kurup, his brother, seeing this
Burst into tears.
But Odēnan remained bold and said—
"Brother? don't you show your weekness
"In the midst of these thousands of men.
"How simple you are!
"Has anybody as yet died
"From arrows on the neck?
"Or from bullets on the forehead?
They then began retreat
Through the Chambāt field
And reached home—Mēppayil in Kadattanād—that day."

It will be observed that this ballard illustrates many of the peculiarities of Malayalee life.

Of the war songs in use in his time Bartolomeo says, "They contain panegyrics on the first Indian warriors and heroes, on the love of one's own country, on the virtues of the people and the happy condition of India during remotest periods; all objects which give full scope to the imagination, and animate the soul with a desire of achieving splendid actions." He gives some specimens of the "War song in the Malabar language." One or two of these may be sub-joined

"Asurer aver aḍhika śaṭhar avani paṭi vīrerai
Āṭyanṭa duṣṭarai ulbhavichchīṭinār
Avani bhara—makaluvaṭin-averkaḷe oṭukkuvān
Āḍi ḍēven muḍṛṭṭan oru yōḍhanam."

"The giants, a horrid race, endowed with irresistible strength, immediately after their birth, became exceedingly arrogant, and exercised the most detestable violence. They made themselves masters of the globe; and the earth groaned under their insupportable burden. To combat and extirpate them a god appeared. It was the supreme God, the God Krishna who took the field against them."

"This poem" says Bartolomeo "has great beauties; the versification is smooth, easy harmonious and lively; and expresses, as it were, the march of an army. The first verse, in each strophe, consists of eighteen syllables or feet which are called *Pada*. The second worse has always twelve such *Pada*. The melody to this song is rather quick than slow; and holds a medium between the alt and bass. The tone always lies on the first syllable of the three or four first words with which the verse begins; and, altogether contrary to the European manner, never on the final words. In the Samscred song, which occurs hereafter, each verse consists of fifteen *Pada*. There are, however, other kinds of verse, the quantity of which is sometimes longer. For example:

Aghila sastra cirtram parama gnana mitram
Agghana gunna matram carunam purna patram

The first of these two verses contains fifteen, and the other only fourteen syllables. The metre is called *Parra* and not *Porb*, as Anquetil du Perron asserts. It serves as a proof that our so called Leonine verses, which rhyme in the middle and at the end, are not unknown to the Indians. Their public songs are always sung with an instrumental accompaniment. Their singing voices, of which they reckon six, have very singular names and are as follows:—

1. Shlagia, the peacock voice
2. Nishada, The elephant voice
3. Irshubha, the ox voice
4. Sandhara, the sheep's voice
5. Madhyama, A voice of certain bird called Anilapakshi.

6. Dhevivada, the horse voice."[1]

38. No materials for cannonading. The Zamorin's seiges of the Portuguese forts of Calicut and Chāliaṭ described by Sheik Zeen-ud-deen as well by the Portuguese historians make it clear that the Malayalees were not altogether ignorant of the science of beleaguering. The attack on the Portuguese Fort of Quilon is also an instance in point. It is also not quite correct to say that they had no materials for cannonading. Before the arrival of the Portuguese, they were ignorant of the use of fire arms; but we have found that the two Milanese deserters supplied the Zamorin with cannon and large pieces of artillery. Rockets and hand grenades were also not unknown, for we read of armies marching to the attack with letting of fireworks in front of them. Baldeus informs us that, when the Dutch beseiged the city of Coulang(Quilon) in 1661, they were met by 7,000 or 8,000 Nāyars of Malabar who were well acquainted with the use of bows, and arrows and muskets and great cannon. He further tells us that "they make their own gun-barrels, gunpowder, and matches." In the wars with the Portuguese, the Zamorin seems to have brought into the field a large number of brass guns.

1 Bartolomeo, pages 365 to 369.

(1) Shadja—the fourth note (according to some, the first), so called as it is derived from the six organs. (നാസാം കണ്ഠമുരസ്താലു ജിഹ്വാം ദന്താംശ്ച സംസ്പൃശൻ).

(2) Nishadah—the first note (properly the seventh).

(3) Rishabhah—the second of the seven primary notes of the Indian gamut (said to be uttered by cows).

(4) Gandharah—the third note.

(5) Madhyamah—the fifth note.

(6) Dhaivatah—the sixth note.

(7) Panchamah—the fifth-(or in later times the seventh)-note, said to be produced by the cuckoo. It is so called because it is produced from five parts of the body. (വായുഃസമുത്ഥിതോ നാഭേരുരോ ഹൃത്കണ്ഠമൂർധസു॥ വിചരൻ പഞ്ചമസ്ഥാനപ്രാപ്ത്യാ പഞ്ചമ ഉച്യതേ).

39. **Entice our men.** European deserters were often employed by Malabar Rajas to instruct their armies in the western system of fighting. We have seen the use made by the Zamorin of the Milanese deserters from the Portuguese. Later, Travancore maintained a considerable army, partly trained by Dutch deserters of whom Lanoy and Duyvenschot are specially mentioned by Moens as the most important. Fra Bartolomeo mentions M. Donaudi, a native of Turin, as a Captain in the Raja's service in 1787. The Dutch Commandeur Gollenesse's administration regarded the reported appointment of Duyvenschot to command the King of Travancore's forces as a most serious danger, and an attempt by Travancore to storm Quilon in July 1742 was attributed to his influence. Lanoy was afterwards appointed Commander-in-Chief of Marthanda Varma's disciplined forces, and he served him and his successor for 37 years, and fortified the frontiers of the State.[1]

40. **Not much bloodshed.** In addition to the reasons mentioned by our author for Malabar wars being less productive of bloodshed, it may be remembered that fire-arms were not of constant use and that the peculiar rules of war, which were accepted as binding on the parties and which have been already referred to, were calculated to diminish the death-roll. In the wars with the Portuguese, we often read in their histories of huge armies being polished off in little or no time; and yet the fighting on either side is described as fierce. Mr. Whiteway tells us that "None of the battles, however, described by the Portuguese historians—and they are numerous and told in great detail—sound much more than magnified street brawls".[2]

41. **Places unprotected.** Till the foundations of Malabar society, political and social, broke up, there was no use of having walled towns and fortified villages. The several chiefs had their territories sharply marked

1. *The Dutch in Malabar.* Introduction, page 25.
2. Page 36.

out and were content to abide within those limits and pass the even tenor of their lives in peace and plenty. But, as time passed on, the avarice of man got the better part of his nature, and the result was greed of power, landgrabbing, earth hunger, internecine wars and aggrandisement by the powerful chiefs on the territories of their powerless neighbours. From the Arab traveller, Ibn Batuta, we learn that the boundaries of the several chiefs were religiously respected and that even criminals found safety when flying from justice. Batuta observes, "In the country of Malabar are 12 kings; * *. That which separates the district of one king from that of another is a wooden gate upon which is written, 'The gate of safety of such a one'. For when any criminal escapes from the district of one king, and gets safety into that of another he is quite safe; so that no one has the least desire to take him, so long as he remains there". The translator of Ibn finds a parallel to this in the custom which obtained among the early Israelites, by which the man who happened to accidently kill another saved his life by escaping to one of the cities of refuge, and remaining there until the death of the high priest.[1]

42. **Pay fine for the slain.** By the time our author wrote, matters must have considerably improved in Malabar regarding the idea of revenge entertained by the Malayalees when any of their Rajas happened to be killed by the enemy, we have already seen that the followers of the Raja were obliged to take as many lives of the enemy as possible, and for this purpose they risk their own. A somewhat similar custom is mentioned by the Arab chronicler, Zeen-ud-deen Mukhdom, who had exceptional opportunities of observing facts and who visited Malabar about the middle of the sixteenth century. "Should the Ray, or chieftain of any tribe of them be slain in battle, his troops continue a

1. Lees' Travels, page 167.

war of extermination against those who were the occasion of his death, attacking them and their cities, until they have succeeded in annihilating the one and laid desolate the other. From this cause, therefore it happens, that their enemies cautiously avoid killing any of their Rays, dreading the consequences which from this ancient custom are inevitable; although in latter days, less apprehension is shown by those opposed to them in this particular."[1] Those who had declared themselves "Amochi" and pledged to guard the lives of the deceased chiefs had to see that they kill an equal number of Princes of the enemies' family. Latterly, a heavy fine or cession of territory seem to have come to be regarded as sufficient satisfaction. Della Vella tells us that 'when two kings happen to war together, each army takes great heed not to kill the contrary king; nor so much as to strike his umbrella which is amongst them the ensign of Royalty: because, besides that it would be a great sin to have a hand in Royal blood, the party or side which should kill or wound him, would expose themselves to great and irreparable mischiefs, in regard of the obligation on the whole kingdom of the wounded or slain king hath to revenge him in the greatest destruction of their enemies, even with the certain loss of their lives if it be needful".[2]

43. **Boast of numbers.** The Malabar calculation of the number of Nāyars in the country might be a good deal exaggerated. According to the *Keralolpathi*, on the alleged distribution of Kērala by the last Perumāl to the various chiefs of Malabar, he is said to have assigned to Travancore and Kōlaṭṭiri 350,000 Nāyars each. There were Cochin, Calicut and a number of other chiefs also to whom large numbers of Nāyars were given. Anyhow we see that the Zamorin was able to bring about 50,000 Nāyars to fight Pacheco at the Cochin ford. In 1510, when Albuquerque

1. Tohfut, page 61.

2. Page 192.

assaulted Calicut, it is said that "the Indians were surprised, but the chief Nairs uttered a cry which repeated from mouth to mouth to the distance of several miles drew quickly around him 30,000 men well armed." Caesor Frederick (1563—1581) tells us that the King of Cochin was considered "a small power in respect of the other kings of the Indies, for he can make but seventy-thousand, men of armes in his camp." The *Tohfut-ul Mujahideen* speaks of the Nāyars "being very numerous and possessed of great power." In Bartolomeo's time, though the Zamorin had been shorn of a good deal of his glory, he was able to bring into the field 100,000 men, while the Travancore King maintained a standing army 50,000, besides a militia of 100,000 men. Malabar has always been a very populous tract though a large portion of it is covered by water and forest lands. In the latter half of the 18th century, Bartolomeo calculated the population of Malabar to be about 2 millions. According to him, in the year 1771, M. Florentius, a Jesuit Bishop and Vicar Apostolic, gave the number of Christians of St. Thomas as 94,600. In the year 1787, when a poll tax was about to be imposed on them by the King of Travancore, they estimated their number at 100,000. Certainly, on such an occasion and for such a purpose, it was not likely that they would have exaggerated their numbers. There were about 50,000 Jacobites whom the Carmelite Father classes as Schismatics. Of new converts to the Romish faith, there were about 100,000. The number of Jews he calculates as being about 15 to 20,000 men. To these are added 100,000 Arabs, 30,000 Koncanies, Chetties, Banians and Komatties besides 15,000 Europeans, Creols, Mestifs and Topasses. The number of the original inhabitants of the country, he says, is far greater than the sum total of all these put together. He estimates the foreigners to number about 400,000, while the original inhabitants amounted to 1,600,000, that in all there were about 2 million inhabitants in Malabar. He adds that this calculation was made at a time when the population of the country had greatly suffered by the war with Hyder and Tippu.[1]

1. Pp. 149—150.

The actual population of Malabar according to the latest Census 1931 is as follows:—

	1931			1921		
	Persons	Males	Females	Persons	Males	Females
Malabar ...	35,33,944	17,16,138	18,17,806	30,98,871	15,10,732	15,88,139
Travancore ...	50,95,973	25,65,073	25,30,900	40,06,062	20,32,553	19,73,509
Cochin ...	12,05,016	5,89,813	6,15,203	9,79,080	4,82,959	4,96,121
Cochin State (Nayars) ...	1,42,637	66,225	76,412	1,31,054	62,977	68,07

LETTER XXI.

Castes of lower orders.

1. Among early travellers, Varthema mentions three classes who may be considered as coming under the heading of lower orders, *viz.* "The Tiva, who are artizans, the Mechuva and these are fishermen, the Polia, who collect pepper, wine and nuts, and the Hirava, and these plant and gather in rice."[1] Barbose, Castenheda and others mention in all 18 classes, of whom about 7 may be said to come under this head. These are—"The Mucoa, Betua, Panen, Canion, Renoleni, Puler and Pareas". Linschoten knew only of two classes. "Of these Malabarres, there are two manner of people, the one Noblemen or Gentlemen called Nayros......, the other is the common people called Polayas."[2] He describes these to be "such as are the country Husbandmen and Labourers, men of occupations, Fishers and such like, those are much condemned and despised, they live miserably and may wear no kind of weapon, neither yet touch or be conversant with the Nayros."[3] Dr. Fryer mentions three classes in all. "The nation is distinguished by three ranks. The Priests make the first ..... The second form is that of the Nobiles ..... The last and lowest are the Artisans and Tillers of the Earth." Hamilton, in the 17th century, mentions "the Tyvees, the Poulias, the Muckavas and the Poulichees" among the lower orders. The *Tohfut ul-Mujahideen* mentions "the Shanars, the carpenters, iron-smiths, painters, fishermen, and numerous other classes who are labourers generally; also those whose occupation consists in the cultivation

1. P. 142.
2. P. 210.
3. P. 213.

of the ground."[1] It does not however mention the class or caste names of any of these. In fact, the author seems to know of the Nāyars alone by caste name, for the term 'Shanar', used to indicate the Chogans or Īluvas, is not a Malayalam one.

2. **Chegos.** (*The Iluvas*) Next after the Nāyars, the Chōgas form an important section of the population of Malabar.

Designation. In South Malabar, on the coast and in North Malabar, this class is known by the name of *Tiyyers*, while in the Palghat and Valluvanad Taluks and in the States of Cochin and Travancore they are called *Ezhuvas* add *Chogas*. The *Shannars* of South Travancore are not far removed from them. The names by which the caste is designated are supposed to indicate the place of their origin and their occupation as a body. The word *Tiya* is said to be a corruption of the Sanskrit word *Dwipa* or Island, showing that the *Tiyer* or *Dwiper* had their origin in an island while the word *Izhuva* is supposed to indicate that island, to be *Izham* a corruption of *Simhalam*, the name by which Ceylon had been known tō Hindus for many centuries. The word *Chogan*, *Chovan* or *Chekavan* is said to have for its original in Sanskrit "*Sevakan*", *i. e.*, one who works or serves, a servant or workman. The corrupt form *Chevaka* or *Chekava* appears in some old boat-songs of Malabar and is commonly used among the lower castes. The term *Shannar* or *Channar* is made use of in some parts of Travancore as an honorofic title, though the analogous class in South Travancore is known as *Shannars*, and these bear a close affinity to the Tinnevelly Shannars. They get honorofic titles from the Rajas and local chiefs such as *Thandan*, *Punampan*, *Panikkan*, etc. In social position, the *Ezhuvas* (Īluvas) come immediately after the artizan classes. They are a thrifty, industrious and pushing community who seem to have

1. P. 69.

made up their mind to win in the race for social, industrial and intellectual advancement. At present they cannot compete with the Nāyars in Travancore, Cochin and British Malabar in point of education. Neither could those of the class, in the Native States specially and in Malabar generally, do so for they were to some extent handicapped with social disabilities. It has been so from remote ages. Barbosa speaks of them as belonging to a sect "which no respectable people touch on pain of death". He adds that "most of them are serfs to Nairs to whom the kings give them, so that their masters may be supported by their labour and these protect and show favour to these slaves".[1] The higher classes have not been, from selfish motives, perhaps, unkind to them. They themselves have opened their eyes and are making a determined effort to free themselves from all social disabilities. Educated people of the higher classes are assisting them in these attempts of theirs. Even the Native States have begun to break through hoary traditions and allow Īlavas who are qualified by their education to enter the public service. In British Malabar they early attained a comparatively high degree of education and advancement, and there have been notable instances of Īlava gentlemen occupying the higher grades of the service such as Deputy Collectors, Sub-Judges, etc.

History of the caste. Regarding their early history, several traditions are extant. The Mackenzi Mss. refer to a tradition that the Īlavas are descended from a *Gandharva* woman who had seven sons. Another story says that a Pandyan Princess named *Alli* married Narasimha, a Raja of the Carnatic. The couple migrated to Ceylon and there settled themselves as the sovereigns of the country. In their train came the Īlavas to the Peninsula. We have already observed that it is generally supposed that they came from

1. Pages 138—9.

Ceylon, and some say that they formed the first wave of emigrants to Malabar. But if the term Īlavas is to be derived from *Izham* or *Silam* or *Simhalam*, *i. e.*, Ceylon, then the reason of their being recognised as the earliest settlers is not apparent; for the name by which Ceylon was known to the ancients was *Taprobane* (Ṭāmraparṇi) and *Lanka* and not *Simhalam* or *Izham*. But it is possible that Ceylon was their original home and that they migrated to the continent in early times as the etymology of their caste name goes to show. Dr. Caldwell has observed that "The general and natural course of migration would, doubtless, be from the main-land to the Island: but there may occasionally have been reflex waves of migration even in the earliest times, as there certainly were later; traces of which survive in the existence in Tinnevelly and the western coast of castes whose traditions, and even in some instances whose names connect them with Ceylon." Again "It is tolerably certain that the Izhavas and Tiyas, who cultivate the cocoanut palm of Travancore are descendants of Shanar colonies from Ceylon. There are traces of a common origin among them all, 'Shanar' for instance, being a title of honour among the Travancore Ezhavas * * * The other portions of the immigrants esteemed a lower division of the caste, came by sea to the south of Travancore, where vast numbers of them are still found and whence having but little land of their own they have gradually spread themselves over Tinnevelly on the invitation of the Natans and other proprietors of land, who, without the help of their poorer neighbours, as climbers, could derive but little profit from their immense forests of palmyra."

It is hardly possible to suggest the period of their imigration into Malabar or to the Tinnevelly coast. According to Singalese traditions, the Cholas invaded Ceylon so early as the 3rd century B. C. and again in the 2nd century B. C. and for a time in the 2nd century A. D. The Singalese retaliated and invaded the mainland and after the 2nd century A. D., there were constant wars between the two races. "These dates" observes Mr. Logan, "are quite uncertain, but it is to be inferred that the inlanders obtained possession of some portion of the mainland and were in turn brought under subjection by an erruption of a Tamil race Nāyars) under Kshetrya leaders from the East Coast."[1]

Mr. Logan adverts to a tradition that the 'Ezhavars' brought the cocoanut tree, the *ten-kay-maram*, i. e., "the southern fruit tree," and introduced it into Malabar from Ceylon. But, as remarked by the Cochin Census Reporter, "Except that Ceylon, lying to the south of Kerala, is known as *Ezham*, and that cocoanut is known in Malayalam as *Thenga*, *Thenkayi* or the southern fruit, there is not much to substantiate the tradition of the Chogans having come from Ceylon and brought with them the cocoanut tree." If they did actually come from Ceylon and bring with them the cocoanut tree, when could they have done so? It is significant that the inventory of articles contained in the *Periplus* [2], as forming the staple of commerce between the East and West, does not make mention of the tree or its produce. It has been described as the "great nut of India" and more than one author has remarked that it is sufficient to build, rig and freight, a vessel with bread, wine, water, oil, vinegar, sugar and other commodities. A mediaeval couplet referring to the cocoanut palm says that it

> "Yields clothing, meat, trencher, drink and can,
> Boat sail, oar, mast, needle, all in one."

If the tree had existed in Malabar at the time the *Periplus* was written, it is difficult to believe that its noteworthy products would have escaped the attention of the shrewd early Greek merchants. In Photio's abridgement of the *Indika* of Ktesias, about B. C. 400, reference is made to "palm trees and their dates" which were said to "be thrice the size of those in

1. P. 257.
2. 1st Century, A. D.

Babylon", and in another abridgement of the same author by a different editor, the palm fruits are referred to as the "largest nuts", It may be conjectured that the reference is to the cocoanut tree and its fruit. Later on, we have an accurate description of the tree given by Kosmos Indi Kopleustus (525 to 547 A. D.) in his *Topographia Christiana* under the name *Argellia*. The word *Argellia* is evidently an erroneous transliteration of the Sanskrit word *Nari-Kelam* or *Nali-Keram*, denoting the cocoanut. It would not be far wrong to say that the tree must have been introduced into Malabar between the dates of the *Periplus* and of Kosmos. If then the Īluvas brought the cocoanut tree, they must have arrived between the 1st and 6th centuries A. D. It is noteworthy that the Īluvas are recognised as an organised civic guild in the Syrian copper-plate deed of 8th century A.D. with a head-man of their own. Two of their specific privileges, "the fetter right" (i. e. the foot-rope for mounting cocoanut trees) and the "ladder right" (for reaping pepper) are also mentioned in the deed, and these indicate the occupation they pursued even then. To have entitled them to a prominent mention in the Syrian deed and allowed them sufficient time to form themselves into a guild with a head-man of their own and to secure exclusive privileges, much valued at the time, the Īluvas must have established themselves in Malabar considerably long before the date of their deed. This document, according to Dr. Burnell, must have been drawn up later than the first Syrian deed, the date of which he says can only possibly be A. D. 774. There is therefore very little to support the tradition mentioned by our author that the Īluvas established themselves in Malabar during the time of the Great Cheraman Perumal.

Appearance, dress and ornaments. In physique and general appearance, they look very much like Nāyars. Buchanan speaks of them as "a stout handsome industrious race". The males of the middle and richer classes especially resemble the Nāyars in comeliness and cleanliness. But they are however distinguishable from their Nāyar brethren by a certain feature of their dress as also by their manners, etc. Their women in the south are seldom well favoured and in this respect furnish a strong contrast to the Ṭiyya women of North Malabar who are reputed to be of "remarkable beauty." [1]. It has been remarked that "in appearance some of the women are almost as fair as Europeans, and it may be said in a general way to a European eye the best favoured men and women are the inhabitants of Kadathanad, Iruvalinad, and Kottayam a large majority of whom belong to the Tiyya or planting community."[2]. The dress of the men resembles that of the Nāyars. But not so that of the women. The *Tattu* form of dressing is not prevalent among the Īḷuva women, while the Nāyar women in South Malabar, Cochin and Travancore, except in the extreme south, dress in that manner. Both however eschew coloured apparel, though both were once in the habit of wearing coloured cloths on festive occasions. In the matter of ornaments also, there was a good deal of difference between the two classes till but recently. The Īḷuva women used to be satisfied with brass and silver ornaments. In Travancore, all the old fashioned restrictions as to dress and ornaments have been removed by a Royal Proclamation and every one of whatever class or creed is now allowed freely the use of all kinds of dresses and ornaments. In practice it is so in Cochin also. As a result we see the Īḷuva women fast adopting the dress and ornaments of the Nāyars. The *Pampattam* or *Katila*, a Tamil ear-jewel, has already given place to the *Toda* of the Nāyar. But the Mūkkuṭṭi and Gnāṭṭu or the nose-screw and its pendant have happily not come into use still. The way in which they dress their hair also differs from that of

1. Buchanan, Vol. 2, p. 98.
2. Logan, Vol. 1, p. 143.

the Nāyar women. While the latter tie their hair into a knot of peculiar form and bring it coquetishly on one side of the head, the former gathers them into a knot in the centre of the forehead. This distinction is also fast vanishing. It is now no uncommon sight to see young Īluva women dressed in cloths of fine texture wearing the Rowki or bodice and decked with precious jewels walking publicly in the thoroughfares, which was a rare sight a quarter of a century ago.

Occupation. Their traditional occupation is to plant and rear the cocoanut tree and gather its produce, to make toddy and to distil arrack. We see that, so early as the 8th century A. D., they had formed themselves into a guild and exercised certain specific functions in the body politic. Varthema tells us that the third class of Pagans are called *Tiva* who are artizans.[1] According to Barbosa, when the Portuguese arrived on the coast, their employment was "to till the palm trees and gather their fruits and carry for hire from one point to another. They hew stones and gain their livelihood by all kinds of labour."[2] The Lisbon edition of Barbosa says, "The clearest of these low and rustic people are called *Tivas* who are great labourers, and their chief business is to look after the palm trees and gather their fruit, and carry everything for hire, because there are no draught cattle in the country."[3]

According to Zeen-ud-deen, their occupation was "to climbe the cocoanut trees, gather the fruit, and extract the juice from its branches, which becomes a fermented liquor of an intoxicating nature."[4] The Īluvas were never known as stone-hewers. Evidently, Barbosa is mistaking them with some other class, probably the Kallāšāri or the stone mason. Alexander Hamilton says that "the Teyvees are the farmers of cocoanut trees

1. P. 142.
2. P. 137.
3. P. 335.
4. P. 68,

IZHUVAS WITH TODDY-DRAWING POTS.

(*To face p.* 430.

and are next to the gentry." Nieuhoff correctly states their occupation. He says, " There is another kind among the vulgar sort, called by some Tivas whose employment is to draw the liquor from the cocoanut trees." The Īluvas, more or less still hold the monopoly of toddy drawing. Many of them are agriculturists and some have recently taken to trade. There are also among them boatmen and weavers. Their women are as much earning members of the family as their men. They are a progressive race advancing with rapid strides. They have taken to the study of Sanskrit, and a goodly number of Sanskrit scholars adorn the caste. Amongst them there are teachers, astrologers and doctors, who go by the names of *Asans*, *Jyolsians* and *Vydyans*. There are officers and poets among them. Some are studying English and, it is hoped, the number of these will gradually be on the increase. Barbosa tells us that " some of them learn the use of arms." In later years, Īluvas were employed by some of the Kērala Rajas as soldiers. They formed separate companies by themselves. According to Barbosa, " the Raja of Porkad (Ampalappuḷa) has not many Nairs, in the place of whom be is served by Chogas".

Sects and sub-divisions. According to Barbosa, in his time, there were eleven sects among the Īluvas, but from the manner in which he sepaks of their occupation, one is inclined to think that he includes the artisan classes also as Īluvas as Varthema does. Though there is not much difference between the two, still, for social purposes, they stand distinctly apart. In Travancore the Īlluvas are divided into Illams or family groups, such as *Mutillam*, *Choti illam*, *Marirvanat illam*, etc. The real significance of this division is not clear. Besides this there is a further division into four classes, viz., the Īluva proper, the Pandi Īluvas, Kollathi Īluvas and the Pachili Īluvas. Their precedence in society is in the order in which they are named. The Ṭiyyas of North Malabar say that they belong to 8 Illams and 32 Kiriyams.

The names of these Illams are:—

1. *Nellikka*; 2. *Pullanni*; 3. *Vangeri*; 4. *Kozhikalan*; 5. *Patiyanguti*; 6. *Manankuti*; 7. *Thenan-kuti*; 8. *Velakkamkuti*.

In Cochin, *the Census Report* of 1891 classified them under five sub-divisions:—

1. *Ezhuvas* ; 2. *Tandan* ; 3. *Vathi* ; 4. *Kavutyan*; 5. *Teyyan*.

In the Census of 1901, however, they are brought under three heads:—

(1) *Ezhuvan*; (2) *Tiyan*; (3) *Kavitiyan*.

In fact there is no real sub-division into sects in the community. For Īluvan and Ṭiyyan are but designations denoting the same class inhabiting different localities. Ṭaṇṭān is the title given to the headman of the caste though, in some parts, the term indicates a sub-caste, only locally known. Vāthi and Kāvuthiyan are almost synonymous terms. These are both the barber and priest of the Īluvas who do not intermess or intermarry with them.

Social Organisation. The internal economy of the caste is regulated by the headmen who receive their title of Ṭaṇṭān or Ponampan or Paṇikkan from the Rajas and local chiefs. In the State of Cochin, the titles give the holder the right to be the headman of his caste living within prescribed limits. He has the privilege of wearing a gold knife and style, may put on a head dress, may ride on a horse, carry a silk umbrella, a gold or silver mounted stick, have a brass lamp borne before him and enjoy various other privileges that are generally specified in the grant.

A Ṭaṇṭān is generally prohibited from doing any menial work, such as ploughing, or climbing cocoanut trees, &c. These headmen have charge of a certain number of houses situated within the limits of their jurisdiction and they preside at the caste ceremonies, for which certain perquisites are due to them. They, together with the elders of the families in a village, decide disputes arising within the community. In former days, they had a council of 31 or 61 elderly men of the caste, according as it represented the sect to which they belonged, that settled all caste disputes. Its decision was final. This authority has latterly become vested in the headman. In the Palghat Taluk the Īluvas of the various villages used to meet under a *Pandalil Elippa* in Tenkurissi for discussing caste matters. As the community increased in numbers, local assemblies were arranged for in place of the general assembly. Besides these, in certain localities, the people elect four of their own castemen whose function is to decide all disputes, preside at all ceremonies and convene meetings for the settlement of all important matters relating to the welfare of the community. The decisions of the assemblies and of the headmen are enforced by imposition of fines which, if not paid, the defaulting delinquent is subjected to social penalties such as excommunication, interdiction from social ceremonies, etc.

In Travancore, as among several other castes, the Īluvas have their social headmen who are known as Chānnārmār, mutul pattukar, and Perambanmār. In each circle or Praṭikraṇam consisting of a certain number of Karas and Muṙis, *i. e.*, villages and sub-divisions of villages, there are a few of these headmen, not less than five or six in number, whose business it is to make preliminary enquiries about social disputes and convene meetings for the arbitration and settlement of all such disputes. Marriage and other important ceremonies unless performed with the knowledge or permission of these headmen are not considered to have been done 'in due and proper form according to the usages of the caste,' and have therefore no validity. They are charged with the distribution of a deceased man's property to his heirs, and they attest the documents relating thereto. They make changes in the customs and usages, and the excommunication of any one offending the caste rules or the re-admission of one put out of caste, after due prāyaschiṭṭam, has to be done by them. The headmen meet every month in some places, while elsewhere their meetings take place only on occasions of some important ceremony. The management of their village temples and institutions is entrusted to them.[1]

Marrige. The Īluvas go through both forms of ceremony, the Ṭālikeṭṭu Kalyāṇam and the Mangalam, *i. e.*, the real wedding. The former is performed more or less on the lines adopted by the Nāyars, with some variations in details. Neglect to perform the Ṭālikeṭṭu Kalyāṇam in time, *i. e.*, generally before the girl attains puberty, entails social disgrace in most parts of Malabar. First comes the Chāṟṭṭu piḍi which corresponds to the Polūṭṭōṇiṭuka of the Nāyars and consists in fixing the first pole of the marriage pandal at an auspicious hour. This is followed by the Aṣhṭa-mangalyam or the ceremony of placing the eight auspicions things in the presence of the caste headmen, the Ṭaṇṭān, or Ponampan. After this, some paddy is boiled over the fire set up for Aṣhṭamangalyam. This is called Polunellu Pulunguka, *i. e.*, boiling the ceremonial paddy. The astrologer (Kaṇiyān) is asked to compare the horoscopes of the bride and the bride-groom designate and appoint an auspicious hour for the marriage ceremony. The day is fixed and written on a piece of cadjan handed over to the father or kāraṇavan of the girl. The girl undergoes *Shandan-guzhika* or a sort of exorcism by the Īluvāṭṭi or the barber priest. Another important ceremony is the Kāppu Keṭṭuka or the tying of the sacred thread, dyed yellow with turmeric, round the wrist of the girl. She is then smeared with oil and adorned with ornaments made of the tender leaves of the cocoanut palm, taken in procession with tom-toms, music and pop-guns to a tank, bathed and brought back in her best attire, and

1. *Travancore State Manual*, Vol. II, pp. 400—401.

adorned with jewels and ornaments from head to foot. In the evening, there is the Aṭṭālam Ūṭṭu or grand supper. Next morning, amidst music, tom-toms, and shouts, she worships the sun, standing on a pedastal. This is called Ādiṭyan Ṭoluka. The bridegroom is brought in great state and is met at the gate by the relatives of the bride with lamps, etc. He is led to his seat in the pandal. So also the bride. The former, standing behind the bride, ties the ṭāli or the badge of marriage with a yellow coloured thread round the neck of the girl amidst the din of music and drums and pop-gun firing. He then sits on the right side of the bride and the female guests who are invited sprinkle some water over them from potful of water placed before him with a few mango leaves. This is called Vachu-ṭāli. Presents are then made after which a grand feast is given. The festivities continue for four days on the last of which comes the Nālām Kuli or the fourth day's bath. The ceremonies close with the couple dressed in *gala* attire going to worship in a neighbouring temple. A good lot of money is wasted on this 'mock marriage', and the vicarious husband is, after a few days, dismissed with presents of a pair of cloths and a couple of rupees, the marriage badge or ṭāli being, in the meanwhile, removed from the neck of the bride and the expensive farce closes!

The real marriage comes on later. The father and kāraṇavan of the bridegroom arrange the match with those of the bride. Horoscopes are consulted and a day fixed. The parents exchange vessels of water in token of their agreement. The castemen assemble at the bride's house and are treated to a feast. The actual ceremony is preceded by the Kāṇam Koṭukkal or the payment of 'bride's price' which consists of the wedding garments along with Rs. 5/4, Rs. 10/8, Rs. 15/8, in North Malabar, Rs. 3, Rs. 6/4, Rs. 18/12, Rs. 31/5, in the Cochin State, and 8 16, 21 or 32 Kali fanams (7 fanams=1 Rupee) in Travancore.

The bride's parents present her with ornaments. In some places the Ṭaṇṭān or headman is a conspicuous figure in these transactions. When the matter is arranged, the bridegroom's Ṭaṇṭān, *i.e.*, the headman of the locality to which he belongs, gives to the bride's Ṭaṇṭān 2 betel-leaves and tells him, "we shall be coming with such and such a number of men and women for the wedding'," to which the other would reply "if you will satisfy our claims with five and a half or ten and a half rupees, six new pieces of cloth (*muri*) and two fanams for the uncle's son, we shall hand over the girl". This last has allusion to the preferential claim that the uncle's son always has to the hand of the niece.

On the day of the marriage, the bridegroom and party proceeds in state to the bride's house and are received ceremoniously at the entrance by the bride's father and kāraṇavan. All along the way there is a display of sword play and athletic feats in front of the bridegroom. The party assemble in the marriage pandal. There is a free distribution of *Pansupari* and sprinkling of rose-water. The two kāraṇavans stand face to face, east and west, and with the permission of the assembly the one gives the bride's price and the other receives it. The bridegroom's Eṇangan (clan's man) takes a plate on which are placed the wedding garments along with eight annas and hands it over to the bride's Eṇangan who in his turn passes it on to the bride's Ammāyi or uncle's wife. After this follows the wedding feast and the distribution of tobacco and betel-leaf. The party assembles once more in the pandal where in the presence of a well-lighted lamp and in the full face of the assembly, the bride's kāraṇavan brings her to the door and makes the following declaration "I offer thee this girl, and thou mayest protect her and punish her when necessary. Thou mayest send her back when thou does not wish to have her as wife". This form of declaration is made when the parties are followers of the Marumakkaṭṭāyam system of inheritance. If they are Makkaṭṭāyees, the declaration would run thus, "I offer thee this girl so that thou mayest protect her and punish her when occasion necessitates it. It is further incumbent upon thee to have her children as heirs to thy property as well as to thy Tarawad (Family)". She is then handed over to the bridegroom. After this, the bride and bridegroom depart to their future home where they are received with great ceremony.

The ceremonies of course vary somewhat as localities vary. In North Malabar, the bridegroom winds the ṭāli round the neck of the girl and his sister completes the knot in imitation of the Brahman custom. The bride's mother receives the bride-price. The bride will be accompanied by two friends dressed like himself and just as the couple leaves the house to their future home, the bride's maternal uncle's son or Machān as he is termed, who has a prior claim to her hand meets them in the way and obstructs their passage. The friends oppose him and the mock fray is closed with a compromise by the Machān being compensated with the payment of two fanams. This custom prevails among numerous other races inhabiting various parts of the world. In Palghat, there is a custom of marriage by proxy, the bridegroom's sister performing the ceremony of tying the ṭāli and bringing over the bride to the bridegroom's house.

There are remnants of polyandrous marriage still existing in certain parts of the country among the Īluvas for instance in the Talapilli Taluk of the Cochin State, the Valluvanad Taluk of South Malabar and in remote corners of Travancore. The following account adapted from the description of such marriages by Mr. L. K. Anantakrishna Ayyar in his work on *Cochin Tribes and Castes* will be found interesting.

In the Northern parts of the State especially in the Talapilli Taluk and in the Valluvanad Taluk of

South Malabar, there is a peculiar form of marriage prevailing among the Īluvas who are called Ṭaṇṭāns. In a family in which there are four or five brothers living together, the eldest of them marries an adult woman, who by a simple ceremony becomes the wife of all. The bridegroom, with his sister and others, goes to the hut of the bride-elect, where they are well received. The sister or some other relation of the bridegroom, hands over to the eṇangan or to the uncle of the bride a plate with a wedding garment and 31 or 101 puṭṭans (Rs. 1—10—0 or 5—4—0) as the price of the bride, reciting certain verses in Malayalam.

The person, with the plate in hand makes obeisance to the good old men assembled in the shed, and says, "I invoke your blessings for the unobstructed celebrations of the marriage which has to be solemnised in your presence, in obedience to the time honoured customs of our ancestors". The relations of the bride, her eṇangan her caste-men are there. The lamp in the shed is trimmed to produce a bright light. The eṇangan, unites the groom's father and the bride's uncle. Placing a few packets of betel-leaf and nuts in a metal plate, the two parties mention their gōṭras (clanship) and the bride's price to be fixed together with the wedding garment is also placed therein. He finally says "I may be excused for any fault, committed by me in my request before the assembly".

Receiving the plate, the bride's eṇangan gives the following reply:—

"You may beat her but not with a stick. You should not accuse her of bad conduct. You should not cut off her ears, breasts, and tuft of hair. You should not take her to a tank or a Kāvu (belonging to high caste-men.) You may keep and protect her, as long as you wish. When you wish to give her up we shall take her back without fail if she is brought along with a third man (*i. e.*, a witness) and the eṇangan of this day, even if she had born 10 sons, provided you satisfy Ḍaṭṭāvakāśam, *i. e.*, claim for maintenance".

The bride and bridegroom are then seated on a mat and given sweets, *i. e.*, some milk, plantain fruits and sugar. This completes the union. The guests are entertained at a dinner, after which the bridegroom returns home with the bride. At this stage, the bride is the wife only of the eldest brother. If she is however intended as the wife of his brothers, the sweet preparation is served to them and the bride, either in the hut of the bridegroom by their mother, or in that of the bride by their mother-in-law. Thence forward she becomes the wife of all. It is the custom even now for four or five brothers to marry a young woman. They follow the conduct of the Pāṇḍavas. They associate with her by turns, and keep a vessel of water at the door to let the others know that one of them is in. Should this be proved to be unpleasant or inconvenient, one of them marries again and keeps her either himself or allows her to be the wife of others also. The sons or daughters are the common property of all of them.

Mr. Logan observes that, "it is said that (Tiya) women are not as a rule liable to any excommunication, if they live with Europeans and the consequence is that there has been a large admixture of European blood, and the caste itself has been materially raised in the social scale."[1] But this statement is thought to be too wide and it is asserted with undoubted truth that such an alliance as mentioned by Mr. Logan is looked upon with contempt by the respectable classes as well as the orthodox community who form the majority. Those who form such alliances and those who associate with such people are regarded as outcastes and tabooed from caste and society.

Divorce is not unusual but of rare occurrence. It is known as Achāram Koṭukkal. Causes for which divorce is allowed are:—want of affection between the

1 Vol. I, p. 143.

parties, unchaste conduct on the part of the wife, faithlessness on the part of the husband, impotency, barrenness, insanity and other like causes. The elders enquire into the allegations and decide. If the husband is the party divorcing, he should take the wife back to her parents and leave her there. He will get half the bride-price he had paid or he may have to give up the whole. If the wife leaves the husband, she has to go back to her parents herself and they return the husband's dues. Re-marriage may take place. The children live with the father or the uncle according as their father is a follower of Makkaṭṭāyam or Marumakkaṭṭāyam law of inheritance.

Inheritance. Among the Īluvas both forms of inheritance prevail, *viz.*, the Makkaṭṭāyam and the Marumakkaṭṭāyam. Those of North Malabar, southern parts of the Cochin State and of Travancore as far as Quilon follow the Marumakkaṭṭāyam, while in South Malabar, the northern parts of the Cochin State and south of Quilon in Travancore, Makkaṭṭāyam prevails. The Makkaṭṭāyam they follow is however not that of the Hindu Law pure and simple. They are guided more by customary law than by any written texts. The rule of impartibility, the lapse of one's undisposed of self-acquisition to the ṭarawād without devolving by inheritance on one's nearest heirs differentiate Ṭiyya Makkaṭṭāyam from that of the ordinary Hindu law. In North Malabar there is a mixed system of Makkaṭṭāyam and Marumakkaṭṭāyam. The issue of parents of this class take the benefit of both systems. But custom varies in different localities. In the Calicut Taluk the self-acquisition of an undivided intestate, Ṭiyya passes on to his brother in preference to his widow. When however the brothers are divided, the property acquired by the deceased and his father go to his widow and daughter in preference to his father's divided brothers. In the Palghat Taluk partition is allowed; where partition takes place no separate share is given to females, their right being only to be maintained out of the family property. From Quilon to Trivandrum, the sons and nephews equally share the Kāraṇavan's self-acquisition.

Ceremonies after marriage. During pregnancy, an Īluva woman has to perform the Pulikuṭi ceremony either in the fifth or the nineth month. In Travancore, this is observed in the 7th month. With slight difference in detail, it is the same as the Nāyar Pulikuṭi. In the fifth month is performed another ceremony which is somewhat peculiar to this community, *viz.*, Ṭiyyāṭṭam or Ḍēvāṭṭam. In front of a leafy arbour, the figure of Chāmuṇḍi, the queen of the demons, is drawn with rice flour, turmeric and charcoal powder. Eighteen washermen dressed as demons appear on the stage before this figure in pairs, dance, caper, jump, roar, fight and throw at each other quantities of saffron water. They work themselves up to a frenzy and are given fowls and goats which they kill and drink the blood. After this the convulsions cease and the dance is over. The din of tom-tom beating and the shouting of those gathered coupled with the strange doings of the dancers make a hell of the place. This sort of dance is peculiar to the northern parts of the Cochin State.

Child-birth. The confinement takes place in a separate room attended by a mid-wife. If the woman is delivered of a male child, the women of the house make Vāikaḷa or Kuṛava, a peculiar shout or ululation made by women in Malabar indicating joy. If a female child, a woman strikes the earth with the mid-rib of a cocoanut palm bough. With the Nāyars, the birth of a male child is announced by the Āṛappu or the hurraing of men, and that of a female by the Kuṛava of women. A female relative would put a few drops of a mixture of palm sugar and onion into the mouth of the babe, and it is believed that the infant acquires the habits of this individual. Instead of this mixture, some give the water of a tender cocoanut, whilst others use water in which some gold dust is mixed. The mother observes pollution for 15 days, and is purified by the *Panchagavyam.* In some parts the pollution is removed by the barber woman who breaks a cocoanut, scrapes it into fine flakes, which she throws about the house. The child is named on the 28th day. Names of Puranic deities have now come into use. Formerly, the names commonly used were Dravidian. For males, Chāṭṭan, Kōnṭan, Iṭṭyāṭi, Mākki, etc.; for females, Kāli, Ūli, Kōṭa, Chakki, etc. Pet names in vogue are Uṇṇi, Kuṭṭan, Kuṭṭi for males, Kuṭṭi-peṇṇu, Kunji-pyṭal for females.

The first rice-giving takes place when the child is six months old. When the first tooth appears, a kind of sweet meat called Pālaṭa, a preparation of rice flour paste in milk with sugar and cocoanut, is given to relatives. The first cutting of the heir or tonsure, ear-boring and Viḍyārambham or initiation into letters all are observed in succession.

Religion. The religion of the Īluvas is professedly Hinduism, but of the Dravidian type rather than the Aryan. It is mixed up a good deal with animism. The worship of the much dreaded Kāli under the form of Aghōraśakṭi is very popular and her shrines are frequently resorted to. The form in which she is worshipped has been thus described: "She is represented as wearing on her head a fiery snake encircled by serpants. Śiva's signs are also marked on her forehead. Lion-fangs protrude from her mouth, and she possesses ten hands, two of which are clasped together and two empty, while three on the right side carry respectively, a rope, a parrot, and a spear and three on the left side a drum with a snake, fire and trident." Her shrine at Kodungallūr (Cranganur) in the Cochin State is a favourite resort of worship, and a great number of Īluvas congregate there for the Bharaṇi festival, and the number of fowls sacrificed on the occasion is so great that the festival goes by the name of '*cock festival.*'

SRI NARAYANA GURU SWAMI.

(*To face p. 443.*

The Īluvas resort to the Brahman temples also for worship, but have to stand at a distance, not being allowed to approach the shrine. They seem to feel the indignity and have begun to build their own temples where priests of their own class officiate. These temples have been up to this consecrated by a well-known preceptor of their community, Śrī Nārāyaṇa Gurukkal under whose guidance and aided by other prominent men as well, the community is making rapid strides.

The Īluvas worship Gaṇapaṭi, Subramaṇian, Ayyappan or Śāsṭa and Vīrabhaḍra, all Saiva deities. They are more Saivite than Vaishnavite, but they do not eschew the worship of Vishṇu altogether. Ancestor-worship and Serpent worship are also in vogue.

Death ceremonies. There is not much difference as regards funeral ceremonies between the Nāyars and Īluvas. The main lines are the same. It is not all that are cremated. The dead bodies of the poor are buried. As soon as death takes place, the body is washed, dressed in neat cloths, smeared with sandal paste on the forehead, breast and shoulders and removed to the front door. The Ṭaṇṭan or headman is sent for, and he on coming puts up a shed of cocoanut palm leaves in the yard and the body is placed in it. The barber prepares a mixture of newly beaten paddy with the husk removed and cocoanut scraping. Those who are closely related to the deceased put a pinch of the mixture into the mouth of the corpse. This is called Vāykkari Iṭuka. They also put new cloths on the body which together with the ear-rings of the deceased form the perquisites of the barber. The shed remains for 7 days and a lamp is kept burning in it. The body with a winding sheet of new cloth is removed to the Paṭṭara Sṭānam, *i. e.*, the eastern side of the main entrance, removed a little to the south. Some ceremonies are performed here after which it is either cremated or buried. A tender cocoanut is placed at each end of the grave. The Uḍaka Kṛiya and Sanchayanam already described in the case of the Nāyars are also performed. The bones are collected in a pot and thrown into the sea or a river at some convenient time.

The death pollution lasts for 15 days. The mourners fast on the night previous to the Pulakuḷi, and on the next morning bathe with a few drops of oil on their body and perform the ceremony of *Shadangam*. Rice balls are offered to the manes of the deceased which are afterwards thrown into the water. They then bathe once more and an Eṇangan sprinkles some water mixed with cow-dung on them. Castemen are entertained to a feast on the night of the 15th day and on the 16th day a ceremony called Shoḍajem is performed. The rice ball offerings (Māna piṇḍam) and the bones of the departed are placed in a metal plate and covered with a piece of silk. It is carried by the chief mourner who goes to the nearest piece of water, whether tank or river, riding on an elephant or a horse (this is a special privilege granted by local chiefs or Rajas and can be exercised only under grant) or walking, and dips himself with it in the water. The procession is accompanied by music and drums. On return, the 16th day feast is celebrated sumptuously, and rich men spent much money on this. The Ḍīkṣha and Śrāḍhas are also regularly observed.

There are various superstitious beliefs regarding dead persons. The graves of virgins dying young are used as places of worship, some tree such as Pāla (*Alstonia scholaris*) being planted over the grave and a lamp kept burning. Pregnant women dying or those dying in child birth are supposed to become demons (this is believed in by the Nāyars also) and are therefore buried at a distance with manṭrams repeated over the grave to prevent their spirits from returning to the house to injure its inmates. Those who die "of fever" (rather of small-pox) are supposed to become *Maruthas* and are strangely enough "buried inside the house, *mantrams* being said over them also, to hinder their attacking the survivors." This was so with Nāyars also in former days. For those who die violent deaths, the regular funeral ceremonies are performed only after their souls have been purified by the manṭravāḍies or sorcerers.

The recognized priests of the Īluvas are their barbers who are known as Īluvāṭṭies. They take part in the funeral ceremonies. Their women tie the *Prathi Saram* or the ḍīkṣha string round the wrist of the bride at a marriage and they finally hand over the ṭāli or marriage badge to the bride-groom which he has to tie round the neck of the bride.

Food and drink. Rice is their staple food. They eat fish and meat, beef excepted. As for drink, the better classes do not take intoxicating liquors, though the lower classes cannot be expected to be free from the temptation of partaking of the toddy and arrack they themselves draw and distil. Dr. Buchanan informs us that in his day the Ṭiyyans of Malabar may "drink distilled liquors but not palm wine".

General condition and position in society. The accounts we have from early writers to which reference has already been made show that in former times their position in society was very low. Ward and Conner in their *Memoir of the Survey of Travancore and Cochin* say that "they were treated with contempt by the higher castes and were owned in a kind of servitude, mitigated to be sure, when contrasted with the proedial slaves." Day says that "they are a people despised by the higher castes such as the Brahmans and Nairs, who, whenever they required money, invariably looked to these classes, whence to obtain it. Always destitute of literature, both sacred and profane, they were not solicitous of education. Fearful of losing money, they often buried their savings. Suspicious of not obtaining justice from the laws of the realm, they often resorted to ordeals. They were not allowed to enter within a native court of justice as they might pollute the judges who were members of the higher castes". All this may now be classed as past history. The high-roads are declared free for all. There has been a gradual elevation of the Īluvas. The repeal of the poll-tax, the abrogation of the Ūliyam or impressed service, the liberty to attend public offices—all these have conduced towards the improvement of their community. Above all, their own endeavours to raise themselves up stand as a beacon light to others still stuck in the slough of despond. The Īluvas have recently organised a registered association called *Sri Narayana Dharma Paripalana Sabha* of over 1,000 members with the object of working for the religious, social, educational and industrial advancement of the caste in Malabar, Cochin and Travancore. It has organised industrial exhibitions, the first of which was opened in January 1905 at Quilon in Travancore when agricultural products of various kinds were exhibited by them. Among other exhibits there were good specimens of ivory and cocoanut shell carving. They are establishing educational institutions and are also organising Panchayats or arbitration courts with a view to wean the litigant class among them from the evils of protracted litigation in courts and consequent waste of money. There is indeed a bright future before them.

3. **Coelgoeryp**—Malayalam Kōlekurups—who are better known as Vilkurups, *i. e.*, those who make bows and arrows, shields and other weapons of war. They are also dyers. While some consider them to be below the Chōgas in social precedence others think that the Chōgas come a long way after them. In these days of piping peace and more especially, when fire arms have superseded the primitive bow and arrow the Vilkurup has lost his traditional occupation and has taken to other walks of life. The bow and the arrow

seem to have stood their ground as military weapons almost till the beginning of the 19th century; for we read that the irregulars of the Travancore Militia who, with the Travancore army, raised the rebellion, known as the 'Nair war' in 1809, were all armed with these weapons. Even in Europe, it is said that there were bowmen in the battle of Leipsic.

Pyrard d Laval gives us the following description of the shields made by this class of people for the Nāyar soldiers to be armed with. "These shields and arms are made by the gentle artizans and are very beautiful being worked in designs of all colours, gold, silver, and azure, varnish and lacquer. They are studded, too, with large gilt nails. The beautiful workmanship of this idolater Indians is indeed wonderful. Their children are taught to work from the age of five or six, and they have the keenest aptitude possible, understanding in but a short time all they see done. It may be remarked, however, that they follow their crafts from father to son, and marry their children to others of their own condition"

The marriage, funeral ceremonies, etc., of the Vilkuṛup and the remaining classes akin to them do not differ much from those of the Īluvas and therefore do not require separate description.

There is another kind of bow which the Vilkuṛup makes for more peaceful purposes. It is formed of a strong and slightly elastic wood with a small cord made of bamboo materials and attached to both ends of the bow by means of two knots, which when played on by means of a small stick produces a very dulcet musical tone. This instrument is used by children during the Ōṇam festival when companies of them may be seen singing and playing merrily on these bows. Experts attempt on these even Ṭāyampaka.

4. **Canniargoeryp**—Malayalam Kaṇiyāra Kuṛup. The prefix Kaṇiyar is generally used to designate

this class. From this class come the fencing masters who, besides being experts in the use of arms study methods of shampooing and training the body to enable it to make difficult evolutions. They are supposed to study anatomy and are held to be experts in setting right dislocations, etc. The Kuṟup is also known as *Gurukal* or teacher.

5. **Cootady**—Malayalam Kūṭṭaṭi—a dancer.

6. **Canianool**—Malayalam Kaṉiyān—correctly so named by our author in Letter 24. Other names by which the class is known are: Kaṉiśan and Kaṉiyāra Paṉikkan. Two different origins are attributed to the term Kaṉiyān each of which is supposed to point to the origin of the class, and each of which is based on a legend of interest, having regard to the anomaly of the Kaṉiyan's position in the caste scale and the learned profession he follows. The Kaṉiyans are a polluting caste whose approach to within 36 feet has the effect of defiling the higher classes, and yet there is no important occasion or incident in the family life of the Brahman, the Kṣheṭṟiya, or the Nāyar at which the presence of this apparently degraded class is not absolutely necessary. This anomaly is accounted for by appealing to their traditionary origin. According to the legend supplied to Col. Mackenzie and preserved in the *Mackenzie Mss.*, the science of Astrology was established by Subramaṉian, son of the God Śiva, with the help of Āḍiṭyar (the Sun), and the Brahmans, as the most favoured of the gods, were initiated into the mysteries of the new learning. It so happened that on one occasion Subṟamaṉian was asked by Śiva to forecast some important incident in his life, and the former declared that Śiva was destined to become a mendicant, walking about with the beggar's bowl, and soliciting alms. The father was enraged at this and straightway uttered a curse on the new science that it might be discredited. Subṟamaṉian could not endure this and his mother Pāṟvaṭi interceded in his behalf with her irate husband and prevailed upon the God to afford him

some relief. It was then decreed that the science will not become absolutely useless and, in order to give it some scope in this world, Śiva sent for the Gandharva Viśwarathan and directed him to be born on this earth as a Brahman and teach the science to the denizens of this sphere and form a new caste of those who take it. The Gandharva did accordingly. The incarnate Brahman married a Tuḷu Nambi woman of the Keṭṭipāṭṭu Illam and had issue by her. Early one morning as the wife of the Brahman entered, with a lamp in her hand, the Kaḷari, the place of worship, to perform her devotions, she was astonished to see Śiva himself emerging from the Kaḷari. Surprised at her appearance there at so early an hour, the God interrogated her as to whether she was not his Kaṇi (*i. e.*, the first object seen on waking from sleep) that day. This was overheard by her husband who at once summoned the Brahmans of the locality and informed them that the woman was a fallen woman and that the inmates of the Keṭṭipāṭṭu Illam were hence forward outcastes. The family was accordingly excommunicated, whereupon Koupi, the son of Viśwaraṭha begged that the family may be afforded some means of livelihood. The Brahmans then replied—"Behave yourself properly, look after the Kaḷari and serve the gods and goddesses; educate the Śūdras and live upon the income from Āyudha pūjah; worship Kandakaman (a devil) and the nine planets and eke out a livelihood by the practice of astrology." These outcastes were known as Kaṇiyāns and were classed among the lower castes. Others joined them later on till at last the caste came to consist of five Illams and were known as Anjillakār or those of the five houses. The names of these are *Velambau*, *Perumana*, *Vallikara*, *Abmadu* and *Nadu*.

The other legend is no less interesting. According to it, astrology was at first a monopoly of the Brahmans, and a Nampūṭiri Brahman known as Pālūr Bhaṭṭaṭiri, a great master of the science, foreseeing an evil conjunction of the planets foreboding his disgrace, forsook his home and relatives and wandered abroad to avoid his adverse fate. But the fates were relentless and pursued him wherever he went. Crossing the bed of a stream, he was carried away by sudden freshes into an unknown region and was thrown on the banks of the stream. Scrambling ashore in torrents of rain and in darkness, he saw a glimmering light in the distance, and at once made for it. Here he found a lowly hut in the veranda of which he laid himself drenched and exhausted, musing on the untoward events of the day and on his affectionate family whom he had so unceremoniously left behind. The hut belonged to a Ṭiyya who had on that day quarreled with his wife and deserted her. The sorrow-stricken woman was anxiously expecting her spouse to return every moment. About mid-night she opened the door of the hut and seeing the man lying in the verandah mistook him for her husband and the weary Brahman was so wrapt in his thoughts about his house and family, that he in his turn mistook the Ṭiyya woman for his own wife—so the tradition goes. In the morning, the truth was revealed and the Brahman accepted his degradation and lived with the woman who bore him a son. This son the Brahman educated in astrology and secured for him an important place in the Hindu constitution as Gaṇakan or astrologer subsequently corrupted into Kaṇiyān or Kaṇiśan. The incident is alleged to have occurred at the village of Pālūr in Travancore where the descendants of the original Kaṇiyān still live and carry on their profession of astrology. He is known as the Pālūr Kaṇiyān and, from all Malabar, people still flock to his house where there is a particular place, Paṭippura or gatehouse, set apart as sacred to the memory of the Brahman progenitor where he is worshipped and where his descendant still practises his profession.

Both the traditions place it beyond doubt that the founder of the caste was a Brahman who had fallen from his caste on account of a misalliance or some misfortune of the kind. The science of astrology came henceforward to be studied exclusively by the Kaṇiyān caste with the result that its professors soon came to occupy an important position in the Hindu constitution. It is most probable that the Kaṇiyān's profession will survive all other relics of the old constitution as his services are required at every turn in the life of a Malayāḷi family. Birth, marriage, sickness, death—he is wanted at all these. He has to ascertain the auspicious moment for starting on a journey, celebrating a marriage, sowing seeds in the fields, planting a tree, giving a loan, executing a document, shaving the head—almost anything that may be imagined. He has to foretell lucky days and lucky hours, cast horoscopes, explain causes of calamities, prescribe remedies for untoward events—in short, his work mixes him up with the gravest as well as the most trivial of the domestic events of the people, and his influence and position are exceedingly great. Of course, his profession is a very remunerative one and, though he thinks it out of form to demand a fee, no one employs him without paying him something. His most lucrative business lies in casting horoscopes, recording in considerable detail the events of the man's life from birth to death, pointing out dangerous periods of life and prescribing rules and ceremonies to be observed by individuals for the purpose of propitiating the gods and planets and so averting the calamities of dangerous times.

"His astrology he will tell you," says Mr. Fawcett, "is divided into three parts—

(1) *Ganita* (Gaṇiṭa), which treats of constellations;

(2) *Samkita* (Samkiṭa), which explains the origin of the constellations, comets, falling stars, earthquakes;

(3) *Hora* (Hōra), by which the fate of man is explained."

The Kaṇiyān's chief occupation is the casting of horoscopes.

"The Paṇikkar, (for he is generally called Kaṇiāra Paṇikkar), who follows in the footsteps of his fathers, should have a thorough knowledge of astrology and of mathematics and be learned in the Vēḍas. (How can a low caste man be expected to be learned in the Vēḍas which none but the twice-born can hear repeated but on penalty of melted lead being poured into the ears?) He should be sound in mind and body, truthful and patient. He should look after his family, and he should worship regularly the nine planets: Sūryan—the sun; Chanḍran—moon; Chovva—Mars; Buḍhan—Mercury; Vyālam, or Guru or Bṛhaspaṭi—Jupiter; Śukran or Śani—Venus; Rāhu and Kēṭu. The two last, though not visible, are oddly enough, classed as planets by the Paṇikkar. They are said to be two parts of an Asura who was cut in two by Viṣhṇu.

"I here produce a diagram made for me by a Paṇikkar showing the relative positions of the planets on the 7th of April 1895.

Suryan, Budhan	Sukran	Chovva	Brihaspati
Rahu			
			Ketu
		Sani	Chandran

N. B.—Chandran remains 2½ days in each of the 12 Rasis or celestial chambers."[1]

Besides being astrologer he is often the village schoolmaster also.

Generally the Kaṇiyān and the castes akin to it follow customs more or less similar to those of the Chōgans or Ṭiyyas. But, in British Malabar, the Kaṇiyān's marriage ceremony assumes a more elaborate ceremonial than in the adjoining States.

"The marriage and other important ceremonial expenses of the village (ḍēśam) astrologer and school-

1 *Museum Bulletin* Vol. III, No. 3, page 305.

master are always provided by the people of his village and the headman and others take a proper pride in celebrating the marriage and other ceremonies in good style. At his wedding, he is decked out for the occasion in valuable ornaments, conspicuous among which is the combined style (for writing on palmyra leaves) and knife which is thrust into the girdle, and which is highly embellished with inlaid silver and gold work. On setting out on his wedding journey he is accompanied by a party of Nāyars as escort, who fire guns, blow horns and beat tom-toms as the procession sets forth from the bridegroom's house, and the same proceeding is followed on arrival at the bride's house. One of the bride's female relatives, who is styled Eṇangaṭṭi has a conspicuous part to play in the ceremony. She seats the bride on seven and a half measures of white rice spread on the floor. The bride is either carried or led in by her with her eyes closed, two betel-leaves being held firmly pressed by her against her eyelids. The ṭāli is placed round her neck by the Eṇangaṭṭi while the bride is seated on the rice, with her back to the bridegroom, and the bridegroom knots the string at the back of the bride's neck at the precise moment when a neighbouring astrologer called in for the occasion declares that the moment is auspicious. The phrase he uses is as follows:—'The auspicious time is come and it greets you with offers of beauty, long life, wealth, sweet wedlock, posterity, and happiness. Seize thou the occasion and marry the bride, and posterity will attend you'. The wedding guests here break in with a solemn twang of "Aha! Aha!" The ṭāli string is thereupon promptly tied by the bridegroom. After reading of a portion of the Rāmāyaṇam, the Eṇangaṭṭi seats the bride by the groom and joins their hands. The rice on which the bride was seated becomes astrologer's fee with eight annas added in money. The Eṇangaṭṭi next feeds the youthful pair with sweets, and practises on the bridegroom various little jokes while so doing. Finally she comes behind the pair with rice in both hands and sprinkles it over their heads with prayers and good wishes, and this is done in turn by all the relations beginning with the parents. The wedding ceremony concludes with the pair making obeisance to their elders. The festivities, however, last for four days, and on the third day the party adjourns to the bridegroom's home, and on the fifth it finally disperses".[1]

Without the consent of the people of the village the parties are not permitted to divorce each other. With this consent the parties have simply to pronounce the divorce in a caste assembly. The children, if any, in that case belongs to the father. They maintain that widow marriage is forbidden by the customs of their caste, but all the same such marriages are by no means uncommon.

Their system of inheritance is mostly Makkaṭṭāyam, *i. e.*, descent from father to son, though in parts of South Malabar as well as in other places descent in the female line is to be found.

They at one time largely practised polyandry of the adelphec or fraternal type two or more brothers marrying one wife. Under this arrangement the first-born child was fathered on the eldest brother, the second on the next brother and so on.

Their peculiar manners distinctly mark them out as belonging to the Kaṇiyān class in the midst of a number of other classes. If they happen to see one of the higher classes on the roadway, they of course keep off from the path at the prescribed distance. Besides doing this, they lower their cadjan or palmyra leaf umbrellas, bow down worshipping him of the higher caste and wish him by saying Nallōṇam Varaṭṭay—"Let all good enure to you". Of all Malabar castes, the Kaṇiyāns are said to be endowed with the least common sense, strange indeed for a class which combines in itself the profession of the astrologer and the schoolmaster, and many droll stories are extant about the

1. *Malabar*. Vol. I, pages 141-2.

curious mistakes they are supposed to make. Barbosa notices this caste as "Canion". "Their business" he says, "is to make shields and shades. They learn letters and astronomy and some of them are great astrologers".

7. **The Corwas**—Malayalam Kuṟavars. These seem to be identical in race with the *Kuranbar* or *Korava* caste in Madras and Mysore and on the slopes of the Nilgiris and closely allied to the Vēṭan or hunting caste. The Odombaerae of Megasthenes, have been taken by some to represent the Kurambers, though Cunningham, Mac Crindle and others are not disposed to accept this identification. However, there can be no dispute that the Kurambers made early settlements in Malabar for they have given their name to their local habitation in the low country which is still called Kurambarnad or Kurambar's land, now a Taluk of the Malabar Collectorate. The Kuṟavas were originally, and are to the present day in districts east of the ghauts, shepherds and herdsmen and are a predatory class who prefer a roving and free life in the jungles to a sedantry one in subjection on the plains. They are usually regarded as of superior rank to the huntsmen who abound on the slopes of the Western Ghauts and in Wynad. They are generally snake charmers and carry with them poisonous snakes whose fangs they extract. These reptiles dance to their piping. They are reputed to possess powerful and efficacious antedotes to snake poison. They wander about in gangs and have the evil reputation to belong to the robber class and are always under the strict surveillance of the Police. They are higher in the caste system than the Pulayers, Paraiars and Vedars.

8. **The Cuka Corwas** — Malayalam Kākka Kuṟavan-is a sub-division of the Kuṟava caste. They are no other than a variety of Kākkālans and are so called because they are said to eat Kākka (crows), vultures, alligators and such like, though they will not touch beef. The Kākka Kuṟavas are but few in

number, and are chiefly beggars, ear-borers, sooth-sayers, gymnasts or thiefs. They often practise palmistry. They dress like the Tamilians. Others are called Kuṇḍa, "low or mean" Kuravers; and are in fact slaves. They used to be sold formerly and were agricultural labourers who are not allowed to approach bazaars and market places or to approach the higher classes. These constitute the most important division and, like the Nāyars, are divided into Illam, Swarūpam, etc. There is no regular marriage amongst the Kuravers, the couple forming but temporary connexions, performing ṭāli tying and Sambandham. They follow the Marumakkaṭṭāyam system of inheritance. Divorce is permitted but only with the permission of the elders. They are demon worshippers who have no regular temples. They perform their devotions in groves and having no images, set up stones to represent the spirit they worship. They bury the dead and observe pollution for 16 days.

9. **The Poenen Poeloo.** Malayalam Pāṇan, Pullon. They are usually known as Pullavans. The term Pullavan is said to have its derivation from Pullu (a hawk). The Pulluvan is said to be clever in remedying disorders which pregnant women and babies are supposed to be subjected to by the evil influence of these birds. They trace their origin to a legend more or less imaginary. It is given in the chapter on Pulluvans in *the Cochin Castes and Tribes*. They say that, when the Pāṇḍavas had set fire to the Khāṇḍava forest, in the conflagration of which the serpent race was almost extinguished, a five-hooded one flew in agony, half scalded and half burnt, and fell somewhere near Alleppey. Two women, who were going to fetch water, chanced to pass by and the serpent in its agony requested them to pour some water on its burning body and afford it shelter in one of the pots they were carrying. The guileless women did as requested. The serpent crept into one of the pots and would not go in spite of their entreaties. They removed

A PANAN DANCE

PULLUVANS WITH THEIR MUSICAL INSTRUMENTS.

(To face p. 2[illegible]7

the pot with the reptile in it and shut it up in a room to the west of their house. A week passed and the husband of the woman in whose room the pot was kept opened the room on returning from where he had gone. He was surprised to see an ant-hill in the middle of the room with a gaping mouth. He broke down the ant-hill and the snake bit him and he died at once. The bereaved wife was inconsolable as she was left without any means of support, and the snake devised a plan by which she could find her livelihood without difficulty. She was asked to go to every house with a Pulluva Kuṭam or Pulluvan's pot singing a song which she was assured would procure immunity from annoyance from snakes. She did so and she was well received. Ever after the Pulluvan and Pulluvaṭṭi go about with their Pulluva Kuṭam reciting the ditty taught by the serpent and every house owner gladly gives them alms.

The caste has no sub-division, but the Pulluvans say that they originally formed 31 families and that the members of the caste are all descended from those families. It is said that in former times the Pulluvans used to marry their sisters, but the practice is unheard of at present.

They observe and perform ceremonies in connection with the attainment of maturity in girls, marriage, pregnancy and child birth.

When a girl attains puberty, she is bathed on the seventh day till which she is confined to a room in the house. At the bath in the morning, seven damsels make offerings to the demons as if the girl is possessed of them. These consist of a triangle formed of the plantain bark on which are stuck small torches and bits of the tender leaves of the cocoanut palm. This is waved over the girl's head several times and then floated in water. The triangle is called *Bali Patam*. After thus relieved of the evil influence of the demons, she is taken home where relatives and friends are fed sumptuously according to the means of the parents.

The Ṭāli marriage, which of course is not the real marriage, may take place before or after puberty. It is said that this is not considered to be an indispensible ceremony and that many fail to celebrate it. However, when it is performed, an auspicious day is chosen on which the father of the girl invites his nephew or some relative of his to tie the ṭāli round her neck. The couple bathe and worship in the nearest temple on the fourth day of the ceremony after which comes the Achchāram Koṭukkal, *i. e.*, the making of a present of a cloth or a few annas to the so-called bridegroom and dismissing him.

The real marriage follows the above ceremony. An auspicious day is selected on which the parents of the bridegroom produce the ṭāli and the wedding dress. At the auspicious hour, the bridegroom accompanied by his friends and relatives come to the Pandal erected for the occasion. The bride neatly dressed is brought thither and the ṭāli tying takes place. A feast follows and each guest makes a small present in money which is put into a plate placed for the purpose. The couple then leave for the bridegroom's house. The other ceremonies they observe are in imitation of the higher classes.

Their dress and ornaments are very simple. Cheṭṭimoṇi, an ornament worn round the neck, and Mūkkuṭṭi or the nose-screw and ṭoḍa for the ears with a piece of cloth tied round the loins complete their outfit. The women wear their hair gathered in a knot on the top of the head slightly inclined to the right hand corner of the forehead. The males dress like the Īḻuvas.

A Pulluva husband can divorce his wife for adultery, sterility, immodesty, disobedience or loquacity. He must in that case leave her in charge of her parents. The couple may separate by mutual consent. Each side has the right of repudiation or divorce. If divorce is effected at the instance of the parents of the woman, they give the husband a piece of cloth which is called Muṙikoṭukkuka. The children sometimes follow the father and sometimes the mother.

As a rule they possess little or no property. So there is little use of enquiring into their law of inheritance. Still they may be said to follow the Makkaṭṭāyam system. All disputes arising in the caste whether from conjugal differences or not are settled at caste assemblies known as *Parishas* the members of which are known as *Parishakkar*. They enforce their decision by levy of fines, by excommunication from caste, etc.

They profess to follow the Hindu religion and worship the deities of the Brahman temples from a distance, not being allowed to approach them lest they may defile the temples by atmospheric pollution. They believe in spirits and, in addition to the adoration of the demons and lesser spirits, they worship their ancestors also. They offer boiled rice, parched rice, plantain flowers and cocoanuts to the lesser deities while they propitiate the demons by sacrificing at their altar sheep, fowls, etc.

The ancestors are remembered, worshipped and their assistance supplicated on certain specified occasions, such as on all new moon days, Sankṙānṭi in the months of Kaṙkaṭakam and Ṭulam, etc. On these days offerings of mutton, fowls, toddy and other preparations are spread on a plantain leaf at which they prostrate themselves and pray to the souls of the departed in this wise: "Ye dead ancestors, we offer what we can afford. May ye take them and be pleased to protect us."

The Pulluvans bury their dead either near a riverside or in a retired spot not far from their habitation. They observe death pollution for 15 days during which they offer rice-ball oblations to the spirit of the deceased. On the 16th day they purify themselves and invite friends and relatives to a feast. Their priest is one of their own caste.

10. **These four castes.**—These four classes, namely Kaṉiyān, Kuṟavan, Kākkakuṟavan and Pulloan, affect to profess sorcery, witchcraft and practise them to a large extent. In fact they earn their livelihood, as our author tells us, by exorcisms, jugglery, snake charming, etc. Noticing the last class, Barbosa says, "they are great practisers of witchcraft and they do not gain their living by anything else than charms." Malabar is *par excellence* the country of magic and of the black art. Those who profess to practise these are by no means confined to the lower classes. There are past masters of the art among the Nambūṭiris themselves some of whom claim to be hereditary professors of the art.

11. **The Macquaas.**—Malayalam Mukkuvan, a 'diver'. These are fishermen by profession and inhabit the sea coast. Classes akin to this are the Vālans and Arayans who ply their trade in the backwaters. They also employ themselves as boatmen, while the Mukkavars, in addition to fishing, do the work of bearers or porters, carrying loads for travellers. Some of them go by the name of Marakkāns. Among their own community in the Cochin State, they distinguish themselves by four distinctive appellations; such as *Sankhan*, *Bharatan*, *Ammukkavan* and *Mukkavan*. The Arayans, called also Kaṭalarayans (sea Arayans), belong to the first group. The Vālans are of the Bharaṭan group. Ammukkavans are a sub-caste of Kaṭalarayans doing priestly functions to both Vālans and Arayans. They recognise four Illams or houses among them, perhaps clans.

The Mukkavans have been noticed as early as A.D. 1409 by Ma Huan, the Chinese traveller. Speaking of Cochin, he observes that they formed the lowest and poorest in the country. "The Mukkuvas live in houses which are forbidden of the Government to be more than three feet high and they are not allowed to wear long garments; when abroad, if they happen to meet a

Nair or a Chetti they at once prostrate themselves on the ground and dare not rise until they have passed by; these Mukuvas get their living by fishing and carrying burden".

Nicolo Conti also mentions the fishermen of Cochin but with him, as we have found, they were extraordinary beings belonging more to the mermaid class than to the human species. Varthema observes, "the fourth class are called Mechua and these are fishers". With Barbosa "these (Mucoa) are fishermen and mariners without other business." But he mentions another class whom he designates "Moguer" who "are people who transport the King's property from one place to another when he moves". He adds that they are mariners and fishermen and they are "slaves of the Kings, Nairs and Brahmans". There can be no doubt that he is referring to the same class under different names. The "Moguers" of Barbosa were perhaps those foreign fishermen, some of whom spoke Canarese and others Malayalam. The Mukkavas are still carriers used by travellers to carry burdens for them. The recent development of easy means of communication has superseded ancient modes of carriage. Ibn Batuta, in 1324, says that "when the nobles pass from place to place they ride in a *dula* (Mal: Ḍōli) made of wood something like a box and which is carried upon the shoulders of slaves and hirelings". Five centuries later, Col. Welsh, travelling in Malabar in 1818, had to be carried in a similar contrivance which he describes, in this *Reminiscenes*, as "a rude misshapen box, an awkward and unseemingly structure, so made as to have a square frame over the head and placed on an oblong platform, projecting about two feet in front, to form a foot broad and from the front of this platform two upright supports are carried to the frame above, over which is fixed an enormous mat umbrella, without a handle; and to finish the concern two thick bamboos about 7 feet long are attached horizontally on either side of the seat, for the purpose of carrying. The rider of this veritable bonesetter gets in by the front. The Mukkavas, being the fishermen of the coast, are the bearers, and four of them in regular service will carry a person about the station and do little jobs besides. They carry on their shoulders and in, changing with a preconcerted signal, they lift the chair over the heads and bring it down with a sudden jerk on the opposite shoulder, the most unpleasant and sea-sickening motion I ever experienced and, if one of them stumble on going over stony or pough ground, the rider may get a fall, easier imagined thân described." But these were not the only conveyances used in Malabar. The *Manjal*, a kind of hammock-litter, used on the coast is thus described by Correa; (A. D. 1561). "He came to the factory in a litter which men carried on their shoulders. These are made with thick canes bent upward and arched, and from them are suspended some cloths half a fathom in width, and a fathom and a half in length and at the extremities pieces of wood to sustain the cloth hanging from the pole; and upon this cloth a mattress of the same size as the cloth * * the whole very splendid and as rich as the gentlemen * * may desire."[1] Col: Welsh gives almost the same description of the *manjal* of his day and adds, "six men will run with one from one end of the Malabar coast to the other, while 12 are necessary for the lightest palanquin"[2]. The *Manjal* as the lightest of the two has stood its ground even to this day, and the descendants of the Mukkuvas who carried Ibn Batuta and Col: Welsh are ready to-day to carry any traveller for hire.

Purchas (A. D. 1626) says. "The Muchoa or Mechoe are fishers, dwelling in villages by themselves; the men thieves, the women harlots, with whom they please"[3]. Alexander Hamilton speaks of them as "Mukkuvas or fishers, who I think are a higher tribe

1. *Three Voyages*, p. 199.
2 Vol. 2, p. 142
3. Purchas *Pilgrimage*, p. 553. The latter part is not correct; at any rate, not now.

than the Poulias".[1] Norbert in 1745 refers to them as "the Macoas a kind of Malabars: who have specially this business (that of fishing) and as we might say the exclusive privilege in all that concerns sea-farming".[2] The Malayalam Mukkuvar is also found on the Canarese Coast. There they are divided into four exogamous septs or *Illams* called *Ponnillam*, *Chembillam*, *Kachillam* and *Karillam*.

The Mukkuvas naturally confine themselves to the sea-coast and are to be found in great numbers on the Travancore Coast and towards the north but are not so numerous in Cochin where their place is taken by Kaṭal Arayans who belong perhaps to the same section but bear a different name. The labours of the Roman Catholic Missionary, St. Francis Xavier, were almost confined to the Mukkuvas of the Malabar and the Paravars of the Coromandel Coasts and he reaped a plentiful harvest among them. A vast majority of the Latin Christians inhabiting the Western Coast come from this class and, as one passes along the sea-shore, one sees churches aud chapels dotting the coast all along the line near one another. "Those who gave the best reception to the Gospel" says Lucenna in his *Life of Xavier*, "were the Macoas; and as they had no church in which to assemble they did so in the fields and on the shores and with such fervour that the Father found himself at times with 5,000 or 6,000 souls about him". In the 18th century, Fra Bartolomeo calculates that "there were 75 Churches of the Muckavas and Paravas on the Travancore Coast and there were 20 Churches belonging to the Latin ritual lying between Poracaud and Cape D'Illy. These Churches mustered about 100,000 Christians newly converted to the Romish faith".[3]

Valans and Arayans. These too are not wanting in tracing their origin to a legend. Their tradition

1. Vol. 1, page 310.
2. Vol. 1, pp. 227-8.
3. Vol. 1, p. 117.

is that, while the God Śiva and his spouse Pārvaṭi were crossing a brook, Śiva lost a ring he wore on his finger. The God created a man from the thigh of Pārvaṭi and he at once plunged into the water and brought up the ring. Śiva then ordained that he and his descendants should henceforward make their living by labouring in the water. Hence their occupation of fishing.

These sub-castes are distinct from the Mukkuvans and Marakkans before mentioned. In certain important respects they differ also from one another. The Vālans assume an air of superiority over the Arayans and attribute it to the distinction conferred on them by one of the Perumāls or early kings of Malabar in selecting their ancestors for his boat service. The Vālans are generally regarded as possessing a higher status than the Arayans and do enjoy certain special privileges. The two divisions do not generally intermess or intermarry. Yet it is significant that it is a sub-caste of the Arayans who minister priestly functions to the Vālans as well. Among Valans the division into Illams or families or houses appertain. There are four exogamous divisions or *Illams*, *Alayakad*, *Eunalu*, *Vaisya*, *gireyam* and *Vazhapilly*. These divisions the Vālans say arose from the various families composing them having originally been attached to four Nambūṭiri Illams or even descended from them. To keep up this tradition, or perhaps in memory of it, when afflicted with family calamities, they still visit the respective Illams with presents and offerings and receive blessings from the Nambūṭiris. Though this may lend some colour to the tradition, it has to be observed that the division of a caste or section into Illams is no exclusive peculiarity of the Vālans. Among the lower classes even the Mukkavas and Pulayas are so divided. There are the Nālillakkār among the Mukkavas and the Paṭṭillakkār among the Pulayas. Perhaps the Illams correspond to the Gōṭras of the higher caste and point to a common origin or clanship.

Each class has its own head-man styled Arayan or honorifically Aravar who derives his authority from the Raja or local chief. In Cochin he is appointed by a Ṭīṭṭūram or royal writ issued by the Raja defining his authority and securing to him certain special privilege and perquisites.

The Aravar appoints Ponambans (*lit*: road-bearers) subordinate to him as sub-heads over each village, ḍēśam or Kaṭavu. (literally, landing-place). These heads exercise great authority, and their influence is such that the community still submits, to their arbitration, disputes, civil and criminal, in spite of the existence of duly constituted courts and tribunals. For all social functions, matrimonial, funeral, etc., their permission has to be obtained and paid for. On these occasions, the head-men have to be approached with presents in money, betel-leaf and sometimes rice and paddy. The Ponambans have also to be paid certain perquisites on ceremonial occasions. These have to carry out the directions of the head-men regarding the conduct of all ceremonies.

The head-man in Cochin of the sea-fishermen is also styled Valia Aravan, and the Ṭīṭṭūram granted to him directs him to preside over the community, realise the perquisities of his and see that the sea-fishermen render proper service at the Port of Malippuram.

In virtue of his office, the Valia Aravan has to lead the way as escort in a snake boat whenever the Raja travels in the backwaters. He has to find the requisite number of boatmen when the Maharaja, the Governor, the British Resident and others travel along the backwaters. It is also his peculiar privilege much prized by the community, to be the first to obtain audience with the successor of a demised Maharaja or Rāṇi of Cochin. He is the first to present his Ṭirumulkāīcha or Nuzzer to the new Sovereign, which consists of a small quantity of salt packed in a plantain leaf and tied round with coir-rope and a gold coin generally a Venetian sequin. Our author himself mentions this in his 8th letter. But he speaks of a golden fish, a silver net and an earthern dish containing sand and salt. The head-man of the caste in Travancore is also called Arayan and has a sword of honour and authority presented by the Maharaja. He too has to escort Royal parties journeying along the backwaters.

The Vālans observe the ṭāli marriage and the real marriage like the Nāyars and the Īluvas while, with the Arayans, the two ceremonies come on together. The Vālans perform the ṭāli ceremony before the girl attains maturity, while the Arayans have both ceremonies together after puberty. In both ceremonies the bride and bridegroom must belong to different Illams. In Ṭālikeṭṭu Kallyāṇam, as soon as an auspicious day is fixed, the girl's relatives go to the head-man to seek his permission with a small present. On granting permission, he issues orders to the Ponamban of the Kaṭavu to see that the ceremony is properly conducted. The Ponamban, the bridegroom and at least four men of the Kaṭavu go to the house of the bride. At the appointed hour, the Ponamban and the men of the two Kaṭavus assemble and the unseen presence of the head-man is recognised by the deposit of a few annas and a bundle of betel leaf with areca nuts at a particular place in the assembly. The ṭāli is then handed over by the priest to the bridegroom who ties it round the neck of the bride amidst the acclamation of those assembled. The festivities last for a couple of days. This is by way of preliminary to the real marriage which follows and which is more ceremonial in its nature. It is thus described in *the Cochin Census Report*. "The maternal uncle or father of a Valan first visits the girl, and if he approves of the match for his nephew or son, the Illam is ascertained and the astrologer consulted to assure themselves that

A VALA MARRIAGE PARTY.

(To face p. 252.

the horoscopes agree. If astrology does not stand in the way, they forthwith proceed to the girl's house, where they are feasted. The bride's relatives then return the visit to the bridegroom's house, where they likewise entertained. The two parties then fix a day for formal declaration of the proposed union. On that day, a Valan from the bridegroom's Kaṭavu, seven to nine elders and the Ponamban go to the house of the Ponamban under whom the bride is, and, in the presence of the assembled multitude, a Valan from each party deposits on a plank 6 and 4 puthans respectively and betel-leaf in token of Eṇangumāṯṯam or exchange of a co-caste man from each party for the due fulfilment of the contract thus publicly entered into. They then fix the date of marriage and retire after a sumptuous meal from the bride's house. On the appointed day, the bridegroom's party proceed to the bride's house with two pieces of cloth, 4 to 32 puthans, rice, betel-leaf, etc. The bride is dressed in the new cloth and decked with such ornaments as she can afford. One piece of cloth, rice, money, etc., are given to the would-be mother-in-law and after the usual feasts the bridal party returns to the bridegroom's house which is entered at an auspicious hour. They are received at the gate with a lighted lamp and a vessel of water. Water is sprinkled on the married couple. After their feet being washed, they are welcomed in by the seniors of the house. They are then given sweets. With the usual feasts the ceremony closes." [1]

Divorce can be effected only with the sanction of the headman whose fee on such occasions ranges from 16 to 120 Puthans *i. e.* 13 as. 4 p. to 6 Rs. 4 as., according to the means of the party applying. The sanction of course presupposes an enquiry into the causes alleged for the divorce. If dissolution is allowed, the Aravan issues his writ and the person obtaining it, whether man or woman, has to pay a few annas to the

1. Pages 171-2.

castemen of the Kaṭavu he or she may belong to. A widow has to obtain the consent of the Aravan before she remarries.

As regards marriage and divorce, there is but little difference between the Vālan and the Arayan. The latter have their own Aravan or headman and Ponamban exercising similar functions as the head-man of the Vālans. To them they owe social allegiance and pay customary dues on ceremonial occasions.

While the Vālans follow a mixed form of inheritance, the Arayans observe Makkaṭṭāyam. The Vālans divide their self-acquired property equally among their nephews or Ananṭravans and sons. They have but little property which they can call their own, being but day labourers and fishermen, acquiring something sufficient for the needs of the day and eking out a somewhat miserable existence. But it is delightful to note that there are signs to their advancement in life. A few have acquired landed property and have taken to agricultural pursuits. The Vālans observe birth and death pollution for 13 and Arayans 11 days.

Their traditional occupation is fishing and boat service. In view of this, they invariably live in small wretched huts on the shores of the backwaters which abound in fish. Their food is scanty, their dress unclean and extremely poor. The women can ill afford to wear ornaments of gold or silver and wear but a loin cloth with a small one on the shoulders, but not covering the breast which would offend custom. In these days one could see a change for the better among them. The women engage themselves in a small way in spinning coir yarn, buying green cocoanut husks from the farmers. The men fish in the backwaters, not in the sea, using large nets which catch the fish at the ebb and flow of the tide as it affects the backwaters, and raising the nets every night to gather the fish. They tie their nets to the fishing stakes in various parts of the lagoons which in former days were rent

MARARS WITH THEIR INSTRUMENTS.

(To face p. 2[illegible]7

free. While the males catch fish, the females carry them to the market for sale. The nets are of cotton-thread of their own make and repaired by themselves. The most they get at a haul is worth but a quarter of a Rupee. They are addicted to drinking and often-times waste the little they acquire on drink.

The other occupation they follow is that of boat service. They are employed to row boats for travellers, also to carry goods in baggage boats. They are as a class expert rowers capable of great endurance. They are great at boat racing. Malabar is intersected by so many canals, rivers, creeks, and lagoons that water communication between long distances is readily available. In fact in certain localities that is the only means of communication. In the Kuttanad, in Travancore *i. e.*, the tract round Alleppy and Ambalapuzhay, without the use of tiny canoes a few feet in length and lightly paddled by a single individual, it is impossible to go about or even to get out of one's house.

The boats in general use are:—(1) cabin boats for the use of the better classes, (2) long narrow canoes for ordinary passengers, (3) slower baggage boats for heavy merchandise. These are employed on the line on traffic from north to south along the backwaters and the junction canals. On the sea coast there are fishing canoes and rafts.

The cabin boats are a sort of house-boats comparatively large, comfortable things swift in their passage and invaluable to travellers. They ply on the backwaters and can go up most of the rivers also. Built of teak, ānnili, and jackwood, they last long and require only frequent oiling and painting. They are usually about 30 feet long and 6 feet in beam. In the front half of the boat are seats for 10 to 16 rowers; the stern part is covered in as a little cabin with wooden roof, windows, doors and seats, which latter are more frequently fitted with planks so as to make a level floor on which the mattresses are spread for reclining or sleeping, while boxes and other luggage are neatly arranged underneath the seats. A second little box-cabin, with a necessary compartment and other accommodation are frequently attached for females and children or servants. Seats are sometimes placed on the top of the cabin with an awning to protect oneself from the rays of the sun. The steersman who sometimes goes by the name of *Marakkan* or *Srang* occupies one seat outside the cabin door while a servant may occupy the other. The steersman is often the owner of the boat. The Vālans ply the oars which they pull lustily and as a relief indulge in boat songs. The paddles are of bamboo with a flat saucer shaped piece of wood secured at the end of each. An awning can be spread over the rowers in the heat of the day to ward off the sun. From their youth the Vālans and Arayans learn the songs and many of the class are said to be tolerable versifiers able to extemporise songs. One man leads off by singing the first line, and then all the rest take it up and sing after him in chorus and so on for every line of the song.

The effect produced in the mind of a European new to these songs is thus described by the Rev. J. O'Connel in the pages of *the Malabar Quarterly Review*. "We approached Ernakulam by Trichur and the long chain of lakes that make a safe and beautiful water-way. For sometimes we enjoyed in silence the unaccustomed scene. Then suddenly the voice of sixteen rowers broke out in song. This astonished me more than the oriental scenery. Sometimes it was a cantata such as we hear at an opera, more rude but more masculine; sometimes a short solo oftentimes consisting of but two or three syllables ; again it became a spirited declamation. Each knew his part perfectly, joining in just at the proper moment ; and, in all this intermingling of solos, duets and choruses, there was not one single hitch. We had never heard anything like these boat-songs. Heard in the silent night, they assume a warlike character very different from the peaceful dispositions of the performers."

They select their subjects from the Rāmāyaṇa, the Bhāraṭa or from other religious poems. Passing events of the day also attract their attention. There are songs on the "Nāyar war", the fall of Diwan Vēlu Ṭampi, the great fire at Alleppey, the inundation at Trivandrum as also in praise of popular favourites such as Naṭavarampaṭṭ Kunju Kṛshṇa Mēnōn, Sarvāḍhi-Kāriakkār, a late minister of Cochin. The convert fishermen have also supplied their quota in the shape of songs on the foundation and consecration of the Venduruthy Church and other subjects of a religious character. Having no education whatever, they express themselves so awkwardly that it is often difficult to distinguish the words themselves. The Rev. Richard Collins has reduced into musical notation one of their songs:—

"Pan-du-bhū-mi-ṭa-ni-lo-ru
Wan-du-ṭa-num-pa-ran-nan-gu
Man-di-na-dak-kun-nan-ē-ram
Kan-da-wa-num-o-ru-push-pam."

He gives also a free translation of the song:—

"Once upon this earth of ours
A bee flew out at evening hour;
And as he hastened here and there,
It chanced he spied a beauteous flower.

The flower it was a moon-faced lotus;
Glad he was to enter in;
Waiting not he sipped the honey;
He cared not for the world a pin.

He knew not that the sun was setting,
While he sucked the nectar pure;
And if we know not what is doing,
We shall find misfortune sure.
Then that fair flower too closed its petals,
And the bee was roused at last—

Alas! but soon the hours will hasten,
Soon the night that's come be past.

Soon will the day again be dawning,
The sun will flood the eastern sky,
And this fair flower that's now my prison
O'er the tank will open lie.

An elephant, while thus he mused,
The tempting lotus chanced to see,
With hungry maw he cropped and ate,
And crunched the too presumptuous bee." [1]

The ordinary canoe or Vaḷḷam or Vanchi is dug out of a single large log and trimmed by carpenters. The wood used is generally of the āññili tree, but pine, mango, elavu and other trees are also used. They range from the smallest size of a few feet in length to the largest measuring sometimes 43 feet long and 3¾ in width. The commonest size for a passenger boat is from 20 to 30 feet long and 2½ to 3 feet broad. They are propelled by a man standing at the stern with a long bamboo pole and slowly move along the shallow parts, sometimes a second man rows with a paddle at the bow and sails are also spread if the wind is favourable. There is a thatch overhead to protect passengers from sun, wind and rain. Its progress is very slow. Besides these, known as Kēvu Vaḷḷams, there are others called Ōṭṭis which are lighter and propelled by means of oars and with a small cabin at the stern made of bamboo mats. These go faster. Those that carry goods are called Keṭṭu Vallams or "sewn boats" because they are made of planks sewn together with coir cordage through holes drilled in the edges, the seams being caulked to make them water tight with coir fibre and yarn round and over which the stitching goes. The general outline is the same as that of the canoe but they can be made of much larger size. Those that are used generally by passengers for travel are about 5½ feet wide and 25 to 30 feet

1. *Missionary Enterprise in the East*, p. 186.

BOATS OF RECENT TIMES.

(To face p. 472.

long and are roomy and comparatively cool though very slow in their progress. These are protected with a semicircular waggon-like cover of thatch or matting which rises to the height of 6 feet above the bottom of the boat, so that one can almost stand upright or lie crosswise in it. A cot, table and chair can also be put in, so that travelling though slow is not very uncomfortable. Boats of a larger size than these are used for the carriage of goods, and scores of these may be seen scudding along in the back-waters, freighted to the brim with their large sails spread, bulging against the wind. When the sail cannot be spread, the bamboo punting-pole is taken up, and two will work at it in turns from morn to eve and the night throughout. At times, when in a hurry, the boats will carry a complement of four men or more working at the poles by two in turn.

There is yet another class of boats that are used almost exclusively for racing. They go by the name Chūṇḍan Vaḷḷams or snake boats. They are long things lying low in the water with ornamental bow and stern curving upwards (hence the name Chūṇḍan in the vernacular). These are paddled by men who keep good time in singing and become greatly excited, yelling and shouting when warmed up with the race. In parts of central Travancore, these boats are a great feature at temple festivals. But those that ply the paddle are Nāyars and not Vālans. There is a striking description of the scene given by the Rev. W. J. Richards:—"Āramula, 18th August at 5 A. M., finds us opposite the great temple steps, on which an immense and excited crowd stands some holding long lighted cressets which are reflected in the water making a weird appearance in the grey light of morning. The river is alive with canoes, big and little, which are objects of great interest to those on the bank. There goes a stately racing-boat with its prow nine feet out of the water, and manned by a hundred rowers, besides a large number of singers standing up, and keeping time with hands and feet to the plash of the oars. These boats are reported when full to contain 200 persons each. How proudly they stand, how exultingly they sing, how gracefully they sway to and fro! Mark the feathering of the oars, and the musical motion of the paddles stretched far from the boats and brought to the water at the end of a circular sweep. How fine the boat looks ornamented at head and stern by plates of burnished brass and large silver headed nails, which they call 'bubbles'? This is Onam, the great festival season of Travancore, and these are high caste people performing their national boat game. These five great boats abreast make the air ring with their songs as they glide in state down the river. If we could but wait till next Monday, the 23rd, we should see twenty-five to-gether."[1]

Fra Bartolomeo speaks of *Tonies*, *Manji* or *Vallam* being used in the Malabar rivers in the 18th century. He also mentions that boat builders "join the planks together with the greatest ingenuity; pay the seams with different kinds of gum, and fill them with fine fibres of the cocoanut tree so as to be impenetrable to water. On the outside they daub them over with oil procured from pilchards and other fat substances which make the wood smooth and at the same time defend it from the saline particles of sea water, and from being destroyed by warms." He names the following as the different kinds of vessels employed for navigation on the coast, and the rivers of Malabar:—

Candimaram. It consists of two pieces of wood closely joined, and strongly fastened together. With this frail and simple vessel the Indians venture even out to sea. It is indeed often over-set; but, as the person who directs it rows quite naked and on his knees, he soon clambers back into his *Candimaram* and the fury of the waves. These *Catamarams* have been explained to mean *Catamarams*" (Mal: Keṭṭu maram= logs tied together).

1. *Native life in Travancore*, p. 250.

Toni, Manji or Vallam. These are canoes, which consist of the trunk of a tree made hollow.

Ciangada. This is the name given to a certain number of planks joined together so as to form a kind of raft.

Cemboca. Is a broad boat or wherry, perfectly flat at the bottom. This has apparently gone out of use now.

This is also a kind of wherry, nearly of a square form, and so narrow at the top that the apperture through which people enter it is scarcely a foot in diameter. These vessels are built on this pattern, because they are employed for transporting the *nellu* (paddy) and other articles, which would be invariably spoiled if the sea-water should find admittance into them.

Koppel or Padava. This is the name given in the Malabar language to large ships which have from two to three masts, and are furnished with anchors, ropes and sails.[1]

In Astby's *New Collection of Voyages*, there is a plate containing an illustration of the boats used in the Cochin Backwaters when the Portuguese were in Cochin, and it will be interesting to compare them with specimens of modern boats.

The boats used by the Mukkuvas and Kaṭal Arayans who fish in the sea are of course of a different type. Ṭhey are (1) Caṭṭamarams consisting of logs of wood tied together with cross bars and ropes near the ends and (2) the fishing boat which is like the ordinary canoe not so long but narrower and deeper with a plank on either side as a kind of gunwale.

Religion. The religion of the Vālan or Arayan is a low form of Brahmanism not far removed from demon worship. They have a few small temples of Bhagavaṭi at which Vālans officiate. They dread demons specially the water-demon. They attend and worship at Brahman temples, but this they can do only standing

1. Pages 206—207.

at a distance. They are becoming more and more Brahmanised, and they make it a point now to observe Hindu festivals, feasts and fasts, and many of them are regular worshippers at Brahman temples.

12. **Cannekaas, Bettoas.** Our author names the Kanakkans and Vettuvans as forming the slave castes of Malabar. The enumeration is not exhaustive. *The Cochin Census Report* mentions the various classes of agricultural serfs, who were but recently slaves, as being (1) Kaṉakkar, (1) Kūṭar (3) Pulayar or Cheṙumar (4) Paṙayar and (5) Veṭṭuvar. These represent the types of various grades in the process of evolution from the highest to the lowest. Of these, Kaṉakkar and Kūṭar are superior to the rest in caste status, and the rest come in order. Dr. Day observes that the soil slaves are sometimes called Cheṙumars (Mal. Chēr=mud) as a whole, and divides them into four classes: (1) Pulayar, (2) Paṙayar, (3) Uḷḷāṭar and (4) Kaṉakkar.

13. **Caste Precedence.** Human nature is such that even among these classes, miserable as they are in every respect, disputes as to social precedence, etc., of caste superiority cause considerable commotion in the community and lead to disastrous results. The slave castes as a whole have to stand at a distance of 64 feet from Brahmans. Their approach within that distance pollutes all castes above them. Next comes the distinction as between themselves. While a Paṙayan pollutes a Pulayan only by touch, a Veṭṭuvan pollutes him by approach; an Uḷḷāṭan (a caste not far removed from these) has to stand as far away from a Pulayan as the Pulayan has to do to castes above him. If polluted by the approach of an Uḷḷāṭan, a Pulayan has to take seven baths and to shed a small quantity of blood from his little finger to remove the pollution. Not only is there a dispute between the Kaṉakkar and the Pulayar, but there is difference of opinion in their respective communities as to the relative status of the Pulayan and the Veṭṭuvan, each claiming superiority over the other.

There is very little difference between the manners and customs of these various classes, so that a detailed account of one of them would be sufficient to give one an idea of the entire class. Still we may make a cursory glance over all or many of them while dealing somewhat in detail with some.

We have already observed that the Kaṇakkar and Kūṭar are superior to the rest in status. The former have almost given up their traditional occupation, and many have taken to fishing and boat service. As a result, they have risen socially and are much better off now than other classes. In regard to the ceremonies of Ṭālikeṭṭu, nuptials, funeral, etc., the Kaṇakkans, Kūṭans, Paṛayans and Veṭṭuvans follow customs more or less similar to those of the Pulayans.

14. **The Pulleahs.** The Pulayans may be treated as the type of the class of soil slaves. They are differently designated in different localities. In the District of Malabar and in the northern Taluks of the Cochin State, they go more generally by the names of Cheṛumakkaḷ, Mulayan and Valliyāḷ. In Travancore and the southern Taluks of Cochin, they are designated Pulayans.

The word Pulaya is supposed to be derived from the Malayalam term Pula meaning pollution and was applied to the class because, under the conventional idea of atmospheric pollution supposed to be caused to the higher classes by proximity of most of the indigenous inhabitants of Malabar, this class was held to cause the greatest impurity by approaching the higher classes.

More than one derivation is attributed to the word Cheṛumakkaḷ. It is said that it is a compound of Chēr + Makkaḷ, Chēr in Malayalam meaning 'wet soil' or mud and Makkaḷ, children. 'Children of the soil' indicates at once their indigenous origin and their occupation, *viz.*, working in the fields. Another derivation is that the compound Cheṛu + Makkal means little children or short-sized people. Yet a third is that of Chiṛa + Makkaḷ, *i. e.*, those who live on the bunds of fields, Chiṛa meaning a bund. These people are also called Cheṛumars.

The term Valliyāl is traced to the practice in many places of giving them in the evening, as the wages of their day's labour, Valli (wages) paddy; hence those who receive this are called Valliāl, (one receiving wages in paddy).

Origin. The Pulayans of Malabar appear to be identical with the *Holyas* of Coorg, Canara and Mysore whose name Mr. Lewis Rice of Mysore derives from *Hola* a field. In Canara they were agrestic serfs in former days and are still the field labourers like the Pulayans of Malabar. The Brahmans derive the name *Holya*, from *hole*, pollution, just as the word Pulaya is derived from Pula, pollution. Others derive it from *hola*, land or soil just as in Malabar the word Cheṛuman or Cheṛumakkaḷ is traced to Chēṛu, soil. Both in Canara and in Malabar, the Pulayas and the Holyas claim to have been once masters of the soil, and there are customs still extant which lend colour to the claim. There can be no doubt that they formed part of the indigenous inhabitants of the country. Though they are regarded by some as descendants of the early Dravidian immigrants, others there are who think that they belong by almost pure descent to the Turanian race that peopled India before the Aryan invasion. The Rev. Richard Collins remarks, "I have observed that some caste or races of the Himalayan tribes which are in the Madras Museum exhibit exactly similar features to those of many Travancore slaves." But Professor Monier Williams observes, "If the term Turanian is to embrace races so widely separated by custom and long usage as the Dravidian and various hill tribes of India, the sooner it is expelled from the vocabulary of philologists and ethnologists, the better". Bishop Caldwell regards the Pulayas as representatives of the same class as the Paṛayas and Pallar of Tinnevelly. He remarks, "perhaps the best representatives at present of the earliest race of inhabitants are those oppressed tribe now considered the lowest in the social scale. It is a noticeable circumstance that there is no tradition whatever of the arrival in the country at any time of the Pallars and Parayans", nor of the Pulayas or Cherumas in Malabar. The learned Bishop considers "the black, low-caste races of southern India not Turanians or immigrants of any sort but aboriginies of the Eastern Islands and Australia." The Pulaya features confirm this view. The type seems to be the Negroid as embracing the Kaffir, the Andamanese and the Papuan. There is distinctly noticeable the short stature, the low forehead, the high cheek bones, the large mouth, the broad nose and the large thick lips of the Negroid type. The hair in some cases is slightly wooly.

The Pulayas about Trivandrum gave the Rev. Mr. Mateer the following tradition of their origin, no doubt as the result of the lesson taught them by the higher classes. "We are content to remain in our present circumstances for Bhagavan (God), after having created the higher castes, considered what to do with the surplus earth, when Parvathi advised him to create therewith a low class to serve the higher ones." Such is the imposition drilled into the untutored minds of these wretched people by the higher castes. Those living at Kanjirapilly, in the interior of Travancore, about the forest tracts where high class arrogance penetrates only with some difficulty have a higher notion of their origin. In an account preserved in *the Mackenzie Mss.*, the people are said to hold that when Paraśu Rāma had made slaughter in his wars, the widows lamented their being without husbands and besought him to supply others, which he effected by calling in strangers, from which origin the Pulayars are derived.

Under the Hindu system they belong to one of the eight Nīcha or polluted castes and are said to have been brought into Malabar by Paraśu Rāma for the service of the Brahman and others. There can however be little doubt that they were the original inhabitants of Malabar along with other analogous tribes, and there are indeed traces of their once having held considerable power in the land. Tradition current among the caste speaks of their having once upon a time held dominion over parts of the country. In the south near Trivandrum, they are said to have had a Raja or chieftain of their own caste who resided in a fort situated on the banks of the Vēli lake, called Pulayanār Kōṭṭa *i e.*, the fort of the Pulaya chief. There are still some remains on the summit of the hill near Vēli of a mud wall and ditch some 60 or 70 feet square enclosing a small level plot of ground now overgrown with shrub and with a deep well inside. It is further said that a Śūḍra family in the neighbourhood are still called by their fellows "the Pulayan's accountant." and these freely admit that their ancestors did hold that office. The Pulayas of North Travancore acknowledge a person called *Aikkara Yajamanan*, whose ancestors are reputed to have been Pulaya kings, as their head and show considerable respect to him and their Ṅād or country, still known as Aikkaraṅād in the Kuṅṅaṭṭunād Taluk Travancore. It is supposed to point to their whilom prosperity. Mr. Mateer thinks that it is impossible to believe that any of this unfortunate race could have been within the last few centuries in possession of independent authority. He therefore suggests that the chieftains or kings referred to were perhaps the headmen of Pulayars appointed by the Travancore Government to be responsible for the others in all matters of business. There may have been one chief, head of all, near the capital, to whom, as a politic means of ruling the others, some special privileges, and *a small mud-walled fort* might have been allowed, as was done to the head of the Shāṉṉārs at Agasṭīśwaram. Even at present, in the Cochin State, the Raja grants royal writs or *Theettoorams*, appointing headmen in the Pulaya community securing to them authority over the people within certain specified jurisdictions and conferring privileges on them. These headmen are called *Kuruppan*, *Elaya Kanakkan*, *Vallon*, etc. Looking however to the tradition not simply of the Pulayas but also of other communities on the East Coast akin to them, it is probable that, though not in the near past, still, far, far in the background, Pulayas had posed themselves as a ruling race holding independent authority, at any rate over their own community. The Parayas claim to have been once an independent community with territorial sway. So also the Kuravas, *e.g.*, the Nānjakuravas who were, they say, ruling over Nānjanād in South Travancore till a couple of centuries ago. The Chakkalian or Shoe-maker's Fort in North Arcot also suggests a similar probability.

Sub-divisions. In Travancore, there is the main division of the Pulayas into the Kilakkan or Eastern and the Paṭinnāran or Western, the former living in the eastern and the latter in the western Taluks of the State. The caste has many sub-divisions some of which may be mentioned here: (1) *Kannappulayas* (2) *Vettupulayas* (3) *Kanakkapulayas*—found in Cochin and to the north of Cranganore. They are polluted by the touch of other Pulayas. (4) *Inapulayans* — do not eat or intermarry with other Pulayas. In Travancore, these live between Quilon and Alleppey. The great difference between the Eastern and the Western Pulayas is that the latter rank above the former on the ground that the Eastern Pulayas are beef-eaters and therefore a degraded class. The beef-eaters are sometimes called Paśu (cow) Pulayas and Eruma (buffalo) Pulayas. The difference is so pronounced that the Westerners consider even the approach of the Easterners polluting. The customs of the Eastern Pulayas seem to point them out as virtually Parayas, as the Pallar colonies in Travancore are often called Pulayars. The term may also be regarded as pointing to the direction whence they came,

Their tradition is that they were the slaves of Ḍuryōḍhana and his brothers while their Western brethren belonged to the Pāṇḍavās—the rival parties in the great war of the Mahābhāraṭa—and the defeat of Ḍuryōḍhana is also alleged to be the cause of the greater degradation of the former. There are other divisions of note such as (1) the *Pichchātan* (2) The *Kuruppan* and (3) the *Valluvan*. In Cochin, the last class the *Valluvan* is said to be the highest class among Pulayas while the term Valluvan is well known to be a title belonging to the Paṟaya caste.

The whole caste is divided into *Illams*, and these *Illams* are numerous. Some may be named here. *e.g.*, *Brahmakotta*, *Velli*, *Pallikutachan*, etc.

General appearance. In appearance they are inferior to the Paṟayas. The men are small, short in stature, and their complexion not simply dark but at times jet black. The women are quite dimunitive and very plain looking, seldom handsome, but a few of them are passable looking when young.

Of these people Barbosa remarks, "They are a very low class living in swamps—Any man or woman touching these is killed immediately by the relations and the Pulers are also killed * * These people are great charmers, thieves and very vile people."

Clothing and Ornaments. As might be expected of such a degraded class, their clothing and ornaments are of the simplest nature. The men generally wear a short Muṇḍu or piece of cloth round the loins seldom reaching to the knees. The Ṭaṇḍapulayas or Veṭṭupulayas or Kāṇapulayas who are found south of Alleppey and extend to the Cochin State, living between the sea and the backwater, are a peculiarly degraded class whose women cloth themselves in a leafy garment. The Rev: W. J. Richards gives the following account of a tradition extant among these people: "The men of these Tanda Pulayans (who wear the *tandu* grass) wear the ordinary lower cloth of the kind worn in this

UMBRELLA - MAKERS.

(To face p. 486.

DULAYAS.

(To face p 483.

THANDAPULAYA WOMEN.

(To face p 483.

country but the distinctive name of the tribe comes from the women's dress, which is a very primitive article indeed. The leaves of a certain water plant (*Isolepis articulata Nees*) are cut into lengths of a foot long and tied round the waist in such a fashion that the strings unwoven hang in a bushy tail behind, and present the same appearance in front reaching nearly to the knees. This dress is accounted for by a tradition that in former days a certain high casteman of that region had been sowing grains and planting vegetables in his fields but found that his daily work was in some unknown way frustrated; for whatever he planted or sowed in the day was carefully picked up and taken 'when men slept'. So he set a watch, and one night he saw coming out of a hole hitherto unknown to him certain beings like men but quite naked, who set to work destroying his hopes of a crop. Pursuing them he succeeded in catching a man and a woman; and he was so impressed with shame at their condition that he gave the man his own upper cloth which was hanging on his shoulder and made him put it on but not having one to spare for the woman, she made herself an apron of grass as above described. These were the progenitors of the numerous slaves who are found there at this day. They are called "Kuzhi" or 'Pit' Pulayans from having originated as above said. These leafy aprons are of rather curious make and occupy the women ten whole days with close application to make their whole grass attire. The Tandapulayas resemble a good deal the Juangs of Orissa who are Kolarians in race and are called Patuas (literally the "leaf wearers") whose women wear no clothes, but only a few strings of beads round the waist and a bunch of leaves tied in front and behind. The British Government shocked at this state of things provided a cotton cloth for each of the women. They passed in their newly acquired garments in single file before the English officer who made the distribution of cloths, made their obeisance as a sign of submission and were afterwards marked on the forehead with vermilion. But this enforced submission to the highly advanced ideas of a civilized Government was too much for the poor beings, for before long many of the young women had gone back to their leaves. Their sisters, the Tandapulaya women of Malabar, share with them similar ideas for they too are much opposed to the change of grass for cloth and maintain that they might as well be out of the world as out of the fashion."

The Pulaya women wear round their neck and hanging on the breast bunches and strings of beads and small shells. Gold and silver ornaments they cannot of course afford to get and, even if they could, till recently, they would not have been allowed to wear them by the higher castes. Thin flat pieces of brass about an inch in diameter with a small dot pattern are strung round the neck and, of late, there are rare instances of a Rāsi (a small gold coin) being also used. Brass bangles are also in use. They purchase bangles, beads, shells, rings, etc., of trifling value which are crowded on their fingers, arms, necks and ears in such quantity as to be almost a burden. The front teeth are filed sharp like canine teeth.

The eastern Pulayars went about in former days, and some even now, without any other clothing than a string of large thick leaves round the loins; or if they got a cotton cloth, they wore it over this or as head cloth. They hang a large quantity of strings of beads or cowries round the neck. The Kuṭimi or top knot of hair is not worn. In Cochin, as a rule, the Pulayas of the northern taluks wear the Kuṭumi like other Malayalees, while those of the southern taluks shave their heads clean like Jōnaka Māppillas and Christians.

Food, drink and habitation. Their food is chiefly rice which they are able to get during a few months of the year. The rice is boiled and eaten with coarse curry made of fish, and vegetables which they sometimes grow on the patch of ground allotted to them by their masters. During the remaining portion of the year, when harvest is distant, they have to content themselves with fruits and roots. Even when they get milk or eggs, they prefer to sell them rather than use them themselves. They indulge freely in drink partly to make up the want of sufficient food so that they may satisfy cravings of hunger. Toddy is their favourite drink and, after a day's labour in the fields and marshes; they may be pardoned if they quaff a quantity of arrack to appease their hunger and thirst before going to rest. Tobacco is also freely used both by men and women. Badly fed, and living on the bunds and in the fields and marshes, the effects of liquor and narcotics like tobacco make the Pulayas soon to succumb to all sorts of ills. The children especially are too prone to suffer from diarrhoea, debility and intestinal worms arising from innutritious foods many of them die young from want of proper care and attention. If the rate of mortality among them is not so high as one is apt to consider from their environments and modes of life, it is entirely due to their hardy life and work in the open air. In the rainy season, small fish, snails and shell-fish are sought for from the tanks and channels that irrigate the fields. Crabs and rats are also eaten. These appease the hunger of the poor children in the wet weather. But as the hot season approaches, they often faint with hunger and are obliged to wander into the jungles in the search of wild roots and fruits.

The Rev. Richard Collins has drawn a correct and striking picture of the dwelling of a Pulaya. "It was built so far as I remember, of five sticks, four of which were stuck into the ground two in front and two behind and tied together so as to form two little forks at the top, on which was laid the fifth; over all were tied some leaves of the cocoanut palm which forms an excellent thatch. Two naked black children were crawling about making mud puddings, just after the fashion of their brothers and sisters in Europe, and a woman was boiling some rice in an earthern-ware pot, here called a codum or chatty, which was supported over the fire upon a few pieces of stone. The pitcher was garnished with two or three fish that lay about and which had been caught by means of a fishing basket in a little canal hard by."[1]

Occupation. From time immemorial they have been field labourers. They were agrestic slaves attached to the lands passing with the land from owner to owner by sale, mortgage, etc., of the land. Their work lies almost exclusively in the rice fields pumping them dry by means of water-wheels, making up embankments, hedging, dipping, manuring, ploughing, weeding, transplanting and reaping. Men, women and children work together during harvest time. In the nights they have to guard their master's field from the encroachments of cattle or the depredations of wild animals. In the evening, their masters dole out 2 Edangalies of paddy barely sufficient to keep body and soul together. After the harvest season, they can seldom find work and are thrown back upon lean resources to find their subsistence, with the inevitable result that they have to starve till the next harvest comes round. Not suffered to leave the fields and approach cities and towns, it is almost impossible for them to find work. They possess no weapons, and have no manufactures save of palm-leaf umbrellas, baskets made of reeds and mats for which they can seldom find markets.

Varthema mentions the Poliar as forming the fifth class coming immediately after the 'Mechura' and their occupation is said to be, "to collect pepper, wine and nuts." We read in Purchas that "the Puler are as excommunicate persons, and live in deserts, where the Nayros have no occasion to pass," also that they are "thieves and sorcerers." Barbosa adds "these people are great charmers, thieves and very vile." Linschoten as already observed knows only of "two manner of

1. *Missionary Enterprise*, p. 178.

people in Malabar, the one Noblemen or Gentlemen, called Nayros * * * the other is the common people, called Polayas". He describes them as "such as are the country husbandmen and labourers, men of occupations, Fishers and such like. Those are much condemned and despised, they live miserably and may wear no kind of weapon, neither yet touch nor be conversant with the Nayros". Hamilton would have it that "the Poulias produce the labourers and mechanics"

General condition. Their position in society ought to excite pity in any one. Warned off from all haunts of human beings, subjected to every possible sort of oppression, denied sufficient and wholesome food, clad in filthy habiliments, living in the marshes and in miserable huts not capable of keeping out sun, rain, or dew, they are a wretched lot of humanity deserving the attention of philanthropists. In early days, no one extended to them the right hand of fellowship except the Christian Missionary. In Travancore, and to a certain extent in Cochin also, the various Missionary bodies have tried and succeeded in a way in alleviating the miseries of these unfortunate beings. Mahomedanism has also come to their assistance specially in the District of Malabar but of course not with the organised machinery of the Christian Missions. Conversion to Christianity or Mahomedanism at once lifts the Pulaya in the social scale and gives him a passport to tread over ground hitherto forbidden. Their approach no longer pollutes higher castes. Only the touch pollution remains. The Crescent and the Cross enable those dark skinned sons of the soil to rise by one bound from the most degraded position to one of equality with most others. But yesterday a wretched slave, compelled to stand and even to prostrate himself on the ground at a distance of 64 feet from his Brahman or Nāyar master, even from castes below these, and always restricted to the field from which he can step out only with loud warnings of his approach lest he may not taint the sacred presence of his lord with his too close proximity, to-day he walks erect on the public road almost shoulder to shoulder with the most orthodox Brahman and approaches within reasonable distance of the sacred edifice of the latter. With the badge of Christianity or Islam on him, he is able to engage himself in whatever honest work he can do, earn higher ways and lead a comparatively easy and comfortable life. The Rev. Richard Collins gives us an account of an amusing conversation between two slave converts and a Brahman. "The slave converts were walking along the highway, when the Brahman meeting them, stopped at some distance and cried out in an authoritative manner the usual 'Po', 'Po', "Go away", "Go away". But the men were not willing to go and marched onwards with a rather determined and careless air. The Brahmin raised his 'Po', 'Po' with a still higher and angry tone. 'But' said the slaves 'we are not going to go; we have as much right *now* to the road as you; we are Christians'. 'Ho, ho'! exclaimed the Brahman, softening his voice a little, 'but it has not quite come to that yet, that I should have to get out of the way for you, times are changing it is true and perhaps before long we shall be obliged to yield to another state of things; but for the present while the custom lasts, you had better move out of the way'. The slaves laughed, but did not move out of the way, and the Brahman was obliged to go into the hedge himself, while they passed, though quite respectfully by on the other side."

Their environments have in no small degree contributed towards their low social position. As a rule the people of the west coast are extremely superstitious and bigoted to a degree and are more tenacious of holding fast to their primitive customs and habits than people on the other coast. This is due a good deal to the physical conformation of the country, and the scrupulous cleanliness of the high class people there. Hemmed in all sides by natural barriers that prevent them from having intercourse with people outside, they have become an extremely conservative lot. While, as observed by Mr. Mateer, the Carnatic serfs could run away from one King to another (as some Parayas are known to have come seven generations ago to Nānjanād for greater freedom and safety); here in Malabar they were hemmed in by impassable mountains and forests and by the sea, deep rivers to cross, Nāyars everywhere on the watch and no possibility of escape. So they sank from generation to generation. Very few can pretend to have gone beyond the bounds of the fields in which they live. Neither will they be permitted to wander by their masters if they have even the mind to do so. They are, no doubt, an unfortunate, wretched race. There is, however, a silver lining to the cloud. Let us hear what a Missionary, who had to do a great deal with them, has to say:—

The Rev. S. Mateer says:—"Yet these poor people are fairly intelligent and readily capable of instruction. They are sharp enough in comprehension, and heartily enjoy any good thing that is said"...... "Even the degraded Pulayars have some excellent qualities. From lengthened and intimate acquaintance, we have found them just like other men under the power of many evils engrained in them through long continued ignorance, superstition and oppression, but simple-hearted, grateful for kindness, deeply attached to those who show themselves their friends and improving with marked rapidity under instruction. It is sometimes difficult to make the young truthful and honest in small things, but this is a defect observable in many Hindus, and it may be expected to take two or three generations to improve and establish their moral stamina. Already some Pulayars, under the operation of Christian teaching and guidance, have become admirable characters,—gentle, honourable, devout, and loving; and probably they will display a very beautiful type of character when fully christianized."

A remarkable testimony is borne to them in *the Cochin Census Report*:—"They are an extremely useful and hard-working race and are sometimes distinguished by a rare character for truth and honour, which their superiors in the caste scale might well emulate."[1]

"Some of the masters appear to appreciate individuals of this tribe as valuable servants: and the Mission teachers like them very much. One expressed the opinion that the Pariahs have more worldly cunning and intelligence, but the Pulayars are more frequently, truly pious." A native Missionary wrote, "The Pulayar Christians are earnest in learning to read and in giving contributions for benevolent objects. Their desire to learn and repeat their lessons is remarkable and they complain if instruction is not duly supplied to them. Some children glean and sell scattered stalks of rice to purchase the Scriptures. The elders sell plantains and fowls in order to be able to contribute for religious purposes." And one European Missionary remarked, "There is a good deal of heart amongst Pariahs and Pulayars such as we do not often see in the Shanars."[2]

The Pulayars are naturally shy and timid. They always avoid being even seen in the proximity of high-castemen, and few will have the hardihood to associate with them.

We have seen that Christianity is doing much to ameliorate the condition of those who are willing to come within its fold. These form but a small minority, and there still remain the great majority of them, eagerly looking forward to be rescued from the mire in which they are stuck. Cannot Hindu philanthropists undertake this benevolent work? Does the Hindu religion stand in the way? Hinduism correctly understood, shorn of the innumerable meaningless accessories which have gone to deform and debase it, will certainly allow, yea, even afford facilities to raise these poor unhappy creatures from their present degraded condition. But Brahmanism would not raise a finger

1. Page 206.
2. *Native Life in Travancore*, pp. 42 to 45.

to effect this philanthropic work. It would present a dead front to all efforts in that direction, and Malabar is priest--ridden and caste-ridden to so great an extent that the Hindus, as if to make decent amends for the past, are doing their best, to pity the lot of these, to improve their condition and in every way to help them to lead better, happier and more godly lives. There is but little hope that any effort will be made by the so-called Hindus of Malabar in the near future with the inevitable result that, sooner or later, the whole class will be lost to the Hindu world.

It is gratifying to note that a change for the better has begun to work. Both in Travancore and in Cochin, the Darbars have started schools for the Depressed classes and facilities are being afforded for their uplift. Private enterprise is also at work. There are Pulaya associations, a Pulaya journal and Pulaya representative sits in the Srīmūlam Popular Assembly being nominated by the Darbar to represent Pulaya grievances, by the side of the highest class Nampūṭiri and the lordly Nāyar. [1]

Religion and worship. The Pulayas are, as a rule, spirit worshippers. The spirits of deceased ancestors called Chavers receive most attention. These are propitiated by offerings of such things as are supposed to please them. The Māṭan and the Panchavar or Anchu *Tampurakkal*, believed to be the five Pāṇḍavas of the Mahā Bhāraṭa, are specially adored. While they hold that these are greater than the sun, there is one other greater than even these, and that is Uḍāya Ṭampurān or Paraḍēvaṭa, the great God—Possessor of all. They have no temples of their own. But they erect temporary

1. In Cochin too there are Pulaya societies working for the uplift of the class. A representative of theirs sits in the Council. They have access to public roads, public offices, schools and hospitals. The Darbar have appointed a highly paid officer, called the Protector of the Depressed Classes, and they have also placed funds at his disposal to look after the interests of these. The Hindus, including Brahmins, are warmly co-operating with he Government in their work for the uplift of all Depressed Classes. *Ed.*

places of worship by raising platforms on trees planted in a square, one at each corner. Such tree as *Odina Odier* Silk-cotton, *Rottlera* and *Erythrina*. On these platforms shrines are put up and offerings of rice, grain, parched rice and flowers are made. Occasionally a fowl is slaughtered and its blood sprinkled over the shrine. They also attend Hindu temples as far as permitted, and worship Hindu divinities who form part of their pantheon. This however is always on sufferance, for they have to stand a good way off from the temples. Yet there are remarkable instances of special privileges being accorded them at particular festivals at certain temples. For instance, at the Mahāḍēva temple at Parachalay in Travancore. Again at Ōchira, they are allowed to take part in the great shạm-fight, give and receive blows equally with the Nāyars. At Śāsṭāmkōṭṭas, a special Saturday in the year is reserved for the Pulayas, and is known as *Pulaṣeniyazhcha* or Pulayas' Saturday. At Kumạranellūr at the annual festival, little beaten gold images of the goddeṣs Bhagavaṭi are offered for sale to the Pulayas outside, who make an offering of them after purchase. "At the Neduvengaud Temple," says Rev. Mateer, "where two or three thousand people, mostly Sudras and Ilavars, attend for the annual festival in March, one-third of the whole are Pariahs, Kuravars, Vedars, Kanikars, and Pulayars who come from all parts around. They bring with them wooden models of cows, neatly hung over and covered, in imitation of shaggy hair with ears of rice. Many of these images are brought each with a separate procession from its own place. The headmen are finely dressed with clothes stained purple at the edge. The image is borne on a bamboo frame, accompanied by a drum, and men and women in procession—the latter wearing quantities of beads, such as several strings of red, then several of white; or strings of beads and then a row of brass ornaments like rupees—and all uttering the Kurava cry. These images are carried round the temple and all amuse themselves for the day".[1] At the great Bharaṇi festival at Çranganur, on the day previous to Bharaṇi, at a given signal, all classes, irrespective of caste, are allowed to circumambulate the temple, and the great unwashed do so with an uproarious rush.

We have an analogue of this on the Eastern Coast where many shrines make similar provision as regards corresponding classes. So also in Mysore, where, as pointed out, in the *Indian Antiquary* for March 1873, by Captain Mackenzie, the Holyars, who correspond to our Pulayars, enjoy special privileges. It is said that a Holyar is even now generally the priest to the village goddess and, as such, the annual offerings of Holyars take precedence of those of the Brahmans. Again at Mailkotta and at Bailur, the Holyars have the privilege of entering the temple during three days in the year specially set apart for them.

Exorcism and devil dancing. Exorcism is in great favour with the Pulayars and, as all ailments are attributed to the agency of demons, it is the business of the Pūjāri or priest to discover it and apply the proper remedy. He is master of the proper manṭrams or incantations and has an iron-nattle called *Kokkara* by the sound of which he divines. It will be revealed to him by a kind of inspiration or possession which demon it is that has caused the sickness, and he will declare, who it is, and what is to be done in the particular case. The following account given by the Rev. Mr. Mateer of their practice of exorcism and devil dancing is faithful and interesting. "The Kokkara is formed of a plate of iron turned into a tube, the edges strongly serrated and not closely united. It is about nine inches in length and one and a half in diameter. From it hangs a chain and an iron pin or spike, which is rubbed along the dentate edges of the iron cylinder, making a horrid grating noise. This instrument is used by sorcerers amongst Pariahs, Vēṭars and

1. *Native Life in Travancore*, p.56.

Kuravars, but it seems more especially to belong to Pulayars. It is used in seeking demoniac possession, in exorcising demons in divination and in cases of sickness. The instrument costs from three-quarters to one rupee and is made by the ordinary blacksmith.

"When a youth wishes to learn this black art, he goes to some one accomplished in it and presents a parah of paddy, three fanams in money, seven cocoanuts, and two chuckrams' worth of betel leaf. A feast is also given to his relatives, costing, say twenty-five fanams. He learns for about a week the names of all the demons and the charms with which the teacher is acquainted. When fully instructed, he receives from the teacher a Kokkara and a cowry shell, and pays a further fee. It costs about 100 (about 16 Rs.) fanams to learn the business.

"He is then called to cure patients, young and old, of various diseases by playing this instrument, and, with the addition of a conch shell, a cocoanut and a cowry, he may make a reputation for himself and much gain by deceiving the people. All Pulayars honour and fear him; Sudras also employ him in various matters. When he goes to find omens for fortune-telling, he is paid one fanam, for casting out demons, three fanams and three *Edungalies* of paddy, for rescuing a pregnant woman from a demon, seven fanams for offering sacrifices, ten fanams and the flesh of the fowls slain and some toddy, and for destroying enemies or detecting robbers, twelve fanams.

"In times of sickness, these dancers frighten the people by announcing the wrath of the demons and the necessity of further propitiatory offerings in order to get rid of the disease. They also give sacred ashes to patients for their recovery.

"When the priest is called to a house for a case of sickness, he generally comes in the evening, and is first entertained with food, toddy to drink, and betel to chew. He then prepares a tender cocoanut, the flower of areca palm, and some parched rice powdered—

these he lays down and covers over with a young palm leaf. Bringing the sick person forward, the priest draws a circle with an iron pen or stylus round the patient, then sticks the stylus outside the circle. This is called 'putting in fetters' and by this the demon is supposed to be arrested. The demon sometimes causes the patient to cry out 'oh, I am in pain, he is beating me, and such like; but the patient does not know who it is that is afflicting him. Sometimes the priest will make the demon speak. The sick man makes a vow, which is to be fulfilled in due course promising sheep, rice, flowers, palm leaf, and arrack. All such vows are paid at their annual festivals in February or March.

"Or, on visiting the sick house, a rice fan or sieve containing three betel leaves with areca nuts, three *nari* of paddy, Ocimum flowers, sacred ashes, and the couch and cowry shells, is laid in the yard; sitting before this fan and facing the sun, the officiator begins to worship the demons. While doing so, he holds the shells in his hand, and turns to the four points. After noticing some omen, he takes the Kokkara and sounds it, chanting the names of terrible demons, such as Mallan, Karunkali, Kottu-tamburan, Ayiravilli, the five virgins; and repeating incantations. This is varied with dancing also.

"The performer plays on an iron instrument, sometimes from evening till noon of the next day; and it is no wonder that the nerves of the tortured patient are unstrung by a whole night's incessant grating of this harsh file. The sick person is often terrified into confession of some sin (possibly, in the case of hysteric females, a purely imaginary one), when a fine of three fanams is imposed, and at once spent for toddy which is drunk by the assembled party.

"If death unexpectedly occurs, he consoles the bereaved, and warns them that their offerings to the spirits have been insufficient.

"Sometimes affliction is supposed to be brought n by the enmity of others who have got incantations written on palm leaf or potsherds, and buried in the earth near the house or by the side of the well. Another sorcerer will be called to find out and counteract such evil charms, for which he digs, destroying them when found. Of course this pretence affords great opportunity for imposition".[1]

"For devil dancing there is a special dress and ornaments. Any one may become a priest by practice, but the profession is often, as might be expected, hereditary. The head-dress is a helmet of basket work with red cords hanging down from either side. A cotton scarf is worn round the waist and bells tied on the legs. In one hand an old sword is held, in the other a bell. At first the dancer goes round slowly, then quickly quickens his motion. He stamps heavily on the ground with the feet alternately, trembling and greatly agitated.

"On one occasion in March, I had the opportunity of witnessing a little of their dancing at Trivandrum during the prevalence of small-pox, when similar scenes were enacted generally through the country. They had been engaged in this festival all night and the noise of their drumming and cheering was still heard in the early morning. The scrub and weeds had been cleared off a raised bank by the side of the rice-fields and a kind of temporary altar, as above described, made on the stem of a tree cut off at the height of ten or twelve feet. On this was a small platform with a rude ladder leading up to it, and offerings laid upon it. At the base of this frail structure stood two or three painted boards, one of them the figure of a Cobra's hood very clearly represented. At one side was a shed for the accommodation of the people and at the other side a miniature house, about two feet high, which was supposed to be the residence of the demon, and in which offerings of cocoanuts and other things were

1. Pages 49, 50, 51.

placed. Women were beating rice for the feast; others selling provisions; altogether about a hundred people were then present.

"Some of the principal officiators were adorned with fringes of young palm leaves tied round the waist and with the usual brass bells around the ankles and calves of the legs. Several had plaited bundles of palm leaves to represent horses, on which they pretended to gallop round the altar, whipping the horses and shouting. A fire was alight and they galloped through and over this until it was extinguished. On such occasions dancing and singing are sometimes carried on for several days with great enjoyment and enthusiasm.

"In the North a curious 'club dance' is practised at night by the light of a large fire. The dancers, men with clubs a foot long, one in each hand go in concentric circles in different directions, and meeting each other very prettily strike each other's clubs, keeping time to the songs they sing—now bending to catch the blow made towards the feet and then rising to ward off or meet one directed towards the head"[1].

Ceremonies. Degraded as their general condition is, the Pulayas are as a class ceremonious in their habits—every important event in a Pulaya's life being attended with some sort of ceremony. When a child is ushered into the world, the mother observes ceremonial pollution for at least 6 or 7 days, during which she lives separate in a hut put up for the occasion and burnt after her leaving it. There she is attended by her mother-in-law or some female friend, no male being permitted to go in. When recovered, she rubs her body with turmeric and oil, and washes herself before re-entering her house. The husband also has to take a sea or river bath to wash off pollution. The child as soon as it is born is given a little cocoanut water and bathed in hot water. In the sixth month solid food is

1. p. 55.

given when friends and relatives are invited and regaled with toddy. At this ceremony the child receives its name, usually the name of the grandfather or father, or grand-mother or mother or other relative. The names in common use are: For males—Aiyan (Father or lord), Chāṭṭan (Śāsṭāvu), Veluṭṭān (white one), Cheṭayan (hairy), etc. For females, Kāli, Chāṭṭa, Aiyi, Veluṭṭa, Chakki, etc. The child's hair is cut as soon as it begins to walk, and the ears of the girls are also bored, these two being attended with some ceremony. When a girl attains puberty, she is removed to a separate hut put up for the occasion, and is confined there for seven days, even her mother being prohibited from entering it. After seven days, she is bathed, attired in new clothes, and brought back into the house, where friends and relatives meet her and are treated with betel-nut, toddy and arrack. If it happens to be harvest time when rice is plentiful, rice flour is put on the forehead, arms and cheeks of the girl.

There is a curious ceremony among them, specially amongst the Kaṇṇa Pulayas of Travancore. It is called the ceremonial entering into friendship. The following account of it is taken from a paper on the Pulayas of Travancore, published in the *Madras Review*.[1]

"The most important ceremony after a child is born is the ceremonial entrance into friendship, the binding of the tie which unites man with man until death. It gave me pleasure to find that the ceremonial friendship, instances of which are to be met with among many races, exists among these degraded people even now. The Christian master never dreams that among his serfs is a custom which sheds a world of light on the verse in his *Bible* which says that there is a friend which sticketh closer than a brother. Here is some small shred of evidence for the primitive identity of the human race, and here is morality, yet entirely distinct from the family. There is real

1. Vol, 2, p. 250.

affection in the relation and the tie is dissolvable only with death.

"A Pulaya can have only a single friend and he should be a member of a different Illam, as all illamites are held to be relatives. A man loses his title, if he marries into the family of his friend.

"A Pulaya boy, when he is between ten and fifteen years of age, contracts a voluntary friendship with some other boy of the same age and locality, and when the friendship has ripened, the parents are informed of it. If the boy is not socially inclined, his father selects a friend for him from a family of his own standing or, if practicable, of a higher standing. The father may of course overrule the will of the boy. The two parents agree among themselves to meet in the house of either of them for the purpose of solemnizing the friendship. On the fixed day, the Vallon and some other officials and thirty-two men of the Kara, go with the parent-guest to the house of the parent-host. The latter takes them first to the toddy shop and then back to his house. The parents walk with their arms over each other's shoulder. The guests are feasted in the regular Pulaya fashion. Both for the dinner and the preliminary refreshments, the parents have to eat from the same dish. After the feast is over, the host asks 'I ask of my lords (*i. e.*, Vallon, etc.) and others assembled whether I may be permitted to buy friendship by paying money.' When he says, 'yes', he gives 120 chs.[1] to the other parent and declares that he has got a friend for his son. The two boys then clasp hands, and they are henceforth never to quarrel. The parent guest has some other day to become host and go through identically the same forms.

"The friend is now regarded as a member of the family. In theory all that the two friends possess are to be enjoyed in common. The friend comes in and goes out as he pleases. There is no important thing

1. Chakram—a small Travancore silver coin worth 7 pies.

done without consulting him. He is an important factor in all ceremonies especially in marriage. I suspect also, that the friend has some claim over a man's wife. In theory the two friends have but one life. The place he fills in marriage will be described later on. The Vallon gets a consideration for his presence."

We find an analogue of this custom of entering into friendship existing in Nepal, and it is curious that practices bearing such close resemblance should exist in countries lying so far apart as Nepal and Travancore, the one in the extreme north and the other in the extreme south of India. It is still more curious that similar practices should obtain amongst the aboriginal races of South India and those that inhabit the Himalayan ranges. Here we may remember the striking similarity between the terms 'Newars' and 'Nairs' and the no less striking similarity in the relations between the sexes amongst the 'Newars' of Nepal and the Nāyars of Malabar. Mr. Shramana Ekai Kawaguchi, the Japanese explorer, in his *Three Years in Tibet* says:—

"I may here observe that in Nepal, as I found out afterwards, the word friend conveys a much deeper meaning, is probably, than in any other country. To be a friend there means practically the same thing as being a brother, and the natives have a curious custom of observing a special ceremony when any two of them tie the knot of friendship between them. The ceremony resembles very much that of marriage, and its celebration is made an occasion for a great festival, in which the relatives and connexions of the parties concerned take part. To be brief, the ceremony generally takes the form of exchanging glasses of the native drink between the mutually chosen two, and they each have to extend their liberalities even to their servants in honor of the occasion. It is only after the observance of these formalities which signify a great deal to the natives that any two Nepalese may each call themselves the friend of the other." [1]. Verily, an illustration of the well-known saying, "Too far east is west"—in the present instance, "Too far north is south."

Marriage. The Pulayas like other Malayāli castes have both forms of marriage the Ṭālikeṭṭu and the nuptials. With some the Ṭāli ceremony must be performed before attaining puberty, otherwise they loose caste. But with others it is not so. Those that thus loose caste among the Kaṉṉa Pulayas in the south become the property of the Valluvan who may sell them and receive the price or banish them beyond Cochin. Before marriage, the astrologer is consulted, and he prescribes the day. Marriage is always preceded by frequent interchange of visits between the bridegroom's and the bride's relatives. When the boy's father first visits the girl's father to make the proposal, the matter is put off for some other day unless the visit had been previously arranged. On some other auspicious day, the betrothal is made when the bride's father is paid some little money and, in return, he sends the bridegroom's father a pot of toddy and a few measures of rice, acceptance of which confirms the betrothal. On the wedding day, some more money has to be paid, which is divided between the bride's relatives. The relatives and friends of both parties assemble in the marriage pandal (shed) put up at the bride's house. The bridegroom's party proceeds in procession to the house of the bride on the morning of the wedding day accompanied by music and the beating of drums. Before he enters the pandal, the bride has to go seven times around it, seven bride's maids going with the lighted lamps in front of her. After several preliminary ceremonies, the ṭāli is tied round the neck of the bride, amongst some by the husband himself, amongst others by his sister. There is a curious custom which prevents the mother of the bride from approaching the bridegroom any time on the wedding day or after on

1. Pages 29—30.

pain of entailing ceremonial pollution. Of course, there is the inevitable feasting at which a large quantity of toddy and arrack is quaffed. Dancing is kept up to the strain of music all the night. In the early morning, the couple worship the sun-god, and leave for the bridegroom's house, invoking the blessing of that deity. But, before leaving, a curious ceremony is observed. A conch-shell is put in a sieve and spun round to discover whether the union will turn out a happy one or not. The wise men of the caste give the interpretation according as the shell points to the various points of the compass. If it points to the east, it is very lucky, if to the north, lucky; the west is not considered specially preferrable but passable. If it falls to the south, the marriage is pronounced to be the most unpropitious.

There are certain interesting marriage observances prevalent among the Pulayas worth noticing, but it is difficult to know if they are observed by all of them. Even two Pulayas from the same place give inconsistent accounts.

(1) The first ceremony before marriage is what is called *seeing the woman*. (*cf*. the observance known as Mukha Darśanam—'seeing the face'—of the Nambūṭiri Brahmans.) This ought theoretically to be four years before marriage. The husband-elect, his 'friend', father and maternal uncle go to the girl's house to see her for themselves and be satisfied. Then for four years annually, at the Oṇam festival, the male party have to keep up their claim on the girl by giving presents of 4 parahs of rice and 40 cocoanuts to her guardians. The boy and his 'friend' take the present to the girl's hut and are feasted and sent back with a few *necessaries*, *viz*., 2 Puṭṭils, a big mat-like basket used both as mattress and blanket, also for putting things in, or as a head-cover; and 2 Vaṭṭis or smaller baskets made of grass.

(2) The next observance is what is known as the *Kuri Manjada* or marriage arrangement. The boy,

his 'friend', father and guardian go to the girl's house and make arrangements about fixing the day and hour of marriage. Here too presents have to be given. This ceremony is also known by other names which are curious and significant: *Mekkanam Iduka* which probably means taking possession of the person by giving a due rent, (the same word is used for buying lands of jenmies—landlords); *Parakallu Erika* (throw stones), probably a 'decayed metaphor', a relic of some old world symbolic action whereby it was made visible that possession was taken; *Mundu Veyka* (put or give clothes) corresponding to the Nāyar custom.

(3) Another observance consists in the boy and his 'friend' giving a rupee and odd to the girl four weeks before marriage, for defraying the expenses of her oil-bath, for the weeks that intervene between the betrothal and the marriage.

(4) Then follows the important custom of fixing on the auspicious hour of marriage, known as Muhūrṭṭam by one astrologer. The 'friend' takes no part in this ceremony. It is the Kaṇiyān or Hindu Astrologer who officiates. He goes through his usual calculations and appoints an hour. By comparing the stars under which the parties are born, he sees whether there is affinity between their nativities. If there is not, some brother of the bridegroom-elect will be found to possess the affinity, and he marries the girl and gives her to the real husband and the relatives are cheated! The astrologer also prescribes how the gods and spirits of ancestors are to be propitiated. He likewise fixes the time for erecting the marriage pandal—when a pillar has to be fixed (*cf.* the *Pozhuloon Iduka* of the Nāyars), and the time for boiling paddy (*cf.* the *Pozhu nel Puzhunguka* of the Nāyars).

(5) On the evening previous to the marriage, the bridegroom's 'friend' and his guardian and about 12 men of the village are invited to *the boy's house*. There some interesting ceremonies are gone through, which befit the boy and 'friend' to enter on the married

estate. In the first place, the two guardians take some water in two brass vessels, put 51 pieces of plantain leaves therein, and taking out one piece at a time, rub each his own boy's body with it from head to sole. The boys stand facing each other. This is known as *Kudumbi Polutu Tirka* and probably symbolises the washing away of the young people's crudeness and foibles of youth, before admitting them to the dignity of manhood. The next ceremony is called *Mayyi Kura Tirka*, which probably means wiping off the deficiencies of the body. The guardians take fire and the husks of rice in the outer shell of a cocoanut, and when it begins to smoke, turns it *seven* times simultaneously round the waist of the boys and then themselves go round them once. This certainly symbolises the purification of the body, perhaps of the loins.

It is very interesting that we have in these customs a symbolic illustration of the *purification by fire and water*, so often referred to in the *Bible*. Fire and water are regarded as emblems of purification among many peoples.

(6) After the ceremony of purification is over, the boys are dressed with a clean white cloth, a black handkerchief is tied round the waist, and a knife, the emblem of manhood, stuck in. The forehead and breast are painted with wetted flour, just as the higher classes do with an odoriferous mixture of sandal paste, rose-water, etc. The guardians then whisper in the ears of the boys *seven* times the word *Kshama*, which means 'forbearance' and 'forgiveness', which is certainly one of the chief qualities which ought to distinguish a man from a boy. This ceremony is called *ear-incantation* (Cheviyil manṭṟam), possibly intended originally to impress on the aspirant for manhood the necessity of possessing the quality aforesaid.

(7) After the ceremonies at the boy's house, the male party proceed to the house of the bride. The boy and his 'friend' are dressed with two cloths tied round

the waist, one over the other with a knife and style stuck in. The bride goes round the marriage pandal *seven* times with *seven* married women holding lamps going in front of her. She is then seated in the pandal with 3 measures of rice, a cocoanut and a lamp placed in a brass plate in front of her. The bridegroom also on arrival goes round the pandal *seven* times and sits outside. A functionary called the *Kudummi Chumki* breaks the cocoanut open and sprinkles the contents with some fresh water added, on the head of the bride-groom and the bride three times.

(8) Next they go to bath in some neighbouring pool or stream, first the man, and next the bride; when they have gone out, the bride's mother spreads a mat specially made by her for the occasion in the middle of the pandal. On it she places 3 measures of rice and some minute particles of gold; over it is put, according to the importance of the Illam, a big brass plate a plank covered with white and black cloth, a simple plank, or lastly a plantain leaf. The bridegroom now returns from the bath and, after making *seven* rounds, enters and stands on the plank. The bride soon follows and makes *three* rounds, when four women hold a canopy of cloth over her head and *seven* virgins go in front of her. The foremost virgin holds a lamp in one hand and a plate of rice and leaves in the other. Her circuit over, the bride enters in and stands beside her man. Four persons raise them up, with the plank, in their hands and set them down. The man faces to the east and the woman to the west. According to another account, the 'friend' is also raised, and he stands *behind* the bride facing west. The girl's guardian puts the 'wedding neck-lace'—a gold bead on a string—on the head of his ward, and then hands it over to the boy.

Now the drummers begin to drum and the *Komarattan* and others sing the song for blessing the neck-lace. When they sing "O Sun-God, who rises in the east, bless this neck-lace and this string", the bride-groom holds the string with his two hands and raises it a little and when, in the same words, they ask a blessing of the Moon-God who sets in the west, the Earth Goddess who is below, and the God of Thunder who is above, he turns the neck-lace to the west, lowers it, and holds it high above the head. Next he makes a circle with it and then straightens it again, when different virtues from above are supposed to descend on it. Repeating the ceremonial words of rejection and so rejecting, one by one, the neck-laces or virtues of death, quarrel, blackness, stagnancy and blood, he jumps and catches hold of the neck-lace when the *diamond virtue* descends on it, and immediately transfers it to the neck of his bride. That is, he puts the string on her neck, and makes one woof of it. Then, he leisurely goes behind and hardens the knot, or the 'friend', who is standing behind, does it for him. This closes the religious part of the ceremony. The husband is raised up in the arms of his brother-in-law or 'friend', and the wife in the arms of her guardian and taken inside the house. Can the Aryan Naṃbūṭiri Brahman steeped in his rituals and ceremonies be more ceremonial than these uncouth aboriginal Pulayas?

When the marriage ceremony is going on or just after it, four sisters of the bride-groom come to the door with music and songs. They are received with presents by their husbands and taken inside the house. They eat rice all together out of the very pot in which it was boiled. When the husband and wife have come back to the pandal, the wife's sister and husband spread *seven* measures and a half of boiled rice and curry on leaves before them. The 'friend' gives *seven* big mouthfuls out of it, first to the wife and then to the man. What remains is eaten by *seven* bachelors who are styled the young men who came to see the marriage (probably), in the place of the unmarried. They sit on one leg, stretch out the other, and shout aloud, *Ittchoyiye*, when eating.

Next the guests are fed and the last item is the subscription. The relatives of the bride and the men of the village put their subscriptions into a plate or piece of cloth placed before the husband. The amount is distributed among those who took part in the ceremonies.

These observances are more prevalent among the Pulayas of Travancore than elsewhere. Also we may note the prominent part taken by the 'friend' throughout.[1]

Tandu Marriage. Among the Ṭaṇḍa Pulayas, there is a special ceremony called the Ṭaṇḍu marriage, performed for every girl during her 7th or 8th year. It consists in dressing the girl on an auspicious day, generally at midday, with the leafy garment made of the Ṭaṇḍu plant. This ceremony too is attended with feasting rice, curry, toddy and fish being largely used. Until the Ṭaṇḍu marriage is over, the girl is not permitted to wear this garment.

Polygamy, Polyandry and Divorce. Polygamy is not only not interdicted but is practised; often a single Pulaya has 4 or 5 wives. But polyandry, even of the fraternal type, does not exist among them, though a brother is not prohibited from marrying his deceased brother's widow. Divorce is easy enough, each party being allowed to separate as he or she wants. If the bride desires the divorce, the bride's money has to be returned. If the bride-groom, he has only to take the girl back to her parents and leave her there. Adultery is severely punished by the castemen, and it is believed that the spirits of the dead virgins will wreck severe vengeance on the sinning woman.

Ceremonies after marriage. The *Vayattu Ponkala*, an imitation of the Hindu *Pumsavanam* and the Nāyar Pulikuṭi, is observed in the 7th month after pregnancy, when an oblation of rice is offered to the rising sun, and the assembled Pulayas feasted. The exorcisor performs various incantations for the safe delivery of the child. A few drops of tamarind juice are also poured into the mouth of the pregnant woman.

1. See Vol. 2, *The Madras Review*, p. 256 *et seq.*

Inheritance. The class is so poor that there will be nothing to inherit. Still there are among them those who follow the Makkaṭṭāyam and Marumakkaṭṭāyam system of inheritance.

Death and succeeding ceremonies. The dying man is given by his relatives some rice water or *Kanjee* "because the soul is leaving". The body is washed, cocoanut oil and turmeric are rubbed over the corpse and it is covered with an unbleached cloth. Vāykkari or a pinch of rice along with a small coin is also put into the mouth. The body is buried in some retired place. The grave is levelled and smeared with cowdung. After the corpse is laid down, a short prayer is made to *Utaya Tampuran*. Pollution lasts for 7 days. On the seventh day, the priest brings a handful of earth from the grave with which he moulds a rude image of the dead man. Turmeric, rice-flour, etc., are put on it and the spirit of the deceased is invoked to enter it. The spirit is supposed to pass from the image to the priest and from him to a cloth which a man standing by holds like a sheet. The priest and the man then go and bathe, dipping the cloth in water and folding it returns to the house. The cloth is then placed on a plaited palm leaf and offerings of rice, paddy, toddy and arrack, betel-leaf and areca-nut are placed round it. The conch is spun to ascertain if the spirit had accepted the offering and if the spira of the conch points to the spirit in the cloth, the offering is taken as accepted. The cloth is afterwards taken to the yard and is sprinkled with water and oil mixed with turmeric. Some food is then presented to the spirit and the priest repeats manṭrams with a view to retain the spirit in the house. It is supposed to have left the cloth which is taken to the yard and opened. After this no further Śrāḍha or funeral ceremony is performed.

Family etiquette. The Pulayas show great respect to their elders and strictly enforce rules with regard to their conduct at home. In the presence of an elder brother a younger brother cannot sit down. Before a father, grown-up daughters cannot sit. Sons sit on a somewhat lower level. Nephews and nieces should not sit on the same level with the maternal uncle. No one sits on the same level with the head Pulayan or the chief, appointed by the ruling power, of whom there is one in every village.

Caste government. The internal economy of the community is regulated by the Vallōns who preside over caste assemblies. We have already observed that formerly there were, it is alleged, kings among them, though the Rev: Mr. Mateer thinks, that it is impossible that such a degraded race could have ever exercised territorial sovereignty, or even independent authority in the community itself. The Pulayas of Cochin and Travancore have their respective chiefs—those of Travancore as already observed acknowledge Aykkara yajamānan, while those in Cochin have a chief called Ālanchēri Kuṛupa. Aykkara yajamānan is also known as Aykkara Tamar; yajamānan means lord, and is the title which people generally use in addressing those who hold authority over them. And Tamar, Dr. Gundhert says, "means one's own people, an owner" clearly indicating the relationship between the lord and his following. He lives in Ṭykāṭṭuśśēri in Travancore and claims to be descended from men who had been once rulers of the land. He held authority over the strip of country lying between the sea and the backwater, to the north of Alleppey and south of Arūkuṟṟi, where he had some private property. He used to derive a very trifling revenue of a sixtieth part of income (perhaps in analogy to the *Shadbhagam* due to kings according to the śāsṭras); according to other accounts a Karavāram of 3 pies from each Pulaya (a poll tax). There are other perquisites due to him on ceremonial occasions such as marriages, etc. These and other revenues he used to exact even within living memory. The present representative of Aykkara yajamānan has private lands of his own, and such of the headmen who live within his jurisdiction still pay him a portion of their income. It is significant that while all Malabar Rajas trace their authority to the gift made by Chēramān Perumāl, the Pulaya kings curiously say that they were independent of the Perumāl and only acknowledged him as their suzerain, receiving a lace cap said to be still preserved by their representatives. They preserve to the present day some of the insignia of royalty such as a gold-handled sword, a lace cap (in addition to the one presented by Perumāl), a silver plated rod of office, a shield of leopard's skin, lance, bows and arrows. The king lives in a big house and not in a hut like other Pulayas. A Pulaya fishing basket, placed in front of the gate, keeps off the unwary wayfarer from mistaking the house for a casteman's, for the house being a substantially built one is apt to be mistaken for a casteman's house, as no Pulaya is allowed by the higher castes to live except in a low hut. The king's family is still held in honour, all Pulayas and Paṙayas do obeisance before the king, speaking in his presence only with the mouth covered as a sign of respect. He still wields the power of excommunication and absolution. He has a minister called *Ponnillattu Vallon* who lives close by, and whose badges of office are a gold knife and style, a short umbrella and a rod of office, all presented by the king. Under the king are two chiefs, one for the north called *Tatteri Acchen* (father or master of Ṭaṭṭēri).and one for the south called *Mannath Koil Vallon* (King Vallōn of Maṅṅaṭṭ). Under them are, or were, Head Vallōns who held authority over small pieces of territory. Subordinate to these were Vallōns or headman of each *Kara* or village, who at present do really exercise authority. The office was hereditary and, when such appointments came to be made by the local Rajas, the choice fell ordinarily on the heir of the previous Vallōn.

At present, the Kara is the social unit of the Pulayas and the Vallōn of each Kara is practically independent. The office-bearers of a Kara are called

Sthanikal or those who hold delegated authority. According to some there are eight such officers and according to others ten. The more important are the *Vallon*, the *Kuruppa*, two *Kaikkarans*, the *Vatikkaran*, the *Komarattan* and the *santi*. There are besides, the *Edapakal*, the *Nattil Sthani* and the *Desavazhi*.

The Vallōn was the *Valia avan* or the 'great man', originally appointed by the Pulaya King, but who now derives his authority from the local Raja who grants him certain privileges. Originally, he had, by virtue of his office the following five privileges conferred on him:—(1) The long umbrella, a circular and slightly concave umbrella, made of palm leaves and raised on a very long bamboo handle. The length of the handle bears a direct ratio to the dignity of the bearer. (2) The dignity of holding the umbrella with five colours. (3) The bracelet of honour. (4) The box for keeping betel leaves, etc. (5) A long ear-ring made of gold. No other Pulaya may use any of these things. His functions are thus described:—

He, as President of the Council of Elders, is the supreme judge and law-giver or, to speak more accurately, the depositary and declarer of custom. His verdict is binding in charges of adultery, wife stealing, etc. His presence and sanction is required for marriage, burial, the entering into friendship and, in fine, all social acts. He has customary fees. He is responsible for the discipline and good behaviour of his people, and is the judicial and social head of the society which he rules. The Pulayan calls him lord, and has to do him obeisance.

(2) Next in dignity comes the Kuruppu supposed to be a corruption of Kurippan (one who makes notes or writes) or accountant. It may be remembered that one of the slave classes goes by the name of Kaṇakkan which means literally accountant. The Kuruppu assists the Vallōn in the exercise of authority. In the trial of offences, he takes the chief part in sifting evidence. He

declares on the facts of the case. The Vallōn who sits by in solemn silence then gives the judgment.

(3) Kaikkārans *or Wardens.* To each Kara two such are elected at a popular assembly. Often the office is hereditary. They are representatives of the people keeping the other officers in discipline and assisting the Kuṛuppu in investigating the facts of the case in trials.

(4) The Vaṭikkāran (the rod-holder). He is the constable who brings parties to a suit, keeps order and executes sentences.

(5) The Kōmaraṭṭān or Devil Exorcisor is a most important functionary who is in evidence at all important ceremonies, from before birth to after burial. These six constitute the Council.

(6) The other Sṭhānikals or dignitaries are (1) the Śānṭi or priest who attends to the temple and feeds the gods; (2) the Nāṭṭilsṭhāni who is chosen from among the people and whose permission (for which he has to be paid) is necessary for a Pulayan of another Kara to marry into the Kara; (3) the Ḍēśavāli, who settles some disputes; and (4) the Eṭapakal, who is supposed to know the ins and outs of the people and who helps the Council.

Of course in these days of centralised government, with duly constituted officers to administer justice in its various forms, an organisation like the above can exercise but little authority. But it is tolerably certain that formerly it had exercised much larger authority than at present. In the Cochin State, the Rajas still appoint Vallōns and Kuṛup.

15. **The Parayas.** The Paṛayas of Malabar belong to the slave class. They are the out-castes of society, so much so that the term Paṛaya has come to mean an out-caste. The word is supposed to be derived from a Sanskrit root meaning, 'abandoned'. Some derive it from Paṛa, a 'drum', and the caste is said to delight in drum-beating and are generally called on

to beat the drum at the funeral procession of the Tamil Śūḍṙas in the Tamil districts. The Malayāḷi section being emigrants from the Eastern Coast retain their Tamil caste name. In Malabar, however, they are not drummers. Though belonging to the same class as the Tamil Paṙayas, the customs of the Malayāḷi and the Tamil sections are by no means the same.

Origin of the caste. There can be no doubt that the Paṙayas along with the Pulayas and other lower classes are descendants of indigenous or original inhabitants of South India. The Hill tribes, we shall have to mention later on, have also been resident in South India ever since the world's history. Of course, Brahman tradition, as usual, gives the class a start in keeping with their own supremacy. The Brahmans say that the Paṙayas had their origin in the connection of a Brahman woman with a low caste man. There is nothing unlikely in this. But when they proceed to add that the degradation of the class was due not simply to this but also to the curse pronounced by the irate Viśwāmiṭṙa against his own flesh and blood, and against those who happened to cross his will, we begin to suspect the truth of the story. According to another legend, it was not Viśwāmiṭṙa who cursed his progeny but Vasishṭa, the son of Uṙvaśi, (a heavenly nymph) and husband of Arunḍhaṭi, born as a Chaṇḍāla woman of the Chakkali (shoe-maker) caste. He had by her 100 sons, 96 of whom disobeyed their father and were on that account degraded to the Panchama (fifth) caste while the four others remained Brahmans.

Sub-divisions. Our author refers to two sub-divisions of the caste; (1) the *Canni* Paṙayas and (2) the *Asse* Paṙayas which divisions seem not to be extant at present. According to Buchanan, there are three kinds of Paṙayas, *viz.*, (1) The 'Paṙayan' properly so called, the Perum Paṙayan and the Mutrava Paṙayan. The Ethnographical survey of the Cochin State says, that they are divided into 18 sub-castes like the Vellālas.

The highest of them is the Valluva Parayan. Valluvan is also the highest sub-caste among the Pulayas of the State. A large number of Parayas seem originally to have migrated to the hills, while some returned and settled down on the plains. Thus there are two classes, *viz.*, the Hill Parayas and (2) Parayas of the plains with different modes of living.

Varthema does not mention the Parayas by name, but he notices a sixth class coming immediately after the Pulaya which he calls 'Hirava', "and these he says plant and gather in rice". Evidently he refers to the Parayas, agriculture being still part of their occupation. Barbosa speaks of the 'Pareni', *i. e.*, 'Pareas' as living in "desert places." "Their very look" he adds, "is contamination. They live on fruits, roots, etc." The account given in Purchas is that "the Pareas are of worse esteem, and live in deserts without commerce of any, reputed worse than the Devil".

General appearance. Physically, the Parayas are stronger than the Pulayas, probably because of their diet. They are inveterate flesh eaters, not disdaining even the dead bodies of cows, etc., that lie about rotting. In fact they claim such dead bodies as belonging to them by right. Their bodies are better developed. They are either dark coloured or brown often verging on black. They have black hair rarely treated with oil. Their nose is mostly large, round and black. They seldom have a wash and are dirty in their dress. Those about Trivandrum are said to be of strong physique and bold. The females there are rather fair and licentious. They rub turmeric on their bodies and faces and wear numerous heavy ornaments.

Clothing and Ornaments. The males wear small *mundus* or pieces of cloth round the loins scarcely reaching down to the knees. Broader pieces of cloth, or even a second one on their shoulders are not used, because of fear or respect for higher castes. The hill Parayas used to wear the barks of trees for their

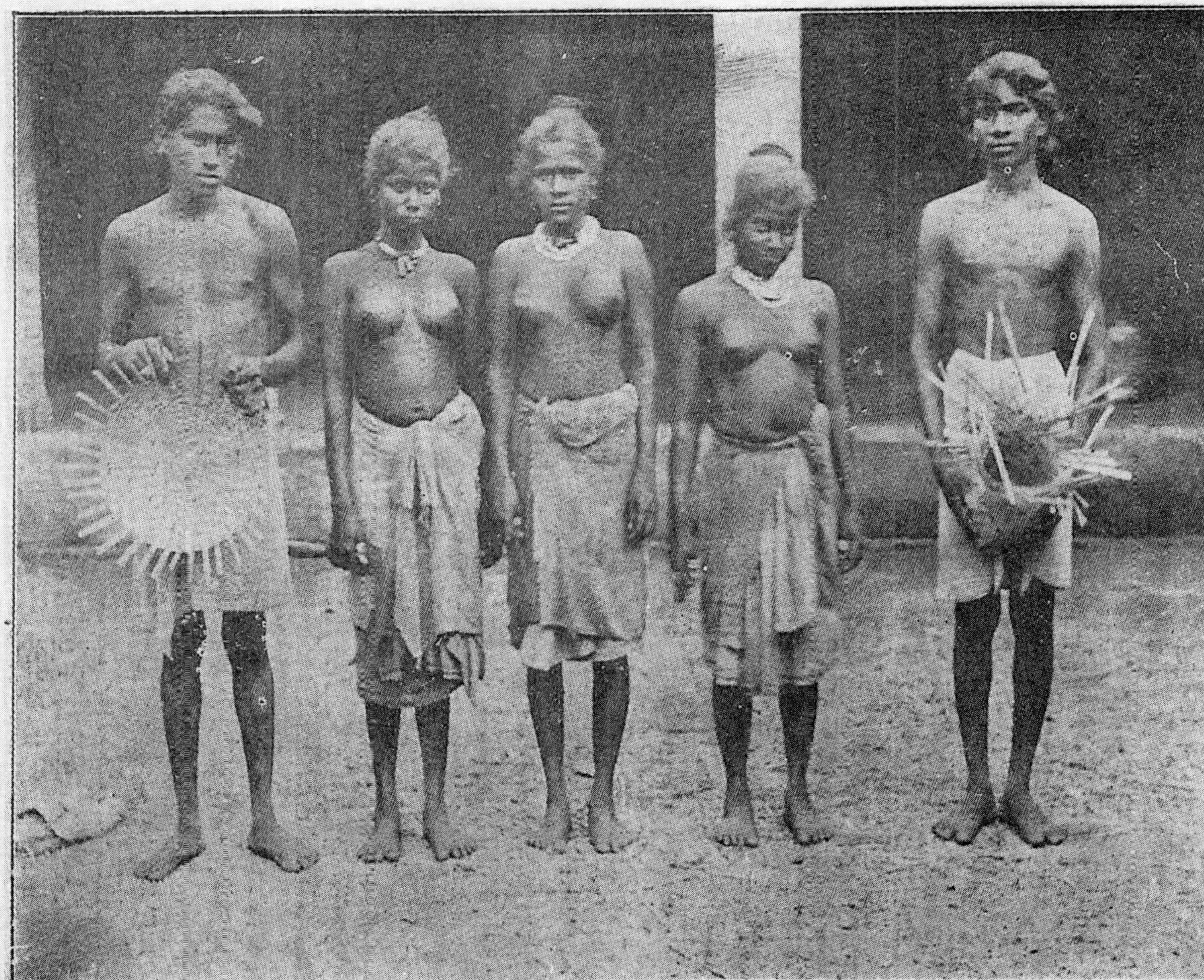

PARAYANS AT WICKER WORK

(To face p. 515

garments but now use cotton cloths. Their ears are bored and sometimes the holes are large enough to admit of four or five ear-rings in each ear. They adorn their fingers with brass rings. Some allow the hair on the head to grow and some crop it and do not shave their face. The women dress somewhat similarly to the men. They fold round their waist a tougher and thicker piece of cloth slightly longer than those of the men, but never going beyond the knees. The rest of the body is bare. The hair is tied in a knot on the top of the head slightly inclined to the back. A wooden disc for the ear which is made wide enough to insert a large heavy thing, neck-laces of glass beads for the neck, brass bangles for the arm, and brass rings for the fingers are their favourite ornaments.

Habitation. Their habitations are of the simplest kind. They are mere huts propped upon sticks. In the south they live in hamlets. They sleep on the bare floor or on plaited cocoanut leaves or old mats. Dress, food and dwelling are all alike uncleanly.

Food and drink. The food of the Parayas like that of the Pulayas is rice when they can afford to get it. The hill men live upon wild roots almost wholly. The flesh of cattle left dead by the road-side is their perquisite. The death of a cow or bullock is with them the season of jubilee, never stopping to enquire into its cause. They are known even to eat the raw carrion. They may indulge in spirituous liquors and freely imbibe arrack and toddy.

Occupation. The Parayas originally formed a very considerable number of the slaves and were employed chiefly in field labour. But though they still engage themselves in all sorts of agricultural work, they have now adopted other occupations. They are ingenious in wicker work. The women make baskets and bamboo mats and the men supply them with bamboos. The process is as follows:—The tools of the basket maker are of the simplest character, those necessary for the harvesting of the material and those used in the manufacture. Fine splints of bamboo are made by the males and the women weave them. In making baskets, the woman starts from the centre of the bottom, coiling and warping the splints as she proceeds with the split pieces, so as to bind it to the preceding turn, drawing her splints between the spirals. When the splint is exhausted, the end is tucked in behind the spiral and another one started in the same manner but so carefully joined as to escape detection. These baskets and mats are used largely in the country, and merchants engage the services of the Parayas in manufacturing them by making advances and derive large profits by their sale. The Parayas themselves are but mere day labourers, receiving from one and a half to two annas in coin or its worth in paddy a day as wages. They also employ themselves, at least a few of them, as trackers and beaters. They pretend to be great necromancers and are said to be notorious masters of the black art. They are often employed in casting out devils and counteracting enchantments. They along with the Malayers, enjoy the reputation of being the sole custodians of the Oṭi cult of which more later on. The Revd. Mr. Mateer tells us that a Christian convert of Paraya caste, who had been a devil dancer, being asked concerning of his former practices, replied that they were tricks to obtain money.

Their general condition and status among Hindus. The Parayas of the south, who resemble their brethren of the Tamil district, stood socially higher than those of the north. In north Travancore, Cochin and British Malabar, their condition was at the lowest. The farther you went into the Malayālam country, their degradation had been more and more pronounced. The southern Parayas profess to have been once free and powerful, and this was not unlikely. For, we know that the Tamil Parayas had produced poets, philosophers, and saints who were reckoned eminent by the Hindus. Ṭiruvalluvar Naynār, the author of *Kural* and his so-called sister the famous poetess *Avvai*, the *Vaishnava Alwar*, were the most famous of them. The great Sivite saint Nanda is well-known to all. Malabar also claim to have produced the Paraya Pākkanār. To this day Pākkanār's residence is pointed out at Tṛttāla, (6 miles west of the Pattambi Railway Station) where his image is worshipped by the members of the family. Pākkanār's brother known as Nārāṇattu Bhrānṭan was also considered a profound philosopher and a saintly devotee. The origin of the temple at Elankunnappula in the Cochin State traced to a Paraya finding an idol of remarkable effulgence. The incident is referred to in a State document presented by the Cochin Sirkar before the Arbitrator appointed to settle territorial and boundary disputes, then existing between the States of Cochin and Travancore. The descendant of the Paraya who discovered the idol is still known as Perum Parayan or the 'great Parayan' and enjoys peculiar privileges and receives valuable perquisites from the temple. His office in the temple constitution was so important that one of the great dignitaries of the pagoda had in the early part of the 16th century to forfeit his rights for killing a Perum Parayan. The incident is referred to in a statement presented by the Cochin Darbar to the British Resident.

The Elankunnappula temple chronicles (*Grandhavari*) say:—"At half past 9 on the night of the 18th of Vrischigam of the Puthuvayppu year 188 (704 M. E.*) Thekkenkoor killed Devaswam (*i.e.* belonging to God) Perum Parayan. That day the Sanketham (*i.e.* the pagoda guild or constitution) was dissolved. Know that when 12 months had passed (*i.e.* at the advent of the next Utsavam), Thekkenkoor had to forfeit his Koima Sthanam (office). For this and his other encroachments within the Sanketham (temple jurisdiction) it was decided by the arbitrators nominated by Perumpadapil Swaroopam (*i.e.* the Raja of Cochin), Porkala Mattathu Vasudevan, Pariyalil Narayanan Kumaran and the

1 A. D. 1529.

other. arbitrators who had assembled for the purpose, that a statue of the Paraiah must be made, that paddy fields and lands must be given for the expenses of the Paraiahs during their fasting, that an offering of a silver pot must be made and that the Perimpadippil Swaroopam, as the suzerain of Thekkenkoor, must, by way of penalty for the outrageous acts of the latter, present to the pagoda an elephant and its stick and Thotty (a kind of sharp headed stick to manage an elephant) and that the Sanketham (*i.e.* the temple guild) may then be renewed."

The Paṙayas are now a very inferior race reckoned so very vile that their proximity or contact would entail the most alarming contamination. According to Barbosa, "their very look is contamination." They have to stand away at a great distance from the higher castes. Some say 72 feet. Their taste for carrion, especially for that of the cow, the animal most venerated by the Hindus, has doubtless caused this prejudice. They are said to emit a fetid odour. Their filthy habits, food and dirty environments may be the cause of the strong stench they produce. They are treated as the lowest of low castes. They were not allowed to walk along the public roads, nor were they permitted to approach the vicinity of the houses belonging to the higher classes. The Cochin Sirkar Ethnographical Reporter, a Brahman gentleman, observes that even at the Police station where some years ago, he was questioning them and taking notes, they stood at such a long distance that he could not distinctly hear them. Evidently he did not venture to seek information at close quarters. No other caste will eat with them. They themselves eat at the hands of all castes except those of Ullāṭans, Nāyāṭis and Pulayas. But they freely take water from the well of Mahomedans, Christians and Pulayas. Pulayas consider themselves superior in social standing to the Paṙayas, and strictly orthodox men of the caste have to bathe five times and let blood flow in order to be purified from contamination caused by the touch of of a Paṙaya. If high caste men have to pass by a Paṙaya hut, situated far away in the hills, these innocent creatures, on the sight of the high caste wayfarer, desert their huts and run away into the jungles. Witchcraft, however, is a power in their possession which mitigate their sufferings a good deal. Their masters fear their spells and their intervention is often called in rural parts either to ward off the spells caused by the enemies or to take revenge on them. It is said that they sometimes waylay and carry away children of higher castes and bring them up as Paṙayas, and we have already referred to what is called Paṙapēṭi or 'the fear of Paṙayas' to which early travellers often allude.

Many Paṙayas have become converts to Christianity and some have become Mahomedans also. Under Christian instruction, they readily improve and leave off their thieving propensity and become good members of society. They strive to learn and are said to show great aptitude for singing. Such of them who have adopted the Christian religion have certainly improved their position.

Religion and Worship. The Paṙayas profess to follow a low form of Hinduism, but are in effect demon worshippers. The Tamil Paṙayas adore Vişhņu and Śiva, and their goddess Athaḷ is said to represent Pāṙvaṭi, the spouse of Śiva. They also worship Piṭāri who in her evil inclination is called Kāli. In the worship of Kāli, the Malayāli Paṙayas follow their Tamil brethren. The Tamil Paṙayas enjoy in the Tamil districts many privileges which are denied to Malayāli Paṙayas in Malabar. The Tamil Paṙayas as already observed have the privilege of pulling the ropes of the car at Kānchīpuram, Kumbhakōṇam, Śrīvalliputṭūr and other places, when the deity is taken round the town in procession during the festival. A Paṙaya still acts the part of a bridegroom to tie a ṭāli round the neck of a tutelary deity of the Black Town, Madras. In Mysore, a Holeya is a priest for every village goddess. They profess the right of entering temples for three days in the year. The origin of the great temple of Jagannath is closely associated with a low caste Paṛaya. In Malabar, the Paṛayas are out-castes of society. And yet the origin of the temple of Elankuṉṉappuḻa like that of Jagannath is closely connected with a Paṛaya who still enjoys rights and privileges in the pagoda. Though the Paṛayas have no temples of their own for the higher deities, they worship them and repeat the name of Śiva as also of Kāli in pious reverence. The present generation in keeping with its filthy habits and surroundings delight in worshipping Kāli in her low forms. Koṭungallūr Bhagavaṭi is their guardian deity in Malabar. They have a Velichappād, or person who pretends that he is possessed of the spirit of Kāli and who, dressed in quaint attire and with small tingling bells attached to his legs and carrying a curved sword in his hand, go about accompanied by drummers beating the drum before him, and collect paddy for their festivals. A shed is put up for the occasion of the festival where they gather and keep on dancing and singing to the accompaniment of the drum and the flute. Some put on the guise of ghosts and dance before the deity. All drink large quantities of toddy. This festival is called Vēla. On the first of every month, they perform a ceremony called Kalaśam for the spirit of the departed. They place on a long plantain leaf, fish, meat, toddy, rice, parched grain, plantain fruits, cocoanuts, etc., and, standing in front in the attitude of prayer, beseech the spirits of the departed to accept these offerings. They pray "Ye dead ancestors, come and take what we have procured for you with much difficulty, and protect us" They also worship minor deities or demons, such as Paṛakuṭṭi and Chāṭṭan. They have no regular temples but have small thatched sheds containing a few stones in it and erected in front of their huts which they call *Daivapura* or 'God's house'. There are no regular priests amongst them. He who can peform the Kalaśam ceremony acts as priest.

THE DEVIL - DANCE OF PARAYANS.

(To face p. 520.

According to Dr. Buchanan, the deity worshipped by the Parayas of British Malabar is named Māriṭi. The Parayas there consider that after death the spirits of the good become like God, while those of bad men become *Culis* or devils. There are small temples or rather huts in which a stone is placed to represent Māriṭi. Individuals at an annual festival present the idol with offerings of fruits and bloody sacrifices. There is a kind of priest belonging to this tribe. He is called *Velatum Parian*; but is of a different race. When any sickness happens, he is consulted, and informs the votary what spirit must be invoked, whether the protection of Māriṭi ought to be solicited, or the wrath of Kūli appeased. This he determines by looking on a heap of rice. He also possesses a jurisdiction over the Parayan in all matters of caste and punishes all transgressers by fine; but he never proceeds to such an extremity as to excommunicate. [1]

Marriage. Girls are married before and after puberty. The Parayas observe the ṭāli marriage as well as the real nuptial ceremony which is called Peṇkoṭa or the giving away of the girl, a term used by the Āryan Nambūṭiries to denote marriage. The ṭāli marriage is generally performed when the girl is about 10 or 12 years of age. The ṭāli is tied round the neck of the girl by the maternal nephew of the girl's father or some other close relative. The ceremony lasts for four days, when friends and relatives invited for the occasion are feasted. The ṭāli tier is afterwards dismissed with the present of a piece of cloth and a few annas. The real marriage is the Peṇkoṭa. The preliminaries resemble those of the Pulayas. On the day the marriage is settled, a Rupee and two cloths are given to the parents of the bride-elect. The bridegroom together with his relatives proceed to the bride's house on the day previous to the marriage, and are regaled with Kaññi and toddy. At the auspicious moment selected, a ṭāli is tied round the neck of the girl, after

1. Vol. 2, p. 152.

which she takes a bath to purify herself. The inevitable feast with copious libations of toddy follows. The pipe and the drum are ever present. The ceremony and the feasting last for a couple of days after which the husband and wife go to the husband's house where the bride's party is feasted. The marriage is generally celebrated on a Monday. Sunday is deemed an inauspicious day for the ceremony itself; cohabitation may begin on a Sunday, Tuesday or Friday. The parents arrange the marriage and the parties have no voice in the matter, with the result that early marriage has been a long standing practice amongst them. A man can marry more than one wife. At present they do not practice polyandry. It is censured and counted a crime.

A widow is allowed to remarry a year after the death of her husband, but not before. If she does not remarry, she remains in her husband's house and is there maintained. Though she cannot marry her brother-in-law, there is nothing to prevent a Paraya from marrying his deceased wife's sister.

Both husband and wife have the liberty to divorce each other. If the husband puts off his wife, he gets back his bride's money and the wedding dress supplied by him. If the wife desires to separate, the separation is effected through the intervention of her parents. In no case is the dowry returned by the husband, but the wife is entitled to half the bride's money.

Pregnancy and child birth. The first delivery generally takes place in the wife's parent's house. A special hut is put up in which the woman is confined after delivery for 15 days, during which period she is not allowed to touch anything lest she may pollute. She is fed from outside the hut. After the 15 days, some water and milk is obtained from a Brahman or Nāyar, and she is sprinkled with it and purified. The temporary hut is burned to ashes and after the 28th day she rejoins her husband. All subsequent deliveries take place in her husband's hut.

Ceremonies after death. On death, relatives and friends assemble and remove the body on a bier to the burial ground in one's own compound or in the neighbourhood. There the grave is dug and the body placed in it on a mat. It is then filled up after putting some rice into it. The party then bathes and returns. The son or the maternal nephew is the chief mourner and performs the same ceremonies as are performed by other low castes. The pollution lasts for 16 days.

Internal economy. The affairs of the community are regulated at caste assemblies of the seniors, which meet on occasions requiring enquiry into allegations of adultery or of the misconduct of unmarried women or infringement of caste rules, etc. There they carry on their deliberations and pass decisions which are final.

16. **Jungle Castes.** There are various jungle tribes that inhabit the hills of Malabar. The Travancore Census Report names the following among the chief Hill tribes as being inhabitants of the Eastern Taluks of Travancore:—

(1) The Kāṇikkar;
(2) The Mala Arayans;
(3) The Mala Urālis;
(4) The Hill Panṭārams;
(5) Maṇṇāns;
(6) Muṭavans;
(7) The Ullāṭans;
(8) The Nāyāṭis.

To this list may be added the Mala Aḍiyārs of the Lower Periyar Valley.

"Viewed from an ethnical stand point" says the Cochin *Census Report* "Kāṇikkars, Pulayans, Paṛayans, Veṭṭuvans, Ullāṭans, Nāyāṭis, Yerravālas, Mudgars, Malayans and Kāṭans are perhaps to be classed together" as 'Hill Tribes'. The last two are the 'Hill Tribe' proper.

The Hill Tribes are all a set of quite inoffensive people who are nomadic in their habits, carrying on migratory cultivation and living mainly upon hunting and forest produce. Their rude and primitive manners, and the marked negroid features of some of them, have led them to be generally regarded as the aboriginies of the country. Bishop Caldwell, however, considers that they are not like the Todas of the Nelgheries, the surviving representatives of the earliest inhabitants of the plains, but like the hill tribes of the 'Pulnys' the descendants of some hinduised low country people, who were driven to the hills by oppression or who voluntarily migrated thither. Perhaps, it is to these hill tribes as a class that Barbosa refers as the "Renoleni". "These" he says "live in the mountains very poorly and miserably. They have no other occupation than bringing wood and grass to the city for sale to support themselves. They go naked, covering only their middle with leaves of trees etc."

The earliest notice we have of these hill tribes is in Purchas *His Pilgrims* and in Nieuhoff's *Travels.* "*Stephanus de Brito* speaketh". says Purchas, "of the *Maleas* (*i.e.*, the Malayars or Hill tribes) which inhabit small villages in the mountains, which are hunters of elephants: amongst whom are no thefts or robberies; and therefore they leave their doors open when they go abroad. They have no idol amongst them; only they observe their ancestor's sepulchres. These have no commerce with their neighbours, nor are much subject to Kings, only pay them a kind of tribute having *Arelli* set over them as judges or magistrates under each of them five or six thousand men. Their houses are made of Indian canes daubed with earth, and some live on trees laying beams from one tree to another, and so building them lofty cottages free from tigers and wild elephants, whereof the mountains are full, which they take in Pits covered over with leaves. They have fertile fields and valleys, but not diligently husbanded. They are content with one wife, which they carry with them whithersoever they go, though but a hunting voyage. They are as other Malabars, naked from the waist upwards, a long garment hangs thence to the ankles; and on their heads a turband as the Moors. Their neck, ears and nostrils are laden with gold. For the Malabars wear gold as well for nose-rings, as ear-rings. These *Maleas* are of better estimation than the base vulgar, nor is it accounted a pollution to touch them, no more than other Nairos or Thomaen Christians. They have their Pipes and Tabors on their feasts. They are also sorcerers and divine by familiar spirits, but use not to kill or hurt men by witchcraft, as other Indians and Malabars do. A witty, docile, honest people, perhaps descended of those Malliani, which *Plutarch* and *Curtins* mention in the life of *Alexander*."

" On the tops of the high rocky mountains of Malabar", writes Nieuhoff, "on the top of which live Christians of St. Thomas—dwells a certain nation called the Malleans they have a pretty good tillage, about thirteen or fourteen leagues from Madura called Priata. * * * Now-a-days they do not inhabit any cities, towns or villages, but only certain enclosures in the valleys betwixt the rocks; their houses are built of canes very low, and plastered up with loom or clay. Some of them live in the woods; these make their houses of wood, which they remove from tree to tree to secure themselves against the elephants and tigers. The first they catch in holes covered with the branches of trees with some earth on the top. They also cultivate the ground, but in a very slender manner, though their valleys would be very fruitful if they were duly managed. They have but one wife at a time who goes abroad a-hunting with them or wherever they go; whereas the pagan Malabars marry, generally several women. They chiefly differ from the other Malabars in their complexion, are just and honest, good natured, charitable and without deceit. For the rest, courageous, ingenious and cunning, they pretend to converse with the devils only out of curiosity to know the event of things; the custom of the other Malabars and Indians, who hurt others by their sorceries being unknown to them.

"Part of the Malleans acknowledge the king of Turbula (Ṭiruwella), part the king of Pugnati (Pūnjaṭṭi), Perimal, for their superiors unto whom they pay tribute, yet with the entire preservation of their liberty, they being governed by their own laws under Captains or Judges of their nation called by them *Arley*, each of them has commonly five or six thousand under his district; besides which each enclosure is governed by its own judges called Pandera; unto them they pay strict obedience".

"Before 1599, when they first began to be instructed in the Romish religion by the assiduity of the then Archbishop of Goa, they were all pagans, but since that time a good number of them have embraced Christianity. Eight of their best men, among whom were three Pandares, with their whole families first received baptism, who being followed by many others, a Church dedicated to St. Michael was built in the village of Priata. Before their conversion they had no temples erected in honour of their idols, neither did they sacrifice with feasting, dancing and such like ceremonies, but each family had its domestic god unto whom they paid their devotions. They are much more esteemed among the Malabars than their common people, neither are they looked upon as unclean by them, no more than the Christians of St. Thomas if they happen to touch a Nayros (Nair). They keep scarce any commerce with the neighbouring nations, even not with the Thomists themselves who live at the foot of the same mountains."

17. **Ollares.** Malayalam Ullāṭers. These, if at all, are only a shade higher than the next succeeding class the Nāyāṭis. They are found in the low country as well as on the hills.

AN ULLADAN'S FAMILY.

(To face p. 527.

The word Uḷḷāṭan is sometimes given a strange derivation which is supposed to indicate the origin of the caste. It is said that when a Naṃbūṭiri Brahman woman was accused of adultery and outcasted, she answered to the accusation saying Uḷḷāṭāṇay, (i. e., Mal:, "It is true"). She is supposed to be the progenitor of this degraded class. Another and more likely derivation that has been suggested is, from *Ul*: 'within' and *Oatana*: running or wandering=Uḷḷāṭan, a person who runs into the forest on the sight of men—apparently of the higher castes. They belong to the lowest class of soil-slaves. They are a true jungle tribe of wild and timid savages whose subsistence and life are truly pitiable. They are good hunters being adepts in the use of the bow and arrow and are excellent shots when trained. They obtain their living by gathering gum, honey, wax and other forest produce. They can gather these only from bushes, shrubs, etc., for they are prevented from climbing trees and driving pegs into them. They chiefly cultivate the ragi and subsist principally on fruits, wild yams, etc., and eke out a wretched existence. They have no settled abode. They snare birds and small game by day and watch crops by night. They may not touch water and if they do so must fast for a day. It follows that they are extremely filthy. Their clothes are merely leaves of trees.

Marriage. Dr. Day gives us a curious description of their marriage ceremony. "Their marriage ceremony is very simple, but it is also employed by some of the other inferior tribes, at certain times, although quite contrary to their rites. A large round building is made of leaves, and inside this the bride is ensconced. All the eligible young men of the village then assemble, and form a ring around this hut. At a short distance sits the girl's father or nearest male relative, with a tom-tom in his hands, and a few more such musical instruments complete the scene. Presently the music begins and a chant which may be translated as follows, is sung by the father.

"Take the stick my sweetest daughter,
Now seize the stick, my dearest love,
Should you not capture the husband you wish for,
Remember 'tis fate decides whom you shall have."

"The young men each armed with a bamboo, commence dancing round the hut, into which each of them thrusts his stick. This continues about an hour, when the owner of whichever bamboo she seizes, become the fortunate husband of the concealed bride. A feast then follows, the ceremony is now complete, whilst there is no divorce."[1] Some attribute this ceremony to the Nāyāṭis also. When an Uḷḷāṭan brings home his wife, some money, a brass vessel and a brass-box are given as dowry. But ofcourse this is only among those who are comparatively well-to-do.

The Vēṭan claims superiority over the Uḷḷāṭan, but the existence and subsistence of both is indescribably miserable. Both however are not insensible to the vanity of ornaments, the neck being hung round with shells in profusion. A dark complexion, restless glance, and exuberance of hair gives them a wild appearance; but they are extremely gentle and so timid that, on the lowest sound of approach, they fly into the woods.

18. **Wedden**. Malayalam Vēṭan or hunter. The Rev. Mr. Mateer observes that though the caste name means "hunter" these people are in a condition very similar to that of the Pulayars, living in jungle clearings or working in the rice-fields and formerly sold and bought as slaves. Their usages, worship and superstitions greatly resemble those of the Pulayars. They are in deep poverty, very timid, and destitute of temporal comfort and conveniences. They have to wander about in seasons of scarcity in search of wild yams, which they boil and eat on the spot and are thorough gluttons, eating all they can get at any time, then suffering want for days. Women are filthy in their habits, the sick are uncared for, and mortality

1. *Land of the Perumals*, p. 329.

VETANS.

(To face p. 528.

amongst the children is great. Polygamy is common as men are not required to provide for the support of their wives. But some who have been converted to Christianity show wonderful and rapid improvement in moral character, civilization and diligence.[1]

A party of Hill Vēṭars came to visit Mr. Baker and spoke with peculiar words and in a curious tone rendering it very difficult to converse with them. Their women had immense necklaces of beads, pieces of lead and brass, one had a broad chain of brass round her neck. These people were coal-black and many quite curly-headed.

19. **Naiaddy.** Malayalam Nāyāṭi—'hunter'. In the Hindu heirarchy of castes in Malabar, the Nāyāṭis are placed on the lowest rung. They are at the very last step of vileness. The following description of them is very apt. "This wretched race is only found in the Northern parts of Cochin, they are banished the villages, and live on the low hills near the cultivated lands—a bush or rock being their only shelter. The Nāyāṭis present a state of society not seen in any other part of India; wild amidst civilized inhabitants, starving amongst cultivation, nearly naked; they wander about in search of a few roots, but depend more on charity, which the traveller is surprised at their clamorous impetuosity in soliciting, ascending the little slopes that overlook the village or road. Whatever charity they receive is placed on the ground near where they stand, but on observing their petitions are heard they retire from the spot, that they may not defile by their presence those coming to their relief."[3]

It is thought that the "Poulichees" mentioned by Captain Hamilton are the same with those whom Buchanan describes under the name of 'Nāyāṭis', and both bear a general resemblance to Varthema's 'Hirava',

1. *Native Life in Travancore*, p. 60.
2. *Ibid*, p. 62.
3. *The Madras Journal of Literature and Science* Vol. I, p 7.

though he describes them as cultivators of rice, whereas the former are not allowed to till the ground but have to dwell in woods and marshes, and subsist chiefly on hunting and begging. According to Hamilton, the 'Poulichees' are the lowest order of human creatures, and are excluded from the benefit of divine and human laws.

The caste has no sub-divisions. Their very look is most unprepossessing. Dark in complexion, stunted in growth, lean and gaunt in appearance, filthy in habits, timid by nature, these wretched specimens of humanity are no better than the wild beasts who are their companions in their forest home.

Clothing and Ornaments. The Nāyāṭis generally cover their nakedness by tying round their waist long strings made of leaves and plants. Some however use a small piece of dirty cloth which hangs on till it drops down in rags. This never goes down the knees. The men wear a number of brass ear-rings sometimes as many as 13 in one lobe. Sometimes a string with brass rings is worn round the loins or the arm as a charm for the cure of diseases or to ward off demons. The women wear a dirty cloth round the waist which is twice folded. The upper cloth is seldom or never worn. The lobes of the ears are dilated and wooden plugs or Ṭōḍa are inserted into them. Bracelets are not generally worn, but round the neck are seen many rows of beads with shells and pendants hanging over their bosoms. These are not removed on the death of their husbands. Ear ornaments are, as a rule, not worn after they have given birth to a child, for they say that after child birth a woman loses her youth and beauty, and with the care of a child to bring up, her days of merriment are at an end. As a sign of mourning, they wear no ornaments for a year after the death of the husband.

Habitations. The Nāyāṭis live on hill tops and valleys isolated from all other human habitations. They generally select a *shola* or valley where there is a pond or small stream. There they erect their huts with small roofs supported on four bamboo posts connected by bamboo beams and protected from wind and rain by palm leaf walls. A few earthen pots and a chopper constitute a Nāyāṭi's property.

Food and Drink. They subsist mainly upon yams and wild roots and possess no knowledge of trapping animals or snaring birds. They are however flesh-eaters and will eat pigs, dear, hares, monkeys, goats, wild squirrel, rats, doves, quails, fowls, etc. They hunt animals by means of the bow and arrow, in the use of which they are adepts. They also eat oysters, tortoises and crocodiles which latter they capture by means of ropes and hooks. They bake the flesh of animals by means of fire which they produce by friction and eat without salt and chillies. These are however but delicacies. Their common food is Kaññi and boiled rice. The rice or paddy they obtain mainly by way of alms. They are averse to manual labour, and work they can seldom get. The result is, that, should they fail to get any alms in the day, they have to starve in the evening. They yell out for charity in their stentorian voice from a distance and follow passers-by miles and miles together, taking care to keep at a respectful distance, beseaching piteously for alms. It is a common sight to see on the road-side in Malabar a dirty piece of rag spread out with a few piece of copper lying on it, and a Nāyāṭi crying out for alms from a long distance. Like other slave castes, the Nāyāṭi is a habitual drinker. Large quantities of toddy are consumed when they can procure the same, but they cannot afford to get so much toddy as the Cheṛuman who regularly works, obtains wages and can pay for his drink.

Occupation. As a rule, the Nāyāṭis are averse to manual labour of any kind. Living round the mountains, valleys and hill tops, they occupy themselves with collecting honey, bee's wax, and Maṭṭippaśa from the Maṭṭipāl tree. Maṭṭippaśa is a resin with a strong balsamic odour which the bark of *Abanthus Malabarica* yields. When placed in the fire, it emits a sweet smell and is used by Malayālis to fumigate their bed chambers and clothes. These articles they sell for a few copper coins, very much below their market price. Sometimes they exchange them for articles of daily consumption. Thus ṅāli of honey is exchanged for six ṅālies of toddy and so on. They also make ropes and slings and, on occasions of national festivals, such as Ōṇam and Vishu, they present four of these ropes to every Nambūṭiri Illam and two to every Nāyar house near their village. In return they get some paddy, a few copper coins and a piece of cloth. They also employ themselves as agricultural labourers, but this very seldom. The Nāyāṭi enjoys certain privileges. Superstition envelopes the Nāyāṭi with certain virtues which he and he alone can impart. The higher classes believe that to feed the Nāyāṭis on birthdays, anniversaries of deaths and festive occasions ensures long life and prosperity to those who do so. Hence the Nāyāṭis get their share of curry and rice on such occasions. Again, when the inmates of a house hear the howling of a Nāyāṭi at a distance, and he goes about howling when he has no work to do, they take a handful of rice, salt, chillies, tamarind, oil, mustard, cocoanut—in short every thing necessary for culinary purposes—put them into a vessel with a few pice added to them, move the vessel round the head of a child or adult supposed to be under the influence of a demon or the potency of some evil eye and hand them over to the Nāyāṭi. He would of course be thankful for the gift and be inclined to bless the hand that gave it. But superstition would prefer the curse of the Nāyāṭi to his blessing, and he is earnestly requested to curse the giver. It is believed that a Nāyāṭi's Prākku or curse will have always its opposite effect and, when he is asked to curse, he pours forth imprecations and invokes all sorts of evil and misery to the person who gave him the alms.

NAYADIS ON A BEGGING TOUR.

To face p. 532.

General condition. As to their general condition, they are almost in a state beyond redemption. Life cannot be lower than theirs. These miserable specimens of humanity, who are no better than two legged animals, pass their days howling for charity under the midday sun in summer, and in storm and rain during the wintry season. They are the Nīcha Jāṭi or Chaṇḍālas of the plains, the helots and bondsmen of society, under the Hindu system. They cannot approach the person or the abodes of higher classes. At any distance shorter than 300 feet they pollute the Brahman, who has to bathe and renew his sacred thread and drink *Panchagavyam* or the five products of the cow to keep off the contamination caused by the approach of a Nāyāṭi. The highways and by-ways were till within living memory closed to them. They could not then approach the markets and bazaars. The very necessaries of life are denied by a cruel and unsympathetic system which aims on the subjection of the lower classes to the higher. Dr. Buchanan observes of the Nāyāṭis that:—"A wretched tribe of this kind, buffeted and abused by every one, and subsisting on the labour of the industrious is a disgrace to any country, and both compassion and justice seem to require, that they should be compelled to gain a livelihood by honest industry, and be elevated somewhat more nearly to the rank of men * * * In the execution of such a plan it would be necessary to transport the Niadis to some country east from Malabar, in order to remove them from the contempt in which they will always be held by the higher ranks of that country."[1] The idea is good and deserves the serious attention of those who are kindly disposed towards this despised and wretched class. They are a timid, truthful and religiously inclined people. The degraded life to which they have been condemned by their dirty habits and by the caste system for ages together has driven some to embrace the Christian and Muhammadan religions which apparently

1. Vol. 2, p. 97.

offer equality and fraternity to all alike. Perhaps there are more converts to Islamism than to Christianity. Great in numbers, their extremely wretched condition deserves the close and sympathetic attention of the enlightened higher classes who should not forget that they too are human beings and fellow creatures.

Religion and Worship. The Nāyāṭis are said to follow a low form of the Hindu Religion. But it is clearly a mistake to say that these low tribes along with their brethren have any idea of Hinduism. All those who constitute the Nīcha Jāṭi or the low castes, according to the Hindu classification of castes, are mere Animists who the plastic side of Hinduism is gradually endeavouring to engraft on it. Living in the forests and oppressed by the vastness of the natural phenomena around them, these simple people believe more in the existence of mountain deities who, if propitiated in season, will watch over their welfare and protect them against wild beasts than in the philosophical abstractions of the Hindu Religion. To the Nāyāṭi rain, thunder and storm, the depredations of wild beasts, etc., are dispensations of some forest deity or other haunting the mountains. The Nāyāṭis are also ancestor worshippers keeping representations of the departed near their huts. To these stones they make offerings of rice, toddy and arrack on

Kar̄kaṭaka Saṃkr̄ānṭi (in July),
Vṛschika Saṃkr̄ānṭi (in November),
Ōṇam (in August),
Viṣhu (in May) and
Kumbha Bhar̄aṇi (in March).

The gods worshipped by them, chiefly, are Mallan Malavāli and Par̄akkuṭṭi—all mala-ḏēvaṭās or mountain deities. The last of these they say aids them in their hunting expeditions. He brings them the game and secures them from molestation from wild animals. They pray to him to render them assistance and, if they have occasion to feel that he has failed to listen to their supplications, they fall to abuse him for ingratitude and for betraying the trust they had reposed in him. In worshipping the spirits of their ancestors and their gods, they resort to bloody sacrifices. Sheep or fowl is killed and the blood spilt on the images. The flesh is cooked. The priest performs a Pūja with offerings of flesh, boiled rice, toddy and other things. The worshippers stand at a distance during the Pūja and approach the images only on the priest clapping his hands after he has finished ministering to the gods. All pray and partake of the offerings. The prayer is generally of this form:—"O my Malla! My Malavāli! My Parakuṭṭi! My father! My mother! My dead ancestor! I give these offerings which I have with difficulty obtained from Ṭampurākkal (members of higher classes) as alms. May you accept them and protect us against wild beasts, as we are wandering through the forests. May you protect our children!"—poor innocent creatures!. They believe in magic and sorcery and the Parayan who is their astrologer, sorcerer and magician is often consulted.

Ceremonies, Puberty, Marriage. Girls are given in marriage before and after puberty. When a girl attains puberty, she is led by a female relation to a tank in which she bathes after a panṭi or frame work composed of several pieces of plantain leaves plaited together has been moved round her three or four times. She is removed to a separate shed for 10 days during which she is considered impure and no one touches her. Her meals are served from a distance. On the 11th day, she bathes and casts off her impurity and a feast is given in honour of it. At every subsequent menstural period, she observes pollution for three days bathing on the fourth day.

The Nāyāṭi generally gives his daughter in marriage to his sister's son, or his mother's sister's daughter's son. The bridegroom's parents and relatives look for a bride. The bride's parents and relatives consider over the matter, and, if the match is accepted, the young man's father pays a few annas and the matter is finally settled. On the auspicious day, the bridegroom and party arrives and a modest feast is given. The bride is dressed in the Kacha (cloth) brought by the bridegroom and is decked with the necklace of glass beads supplied by him. The bridegroom wears a skull cap made of the bark of the areca palm. In some parts there is no further ceremony. Each of the contracting couple is presented with a mat and the union is said to be complete. In some parts the necklace of glass beads is tied as the equivalent of the ṭāli round the bride's neck by the bridegroom's sister. On the following day the wedding party breaks up and the relations return home. The Nāyāṭis are monogamists. Conjugal fidelity is the rule and the adultery is not heard of. Both divorce and widow marriage are allowed. If the husband divorces his wife on account of any moral offence on her part, she is taken to her father's house and left there, and the father returns half the dowry which in full is not more than a rupee. If the wife seeks the divorce owing to the misdeeds of the husband, she is taken back to her father's house, and the full dowry is returned to the husband. The elder children remain with the father while the younger ones and the babies are taken by the mother. The woman is free to marry again.

Pregnancy and Child birth. During the 7th month of pregnancy, certain ceremonies are performed to keep off the influence of demons; a magic thread is worn round the neck as a charm against the malignant influences of evil spirits. The delivery takes place in a hut put up for the occasion. The birth pollution lasts for ten days during which the husband avoids seeing her. For a period of seven months, she does not go out to work.

Inheritance. To speak of inheritance in the case of Nāyāṭis is absolutely useless. For they have nothing to leave to their successors except their huts, earthen pots and chopper which are not likely to excite the ambition of others who may possess such things of their own.

Death and after ceremonies. Both burial and cremation are practised, the former being the rule and the latter the exception. Custom requires the burning of the bodies of the old, but want of funds more often leads them to bury them. They have a fixed burial ground to which dead bodies are taken after being washed and anointed. The Eṉangans carry the corpse on a bamboo bier. A pit is dug due north to south and the body is let in with heads towards the south. The sons and relatives throw earth into it and, when the grave is partly filled, seven layers of small stones are placed in it. More earth is then thrown in and seven more layers are added. The grave is finally filled up with earth. Three big stones are then planted, one at each end and one in the middle. From the time of death till the burial is over, the family has to fast. They then bathe and eat fruits and other articles, but may not take cooked food till the following day. The death pollution lasts for 10 days, during which they are prohibited from meat. From the second day forwards the son or other relative who performed the funeral rites bathes every morning and offers oblations of balls of rice and water to the spirit of the deceased. He has to cook his food for himself. If he cannot do this, only an Eṉangan can do it for him, and none else. On the 11th day they take a quantity of rice, some Kaṟuka grass, some water in a cocoanut shell, a plantain leaf with the tips entire and a lighted wick. The agnates assembled go to a reservoir and bathe. A figure is made of sand to represent the deceased before which the plantain leaf is spread with the tip towards the east. The other articles are placed on the leaf. The eldest son or other relative commences the ceremony by standing in front of the leaf, his face turned towards the east, and throws the water with his right hand towards the east, according to some, three times, while, according to others, ten times. He then raises his hands above his head and salutes the deceased and prostrates himself. All the agnates follow him in this. They then retire, leaving the rice to be eaten by crows. The party then returns home and the Eṇangan purifies them by sprinkling on each a mixture of cow-dung and water. The eldest son observes Ḍīkṣha or penance, growing his hair for one year during which period he abstains from eating meat. At the close of the year, he performs Śṛāḍha and terminates his Ḍīkṣhā. After this at certain fixed days, such as Kaṛkaṭaka Saṃkṛānṭi, he makes oblations. If the body had been cremated, the bones are collected on the seventh day and preserved in a pot to be finally consigned into a stream or river. In cases of burial, after some time, the grave is dug up, the bones are taken and burnt. The ashes are collected and buried by the side of the stream. On this the agnates pour water three times reverentially, prostrate themselves and retire. Of course there is the funeral repast. It is indeed curious that in all this the Nāyāṭis closely imitate, so far as they can, the higher classes. But why they should do this in the matter of the death ceremonies alone is not apparent except that they are being gradually caught in the eddy of Hinduism.

Caste government. The senior members of the community are known as Pṛamāṇies. The priest is called Mūppen whose function is hereditary. There is another officer called Avakāśi who is entitled to two-thirds of the shares in all domestic ceremonies, rather a large slice in the case of such poor people. The Mūppen has the power to enquire into all matters affecting the community and can excommunicate any guilty person.

Hill Tribes, *not noticed by our author*. The hill tribes of Travancore may broadly be divided into two sections, viz., those living towards the south known as Kāṇikkar and those living towards the north known as Mala Arayans. Similarly the hill tribes of the Cochin State may also be divided into Kāṭar and Malayar

A GROUP OF KADARS.

(*To face p.* 538

signifying 'jungle-dwellers' and 'hill-men'. The Kāṭar are found in the forests of the Nelliāmpaṭi, Parampikuḷam and Aṭirappiḷḷi hills, while the Malayar are confined to the regions of Paravaṭṭāni, Pālappiḷḷi, Kōṭaśśēri, Machād and Elanād. The differences between the several classes of hill tribes are due more to their isolated living in distant tracts of hills and forests which present physical difficulties for intercourse with each other than to any variety in origin.

According to Mr. Bourdillon, late of the Travancore Forest Department, the Travancore hillmen are divided into 12 or 14 tribes, who live apart, and whose members do not inter-marry with those of other tribes. Each tribe or clan has a certain tract of country which is considered to belong to it, and even each village of a tribe has its land allotted to it; and no one would dare to encroach on the land assigned to another clan or another village without permission. These hillmen live scattered through the forest of the State from the extreme south to the confines of the Cochin State.

Though split into so many tribes, living apart and not intermarrying with one another, they probably sprang from 2 or at most 3 sources. They are all dark skinned and many of them have short noses and thick lips and possess African features. It is probable, therefore, that they are descendants of the aboriginal inhabitants of the country and they took refuge in the forests to avoid the oppression and slavery imposed upon them by early foreign settlers.

Designation. The term Kāṇikkāran means, according to Dr. Gundhert, "one who has some claim to an estate." In popular language, it means "hereditary proprietor of land" and the Kāṇikkar claim proprietorship over the forest tracts they inhabit. They refer to a tradition that "there were once two hill-kings, Śrī Rangan and Vīrappan and that their descendants emigrated from the Pandyan territories beyond Agasṭyakūṭam under pressure from superior force and never returned to the low country." The Kāṇikkars abound in the Taluks of Neyyāttinkara, Vilavancōde and Kalculam. To this has to be added the few Malavēlans who are only Kāṇies that live near the lowlands in the Taluks of Vilavancōde and Neyyāttinkara.

Appearance, Clothing and Ornaments. The Kāṇis are generally of short stature, spare body and of dark colour. Their habits are active. Some have markedly Negroid features. They have but little clothing and that unclean, the men going about almost naked, having only a strip of cloth round their waist; the women are better clad. Both men and women wear their hair long and tie it into a round knot behind the head. The women indulge in strings of beads and shells which they wear round their necks as ornaments. Round their wrists bracelets of iron and brass, and in the ears leaden rings are worn, the lobes of the ears being artificially distended. The men carry with them, when they go out, a cane basket containing their food, necessary utensils, etc., a long staff, a heavy knife which is stuck in the waist cloth and sometimes a bow and arrows.

Food and Drink. Their food is but scanty and consists of what they can gather on the hills. They seldom come down to the plains, so that they have to confine themselves to fruits and roots and the animals and birds they can entrap or shoot with their bows and arrows. The traps for the wild boar and tiger are made with rough timber supported on a spring which falls and lets down the whole weight upon the animal's back. They eat most kinds of fish. Till but recently, they were strangers to liquor, but they have now contracted the vice of drink from their civilized neighbours on the plains. Cow life is scrupulously honoured. They do not eat the wild ox or buffalo, nor the grey or Hanuman monkey, but only the black species. They will not eat with the Ṣhāṇārs or Īluvas or still lower castes but will take food cooked by Nāyars.

Occupation and Living. They form a migratory population, cutting down patches of forests, burning and clearing them for purposes of cultivation. On these patches of land, they sow a crop with little or no tillage and continue raising the crop for 3 or 4 years. When they find the soil exhausted, they move on to other patches, thus employing the whole forest in time for agricultural purposes. They do not, however, go long distances. They grow rice and millet, tapioca and sweet potatoes, raggi, plantains, ganja, tobacco and pulses of sorts. Generally the clearing of the jungle for agricultural purposes is commenced on a Friday in the months of November, December and January. The felled wood and undergrowth is allowed to dry up before they are burnt, and the seeds are sown almost invariably on a Monday or Friday in April, May and June. The Kāṇis have had recently to give up their habit of migratory cultivation as the new Forest Laws prevent them from clearing and setting fire to patches of their selection in the forests, and they have resigned themselves to the new order of things. They console themselves by saying "as the sovereign has commanded that no jungle should be burnt nor any trees felled, we have had to resolve on giving up the migratory cultivation." At present each Kāṇi village has its own forest block for cultivation with which other villagers are not to interfere. The Kāṇis do not pay any tax to Government. They occasionally go in a body to pay homage to the Maharaja at Trivandrum. They are received very kindly and the Maharaja accepts the Nazzur they offer. These consist of (1) the bamboo plantain with large though few fruits, (2) a parcel of *Muttucheri* hill paddy seed, (3) bamboo joints holding honey of different varieties and (4) *Virukachattam* or a parcel of civet. The Kāṇis fancy that the large bamboo plantain is reserved for the use of the Raja only, and Mr. Mateer tells us that he had great difficulty in inducing them to part with a sucker of this curious plant. At the interview they have with the Maharaja, the customary modes of court address and court etiquette are dispensed with. They address the Maharaja without the usual honorifics, and their boorish ways are good naturedly excused. The Maharaja, pleased with their simplicity, unsophisticated manners and unaffected homage, make them presents of cloth, money, salt and tobacco. The Kāṉis are employed by Government to collect forest produce, such as honey, cardamoms, wax, ginger, dammer, Kunṯirikkam, and elephant tusks in return for a small remuneration known as Kuṯivāram. They also occupy themselves in the capture of wild animals, such as the elephant, the tiger and the wild boar, and the making of wicker work of bamboo, rattan and reed. They are very ingenious at wicker work of bamboo and reed. Mr. Mateer says that he has seen a bridge over a river, a hundred feet wide, constructed by the Kāṉikkar, of wicker work made of bamboo materials over which a pony could pass. They are of service to sportsmen and travellers. From their intimate acquaintance with the forests and hills, they can readily point out the places haunted by wild animals which they recognise by the smell. They thus warn the traveller against danger or guide sportsmen to their game. Referring to the faculty of observation developed in these hill tribes from their mode of life, Sir William Crooks, the Great Indian Ethnologist, observes,—"One thing the jungle dweller acquires by this course of life, is a marvellous insight into nature and her secrets. His eyesight and power of hearing are wonderful. He sees or hears a tiger creeping down a ravine long before sportsmen will. Every thing in the forest has a meaning for him—the grunt of the monkey, as the tiger comes beneath his tree, the hoarse alarm bark of the stag. From the way the vultures hover in the air, he will tell whether the tiger has finished his meal, or is still tearing the carcase. Every foot mark, a displaced pebble, a broken grass stalk will tell him something."

The method of their making fire is thus described by Mr. Mateer. "A peg of the wood of *Isora Corylifolia* (or of bamboo) is taken and inserted in a small reed which is rapidly revolved on another piece of the same wood, this being the best for the purpose: in a few minutes smoke is evolved, then fire, which is caught in tinder contained in a small joint of bamboo, and can then easily be preserved or carried about."

The Kāṇis live together in small bodies, each hamlet being under the rule of a headman or Mūṭṭakāṇi (=the eldest Kāṇi) who wields considerable authority over them. Their huts are neatly made of bamboos and the elephant reed, the leaves and stems being interwoven for walls as well as roof. Besides the huts on the ground, a number of booths are built on trees with large branches, a platform being made of sticks and the hut built on this in order to be out of the way of mischievous elephants, tigers, etc. Access is obtained by a ladder or a single bamboo with the side shoots cut off on either side at a distance of a few inches.

Caste government. The Kāṇi community is governed in the patriarchal method by the Mūṭṭa Kāṇi who is entitled to certain perquisites. He is, as the very term imports, the eldest member of the village councils, and can be removed only by constitutional methods. Questions relating to marriage, divorce, etc., are discussed at village Panchayats.

Language. The Kāṇis call their language *Malampashai, i. e.*, the language of the mountains. It is a dialectic form of Malayalam with a large admixture of Tamil. The southern Kāṇis speak Tamil, and it is the northerns that use Malampāṣhai. Their pronounciation is very bad. As observed by Mr. Mateer, "Words strange to the people of the coast, or archaic, are intermingled with their speech as 'Kāla' (Kalayi, second cultivation of a rice field), for a place where they have remained for two years; 'Kuruma' (Kurumba) a child ; 'yengachi' (where ?) for 'yevide' and 'pati' (a fold) or 'wadi' (an enclosure, entrenchment) for house; with other oddities in talk which it required some time to become familiar with". It will be observed that the terms mentioned in the above extract are all Malayalam words. *Kalay* means a second cultivation of a rice field and the tax on this cultivation goes by the name of *Kalay nikuthi* in the official language of the Cochin State. Again, according to Dr. Gundhert, Kuṙumba means, an infant and the Goddess of Cranganore goes by the name of Śrī Kuṙumba. Wādi is still used for 'house' as in Ṭachchu wādi a carpenter's house.

Sub-divisions. There are amongst them two sub-divisions of 5 Illams in each, one being exogamous and the other endogamous as Machchampi or brother-in-law Illams. The names of the former are (1) Kali, (2) 3) Talamala, (4) Kurumilla and (5) Perim. The names of the latter are (1) Mangot, (2). Moot, (3) Peringalatti, (4) Vel and (5) Vellanat.

Marriage. Girls are married between the ages of 7 and 12, and boys above 16. But girls remain unmarried even beyond the age of 16, "because no bridegroom has offered." The husband need not be older than the wife, instances of women of 30 and 35 years old being married to adults of 20 being not rare. A Kāṇi youth desirous of marrying a girl visits the uncle or parents accompanied by four of his relatives who make the proposal. They consult their relations and give an answer. The matter is then submitted for the consideration of the village council, and after it is settled there, the marriage day is fixed and guests are invited by both parties. It is indispensible that the invitations should be accompanied with presents of betel and spice. Otherwise the invited guest will not attend. When the bridegroom and party arrives at the bride's house where the marriage takes place, the headman or the Mūṭṭa Kāṇi declares in the presence of those assembled that so and so is to be married to so and so. The bridegroom presents a cloth to the bride's mother which is called Amma Vīṭu Muṇḍu—'Mother's house cloth' and five and a half fanams (12as. 10 ps.) to her uncle, if she has become marriageable; if otherwise, seven and a half fanams (*i. e.*, Re. 1 a. 1 ps. 6). He also gives betel and nut to the bride who is brought into the marriage shed amongst the company assembled. The bridegroom then takes the ṭāli in his hand, worships the sun and holds the string to which the ṭāli is attached round the neck of the bride and his sister standing behind ties it on. He also hands over a cloth to his sister who puts it on the bride. Marriage presents are given by friends and relatives. The headman, according to Mr. Mateer, offers some "advice" to the husband as to the management of his wife, beginning his rule with mild measures and proceeding to extremities only by degrees as required. The heads of his discourse are drawn from a well-known Malayālam saying and are as follows:—

1. Cholli Koṭu—teach by words, 2. Nulli Koṭu—teach by pinching—slight punishment, 3. Ṭalli Koṭu—teach by blows—and lastly, 4. Ṭalli Kaḷa—cast her away (that is if she will not obey).

The higher classes that dwell on the plains and pretend to a higher civilization than these simple hillmen will do well to take a lesson from the discourse of the Muṭṭa Kāṇi.

On the marriage day, those who can afford to do so, hold a feast at the bride's house, and another on the next day at the bridegroom's. Others satisfy themselves with entertaining their guests with betel and nut to chew and Indian hemp to smoke.

The dowry consists generally of brass vessels, earthen ones, mattocks, a large chopper, an axe, pulses and grains, etc.

Lapses from virtue in women are severely dealt with. If such occur before marriage, the Kāṇi society will compel the man, if found out, to make amends by legalising the union into a formal alliance. Adultery used to be punished with death; but now the culprit is subjected in some places to four lashes on the back and often a money penalty alone is enacted. Widow marriage is permitted, the new bridegroom presenting cloth to the widow with the consent of the village council and the guardians of the widow. Divorce also is permitted, but is of very rare occurrence, and is effected by the village council after due consideration. The separated husband will have to give back the wife's dowry.

Inheritance. In the matter of inheritance, there is some difference between the Kāṇis who live in the interior of the hills and those living near the plains. The former follow Makkaṭṭāyam, the sons taking the fathers' property, if any. And yet it is not Makkaṭṭāyam pure and simple, for a moiety of the personal property goes to the sister's son, *i. e.*, the nephews. With those living on or near the plains, the self-acquired property is distributed equally between the sons and the nephews. If there are no sons, the nephews inherit the whole property, the right of the widow being confined to maintenance alone.

Ceremonies. The most important ceremony after marriage is the *Vayaru Ponkala* which is performed at an advanced stage of pregnancy. It consists in boiling some rice before an image of Gaṇapaṭi and then offering it to the sun. Offerings are also made at the same time of beaten rice, fried rice, cakes, plantain fruits, tender cocoanuts, etc. The headman performs a dance repeating Manṭrams. He waves the offerings to the sun. The first rice giving to a child is celebrated with a feast, at least to four of the villages. Offerings are also given to the village demons. The child receives its name when able to sit on the ground, generally three or four months after birth. The usual names are *Parappankani, Sattan, Eiyan, Madappan, Vikkaran*, for men;

and for women—*Echchi*, *Valli*, *Kannamier*, *Poomalie*, *Parappi*, etc.

Sickness and Death. When the Kāṇi takes ill, the headman is at once consulted; he visits the sick and orders two drumming and singing ceremonies to be performed. A whole night is spent in dancing, singing and drumming and in offering prayers for the recovery of the patients. The offerings consist of tapioca, flour and cocoanuts, etc. After some time, the headman, with manifestations of demoniac possession, reveals whether the sufferer will die or not. If he will die, he repeats a Manṭram (Kuṭumi Veṭṭu Manṭram; formula on cutting off the top-knot) and cuts off the sick man's Kuṭumi. This being a sign of approaching death, the relatives and others pay their last visits to the sick.

After death, a mixture of ganja (hemp), raw rice and cocoanut is put into the mouth of the corpse by the sons and nephews; and it is buried at some distance from their abode, Manṭrams being repeated over the body. Occasionally one is cremated. The relatives bathe before returning home, and cannot take any of the produce of their lands till the death pollution is removed and ceremonies are performed lest that wild beasts will attack them or destroy their crops. To avoid this, a small shed is built outside their clearing. On the third day, three measures of rice are boiled and placed in a cup or on a plantain leaf inside the shed: then all bathe once more and return home On the seventh day, all this is repeated, the old shed being pulled down and a new one put up. On returning to their dwelling, they sprinkle cowdung on their houses and in the yard which finally removes the defilement. People in better circumstances make a feast of curry and rice for all present.

We gather from the *Travancore Census Report* that the cremation of dead bodies generally takes place on the bank of a stream or river and that all the neighbouring villagers, both male and female, have to pour water over the corpse with both hands. Some of the cooking utensils of the house-hold of the deceased person are broken, as typifying the end of his connection with earthly things. Dr. Subramania Ayyar remarks "it is significant to note that many of these form part of the Brahmanical funeral ceremonial".

Ceremonies with reference to cultivation. Here also we cannot do better than quote Mr. Mateer. "When intending to clear some land, the headman is invited Three edungaly measures of rice and six cocoanuts are presented to him. These he takes to a suitable plot of forest-land, makes an offering and first clears a small portion with his own hand; then the others follow. These offerings are repeated at the burning of the felled timber, and the sowing of the seed, plantain fruits and other articles being added. On the first appearance of the ear, they spend two nights in drumming, singing and repeating Mantrams at the field, putting up a *tattu* or platform, on four sticks as a shrine for the spirits, where they offer raw rice, tender cocoanuts,flowers, etc.

" At harvest time a sufficient quantity of rice being eaten, sweet-meats are prepared, and cocoanuts,plantain fruits and flowers added to these for a general offering to the various spirits such as Ayiravilli, 'he of a thousand bows'; Madan Tamburan, 'the cow-like Lord'; Mallan Tamburan, 'the Giant Lord'; Mathandan Pey, 'the Sun Demon';, Pucha Mallan Pey, 'the Cat Giant Demon, Athirakodi Pay, 'the Boundary flag Demon;" and a great many others whom they regard as deities. They wait upon the headman for the manifestations of the gods, then devour the offerings"[1].

Religion. The Kaṉikkars are demon worshippers. Some of the demons whom they adore have already

1. *Native Life in Travancore*, pages 68—69.

been named. These demons are said to be peculiarly hill deities whose function is to rule the wild beasts and restrain them from doing mischief. They are supposed to reside in large trees. There are no distinctive images used for worship, but any stone is good enough as an idol or fetish when occasion required one. "The Kanikkars have no much idea", observes Mr. Mateer, "of the soul or immortality. When asked they say 'Who can tell?'. Some with whom we conversed said they knew nothing of a hell, or of the wicked going there."

Sorcery and Witchcraft. The Kāṇikkars are addicted to sorcery and witchcraft. They have little faith in medicine. Their medicine-man is the sorcerer. It is his songs and dances that propitiate the demons that cause illness and lead to cures. One of their curious dances has been graphically described by Mr. A. P. Smith who witnessed it. He says:—"The propitiatory ceremony should ordinarily be done every year just before the harvesting of the grain commences. It is commonly called the *Oattu*, feeding ceremony. The officiating Kani is generally an elderly and influential man who professes inspiration and knowledge obtained when asleep. The articles necessary to perform the ceremony are called *Padukka* or sacrifice, and *Ashtamangalyam*. *Padukka* is for the adult gods or manes, male or female, called *Chavu*, and *Ashtamangalyam* is for the virgins who have died, called Kanyakas. A temporary pavilion or *pandal* had been erected in front of the house and the courtyard known as the *mittam*—and from the canopy long streamers of tender cocoanut leaves, plantain bunches, the tender cocoanuts with their husk on, were hung. Bunches of arecanuts and flowers adorned the posts and pillars and gave an air of festivity to the scene. Fires were burning outside, round which—for the nights were dewy and the air keen—were groups of people enjoying the warmth, and gossiping. The primitive oil lamp appeared in places, while the smoky kerosene tin lamp, without chimney, was much in evidence and tainted the pure atmosphere. Small heaps consisting of boiled rice (*pori*), paddy, one tender cocoanut, a spring of arecanut flowers, betel, nut were placed on plantain leaves in seven definite spots. The officiating Kanikaran, dressed in his usual every day costume, except his covering cloth, after formally getting the permission of the assembled spectators and persons interested in the ceremony, and especially of one who subsequently appeared in the scene as the chief dancer, began a monotonous chant, in what appeared to be a mixed language. Parts of this singing were wholly unintelligible, but it was understood to be a history of the beginning of earthly things, a record of the life and doings of the souls departed this life whose protection was prayed for, and a prayer for the souls of those persons for whose benefit the ceremony of propitiation was in progress. Now and again the feelings of the narrator or singer would overcome him, and he would indulge in a shout, or an emphatic gesticulation. This went on for about three or four hours, punctuated at intervals by the firing of petards or of old smooth bore guns, shouts and *Kurava* cries. The *Kurava* cry is the ululation, in a shrill tone by Malayalee women at all important ceremonies. The crowd of people present did not mind the chanting much, but talked apart in groups, gossiped, warmed themselves at the various fires and seemed to enjoy the midnight picnic immensely. Before the chanting terminated, a large heap of the red *thetti poo* (*Ixora coccinca*) about a yard square at the base, had been raised in the centre of the pandal and it was prettily picked out with areca flowers in artistic designs. I was getting tired of this endless noise and was expecting to see the old Kanikar begin his attitudinising and dancing when the horrible sound of a human voice roaring like a wild beast aroused every one to a sense of activity. From behind the hut came the man mentioned earlier in this paper and he was very primitively clothed indeed, his hair hanging loose, his eyes staring and what appeared like foam at his mouth. He would stand, run short distances, leap, sit, agitate his body and dance, keeping step to the rythmic and muffled beating of the drum, and this he did for ten minutes or so. Suddenly, with a shout, he dived into the hut specially set apart as the feeding place of the god Madan and presently appeared with two long sticks adorned at their ends with bells which emitted a jingling sound. The frenzy of motion, ecstatic, unregulated and ungovernable was apparently infectious, for a young man, hitherto a silent spectator of the scene, gave a shout and began to dance wildly, throwing up his arms and stepping out quite actively. This encouragement stimulated the original performer, for he caught a man standing near, by the neck, thrust the stick with the bells into his hand and he thereupon started dancing as well. In about ten minutes there were about half a dozen wild dancing dervishes, shouting, gesticulating, revolving, and most certainly in an abnormal state of excitement. Not contented with this, a dying but still glowing heap of fire and ashes became the centre of attraction, for the chief dancer danced over the fire and sent the sparks flying and scattered the wood and evoked the admiration and eulogics of the crowd. Streaming with perspiration, spotted with wood ashes, wild, dishevelled and exhausted, the chief dancing demoniac stepped under the pandal and finally sat himself before the heap of the red *thetti poo* and tossed the cool red dewy blossoms over his head in a kind of shower bath. He was assisted in this by the old Kanikar and other bystanders. Sitting thus, a little boy was brought before him and he (the man in the flowers) called the lad by a name. And this was his christening ceremony, for the lad assumed the name from that date. The chief dancer then stood up and appeared to be in a possessed state still, and immediately, a fine old rooster was brought in, and its throat was cut by the Kanikar and handed to the dancer who eagerly applied his lips to the gaping wound and drained the blood, swallowing the fluid audibly. Before relinquishing his hold of the bird, he swayed and fell on the ground in what seemed to be a swoon. This indicated that the sacrifice had been acceptable, that the propitiation was perfected and that all the wishes of the persons interested in them would be granted. The crowd then set to eating and drinking the sacrificial elements and dispersed an hour or two after—the drums for a wonder remaining silent after the ceremony" [1].

General character and present condition. The Kāṉikkar maintain a reputation for a high standard of domestic honour and morality. They are thoroughly straight-forward, honest and truthful, so much so, that they afford an interesting object lesson to the more civilized people on the plains. Rude, hardy and courageous, as they are, they are altogether inoffensive. They are hospitable to strangers and afford them every assistance during their sojourn on the hills. The vice of drunkenness is their besetting sin. It is of almost universal prevalence and it is difficult to wean them from it. Christian Missionary endeavours have not had much success among these simple people. Of their present condition, Mr. Honiss observes, "The fate of the hill kings is rather sad. For ages past they have boasted of being the undisputed lords of the primeval forests. The elephant and tiger were their only foes; but with snares and traps they could hold their own against these enemies. But they could not resist the onward march of a superior race. The planter approaches them in a peaceable way offering wages for their hire, but demanding as his right the land he has purchased. The proud men of the woods decline to herd with coolies, and work like common people. As soon as the planter's axe is heard, the hill kings pack their traps and desert their homes to establish themselves in another valley. In this way they have been

1. *Malabar Quarterly Review*, Vol. IV, pp. 81—3.

driven from hill to hill and from valley to valley, until some have found now a safe resting place in the dense jungles of the low lands of Travancore. If the planter wishes to penetrate some unexplored jungle, or cut a path in some out-of-the-way place, the hill men are ready to assist, and it is the universal testimony that they are more faithful to their engagements than their more civilized brethren from the plains".[1]

The Mala Arayans. The Mala Arayans of Travancore are a much more civilized class than other hill tribes. They are not a migratory population like the others. They live in settled villages and have their cultivated lands and pastures which they own for themselves. They are a Dravidian people who live on the western slope of the Western Ghats between Quilon in the South and the Travancore-Cochin boundary line on the north.

Designation. Though the tribe is called Arayan, they have no affinity whatever with the Arayans of the coast who are fishermen. The coincidence in name is but an accident. The Mala Arayans inhabit the Koṭṭārakkara, Changanāssēri and Paṭṭānāpuram Taluks. They number 2,048 men. The word Mala Arayan is not definite in its denotation and often applies to the Kāṉis as well.

Appearance, clothing and ornaments. The Arayans are for the most part short in stature. The men average 5 feet 6 inches in height. They are generally not a very long lived race. The feverishness of the climate in the districts they inhabit is enough to account for any physical degeneracy of race. They are in colour as fair as the high caste Hindus, the women frequently beautiful, showing that the aboriginies of India are not black from race peculiarities, but only sometimes black through circumstances. Their features are as a rule, well formed. The lips are thin and the nose frequently aquiline. They wear the Kuṭumi in the front like

1. *Quoted in Native Life in Travancore*, page 66—67.

Nāyars. They are addicted to drunkenness and this makes the middle aged look older than they really are; while the young men, from exercise in the clear mountain airs, have a healthy look. They are rich enough to possess some gold ornaments and, deck themselves in these, and make use of better clothing than others.

Food and drink. Being large cultivators of hill slopes, some of them are rich, and most of them have plenty of paddy to live upon. They are great hunters of wild beasts and have a partiality for monkey flesh. From this they are called by the low country people *Kurangan Teeni*, i. e., "monkey eaters." They draw toddy from two wild palms of the hills, and much arrack is taken to them from the low country. Drunkenness is their great drawback and drunken fits and quarrels are of frequent occurrence among them. They chew tobacco, which they grow themselves, along with the bark of a tree in place of arecanut.

Living and occupation. Their villages consist of houses scattered all over the steep hill sides like bird's nests perched among the rocks. These are often lovely spots, in a ravine not accessible to elephants, near to some rushing rivulet falling over granite rocks, and surrounded by gigantic trees and palms. Their villages are often situated between 500 and 2,000 feet above the sea level. Many of their houses are good, substantial erections of wood and stone, built by workmen from the plains, and after the fashion common to the western coast, but in many cases they prefer temporary huts of mud, bamboo and grass thatch, as the survivors often dislike living in a dwelling in which the head of the family has died. Small huts are also built on trees for watching and for security against wild beasts. Every son has his own room in the family house, into which no one intrudes excepting himself and his wife. There is a general store for provisions for the family, which is provided by all in common, but each individual has, in addition his own cultivation and store, to provide for his private wants.

They will not work for hire generally and are very averse to carrying loads. They carry their produce in baskets slung on their shoulders. They are large cultivators of the hill slopes, which they clear of jungle in the dry season, sowing during the rains. This gives them abundance of rice. The Arayans have certain signs to be observed when fixing on land for cultivation or site of a house, but no other elaborate religious rites. In choosing a piece of ground for cultivation, before cutting the jungle, they take five strips of bark of equal length, and knot all the ends together, holding them in the left hand by the middle. If all, when tied, form a perfect circle, the omen is lucky and the position in which the cord falls on the ground is carefully noted by the bystanders. Little terraces are cut out on the steep ascents to prevent elephants from getting at them, and some protection is obtained by high and strong fences made of wood from the trees that have been felled. Every man has, however, to be on the look out with loaded guns, during seed and harvest times, to protect the crops from elephants, deer and other animals as well as from the swarms of birds which destroy the crops, and tigers and leopards which kill the cattle. They are also frequently exposed to drowning in the swollen torrents during the monsoon, to falls from trees and precipices which they climb to procure fruits and honey. The headman of the village is considered very wealthy, his annual crops yielding him ten or twelve thousand paras (say four or five thousand bushels) of paddy besides other grains, pulses and roots.

Caste, position, etc. Though sometimes spoken of as an inferior race by the Hindus, they are considered to rank in caste above all mechanics and artizans. They keep themselves off from Chōgans or Īluvans for fear of defilement. The Chōgans however consider themselves superior to the Arayans. The more degraded *Mala Arasirs* of the south are not allowed by them to be of the same race. Their language is a corrupt form of Malayalam with several words which are not known on the coast. The southern *Mala Arasirs* speak Tamil.

Marriage. The marriage ceremony of the Arayans is simple. The bridegroom and the bride sit together and eat off the same plantain leaf, which shows their relationship. After this, the bridegroom ties the Ṭāli round the bride's neck, and a collection is made for the happy couple, which is concluded by the bride taking possession of any brass cooking vessels or gold ornaments in the house saying "this is my father's", then her husband appropriates them.

Marriage takes place generally when the woman is 17 or 18 years of age. Before the ceremony, the horoscopes of the parties are examined and the day fixed by the Kaṇiyāṇ or astrologer, invitations are issued and a pandal erected and the bride is placed seated inside. The bridegroom is then brought up by his friends who demand to know who is inside. The reply is such and such Illakkār, as the case may be. If the reply is satisfactory, they enter and the bride is brought and placed in the centre. The conductor of the ceremonies on the bride's behalf proclaims in a loud voice. "I am to give a woman of such Illam to a man of such Illam". On the bridegroom's behalf, a similar announcement is made. A set of new clothes is presented by the bridegroom to the bride, and afterwards the happy pair sit to eat, out of the same vessel or leaf. Then follows the ṭāli tying.

The marriage tie is held sacred and indissoluble. Polygamy is almost unknown and considered disgraceful. Adultery is considered a great crime. Infant marriage is unknown among them, but the Keṭṭu Kallyāṇam has been copied from the Nāyars and Īluvas of the plains though differing in particulars. As soon as a woman attains maturity, relatives and friends are summoned to a feast. The Pūśāri or the priest having fixed the propitious hour, the girl is brought in and made to stand on a plank of jack-wood (a tree considered sacred by the Arayans), the father's sister then ties the ṭāli or thread round the neck, the feast is then partaken of and the ceremony is considered complete. The prevailing system of inheritance is Makkaṭṭāyam. There are however three Arayan villages which follow Marumakkaṭṭāyam said to be forced on them by a local chief.

They are divided into Illams or clans. There can be no marriage between members of the same Illam. Men of a superior Illam may marry a woman of an inferior Illam, but not the other way, *i. e.*, they observe the Malayāli rule of Anulōma and Pratilōma. The chief Illams are the Pūṭāni and Maṇḍa. Inferior to these are the Walla etc., But lowest of all are those known as the "Three Thousand." All the Illams eat together, the objection is only as to intermarriage. Women occupy a much better position among the Arayans than among the higher classes. They are regarded as equal to men, move about unrestrictedly and eat with their husbands, especially at feasts.

Other ceremonies. The birth of a child renders the mother impure for a month, when she must reside outside the village and cannot cook or go near springs or enter the provision grounds or touch any implements or vessels. She generally lives in a hut on a tree. The father also is impure for a week and must not eat rice ; but like the mother, must live on roasted roots and water.

A child, when a month old, is seated in the father's lap and fed with a little sweetened rice; the omission of this ceremony implies it to be illegitimate. The maternal grand-father and other near relatives repeat the ceremony.

As a rule, the names of individuals among the Arayans are not Hindu. They signify some personal peculiarity such as Kaṇṇan—"the eyed one"; Poṭṭan—"the deaf one"; Ṭaṭiyan—"the fat one". For females, Maḍhura—"the sweet one"; Ponna—"the gold one"; Chakkara—"the sugar one". Puranic names are however coming into use, specially among those of them who are under the influence of Nāyars.

Death ceremonies. "The Arayans bury their dead; consequently there are many ancient tumuli in these hills, evidently graves of chiefs, showing just the same fragments of pottery, brass figures, iron weapons, etc.. as are found in other similar places. These tumuli are often surrounded with long splintered pieces of granite, from eight to twelve or fifteen in length, set upon end, with sacrificial altars and other remains, evidently centuries old. Numerous vaults too, called *Pandi Kuzhi*, are seen in all these hills. They stand north and south, the circular opening being to the south; a round stone is fitted to this aperture with another acting as a long lever, to prevent its falling out; the stones at the sides, as also those at the top and bottom, are single slabs. To this day the Arayans make similar little cells of pieces of stone, the whole forming a box a few inches square; and on the death of a member of any family, the spirit is supposed to pass, as the body is being buried, into a brass or silver image, which is shut into this vault; if the parties are very poor, an oblong smooth stone suffices. A few offerings of milk, rice, toddy and ghee are made, a torch lighted and extinguished, the figure placed inside the cell and the covering stone hastily placed on; then all leave. On the anniversary, similar offerings being made, the stone is lifted off, and again hastily closed. The spirit is thus supposed to be enclosed; no one ventures to touch the cell at any other time".[1]

The Rev: A. F. Painter, discoursing before the Bombay Anthropological Society on the Hill Arrians of Travancore, gives a long account of the ceremonies

1. *Native Life in Travancore*, page 74.

observed on death which, he says, are the most elaborate and important. Death brings defilement to the members of the family and none may eat until after the funeral. The body is bathed and betel-nut placed in the mouth. A member of the deceased's Illam is chosen as master of the ceremonies. He bathes, wears a strip of new cloth after the fashion of the Brahmanical thread, proceeds to the place where the grave is to be dug and calls upon the earth to give up six feet. Advancing backwards he digs with a hoe and removes three hoesful of earth after which the grave is dug by others. The body is laid in it with the head always to the south, and earth is thrown in. He then advances backwards and draws with a knife three lines round the grave, which is supposed to protect it from evil spirits. A cocoanut is broken over the grave, some paddy strewn on the top and lights placed at its head and foot. The master of the ceremonies returns to the house round which he walks three times, with two sticks tied crossways with rags soked with oil tied in the ends and lighted, attended by the members of the houses. The sticks are then placed one at the head and the other at the foot of the grave. A tiny shed of cocoanut leaves is next made on the eastern side of the house. Here *Bali* is offered for the first ten or fifteen days according to the custom of the locality. A small quantity of unboiled paddy is taken and beaten carefully, then boiled and pressed into the shape of a ball; a cocoanut is broken and these together are placed before the small hut; the master of the ceremonies bending forward on one knee, twists his hands round each other seven times and then places them beneath his knee, bowing his forehead to the ground. The rice is then thrown at the foot of a jack tree. Small lamps made of leaves are lighted on four sides of the hut. In some places, on the 10th and 11th, in others on the 15th and 16th days, the chief ceremonies are performed. Early in the morning, the relatives of the deceased having bathed, the master of the ceremonies, still retaining the strip of cloth tied as a sacred thread, takes up the small hut and carries it thrice round the house, then to the grave where it is placed. A new cloth and (in some places) the dead man's property—gun, knife, topee, betel-box—are placed upon the grave. A plantain leaf is cut up into five small pieces, which are placed opposite the hands, feet and head; a little rice is placed in each and pūja done. The cloth and dead-man's property are then carried into the house. There is much divergence of practice in this respect. In some places only a cloth is placed in the grave, a white stone is taken from the earth and wrapped in it and then conveyed to the house. In others the cloth is not taken back to the house at all, but becomes the property of the washerman. In all places, after the ceremonies at the grave are all over, all bathe, a clean new cloth is placed in an inner room of the house and on it the dead man's property, knife topee, betel-box etc., etc. A feast is prepared, plantain leaf is cut into narrow strips, rice, boiled fowl, plantain, fish, toddy, arrack and parched rice are placed upon the leaves, lights are lighted, the master of the ceremonies then does pūja to the spirit which is now supposed to be in the house. The door is closed and the spirit is left to feast. After half an hour it is opened and the things taken forth. At the conclusion of the ceremony, the whole assembly partake of a feast consisting of fish, rice and arrack (the latter in abundance). The spirit is then said to have become a Nāṭṭu Ḍēvaṭa. As soon as possible, an image of the deceased is prepared, which is brought into the house. Similar offerings of those mentioned above are offered before it, and it is then placed, among others, under a tree in a little niche of laterite. Twice a year similar offerings are presented and in times of drought, ravages by wild beasts or sickness, vows are made and prayers such as "O Ancestor, be not angry with us", are offered.

Religion. The objects of Arayan worship are the spirits of their deceased ancestors or local demons supposed to reside in rocks or peaks and having influence only over particular villages or families. Female ancestors receive equal honour with males. The religious services rendered to these are intended to prevent or avoid anger rather than to seek benefits; but in no case is lust to be gratified or wickedness practised, as pleasing to these deities. Each family keeps an image of a demonized ancestor which is worshipped with great reverence. Lamps are kept burning to the memory of their ancestors. In cases of sickness, sometimes, Arayans make offerings to Hindu gods. The Hindu deities worshipped are the god Ayyappan or Śāsṭa and the goddess Bhaḍra Kāli. They go in large numbers to the chief shrine of the former at Śowri Mala, and even human sacrifices are said to be offered to the latter elsewhere. They also attend the great Hindu feasts occasionally; but in no case do they believe that they are under any obligation to do so, their own spirits being held fully equal to the Hindu gods. These are known as Malla Mūṛṭi Nāyāṭṭū Pey, etc. Each village has its priest who, when required, calls on the "Hill" (Mala) which means the demon resident there or the Prēṭam, ghost. If he gets the afflatus, he acts in the usual way, yelling and screeming out the answers sought. They have some sacred groves, where they will not fire a gun or speak about or breathe.

Of the religion and worship of these primitive people, the Rev. Richard Collins makes the following interesting observation: "Cast upon the desolate wilds and primeval forests of India, they seem long since to have lost almost every trace of a Divine law. They do, indeed, acknowledge a supreme spirit, whom they originally named Kō, or Kōn, the King; but whatever the case may have been once, they now offer him no worship. While the Sanskrit language is rich in theological terms, the aboriginal language, of which our Malayalam is a branch, contained or retained scarcely any. The religion of these ancient tribes consists in the worship, if it can be so called, of their ancestors, which is an offering made yearly, on the anniversary of death, before a rude image, generally of bronze or brass, the effigy of the ancestors; and they worship demons through the intervention of a devil-dancer. The man who is to perform this unenviable office, generally the headman of the village, puts on a brazen belt covered with a number of small bells, and hollow bangles, with pieces of copper inside to rattle, round his ankles. With a staff in his hand, also hung with small bells, and other paraphernalia, the man then begins to jump and dance to the increasing sound of tom-toms, cymbals, and like noisy affairs, sometimes even lacerating his flesh till he is apparently in a frenzy, and is thought to be, perhaps is, possessed by the demons; when a terrific shout is raised by the people, and he is supposed to be able to give an oracular response to any question that may be put to him."[1]

Sorcery and Witchcraft. The Arayans are supposed to be great sorcerers. They are looked upon as beings in alliance with some powerful demons. Presents are often given them in order to prevent their curses producing ill effects.

General character and present condition. The Arayans are a set of independent, respectable people free and somewhat intelligent in their manners, more truthful and generally moral in their habits than the people of the plains. "These mountain-men" says Mr. Mateer "were in former times terribly fleeced and oppressed by their rulers and by powerful neighbours. The Sirkar required each individual to furnish a certain quantity of wax and wild honey and firewood for temples without remuneration, also to assist in catching elephants. They were otherwise free even from paying land-tax. The Kānikar people, though freemen, paid head money for themselves and all males who had died within the previous ten years, besides the usual land-

1, *Missionary Enterprise in the East*, pages 240—41.

tax and ground rents and taxes on fruit trees; and were besides fleeced by the local petty officers. The services required furnished occasion for continual annoyance and exactions. The Arayans of Todupuley, it is said, are still much oppressed by their Mahammadan neighbours.

"The Puniathu Rajah who ruled over those at Mundapalli, made them pay head-money—two chakrams a head monthly as soon as they were able to work—and a similar sum as "presence money", besides certain quotas of fruit and vegetables, and feudal service. They are also forced to lend money, if they possessed any, and to bring leaves and other articles without any pretext of paying them, and that for days. The men of these villages were thus placed in a worse condition than the slaves. This petty Raja used to give a silver headed cane to the principal hill-man who was then called Perumban, cane man".[1]

The condition of the Mala Arayans has been considerably improved by the proseletysing endeavours of Christian Missionaries. About 1849, the late Rev. Henry Baker, Junior, began the work of evangelizing and civil sing these interesting tribes and the good work is still kept up by the Kottayam Mission much to their own credit and to the benefit of these wild men.

Long before the Protestant Missionaries entered on the task of converting the *Malayars* or Hill tribes to Christianity, the Portuguese had made a successful attempt to bring them into the fold of the Romish Church. But their endeavours being not sustained, their so-called converts soon relapsed to their old beliefs. In the year 1599, Archbishop Menezes sent out a mission to these Hill men. The mission started on their journey on the 16th of July and reached the foot of the Ghauts in eight days. Gouvea calls this place, "Carathnarat, in the kingdom of Canarate—a territory little known in Malabar." Nieuhoff

1. *Native Life in Travancore*, page 78.

calls the place, "Karatkara, bordering on the kingdom of Karnata". Whitehouse supposes this to be identical with Karōṭṭukara (the higher land) a name by which the hills in that part are occasionally called. Here they met some isolated Christian settlers with whom they stayed for ten days, after which they proceeded on their errand, taking one of the Christians as their guide to the summit of the mountain range. They were taken to a 'Malean' chief who is said to have had under his jurisdiction '5,000 Malears.' The object of the Mission was explained to him by Simon, the elder of the two Caṭṭanārs or native priests who headed the Mission. The Malayans could, however, do nothing without the previous sanction of their Rajas, the chiefs of Ṭiruvella and Pūññāt, to whom they were subject. The Caṭṭanārs therefore simply planted the cross and prepared to return and report the results to the Archbishop. The Malayan chief accompanied the Mission on their return journey to the foot of the ghauts and parted with them at the Church of Corolangād promising to repair thither when the Archbishop would visit the place and bring with him the consent of the Raja to whom he was subject. On the return of the Mission, Menezes approached the Rajas of Ṭiruvella and Pūññāt with handsome and valuable presents of precious stones and obtained formal permission for the baptism of the Head Malayas and his followers being converted to Christianity. The Archbishop then deputed the Syrian Archdeacon George and Stephen de Brito, Rector of the Vaipicotta College, and other Caṭṭanārs to administer the initiatory rite. Eight of the chiefs with their families received baptism, the first three of them being heads of district clans. Of the latter, one called Collegeira Paṇḍārā was christened Don Alexis after the Archbishop, the second Canaque Paṇḍāra, was named Don Stephen after the Rector of Vaippicōṭṭa; and the last Don George after the Archdeacon. The authorities having given their permission, a Church was also erected for them dedicated to

St. Michael. Such was the first Christian Mission to these wild men. They seem to have been afterwards neglected altogether by the Romanists till the Protestant Missionaries took them in hand almost three centuries after.

Other Hill tribes of Travancore. The other hill tribes of Travancore need not detain us long. As regards appearance, the *Mutuvans*, who claim superiority over all the other tribes, are probably the tallest and have the best features of all, with aquiline noses, beards and mustachios. The *Mannans* have as a rule little hair on their faces, but they are pleasant looking, bright and quick.

The Mannans, Mutavans, and Uralis all say that they were originally dependants of the king of Madura whence they emigrated into the Travancore hills. The Pūññāt Raja, a Pandyan chief, who settled himself among the hills is said to have nominated three of these Maṇṇans as his agents at three different centres in his dominions. To one he gave a silver sword and called him Varayilkīl Maṇṇān, to the second a bracelet and called him Gōpura Maṇṇān, and to the third a silver cane and called him Ṭaḷamala Maṇṇan. The Muṭavans believe that they were driven to the hills in the latter part of the 18th century by the Muhammadan invaders. They say that, on their coming away, they carried on their Muṭu, back, the goddess Mīnākṣhi of Madura, hence their name Muṭavan, *i. e.*, those who carried something on their back. The chief of the Muṭavan is known as *Vakka*. The Urālis according to tradition were dependants of the King of Madura and their duty was to hold umbrellas in times of state procession. Their ancestors are said to have accompanied the king while on a visit to the hilly tracts which were then under his sway, and were left behind to rule, hence Ūrāli (Ūr=village and Āli=one who rules). Their headmen are called Kāṇikkāran. The headmen of all these communities exact a lot of miscellaneous service from those under them. It is only with their consent that marriages can be performed. With Maṉṉāns marriage takes the form of ṯāli-tying, the ṯāli being removed on the death of the husband, while with the Muṯavans the bridegroom only presents new cloths to the bride. The Urālis dispense with this even. With them, after the marriage is settled, the girl is merely sent to the pandal or the hut of the husband. There is with the Muṯavans the peculiar practice of carrying away the bride by force from her mother's house after the marriage is settled. She is forcibly taken away and the couple live by themselves in some secluded part of the forest for a few days whence they are either brough t back or return themselves. The Urālis inter-marry with Ullāṯans and in rare cases with the Muṯavans. A Maṉṉān always claims the hand of his maternal uncle's daughter.

Remarriage is permitted to the Maṉṉān and the Urāli. Widows of the former class generally wait for two years before they marry again. With all the three tribes Marumakkaṯṯāyam is the prevailing form of inheritance; but a portion is given to the sons also.

Dress and Ornaments. The males among the Maṉṉāns and Muṯavans and the females among the former dress like the Maṟavans of the plains. With the Muṯavan male, a huge turban is indispensible and, before such turban can be worn, the consent of the head-man has to be obtained. A Muṯavan female dresses herself with 10 or 12 cubits of white or coloured cloth. The males of the Urālis dress like the low country people with cloths about 4 cubits long extending from the hip to the knee. Another cloth, about one or two cubits in length, is put over their back, one end of which passes under their right arm and another over the shoulder, both meeting in front, over the chest where they are tied together in a peculiar knot by folding the extremities, thus forming a bag wherein to contain their way-side necessaries. Females wear two pieces of cloth nine and two and a half cubits in length respectively and folded in the middle. The larger or lower garment and the smaller or upper garment is worn with the two ends tied round their neck with a brass or iron zone for the waist. In addition to this, Muṭava females have bracelet for the upper arm called *Mutakku*. Both Muṭava and Urāli females have ear and nose ornaments. Those of the former are mostly of brass while the ear ornaments of the latter known as *Kattumani* are rings of metalic wire four or five in number. The Maṉṉāns wear ear rings of silver and brass while the Urāli adorns his fingers and toes with rings of silver. The latter deck themselves in wreaths of coloured leads from 15 to 30 in number. He allows his hair to grow, shaving the face alone.

Habitation, Food and Language. The Maṉṉāns put up the best huts among all the hill tribes. These hill men subsist mostly on roots, fruits, and other forest produce as also on game, but the Urālis, being cultivators of forest land, eat rice for 6 months of the year. But a large portion of the paddy goes to the low country in exchange for clothing and salt. The Maṉṉāns eat the flesh of the monkey but not that of the fox, crocodile, snake, buffalo or cow. The Urālis eat the flesh of most animals; but the elephant and buffalo are held in such great respect that no Urāli will even venture to hurt them. Even the approach of the buffalo is religiously avoided. The Urālis speak a kind of corrupt Malayalam while the language of the Maṉṉāns is Tamil and that of Muṭavans has no connection with Malayalam but is a corruption of Tamil having a peculiar intonation.

Occupation. The Maṉṉāns really cultivate any thing but ragi. They are employed by the Sirkar to collect honey, in which they are experts, cardamoms, and keep watch, etc. The Muṭavans cultivate some land and to pay no taxes to Government, but have to serve the Sirkar when called on, at favourable rates of wages, in gathering forest produce. The Urālis occupy themselves in migratory cultivation in a rude way, using only a Kaṭṭi, a kind of chopping knife, for purposes of ploughing. They make excellent mats of reeds. They hoard their grains in wicker baskets called *Virivallams*. They are clever huntsmen and are passionately attached to their hunting dogs. They possess copper and brass vessels, mortar, chopping knives, axes, sickles, spades, flint and steel.

Ceremonial Pollution. Both the Muṭavan and the Urāli observe pollution of a very aggravated kind during the menstural and pureperal periods. With the Maṉṉāns it is not so repelling. At both periods the woman is lodged in a separate Māṭam or hut at a distance from the main one where she has to stay for three days. After bathing on the fourth day, she shifts to another Māṭam, nearer and stays there for one or two days. On the seventh day she rejoins the family. In cases of confinement, 12 days are spent in the remotest hut and 5 days in the nearer one. But, for a period of another 20 days, she is not permitted to touch any one in the house or even the roofing of the hut. During these days, food is prepared by others and given her. The water in which those who are confined and those who are in their menses bathe is considered to be defiled beyond remedy. Hence, for bathing purposes, some secluded and out of the way pool called Pattuvellam is selected. Urālis coming to the low country hesitate to drink water on suspicion that it might be thus polluted. When the woman delivers herself of her first child, her husband observes three days pollution but more for subsequent confinement.

Death and Burial.—The Maṉṉāns bury their dead in a coffin made of bamboo and reeds and the corpse is taken to the grave with music and beating of drums. The personal ornaments, if any, are not removed. Before covering the grave a quantity of rice is put into the mouth of the deceased. A shed is erected over the site of the burial. After a year is past, an offering of food and drink is made to the dead. The Urālis also bury their dead, but not in a coffin. Each relative has to put a cloth into the grave. After covering the grave, they erect a shed over it like the Maṉṉāns and place within it the chopping knife of the deceased, a quantity of boiled rice and some betel and nuts. After the lapse of 7 years, an offering of food and drink is made to the departed soul. Death pollution lasts for 16 days.

Religion. Sorcery. All the three tribes are demon worshippers and dabble much in sorcery and witchcraft. The would-be sorcerers of the Urālis have to leave the community and wander over the forests alone for a number of months to enable their masters to initiate them in the mystic art. While so wandering, they are said to go into a trance when their ancestors appear before them as maidens and initiate them. The Urālis as well as the Maṉṉāns have more faith in enchantments called *Cheppuka* and *Chattuka* for the cure of diseases than in medicine, though the Maṉṉāns have the reputation to stand ahead of all other hillmen in the knowledge of the latter. The principal deities worshipped by the Muṭavans are Chānṭiāṭṭu Bhagavaṭi and Neriamangalam Śāsṭa. The Maṉṉān worships the Śāsṭa of Śabarimala and Periyar.

Location. The Maṉṉāns inhabit the Cardamom Hills and their number is 1,172. The Muṭavans number 808 souls and are to be found in the Cardamom Hills and the Taluks of Muvvāṟṟupuḻa and Ṭoṭupuḻa. Only 220 Mala Urālis have been returned for the State at the last Census and they reside in the Ṭoṭupuḻa Taluk.

There are a few other hill tribes of Travancore who may be named here: Mala Pulayans, Hill Panṭarams and Kāṭar. The Mala Pulayans are a hunting class who are not far removed from the Urālis and speak Tamil. The Hill Panṭārams go about, almost naked, without implements or huts, living in the holes, rocks or trees. They collect honey, wax, ivory and other forest produce and exchange them for salt, tobacco, etc., with the Arayans. They dig roots, snare the ibex and jungle fowls, eat rats and snakes and even crocodiles found in the pools amongst the hill streams. They are filthy to a great extent. They speak a sort of corrupt Malayalam. All those jungle tribes have generally the same rules and notions respecting women, property, demonology, etc., as the Arayans.

The Mala Aṭiyars. The Mala Aṭiyars are an interesting tribe inhabiting the Lower Periyar Valley. The term Mala Aṭiyar means "Mountain slaves" (aṭi-foot) and they resemble the Urālis in many respects such as stature, physique, colour, facial contour, dress, habits, language, customs and manners.

Appearance, Dress and Ornaments. Mr. Sawyer, late of the Travancore Forest Department, describes them as of middle height, fairly thickset, dark brown in colour, with brownish-to-black eyes, curly hair, flat noses, protruding upper lips, receding foreheads and chins, prominent cheek bones and generally smooth faces. Both men and women wear the hair long, either loose or knotted on the top of the head. The men ordinarily wear a loin-cloth reaching down to the knees, while another, thrown over the body, is passed over the right shoulder and under the left arm, the ends being tied into a knot over the chest. The women wear a single cloth, the upper end of which is passed under the arms and covers the bosom. The lower end reaches above the knee. The men wear finger and toe rings also ear-rings of iron or brass, and frequently as many as six pairs are worn in the same ear-hole. The earlobes of the women are artificially distended and discs of the soft white wood or flattened rolls of lead are worn. Several wreaths of glass beads of many colours are worn round the neck. They have also finger and toe rings, and round their waists they wear zones of iron and brass.

Habits. Their habits are extremely filthy. They seldom bathe, and their dark skins are frequently coated over with an ashen incrustation of dirt and mud. From want of due attention to the hair, it turns a reddish-yellow in colour, particularly at the far ends and is sometimes matted. Their cloths are invariably dirty and emit an offensive odour.

Occupation. The chief occupations of the tribe are shifting cultivation, hunting with dogs and fishing. Besides living upon the indigenous wild yams, roots and fruits, and the smaller animals of the forest, such as the Iguana lizard, tortoise, arm-adillo, hedghog, etc., they cultivate in small patches all the commoner crops raised in the low country. A portion of the produce is bartered in the plains in exchange for salt, cloths, knives, tobacco, arrack, bhang and opium. They are adicted to drinking. Some of them smoke bhang, but the majority of the men, as well as a large number of the elderly women are slaves to opium eating. They however keep within bounds.

Amusements. The Mala Aṭiyans like the Urālis are fond of singing and dancing. On special occasions, both men and women dance round a bonfire to the accompaniment of loud chanting, tom-toming, the clapping of hands and dry tamboo slips and the jingling of tiny brass bells tied on to the arms and legs. When dancing they put on their cleanest cloths. Girdles of sambir or deer-skin with the hair on, are worn over the waists from which their ends descend as down as the knees. Cloths are sometimes tied over the head or folded and thrown over the shoulders. In the latter case, the ends are held in the hands while dancing.

The language of the Mala Aṭiyar is Malayalam, which is however spoken with a quaint Tamil intonation. They live in meagre huts situated in the dense and ever green wilds they have selected for their dreary abode.

Marriage. Their marriage ceremony is very simple with no trace of any religious element in it. The betrothal is made when the girl is 3 or 4 and the boy 8 or 10 years old. A maternal uncle's son is the most eligible match for a girl. The betrothal consists in the mothers of the girl receiving a string of red glass bead from the bridegroom and tying it round the neck of her daughter. This corresponds to the *Kettu Kallyanam* of the Nāyars. A loin cloth is at the same time accepted and worn by the girl. The real marriage takes place on the girl attaining maturity when an auspicious day is selected on which the members of the tribe assemble in a pandal at the bride's house. The mother of the bridegroom stands up in the assembly and declares her willingness to take care of the bride as if she were her own child. The bridegroom, in his turn, then stands up and declares that, in sickness or health, sunshine or storm, in plenty or famine, he would support his bride, as best he could then, and ever after. The bride, who sometimes has as many as ten companions or bride's maids, then promises, in return, for the assurances already received, that, so long as her husband lives, she will not hold the hand of another man. This is the ceremony, pure and simple, yet solemn enough without any incantations or prayers. A feast follows and the next day the bride is taken to the bridegroom's house, her parents and other relatives accompanying her. The party is accommodated in a pandal erected for the occasion. Here another feast is given by the bridegroom. Singing and dancing follow and are kept up till morning. The bride, it is interesting to note, does not speak to the bridegroom for two or three days; if necessary, she communicates with him through his or her mother or other elderly female of the family. Both bride and bridegroom are well dressed and the bride's hair is ornamented with wild flowers, chiefly jasmine. Such is the simple, yet solemn marriage ceremony of these wild unsophisticated men, a life-long union is effected without the interference of any priest and without having recourse to *mantrams*, bell ringings, *homams* and prayers. The civilised Marumakkaṭṭāyam Malayalees of the plains who are on the look-out for a simple form of marriage need not at all be ashamed to take a lesson from these 'barbarians'. Widow marriage is allowed and polygamy is seldom practised. If a man commits adultery, he has to compensate the woman and her relatives with presents of money and grain—a severe drain on their scanty resources, and therefore a heavy punishment for the offence. If a woman be guilty of the offence, she is discarded by the tribe; she may, however, be received back into her father's house, where she remains until remarried by a man of a kindred tribe or clan, for no one of her own tribe or clan will marry her again. The Mala Aṭiyars follow the Marumakkaṭṭayam system of inheritance.

Observances at birth. The observances attending birth are like those of the Urālis, with the main difference that, when the woman is advanced in pregnancy, she is taken to her father's hut and the delivery takes place there. The husband leaves the woman there, giving her all necessaries and returns home. On being apprised of the birth of the child he goes with a supply of provisions and things, some of which are presented to the midwife. The same practices with regard to pollution, uncleanliness, living in separate huts, bath, etc., as among Urālis prevail among the Mala Aṭiyars also. The child is named on the fourth day after birth, the name being announced by its maternal grandmother in the presence of the assembled tribesmen. The names commonly in use for men are Kuññu Kōṭa Kaṇḍen, Moli Kaṇṇan Rāman, and Vēlayuḍhan. Of these only the last two names are Hindu and Puranic. The names of females are Kochi, Kaychi, Pankachi, Kuṙumba, Kāli, Kōṭamma, Kuññama, and Māli, all Dravidian names.

Illness—Death. All illness is attributed to the influence of the spirits of ancestors, so that when one falls ill, it is the exercisor whose aid is sought, and not that of the physician. He practises his art, goes through many tedious gesticulations, croonings and incantations and the whole proceedings are enlivened by tom-tom beating and other noisy accompaniments. In bad cases the manes are propitiated by the sacrifice of fowls.

When a man dies, the calamity is attributed to the anger of the manes or of a malignant spirit who is forthwith propitiated with sacrifices. No member of the family partakes of food for 24 hours succeeding the funeral. The body is enshrouded in a new cloth and is rolled up in the mat on which the person died. It is carried to the grave on a rude bier improvised of reeds and sticks. An elder, often not a relative of the deceased, is selected by the bereaved family as the celebrant of the funeral obsequies. The funeral cortege ordinarily consists of ten men, not counting the celebrant; only these eleven men are permitted to go to the burial ground. The grave is large and deep, its bottom and sides are neatly paved with cross-sticks and split bamboos and two new cloths are spread over the former. The body, bier and all, is lowered into it and the whole covered with two more new cloths. Before internment, however, that portion of the shroud, covering the face of the dead, is tenderly and carefully torn out and kept by the celebrant. The bier is then once more covered and fastened. The funeral party now arrange themselves, five on each side of the grave, and sit down near its margin with their backs towards it and their faces away from it. The body is laid with the head to the east. Directly above it, the celebrant sits, with reverently-bowed head and clasped hands, and while he utters incantations to the spirit of the dead, the earth is slowly thrown in by the silent tearful party of ten. Hands alone are used throughout the tedious function and, when the grave is completely filled in, the party turns round, and facing it, finishes by packing the earth over it in a compact mound. Three stones are then placed over the grave, one at each end and the third in the middle. An Ītta reed, about 6 feet long, is now stuck firmly over the grave; the party once more arrange themselves on both sides of it and successively placing their upturned hands one above the other in such a manner that the reed passes between each one's fingers, sway up and down four times. The reed is then taken up by the celebrant and thurst into the mound over the grave obliquely from end to end. A handful of paddy is, thereafter, scattered over the grave. A frond of the rattam palm, with leaves (pinnoe) and spines on, is then laid across the head of the grave and the silent party, after slowly walking round the grave four times step over it, and without once looking back, return to the hut of the deceased. On the way, however, and when well out of sight of the grave, they enter a stream, bathe, collect seven leaves of the wild arrow-root plant. These are taken and carefully placed in the caves of the hut in which the person died. On arriving at the hut, the members of the deceased's family who will have bathed and swept out the hut and premises, sprinkle the funeral party with cow-dung water. The celebrant, then entering the hut of the deceased, procures a new mat which he spreads in it. Over the middle of this mat, the piece of cloth that formed part of the torn shroud is neatly folded and laid lengthwise. A cocoa-nut shell containing cold water is placed over the cloth at one end of it. The celebrant then sits beside the mat, and dipping the knuckles of the little finger of his left hand into the water, touches the cloth with it. After this, he touches the shell with the fingers of the one hand and the end of the cloth with those of the other and gently approximates both palms until they meet before his chest in an attitude of devout and reverential adoration. This is repeated three times. Early the next morning, the funeral party of ten, accompanied by the celebrant, go to the nearest stream, cook a handful of rice, and, after bathing, stand side by side in a line facing east. Each one then crosses his hands with the palms downwards in such a manner that the right hand is uppermost. On the back of the latter, a little of the hot broth from the boiling rice, with a grain of salt, is placed by the celebrant. Each of the party then raises his still crossed hand to his lips and licking up the salt spits out before him. The cooked rice itself is taken and placed over a leaf near the water in the stream and the party returns to the hut. Late in the evening of the same day, boiled rice is served on one of the seven arrow-root leaves placed over the mat in the hut of the deceased, and, after the bereaved family mourns over it, a little child, boy or girl, is asked to eat it. The child readily obeys, and for the succeeding six evenings, the ceremony is repeated. On the eighth day, a feast is given, the shell and water are thrown away, and the strip of cloth torn into shreds, is twisted into a cord and worn by the child around its neck for one year. This strange practice is all the more interesting when it is remembered that the child, like the celebrant elder, is frequently no relative or connection of the deceased. The mat on which the ceremony is performed may be used by any member of the family, but it is usually given to the child. On the anniversary of the death, the male and female members of the deceased's family, shave a narrow ring of hair right round their heads, and bathe. The celebrant is presented with grain and provisions to the value of a rupee, a feast is given to the assembled tribesmen, and the mourning is considered at an end. [1]

Religion. The Mala Aṭiyạrs are ancestor and spirit worshippers. They however adore the Hindu divinities Śāsṭa and Bhagavaṭi both of whom are Dravidian deities rather than Aryan. They also adore the stone at Athirapilly under the name of *Cherthavu* (probably Śāsṭāvu). They have sacred groves; and even individual trees and rocks are looked upon with

1. *Malabar Quarterly Review*, Vol. III, pp. 256.

sentiments of awe and reverence. Evil spirits are dreaded and propitiated with sacrifice and incantations more than good ones.

General condition. It need scarcely be added that the general condition of these primitive people is very low. Living in the recesses of forests, hidden from the sight of civilization, they are impervious to all ideas of improvement, yet not having come in contact with the cunning and chicane of the low country, they are an honest lot, trying to eke out an existence in their own humble way. Any attempt to ameliorate their condition is highly necessary. The Christian Missionary has yet not reached them, and the Hindus of the plains rarely meet them as they live far away in the hills.

Malayar and Katar.

Designation and appearance. Amongst the hill tribes that inhabit the Cochin forests is a class called Malayar and another called Kāṭar. The terms Malayar and Kāṭar mean "hill men" and "jungle men." Except that they live in different localities in the Cochin forests, there is little or no difference between them. The Malayar are perhaps fairer in colour, thinner and less muscular, and more civilized in appearance than the Kāṭar who are dark, short and muscular with pointed thick lips and curly hair and less civilized in appearance. Both of them have great power of endurance.

Habitation. They live in groups of 8 to 20 huts, forming a village situated on the banks of a stream, or in an open glade in a dense forest and in the vicinity of a water supply. These villages are called Paṭis. The huts are made of bamboos, strong saplings and reeds, and thatched with teaks, date or reed leaves and leafy twigs and branches. The doors form sliding panels of bamboo work. A part of the floor inside is raised for them to sleep on. In some places, these huts are built on clumps of bamboos upon which a platform is first put up and the huts built on them. Entrance is afforded by means of a ladder made by cutting away the knots from a single bamboo outside the clump and leaving the root ends to serve as steps to ascend. Very often huts are constructed on trees as a means of security against the depradations of wild beasts. Their domestic utensils are of the simplest description; excepting a few earthen pots for cooking, all the rest is made of bamboo such as mats, vessels for holding water etc. They are very ingenious in adapting things found round them in the forests for their domestic purposes. They make fire by striking a piece of flint with a piece of steel; the sparks fall on a kind of pith which is like cotton.

Village organisation. Every village has a *Moopen* or headman who is elected by the villagers from among themselves. Sometimes the Mūpen derives his authority from the Raja, specially where the villages are situated in the Sirkar forests. The Mūpen is in such cases given a rod of office, tipped with silver at one end. Otherwise, the office is hereditary and descends from maternal uncle to nephew. He has considerable authority which, if properly exercised, are unlimited. If he abuses it, he is displaced by the villagers, and another elected. He has many privileges and perquisites. He presides at marriages, funerals and other ceremonies. He decides tribal altercations and family disputes and quarrels. His consent has to be obtained before anything out of the ordinary groove can be done. The Mūpen's wife is known as Mūppaṭṭi and her position, specially in the case of Kāṭars, among women, corresponds to that of her husband among men. The Malayars are said to be divided into certain clans which derive their designation either from the place-names of the localities they inhabit or from the personal names of some among them who have distinguished themselves in former times or from their occupations. The names of the clans are :—

(1) Kaṭaṭṭukkar; (2) Ṭōṇikar; (3) Pokenkar; (4) Eranāṭṭukar; (5) Ayambakar; (6) Nellakkar; (7) Chākkenkar; (8) Kutenkar; (9) Kuṇṇikar.

The Malayar are also divided into two sub-tribes:—

(1) The Kongu (Tamil) Malayar and (2) the Ṅāṭṭu (Native) Malayar.

The former are emigrants from the forests of the Coimbatore District. While Mr. Anantha Krishna Aiyar, the Cochin Ethnographic Surveyor, tells us that "these two sub-tribes widely differ in their customs and manners", Mr. K. Govinda Menon of the Cochin Forest department assures us, and he must know better, in a very interesting account of the hill tribes of Cochin given by him in the *Malabar Quarterly Review*, that "their religious and social observances, their customs and manners are all alike, except their form of mariage which is rather unique among the Kongu Malayars."[1]

Language. The Kongu Malayars speak Tamil while the rest of the tribe as well as the Kāṭar speak a mixture of slang Malayalam and Tamil. The Kāṭar's language contains more Tamil words. All speak with a peculiar intonation and their pronounciation is curious.

Dress and ornaments. The dress of both male and female members of the tribes is very simple. Males simply tie a piece of cloth round their loins while the females have one hanging from their chests to the knees. The Kāṭar of the Nelliampathies are now better dressed in dhoties, coats, petticoats etc. This is due to their being employed by European coffee planters who have extended their enterprise to these hills. The hair of the females, like that of the males, is wavy and is combed, oiled and neatly parted and tied behind with a comb stuck into it. It is said that the comb is not added to beautify but to be

1. Vol. 5, p. 295.

utilised in combing their hair when out in the jungles where they frequently stay for days and days together. The males wear ear-rings of brass. The females wear discs thrust into their ears the lobes of which are artificially distended. Round the neck they wear necklaces of brass and glass beads. Some wear brass nose rings and brass and bell-metal bangles and toe rings. There is an interesting custom observed by the Kāṭar that is not found with other classes, the chipping of all or some of the incisor teeth, both upper and lower, into the form of sharp pointed, but not serrated cones. The operation is performed with a chisel or bill hook and file by the members of the tribe skilled thereat, on boys at the age of eighteen and girls at the age of ten or thereabouts. The girl to be operated upon lies down and places her head against a female friend who holds the head firmly. A third woman takes a sharpened bill hook and chips away the teeth till they are shaded to a point, the girl operated on, writhing and groaning with the pain. After the operation, she looks dazed and, in a few hours, the face begins to swell. Swelling and pain last for a day or two accompanied by severe headache. The custom of deforming the teeth is not confined to Southern India, but is found prevailing among different tribes in Africa and Australia, where the practice is in general confined to the chipping of the incisor teeth.[1]

Occupation. The chief occupation of these tribes consists in gathering minor forest produce, such as honey, wax, dammer, ginger etc. The Sirkar employs them in this and in other works such as catching elephants and the like. They also work for the contractors of the low country who, in exchange for the honey etc. they supply, give them rice, tobacco, sundry provisions, cloth, opium, etc. They also do cooly work, while some have turned to agriculture. They are good trackers and huntsmen. They follow a wounded animal

1. *Ethnographical Survey of the Cochin State, Monograph No. 6, Kadars*, pp. 14—15.

with wonderful agility and find it out even from the densest recesses of the forest. They trace as if by instinct the devious paths of the forest and decide with almost unerring certainty on the number and variety of animals that may have traversed them. They know the animal by their foot prints and find out their whereabouts, probably by the peculiar and wonderful development of their olfactory nerves. They hunt tigers, bison and bears. Deer and wild hogs are caught in snares. During the summer months, they dam up mountain streams, poison the water and take the dead fish. The Kāṭars are peculiarly expert in climbing trees of great height. Honey gathering is a favourite occupation with them. They approach the honey combs on the top of the trees during the night, carring torches with them to burn the bees. This they easily do, but their greatest feat consists in gathering the honey of the rock bee which requires considerable daring and courage. The process is thus described by Mr. Anantha Krishna Iyer: "The honey of the rock-bee (Malānṭen) is of a superior quality. It is a large bee that builds its large nest in the cavities of rocks and on the edges of appalling precipices. It is a most fearful adversary, so much so that the native bee-collectors dare not attack it in the day time. If their nest is attacked by an intruder, the bees begin a united, persistent attack and, as their sting is severe, it is almost impossible to escape from the attack; it is most dangerous to go near them. The natives take the combs at night, and the mode of procedure evinces a cool daring which one would never expect even in such a daring race. At sunset the Kadar performs puja to his sylvan deity. He makes a chain of rings of rattan or bamboo ladder, and this chain, over 100 feet in length, is lowered from the top of the precipice until it reaches a point where the bee's nests are. This being done, a dark windy night is chosen, and the honey hunter, either alone or accompanied by his wife, brother or son and, in the pitch of darkness, descends this loosely hanging ladder with a fire brand, and chasing away the bees by means of his torch he collects the honey and thus secures the prize. To look at one of these ladders as it hangs over the face of some fearful cliff and to imagine the scene is to make one's flesh creep. For the horrible feast of daring he feels amply rewarded if a rupee is given. The bees appear to be sluggishly stupid on dark nights and hence the rationale of this method of procedure."

Those who work for the landlords as also those working for the forest department are given Ōṇam presents in the shape of rice, cloths, caps, coats, turban, ear rings, tobacco, opium, salt oil, cocoanuts etc. A large number of Kāṭars now work as maistries and coolies under coffee planters.

Food and Drink. These tribes live mostly on wild yams, roots and fruits of the forests. Rice is a luxury with the Kāṭars and the occasions on which they go in for it are very few. They rarely indulge in animal food. They however eat fish. They have a mortal aversion to the flesh of the bison. The Malayars live on rice so long as they could find the means of getting it in exchange for forest produce from the low country traders and contractors. In the morning before setting out for the day's work, the Malayar takes *Kanji* (gruel) prepared from the chama, Kora and Kambu. Their evening meal is the same accompanied with curries made of roots, yams etc. "Sometimes they make a delicious preparation out of bamboo seeds. They fill a hollow bamboo, two feet in length and four or five inches in diameter, with the seed above referred to, and fill it with honey and then close the mouth of the bamboo air-tight. This is then coated with a layer of earth and placed in a bright red hot fire, allowing sufficient time for the grain to be well boiled in honey. The bamboo splits, when quite red hot, and in the inside is seen a cylindrical soft and sweet mass, which forms

1. *Ethnographical Survey of the Cochin State. Monograph No. 6, Kadars, pp. 11 and 12.*

their dainty meal with which they welcome high castemen, who happen to stay in their midst for a night. This they consume with a deep draught of water. They eat the remains of carcase left by tigers, as also the flesh of deer, bison and goat but abstain from touching the flesh of the cow, wolf, elephant and tiger.

Menses—Marriage. Marriage takes place before and after puberty, but generally after. The match is arranged by the parents of the parties assisted by the Mūpen. The period of pollution caused by the appearance of the menses for the first time is 7 days with Malayars and 10 with Kāṭars. During this period they have to live in a separate hut and can join the family only after the ceremonial bath is over at the end of the period. The day is one of festivity to which castemen are invited. The Kāṭar women observe pollution to a greater extent than the Malayar; during their monthly periods, they are kept apart in a separate hut and no one is permitted to approach them within a certain distance. Like the Mala Aṭiyars, their idea of this species of impurity is so strong that they would not touch or take water from a reservoir or a stream in which a woman in her periods has bathed. Their marriage ceremony is simple enough. When the match has been arranged between the parents of the couple the boy's father gives a dinner to all his relations, as also two fanams to the girl for a new dress and one fanam (4 as. 7 ps.) worth of spirituous liquor to the guests. The girl is then delivered over to the boy and this constitutes a valid marriage among the Kongu Malayars. In some cases a wedding garment is given to the bride and a string dyed yellow to which a brass ring is attached is tied round her neck. Among Ñāṭṭu Malayars marriage is effected by a somewhat similar observance. The bridegroom's party goes to the bride's house where the guests are entertained. The wedding

1. *Ethnographical Survey of the Cochin State, Monograph No. 9, Malayers, p: 20.*

garment is given to the bride and the party leaves. Two or three weeks after this, the bride's party returns the visit and is in turn entertained after which the girl is handed over to the boy. The Kāṭars observe the rule of exogamy and a man is not permitted to marry a girl related to him on the male side. As a rule marriages between persons descended in a direct line from the same parents is forbidden. No bride price is paid but presents of cloths are given to the bride's relatives. There is no formal ceremony performed for the wedding. On the day appointed, the bridegroom goes to the hut of the bride escorted by friends and relatives who are given a cordial welcome and seated on mats. The couple stand face to face in a decorated pandal in front of the hut. Men and women keep dancing, separately, to the music of pipe and drum. The bridegroom's mother ties the ṭāli of gold or silver round the bride's neck and her father places a turban on the head of the boy. The little fingers of the right hands of the contracting parties are linked together as a token of their union and they walk in procession round the pandal. Then sitting on a mat of Kāṭar manufacture, they exchange betel. Another custom is for the person desirous of marrying to seek a wife in another village where he dwells for a whole year. When he has found a suitable match, he returns to his village gives her a dowry and ties the ṭāli round the neck of the bride. After the usual feast, the couple proceed to the husband's hut where his friends and relations are treated to a feast. After a few weeks, a new hut is erected where they reside and maintain themselves. With the Malayarṣ as well as the Kāṭars the ṭāli is cut and cast off on the death of the husband or on the severance of the connection between the two. Widow marriages are allowed. Divorce is resorted to only when the charge of prostitution is laid at the door of the woman who is at once sent back to her parents. A divorced female is never remarried by a member of the village to which the husband belonged and rarely by any member of the tribe. The poor wretch is shunned by all except her parents to whose lot it falls to maintain her. Invariably such females are carried away and kept by low caste people from the plains. Polygamy is sanctioned by society but is seldom practised. Polyandry is never heard of and is regarded with the greatest contempt. Prostitution is never tolerated and the female in such cases is obstracised. Sexual license prior to marriage is looked upon with the greatest contempt and the parties concerned therein are outcasted. The Kāṭar girls are described as "modest and child-like in their behaviour and when married they make good wives and become models of constancy." The women are said "to be treated with affection and respect and enjoy a certain amount of freedom. They tend children, cook the family meals, bring water from the spring or stream close by and sometimes accompany their husbands for some out-door work and keep the hut in order.

Birth. Though Mr. Ananthakrishna Ayyar says that these tribes do not perform any ceremony in connection with pregnancy, we read in Mr. Govinda Menon's account that "the tribes observe the usual Puli-kuti ceremony during the course of the month when a small feast is given to the relatives of the husband and wife." The mūppen presides at it and receives a present for his trouble. A separate hut is put up for delivery and the young mother is attended by an old woman during confinement, generally her mother. The lying-in-woman bathes on the third and the 7th day. With the Malayar, pollution lasts for a month. The Kāṭars think that for three months after birth the woman is unclean. For 2 or 3 weeks after birth, in the morning and evening, the Kāṭar woman takes a decoction of anise, ginger, pepper, mustard, calamus and asafoetida which are all well fried and boiled in water. The naming of the child generally takes place in the third month, among the Malayars, and the 6th month among the Kāṭars. The Malayan parents sit side by side, after bathing and putting on new garments, and one of them holds the child on a rice pan. A member of the caste who acts the part of Pūjari goes into a trance and gives out in hysterical tone a name, and this is borne by the child henceforward. The Kāṭar father simply calls the child by a name. The names in common use among Kāṭars are:—

For males: Vēlānṭi, Kuñchī, Kiṭṭu, Piḷḷa, Chelamban, Chōṇṭan, Alakku Piḷḷa and Moyali Mūppan.

For females: Kaṛuppāyi, Rāmāyi, Ponnāyi, Nelli, Kaṛambi, and Veḷḷayammāl.

Names in common use among the Konga Malayars are:—

For males: (1) Mallan Mūppan, (2) Kaṛuppan Mūppan, (3) Ṭamman, (4) Chaṭayan, (5) Veḷḷi, (6) Piṭāri (7) Karumala Mūppan.

For females: (1) Kāḷi, (2) Araśi, (3) Malli, (4) Kathi, (5) Mayal, (6) Cheṭṭichi, (7) Nāyiṭṭi.

The ears and, if a girl, the nose as well of the child are bored through, usually on the date of naming.

Inheritance. The Konga Malayars and the Kāṭars follow the Makkaṭṭāyam, while the Nāṭṭu Malayars follow the Marumakkaṭṭāyam law of inheritance.

Death. The Malayars and Kāṭars both bury their dead. There is very little ceremony attending the burial. When a Malayar dies, his son or nephew procures some toddy. Those present drink it and dance round in honour of the deceased. The body is taken on a bamboo bier. It is placed on the grave which is filled in with earth and stone. They observe pollution for 3 days and, on the morning of the fourth, friends and relatives are invited to a feast at which toddy is freely used. The Nāṭṭu Malayars observe pollution for 16 days. The Kāṭars wash the body before burial. After the usual wailing, a funeral dance is performed. The body is covered with a neat cloth and carried to its resting place on a bamboo bier. As it leaves the hut, rice is thrown over it. The corpse is laid in the grave with the head to the east. Pollution is observed for 10 days. On the 11th day, they take a plunge-bath and invite friends and relatives to a feast. We learn from Mr. Govinda Menon that the ceremony of Śrāḍḍha is very rigidly observed by these tribes It is reckoned by the first new moon of the month in which death took place. Śrāḍḍha is performed only by the eldest son of the deceased and, in the absence of a son, by the brother or nephew.

Religion. The Malayars and Kāṭars are animists and are generally being absorbed into Hinduism, i. e., Brahmanism. They now worship deities borrowed from the lower classes on the plains, such as Kāli, Ayyappan, etc. The Malayars of the Chittur forests worship the following demons:

(1) Karumala Mūppan, (2) Mallampāra Āṇṭan, (3) Nāyiṭṭi Aṭṭal, Manakkaṇṭamma, (5) Paliyamma (6) Kāli.

Those of the Kollenkode forest worship Bhagavaṭi, Nāgaswāmi, Muniyappan, Karumala, Vēṭṭakkāran, Mallan and Bhaḍra Kāli. The stones and images worshipped are regarded not simply as symbols but as deities themselves capable of giving health and prosperity to man. They believe in the existence of spirits with power to work good or evil. Their principal objects of adoration are a few wild animals, ancestors, and a demon called Malavāli, i. e., "he who lives on the mountain". The blessing of ancestors is invoked on all occasions and undertakings. Ancestors occupy among the tribes the same position as that given by Hindus to Gaṇapaṭi. Offerings of boiled and beaten rice, fowls, and arrack are given to ancestors and deities to invoke their blessing. The Mūppen generally acts as priest.

The following extract from the *Imperial Census Report* will give us some idea of the religion of the Kāṭars and how they are approximating towards

Brahmanism. "Special interest attaches to the religion of the Kadars as representing a comparatively early stage in the process of conversion to Brahmanism which the aboriginal races of Bengal are undergoing. The real working religion of the caste is pure animism of the type which still survives, comparatively untouched by Hindu influences among the Santals, Mundas and Orans of Chota Nagpur. Like these, Kadars believe themselves to be encompassed about by a host of invisible powers, some of whom are thought to be the ancestors, while others seem to embody nothing more definite than the vague sense of the mysterious uncanny with which the hills, streams and the lonely forests inspire the savage imagination. Of these shadowy forms, no images are made, nor are they conceived of as wearing any bodily shape. A roughly moulded lump of clay in an open glade, a queer shaped stone bedaubed with vermillion which is all the visible presentiment that does duty for all. Their names are legion and their attributes are barely known. But so much is certain that to neglect their worship brings disaster to the offender, death or disorder to the household, murrian among the cattle and blight on his crops. In order to avert these ills, but so far as I can gather without the hope of any benefit from Gods who are active only to do evil, the Kadar sacrifices pigs, fowls, goats and pigeons and offers ghee, molasses and heads of Indian corn in the sacred groves in which his deities are supposed to dwell. The priest is a man of the caste who combines the sacred functions with those of the barber to the Kadars of the villages of the neighbourhood. The offerings are eaten by the worshippers. For all this, the Kadars, if questioned about their religion, will reply that they are Hindus and will talk vaguely about their Hindu gods (Parameswar, Vishnu), as if they live in the very odour of orthodoxy instead of being in fact they are wholly outside the sphere of the Brahmanical system. To talk about the Hindu gods is usually the first step towards that insensible adoption of the externals of Hinduism which takes the place of formal and open conversion which sterner and less adaptive creeds demand. The next step is to set up Brahmans whose influence furthered by a variety of social forces gradually disposes the tribal gods and transforms them into orthodox shapes and gives them places in the regular pantheon as local manifestations of this or that well known principle and relegates them to a decent and offensive obscurity as household or village deities. Last of all if the tribe is an influential one it gives itself brevet rank as the Rajaputs".

Caste position. The Malayar and the Kāṭar, each affirms his own superiority over the other in social position. The one regards the touch of the other as polluting. Among the Malayars, the Nāṭṭu Malayars possess a social superiority over the Konga Malayars who are not allowed to approach them within a certain distance. Malayars would not eat at the hands of the Kāṭars, Eravallers, Pulayars and Parayars. The Kāṭar will eat at the hands of all castes except the Malayar, Parayar, Pulayar, and Ullāṭar.

The hill tribes are to a great extent under the protection and control of the Forest Department. They are bound to serve it on nominal wages whenever and wherever they are called on to do so. In return they are granted lands for cultivation free of tax, presents for the Oṇam festival, and bamboos, branch wood, etc., free for constructing their huts and similar gifts and concessions which are never allowed to the low country people.

Occasionally, disputes and quarrels among them, when not settled by themselves, are mediated upon by the Forest Department and amicably settled.

The Eravallers. The Eravallers who live in the Chittur forests are a hill tribe of inoffensive men, known also by the name of Villuvēṭan (hunters using the bow). They are an extremely poor class dependent altogether on the landlords under whom they work for very low wages. They live in huts similar to those of the Malayars and Kāṭars in Pathies or villages. "Both men and women are decently clad and the latter are shy of strangers. Males wear *Veshties*, one end of which hangs loose and the other is tucked in between the legs. They have a shoulder cloth either hanging loosely over their shoulders or sometimes tied to the turbans. They allow their hair to grow like women, but do not, for want of means, anoint it with oil. They grow mustaches. They wear round the neck a necklace of small white beads to distinguish them from Malayars, who are always afraid of them. Some bear brass finger rings. Women wear a *potava*, a coloured cloth, 8 yards in length, half of which is worn round the loins, while the other half serves to cover the body. The hair is not smoothened with oil. It is twisted into a knot on the back It is said that they take oil bath once a week. Their ear ornament is made of a long palmyra leaf rolled into a disc and the ear lobes are sufficiently diliated to contain them.

Food and drink. Their food ordinarily consists of Chāma in the form of Kanji (gruel) with salt, tamarind and chillies added. They do not eat from the hands of Maṉṉāns, Pāṉans, Paṟayans, and Cheṟumans.

Occupation. Their occupation is chiefly agriculture. They also employ themselves in gardening, fencing, thatching, etc. As they know the forests well enough they are employed by sportsmen to beat game. They themselves are good bow men. Ten or fifteen of them form a party and are armed with knives, bows and arrows. Some of them beat up and corner the game when they are caught in a net or are shot with arrows or beaten to death. Animals hunted generally are hogs, porcupines hares and such other small game. They skilfully aim at birds and kill them while flying.

Marriage etc. Marriage takes place only when the husband is in a position to work and maintain his wife, a lesson which the early marrying civilized Hindu may well learn. A girl may be married before puberty; but then she lives with her parents till she comes of age. Menstural pollution is very rigidly observed. The girl is lodged in a separate hut at some distance and only girls of her age are allowed to go near her. Food is served at a distance and all grown-up members of the family keep away from her. This seclusion continues for 7 days. She bathes on the morning of the 7th and is then allowed ingress to her hut. The 7th day after the 1st menses is observed as a day of festivity towards which her husband has to contribute, if she is already married. Subsequent menstural period are for 3 days and the ceremonial bath takes place on the fourth day. Marriage is arranged by the parents. When the day is fixed, the parents of the couple wait on their land-lords with a present of betel, nut and tobacco and inform them of the proposed interesting event. He generally gives a para of paddy towards the marriage expenses. The wedding takes place on a Monday. On a Monday previous to the marriage, the sister of the bridegroom visits the parents of the bride accompanied by friends and relatives, and presents them with the bride's price which is never more than a rupee. Along with it a brass ring is also given for the bride. On the Monday selected for the wedding, a similar party proceeds to the bride's house and decks her in new clothing. They get a dinner there, after which they turn homewards with the bride. An entertainment is given at the bridegroom's house also on the bride coming there. On the Monday after this, the bridegroom and bride are taken to the bride's hut where they stay for a week and then return to the bridegroom's hut. There is no ṭāli tying and no presents are given to the bridegroom at the time. But on the Kaṙkaṭaka Saṃkṙānṭi following (about the 15th or 16th of July), the father-in-law invites him and gives him two Vēshṭies or long pieces of cloth after sumptuously feeding him. Widow marriage is permitted but a widow can marry only a widower. When the parties have children by the first marriage, the widower bridegroom must solemnly promise in the presence of the castemen that he would treat them and the issue he may have, alike and impartially. The marriage is effected by the presentation of a brass ring and a cloth, but not with much ceremony. Divorce is allowed, the divorced woman can however marry only a widower. Such cases are very rare among them. Both polygamy and polyandry are absolutely unknown in the community. Should a woman cohabit with a man before marriage and become pregnant, she used, in former times, to be put to death, but is now turned out of caste. Such instances too are very rare. The Eravallers follow Makkaṭṭāyam.

Pregnancy. No ceremonies take place during pregnancy except exorcism if the woman is suspected to be possessed by a demon. On delivery she is located in a separate hut where she is attended by her mother or some old woman. Soon after delivery both mother and child are bathed. She has pollution for 7 days. On the 7th day she bathes and is removed to another hut closer to the main one. Here she stays for a period of 5 months. She returns to the main hut after having her ceremonial bath. That day is one of festivity. During convalesence she is strictly forbidden from taking meat and a medicine consisting of a mixture of pepper, dried ginger and palm sugar mixed with toddy is given her.

The naming of the child comes on two years after birth. The male child receives his grandfather's and the female her grandmother's name. The names in common use are:—*for males,* Kaṇṇan, Oṭukan, Kōṭhaṇḍan, Kēchāran and Āṭṭukaran; *for females,* Kanni, Kēypi, Kaikēyi, Oṭuka and Rāmāyi.

Death. They bury their dead and observe pollution for 5 days. On the 6th day, the son or the younger brother of the deceased, as the case may be, who is the chief mourner gets shaved, bathes, and offers to the spirit of the departed boiled rice, plantains, fowl, and parched rice. A feast is also given to castemen, which is repeated annually if they can afford to do so.

Religion. They are pure animists and centre their belief mostly on demons who are said to reside on the trees, rocks or peaks with which the mountains abound. The demons are worshipped with a view to appease their supposed anger towards these simple people. Their gods, male and female, are Kāli, Muni, Kannimar and Karuppu. The first is a female deity who is worshipped to obtain protection for themselves and their families; the second for the protection of their cattle and for having a good harvest, and the third (who are said to be seven maidens) because they are their family deities always watching over their welfare. Offerings of beaten rice, boiled rice, plantains, etc., are given to propitiate them. Kāli and Muni are worshipped in the forest, and the rest in their huts.

General condition. The general condition of these hill tribes is very low, notwithstanding that a great number of the Nelliampathi Kāṭars have for some years enlisted themselves under the coffee planters as Maistries and coolies, and that the Malayars have recently turned to agriculture and farming. They are bound to serve the Forest Department on mere nominal wages whenever and wherever they are called on to do so. In return, they are allowed to cultivate patches of forest land tax-free. They are also given bamboos and branchwood, etc., for constructing their huts, while similar gifts and concessions are denied to the low country people. They have to do a miscellaneous assortment of work, hard enough, which they do most willingly though not sufficiently remunerated. They have to lead the Sirkar officials through the forests when on duty, to attend to the elephant capturing operations, such as to cover the pits, to see whether elephants have fallen into them, to announce the fall to Forest officials, to water and feed the animals in pits till they are kraaled, and to construct māṭoms (huts) for the Government servants and officers. They get an edangaïi (⅓ of the Madras measure) of rice for covering and watching the pits; while for tracking and for constructing māṭoms they are given five n̄aïies of rice and six pies per day; for feeding the elephants in the pit a similar quantity of rice and three pies per diem. On the kraaling day there is a general distribution of rice. These duties fall to the share of the Malayars specially. It is the privilege of the Kāṭars to serve the Raja when touring in the forests. They carry his Manjel (a hammock-like conveyance in which the Raja travels, and carried by men on their shoulders), his luggage, etc. In return they meet with kindness at the hands of His Highness who feeds them and gives them cloths, ornaments, combes and looking glasses. Of the Kāṭar it has been observed that "these peculiar people could never be frightened into doing anything, and that when any harsh words are used, they simply move away from one place to another. One forest to them is as good as another, and they get their few wants supplied either here or there. They are quite simple, unsophisticated and utter aliens to vice and trickery. They are plain and straightforward in their dealings, never tell a lie, never deceive another. Work they never shirk, and being sturdy and strong they are fit for any kind of physical exertion or endurance. In the carrying of loads and weights, they are very enduring and have a great capacity for rapidly recruiting. Altogether they appear to be a quiet and submissive race obeying the slightest expression of a wish and very grateful for any assistance or attention." The lot of the Eravallers is no better. The men are attached to farmers under whom they work for daily wages of 2 edangaïies of paddy, worth perhaps 2 annas. The women also work for low wages, but never agree to serve in a state of bondage. Notwithstanding their low condition they have been described as "always truthful, honest, faithful, and God-fearing and never, like the Pulayas of the northern parts of the State, running away from their masters."

These simple people have not yet left behind them their ancient landmarks and attempts made by the Christian Missionaries to wean them from primitive barbarism have not hitherto met with much success. It is said that a certain philanthropic Missionary in Cochin made an endeavour to educate the hill tribes, and, if possible, to bring them into the fold of Christianity. With this view he set up a small school in one of the jungle villages and tried his level best to persuade the tribes to send their youths to be educated but to no purpose. They would not swerve an inch from the beaten track of their ancestors. Distribution of sweets and pictorial booklets failed and no inducement of whatever sort would lure them to send their children to be educated. The disheartened philanthropist had at last to give up his attempt. Perhaps one need not be sorry at such failures, for the enlightened philanthropy of such gentlemen is slowly but surely wiping the traces of early tribes. Several forces are working at the annihilation of the remnants of ancient races and unless a full record of the life, manners and customs of those that have hitherto escaped the attention of the philanthropist is made at once, the historian of the future will have no material to trace the evolution of the races that once inhabited this land. "The employment of tiles and kerosine tins in lieu of primitive thatch, the import of cotton piece goods and umbrellas instead of country made goods and umbrellas covered with leaves, the decline of national costume in favour of European costume, the substitution of caps of gaudy hue and pith turbans for national turbans, the replacement of peasant jewelry of indigenous manufacture by beads and imitation jewelry made in Europe, the use of lucifer matches by aboriginal tribes, who formerly made fire by friction, the supply of new forms of food and of beer and spirits in the bazaars, the administration of justice instead of that distributed by the old village panchayats, the attempts of the low castes to elevate themselves by the adoption of the customs and manners of the higher castes, the spread of western education, religious teaching and conversion to Christianity by European Missionaries—these and many other factors are the causes of radical change in the ethnographic conditions of the country."[1] In the words of Professor A. C. Haddon of Cambridge, "Now is the time to record. An infinitude has been lost to us and a very great deal is now rapidly disappearing. The most interesting materials are becoming lost to us not only by their disappearance, but by the apathy of those who should delight in recording them before they have become lost to sight and memory."

It is interesting to know something of the origin of these tribes. Dr. Topiniard in his well-known work on Anthropology classes the hill tribes of the Dekhan and Southern India as coming under the first of the three classes into which he divides the "Hindu type", viz., the Black, the Mongolian and the Aryan. Mr. Denikar regards them as uncivilized Dravidians while Dr. A. H. Keane says, "There is good evidence to show that the first arrivals in India were a black people most probably Negritos, who made their way from Malaysia round the Bay of Bengal to the Himalayan foot hills, and thence spread over the peninsular without ever reaching Ceylon. At present there are no distinctly Negrito communities in the land nor has any clear trace of a distinctly Negrito language yet been discovered. But distinctly Negrito features crop up continually in the uplands from the Himalayan slopes to Cape Comorin over against Ceylon. The Negritos in fact have been absorbed or largely assimilated by the later intruders, and as of these there are four separate stocks we call the Negritos the submerged fifth. There has been

1: *Cochin Tribes and Castes.*

ample evidence for the submergence since they arrived if not in the early, certainly in the Tertiary period, many thousand of years ago." According to Dr. Keane, many of the primitive tribes living in the plateau of the Dekhan and in the uplands of Southern India are of Kolarian race, and to this primitive group belong the Malayar, Kāṭar, Uḷḷāṭan, Eravaller and other tribes who though speaking a Dravidian dialect are not full-booded Dravidians but represent different Negrito, Kolarians, and Arayan blends. These tribes avoiding all contact with the Aryans and Dravidians have preserved many of their primitive customs and manners.

Some of the customs observed by these hill tribes as well as by their more civilized brethren on the plains are to be found outside India among people in a low state of civilization. For instance, the seclusion of girls during puberty and subsequent menses; the various ceremonies performed during puberty by hill tribes and by all castes among Hindus, are not confined entirely to India, but are prevalent among savage races in many parts of the world. There appears to be some sort of uniformity in the observances which are rigidly followed by people in a low state of civilization. Some incidents of the curious custom regarding puberty mentioned hereunder will be found to be interesting. The girls of Loango are at puberty confined in separate huts and they may not touch the ground with any part of their body. Among the Zulus and the kindred tribes, if the first signs of puberty appears, while a girl is walking, gathering wood or working in the field, she hides herself among the reeds for the day so as not to be seen by men. She covers her head with a blanket so as to prevent the rays of the Sun from falling upon her head and returns home during the night. In new Ireland, girls are confined in small cages for four or five years and kept in the dark without being allowed to set foot on the ground. In North Queensland a girl at puberty is to live by herself for a month or six weeks, no man may see her though women may. She stays in a separate hut and will always be lying on the floor. She may not see the Sun, and till Sunset, she must keep her eyes closed, otherwise it is thought that her nose will be diseased. She cannot during her seclusion, eat anything that lives in salt water. If she does, she would die of snake-bite. An old woman, who waits upon her, supplies her with roots and water. Some tribes are wont to bury their girls at such seasons more or less deeply in the ground, probably to hide them from the light of the day. Among some of the American tribes girls after the first bath submit to a flogging by her mother with thin rods without uttering a cry. At the end of the second period, she is again beaten, but not afterwards. She is now clean. It is supposed that the girl is under malign influence at this period. The custom of stinging her with ants or beating her with rods is intended to relieve her from it. The Indian girls of Cayenne subject themselves to excruciating torture from the stings not merely of ants, but also of the most ferocious of wasps.

The reason for this seclusion of girls and women during menses lies in the dread which the primitive man entertains of the menstruous blood. Among the Australian Blacks the boys are told that the sight of the blood turns one's hair grey and causes premature old age. Hence it is, that women live apart and keep away from places frequented by men who in their turn scrupulously avoid paths trodden by women in their menses. In Australia women who infringe these rules are severely punished even into death. In central Australia, women at these times avoid eating fish or bathing in a river, lest they may die and the water dry up. It is the belief of the people of Sumatra that women in the unclean state cannot go near paddy fields, lest the crops may all perish. The Bushmen of Africa believe that the glance of women at this period changes men into trees with power to talk. Cattle-rearing tribes in Africa hold that cattle would die if milk were drunk by women in their menses. According to the Talmud if a woman at the beginning of the period passes between two men, she thereby kills one of them, if she passes between them at the end of the period she causes them to quarrel violently. The Parsees, who worship fire, will not allow menstruous women to see a lighted taper. Among all classes of the Hindus the women at such periods are under seclusion. Men who speak with them, who approach them, who are exposed to the air that blow over them, are all regarded as unclean. They cannot walk by the side of flowering plants, or by the side of the kitchen, nor can they touch any of the vessels. To approach her at this period is to ensure dangerous illness. They may not walk on common paths, cross the track of animals or milk cows, they have to eat as little as possible and remain lying down in a penitential mood. Strict adherence to these rules, it is said, will lead to good health and long life.

The ideas detailed above and deeply ingrained in the savage mind re-appear at a more advanced period of society in the form of elaborate codes which have been drawn up for the guidance of people by lawgivers who claim to have derived their inspirations from God. Manu says that the wisdom, energy, sight and vitality of a man who approaches a woman in her courses, will perish, whereas if he avoids her the same will increase.[1] According to the Persian lawgiver Zoroaster, the flow of menses in women is caused by the evil one known as *Ahriman*. Therefore, as long as it lasts, she is unclean and is possessed of the evil one. She has to be kept confined and not allowed to see the fire, and her diet during the period should be as sparing as possible, lest the strength she may acquire by a rich diet should lead to the harm of her friends. According to Pliny, the touch of a menstruous woman turned wine into vinegar, blighted crops, killed seedlings, blasted gardens, brought down the fruit from trees, dimmed

1. Vide *Sankara Smrithi*.

mirrors, blunted razors, rusted iron and brass, killed bees or drove them from the hives and caused mares to miscarry. In various parts of Europe it is still believed that, if a woman in her courses enters a brewery, the beer will turn sour; if she touches beer, wine, vinegar or milk, it will become bad; if she mounts a mare, she will miscarry; if she touches buds, they will wither; if she climbs a tree it will die; if she helps the touching of a pig, the pork will be putrified. Her presence in a boat is said to raise storms. Therefore the seclusion of women at such times is to minimise the dangerous influences that are supposed to emanate from them.[1]

Another custom which may be referred to here is that of the Kāṭars chipping their incisor teeth. The custom of deforming the teeth is not confined to Southern India, but is found prevailing among different tribes in Africa and Australia, where the practice is, in general, confined to the chipping of the incisor teeth. Westermark in his *History of Human Marriage* says, that, when the age of puberty is drawing near, in several parts of Africa and Australia, they knock out some teeth, knowing that they would otherwise run the risk of being rejected on account of ugliness. In the Malaya Peninsula, the practice of filing the teeth and blackening is a necessary prelude to marriage. Further Darwin, in his *Descent of Man*, writes, that the natives of the Upper Nile knock out the four front teeth, saying that they do not wish to resemble brutes. Some tribes, says Dr. Livingstone, knock out the two incisors, because they give the face a hideous appearance. A writer in the *Madras Journal of Literature and Science* observes. "These little dwarfish people the Kadars file their front teeth in points to facilitate their eating the hardest roots. There is some nerve shown in this and we may look with wonder and respect upon the exiled lords of the ancient land when we see that rather than serve those who usurped the country, they chose to live,

1. See instances collected in *Cochin Tribes and Castes*.

where the food was beyond their natural powers and could be eaten only by such a preparation of their teeth. It is possible, that in the absence of better arms, they reckoned upon these pointed teeth as weapons, in case their conquerors should follow them to their mountain home."[1]

---

1. Monograph No. 9, Kadars, page 15.

LETTER XXII.

1. **Foreigners: three descriptions.** This letter treats mostly of the foreign Brahman element in the population of Malabar. Our author's classification of them is not exhaustive. In the *Mackenzie Manuscripts*[1], it is said that there are fifteen sects of Brahmans in Malabar. In the Cochin State Dr. Day divides them into five. — "the Dravida, Ṭelinga, Carnatic, Maharatta and Guzeratta." A common division into Eṃprāns from Mangalore, Paṭṭars from various districts on the East Coast, and Konkaṇis from Canara may also be mentioned.

2. **The Pattars.** The word Paṭṭar is a corruption of the Sanskrit Bhaṭṭar, and the term is used to denote the Brahmans from the East Coast, who have either permanently settled in Malabar or have made it their temporary abode. The prospect of gain and the great veneration entertained by the Malāyālis for the twice-born class attract crowds of Brahmans from the surrounding countries, such as, Tinnevelly, Tanjore, Coimbatore, etc. The Paṭṭars trace the date of their first emigration to the period of the earliest Kṣheṭriya Princes. There are large colonies of them spread throughout the country. But their chief settlement is in and around Palghat. Wherever they have settled, they live in *Agrahārams* or *Gramams* (villages). The houses of the *Pattar* Brahmans are built contiguous to one another in straight streets, while the Malayālis live in detached houses surrounded by gardens. In other places, where their residence is only temporary, they are collected under *Samooham Madhams*, (communal mutts) or houses belonging to the community, which serve as a point of union. Of these there are many, scattered throughout the country. Every individual attaches himself to one of these

1. No. 17. Countermark 9—10.

A TAMIL BRAHMIN LADY WITH HER DAUGHTERS.

(To face p. 603.

Madhams, and thus the Paṭṭars form themselves into little corporations. The *Madhams* (maṭhams) have generally common funds replenished by contributions made by members of the community. The funds are administered and the affairs of the community looked after by officers elected from among themselves. The Paṭṭars used to be chiefly engaged in the pursuits of commerce, but latterly have devoted themselves to other walks of life as well. Those bent on commerce alone traverse all parts of the interior finding a subsistence at every Pagoda or Ūṭṭupura or feeding house of which there are many in the country, which are designed for their sole benefit. They take full advantage of these institutions, for they congregate and carry on their trade generally in their vicinity, thus turning what was originally intended as resting houses for wayfarers into feeding houses for permanent residents. Their object is only to accumulate as much wealth as possible with which to retire to their families by whom they are rarely accompanied. They are indefatigable in the pursuit of this end which their singular perseverance and economy generally enable them to accomplish soon. They do not generally build their houses in the country but manage to get a room in a Nāyar house, and more often ally themselves in saṃbhandham with the female members of the Nāyar family who, out of their superstitious reverence to their sacred order, minister to them without stint. Thus they live enjoying all comforts of life till they are able to accumulate some wealth, which being accomplished, they coolly retire to their own country, caring little for their offspring they may be leaving behind. Unlike the proud and domineering Malayāli who disdains from pursuing professions other than those that are theirs by tradition, the Paṭṭar Brahman plies his hand to every trade.

The Paṭṭar is found in every walk of life and he makes his presence felt by his superior intelligence, application and industry. This class of Brahmans occupy at present the most important offices in the

Government and are conspicuous in all the learned professions. Sacred as their order is, they do not show any aversion to serve in any department, however low, in the State. Of them it has been remarked, "Ambitious of office they often attain it, but are generally seen performing some of the minor duties of the temples, often in still meaner occupations, frequently of a secular kind, but nearly half are merchants trading in cloth (of which they once had the exclusive privilege) and grain". They are the sowcars of Malabar. But as merchants and money-lenders, their reputation has not been altogether enviable. As cooks and domestic servants, they are largely employed by all aristocratic families. Even under Nāyars, they serve as cooks. In Malabar they have made themselves thoroughly at home by adopting the ways of the Malayāli in regard to minor social matters, such as dress, language, observance of pollution by touch and approach etc., while retaining their distinctive nationality and adhering steadfastly to the customs of their forefathers in all essential respects. Many of them speak Malayalam well enough, while those who have adopted Malabar as their native country use a jargon which is more Malayalam than Tamil.

3. **Pattars no share in administration.** Our author must have been misinformed in this respect. Though the Paṭṭars used not to be so largely employed formerly in the Government services as at present, yet it is certain that they took not an unimportant part in the administration of the country. It may, however, be true that those who spent only three or four years on the coast were regarded as foreigners and for that reason excluded from the Public Service. The celebrated Rama Ayyen Dalavah of Travancore, "the General Ram" mentioned by Col. Wilkes, who worked so admirably with the famous Travancore King Mārṭṭāṇḍa Vuṙmah in resuscitating, unifying and consolidating that State, belonged to this class. Fra Bartolomeo, in referring to the statement of Diodorus

The Late Mr. T. A. Doraswamy Iyer.

(He was a leader of the Bar and of the public in Cochin, and a musician famous in South

Siculus that the Brahmans engaged themselves in no public business and accepted no dignified places, remarks that "this is a palpable falsehood. The kings who hold the reins of government at Edappilly on the Coast of Malabar and also at Parur and Araceri are certainly Brahmans; and the King of Travancore, in the year 1776, had a Delava, a prime minister who also belonged to that class. In States which are under the dominion of Pagan princes, they are still, as in the time of Diodorus Siculus, overseers of religion, high priests, instructors of the people, observers of eclipses of the Sun and Moon, and the King's councillors."[1] But we have to remark that the accounts left us by the Portuguese and the Dutch travellers of the early middle ages do not make mention of any Paṭṭar Brahman as occupying any conspicuous position in the administration of the country. It may be that the Portuguese and the Dutch were not able to differentiate between the home and the foreign Brahmans, or it may be that, by the time that Bartolomeo wrote, the Paṭṭar Brahman had begun to make his presence in Malabar felt. In former times, they were undoubtedly used as confidential messengers and spies[2]. Their sacred order secured immunity from molestation while passing through Hindu States, and both the European and Mahomedan States of Southern India used to employ a large batch of them as messengers who were called *Harikars*, a designation still retained by the *Pattar* Brahman servants attached to the Rajas and high officers of State.

4. **Factories.** These factories and magazines are perhaps the Samūha Maḍhams already mentioned.

5. **Privileges to Pattares.** As regards the first privilege—They have the privilege of being fed free at choultries or Ūṭṭupuras or feeding-houses with which the country abounds. These are generally attached to Pagodas. They were originally designed for wayfarers but has latterly became either asylums

1. P. 296.
2. *Malabar*, p. 129.

for an indigent and idle resident Brahman population, or centres round which shrewd members of the class congregate for purposes of trade and take advantage of the free feeding. The Brahmans who are fed at these institutions are not now called on to sweep and clean the buildings. The States of Cochin and Travancore have recently restricted the feeding of the resident Paṭṭar population in the choultries to a large extent.

6. **Three castes.** These are not castes of Brahmans. The names indicate more or less the localities wherefrom they came into Malabar originally.

Pandy is a term used by the Malayāḷis to denote the country to the East of the Ghauts lying towards the south, comprising the districts of Tanjore, Tinnevelly, Trichinopoly and Madura.

Tole stands for Ṭuḷunāḍ or Canara. The Brahmans who came from Ṭuḷunāḍ are strictly speaking Malayāḷis, for Malabar or Kēraḷa extends to Gōkarṇam in the north. As such they enjoy privileges that are denied to the Paṭṭar Brahmans. While the Emprāns or Ṭuḷu Brahmans are accepted as priests to officiate in Malabar temples, the Paṭṭar Brahmans are not allowed even access to the interior of the chief shrine. In Travancore, they are also called Pōṟṟi. The word signifies in Tamil "worshipful". Besides temporary residents, there are those who have made Malabar their home. There are three sections among them answering to the chronological order in which they arrived in the country. Kēraḷa is said to have been once divided into five Khaṇḍams (Khaṇḍams or divisions with regard to the Brahman communities that held sway over each. These were known as:—

(1) the Pōṟṟi Khaṇḍam which is the southernmost occupied by Pōṟṟis; (2) the Nampi Khaṇḍam, (3) the Nampiṭi Khaṇḍam; (4) the Nampiāṭiri Khaṇḍam; and (5) the Nampūṭiri Khaṇḍam.

In Travancore, the Pōťťis are the largest land-holders corresponding to the Nampūṭiri jenmies of the north.

The seven families of Sṭhānaṭṭil Pōťťis and the Paṭṭillaṭṭu Pōťťis of Travancore come under the first of the three divisions. The Sṭhānaṭṭil Pōťťis are among the traditional trustees of Śrī Paḍmanābha Swāmi's temple at Trivandrum. The names of the seven families are:—

(1) Kūpakkara Pōťťi; (2) Vanchiyūr Aṭṭiyara Pōṭṭi. (3) Kollūr Aṭṭiyara Pōṭṭi; (4) Mūṭṭavila Pōťťi; (5) Nayśśēri Pōťťi; (6) Kaŕuva Pōťťi and (7) Śri Kariyāťťu Pōťťi.

These together with the Maharaja, the Nampūṭiri Swāmiyār attached to the temple, and a Nāyar nobleman, called Karanāṭṭa Kuŕup constitute the Eṭṭara Yōgam or council of 8½ members of the temple corporation. They at one time enjoyed quasi-sovereign powers. The Paṭṭillaṭṭ, Pōťťis who are Purōhiṭas, or family priests of the Travancore Royal house, also come under this head, They are also called Ṭiruveli Pōťťis (Pōťťis that attend at the Śrāḍha rites of the Kings) and enjoy the same rank for purposes of State privileges as Nampūṭiris.

The next division comprisē the Ṭiruvella Ḍēśi Pōťťis who are later emigrants from Ṭuḷuńād and who by lapse of time became assimilated with the general body of the Nampuṭiris in habits, manners and customs. The first batch is said to have come at the invitation of Uḍaya Vaŕma Raja at about 336 A. D. and settled themselves in and around Ṭiruvella. Hence they came to be known as Ṭiruvella Ḍēśis. The grāmams of Chengannur and Veṇmaṇi are two important groups of Ṭiruvella Ḍēśis with the Māmpiḷḷi Panṭāram as the head of the latter. They belong to the Bōḍhāyana Sūṭŕa.

The third division consists of those sojourners who came from the Taluks of Uppinangate and

Kasserkote in South Canara and who are employed as temple priests or Pūjāris.

For all practical purposes, the Pōṭṭis may be classed under Nambūtiris. The Nambūtiri Vaidīkas and Smārttas have the same social and religious control over them as over the Nambutiris themselves. Their rules of caste government are similar and the machinery to enforce them identical. They however perform no yāgas (sacrifices), never enter the ascetic order of Sannyāsis and seldom study the Vēdas, confining themselves to what is called Mutalora, *mutalmura* or formal first recitation. The Tiruveli Pōṭṭis, being the Purōhits of the Travancore Royal family, have however kept up Vedic studies. Hence no Malayāli Pōṭṭi, excepting the Pattillatt Pōṭṭis is eligible to chant Vedic texts during the Murajapam ceremony, celebrated at Trivandrum once in six years.

A Nambutiri, learned in the Vēdas, officiates at their ceremonies as chief priest. The following distinctions in ceremonial observances between the Pōṭṭis and Nambutiris may be noted. The Samavarttanam ceremony among Pōṭṭis takes place three years after the Upanayanam and a Pōṭṭi becomes a Snataka at the latest by his 12th year unlike in the case of Nambutiris. The females of all Nambūtiri classes except the Adhyan wear brass bangles, while the Pōṭṭi women generally put on silver bangles. Consummation takes place on the fourth day of marriage or, if that is inauspicious, on the fifth. The Chengannur Grāmakkār are endogamous in the extreme and never marry out of their village. The other Malayāli Poṭṭis do not observe such a restriction. The chief occupation of the Pōṭṭi is priesthood at temples, but several of them are landlords. In the matter of education on western lines, they occupy almost the same position as the Nampūtiris.

Their laws of inheritance, their habitation, their social ordinances and appellations, their songs and recreations are all exactly the same as those of the

KONKAN BRAHMINS.

(To face p. 609.

Nambūṭiris. In their religious worship too, they resemble the Nambūṭiris.[1]

"Toelegen". Those who came from the Telingāṇa or Telugu country.

" Tanjour". Perhaps a misprint for 'Tanjour', indicating those who came from the district of Tanjore.

"Choolea ". Those who came from the Chōla country. There is a peculiar feature about the Chōlia and Mukkāṇi Brahmans. While all other East Coast Brahmans wear the Kuṭumbi, or tuft of hair, at the back of the head, these like the Malayālis wear it on the crown.

"Mockeramby ". Otherwise Mukkāṇy who are perhaps emigrants from Chōla. They too wear the top-knot. These constitute the "Pattares" of Malabar, i. e., the foreign Brahmans. They have been so well described as regards their manners, customs, daily life etc. by the Abbe Dubois that it is altogether unnecessary to say anything about them here.

7. **The Konkanies.** *Their ornaments and clothing.* Our author gives us a good idea of the dress and ornaments of the Konkaṇies. Though not materially changed, still, to a certain extent, a change has come over them in this respect. At present, men do not generally wear the long white tunic nor do they cover their heads with an 'Roomal' or band. But, in the near past, they did so, and there are still a very few who do so. The present generation of Konkaṇi men adopt the ordinary dress of the people of Malabar when they go out in the public; but, on religious and festive occasions, they wear *Soman* tucked between the legs like the East Coast Brahmans and throw the *Uttariyam* or *veshti* over the shoulders. The women have begun to wear white cloths with silken and laced borders. Their cloths are generally meagre of breadth and seldom extend below the knees, leaving the calves of the legs exposed to view. They wear the *Rowkki* or

1. Travancore Census Report, p. 339.

BY.

bodice. The wedding ornament is a pendant of an oblong form made of pure gold. A silken cord with black beads strung together on either side of the pendant is their neck ornament. Figures of the sun and moon, or rather of the half-moon are engraved on the pendants. They bore the ears and the nose and wear ornaments there. The ornaments of the Konkaṇis are, generally speaking, more massive and interestingly antique in appearance than of elegant workmanship. The women indulge in the use of all sorts of flowers, sweet scented or not, to adorn their hair, which they tie in a knot behind their heads and not twist in a roll on one side as in our author's days. They pluck their hair off their forehead up to above the ears from below.

8. **The Canarese.** These are more properly known as Konkaṇies, or those that have come from the Konkan Coast, being natives of the Konkaṇa country now in the Bombay Presidency. They belong to the Sāraswaṭa section of the Gouda Brahmans as distinguished from the Dravida Brahmans proper who inhabit South India. There are, among the Konkaṇies, Brahmans, Vaisyas and Sudras. Ethnically, the Konkan Brahmans may be classed as belonging to the Aryan stock. They are a tall, handsome race with fair complexion, regular features, thin lips, prominent nose, and broad chest. They are said to take their class name of Sāraswaṭans from their Guru, or first preceptor, Sāraswaṭa. The claim to have originally inhabited Trihatapura, the modern Tirhut in Behar, whence tradition says that Paraśu Rāma brought ten families whom he settled at Gomantaka, the modern Goa, Panchakrōsi and Kuśasṭhali. Others soon followed and the whole population settled themselves in 60 villages and 96 hamlets in and around Goa. When Goa was captured by Vijayanagara, they placed themselves under the protection of the Hindu Kings of Vijayanagar. But, not long after, the Portuguese appeared on the scene and captured Goa. The commercial prosperity that the community enjoyed under the

THE LATE MR. HARI SHENOY.
(Was a leader of his Community and for a long time the Managing Trustee of the Cochin Thirumala Devasvom).

(*To face p. 610.*

Hindu Kings continued for about a quarter of a century more under their Christian masters. King John of Portugal, the successor of King Emmanuel, who established the Portuguese Empire in India, was suddenly seized with a religious frenzy for the propagation of the Gospel in his Indian dominions, and no measures, fair or foul, were left untried to convert the Hindus to Christianity. An order was issued for the forcible conversion of all those round Goa on pain of a general massacre. A humane Governor took pity on the poor suffering Hindus and gave previous intimation of the enforcement of the order, so that those who were so minded may leave the place. A large number of Konkanies took advantage of the kindly warning and ran to neighbouring places. With the establishment of the inquisition in Goa, they deserted their houses and went into voluntary exile. A large body of them fled to the south and made settlements in the Travancore, Cochin and Calicut. The rapacity of the Zamorin drove the settlers still further south into the Cochin and Travancore States. The main body settled in Cochin.

In Cochin, they found a congenial home and set themselves out, at once, to better their condition. Their natural aptitude for trade had scope for full play, and the Rajas of Cochin extended their protection and sympathy to the community. On the advent of the Dutch, they placed themselves under the protection of the Dutch East India Company, as the Raja had latterly begun to molest them at the instigation of the Portuguese who never bore goodwill towards them. We have seen that the first act of the Portuguese on the retirement of the Dutch squadron from Cochin after the first attack was to sack the quarters of the Konkanies on the plea that they had assisted the Dutch. On the Dutch becoming supreme in Cochin, the East India Company at once took the Konkanies under its special protection. One of them was appointed the Company's merchant, and special privileges were granted to him. We have also seen that the murder of one of the Company's merchants Malappa by name, by the Pāliyaṭ Achchen had caused considerable friction between the Company and the Raja. The Konkaṇies lived in the suburbs of Cochin, known as Chellāi and Amarāvaṭi. The ground occupied by these localities had in olden times been the esplanade of the fort which was made over to the Dutch by the Cochin Raja in 1663.

In 1772, disputes arose between the Raja and the Dutch regarding the right of the Dutch to collect the revenues around Cochin. A convention was held and the following terms were finally agreed to by the Dutch Governor. "From this day forward as long as the Government of Cochin exists, I do cede and transfer, unto you and your descendants, the right of collecting the income from Mattancheri and Chellaye. To collect the farms and customs of Amaravaty and to conduct the affairs of Mattancherri, Chellaye, and of the Konkanies and their temple." But, along with this, there was also the following understanding, "that the Raja shall impose no new demands upon the Konkanies, that they shall have full liberty to complain to the Dutch Governor if aggrieved, and that the Raja shall not interfere in any matters of the temple, without the knowledge and consent of the Company". In spite of these special reservations, the Raja was not slow to oppress the Konkaṇies as opportunities occurred. In 1791, the Raja directed the Konkaṇi Pagoda to contribute a large quantity of molasses (Sugarcane-Jaggery) towards a feast at Ṭṛppūniṭṭura. On the Trustees refusing to meet the demand, two of the Raja's Eurasian officers, accompanied by a Kāriakār, went to the shop of Dēvaraśa Kiṇi, one of the Pagoda Trustees, got in on the pretence of having gone to purchase some silks and had his head cut off and carried away to the Raja. The Raja's troops then made a rush on the Konkaṇi Bazaar and sacked it. The priests of the temple, hearing the tumult outside, hastily removed the idol and its jewels in a box and sought refuge under the guns of the Dutch fort. The Raja further loaded the Konkaṇies with new imposts against the spirit of the convention of 1772 with the Dutch. The Cochin Council resisted the attempts of the Raja to encroach on Dutch privileges. The English who were gradually displacing the Dutch from Malabar espoused the Raja's side, but eventually the Raja gave way and admitted the right of the Dutch protection over the Konkaṇies.

9. **Canarese live near forts.** The Canarese were under the special protection of the Dutch, and this protection says Governor Moens, "is a little different from the protection the Company exercises over the Christians, and relates more to the differences as citizens." After referring to the settlement of the disputes regarding the right of levying tolls in Mattancherri and Chellāi, M. Moens observes, "At any rate, the Company has exercised since that time, through this policy, even more authority over the Canarese than it had before, and the King had never made any objections; possibly because discretion was used, and because it was that the King was quite satisfied with being thought to have authority over the Canarese. For although authority over these people in the settling of their cases is left to the King with certain restrictions, and especially with this, namely, that they may make complaints against the King to the Honourable Company, yet it is necessary for us to claim every now and then the supreme authority over the same, which we reserve to ourselves specially in cases, in which it is noticed that the Canarese do not get their rights from the King, either in case of debt or other disputes, in order that it may be clear to all, that right and justice are practised by the Company." The Dutch Government justifies this on the ground that "with the native authorities money goes a great way in obtaining a favourable decision." The Canarese mixed much with the people. They did much retailing in the streets like the Chetties and Moors of Ceylon and the common Jews in the Netherlands. "They are

here" continues M. Moens, "absolutely necessary, and almost the whole of the retail trade is in their hands. They sell even the smallest articles. The necessaries of life (except live-stock, because trading therein is against their religion and, therefore, the black Jews take them to the market) can be had almost only from them. For this purpose they possess in their neighbourhood, not far from town, a bazaar, and besides everywhere, if there is but a little space, anywhere outside or inside the town, little stalls. In this way they buy and sell daily, exchanging, lending or borrowing goes on both among white and black people, and hence it is but natural, that through all this questions and complaints certainly arise, which become at times such a muddle that the greatest patience is required to discover the origin of the dispute. In fine the Canarese are completely mixed up with our inhabitants: they with their affairs and complaints cannot be entrusted to a Court, where for gifts and presents one can obtain a sentence according to one's liking. And as these people here are a *Mallum necessarium* it is necessary to procure them their rights, but to punish severely if they are caught arranging a monopoly or intriguing with slaves, cheating or committing frauds. With regard to other cases, which have reference to old customs and privileges of the King, *e.g.*, the small revenue of their bazaar outside the town, the administration of their pagoda or temple, the part of the inheritance, which after death goes to the King, we ought not to listen to the Canarese but reject them at once, as affairs, in which they cannot hope for a change or assistance."

10. **Two classes of Canarese.** *Religion.* As the majority of the Konkaṇies are Vaishnavites, the Vishnavite sect mark find singular predominance. The *Gopi* is the mark that has to be worn on the forehead. But till *Upanayanam* a boy is not to wear this mark, but merely an impress of Vishnu's Suḍarśana (disc) on the chest. The Vysias being Saivites put on only Vibhūṭi (holy ashes). The

Konkaṇies are mostly Vaishnavites, being followers of Maḍhvāchārya. There are very few Smārṭas or Saivites or followers of Śankarāchārya among them. Their chief deity is Venkeṭaramaṇa of Ṭiruppaṭi (Trippathy) or shrine to which they make pilgrimages. In Malabar they have their own temples and priests. Their temples, known as Konkaṇi Mukkālvaṭṭam in Malayalam, are generally styled *Tirumala Devaswams*, and are managed by trustees chosen from among the community itself. These temples are said to be so called as the divinity that resides on the sacred hill (Ṭirumala) is represented in each. It is also suggested that they take the name after Ṭirumala one of the Kings of Vijayanagara to which dynasty they were once subject. Some of these temples are very rich, such as the one in Cochin and those at Ṭoravūr and Alleppy in Travancore. Their religious services do not differ much from those of the other Brahmans in South India.

The origin and history of the *Bimbam* or image installed in their great Pagoda situate in Cochin is not simply interesting in itself, it also throws a flood of light on their position in Cochin, politically and socially. It is thus related by Day:—"Up to 1589, they possessed in Cochin a small metal idol and, in that year, their High Priest, Coombaconum Madum Swamiyar visited the place, bringing with him a Bhimmum, before which he performed his private devotions. Having remained about six months, he prepared to depart but, at every attempt to leave, he became seriously ill. Alarmed at this, the soothsayers were consulted, and they discovered, that his little god has taken such a fancy to Cochin, that he declined to leave the place. The Swamiyar then offered to give up the Bhimmum, provided he were given as many Venetian gold sequins as would cover the image when placed in a large salver. This was acceded to, but as fast as they heaped up the money, the higher grew the idol's head, until all the sequins in Cochin were expended. Again soothsayers were consulted, and they discovered that, although the Bhimmum wished to reside in Cochin, he had an aversion to lose sight of his former master and his family; so a contract was drawn up, in which the Pagoda worshippers stipulated, that they would always obey the Swamiyar or one of his family as High Priest, and that his decendants should have the right to perform three day's devotion yearly, in the Pagoda.

"The Bhimmum therefore remained peaceably in Cochin until about 1719, when it miraculously disappeared, and was found on the sea beach, and taken to the house of the Dutch Governor. He saw nothing but a little misshapen figure, apparently composed of an admixture of gold, silver and other metals; and thinking it of little value, gave it to his children as a plaything. But hardly it reached the house, when the Governor's wife was attacked with severe colic, which did not cease, until the idol had left their roof, and obtained shelter in the house of a native doctor. The poor man as well as his family were tormented with illness for seven years, when it was fortunately discovered that the idol was the cause of his misfortunes, and that it was the long lost Bhimmum. Again it reached the Pagoda, where it rested quietly until 1791, in which year the Raja of Cochin directed the Pagoda to contribute a large quantity of sugar-cane jaggery, towards a feast at Trippunittura. The trustees refused, one of them being Dagwars Kini, and the "Dagwars Kini war", as it is termed, ensued. About the third week in September, two of the Raja's Eurasian officers, accompanied by a Ragiadoor, went to Dagwar's Kini's shop, and stated that they required some silks; but while serving them, he was murdered, his head cut off, and carried away to the Raja; whose troops made a rush upon the Canarese bazaar. The priests hearing the uproar hastily deposited the idol and its jewels in a box and sought refuge under the guns of the Dutch fort, inside which the Bhimmum was placed. Fearing it might be given up by the Dutch, they the next day sent it by a canoe to Chellāna, and about a month subsequently to Alleppey, where the Travancore Raja permitted it to be placed in an Oottupurah where it remained securely guarded for many years.

"As soon as the British supremacy had caused tranquillity, it was proposed to build a large temple at Cochin, and again install the Bhimmum there. They believed that it was owing to the good will manifested by the idol that Cochin had become a prosperous place; still they agreed that, if a Pagoda were built at Alleppey, and lands yielding Rupees. 12,000 yearly given as an endowment, they would let it remain there; and these terms were acceded to by the Raja of Travancore. The importance of Alleppey is now decreasing, which is attributed by the Hindus, to the Cochin Pagoda having regained possession of the idol, owing to the Bhimmum having been conveyed out of the Alleppey Pagoda, in the bread basket of a Cochin Brahman and thus reached its old abode. It is usual after the Brahmans have been feasted, inside the Pagoda, for the remainder of the food, to be carried outside in long baskets, where persons are awaiting their shares of the precious morsels. In February 1853, after the feast, a Cochin Brahman concealed the God in one of these baskets and thus it was conveyed out of the Temple, and was soon placed in a boat, and rapidly propelled to Cochin. Early the following morning, great was the dismay at Alleppey, the image had disappeared and the Travancore Government protested that the Cochin people had robbed Alleppey of its chief treasure. Communications at last led to angry recriminations and in 1856 troops were ordered from Quilon, to march towards Cochin, and compel the restitution of the highly prized idol.

"The Cochin Dewan now offered to return it; this was acceded to; a day was chosen, on which to receive it and a portion of the Nair Brigade was in readiness to meet it with all honours at Alleppey. At last, on January 28th, 1857, the boat hove in sight and the Priests met at the landing place. Having broken a cocoanut the chief Brahman making profound Salams entered the cabin, but soon in wrath and disgust reappeared, declaring the image was a spurious one, dressed up in the true jewels. Having deposited it in the verandah of the Pagoda, another letter was despatched to Cochin, and another idol declared to be the true one, was sent on January 31st, 1857, but was as false as the first. Finally in 1859 the Madras Government settled this important question, by deciding that as the idol had originally deserted from Cochin, and had now returned to that place, there it was to remain[1] whilst the Travancore officials are said to have finished the business, by resuming the lands they had granted, for the idol's support"[2].

11. **Sancaratchar.** The life and work of Śrī Śankarāchārya are of as much importance in the religious and social history of Malabar as those of Śrī Paraśu Rāma, the Patron Saint of Kērala, and it is therefore necessary to know something of them.

His Life.

Sri Sankaracharya,[3] the great Adwaita philosopher and religious reformer of India, a Nambūtiri, was born in 788 A. D. in Kaippilli illom (4) at Kālaṭi, (5) a small village on the banks of the Alwaye

(1) See Minutes of Consultation. Fort St. George, 24th August 1858.

(2) Day, pp. 309—312.

(3) For the following note on Sankaracharya, I am indebted to my friend Mr. P. Krishna Menon, B. A., L. T., to whom my thanks are due.

(4) "Exactly a thousand years before his Spiritual Kinsman Schanpenhauer" as Professor Deussen puts it.

(*See outline of the Vedanta System of Philosophy according to Shankara* by Paul Deussen. Translated by J. H. Woods and C. B. Runkle with Prefatory note by the Author.)

(5) The insignificant village of Kalati had been left unnoticed and neglected hitherto.

river, six miles to the east of Alwaye, a station on the Cochin State Railway. The place is now situated in the Manjappra Proverthy of the Kuṅṅaṭṭunad Taluk of the Travancore State; but, at the time of the Guru's birth, and until 946 M. E., it formed part of the Cochin State. The river in that part abounded in crocodiles, one of which was, according to tradition, the immediate means of the Teacher's renunciation of the world and entrance into the Order of the Sannyasins, a boon his mother was forced to give, in order to save the future great seer and philosopher from the jaws of a ravenous amphibian. The place where the blessed lady was is still shown to the pious pilgrim who wends his way to the sacred spot.

Śivaguru, Sankara's father, having died before the sage's birth, the Teacher was born a posthumous child and his early education devolved on the shoulders of his maternal uncle. The following Slōkas (verses) embodying a well-known traditional account of Śankar's Life, in Sanskrit, are both interesting and instructive; as, besides giving us the chief incidents in his life time, they serve as a clue to the solution of the question of his, date.

Ḍuṣhṭāchara Vināśaya
Pṛaḍurbhuṭo Mahīṭale
Sa Eva Śankarāchārya
Sākṣhāl Kaivallya Nāyakaḥ!
Niḍhināgē Bhavanyabdē
Vibhave Śankaroḍayah
Aṣhṭavaṛṣhē Chaṭurvēḍān
Ḍwāḍaśē Sarvaśāsṭṛakrit
Ṣhōḍaśē Kṛiṭavan Bhāṣhyam
Ḍwāṭrimśē Munirabhyagāl
Kallyabḍē Chanḍranēṭṛānka
Vanhyabḍē Guhāpravēśah
Vaiśākhē Purṇimāyāmṭu
Śankara Śivaṭamagat*

* See the Travancore State Manual by Mr. V. Nagam Aiya Vol. II., Chap. VIII, p. 99.

"He the same Sankaracharya, verily God Himself (or, The Abode of Bliss Incarnate) manifested Himself on earth for the extermination of wicked ways. The advent of Sankara was in the year called Vibhava 3889 of Kali Era (*i. e.* 788 A. D.). He studied in (his) eighth year the four Vedas. He mastered all the Sastras in his twelfth year. In his sixteenth year, he composed the Bhashya (commentaries on the Gita, the Upanishads and Brahma Sutras). In his thirty-second year the sage ascended (the seat of Learning). In the year 3922 of the Kali Era (821 A. D.) he entered the cave; and on the full-moon day of the Vaishakha of the same year Sankara attained Supreme bliss."

From the above account certain important facts may be deduced—namely—1. that Śankara was born in 788 A. D. as held by Professors Max Muller, Sundram Pillai and others; (2) that he was the author of the Bhāṣhya; (3) that he went to Kashmir and ascended the seat of Learning; and (4) that he died in his thirty-second year or 821 A. D.

The tradition that the death of Śankara synchronized with the commencement of the Kollam Era, *i. e.*, 825 A. D., may have some substantial basis in fact, as it is not difficult to believe that the news of his death which occurred at Kedarnath on the Himalayas took about three years to reach Malabar at a time when all travelling was done on foot.

One important event in the life of Śankara was his initiation into the Sannyāsāśrama by Gōvinḍa Bhaṭṭa. Gouḍapāḍa's desciple, somewhere near the banks of the Narmada. After this, he went to Benares where he wrote his famous commentaries on the *Prasthhanathraya*—the Gīṭa, the Upanishads and the Vēḍānṭa Sūṭras. Then commenced his famous itinerancy or controversial tour through the length and breadth of India. He preached pure Adwaitism as inculcated in the well-known Vedantic aphorisms. Ēkam ēva aḍviṭīyam[1] (one only, without a second); Ṭaṭṭwam

(1) Chandogyopanishad VI. 2, 1.

asi[1] (That thou art); Sarvam Khalvidam brahma [2] (All this is verily Brahman); Aham Brahma asmi [3] (I am Brahman); and many others of a like import. Śankara's victorious tour took him to such distant places as Balkh and the frontiers of Afghanistan on the west, Kashmir and Cis-Himalayan regions in the North, Assam on the east, and Chōla and Pāṇḍya in the South, that to this day his name is affectionately invoked by his followers as "the best of peripatetic teachers", In one of these tours, when he was at Śringēri in Mysore, he heard of the illness of his mother and so he hastened to Malabar to be nearer her in her last moments. The biographer says that, after her death, Śankara had to preform obsequies himself, unaided by the formalist Nambūṭiris of the day, who objected to the Guru's performance of these on the grounds of his being a Sannyāsin [4]. The ingenuity of the priesthood has not failed to take advantage of this, and the institution of the well-known sixty-four Anāchāras or peculiar usages of Kērala has been purposely fathered upon the sacred name of Śankara to give them an authority and sanction which they would otherwise have never had. We shall return to the consideration of the authenticity of this tradition in a later part of this thesis.

The story of Śankara's having met Kumārilla Bhaṭṭa, the hoary advocate of Pūrva Mīmāmsa of Northern India, is not of much historical value, but the incident of Śankara's long controversies with Mandana Misra, and his wife Bhāraṭi— supposed to be an incarnation of the Goddess of Learning—is interesting, as it afterwards led to the conversion of Mandana and his initiation, under the name of Surēswarāchārya, into the Sannyāsa Order.

(1) Chandogyopanishad VI, 8, 7.
(2) Ibid III, 14, 1.
(3) Brishadarnyakopanishad, 1, 4, 10.
(4) Madhava's Sankaravijaya, Poona Edition, pp. 496—7.

The legend that Śankara persecuted the Buddhists is entirely unsupported by facts, and we shall not stop to examine it. On the other hand it is possible, even highly probable that Śankarāchārya by his powerful and irresistible advocacy of theism and the moral trustworthiness of the universe, as opposed to the Buddhistic doctrines of Nihilism and final annihilation current at the time, contributed more than any other man to the final extirpation of the rival faith from the land of its birth.

Sankara had no great respect for mere book learning as such, and the pedantry of the scholiast, and his "Exhortation to a Grammarian" with its musical refrain of "worship the all merciful God (Govind)", is one of the most trenchant criticisms on those who seek to cram their memory with the dry bones of knowledge without seeking true enlightenment and spiritual vision at the same time.

While travelling in north-eastern India, he passed through Assam where he was attacked by a disease said to have been due to Black Magic practised by Abhinava Gupta, the commentator on Sakta works, who was defeated by Śankara in controversy. Although partially cured, the teacher never recovered fully from the effects of the attack and going to the Himalayas, he died at Kedarnath, in his thirty-second year, in 821 A. D.

Kalaṭi was left neglected up till recently. But the occupant of the Śringēri Seat, the 33rd in succession from its founder, the Āḍi Śankarāchāryār, revived it by improving the site and establishing a temple for the worship of Śankara. Kālaṭi is but an obscure village in North Travancore; and so other towns of celebrity, such as Conjeevaram and Chidambaram have put forth claims of having given birth to the great teacher. Anandagiri mentions Chidambaram, while the writer of Maṇimaññary gives it as Kālaṭi and "his testimony in such matters [1] must be held peculiarly valuable for obvious reasons". The Kaippilli illom to which Ṡankara belonged had in its possession till recently a plot of ground which his mother is said to have obtained in her life-time. Her crematorium is in it. The Travancore Government acquired this plot on 27th January 1906. The locality is treated as a Samkēṭam or place of sanctity, none but high caste Hindus being allowed to reside or to acquire land within the Samkēṭam.

After the acquisition of the plot, the Travancore Government has transferred it to the Sringeri Mutt for the erection of a temple for Ṡrī Ṡankarāchārya. Two beautiful temples one to Ṡri Ādi Ṡankarāchārya and the other to the Mutt's tutelary deity Ṡāradāmba have been built, and a magnificent flight of steps leading to the river. The consecration of the temples was performed on Monday the 10th of Kumbham 1085 M. E., corresponding to the 21st of February 1910, in the presence of no less than forty thousand devotees who had come from all parts of India.

The land of Kērala has to be remembered and its memory dearly cherished by the whole civilised world for having given birth to so great a teacher as the great Ṡankarāchārya.

His work.

Ṡri Ṡankarāchārya was a practical reformer. He was not content with giving, from his point, a mere theoretical interpre- own Adwaitic or Non-dualistic stand- tation of the ancient Aryan religion and philosophy. He instituted Mutts, Adwaitāṡramas or monasteries for the teaching and propagation of the principle of the Oneness of Life in some of the most important places in India—at Sringeri in Mysore, at Puri in Orissa, at Badari on the Himalayas (where a

1 Mr. C. N. Krishnaswami Ayyar, M. A., L. T., in his *Sree Sankaracharya, His Life and Times*, p. 13.

Naṃbūṭiri Brahmin has been an officiating priest ever since Ṡankara's time) and Ḍwāraka in the Gaikwar's Dominions in Gujarat. It is this aspect of Ṡankara's character—the combination of the subtle, hair-splitting, speculative philosopher and the clear-eyed, practical reformer that is the most wonderful feature of his sublime personality. In his merciless insistence on keeping strictly to the exact definition of a term, and on unravelling the intricacies of an argument so as to find out the lurking fallacies in it, he is as great as Socrates or Aristotle, if not greater. In his appeal to our Ṡās-ṭras (in the wider sense) as the final repository of the possible spiritual experiences of the race, he out-platoed Plato whose "Doctrine of Ideas" pales before Ṡankara's *Theory of Maya* as a mere well-thought-out guess. There is no other character in History, ancient or modern, in whom the thinker and the doer have been so happily combined as Ṡṙi Ṡankarāchārya; and there is no other personality whose work as both thinker and doer has had such an abiding influence for good. But for Ṡrī Ṡankarāchārya, Hinduism would have been a fossil religion now, like many other religions of the past, and the world of thought would have been poorer for lack of its most powerful champion in the cause of philosophic theism.

Again, by his commentaries on the *Three Prasthanas*, and by his preachings, he not merely revived the ancient religion of the Aryans, but he also gave a new life to the various sects existing at the time, such as the Gaṇāpaṭyas, the Ṡākṭas, the Souryas, etc., by supplying them with a new interpretation of their varying beliefs. All were asked to see behind Manifested Nature and the Unmanifested Personal Deities of the sects, One Unmanifested Being, that which is "beyond the veil" in the language of Tennyson, or "*avyaktovyaktat*", in the language of *Bhagavad Gita*. Hence he was not merely a revivalist, but a purifier as well. He condemned the despicable practices of the Kapālikās of Western India and of the Sākṭās at Kāmrūp in Assam and at Kānchi in South India. Hence he composed after his return to Kērala that magnificent poem Ānanḍalahari, or bliss intoxicant, which is the most superb "Hymn to Intellectual Beauty" extant in the world, which gives an aesthetic interpretation of the universe in some of its recondite aspects, and which follows, in the very first stanza, the interpretation which the position of the images in the northern shrine of the temple at Trichur, is designed to give to the ardent truth-seeker.

The Anachars of Malabar. According to the Kēralōtpaṭṭi, the sixty-four Anāchāras or peculiar usages of Malabar, already enumerated in a former note, were promulgated by Śankarāchārya when he was not assisted by the Nampūṭiris in the cremation of his mother's dead body.

If we want to understand, to get into the spirit of, these Anāchāras, we should do well to classify them under certain headings as follows:—[1]

1. *Rules regarding personal hygiene.* Under this head will come numbers 1, 2, 3, 4, 6, 7, 8, 9, 10, 11, 12, 22, 28;

2. *Rules regarding eating.* We may include in this group Anāchāras Nos. 5, 15, 16, 17, 18, 21, 27;

3. *Rules regarding the worship of the Gods and the Manes.* This class consists of Nos. 13, 14, 19. 20, 31, 32, 33, 34, 35, 36 37, 38, 39, 50, 52, 60;

4. *Rules regarding conduct in society.* This group will comprise Nos. 29, 30, 40, 44, 45, 46, 47, 48, 49, 51, 54, 55, 61, 62, 63, 64;

5. *The four Asramas or stages of Life.* In this class we may include Nos. 23, 24, 25, 26, 41, 42, 43, 53, 56, 57, 58, 59.

In the first place, the so-called Anāchāras or mal-observances of Malabar, are not mal-observances at all. They are sanctioned by the code of honour of the East

1. See the *Travancore Census Report for 1901.* Part I, page 303.

Coast as well as that of the West Coast, though the East Coast Brahmin is not so strict in following them as the Nampūṭiris.[1] Secondly, there is nothing *peculiar* or strange about many of these customs, as they are the most natural that one might expect to find in a country with the like physical and ethnological characteristics of Malabar. In a land where the rainfall is plentiful and tanks are abundant, that bathing should be practised as a fine art and resorted to on every conceivable pretext, is not at all surprising, especially when we take into consideration the wide social gulf that existed between the Aryan emigrants and the Turanian or Dravidian inhabitants at the time when they come in contact with one another. The same fact will account for the rules regarding eating as well as those connected with the ceremonial pollution. In a community so sparsely populated as the Nampūṭiris at the time of their colonisation, as now, it would be difficult to employ other Brahmins as *Purohits*, and unwise to divide themselves into innumerable sects by fruitless controversies about the supremacy of particular Gods. Hence Nampūṭiris are their own priests, and they pay equal veneration to the Gods of the Hindu Pantheon. No doubt this unsectarian character of their religious worship received an impetus and an additional sanction from the Reformation effected by Śrī Śankarāchrāya, whose one object in life was to abolish all sectarian differences and to unite the Hindus in the worship of the one True God, though invoked under the different names and forms. Again, the soil of Malabar being so poor in saline elements compared with the soil of the East Coast and of the surrounding Districts, where, rainfall not being excessive, salinity is better retained, cattle are neither so good nor so many as elsewhere; and this necessitates the introduction of special rules for the employment of cow's milk, ghee, etc., and the

1. A New Study of the Nampuṭiris, by Pandit Natesa Ayyar in *the Madras Mail*. See also *The Travancore State Manual*, Vol. II, page 266.

avoidance of those of buffaloes, for ceremonial purposes. Malabar is a place where snakes are as plentiful as crows and where it could be often dangerous to go out for bathing before sun-rise, not to speak of the inconvenience to the junior members of the Nampuṭiri household to leave the houses of their Nāyar wives and seek a plunge bath in the torrential rain. In the same way, it is not necessary to call in the adventitious sanction of the sacred name of Śankara for the custom of the Nampūṭiris cremating corpses in the vicinity of their houses. It may be the Guru did this himself, as he was compelled to do, because the pharisees of the day refused to help him. But the fact that the Nampuṭiris are the real landlords of the soil, and owned and even now own extensive tracts as their exclusive properties, made them live far apart and not in *agraharams* or in close proximity, as other Brahmin communities do. Their numbers being very small, the Nampūṭiris are not able to carry their corpses to distant crematories, and, even in their own house-yards, they are dependent on the Nayars for the preparation of the funeral pile. [1]

It is needless to pursue the argument further. The physical features of the country and the social status of the Nampūṭiris at the time they migrated into it are sufficient to account for their peculiar customs imposed by necessity and sanctified by time. The Nampūṭiris are pure Aryans who came from different parts of India and colonized Malabar at different intervals. Their civilization was uncontaminated by contact with the surrounding Dravidians or the invading Scythians of the North-west of India. Hence they devoted themselves exclusively to the study of the Vedas and to the conduct of life as revealed in the Four Āśramas. At first probably they practised agriculture, spun cotton, and washed their own clothes. In course of time, by sheer of force intellect, and also,

1. See the observations of our author in para 3 of Letter XX.

perhaps, by the splendour of their position, they compelled the other people to do all these things for them. They disapproved of Saṭi, which is Non-Aryan and which is of Scythious origin. And it is likely that in the very legend of their leader Paraśurāma having killed the Kṣhaṭṭiyas twenty-one times, there is this soul of truth—that the Aryans had to fight, often single-handed, against the barbaric hordes of the Scythian invaders who poured into India through the North-western passes from Western and Central Asia. The story of Paraśurāma's mother having been smitten by the shadow of a passing Ariel, her consequent death at the hands of her son, the assasination of Paraśurāma's father by the Kṣhaṭṭiyas, and Paraśurāman's interminable wars with them—all these show the jealous care with which the ancient Aryans—the ancestors of the present-day Naṃpūṭiris—guarded the purity of their race. The Naṃpūṭiris practise no "Lynch-law". But they impose a number of most stringent restrictions on the movements of their fair sex. A Naṃpūṭiri woman, generally called an Akāyilullaver or Anṭarjanam (occupant of the inner apartment) must not look at any other person besides her own husband, and when she goes out, she is always accompanied by Nāyar maid-servants to shout and keep men out of her way. This anxiety to preserve their racial purity is quite natural and is due to various causes. One of these is the degree of civilization attained by the Aryans who were superior in intelligence and in physical features to the earlier Dravidian inhabitants of the country; another is the fact that the Aryan colonies in Malabar, when they migrated from their original houses, had fewer females among them than males. This latter circumstance also accounts for the fact that the Naṃpūṭiris permit only their eldest sons to marry, and allow alliance for the other male members with the Kṣhaṭṭiya, Vyśia and Nāyar women. A study of past and contemporary history in various parts of the world will lead one to believe that any other community of shrewd people in similar circumstances will do exactly like this.

12. **Marriage.** There is but little difference between the Koṇkaṇis and other Brahmans so far as marriage ceremonials are concerned. Our author has given a fair description of what takes place. His account may be supplemented by a few further details. The status of husband and wife is created by the tying of the ṭāli or Mangalya Sūṭram. So long as the ceremony lasts, the couple eat and sleep in the same apartment. The Kanyakāḍānam or the giving away of the bride takes places on the fourth day of the ceremony and not on the first day as among other Brahmans. The Avabhṛṭasnānam or final bathing is performed on the night of the 5th day. The bridegroom stays in the house of the bride for three months and performs the Śṭhālīpāka sacrifice. The Ḍīkṣha terminates in the third month. The Konkaṇi is divided into several endogamous Gōṭṛās or septs. Custom enjoins that as far as possible a Konkaṇi ought to marry his maternal uncle's or paternal aunt's daughter. Divorce and widow marriage are not allowed. Polygamy is allowed but seldom practised. If the wife proves barren or suffers from an incurable disease, another one may be married, but only with the consent of the first wife. Our author is not correct in saying that "polygamy is forbidden among the Canarese as it is among other Brahmans." Among no class of Brahmans is polygamy forbidden. The Hindu Law allows it, though it is seldom practised.

13. **Solemnities are alike at birth and death.** The ceremonies observed by the Konkaṇis before marriage are the same with those of the other Brahmans, differing, if at all, only in slight local details. They have the Jāṭakaṛmaṃ, Nāmakaṛṇam, Annapṛāśanam, Choulam, and Upanayanam ceremonies in succession. A Kṣhurapūja, or the consecration of the razor, precedes its employment for cutting the umblical cord. On the fifth day after birth, in the case of boys and, on the sixth day, in the case of girls, a golden necklace is tied round the neck of the child after a small ceremony. The naming or

Nāmakarṇam takes place on the 12th day, the eldest male child being named after the paternal grandfather and the first daughter after the maternal grandmother. Annaprāśana and Choula are the first rice-giving and the first cutting of the hair, which present no special features requiring notice. Upanayana or investiture with the sacred thread comes on between the seventh and tenth years of the boy's age. This is a very important ceremony. It is by the investiture of the thread that the boy becomes a Brahman, a member of the twice-born class.

Ceremonies after marriage. When a girl attains puberty, the husband's relations, on information received from her father, arrange to have the nuptials performed in the husband's house, if possible within a fortnight, the fifth day being the most appropriate. Till this ceremony is over, the girl is strictly prohibited from going out of doors. In the third month after conception is the Pumsavanam and, in the seventh, Sīmamṭam. Pollution after death lasts for ten days. Only one Brahman is fed on occasions of Śrāḍḍhas.

Personal names. The names generally in use are:—*for males*, those of Vishṇu, Subramaṇya and Gaṇapaṭi, such as Kṛshṇa, Vāmana, Narasimha, Guṇa Vitlan etc. The names by which the sacred rivers of India are known are generally employed as personal names of females, such as, Ganga, Yamuna, Saraswaṭi, etc. Gouri, Yaśōḍa, Sumiṭra, Saṭyabhāma, Subhaḍra, Rukmaṇi, Nāgāi and Guṇāi are also in general use. The titular suffixes to their names are many; some of them are:—Kammaṭṭi, Pai, Prabhu, Shenai, Nāyken, Vālikan or Bālika, Kiṇi, Paṭiyār, Row, Kilikāran, Paṭṭar, Ayyar, Mallan, Vāḍhyār and Achāryar.

Language. The Shēṇavis speak Maharathi and the Konkaṇis, Konkaṇi. Their written Character is the Maharati. Both the Portuguese and Malayalam languages have contributed largely to the language of their homes. To those who are not their castemen, the Konkaṇis, both males and females, speak Malayālam. But there are women among them who are strangers to that language altogether. Tamil is almost unknown. There is a peculiar intonation which is distinctly characteristic of the caste when the Konkaṇi speaks Malayālam—an intonation which he has probably derived from his native tongue.

14. **Caste and occupation.** The occupation of the Konkaṇies have been commerce ever since they settled in Malabar. Their character as tradesmen has been described by our author in a way not very complimentary to them. The Dutch Governor, M. Van. Adrian Moens, also, speaking of them, observes much in the same manner. Ward and Cornner, however, writing about them, a century later, speak of them as devoted to commerce in all its shapes and deserving the merit of at least a very tolerable share of integrity and fair dealing. Whether for want of integrity or not, they have considerably fallen in their profession as merchants. Their former prosperity in this line has altogether deserted them. In Cochin there is hardly any one at present who can be called a prosperous merchant. Of course there are numerous small traders who vend sundry articles of domestic use. There are some who own lands while others are slowly giving up their traditional occupation and betaking themselves to other professions. The other Brahmans of South India never acknowledge them to be on a par with them in caste status, and do not interdine or intermarry with them, and the Konkaṇis return the compliment by keeping aloof from them altogether. It is said that their occupation as merchants has lowered them in the eyes of their Brahman brethren. But this can hardly be so. For, we know that, in spite of their being members of the twice-born class, these Brahmans themselves are seldom loth to earn an honest penny as a merchant. They do in practice trade in all kinds

of articles, not excepting those which the Ṣāṣṭras denounce as abomination for them even to look at. The Konkaṇis of Malabar have now begun to imitate the example of their castemen in South Canara and Bombay. There the Shēṇavi Brahmans have always been a very intelligent class and some of the greatest scholars of the Bombay Presidency, such as the late Dr. Bhau Daji, the late Justice Kasinath Trimbak Telang, the late Sankar Pandurang Pandit and Professor Rama Krishna Gopal Bhandarkar, whose names will always stand honoured in the literary history of India, are Shēṇavis by caste. The Malabar Konkaṇis are intellectually not in the least behind their kinsmen elsewhere and, if by force of circumstances and occupation, they have not been able to keep pace with their brethren in Western India in intellectual culture till recently, they have now begun to brace themselves up, and are endeavouring to qualify themselves for the learned professions according to the requirements of the modern age. It is gratifying to note that there are at present a few graduates in arts and in law in the community in the Malabar.

Some of them make Pappaṭam or fine thin cakes made of grain flour and a fine species of alkali which gives them an agreeable salt taste and serve the purpose of making them rise and become very crisp when fried.

In their home near Goa, there were two sects called the Shastis (Sanskrit for 60) who settled in Goa and Shanvis or Shenvis (Sanskrit for 96), being those who settled in the districts surrounding Goa. These names evidently indicate the number of families that had originally come down from the north. As observed by our author, the Canarese are divided into several castes which differ in rank and sanctity but have similar customs. There are the Brahmans who, in Malabar, are generally called the Konkaṇis, the Vāniyans who are Vyśias and the Kuṭumikār who are

Śūḍras. Dr. Day says that the Konkaṇies of Cochin are sub-divided into four grades: (1) Ṭaṭṭans or gold-smiths; (2) Vāṇiyans (oil merchants); (3) the Cheṭṭies who are shrops and general merchants; and (4) the Kuṭumies who found rice and perform inferior offices. It is not, however, correct to say that the Vāṇiyans are oil merchants. That class of men as well as the Ṭaṭṭans, Cheṭṭies and Kuṭumies form no part of the Konkaṇi caste.

15. **Sons alone inherit.** The Konkaṇies follow the ordinary Hindu Law of inheritance and succession. The property of those who die without heirs goes by custom to their Devaswams, and an annual ceremony is performed in memory of the deceased and in the interests of their souls.

16. **Wannia—The Vaniyans.** They are Vaiśyas, and wear the sacred thread. In regard to marriage, inheritance, ceremonies, dress, ornaments, etc., there is practically no difference between the Vāṇiyas and the Konkaṇies. But, as the former do not altogether abstain from meat and spirituous liquors, they are not allowed free access to the houses of the Konkaṇies, nor are they permitted to touch their tanks and wells. They are Saivites. They have their own priests, who are called Paṇḍiṭars. They observe birth and death pollution for 10 days, and are like Brahmans in this respect. They are mostly petty merchants and shop-keepers. Some can read and write Malayalam, but they are very backward in English education. The title of Cheṭṭi generally assumed by them points to their being Vaiśyas, and to their merchantile profession.

17. The **Sonar.** The *Sonar* or *Sonagara* from Sonna or Swarṇa, gold, is a gold-smith by caste. Mr. Sturrock, in his *Manual of the District of South Canara*, has the following notice of them: "They speak Konkaṇi which is a dialect of Marathi and are believed to have come from Goa. The community at

each station has one or two Mukhtesars or headmen who enquire into and settle the caste affairs; serious offences are reported to the *Swamy* of Sode, who has authority to excommunicate or to inflict heavy fines. They wear the sacred thread, and employ Brahman priests. Marriages within the same *Gotra* are strictly prohibited. Most of them are Vaishnavites but a few worship Siva. The dead are burned and the ashes are thrown into a river. They eat fish but not flesh. Their title is Setti."[1] There is a large colony of them in Cochin with a temple of their own. They are excellent workmen who are able to turn out any kind of work of which a sample is given them.

18. **The 'Iswwede' and the 'Curronby'**: These perhaps form one and the same class. The equivalent of the first name, Iswwede, it has not been possible to get at. But there can be no doubt that the 'Carronby' stands for Kuṭumbi, Kuṭumpi or Kuṭumi.

The Kutumpi. These are the Konkaṇa Śūdras who serve as the domestic servants of the Konkaṇies in whose midst they are invariably found. Their immigration into Malabar may be taken to have been coeval with that of the Konkaṇies. As usual, a more or less fanciful derivation is attributed to their class name, Kuṭumikār. They are said to be so called from the fact of their having attached themselves to the Kuṭumbams or families of other sections of the Konkaṇi population. As well might we derive the name from the Malayalam Kuṭumi or tuft of hair and say that they are called Kuṭumikār because they wear the Kuṭumi (tuft). Both Kuṭumbam and Kuṭumma are Malayalam terms and the derivation attributed is altogether imaginary. They are said to be Smārtas by persuasion, though their masters are Vaiṣṇavas. In attending to the accessory duties of Konkaṇi temples, the Kuṭumpis may be said to resemble the Ampalavāsies of Malabar, but, like these, they are not allowed to enter into the inner precincts of the temple. They are at the same

1 Page 516.

A GROUP OF KUDUMI CHETTIES.

(To face p. 634.

time domestic servants doing menial work in Konkaṇi houses. In Travancore, they are said to be divided into two broad divisions, Mūppans and Iṭiyans. These do not intermarry. The Mūppans, who claim descent from some old Konkaṇi chieftains, consider themselves higher than all other Kuṭumbies. Two other divisions are also referred to, *viz.*, the Kaṭiyans and the Kuṭumpies (proper), but in practice nothing turns upon this. The Mūppans of Ṭoravūr in Travancore are famous for the fireworks they manufacture for the Konkaṇi temple there. The Iṭiyans employ themselves in the preparation of *Aval* or beaten rice. The Kuṭumpies have the reputation of possessing an uncommon capacity for hard work and are not averse to any form of it. They are boatmen, porters, agricultural labourers, etc. They clean tanks and wells, thatch houses, in short they are willing hands at all kinds of manual labour. They are an altogether illiterate class almost incapable of intelligent work, mother wit and common sense being a great desideratum with them. Animal food and intoxicant drinks are not tabooed. But they eat only fish and abstain from liquor generally. Their dress and ornaments are peculiar. The men dress like the ordinary natives of Malabar, having a Muṇḍu or short piece of cloth tied round the waist and reaching the knees. The women wear a much longer piece of cloth which goes down the knees below and also covers the upper portion of the body by taking it over one of the shoulders, and securing it with a knot at the left shoulder. Bodices are not worn. But strings of coral and red beads, brass and glass bracelets are almost a speciality. Those who can afford use coloured cloth. They tie their hair behind in a peculiar fashion and adorn it with all sorts of fast coloured flowers, little caring for the smell. The girls are married young. The Kuṭumies are generally Makkaṭṭāyis. Death pollution lasts for 15 days. On the 16th day, they are purified by the sprinkling of consecrated water from the Konkaṇi temples. For ceremonial purposes in some places, Konkaṇi Vāḍhyārs officiate as priests, while, in other places, there are priests belonging to their own community. Their tutelary divinity is Bhagavaṭi, and the day on which the Bharaṇi asterism falls is one of great festivity. They attend the Cranganore Bhagavaṭi temple on Makara Saṃkrānṭi day in great numbers. At Alīkkal in Cochin, they have a temple of their own, where their castemen officiate as priests. Their chief amusement is called Kōlaṭi. A dozen people stand in a circle, with sticks, a cubic long, in hand, strike them against one another in unison, so as to keep time with the songs they sing in praise of Kṛshṇa and Bhagavaṭi. The Vāṇiyans and Kuṭumies speak a somewhat corrupt form of a Koṇkani dialect of Maharathi. They have a peculiar intonation in speaking. The Kuṭumies do not take food at the hands of Nāyars. They cannot, as they say, even take water touched by the Nāyars, and the Nāyars in their turn would not allow them to draw water from their tanks and wells. The difficulty is got over by the Kuṭumies accepting water drawn by Nāyars, only they insist on a few drops of buttermilk being poured into it, the idea being that this converts the water into butter-milk which they are not prevented from taking at the hands of the Nāyars. Such are the subterfuges to which simple people are driven to circumvent caste, customs and usages.

19. **Festivals of Canarese.**—(1) *Isamparocah.* This is the Malayalam Samvaṭsarampurakkal or the new year's day which is, as with all Hindus, on the 1st of Mēdam or Chiṭray.

(2) *Tirunal.* This is not a ceremony peculiar to Konkaṇies. It corresponds to the Uṭsavam of Malabar temples. In memory of the foundation of the temples, festivals are celebrated in them annually which last for 7 or 8 days, when the shrines are decorated and the idol is taken in procession daily round the pagoda in great pomp, three times a day, on the back of richly caparisoned elephants, and, in the case of Konkaṇi

temples, in palanquin or on various vāhanams, to the accompaniment of drums and music, and is bathed in the temple tank on the last day. Every night, during the festival, the pagoda and its surroundings are illuminated, and the money spent on pyrotechincs is enormous. Their castemen are daily fed in the temple. This festival is known as Uṭsavam and is no peculiarity with the Canarese. Every temple in Malabar of any consequence celebrates its Uṭsavam annually with more or less grandeur as it can afford.

(3) *The feast of Mantjemy.* This is the Nāga Panchami celebrated in honour of serpents. Serpent worship is held by the Canarese in as much importance as by other Brahmans. Images of serpents are consecrated and worshipped in their temples as also in the serpent groves of private individuals. The pollution and desecration of these groves and the molestation and the killing of the serpents are looked upon with as much abhorence as with other Hindus, and the Canarese with their other Hindu brethren fully believe that such acts would certainly lead to leprosy and barrenness. The Konkaṇa Vyśias and Śūdras are also snake worshippers. In their case, the Pūja is performed by the Konkaṇ Brahmans. Nāga Panchami is the special day for the worship of serpents.

(4) *Tzontam Pounow.* More correctly *Sattam Pounow.* This corresponds to the Āvaṇi Avaṭṭam or Upākarmaṃ of the other Brahmans, solemnised in the month Śrāvaṇa, Chingam or August-September, when all Brahmans change their sacred thread, repeat their Sandhya, Gāyaṭri, etc., a number of times, and make amends for neglect to repeat these daily in the course of the year ending with that day.

(5) *Astamy.* This is the Aṣhṭami Rōhiṇi or Gōkula Aṣhṭami celebrated as the day of the birth of Kṛṣhṇa as Viṣhṇu incarnate.

(6) *Wine Szoute.* More correctly Vināyaka Chaṭurṭhi, a festival observed in honour of Gaṇapaṭi or

Vighneśwara, the issue of Śiva and Pārvaṭi, conceived while they were sporting on the mountains in the form of elephants. The image of Gaṇapaṭi is represented as having the head of an elephant with its trunk and tusks the body being of human shape with four arms and a bulging belly. He is generally spoken of as a voracious eater and a gourmand, and it so happened that, while he was once out on an errand, after a more than usual filling of his huge belly, he happened to trip his foot and have a nasty fall. He got up hastily and looked round to see if any had witnessed the awkward plight in which he was and found none. Glad at not being observed by any one, he was passing on, when he happened to look up and, to his great disgust and mortification, he saw the waxing moon having a hearty laugh at his uncouth figure and his awkward fall. Albiet his claim to be classed as one of the chief among gods, his vanity was wounded and he pronounced a solemn curse on the unfortunate moon that those who happen to see her on that day every year will be subjected to all sorts of culumnies and will become objects of laughter to their brethren. Hence all orthodox Hindus avoid seeing the moon on that day, and worship the gourmand god by placing before his image an immense quantity of delicious eatables. On this day Pūja is also performed to Gaṇapaṭi.

(7) *Tjc Hordesje.* More correctly Ananṭa Chaṭurḍeśi or Ananṭa Vraṭam, a very important festival. At present the Raja of Cochin does not attend this festival, as is mentioned by the author.

(8) *Mannemy or Mahanavami.* Our author has failed to understand the importance of this festival. He describes it as a holiday for school-going children. It is the Nava-Rāṭri, or Durga Pūja or the Dussara in honour of the goddess Saraswaṭi celebrated all over India by all Hindus. The worship goes on for 9 days and with the Bengalees and Maharattas, it is one of the most important national festivals in their calendar. During

the palmy days of Maharatta supremacy, the Maharatta hordes set out on their career of conquest and raid on the last day of this festival. In Bengal, even today, all work is stopped for ten days, the shops, the Law Courts and other Government institutions are closed, and the people make the ten days regular holidays. In Malabar, among classes other than the Brahmans, it is known as Āyuḍha Pūja and all handicrafts men, in imitation of the Nāyars who, as men of the military class, began the worship of their arms, offer worship to their tools and implements and spent the last three days of the festival in great glee. In Malabar, for those three days, no one would write, or even read one's prayer books. Their books are placed before the image of the goddess Saraswaṭi and pūja or worship offered. On the last day, they are received back and solemnly opened and a few lines read. Then some sand is spread on the floor on which the letters of the alphabet are traced in token perhaps of the original initiation into letters and learning. This opportunity is also availed of for the commencement of the education of children.

(9) *Deevali* or *Deepavali* means literally a collection of lights. Nabakasser stands for Narakāsura whom the God Krishna killed to relieve the world from his oppression and tyranny. The festival is observed in honour of the event. It is celebrated with much rejoicing through the whole of India by all classes of Hindus. The Saivites and Vishnavites explain its origin in different ways. Both versions however agree in saying that it is celebrated in commemoration of the killing of the Rakṣhasa Narakasura. The Saivite say that the giant was killed by Subramaṇia, the son of Ṡiva or Mahēṣwara, whose aid was sought by the Dēvas who were being cruelly oppressed by the Rāk-ṣhasa. According to the Vaishnavas, Narakāsura had imprisoned 16,008 Gōpis (women of the cowherd class). Ṡri Krishna out of compassion for them accompanied

by his consort Saṭṭya-Bhāma, went against the Asura, fought with him, and left him dead on the field. The Gōpis were released and they became greatly elated with their success. They illumined their houses with myriads of lamps, and having, at the break of day, just at the hour corresponding to that at which Narakāsura died, partaken of a sumptuous feast, the sons of India have since that day celebrated the feast in the same manner. The festival is also known as Ṇaraka Chaṭurḍeśi.

(10) *Terou* or *Ter* or car. At temple festivals or uṭsavams, the image of the god ('Winke Tapati'= Venkitapati) is placed on a trumphal car beautifully decorated, and dragged round the pagoda. It is peculiar to the Canarese temples in Malabar as also to the Paṭṭar Brahman temples of Palghat. The Malayalees do not observe this in their temples which do not keep cars at all. Their images are always carried on the backs of huge elephants with gold or silver facings. On the East Coast, however, a car is almost an indispensible adjunct to a temple.

(11) *Chigma* or *Sikma*. This corresponds to the Holi festival lasting for a fortnight.

There are other festivals observed by the Canarese not mentioned by our author but which are of sufficient importance to be named here. Along with the Ananṭavṙiṭa may be mentioned Varalakṣhmivṙiṭa as being of paramount importance. In the month of Kāṙṭika (November), fasts are observed for the special propitiation of Ḍāmōḍara (Viṣhṇu). The Uṭhānā Ekāḍeśi day closes the fast days of Kāṙṭika. On that day Viṣhṇu is worshipped by the side of the Ṭulasi plant, (*Ocymum Sanctum*) and Brahmans are entertained.

20. **The Caste Government** The following extract from the Census Report of Travancore gives us an idea of the caste Government of the Canarese. "The Konkaṇies have been said to belong partly to the Vaishnavite and partly to the Saivite sect of Hinduism.

There are eight gramams or villages for the Konkana Brahmans of Travancore. They are known as Ashta-gramas, and consist of one at Alleppey, another at Poracad, a third at Kayamkulam, a fourth at Quilon, a fifth at Shertallay, a sixth at Turavur, a seventh at Kottayam and the eighth at Parur. It is only those who belong to one or other of these eight villages that are said to be strictly entitled to the name of Konkani. In Trivandrum there are many Konkanies. They are not allowed to mix with their fellow castemen who dwell in the north for purposes of commensality. Difference of faith, however, between the Saivites and Vaishnavites is no bar to the interdining and intermarriage. The Smartas owe spiritual allegiance to the ancient Kaivalyamath, situated in the Goanese territory, and founded by a disciple of Govinduyati, the Guru of Sri Sankara. The Vaishnavas have two Maths, offshoots of the Phalimarmath of Udipi founded by Madhava Charya. They are known as the Kasi and Gokarna Mutts from the principal seats of the respective Swamiyars being located at Benares and Goa respectively. (It is the Swamiyar of the Benares Mutt who is styled their Bishop by our author). The present Swamiyar at Benares is called Srimath Varadendratiratha Swamikal. The Swamiyar is the highest authority in all social and religious matters. There are several temples and village priests under his control. The ordinary and emergent affairs of every village are heard and decided by the managing Committee of the temple attached to that village. A portion of the temple is specially set apart as a sort of court-house and is called Yogasala or the Council hall. This Yoga (council) is bound to see that the priests perform their duties with care and attention. Every important decision has to be communicated to the Swamiyar and all facts have to be laid before him".[1]

In Cochin also, all caste disputes are referred to their High Priest the Swamiyar of Kāśi (Benares) Mutt

1. Pages 283—284.

CC.

who resides at Munchēśwar or Basroon. The community is everywhere known as *Pathum-per* or the ten individuals perhaps with reference to the original ten families said to have been brought from Tirhut.

Our author's account of the Konkaṇies shows them to have been, as they still are, to a certain extent, an important section noted for the industry and their enterprise. As merchants, no doubt they are losing ground, but they are steadily advancing on their lines. Ward and Conner's description of the sect informs us that, in their day, "their superior perseverance and industry rendered them productive subjects." Comparing them with the Lubbays who were also immigrants, Ward and Conner say that the Konkaṇies "have all their habits of unwearied diligence, without any of their vices". They are a thriving class and there can be no doubt that ere long they will be able to take their place by the side of their Brahman brethren in every walk of life.

21. **Jogis.** Then, in this letter our author refers to a class of people who wander about from one end of India to the other and have no permanent abode of their own. They are of no particular caste. According to Yule a *Jogee* is a Hindu ascetic, and sometimes a conjuror. From Sanskrit *Yogin* one who practises the *yoga*, a system of meditation combined with austerities which is supposed to induce miraculous power over elementary matter.[1] Dr. Forster, the learned translator of Fra Bartolomeo, derives the word *Yogee* from 'Yoga', community under which name he says, "is understood people who have everything in common. In the Samscred, they are named Goswami, from *Go* a cow and *Swami* a lord, consequently lords of the cow, for they are accustomed to sprinkle and paint their bodies with dried cow's dung. They are known also by a more ancient Samscred name, *viz.*, Samana or Shamana, that is the Mild; for they kill no animals,

1. *Hobson Jobson*, p. 351.

cut no plants, and never eat fish, but feed merely on rice, wild herbs, roots and fruit. They live together in company under a common chief or teacher who in the Samscred is called Guru. As true gymnosophists, they go quite naked and sleep on the ground, having nothing under them but made of palm leaves interwoven with each other. They avoid all intercourse with the world, study philosophy, theogony, botany and astronomy and have written a great many treatises on these sciences in the Indian languages. They are real stoics and often impose upon themselves severest penances. They are mentioned by Cicero, Plutarch, Clemenes of Alexandria and Arrian. The last author says, besides other things respecting them, that they were accustomed to walk down into the Sea at Cape Camari (Camorin) in order to purify themselves, a custom which they have retained to this day."[1] Again, while differentiating the *Bikshu* or the begging monks from the *Yogi*, the same writer observes; "They have nothing in common with the gymnosophists. *Samaneir Yogins*, and *Gosuza* who never eat with them nor enter their pagodas or temples. The last mentioned form also four different classes, for they consist of hermits, members who live in common and possess certain portions of land, mendicants or the gymnosophists properly so called and Sanyasis (Senasseys), who all forsake their wives and run about naked. All the philosophers, who as already said, must not be confounded with the Brahmans, impose upon themselves penances which appear almost incredible. 'Some of these people' says Pallebot de Saint Lubin[2] 'remain sitting on the ground so long that they are not able to move from the spot; others keep their arms so long in an erect posture that an anchilosis is formed between the joint of the arm and the shoulder blade, and they are altogether incapable of holding their arm out straight. Some keep their hands always folded together, so that their

1. Bartolomeo, p. 111.
2. Vol. I, p. 25.

nails grow through the flesh and appear on the other side. Some drag after them monstrous chains; others support heavy beams in the air, and others roll themselves down from the top of the mountains etc.' I myself saw one of these men who had a heavy chain suspended from his foreskin; another had stuck his head up to the neck in an iron cage and a third had held his arm so long over the fire that it was entirely withered."[1]

Marco Polo (1298) refers to them as *Chugi*. Speaking of the people of "The Province of Lar whence the Brahmans come," Polo observes:—"There is another class of people called Chugi, who are indeed properly Abraiaman, but they form a religious order devoted to the Idols. They are extremely long lived, every man of them living to 150 or 200 years. They eat very little, but what they do eat is good rice and milk chiefly. And these people make use of a very strange beverage; for they make a portion of sulphur and quicksilver mixed together and this they drink twice every month. This, they say, gives them long life, and it is a potion they are used to take from their childhood."

"There are certain members of this order who lead the most ascetic life in the world, going stark naked, and these worship the ox. Most of them have a small ox of brass or pewter or gold which they wear tied over the forehead. Moreover they take cow-dung and burn it, and make a powder thereof; and make an ointment of it, and daub themselves withal, doing this with as great devotion as Christians do show in using Holy Water. Also if they meet any one who treats them well, they daub a little of this powder on the middle of his forehead."

"They eat not from bowls or trenchers, but put their victuals on leaves of the Apple of Paradise and other big leaves; these, however, they use dry, never

1 Page 294, Note.

green, for they say the green leaves have a soul in them, and so it would be a sin. And they would rather die than do what they deem their Law pronounces to be sin. If any one asks how it comes that they are not ashamed to go stark naked as they do, they say, 'We go naked because naked we came into the world, and we desire to have nothing about us that is of this world. Moreover we have no sin of the flesh to be conscious of, and therefore we are not ashamed of our nakedness, any more than you are to show your hand or your face, you who are conscious of the sins of the flesh do well to have shame, and to cover your nakedness.

"They would not kill an animal on any account, not even a fly, or a flea, or a louse, or anything in fact that has life; for they say these have all souls, and it would be sin to do so. They eat no vegetable in a green state, only such as are dry. And they sleep on the ground stark naked, without a carp of clothing on them or under them, so that it is a marvel they don't all die, in place of living so long as I have told you. They fast everyday in the year, and drink nought but water. And when a novice has to be received among them, they keep him awhile in their convent, and make him follow their rule of life. And then, when they desire to put him to the test, they send for some of those girls who are devoted to the Idols and make them try the continence of the novice with their blandishments. If he remains indifferent, they retain him, but if he shows any emotion, they expel him from their society. For they say they will have no man of loose desires among them.

"They are such cruel and perfidious Idolators that it is very devilry. They say that they burn the bodies of the dead because, if they were not burnt, worms would be bred which would eat the body and, when no more food remained for them, these worms would die and the soul belonging to that body would bear the sin and the punishment of their death. And that is why they burn, their dead !"[1]

Ibn Batuta (1343) found a yōgi in the Island of Anjedēva, where there was a temple, a grove and a tank of water, leaning against the wall of the temple. Respecting him he tells some remarkable stories. A century and a half after, Ibn Batuta Correa (1498) says that Vasco da Gama's ships put in at Anjedeva, and the men going on shore found that "there were good water springs, and there was in the upper part of the Island a tank built, with stone with very good water and much wood * * * * there were no inhabitants, only a beggarman whom they call *joguedis* of whom further on I will give a long account."[2]

Speaking of the infidels of Calicut, Abdur Razak (1442) says that they "are divided into a great number of classes such as the Brahmans, the yogis and others."

The yōgis seem to have had a king of their own who Yule and Burnell think was perhaps the chief of the Gorakanatha Gosains who were once very numerous on the West Coast and have still a settlement at Kadri near Mangalore. Varthema (1510) referring to their chief observes, "The king of the *Joghe* is a man of great dignity, and has about 30,000 people, and he is a pagan, he and all his subjects, and by the pagan kings he and his people are considered to be saints on account of their lives which you shall hear * * * * *. "[3]

In 1624, Della Vella says. "Finally I went to see the king of the yogis (Gioghi) where he dwelt at that time, under the shade of a cottage, and I found him roughly occupied in his affairs, as a man of the field and husbandman * * they told me his name was Batinata (Badrinatha?) and the hermitage and the place generally was called Cadira (Kadri)."[4]

1. Marco Polo in vol. 2, pp. 365 to 367.
2. Page 239, Stanley's Correa.
3. P. 111.
4. Vol. 2, p. 724.

In course of time, the order of the yogis must have considerably deteriorated. Originally they formed a community of men who had retired from worldly affairs and devoted themselves to philosophy and religion. Barbosa (1516) in noticing them observes, "And many of them noble and respectable people not to be subject to the Moors, go out of the kingdom and take the habit of poverty wandering the world." Thus political causes seem to have contributed to augmenting their number. Barbosa describes them as carrying "very heavy chains round their necks and waists and legs. They smear all their bodies and faces with ashes."[1]

Two and a half centuries before our author wrote, Ma Huan the Chinese Muhammadan (1409), found the yogis in the town of Cochin. Like Marco Polo he calls them Chokis rendered into yogi by his translator. Of them he says:—"Here also is another class of men Chokies (yogis), who lead austere lives like the Taoists of China, but, who, however, are married. These men from the time they are born do not have their heads shaved or combed, but plait their hair into several tails, which hang over their shoulders, they wear no clothes, but round their waist they fasten a strip of rattan, over which they hang a piece of white calico; They carry a conch-shell which they blow as they go along the road. They are accompanied by their wives, who simply wear a small bit of cotton cloth round their loins. Alms of rice and money are given to them by the people whose houses they visit." This picture of the wandering Yogi or Byragi, vairagi (*lit*: one who has renounced all worldly connection) in the streets of Cochin is as true today as when it was drawn. Any one passing through the streets of Mattancherry in Native Cochin can see the naked yogi passing from door to door seeking alms, accompanied by his wife, if he has one, who however is now better clad, perhaps to suit modern notions of decencey. At present there is a perennial stream of wandering pilgrims, yogis, Gosais, Byragis, *et hoc*

1. Pages 99—100.

genus omne passing along from one end of India to the other, some indeed truly bent on holy pilgrimage to sacred shrines. But the majority of them seek by wandering a subsistence which their idleness and indolence cannot find by other means. Many of them are conjurors, jugglers, charlatans and mountebanks, vending glass beads, relics, images and nostrums. Some pretend astrology and divination. De Barros (1553) tells us that "much of the general fear that affected the inhabitants of that city (Goa before its capture by the Portuguese) proceeded from a Gentoo of Bengal by nation, who went about in the habit of a *yogue*, which is the straitest sect of their religion. * * * Saying that the city would speedily have a new Lord, and would be inhabited by a strange people, contrary to the will of the natives." De Barro's *jogue* appears to have been of the true metal, for his prediction was soon fulfilled; for Goa soon had a new Lord, the Portuguese, and came to be inhabited by that strange people to the disgust of the natives who were sorely persecuted. A decade after De Barros, Garcia (1563) speaks of these *jogues* carrying the *Cobras de Capello* while asking alms of the people "and these yogues,' he says "are certain heathens (Gentios) who go begging all about the country, powdered all over with ashes, and are venerated by all the poor heathen and by some of the Moors also."[1]

The yogis or Gosais receive alms all along the line of the way from Nepal to Rameswaram, and their wants are specially attended to in Malabar and more particularly in the Native States of Cochin and Travancore. At every choultry and temple under the management of the Sirkar, and there are many of these, rice is doled out to them regularly and, in the course of their journey, they are carried over ferries free of charge. It has been so all along. They have choultries or Chāvaṭies specially built to accommodate them. Dr. Fryer describing them in 1673 says, "Near the gate in a choultry

1. Pages 156—157.

sate more than forty naked *Jougies* or men united to God covered with ashes and plaited Turbats of their own Hair."[1] Fra Bartolomeo speaking of "the Madams, Ambalams, or inns erected on the public roads for the accommodation of strangers" observes," In these inns those philosophers known under the names of *yogi* and *Goswami*, and by some called Fakirs, who subject themselves to severest penances are treated at the king's expense, though this is done sometimes in some neighbouring temples. They eat nothing but rice, fruits, herbs etc."

---

1. Page 160.

The Transliteration Table followed in the printing of this work.

The Press has accented letters only for 12 point capitals and lower case letters; and, even among these, the sets are not complete.

In spite of great care, a few mistakes have crept in to mar the uniformity attempted to be maintained in spelling the names of places and of persons. For this, the Editor craves the pardon of the reader.

This Press owns no letters of the Nagara alphabet, and so Malayalam characters have to be used.

അ	a	ഖ	kha	പ	pa
ആ	ā	ഗ	ga	ഫ	pha
ഇ	i	ഘ	gha	ബ	ba
ഈ	ī	ങ	nga	ഭ	bha
ഉ	u	ച	cha	മ	ma
ഊ	ū	ഛ	chha	യ	ya
ഋ	ṛ	ജ	ja	ര	ra
ൠ	ṝ	ഝ	jha	ല	la
ഌ	ḷ	ഞ	ña	വ	va
ൡ	ḹ	ട	ṭa	ശ	śa
എ	e	ഠ	ṭha	ഷ	ṣha
ഏ	ē	ഡ	ḍa	സ	sa
ഐ	ai	ഢ	ḍha	ഹ	ha
ഒ	o	ണ	ṇa	ള	ḷa
ഓ	ō	ത	ṭa	ക്ഷ	kṣha
ഔ	au	ഥ	ṭha	റ	ṙa
അം	aṃ	ദ	ḍa	ഴ	ľa
അഃ	aḥ	ധ	ḍha	റ്റ	ťťa
ക	ka	ന	ṅa	ന്റ	ńta

INDEX TO THE NOTES.

A

B

B—*cont.*

C

D

D—*cont.*

I

J

K

K

L

M

M—*cont.*

O

T—*cont.*

U

V

V—*cont.*

W

Y

Z